ELT IN ASIA IN THE DIGITAL ERA: GLOBAL
CITIZENSHIP AND IDENTITY

T0360956

PROCEEDINGS OF THE 15ᵀᴴ ASIA TEFL AND 64ᵀᴴ TEFLIN INTERNATIONAL CONFERENCE ON ENGLISH LANGUAGE TEACHING, JULY 13–15, 2017, YOGYAKARTA, INDONESIA

ELT in Asia in the Digital Era: Global Citizenship and Identity

Editors

Suwarsih Madya
Yogyakarta State University, Indonesia

Fuad Abdul Hamied
Universitas Pendidikan Indonesia, Indonesia

Willy A. Renandya
Nanyang Technological University, Singapore

Christine Coombe
Dubai Men's College, the United Arab Emirates

Yazid Basthomi
Universitas Negeri Malang, Indonesia

Jointly Organized by
Teaching English as a Foreign Language in Asia (Asia TEFL), The Association for the Teaching of English as a Foreign Language in Indonesia (TEFLIN), and English Language Education Department, Yogyakarta State University, Indonesia

LONDON AND NEW YORK

Published 2018 by Routledge
2 Park Square, Milton Park, Abingdon, Oxon OX14 4RN
605 Third Avenue, New York, NY 10017

First issued in paperback 2020

Routledge is an imprint of the Taylor & Francis Group, an informa business

© 2018 Taylor & Francis Group, London, UK

Typeset by V Publishing Solutions Pvt Ltd., Chennai, India

ISBN 13: 978-0-367-73429-9 (pbk)
ISBN 13: 978-0-8153-7900-3 (hbk)

Published by: CRC Press/Balkema
Schipholweg 107C, 2316 XC Leiden, The Netherlands
e-mail: Pub.NL@taylorandfrancis.com
www.crcpress.com – www.taylorandfrancis.com

ELT in Asia in the Digital Era: Global Citizenship and Identity – Madya et al. (Eds)
© 2018 Taylor & Francis Group, London, ISBN 978-0-8153-7900-3

Table of contents

Preface   xi

Acknowledgement   xiii

Organizing committee   xv

Part I: English language teaching and learning developments – what do they
mean in different contexts with different paradigms?

Teacher development for content-based instruction   3
D.J. Tedick

Sustainable professional development programs for English teachers: A case study
in South Sulawesi, Indonesia   15
A. Abduh & R. Rosmaladewi

Teacher efficacy in instructional strategies in classroom among tertiary teachers
in Central Java, Indonesia   21
Muamaroh

Sex-based grouping in English language teaching   29
M. Mahmud & Sahril

The relationship of English proficiency and socioeconomic status with the choice
of language learning strategies among EFL students of Cenderawasih University Papua   37
R.D.B. Rambet

Learners' native language interference in learning English pronunciation: A case
study of Indonesian regional dialects   45
M.N. Jannah, K.H. Hidayati & S. Setiawan

English Language Teaching (ELT) learners' communication strategies in exclusive
and task-based learning   49
B. Kadaryanto, T.H. Febiani & D. Utaminingsih

Exploring English lexical inferencing strategies performed by EFL university students   57
I. Hermagustiana

Digital collaboration and the impact on motivation and identity   65
S. Healy

Interpreting the demand of the curriculum creatively   73
A. Widyantoro

The effectiveness of an ELT model using Curriculum 13 to SMA students in Surakarta   79
Ngadiso

Compromising between the general and specific skills in EAP syllabus development
in Indonesian context   87
Jamilah

Academic reading needs analysis: Preliminary study of Malaysian prospective
higher education students   93
S.M. Damio & N.N. Rosli

Using multi techniques to improve reading fluency in ESL classrooms   103
D.B. Devi & M. Dhamotharan

Collaborative summary writing as an activity to comprehend reading texts   113
L.A. Mauludin

Integrating CEFR, thematic contents, and intensive instruction in developing
speaking materials for first-year English language teacher trainees   119
C.A. Korompot

Developing public speaking materials based on communicative language teaching
for EFL learners in Indonesia   129
M.A.R. Hakim & M.J.Z. Abidin

Improving learners' vocabulary mastery through the use of scaffolding strategies
while storytelling in an EFL multiethnic classroom   135
Istiqamah

The effect of school origins on the grammatical competence of university students   143
C.H. Karjo & R. Djohan

*Part II: Exploring the relationship between the knowledge-based
era and TEFL development*

When ELF meets BELF: Building business communication into
ELF-informed curriculum   153
Y.J. Yujobo

Indonesian English as a foreign language teachers' instructional curriculum design:
Revealing patterns of needs analysis   161
A. Triastuti & M. Riazi

Need analysis of English needs of midwifery students in Indonesia   173
F. Fahriany & N. Nuraeni

Teachers' accountability in the post-method era: Balancing freedom
and responsibility   181
Sugirin

Pre-service teachers' self-reflection on their pedagogical competences upon
joining the *SM-3T* program   189
N.A. Nurichsania & S. Rachmajanti

Exploring types and levels of motivation of Indonesian EFL learners   197
A. Budiman

Influence of motivation and language learning environment on the successful
EFL learning   205
Masyhur

L2 learning motivation from the perspective of self-determination theory: A qualitative
case study of hospitality and tourism students in Taiwan   221
H.T. Hsu

A comparison of gender disparity in East Asian EFL textbooks   229
N. Suezawa

EFL students' perception on the role of target-language culture in CCU class   235
N. Hidayati, Sumardi & S.S. Tarjana

Sundanese local content integration in English for young learners' classroom   241
I.A. Alwasilah

Written corrective feedback in a writing skill development program   249
S. Hidayati, A. Ashadi & S. Mukminatun

Contact with the nature: Field trip strategy in enhancing writing descriptive text   255
Rugaiyah

Inquiring language awareness of TEFL master students in advanced grammar course   265
M.D.A. Rizqan

Part III: Exploring and understanding today's demands for foreign languages: Going beyond English language competencies

Developing fluency   275
I.S.P. Nation

Foregrounding global citizenship in EFL using UNESCO's category of
core values   285
Masulah

Pedagogical movements in teaching English in the emerging issues of World Englishes   293
N. Mukminatien

Considering English varieties in Indonesia's EFL teaching and learning   299
E. Andriyanti & V. Rieschild

Prospective EFL teachers' awareness of varieties of English: Implications for ELT   307
N. Atma & W. Fatmawati

ELT shift: Necessary matters to be taught dealing with pronunciation among
NNS related to English as a Lingua Franca (ELF)   315
Andy & L. Muzammil

Visualizing ideal L2 self and enhancing L2 learning motivation, a pilot study among
Chinese college students   327
C. Zou

The potential of mobile technology in testing and enhancing L2 word recognition
from speech   343
J. Matthews

Does exposure to L2 affect cultural intelligence?   349
Z. Nafissi & N. Salmasi

Indonesian EFL teachers' identities in written discourse: English or
Oriental domination?   361
R.D. Pratama

The construction of imagined identities in two Indonesian English
bilingual adolescents   369
B. Chen & A. Lie

A case study of a seven-year old Indonesian-English bilingual child in a
trilingual school   377
R.Y. Prayitno & A. Lie

The teacher's code-switching in ELT classrooms: Motives and functions 385
D.A. Andawi & N.A. Drajati

Features of teachers' code-switching in Indonesia: How multiple languages are used in tertiary bilingual classrooms 393
H. Cahyani

Code-switching and code-mixing in bilingual communication: Language deficiency or creativity? 401
D.A. Nugraheni

English as a medium of instruction: Issues and challenges for Indonesian university lecturers and students 409
R. Hendryanti & I.N. Kusmayanti

EFL learners' opportunities and problems in literacy strategy implementation 417
N. Christiani & M.A. Latief

An explanatory study on the needs of skill-integrated coursebook for listening and speaking classes 423
S.K. Kurniasih, B.Y. Diyanti & L. Nurhayati

Indonesian teacher's beliefs and practices on teaching listening using songs 429
N.A. Fauzi

More than just vocabulary search: A bibliographic review on the roles of corpora of English in 21st century ELT 437
S. Simbuka

Hyland's model of argument in ESL writers essay 445
W.H. Osman

Investigating students' perceptions of blended learning implementation in an academic writing classroom 453
F. Indratama, N.A. Drajati, D. Rochsantiningsih & J. Nurkamto

Part IV: Transforming TEFL in a fully digital world

Intercultural language teaching and learning in digital era 463
A.J. Liddicoat

Developing multiliteracies for EFL learners in the digital era 471
W. Lei

Exploring the contribution of the school culture and the learner factors to the success of the English e-learners 479
R.C.Y. Setyo, Suharsono & O. Purwati

Perception and ICT usage of students and lecturers of the English study program of the Faculty of Teacher Training and Education, Tridinanti University 487
Y. Hendrety

The story of "Julie": A life history study of the learning experiences of an Indonesian English language teacher in implementing ICT in her classroom 495
D.S. Ciptaningrum

Faculty's attitudes towards the shift to blended learning, challenges faced and its impact 505
K.K. Aye

The incorporation of Facebook in language pedagogy: Merits, defects, and implications 513
T.N.T. Dung & L.T.N. Quynh

Reading enjoyment in the digital age: How does it differ by parents' education, self-expected education, and socio-economic status? 521
N.H.P.S. Putro & J. Lee

'Read-to-Me' story books: Parent-child home English reading activities 531
D.R. Meisani

Utilizing iBooks in teaching EFL reading comprehension 537
D.S. Suharti

The effectiveness of online brain-writing compared to brainstorming as prewriting strategies in teaching writing to students with high frequency and low frequency of Language Learning Strategies (LLS) 555
D. Hermasari

Gallery Walk for teaching a content course 563
I. Maharsi

Assessing speaking by f2f or using a developed application: Are there any differences? 571
M.S. Simatupang, M. Wiannastiti & R. Peter

Author index 577

Preface

This book presents the proceedings of the 15th Asia TEFL and 64th TEFLIN International Conference held in Yogyakarta from 13–15 July 2017 co-hosted by Yogyakarta State University, TEFLIN (the Association for the Teaching of English as a Foreign Language in Indonesia), and Asia TEFL. This conference was designed to provide a forum for EFL teaching and learning researchers, policy makers and practitioners to assemble in the spirit of "learning and growing together" to: (a) engage in an informed, critical and insightful dialogue about enhancing learning for all students in all settings in all countries, a dialogue about what works, how it works, what it takes to make things work, and how to develop thereon a new understanding of the nature of EFL teaching and learning; (b) strengthen national and international EFL education networks to promote powerful research in TEFL effectiveness, improvement, and innovation and to engage EFL learning and teaching researchers, policy makers, and practitioners in ongoing conversations about the interpretation and the application of research in practice; and (c) critically examine the strengths and weaknesses of different theoretical paradigms of language learning and to explore how different conceptions frame and influence the whole business of TEFL, especially in a global, knowledge-based, technologically wired context.

The above purpose was achieved by raising the theme *ELT in Asia in the Digital Era: Global Citizenship and Identity* from which four subthemes were derived: (1) English language teaching and learning developments – What do they mean in different contexts with different paradigms?, (2) Exploring the relationship between the knowledge-based era and TEFL development, (3) Exploring and understanding today's demands for foreign languages: Going beyond English language competencies, and (4) Transforming TEFL in the fully digital world.

This conference presented eleven plenary speakers, 14 workshops, and around 800 concurrent papers, which were enjoyed by around more than 1000 participants from 32 countries. Three of the plenary speakers responded positively to the Committee's request to submit their papers to be published in this book. Among the papers submitted for the proceedings, 68 were regarded as meeting the criteria and these papers have been grouped in four parts according to these four subthemes in this book.

Part I presents 19 papers talking, among others, about teacher development, learners, learning strategies, curriculum, teaching methods, and material development. A paper entitled *Teacher development in content-based instruction* by Diane J. Tedick opens this part. Part II presents 14 papers talking, among others, about needs analysis, gender disparity, teaching creative writing, and language awareness. Part III presents 22 papers, beginning with a paper entitled *Developing fluency* by I.S.P. Nation. Other papers are talking, among others, about global citizenship, world Englishes, English varieties, teacher accountability, ICT-based testing, and code switching. Part IV presents 13 papers, beginning with a paper by Anthony Liddicoat entitled *Intercultural language teaching and learning in the digital era*. So, altogether this book presents 68 papers.

This book will hopefully facilitate the sharing of knowledge between the writers and the readers for purposes of developing the teaching of English as a foreign language in this digital era.

Acknowledgement

Agus Widyantoro, *Yogyakarta State University, Indonesia*
Ali Saukah, *Universitas Negeri Malang, Indonesia*
Andy Bayu Nugroho, *Yogyakarta State University, Indonesia*
Andy Kirkpatrick, *Griffith University, Australia*
Anita Triastuti, *Yogyakarta State University, Indonesia*
Antony John Kunnan, *University of Macau, China*
Ashadi, *Yogyakarta State University, Indonesia*
Asruddin B. Tou, *Yogyakarta State University, Indonesia*
Basikin, *Yogyakarta State University, Indonesia*
Chairil Anwar Karompot, *Universitas Negeri Makassar, Indonesia*
Christine Coombe, *Dubai Men's College, the United Arab Emirates*
David Shaffer, *Chosun University, Korea*
Dewi Nurul Lailatun Mubarokah, *Yogyakarta State University, Indonesia*
Didi Sukyadi, *Universitas Pendidikan Indonesia, Indonesia*
Dyah Setiawati Ciptaningrum, *Yogyakarta State University, Indonesia*
Edwin Vethamani, *Taylor's University, Malaysia*
Erna Andriyanti, *Yogyakarta State University, Indonesia*
Fuad Abdul Hamied, *Universitas Pendidikan Indonesia, Indonesia*
Ganakumaran Subramaniam, *University of Nottingham, Malaysia*
Gunadi Harry Sulistyo, *Universitas Negeri Malang, Indonesia*
Haixiao Wang, *Nanjing Univ., China*
Hee-Kyung Lee, *Yonsei University, Korea*
Helena I. R. Agustien, *Universitas Negeri Semarang, Indonesia*
Hung Soo Lee, *Chonnam National University, Korea*
Hyo Shin Lee, *Konkuk University Glocal Campus, Korea*
Isaiah WonHo Yoo, *Sogang University, Korea*
Jihyeon Jeon, *Ewha Womans University, Korea*
Joko Nurkamto, *Universitas Sebelas Maret, Indonesia*
Joko Priyana, *Yogyakarta State University, Indonesia*
Jong Bai Hwang, *Konkuk University, Korea*
Joo Kyung Park, *Honam University, Korea*
Judy Yin, *Korea National University of Education, Korea*
Kilryoung Lee, *Hankuk University of Foreign Studies, Korea*
Le Van Canh, *Vietnam National University at Hanoi, Vietnam*
Maman Suryaman, *Yogyakarta State University, Indonesia*
Masaki Oda, *Tamagawa University, Japan*
Mauly Halwat Hikmat, *Universitas Muhammadiyah Surakarta, Indonesia*
Muhammad Taufiq al Makmun, *Universitas Sebelas Maret, Indonesia*
Mukhaiyar, *Universitas Negeri Padang, Indonesia*

ELT in Asia in the Digital Era: Global Citizenship and Identity – Madya et al. (Eds)
© 2018 Taylor & Francis Group, London, ISBN 978-0-8153-7900-3

Organizing committee

PATRON

Sutrisna Wibawa

CHAIR

Suwarsih Madya

VICE CHAIRS

Widyastuti Purbani
Sugirin
Sukarno

COMMITTEE

Joko Nurkamto
HyoWoong Lee Asia
Haixiao Wang
Masaki Oda
Fuad Abdul Hamied
Gunakumaran Subramaniam
Hung Soo Lee
Sisilia Halimi S.
Didi Sukyadi
Margana
Edi Purwanta
Sumaryanto
Senam

Moch. Brury Triyono
Satoto Endar Nayono
Joko Priyana
Maman Suryaman
Andy Bayu Nugroho
Asruddin B. Tou
Susana Widyastuti
Basikin
Samsul Maarif
Suhaini M. Saleh
Anita Triastuti
Ashadi
Erna Andriyanti

Part I: English language teaching and learning developments – what do they mean in different contexts with different paradigms?

ELT in Asia in the Digital Era: Global Citizenship and Identity – Madya et al. (Eds)
© 2018 Taylor & Francis Group, London, ISBN 978-0-8153-7900-3

Teacher development for content-based instruction

D.J. Tedick
University of Minnesota, Minneapolis, USA

ABSTRACT: The fundamental premise underlying Content-Based Instruction (CBI) is that students can learn (and teachers can teach) both meaningful content and a new language at the same time. The crux of effective CBI is content and language integration—teachers and students have to attend to both content and language if the language learning benefits of CBI are to be maximized. Yet such integration is challenging for teachers and needs to be systematically addressed through professional development. This paper provides an overview of the features and goals of CBI, types of CBI models, and benefits of CBI. It then identifies key teacher characteristics needed for CBI and illustrates ways that teachers can learn to integrate language and content. It concludes with review of a recent study that explored the types of professional development experiences teachers perceive to have a positive impact on their ability to integrate language and content in their teaching.

1 CONTENT-BASED LANGUAGE INSTRUCTION

1.1 *Definitions and goals*

Content-based language instruction (CBI) is an approach to language teaching in which the second or foreign language serves as the vehicle for teaching content. Different terms are used around the world to refer to CBI, for example, content-based language teaching, or content and language integrated learning (CLIL), widely used in Europe and Asia. CBI is the most common term in North America and will thus be used throughout this paper. The fundamental premise underlying CBI is that students can learn (and teachers can teach) both meaningful content—including academic subject matter content—and a new language at the same time (Lightbown 2014). CBI intends to promote (a) language use and purposeful communication about meaningful content, (b) cognitive engagement, (c) critical and divergent thinking, (d) advanced literacy skills, and (e) students' intellectual sensitivity and motivation (Cammarata, Tedick & Osborn 2016). These goals reflect language learning as a mechanism for lifelong learning, a way to spark in students a desire to want to know more, a curiosity to learn about the unknown and other, and an openness to reflecting on one's own worldviews when they are challenged. CBI aims to help learners to *use language* meaningfully and purposefully, to *learn through language* as they construct knowledge and develop understandings about a topic and learning task, and to *learn about language* when there is a focus on form in the context of learning through language (Gibbons 2015).

1.2 *The nature of content in and types of CBI*

Met (1999) conceptualized different types of CBI programs as falling on a continuum ranging from content-driven models to language-driven models. In content-driven programs, content-trained teachers teach content in the second language (L2), and content learning is the priority, while language learning is secondary. In these programs, the focus is on academic (subject matter) content that is appropriate to the cognitive and linguistic level of the learners. Content objectives are determined by course goals or prescribed curriculum, and teachers may select language objectives that align with the content. Students are evaluated primarily (or solely) on content mastery and get academic credit for content. In language-driven models, language-trained teachers teach the L2 using content, but language learning is priority with content learning considered incidental. Language objectives are determined by the L2 curriculum, and teachers may consider adding content objectives. Students are evaluated primarily (or solely) on language performance, and they earn academic credit for language. In these programs, the content is more thematic in nature. For example, in an elementary Spanish class in the US students learn Spanish as they learn about animal characteristics and habitats. In a middle school in Xi'an, China, students study the classification of living things while learning English (Kong & Hoare 2011). In a US university level, intermediate German class, students improve their German as they explore environmental sustainability (Kautz 2016).

Drawing upon Met's conceptualization, Tedick & Cammarata (2012) organized CBI models within a matrix consisting of two intersecting continua, one reflecting the content-driven versus language-driven range and one corresponding to time intensity. Programs that devote a large percentage of instructional time to teaching the L2 through content (at least 50% of the curriculum) are considered "high time-intensive" and those devoting less than 50% are in the "low time-intensive" range. Language immersion models, in which the L2 is used to teach the regular school curriculum, are content-driven and high time-intensive. They can devote 50% of instructional time to content taught in L2 throughout the program (partial immersion) or over 50% initially (total immersion). English medium instruction (EMI) [subject courses taught through the medium of English (L2) often in post-secondary contexts] may also be considered high time-intensive if over 50% of the courses that students take are taught in English.

Programs that remain content-driven but devote less time to teaching the L2 through curricular content are low time-intensive. For example, EMI programs that represent less than 50% of subject matter courses that students take fall into this category. Similar to EMI models are language across the curriculum (LAC) programs at US universities wherein students take one or a few subject courses in a foreign language. Sheltered English as a second language (ESL) classes in the US and other contexts where English is the majority societal language also are content-driven and low time-intensive. In these courses, English learners are grouped together and taught history or mathematics by a subject-trained teacher who uses sheltered instruction techniques to make the content accessible to students still learning the language.

Language-driven, low time-intensive models include English for academic or specific purposes (EAP/ESP). These language classes develop communicative competence in a specific discipline (e.g., business, medicine), but the emphasis is on language learning rather than the learning of disciplinary concepts. Language-driven, low time-intensive programs also include theme-based and content-related classes. Theme-based courses involve topics that "provide the content from which teachers extract language learning activities" (Snow 2001: 306) and are therefore more language—than content-driven. In content-related classes (typically designed for early language learning programs) the language teacher incorporates some content from the regular curriculum to make language activities more cognitively engaging for children. For instance, a teacher might reinforce math concepts while teaching a unit on food and cooking.

In the Adjunct Model (a type of LAC program), post-secondary students enroll concurrently in a content course and a language course designed to support student learning in the content course (Brinton, Snow & Wesche 2003). Students are sheltered in the language course but often integrated with native speakers in the content course. Thus, this model is both content-and language-driven and would appear in the middle of the content – and language-driven continuum while also being placed towards the low time-intensive end of the time intensity continuum.

Finally, there are few models representing language-driven and high time-intensive programs. Intensive language "camps" that incorporate content would fall into this category. For example, the state of Minnesota offers summer residential language camps. Students in the German camp may opt to live in the *Biohaus*, which uses solar and thermal energy to power appliances, run equipment, and heat water. Students learn and use German as they gain knowledge about energy efficiency and develop STEM (science, technology, engineering, math) skills while earning high school German credit.

As this discussion illustrates, CBI models vary widely. Where they fall on the two intersecting continua will vary depending upon how time-intensive the model is and how content-driven versus language-driven it is. The fact that so many models attempt to combine language learning with meaningful content derives from the research-based benefits of CBI.

1.3   *The benefits of CBI*

Studies have shown that CBI yields better language acquisition (SLA) results than traditional language teaching (e.g., Admiraal, Westoff & de Bot 2006, Center for Applied Language Studies 2011 Genesee 1987, Pessoa, Hendry, Donato, Tucker & Lee 2007, Verspoor, de Bot & Xu 2015). CBI promotes better SLA because students learn language best in contexts where there is an emphasis on relevant, meaningful content rather than on the language itself (Gibbons 2015, Lightbown & Spada 2013). At the same time, both meaning and form are important and are not readily separable in language learning (Lightbown & Spada 2013, Lyster 2007). Lightbown (2014) suggests that separating content and language in instruction "may deprive students of opportunities to focus on specific features of language at the very moment when their motivation to learn them may be at its highest" (p. 30).

In addition, CBI provides affordances that are thought to contribute to SLA, such as participation in the "zone of proximal development" (e.g., Swain, Kinnear & Steinman 2015, Vygotsky 1986). Finally, brain-based research has pointed to the holistic and interconnected nature of brain activities. Kennedy (2006) contends:

> The tendency of the brain to consider the entire experience and to search for meaningful patterns calls for thematic, content-based interdisciplinary language instruction at all levels. (p. 480).

2   TEACHER KNOWLEDGE AND SKILLS FOR CBI

2.1   *A unique knowledge base and pedagogical skill set*

CBI teaching is different from teaching language or content on its own. Scholars agree that CBI teachers require a particular knowledge base and pedagogical skill set (e.g., Cammarata & Tedick 2012, Coyle 2011, Dalton-Puffer 2007, Day & Shapson 1996, Fortune, Tedick & Walker 2008, Kong & Hoare 2011, Lyster 2007, Tedick & Cammarata, 2012, Tedick & Fortune 2013). Regarding the language proficiency that is required for successful CBI teaching, teachers in language-driven programs should be able to maintain L2 use during instruction and have good literacy skills (i.e., B1 level on the Common European Framework of Reference – CEFR) (Council of Europe 2017). For content-driven programs, teachers must have high enough proficiency to be able to maintain L2 to teach the content as well as high L2 literacy skills (i.e., B2 and above on the CEFR).

Among the many knowledge concepts and pedagogical skills recommended for CBI in the literature are knowledge of SLA and teaching (Tedick & Fortune 2013), academic genres and academic language development (Gibbons 2015, Kong & Hoare 2011), strategies for scaffolding comprehension and production (Lyster 2007, 2016), pedagogical strategies eo engage learners in depth of processing content knowledge (Kong & Hoare 2011), and cross-lingual pedagogy and teacher collaboration (Lyster & Tedick 2014). Moreover, pedagogical skills for integrating content and language are paramount. Teachers must learn strategies for integrating language and content in curriculum development, instruction, and assessment (Cammarata & Tedick 2012, Lyster 2007, Tedick & Fortune 2013). Lyster (2007, 2016) recommends that they also adopt a "counterbalanced instructional approach".

The idea behind counterbalanced instruction is that students in largely communicative classroom contexts that focus on meaning (as in content-driven CBI), will benefit from a focus on form (a counterbalance) to improve their target language proficiency. The reverse is also true—students in predominantly form-focused classrooms (i.e., traditional foreign language instruction) will benefit from more of a focus on meaning and on the contextualization of language form within meaningful content (as in language-driven CBI). Counterbalanced instruction requires teachers to alternate the instructional focus between language and content. The effort expended by students to shift attention between form and meaning increases depth of processing and strengthens their metalinguistic awareness. Processing disciplinary content while also attending to the language that encodes the content is one way for students to engage with increasingly complex language, which is key to academic literacy and success in content-driven CBI programs.

2.2 *Focus on content and language integration in CBI*

Swain (1988) noted nearly three decades ago that content teaching on its own is not necessarily good language teaching, and that content teaching needs to be manipulated and complemented to maximize language learning. Yet observations in CBI classrooms have shown that it is rare for teachers to make direct links between content lessons and grammar lessons and to set up content-based activities to focus on form related to meaning (Allen, Swain, Harley & Cummins 1990). Studies in high time-intensive and content-driven immersion classrooms have shown that students' L2 is often underdeveloped, lacking grammatical accuracy, lexical variety, and sociolinguistic appropriateness (e.g., Harley, Cummins, Swain & Allen 1990, Lyster 2004, Tedick & Young 2016). Studies exploring teacher perspectives have reported that primary immersion teachers see themselves first and foremost as content teachers (e.g., Fortune et al. 2008). Secondary CBI teachers perceive themselves as "only content teachers or only language teachers" (Tan 2011: 325). Importantly, studies have demonstrated that teachers have difficulty integrating language and content in their instruction (Cammarata & Tedick 2012, Dalton-Puffer 2007, Fortune et al. 2008, Lyster 2007, Tan 2011).

For these reasons, scholars and teacher educators have developed ways to help CBI teachers learn to counterbalance their instruction and strive toward language and content integration. Such integration is critical if CBI programs are to achieve their language learning potential.

3 TEACHING CBI TEACHERS TO INTEGRATE LANGUAGE AND CONTENT

To achieve an instructional counterbalance between language and content (Lyster 2007), teachers can use both reactive and proactive approaches.

3.1 *Reactive approaches*

Reactive approaches involve teacher reactions to student language production. For example, teachers need to use special questioning techniques and follow up strategies during classroom interaction to enhance student language production (Kong & Hoare 2011, Lyster, 2016). They can use question scaffolds that can ask students, for example, to elaborate – could you tell me more about? what do you mean by? – to justify – why do you think that? how do you know? – or to explain – what do the objects have in common? In addition, teachers need to provide corrective feedback to draw student attention to linguistic errors. In their pioneering study, Lyster & Ranta (1997) identified six different feedback types that language immersion teachers were observed utilizing during classroom interaction. These six types fall into two main categories: reformulations and prompts. Reformulations provide students with the correct form. An example is a recast – in a recast, the teacher repeats what the student has said sans the error. If the student says, "She like to swim," the teacher responds, "She likes to swim" (adding the necessary "s" on the third person singular verb). In contrast, prompts provide hints or clues as to the nature of the errors students have made to push them to self-correct. For instance, if a student says "Mr. Smith travel a lot last year," the teacher might respond with metalinguistic clue: "Do we say travel when we're talking about the last year?" Such a response encourages student self-correction. Teachers also need to be aware of their own use of language and how they interact with students in order to ensure that oral communication is clear and that it serves the dual purpose of supporting both content and language learning.

3.2 *Proactive approaches*

Proactive approaches involve systematic teacher planning for a focus on both content and language in curriculum development, instruction, and assessment. Examples of proactive instructional strategies include: learning objectives that target language and content, teaching activities that scaffold content learning and language production, instructional sequences that bring students' attention to form, and assessments that integrate language and content. Given length limitations, it is not possible to discuss strategy each in depth. Introduced briefly in the following sections are a teaching activity that scaffolds content learning and language production, learning objectives, and an instructional sequence that integrates language and content.

3.2.1 *Scaffolding content learning and language production*

There are many different ways that CBI teachers can incorporate instructional activities that scaffold both content learning and language production. At the University of Minnesota, we developed customizable graphic organizers that scaffold both content and language production (http://carla.umn.edu/cobaltt/modules/strategies/gorganizers/index.html). Graphic organizers (e.g., Venn diagrams, timelines, grids, semantic maps) promote the learning of subject matter and specific thinking skills (e.g., compare/contrast, cause-effect). They can assist learners in processing, comprehending, synthesizing and displaying complex ideas. Yet they emphasize grasp of concepts rather than mastery of language. A Venn diagram helps learners to compare and contrast characteristics of two objects or animals – such as tadpoles and frogs – but it does not help students develop the language needed to describe similarities and differences. The customizable graphic organizers we developed combine both content learning and language practice. The graphic organizer itself helps students summarize their understandings about the content concepts and an additional language task requires that they practice the language needed to explain their understandings.

Figure 1 displays a Comparison/Contrast Chart where students are asked to summarize what they know about reptiles and amphibians with respect to their physical characteristics, behaviors, habitat, and food. This graphic organizer activity is an excellent way for students to pull together content from various sources and see how the two animal classes differ and how they are similar.

Yet the major emphasis is on content learning because to fill in the chart the only language that students need to use is vocabulary and possibly some short phrases in the present tense. To encourage more extended language use and to scaffold compare/contrast language constructions specifically, an additional language task is added to the activity:

> Write at least two sentences in the present tense to compare/contrast the animal classes. Write a sentence describing a similarity and one describing a difference. To describe similarity, use the word "both" in your sentence, and to describe difference use the word "whereas".

	Reptiles	Amphibians
Physical characteristics		
Behaviors		
Habitat		
Food		

Figure 1. Sample comparison/contrast chart.

When using these customized graphic organizers, students reformat the content and, at the same time, practice specific language structures, thereby combining content mastery and language use.

3.2.2 *Learning objectives targeting language and content*

When planning lessons, teachers must consider and articulate what they want to students to learn with respect to both content and language by formulating learning objectives. Content objectives, which should always be written in terms of what students will do, reflect the academic concepts of the lesson. They should describe the what and/or why that underlies the how (the instructional activities that are planned). Sample content objectives are:

1. Students will identify similarities and differences between reptiles and amphibians.
2. Students will describe the stages of the butterfly's life cycle.
3. Students will compare and contrast Hopi tribal and mainstream culture perspectives.

Language objectives derive from the content and reflect the language that students need to learn and use accurately in the lesson. They should be very specific and should contain three linguistic components that are aligned—communicative or academic functions, grammatical structures or forms, and vocabulary (the words, phrases needed to produce the forms). Through our teacher preparation and professional development programs for CBI teachers at the University of Minnesota, we have learned that the clearer teachers are about the language they want students to use, the greater the likelihood students will use it.

As an example, imagine that pairs of students are instructed to complete the graphic organizer shown in Figure 1 and to carry out the additional language task. Sample language objectives for the additional language task include:

1. Students will use the present tense [grammatical structure] of verbs like have, eat, are, can (live, swim, etc.) [vocabulary] to describe similarities and differences between reptiles and amphibians [function].
2. Students will use negative verb forms and contractions [grammatical structure] like can't and don't [vocabulary] to describe similarities and differences between reptiles and amphibians [function].
3. Students will describe similarities and differences between reptiles and amphibians [function] with conjunctions [grammatical structure] such as both, and, whereas, but [vocabulary].

These examples should make clear how the three objective components are aligned. As a teacher educator, I have found that teachers struggle initially to write clear and complete language objectives and that they benefit from a great deal of modeling, practice, and feedback. Content-trained teachers in particular are challenged to articulate language objectives because they tend not to have the requisite linguistic knowledge.

3.2.3 *Instructional sequence to bring students' attention to form*

An instructional sequence comprised of five phases can be used as a means of integrating language and content (Lyster 2007, 2016). In the first phase, teachers must identify a grammatical feature to focus on within the context of the content they're teaching. In the second phase, they develop a noticing activity to draw students' attention to the form by highlighting it in some way and/or making it more salient in a text. Next, they develop awareness activities designed to engage students in some type of meta-linguistic reflection to raise their awareness about linguistic patterns. The fourth phase involves controlled or guided practice activities that push students to use the grammatical form in a meaningful yet controlled context to develop automaticity and accuracy. In the final phase students are encouraged to use the feature in more open-ended ways to develop fluency and confidence through communicative practice activities.

To exemplify this instructional sequence, I will share activities developed by Cari Maguire, a former ESL teacher, now PhD and faculty member who prepares ESL teachers at a college in Minnesota.

Phase 1 – identification of the form in the context of meaningful content. Cari developed this sequence for a middle school (students aged 12–14) ESL science class. The unit theme is "Landforms" and the linguistic feature Cari identified was participial phrases used to indicate cause/effect: The running water of the river wears away the ground, *forming a canyon.* The emphasis is on the present participle that is set off by a comma at the end of the sentence. A focus on form like this helps students to develop academic language proficiency.

Phase 2 – noticing activity. To set up the noticing activity, Cari adapted a text from the students' science textbook to include multiple instances of these participial phrases (to make the form more salient). An excerpt from this text appears in Figure 2.

Volcanos send melted rock, or lava, up to the Earth's surface. Mountains can be formed by volcanos. Lava flows up through a crack in the earth and hardens, creating a mountain.

When volcanos erupt underwater, they can create islands. Lava builds up until it reaches the surface of the ocean, forming an island.

Earthquakes happen when two pieces of Earth's crust move, causing the ground to shake and roll. Mountains can be formed by earthquakes. Two pieces of the earth's crust push against each other, making a mountain.

First, the teacher reads the text with students to ensure that they capture the meaning. According to Nassaji & Fotos (2011) if students cannot comprehend a text, they will most likely not be able to create required form-mapping connections of the language features in the text, even if they are able to notice the form. Beginning instruction by focusing on meaning will increase learners' comprehension of the text and prepare them to use the text to notice the form later.

The teacher then takes sentences containing the target feature from the modified text and matches them with pictures on PowerPoint slides. Each slide shows a picture of a landform accompanied by a descriptive sentence including the focus form. The teacher shows each slide and asks a student to read the sentence aloud. She models how students should say "comma" aloud and draw a comma in the air when they reach the end of the first clause. After drawing the comma, the class and teacher say the participial adjective with extra stress, especially on the 'ing' before completing the rest of the sentence in a normal reading voice. Making a physical gesture to indicate a comma and stressing the 'ing' of the participial adjective make these two features of this type of sentence more salient.

Phase 3 – awareness activities. In the awareness phase, students are instructed to return to the text (Figure 2) and circle all sentences with the participial phrase. They highlight the comma in one color and the participial adjective with another. Together the teacher and students examine the highlighted sentences and have a brief discussion about how they show cause and effect, with the teacher eliciting as much explanation as possible from the students. To continue developing their awareness of how the form works, the teacher has the students work in pairs to complete a graphic organizer asking them to analyze the highlighted sentences and determine which action happened first and which action was caused by the first

> Volcanos send melted rock, or lava, up to the Earth's surface. Mountains can be formed by volcanos. Lava flows up through a crack in the earth and hardens, creating a mountain.
>
> When volcanos erupt underwater, they can create islands. Lava builds up until it reaches the surface of the ocean, forming an island.
>
> Earthquakes happen when two pieces of Earth's crust move, causing the ground to shake and roll. Mountains can be formed by earthquakes. Two pieces of the earth's crust push against each other, making a mountain.

Figure 2. Excerpt of text used for noticing activity.

action. The teacher guides the students in an inductive rule discovery activity, asking them to describe the purpose and rules of the participial phrase. Together the class co-constructs a student-friendly rule for the form: "describe the first action, insert a comma, and then write the second action using the participle ('ing')."

Phase 4 – controlled practice. To engage students in controlled practice, Cari created a game. Students work in teams of five and stand in lines. The first student on each team is given an individual white board and marker and is up first. The teacher shows a brief video clip depicting the formation of a land form—e.g., how over time a river creates a canyon. After the video ends, the teacher gives the signal and the student with the white board on each team races to write an accurate sentence describing what happened in the video—to win they must use the participial phrase accurately. The first student to finish wins a point for his/her team and then the next person in line takes the white board and marker and prepares for the next video. With repeated rounds, the students develop automaticity and greater accuracy in producing the form.

Phase 5 – communicative practice. The teacher assigns each student to create a poster of an assigned landform or natural force to illustrate what they have learned about how the landform might be created or how the natural force might impact Earth's surface. They are instructed to use at least one participial phrase showing cause and effect. As students work the teacher provides corrective feedback as needed to assist them in using the targeted form accurately.

This instructional sequence moves students from a focus on meaning/content (during the initial text reading and noticing activity) to a focus on form/language in the awareness and controlled practice phases back to a focus on meaning/content in the communicative practice activity. In so doing students learn *through* language and *about* language (Gibbons 2015).

3.2.4 *A caveat*

On the surface, the activities introduced in this section appear relatively straightforward and perhaps even simple, but this kind of proactive planning for language and content integration is not easy. A teacher interviewed by Cammarata & Tedick (2012), who had participated in a year-long professional development course to learn to integrate content and language, concluded: "Perhaps my biggest reflection is that it is easy to focus on only content or only language, *but it is a real challenge to effectively intertwine the two and do both well at the same time*" (p. 261, emphasis added). These practices take time to develop and require guided practice. What types of experiences help teachers to learn to integrate content and language effectively?

4 TEACHER PERSPECTIVES ON EXPERIENES THAT HELP THEM INTEGRATE LANGUAGE AND CONTENT

Tedick & Zilmer (2017) conducted a study focused on the professional development experiences that CBI teachers perceive to have a positive impact on their ability to integrate content and language in their teaching. The context was a 15-credit, online, graduate level professional development program designed for practicing CBI educators (immersion, CLIL, ESL, and EFL teachers). The assignments and experiences from four of the five 15-week courses that comprise the program were the focus of the study. Seventy-five teachers were invited to complete an extensive online survey, and 59 (79%) completed it. The survey asked teachers to rate the level of impact that course assignments and experiences had on their practice (low, moderate, low, no) and to provide specific examples in writing. In addition, eight teachers participated in follow up focus group interviews.

The study used a social theory of learning—Communities of Practice (CoP) (Lave & Wenger 1991, Wenger 1998)—as its theoretical framework. CoPs refer to groups of people who share a passion for something they do, and as they interact regularly, they learn how to do it better (Wenger-Trayner & Wenger-Trayner 2015). The CoP in this study was comprised of CBI teachers interacting and learning together within the online classes. They intentionally chose to learn together within the online community, sharing a passion for their work. According to Wenger (1998), The CoP includes four components: community (learning as belonging), practice (learning as doing), meaning (learning as experience), and identity (learning as becoming).

Although a complete description of the study is beyond the scope of this paper, the results related to the CoP components of practice and meaning showed that the assignments and experiences teachers perceive to have a positive impact on their ability to integrate language and content are those that:

1. are *meaningful*, relevant to teachers' practice
2. involve opportunities to give and receive *feedback*, to revise and further refine their work
3. involve *enactment* – opportunities for teachers to put into practice what they are learning
4. result in observable changes in student learning and language production
5. involve collaboration
6. include opportunities for *reflection*

Moreover, in the CoP realm of identity, Tedick & Zilmer identified five salient themes: intentionality, self-awareness/growth, empowerment, becoming a collaborator, and maintaining high expectations for student learning and language use and production. *Intentionality* reflected teachers' need to be deliberate about integrating language and content and to adopt an integrated identity. Related to this concept is *self-awareness and growth*. Teacher identify evolved as teachers became more language aware—able to write language objectives, integrate a focus on form in their lesson planning and assessment, and provide form-focused corrective feedback. Teachers pointed to learning concrete strategies that caused them to change their practices and ultimately led to a feeling of *empowerment*. They also emphasized how *becoming a collaborator* with other teachers contributed to their evolving identities. Finally, teacher identities shifted as they began to develop *high expectations for their learners* specifically related to language production. Tedick & Zilmer (2017) concluded that "Through participation in this CoP, where individual and group meanings are made, these teachers experience, shape, and adopt new identities that are informed by and that transform their practices" (np).

The study results imply that in order to help CBI teachers learn to integrate content and language, teacher educators need to develop experiences and assignments for teachers that are meaningful and relevant and that engage them in applying their understandings by enacting new practices in their classrooms—hopefully these will lead to observable improvements in student learning and language production that will encourage students to make the practices part of their instructional repertoire. Teachers need opportunities to collaborate with each other and to reflect on their learning; these components should be deliberately built into assignments and experiences. Importantly, teacher educators must spend time giving detailed and pointed feedback to teachers and allow them to revise and refine their work. It is through such experiences that CBI teachers adopt new identities and learn to embrace their dual role as content and language teachers.

5   CONCLUSION

CBI is a worthwhile endeavor. While there are many different types of CBI, at the heart of all types is content and language integration. Content and language must be integrated to enhance the language learning potential of CBI. CBI teachers need specific professional development opportunities to help them learn to integrate content and language in their instruction. Learning to integrate language and content takes a great deal of time, guided practice, and feedback. Professional development experiences should be meaningful and relevant, involve enactment (application of new concepts and strategies in practice), collaboration with other teachers, and ongoing feedback from instructors and peers. They should support reflection and involve self-awareness and growth so that CBI teachers' identities evolve over time in ways that encourage them to see themselves as both content and language teachers.

REFERENCES

Admiraal, W., Westhoff G. & de Bot, K. 2006. Evaluation of bilingual secondary education in the Netherlands: Students' language proficiency in English. *Educational Research and Evaluation: An International Journal on Theory and Practice* 12(1): 75–93.

Allen, P., Swain, M., Harley, B. & Cummins J. 1990. Aspects of classroom treatment: Toward a more comprehensive view of second language education. In B. Harley, P. Allen, J. Cummins, & M. Swain (eds.), *The development of second language proficiency*: 57–81. Cambridge: Cambridge University Press.

Brinton, D.M., Snow, M.A. & Wesche, M.B. 2003. *Content-based second language instruction* (Michigan Classics ed.). Ann Arbor, MI: University of Michigan Press.

Cammarata, L. & Tedick, D.J. 2012. Balancing content and language in instruction: The experience of immersion teachers. *Modern Language Journal* 96(2): 251–269. doi:10.1111/j.1540-4781.2012.01330.x

Cammarata, L., Tedick, D.J. & Osborn, T.A. 2016. Content-based instruction and curricular reforms. In L. Cammarata (ed.), *Content-based foreign language teaching: Curriculum and pedagogy for developing advanced thinking and literacy skills*: 1–21. NY: Routledge.

Center for Applied Language Studies. 2011. *What levels of proficiency do immersion students achieve?* Eugene, OR: University of Oregon.

Council of Europe. 2017. *Common European Framework of Reference for Languages.* Retrieved from http://www.coe.int/en/web/common-european-framework-reference-languages/.

Coyle, D. 2011. Post-method pedagogies: Using a second or other language as a learning tool in CLIL settings. In Y. Ruiz de Zarobe, J. Sierra & F. Gallardo (eds.) *Content and foreign language integrated learning: Contributions to multilingualism in European contexts*: 49–73. Bern: Peter Lang.

Dalton-Puffer, C. 2007. *Discourse in content and language integrated learning (CLIL) classrooms.* Amsterdam: John Benjamins.

Day, E.M. & Shapson, S. 1996. Studies in immersion education. Clevedon: Multilingual Matters.

Fortune, T.W., Tedick, D.J. & Walker, C.L. 2008. Integrated language and content teaching: Insights from the language immersion classroom. In T.W. Fortune & D.J. Tedick (eds.). *Pathways to multilingualism: Evolving perspectives on immersion education*: 71–96. Clevedon: Multilingual Matters.

Genesee, F. 1987. *Learning through two languages: Studies of immersion and bilingual education.* Cambridge, MA: Newbury House.

Gibbons, P. 2015. *Scaffolding language, scaffolding learning: Teaching English language learners in the mainstream classroom* (2nd ed.). Portsmouth, NH: Heinemann.

Harley, B., Cummins, J., Swain, M. & Allen, P. 1990. The nature of language proficiency. In B. Harley, P. Allen, J. Cummins & M. Swain (eds.), *The development of second language proficiency*: 7–25). Cambridge: Cambridge University Press.

Kautz, E. 2016. Exploring environmental and sustainability issues in the intermediate-level foreign language curriculum. In L. Cammarata (ed.), *Content-based foreign language teaching: Curriculum and pedagogy for developing advanced thinking and literacy skills*: 234–249. NY: Routledge.

Kennedy, T.J. 2006. Language learning and its impact on the brain: Connecting language learning with the mind through content-based instruction. *Foreign Language Annals* 39(3): 471–486.

Kong, S. & Hoare, P. 2011. Cognitive content engagement in content-based language teaching. *Language Teaching Research* 15(3): 307–324.

Lave, J. & Wenger, E. 1991. *Situated learning: Legitimate peripheral participation.* Cambridge: Cambridge University Press.

Lightbown, P. 2014. *Focus on content-based language teaching.* Oxford: Oxford University Press.

Lightbown, P. & Spada, N. 2013. *How languages are learned* (4th ed.). Oxford: Oxford University Press.

Lyster, R. 2004. Differential effects of prompts and recasts in form-focused instruction. *Studies in Second Language Acquisition* 26: 399–432.

Lyster, R. 2007. *Learning and teaching languages through content: A counterbalanced approach.* Amsterdam: John Benjamins.

Lyster, R. 2016. *Vers une approche intégrée en immersion* [Towards an integrated approach in immersion]. Montréal: Les Éditions CEC.

Lyster, R. & Ranta, L. 1997. Corrective feedback and learner uptake: Negotiation of form in communicative classrooms. *Studies in Second Language Acquisition* 19: 37–66.

Lyster, R. & Tedick, D.J. 2014. Research perspectives on immersion pedagogy: Looking back and looking forward. *Journal of Immersion and Content-Based Language Education* 2(2): 210–224.

Met, M. 1999. *Content-based instruction: Defining terms, making decisions.* Washington, DC: The National Foreign Language Center.

Nassaji, H. & Fotos, S. 2011. *Teaching grammar in second language classrooms: Integrating form-focused instruction in communicative context.* NY: Routledge.

Pessoa, S. Hendry, H., Donato, R., Tucker, G.R., & Lee, H. 2007. Content-based instruction in the foreign language classroom: A discourse perspective. *Foreign Language Annals* 40(1): 102–121.

Snow, M.A. 2001. Content-based and immersion models for second and foreign language teaching. In M. Celce-Murcia (ed.), *Teaching English as a second or foreign language* (3rd ed.): 303–318. Boston: Heinle & Heinle.

Swain, M., Kinnear, P. & Steinman, L. 2015.*Sociocultural theory in second language education: An introduction through narratives* (2nd ed.). Bristol: Multilingual Matters.

Tan, M. 2011. Mathematics and science teachers' beliefs and practices regarding the teaching of language in content learning. *Language Teaching Research* 15: 325–342.

Tedick, D.J. & Cammarata, L. 2012. Content and language integration in K–12 contexts: Student outcomes, teacher practices and stakeholder perspectives. *Foreign Language Annals* 45(1): S8–S53. doi: 10.1111/j.1944–9720.2012.01178.x

Tedick, D.J. & Fortune, T.W. 2013. Bilingual/immersion teacher education. In C.A. Chapelle (ed.), *The Encyclopedia of Applied Linguistics*: 438–443. Hoboken, NJ: Wiley-Blackwell. doi: 10.1002/9781405198431.wbeal0096.

Tedick, D.J. & Young, A.I. 2016. Fifth grade two-way immersion students' responses to form-focused instruction. *Applied Linguistics* 37(6): 784–807. doi: 10.1093/applin/amu066.

Tedick, D.J. & Zilmer, C. 2017. *Teacher perceptions of immersion professional development experiences focused on language and content integration.* Manuscript under review.

Verspoor, M., de Bot, K. & Xu, X. 2015. The effects of English bilingual education in The Netherlands. *Journal of Immersion and Content-Based Language Education* 3(1): 4–27.

Vygotsky, L. 1986. *Thought and language* (rev. ed.). Cambridge, MA: The M.I.T. Press.

Wenger, E. 1998. *Communities of Practice: Learning, meaning, and identity*. Cambridge: Cambridge University Press.

Wenger-Trayner, E. & Wenger-Trayner, B. 2015. Communities of practice: A brief introduction. Retrieved from http://wenger-trayner.com/wp-content/uploads/2015/04/07-Brief-introduction-to-communities-of-practice.pdf.

ELT in Asia in the Digital Era: Global Citizenship and Identity – Madya et al. (Eds)
© 2018 Taylor & Francis Group, London, ISBN 978-0-8153-7900-3

Sustainable professional development programs for English teachers: A case study in South Sulawesi, Indonesia

A. Abduh
Universitas Negeri Makassar, South Sulawesi, Indonesia

R. Rosmaladewi
Politeknik Pertanian Negeri Pangkep, South Sulawesi, Indonesia

ABSTRACT: The goal of this paper is to explore teachers' perception on a more sustainable model of professional development programs for English teachers. A case study research was used in this research which was conducted in South Sulawesi, Indonesia. Multiple methods of data collection were used including Likert-scale questionnaire and interviews. 30 participants completed the online questionnaire and five of them were interviewed to further explore their perceptions of sustainable professional development. The analysis of questionnaire was assisted by Ms excel and the interview data were coded through thematic data analysis. The findings revealed that five sustainable professional development programs were on-going mentoring, gain a degree, series of practical workshop, teachers' exchange program, and bottom up teacher' association program. The implication is that it is essential for the government and educational stakeholders to consider a sustainable professional development program as a way to improve teachers' knowledge and skills that result in improving the quality of teaching and learning.

1   INTRODUCTION

The aim of this paper is to explore English teachers' perceptions of sustainable model of professional development programs. Professional development of English teachers in Indonesia has become the central issue nowadays especially in relation to the lack of many trained and knowledgeable English teachers who teach in primary schools. As found in two studies (Wati 2011, Yuwono 2005), the professional development programs through short workshops, short periods of teacher training and in-site training have failed to improve the quality of English teachers. The research concluded that there are some serious problems in terms of improving teachers' quality in Indonesia; a) unbalanced educational training programs from elementary school level to high school level; b) ineffectiveness of training; c) different concept of what teachers got from training is different from what they applied in the class (Wati 2011, Yuwono 2005). Besides, many of the English teachers who teach in primary schools do not graduate from the English Education study program and this means that they are less trained to teach English (Rosmaladewi 2017) and bring little impact on quality teaching and learning (Widodo et al. 2009). For these reasons, professional development issues are important to be explored.

The professional development of English teachers in Indonesian context has been significantly under researched, particularly in the South Sulawesi contexts. Up until now there has been very little in-depth research that describes the model of sustainable professional programs, how they are implemented and what model of evaluation is used. Therefore, this research study aimed to provide models of sustainable professional development programs for English teachers in Indonesian primary and secondary education. The question to be answered was: What are the English teachers' perceptions on effective and sustainable professional development for primary school teachers?

2 SUSTAINABLE PROFESSIONAL DEVELOPMENT

Bymes (2007) proposed five aspects for sustainable teachers professional development programs: 1) the major objective is to understand systems and the integration of ecology, economics, and societal frameworks that influence teachers' practices; 2) the program creates teams to solve 'real-life' problems; 3) participants also play an active part in managing problems relating to their teaching practices; 4) participants also interviewed educational stakeholders; 5) another objective is to improve English language proficiency for all participants by speaking, reading, and writing English throughout the program.

Shulman (1987) pointed out that it is the subject matter knowledge and the associated pedagogical content knowledge that hold real challenges for teachers who must learn about an innovation and somehow convert their new knowledge into a pedagogical form. He also identifies the disequilibrium that happen to all teacher professional knowledge by the introduction of new ideas and changes in beliefs and practices.

A number of research studies on teachers' professional development were conducted during the last four decades as generic guides for teacher change processes. For example, Sparks & Loucks-Horsley (1989) suggest five models that are useful for accomplishing the goals of staff development. Cook & Rasmussen (1994) designed the effective professional development model for identifying, understanding, planning, carrying out, and evaluating change. Meyers & Salter (2007) identified elements of sustainable professional development as follows: a) flexibility; b) modularized units of study; c) combination of self-directed/paced and collaborative elements; d) utilisation of online tools; e) reduction of isolation; f) relevance to immediate work; and g) task based learning.

Elliot, Macpherson & McLaughlin (2005) urged that while there is increasing interest in the professional development of all educators there is no one approach that seems to have been very successful. In fact, Borko (2004) claimed that approaches are generally fragmented, intellectually superficial, and do not take into account what we know about how teachers learn. The recent research suggests that the majority of teachers need longer and sustainable professional programs (Wati 2011). The model is believed to be one of the effective ways to improve basic English knowledge as the most important aspect for being effective English teachers. Therefore, the goal of the research is to explore teachers' perception on a more sustainable model of professional development programs for English teachers in South Sulawesi, Indonesia.

3 RESEARCH METHOD

A case study research is adopted in this research. Creswell (2012) defined that case study offers the study of the phenomenon in its natural context. The phenomenon in the research was sustainable professional development programs for English teachers. Multiple methods of data collection were used including Likert-scale questionnaire and interviews. The questionnaire contained ten items that was sent through online survey monkey to 50 teachers who teach English from primary to secondary schools in South Sulawesi. However, only 30 participants completed the online questionnaire.

From the total participants, five participants were chosen purposively to be interviewed. The interview questions relate to their perceptions of sustainable models for teachers' professional development. There were three reasons of choosing these five participants: a) they have been teaching English for more than five years; b) they were representative of teachers in three areas: urban, suburb and village areas; c) they provided consent to be interviewed by researchers.

The analysis of questionnaire was assisted by Ms excel and the interview data were coded through thematic data analysis (Gall et al. 2007). The data from interviews were coded thematically based themes from questionnaire, with P1, P2, P3, P4, and P5 (Participant 1, 2, 3, 4, 5).

4 FINDINGS

The findings show that there were five programs of sustainable professional development (Figure 1). They were on-going mentoring, gain a degree, series of practical workshop, teachers' exchange program, and bottom up teacher' association program.

4.1 *Bottom up teachers' association programs*

Button up teachers' association programs are the professional development programs that are initiated and created by teachers at school levels, not the government programs. The majority of participants in this study believe that bottom up teachers' association programs can be one of the sustainable professional development programs. It can be sustainable if it is proposed and designed by teachers themselves that meet their demands. There were three reasons why button up teachers association programs important for teachers: 1) "It gives example how to use technology in teaching" (P1); 2) "It gives me more information about new curriculum" (P2); and 3) "Skills and new information are found in PD, and the skills include the way we create a method in teaching in our class, the information is such as like the use of other technology in teaching in the class" (P3).

4.2 *A series of workshops*

The series of workshops can be very sustainable when it fulfills current future needs of teachers. The reasons why such a series of workshops can be effective for PD because it provided relevant knowledge for teachers, as supported by a participant: "Because the workshop is relevant with my profession that's why it provides new skill for me" (P1). Similarly, workshops can include teaching methodology and skills needed in workplace. These were commented on by two participants: "I get much information from PD like how to teach the students well" (P5), and "The workshop can improve knowledge and skills that can be implemented at workplace" (P2).

4.3 *A degree program*

A degree program can also be effective to enhance teachers' motivation for continuous learning. A degree program can encourage teachers' motivation when it deals with the financial incentives or financial factors for teachers. In this case, teachers may gain promotion after

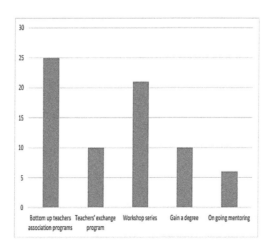

Figure 1. Teachers' perception of sustainable professional development.

receiving their degree. This can result in the increase of teachers' income. A degree is important because it "encouraged teachers to think critically" (P5), and it can "make us self-confident, honest, improve our attitude, act" (P4). In a degree program, teachers can engage and learn a variety of skills such as classroom management and using media for teaching. This was commented on by one participant: "of course that a degree provides me with new skill and information. Through PD we learn many things, especially it relates to how to teach in the class, how to use media, method, and how to manage the classroom (P1).

4.4 *Ongoing mentoring*

Mentoring can be very effective and sustainable under two conditions: a) it provides clear guidelines of the roles of mentor and mentee; b) it is based on the interests of both mentor and mentee. One participant commented: "Mentoring is a friendly mode of sustainable professional development if both parties (mentor and mentee) have the same goals and provide guidelines" (P1). The advantages of mentoring are: "It gives the way and technique to handle students in managing classroom and to train me in the improvement of teaching in a daily basis" (P5); "It provides the ways to utilise materials for teaching" (P4), and "We can share everything about teaching. Automatically our knowledge can improve about how to give the students understanding about teaching material" (P2).

4.5 *Teachers' Exchange Program (TEP)*

TEP can be sustainable under three conditions: a) It should be based on the interests of two institutions; b) it is organized at the school level; and c) it is partially funded by the government. The benefits of TEP are: 1) it provides opportunities for teachers to "witness the best practice in the field" (P4); 2) it "provides chances to share knowledge with other teachers, establish good networking, and experience living within different cultural setting" (P2), and 4) it "can be part of a life time experience in teaching" (P3).

5 DISCUSSION

The context of the study is the sustainable teachers' professional development from primary to secondary schools. The findings of this study further extend Bymes (2007) and Meyers & Salter's (2007) notions on sustainable models of professional development programs for teachers.

The findings add what Bymes (2007) indicated that sustainable professional development provide opportunities for teachers to solve their practical problems through series of workshop and degree programs. In addition, sustainable professional development enables teachers to improve their skills and knowledge that support them to be effective and sustainable teachers in their profession.

The findings in this study also further extend Meyers & Salter's (2007) elements of sustainable professional developments particularly collaborative features. The collaborative elements include bottom up programs that were initiated by teachers at schools and ongoing teacher mentoring programs. These sustainable programs have strong relevance to teachers' roles and responsibilities at schools.

6 CONCLUSION AND RECOMMENDATIONS

It appears from the findings that sustainable teachers' professional development programs vary according to the contexts and the needs of teachers. Sustainable teachers' professional development programs include on-going mentoring, gain a degree, series of practical workshop, teachers' exchange program, and bottom up teacher' association program. Teachers may choose the appropriate options based on their interests and problems they face in practice.

It is recommended that the five sustainable teachers' professional development programs identified in this research can become a guideline for professional development practices, researchers, and trainers. It is also significant for knowledge development and the debate on teachers' professional development. It is suggested that findings can be a resource for professional practice on teachers' development and change for sustainable education.

REFERENCES

Bymes, L. 2007. Swiss International teachers programs in *good practices in education for sustainable development: teacher education institution.* Paris: UNESCO.

Borko, H. 2004. Professional development and teacher learning: Mapping the terrain. *Educational Researcher* 33(8): 3–15.

Creswell, J.W. 2012. *Educational research: Planning, conducting, and evaluating quantitative and qualitative research. Educational Research. New.* California: Sage Publication.

Cook, C. & Rasmussen, C. 1994. *Framework for designing effective professional development: Change-based inquiry process.* Oak Brook, IL: North Central Regional Educational Laboratory.

Elliott, R., Lucas, B., Stewart, E. & Burke, C. 1998. Authenticating a model for sustainable professional development in an international context. *International Journal of Educational Development* 18(2): 119–131.

Elliott, B., Macpherson, I. & McLangliughlin, J. 2005. *Empowering curriculum thinkers and transforming curriculum sites: a need for a hand-in-hand approach.* Paper presented National Curriculum Reform Conference July 13th – 15th 2005 'Sustainable curriculum development – the PNG curriculum reform experience' PNG.

Gall, J.P., Gall, M.D. & Borg, W.R. 2007. *Applying educational research: a practical guide.* Boston: Pearson Education Inc.

Gay, L.R., Mills, G.E. & Airasian, P. 2006. *Educational research: competencies for analysis and applications.* Ohio: Pearson Merrill Prentice Hall.

Meyers, W. & Salter, D. 2007. E-teaching professional development: Designing a sustainable program for multi-location teachers. *In ICT: Providing choices for learners and learning. Proceedings ascilite Singapore 2007.* http://www.ascilite.org.au/conferences/singapore07/procs/meyersposter.pdf.

Rosmaladewi, R. 2017. English language teaching at Makassar primary schools: a case study. *International Journal of Language Education* 1(2): 29–37. Retrieved from http://ojs.unm.ac.id/index.php/ijole/article/view/4312.

Shulman, L.S. 1987. Knowledge and teaching: Foundations of the new reform. *Harvard Educational Review* 57(1): 1–22.

Sparks, D. & Loucks-Horsley, S. 1989. Five models of staff development for teachers. *Journal of Staff Development* 10(4): 40–57.

Wati, H. 2011. The effectiveness of Indonesian English teachers training programs in improving confidence and motivation. *International Journal of Instruction* 4(1): 79–104.

Widodo, A. Riandi & Hana, M.N. 2009. *Dual mode in-service training: An alternative model for teachers' professional development (PD) in Indonesia.* Proceedings of the third International Seminar on Science Education, Bandung, 17 October 2009.

Yin, R.K. 1994. *Case study research: design and method.* Second Edition. California: Sage Publication.

Yuwono, G. 2005. *English language teaching in decentralized Indonesia: Voices from the less privileged schools.* Paper presented at AARE 2005 International Education Research Conference, Sydney Australia, 27 November – 1 December 2015.

ELT in Asia in the Digital Era: Global Citizenship and Identity – Madya et al. (Eds)
© 2018 Taylor & Francis Group, London, ISBN 978-0-8153-7900-3

Teacher efficacy in instructional strategies in classroom among tertiary teachers in Central Java, Indonesia

Muamaroh
Universitas Muhammadiyah Surakarta, Surakarta, Indonesia

ABSTRACT: The present study investigates teacher efficacy in applying instructional strategies among tertiary teachers in Indonesia. The participants were seventy-nine teachers from seven universities in Central Java Indonesia. This study used descriptive design using a quantitative analysis. Questionnaire was used to elicit the data of the study. Descriptive statistics, T-test and ANOVA were applied to analyze the quantitative data of the study. It was found that teacher efficacy in instructional strategies among tertiary teachers based on gender, age, teaching experience, educational background, and teacher's place of work or institution is different based on the results of descriptive statistics analysis. However, those differences were not significant based on the results of T-test and ANOVA with the exception of differences in ages. Its significant was sig = 0.018 based on ANOVA (F = 3.569) statistical analysis.

1 INTRODUCTION

The role of teachers at English language classrooms is important in particular at tertiary education levels (Halim, 2011, p. 103). For instance, since English is hardly spoken in daily basis in Indonesia, English teachers play very important roles as models in conversation or speaking class.

Traditional teaching methods have been applied in most of English classes in Indonesia until now. A study by Supriadi (as cited in Lie, 2007) shows that the majority of teachers use textbooks heavily and thus the teaching and learning depends on textbooks. In addition, teaching tends to be teacher-centered, placing teachers as the only persons who are actively talk in the class while students just listen to them passively and they talk only when they are asked by their teachers (Noel: 2008, p. 80). Other studies (e.g., Martani, 1996; White, 1997; Koesoema, 2009) found that many Indonesian teachers of English still use traditional teaching methods and they are mostly teacher-centered with too much lecturing.

Nowadays however, Indonesian teachers are expected to have a high degree of teacher competences. The act of Republic of Indonesian Number 14/2005 on teachers and lecturers stipulates teachers to have four competences including pedagogical, professional, social, and personality competence. Pedagogical competence covers the ability to understand students, design and process of learning, evaluation, and students' progress. Personality competence covers teachers' personality such as dispassionate, mature, and responsible. Teachers should show good examples for students to have good attitude and behavior. Professional competence covers the mastery of curriculum, syllabus, materials, basic concepts and structures of scientific knowledge. Social competence covers teacher's capability to communicate effectively with students, teachers, parents and members of society.

On the basis of the Indonesian education act above, teachers should have excellent instructional strategies to help students develop their knowledge or competence. In fact, the mastery of instructional strategies is an indispensable component of teachers' pedagogical competence. However, many English teachers in Indonesia still experience difficulties to develop their pedagogical and professional competence. As reported by NCES (cited in de Jong and

Harper, 2005), 42% of English teachers had English Language Learners (ELLs), but only 12% had received more than eight hours of professional development specifically related to ELLs. A similar finding was reported by Muamaroh (2016) that English teachers in Indonesia still lacked professional training to improve their pedagogical competence in particular the abilities to employ and innovate teaching methodologies.

Although there are some supports from Indonesian government to improve their competence, they are different from that of other countries such as Australia, the neighboring country. Australia has systematically monitored arrangements of teaching procedures, and easier accessible supplementary materials. Even teachers in Australia can access online teaching resources easily such as books, plays and poetry (Jenkinson, 2015). Australian education supports teachers for broad-based skills: skills of creative problem solving, independent learning, and critical thinking alongside understanding of the effectiveness of group endeavor and appreciation of cultural differences (Power et al., 2007).

It does not mean at all that the Indonesian government has not provided enough supports to improve the quality of English teaching. The innovation and development of national curriculum is one of the efforts to improve it. The newest curriculum enforced in 2013 named as K 13 uses scientific approaches as the teaching and learning strategies that mainly adopt student centered approach. The Indonesian government also has provided financial support for improving teacher quality. For example, the National Education Act No. 20/2003 states that the Indonesian government is mandated to allocate 20 percent of the annual state expenditure for education. This has been allocated for education strategic plan since 2005 focusing on three strategic issues: (1) increasing more access to education, (2) improving education quality, and (3) achieving better governance (World Bank Group, 2011).

It is generally assumed that a teacher's behavior in class is likely to be influenced by his/ her perceived sense of efficacy and belief that what he/she does in the class will be successful (Palmer and Collins, 2006). Bandura (2006) stated that self-efficacy is concerned with perceived capability. Bandura (1997) in Tschannen-Moran and Hoy (2001) defined perceived self-efficacy as "beliefs in one's capabilities to organize and execute the courses of action required to produce given attainments". Moreover according to Hoy (2000 in Protheroe, 2008) stated that "Teacher efficacy is" teachers' confidence in their ability to promote students' learning. Teacher sense of efficacy means a teacher's sense of competence (Protheroe, 2008). According to Tschannen-Moran and Hoy (2001) teachers' sense of efficacy had a strong positive relation to student performance, to the percent of objective to achieve, to the use of methods and materials and to the amount of teacher change.

A teacher who has high teacher efficacy can enfluence their students efficacy to succeed in their study. The study by Guskey and Passaro (1994) found that students tend to have high learning motivation and high self-efficacy when their teacher also has high teacher efficacy. Some studies show that a teacher who has a higher sense of efficacy demonstrate not only greater enthusiasm for teaching (Allinder, 1994; Guskey, 1984; Hall, Burley, Villeme, & Brockmeier, 1992 in Tschannen-Moran and Hoy, 2001) but also greater commitment for teaching (Coladarci, 1992; Evans & Tribble, 1986; Trentham, Silvern, & Brogdon,1985 in Tschannen-Moran and Hoy, 2001) and they are more likely to stay in teaching (Burley, Hall, Villeme, & Brockmeier, 1991; Glickman & Tamashiro, 1982 in Tschannen-Moran and Hoy, 2001).

However, in some cases, a teacher can affect whether students would be successful in learning a foreign language. For instance, a study by Muamaroh (2013) found that one of the factors that could discourage students' confidence in speaking English was their teachers. Some students participated in her study reported that their teacher's facial expression could affect their confidence positively or negatively. Importantly, teachers' efficacy influences not only students but also the teachers' satisfaction towards their own work. The teachers' belief in their abilities to positively motivate students' learning is critical to the success or failure in the teachers' behavior (Henson in Protheroe, 2008). For example, a study by Wibowo and Brahma (2013) indicated a strong correlation between teacher efficacy and their work satisfaction. A study conducted by Gkolia et al. (2014) found that teachers' job satisfaction had a positive influence on teachers' efficacy. However, Shaukat et al. (2013) reported that there was no correlation between teachers' attitudes and self-efficacy towards inclusive education.

There have been very limited studies that have addressed the self-efficacy of pre-service teachers who will work for students with special needs (Hsien, 2007). In addition, Pendergast et al. (2011) claimed that there has been very limited research that has observed self-efficacy beliefs and identity construction of pre-service teachers when they take teacher training. The following are few studies that have investigated teacher efficacy. A study by Abu-Tineh et al. (2011) focused on teacher self-efficacy and classroom management styles. The participants were Jordanian teachers. The research used a survey design. A study by Sridhar and Javan (2011) focused on the efficacy of secondary school teachers. The participants were teachers in Kigali city, Rwanda. The instrument of the study was questionnaire. In Indonesian context, research on the self-efficacy is also very limited, particularly the one that concerns pre-service teachers or experienced teachers who have taught years at tertiary levels. For instance, a study by Wibowo and Brahma (2013) focused on inclusion class teachers at elementary school. The participants were 77 inclusion elementary school teachers in five cities in West Java Indonesia (Jakarta, Bogor, Depok, Tangerang, and Bekasi). The instrument to elicit the data was questionnaires of Job Satisfaction Survey (JSS) developed by Spector in Wibowo and Brahma (2013). They also used a modified questionnaire of teacher efficacy scale based on Winafaisal (2010 in Wibowo and Brahma (2013). Research that has ever addressed teacher efficacy on teaching English as a foreign language is limited too. The present study was meant to fill in the gap. It examined teacher efficacy at a tertiary education level or university in Central Java, Indonesia.

The present study focused on teacher efficacy in instructional strategies at a tertiary education level. The study explored the effects of some variables such as gender, age, teaching experiences, teacher's background of study, and teacher's institution on teacher efficacy. The participants were lecturers from two state universities and five private universities in Central Java Indonesia. The instruments used to gather data were questionnaire developed based on Tschannen-Moran and Hoy (2001).

2 RESEARCH METHOD

The participants of this study were English lecturers at the Department of English of two state universities and five private universities in Central Java, Indonesia. Seventy-nine (79) lecturers from the seven universities filled in a close questionnaire in the form of Teachers' Sense of Efficacy Scale (TSES) developed by Tschannen-Moran and Hoy (2001) which is sometimes recognized as the Ohio State Teacher Efficacy Scale (OSTES). For the purpose of this study, long form type of the TSES questionnaire was used. Because it is appropriate with the objectives of this study. This instrument covers teacher efficacy in student engagement, instructional strategies, and classroom management. Those three factors are important in the English language classroom. This supported a study by Zheng (2010) who found that the learning situation was one of the strong indicators of motivation which affected language achievement and confidence. Taha & Ming (2014) found that the learning environment is an influencing factor in learning, besides the individual learners' behaviors.

There were 24 items for Teacher's sense of efficacy scale to be filled in by the research participants. A Likert-type scale with nine possible responses (1–9) to each item of the questionnaire was used. The scale ranged from (1), that is for "None at all" to (9) that is for "agreat deal", thus each number in the scale represented a degree on the continuum. The questionnaire of the Teacher Efficacy Scale was written in English since the participants were English teachers. Descriptive statistics was employed to test whether variables such as gender, age, teaching experiences, teacher's background of study, and teacher's institution influence teacher efficacy. T-test was also used to observe whether there are some significant differences between two variables, while ANOVA was used to observe whether there are some significant differences among the variables.

3 FINDINGS AND DISCUSSION

3.1 *Teacher efficacy in instructional strategy based on gender*

The study revealed that male teachers used instructional strategies more effectively (mean = 59.10) than female teachers (mean = 57.75) based on descriptive statistics analysis. Although based on T-test (t = 0,723) the difference was not significant (sig = 0,473).

3.2 *Teacher efficacy in instructional strategy based on age*

Based on descriptive statistics analysis, teachers who were more than fifty-one years employed instructional strategies more effectively than those who were thirty-one to forty years (mean = 58.37), twenty to thirty years (mean = 56.47) and forty-one to fifty years (mean 55.55). This difference was significant (sig = 0.018) based on ANOVA (F = 3.569).

3.3 *Teacher efficacy in instructional strategy based on teaching experience*

Teachers whose teaching experiences were more than twenty-one years employed instructional strategies (mean = 59.50) more efficiently than those with eleven to twenty years (mean = 57.47) and those with one to ten years (mean = 57.26) based on descriptive statistics analysis. Although the difference was not significant (sig = 0.650) using ANOVA (F = 0.434) analysis.

3.4 *Teacher efficacy in instructional strategy based on teacher's background of study*

In view of descriptive statistics analysis, it revealed teachers with doctorate degrees used instructional strategies more effectively (mean = 59.92) than those with master's degrees (mean = 58.06). Teachers who graduated from overseas universities used instructional strategies (mean = 59.17) more efficiently than those from domestic universities (mean = 57.34). Even though the difference was not significant (sig = 0.283) using T-test (t = −1.082).

3.5 *Teacher efficacy in instructional strategy based on teacher's institution*

In relation to teachers' institutions, teachers who taught at private universities used instructional strategies (mean = 58.02) more effectively than those at state universities (mean = 56.76). Despite the facts however, the results of T-test (t = 0.675), its difference is not significant (sig = 0.502).

All variables which analyzed using descriptive statistics (Table 1), T-test and ANOVA (Table 2) are in the following:

The current study investigated the teacher efficacy in instructional strategy at tertiary level in Indonesian context. The result of this study agrees with the finding from the study by Sridhar and Javan (2011) who found that male teachers have higher levels on management than female teachers. However, their study focused on classroom management while the current study related to instructional strategy. Based on T-test (t = 0,723), this study found that differences in gender did not significantly influence teacher efficacy (sig = 0,473). This supported the study by Martin et al. (1997) that no significant differences were found between male and female teachers regarding their attitudes and beliefs on classroom control.

However, teachers' teaching experiences influenced their efficacy in instructional strategy. The more teaching experiences the teachers have, the more efficient they are. This suggests that the length of teaching experience has strong connection with their confidence and thus this improved their efficacy. For example, teachers whose teaching experiences were more than twenty years had the highest scores in the use of instructional strategies. This result of this study is in line with Kissau and Algozzine (2014) who found that to become confident in teaching, teacher candidates need more opportunities in their coursework.

The result of this current study also supports Ghaslani's (2015) finding that teachers' self-efficacy had negative correlation with burnout and differences in some variables such

Table 1. Descriptive statistics.

Aspect	Category	Mean	Standard deviation	Number of people
Gender	Male	59.10	6.569	20
	Female	57.75	6.942	40
Age	20–30 years	56.47	5.055	15
	31–40 years	58.37	6.499	35
	41–50 years	55.55	7.418	22
	51 years and more	64.29	5.187	7
Teaching experience	0–10 years	57.26	4.859	35
	11–20 years	57.47	7.552	32
	21 years and more	59.50	9.992	10
Degree	S2	58.06	6.584	52
	S3	59.92	7.643	13
Educational background	Domestic university	57.34	6.660	50
	Overseas university	59.17	7.081	24
Institution	Private	58.02	6.713	62
	State	56.76	7.005	17

Table 2. T-test and ANOVA.

Aspect	Category	T-test/ANOVA	Significant
Gender	Male	$t = 0.723$	sig = 0.473
	Female		
Age	20–30 years	$F = 3.569$	sig = 0.018*
	31–40 years		
	41–50 years		
	51 years and more		
Teaching experience	0–10 years	$F = 0.434$	sig = 0.650
	11–20 years		
	21 years and more		
Degree	S2	$t = -0.885$	sig = 0.380
	S3		
Educational background	Domestic university	$t = -1.082$	sig = 0.283
	Overseas university		
Institution	Private	$t = 0.675$	sig = 0.502
	State		

*Significantly different.

as academic degree, years of experience and age levels. Furthermore, the result of this study also agrees with the study by Pendergast et al. (2011) who found that characteristics of age, program and gender were not systematically related to the self-efficacy of pre-service teachers. However, there was a significant difference in teachers' level of burnout with respect to their gender. This study found that, based on gender, the differences between male and female teacher efficacy in instructional strategies were not significantly observed (sig = 0,473) based on T-test (t = 0,723). The different might be because this study focused on instructional strategy while Ghaslani's (2015) focused on teachers' self-efficacy in correlation with burnout. The result of this study supported Abolhasanpour (2016) who found that knowledge of teaching/learning context contributed to teachers' sense of efficacy. However, the finding of this study was different from the result of the study by Kurt (2016) that found that distributed leadership directly affected teacher leadership and indirectly affected organizational learning and self-efficacy perception of teachers. This could be because the studies focused on different variables.

4 CONCLUSION

This study had added to the existing literature about teacher efficacy in instructional strategies in Indonesian context. In view on descriptive statistics analysis, it was found that teacher efficacy in instructional strategies based on gender, age, teaching experience, educational background, and teacher's place of work or institution is different. However, those differences were not significant based on the results of T-test and ANOVA with the exception of differences in ages. Its significant was sig = 0.018 based on ANOVA (F = 3.569) statistical analysis.

REFERENCES

Abolhasanpour, F. 2016. Pedagogical knowledge, sense of efficacy, language efficacy and their relationship: a study of Iranian EFL teachers. *Modern Journal of Language Teaching Methods (MJLTM)* 6(4): 477.

Abu-Tineh, A.M., Khasawneh, S.A. & Khalaileh, H.A. 2011. Teacher self-efficacy and classroom management styles in Jordanian schools. *Management in Education* 25(4): 175–181. doi: 10.1177/0892020611420597.

Bandura, A. 2006. Guide for Constructing Self-Efficacy Scales. *Self-Efficacy Beliefs of Adolescents,* 307–337.

De Jong, E.J. & Harper, C.A. 2005. Preparing Mainstream Teachers for English-Language Learners: Is Being a Good Teacher *Good Enough? Teacher Education Quarterly* 32(2): 101–124 spring. Retrieved from: https://eric.ed.gov/?id=EJ795308.

Ghaslani, R. 2015. The relationship between Iranian EFL teachers' self efficacy and burnout and possible differences with respect to demographic variables. *Modern Journal of Language Teaching Methods* 5(3): 164.

Gkolia, A., Belias, D. & Koustelios, A. 2014. Teacher's Job Satisfaction and Self- Efficacy:A Review. *European Scientific Journal August* 10(22). Retrieved from: http://eujournal.org/index.php/esj/article/viewFile/3923/371.

Guskey, T.R & Passaro, P.D. 1994. Teacher efficacy: A study of construct dimensions. *American Educational Research Journal*, 31, 627–643

Halim, T. 2011. Teacher Certification in Indonesia. *International Journal on Social Science, Economics and Art* 1(2): 103–106. Proceeding of the International Conference on Social Science, Economics and Art 2011. Retrieved from: http://ijssea.insightsociety.org.

Hsien, M. 2007.Teacher attitudes towards preparation for inclusion – in support of a unifiedteacher preparation program. *Postgraduate Journal of Education Research* 8(1): 49–60. Retrieved from: http://www.edfac.unimelb.edu.au/research/resources/student_res/pscript_past.html.

Jenkinson, P. 2015. *Discover online teacher resources that help bring Australian stories to life.* Retrieved from: http://search.proquest.com/docview/1764658588/fulltextPDF/53D737E4F7604389PQ/3?accountid=34598.

Kissau, S. & Algozzine, B. 2014. The impact of mode of instructional delivery on second language teacher self-efficacy. *ReCALL* 27(2): 239–256. doi:10.1017/S0958344014000391.

Koesoema, A.D. 2009. *Pendidik Karakter di Zaman Keblinger: Mengembangkan Visi Guru SebagaiPelaku-PerubahandanPendidikKarakter*. Jakarta: Grasindo.

Kurt, T. 2016. A Model to Explain Teacher Leadership: The Effects of Distributed Leadership Model, Organizational Learning and Teachers' Sense of Self-Efficacy on Teacher Leadership. *Education and Science* 41(183): 1–28.

Lie, A. 2007. Education Policy and EFL Curriculum in Indonesia: Between the Commitment to Competence and the Quest for Higher Test Scores. *TEFLIN Journal* 18(1). Retrieved from: http://journal.teflin.org/index.php/teflin/article/viewFile/113/102.

Martani, J.Y. 1996. *Directions for Reform: Perceptions of Indonesian Students towards English Language Curricula.* Retrieved from: http://scholarworks.umass.edu/dissertations/AAI9709625.

Martin, N.K., Yin, Z. & Baldwin, B. 1997. *Attitudes and beliefs regarding classroom management style: Differences between male and female, urban and rural secondary level teachers.* Paper presented at the annual meeting of the American Educational Research Association, Chicago, II.

Tschannen-Moran, M. & Hoy, A.W. 2001 'Teacher efficacy: Capturing an elusive construct' Teaching and Teacher Education 17(7): 783–805.

Muamaroh. 2013. *Improving Indonesian university students' spoken English using group work and cooperative learning.* Dissertation, Charles Darwin University Australia. Retrieved from: https://espace.cdu.edu.au/eserv/cdu:38908/Thesis_CDU_38908_Muamaroh_A.pdf.

Muamaroh. 2016. Why are students reluctant to converse in their speaking class? Proceedings. *The 63nd TEFLIN International Conference 2016*. University of PGRI Adi Buana Surabaya.

Noel, B.R. 2008. *Conflict Resolution Education in Indonesia: Mapping Adaptations and Meanings*. (Ph.D thesis. Ohio University, United States). Retrieved from: http://search.proquest.com/docview/3044884 85?accountid=10424 ProQuest Dissertations & Theses (PQDT) database.

Palmer, A. & Collins, R. 2006. Perceptions of rewarding excellence in teaching: Motivation and the scholarship of teaching. Journal of Further and Higher Education 30(2): 193–205. doi. org/10.1080/03098770600617729.

Pendergast, D., Garvis, S. & Keogh, J. 2011. Pre-Service Student-Teacher Self-Efficacy Beliefs: An Insight into the Making of Teachers. *Australian Journal of Teacher Education* 36(12). Retrieved from: https://files.eric.ed.gov/fulltext/EJ954836.pdf.

Power, A., Southwell, B. & Elliott, R. 2007.Teacher Education for the Future: Some Australian Perspectives. *Journal of Teacher Education for Sustainability* 7: 27–39. doi: 10.2478/v10099–009–0003–8.

Protheroe, N. 2008. Teacher Efficacy: What is it and does it matter? *Principal* 87(5): 42–45. Retrieved from:http://eric.ed.gov/?id=EJ806309.

Shaukat, S., Sharma, U. & Furlonger, B.E. 2013. Pakistani and Australian pre-service teachers' attitudes and self-efficacy towards inclusive education. *Journal of Behavioural Sciences* 23(2): 1–16. Retrieved from: https://research.monash.edu/en/publications/pakistani-and-australian-pre-service-teachers-attitudes-and-self.

Sridhar, Y.N. & Javan, S. 2011. Teacher efficacy and its relationship to classroom managementstyle among secondary school teachers of Kigali city, Rwanda. *Journal of Education and Practice* 2(2).

Taha & Ming. 2014. Exploring motivational design and motivation types facilitated by an online support system for learning literature. *GEMA Online® Journal of Language Studies.* 109 Volume 14(2), June. Retrieved from http://dx.doi.org/10.17576/GEMA-2014-1402-08) ISSN: 1675–8021.

Tschannen-Moran, M. & Hoy, W.A. 2001. *Teacher efficacy*: capturing an elusive construct.

Undang-Undang Sistem Pendidikan Nasional. 2003. *Undang-Undang Republik Indonesia nomor 20 tahun 2003 tentang Sistem Pendidikan Nasional*. Retrieved from: http://www.dikti.go.id/files/atur/UU20–2003Sisdiknas.pdf.

Undang-Undang Republik Indonesia. 2005. *Nomor 14 Tahun 2005 Tentang Guru dan Dosen*. Retrieved From: http://sindikker.dikti.go.id/dok/UU/UUNo142005%28Guru%20&%20Dosen%29.pdf.

White, C. 1997. Indonesian Social Studies Education: A Critical Analysis. *The Social Studies* 88(2): 87–92. Retrieved from: http://tn3tv8rl4l.scholar.serialssolutions.com.

Wibowo, S.S & Brahma, G.H.T. 2013. *Hubungan antara Teacher Efficacy dan Kepuasan Kerjapada Guru Sekolah Dasar Negeri Inklusi*. FPsi UI. Retrieved from: http://lib.ui.ac.id/opac/ui/detail.jsp?id=20331006&lokasi=lokal.

World Bank Group. 2011. *World Bank and Education in Indonesia*. Retrieved from http://web.worldbank.org.

Zheng, Y. 2010. *Chinese University Students' Motivation, Anxiety, Global Awareness, Linguistic Confidence, and English Test Performance: A Correlational and Causal Investigation*. Retrieved from https://catspaw.its.queensu.ca/handle/1974/5378.

ELT in Asia in the Digital Era: Global Citizenship and Identity – Madya et al. (Eds)
© *2018 Taylor & Francis Group, London, ISBN 978-0-8153-7900-3*

Sex-based grouping in English language teaching

M. Mahmud & Sahril
Universitas Negeri Makassar, Makassar, Indonesia

ABSTRACT: The main objective of this paper is to explore the students' perspectives on the use of sex-based grouping in English language teaching. The main idea of the paper is drawn from the literature on the gender differences in communication that has been much discussed in the literature of language and gender (Lakoff 1976, Tannen 1990). This research is based on the interview conducted to 12 students taken randomly from one class at one Senior High School in Makassar, Indonesia. Interviews were recorded and transcribed, and discussed in relation to the issues raised above. The results of this study showed that students have good perception toward the application of sex-based grouping. An important finding from this study was the preference of mixed group of men and women as a choice to accommodate the different learning strategies of female and male students.

1 INTRODUCTION

Discourses on gender remain important in today's society. It can be found in many different areas and it is in fact "the most extensively investigated constructs of the social sciences" (James & Berger 1996). This is in line with Eckert (1998) who states that gender differences can be found in "different cultures, places, and groups". Therefore, gender issues and effects can be found in all aspects of human's life including the communicative styles.

There is a significant relationship between gender and communication in society, in which one of the important factors influencing the communicative styles in a particular society is the gender concerns. Talbot (2010: 15) had confirmed that "language simply reflects society so that social divisions on gender grounds are reflected in patterns of language use". Therefore, gender is an important part of communication. When communicating each others, interactions may take place between men and women, and of course, relations between men and women may influence their communicative styles.

This issue has become important topics for discussion recently since the notion about 'women's language' was elaborated by Lakoff (1976) and followed by Tannen (1990). This notion emphasized that men and women have different styles in using a language to communicate.

As a result, numerous studies on gender differences in communication then flourished in many different countries such as in Saudi Arabia (Hassan 2000), in Malaysia (Mellor & Fung 2012), in Japan (Itakuro & Tsui 2004), and in Indonesia (Mahmud 2008, 2013). Hassan (2000), for example, found that the notion of gender differences in communication had empowered women in Arabic conversation so that they had ability to interact competitively. In the study on sex roles in Malaysian perspective, Mellor & Fung (2012) confirmed that women have higher empathy than men whereas men are less forgiving. Itakuro & Tsui (2004) in their study in Japanese conversation found that "males played a central role in shaping the development of the conversation". Consequently, all the conversation evolved around the interests of the male speakers while "the female speakers were forced to play a subservient role to the conversations". In addition, Mahmud's study (2008) revealed that there are some characteristics of men and women in Bugis society in using a language, such as the tendency of women to use polite forms, to express opinions emotionally, to talk about their own achievement, and like to talk about the bad points of other people. Gender is one aspect influencing the politeness of Bugis people besides other aspects such as age differences, social status, familiarity, and situation (Mahmud 2013).

Gender differences in communication may also be found in another area, such as in education. Teachers and educational practitioners should be aware that students in the class will have different communicative styles. Mahmud (2017)'s study had revealed the number of styles employed by students to communicate in the class. It should also be noted that those different communicative styles can be influenced by many factors including gender differences among the students.

Several studies had been conducted in this issue and found some differences of men and women in terms of learning. Younger, Warrington & Jacquita (1999) stated that the interaction of male student and female student are different in which male students tend to "dominate certain classroom interaction" whereas female students "participate more in teacher-student interaction which support learning". Logan and Johnston (2009) found that women have better reading comprehension than men. Nassab and Motlag (2017) found that girls were speaking without any stress and pause. Female learners were speaking without any interruption with so many verbs, adjectives, coordinators, but the boys had so many interruptions during their speech and sometimes their pronunciation and grammar was wrong with more discourse markers. In terms of English language teaching, Mahmud (2010) mentions that some characteristics of female students such as being "ashamed, nervous, not certain" can influence their English proficiency and therefore they prefer writing as the skill to express their ideas. Mahmud further states that, for men, due to their need to "challenge and maintain strength as men", they mostly choose speaking English ability as the way to show their status as men.

Based on these phenomena, it is important for teachers to consider the various learning styles of students that may be affected by gender differences. One of the strategies is to create a grouping technique which may accommodate those differences. In this paper, the researchers examined the use of sex-based grouping (female single sex, male single sex, or mixed sex) in English language teaching. The focus was to investigate the students' perspectives on the use of this sex-based grouping in the class.

Discussion in this paper becomes precious findings on the literature of English language teaching, in which it can contribute to the innovation of English language teaching. It will also become valuable results on the discussion of gender differences in communication and its effects on educational setting, particularly in English language teaching.

2   RELATED LITERATURE

Tannen (1990) in her book "You Just Don't Understand" has viewed the men and women differences of language style. One example is that there is a tendency for men to use language to "preserve their independence and maintain their position in the group". Conversely, women use language to 'create connection and identity'.

The main focus of their conversation tends to be different. When men and women are interacting, these purposes may have counteracted to each other, leading to different perceptions or opinions. With reference to these ideas, Biber & Burges (2000) confirm that women's focus in conversation is on "personal and interactional aspects of conversation", whereas men's focus is more on "transferring information". According to Stanton (2001), conversations for women are for the sake of "developing and preserving intimacy", while for men, "maintaining power" is more important than other aspects, such as intimacy.

Tymson (1998) mentions some differences of men and women in their conversations. Typically men will talk about "things" while women will talk about how they "feel about things". Gray further (1992) states that, "a man's sense of self is defined through his ability to achieve results…women's sense of self is defined through her feelings and the quality of her relationships".

Several characteristics of women's language are mentioned by Lakoff (1976) that women tend to use "lexical hedges or fillers, taq questions, rising intonations, intensifiers, etc".

Vanfossen (2001) also notices the passiveness of women by the use of "tag questions, disclaimers, or directive statements".

Differences of men and women in communication can also be seen in non verbal communication. It is noted by Griffin et al (1999) that females apply more non verbal communication than males. There are more eye contacts, gestures, and smiles that are used by females (67.5%, 75.5%, and 83.7% respectively) than are used by men.

From all of those studies above, it is important to look at how gender differences in communication exist in a different situation, such as in a setting of education and English language teaching. This study proposes the exploration of how those gender differences affect the process of English language teaching. The application of sex-based grouping in English language teaching in this study could reveal the impacts of gender differences on the learning styles of the students.

3 RESEARCH METHODS

This research used a qualitative research. It was based on the data taken in 2015.The population of the research is one class at one Senior High School in Makassar (SMA 17 Makassar). To collect data, 12 students (6 males and 6 females) were interviewed related to their perspectives toward the use of sex-based grouping in the class. These respondents were chosen based on their active participation during the teaching process applying the sex-based grouping in a discussion (female single sex, male single sex, and mixed sex). Before conducting the interview, students in the class were taught by applying the sex-based grouping in a discussion (female single sex, male single sex, and mixed sex). Interviews were conducted at the end of the meetings.

The data analysis applied the technique of discourse analysis which rely on the data recording, data transcription, data selection, and data interpretation. Jones (2011) states that discourse analysis is a process of "entextualization, in which activities include transforming actions into texts and texts into action". In this study, after the interviews, the results were transcribed, identified, extracted, and interpreted based on the issues raised above.

4 FINDINGS

The following sets of interview, (I = Interviewer; M = Male students; F = Female students), show the perspectives of the students in the use of sex-based grouping in the English class. The first one was about the preferences of working in a group.

Extract 1: Preferences of working in group:

I: "in a group discussion, [do you] prefer [working] with the members who are the same sex, different sex or just mixed?"
F1:   "with the same sex [women]"
I: "[you] with the same sex, right? Why?"
F1:   "because men sometimes want to be easy"
I: "oh, is it?"
F1:   "so we are tired of working, they [men] can have the same score as we [women]"
I: "How about you?"
M1:   "mixed"
I: "mixed? Why?"
M1:   "in order to share the task. Females are sometimes diligent"

From extract 1 above, it can be seen that both of the respondents have different preferences in group discussion. The female respondent (F1) preferred working with the same sex. She enjoyed working with the same sex (female single sex group). According to her, she sometimes worked hard if she worked with male students. Sometimes her male counterparts just wanted the easy way. Usually they did not want to work but wanted the result. On the contrary, the male respondent (M1) preferred the mixed group in which he can work together with his female counterparts. His reason is that mixing the students could give opportunities to share the task. Also, he could share the task with the female students who sometimes are very diligent and careful in doing the work. Another reason can be seen in the following extracts of interview:

Extract 2: Preferences of working in group:

I: "in a group discussion, which one do you prefer, mixed or the same sex only?"
M2:   "mixed"
I: "why?"
M2:   "open the mind, if with the same men, usually just play, not focus, with women, usually..."
I: "more spirit"
M2:   "yes"
I: "how about you"
M3:   "mixed too, to have more insights"

Extract 2 of the interview above confirmed that male respondents preferred the mixed sex group as the way to open their mind. M2 said, "open the mind, if with the same men, usually just play, not focus, with women, usually". They realized that working with the same sex (all males) might not be effective since they sometimes were careless while women were more diligent. Another male respondent (M3) said, "mixed too, to have more insights". The mixing of the group allowed them to obtain more insights of knowledge. Another opinion regarding this can be seen in the following extract of the interview:

Extract 3: Preferences of working in group:

I: "in a group discussion, which one do you prefer, mixed or the same sex only?"
F2:   "I preferred mixed"
I: "why"
F2:   "because men and women are different, if they are united, it can produce better opinion"
I: "okay, what about you?"
F3:   "mixed too, because the power of men and women is not the same, so it is good to be mixed"

In extract 3 above, both female respondents above (F2 and F3) stated that working in a mixed group of men and women actually could also give an advantage as the way to learn together. F2 said, "because men and women are different, if they are united, it can produce better opinion". They also realized that they have weakness which can be supported by the presence of the male students. This is stated by F3, "mixed too, because the power of men and women is not the same, so it is good to be mixed".

The next question was about the preferences to study English. Respondents both male and female students were asked about the preferences to learn or to study English whether with the same sex only or with the mixed sex. Both male and female respondents stated that they wanted to study English by mixing the sexes of males and females. One of the reasons is seen as follows:

Extract 4: Preferences to study English

I: "if you study English, which one can improve your English better, the same sex or mixed sex?"
F6:   "[it's good if [we] are mixed"
I: "why"
F6:   "Because our ability is different. [I am] afraid if [I study with the female only, it is just like that, so [I think] it should be mixed"
I: "and you like mixed, too?"
M6:   "if it can be mixed, so [it can improve our insight]"

Both of the male and female respondents interviewed agreed if they could be mixed between female and male students when they learn English. The female respondent stated that mixing in the class could give opportunities to improve their English achievement well. She said, "Because our ability is different. [I am] afraid if [I study with the female only, it is just like that, so [I think] it should be mixed". The male respondent agreed in the same way as the way to improve their insights in learning English. He said, "if it can be mixed, so [it can improve our insight]". Another opinion can be seen in the following extract:

Extract 5: Preferences to speak English

I: "In speaking English, which one do you prefer, with the same sex or different sex? Or mixed?"
M1:   (Male respondent) "with the same, the same sex"
I: "The same sex, with men as well, why?"
M2:   "because the topic suits"
I: "If you talk to the women?"
M2:   "usually it does not suit. The story will be different. They have their own story"
I: (asking the female respondent) "How about you?"
F1:   "sometimes with men sometimes with women. If talking to the women, it can reach the feel, if talking to men, usually the topic will be different. With the same women, the topic is the same"

The respondents above stated that they preferred to communicate with the same sex. Female respondents liked talking with other women, while men prefer to talk with other men as well. Both also have the same reasons. Speaking with the same sex makes them easy to interact because they generally have the same topic for discussion. Whereas if they talk to the opposite sex, there is often a gap in communication because they have a different topic and a different way of communicating.

5 DISCUSSIONS

Discussion on the above five extracts of interview shows that female and male students have different preferences in working in a group. The topics they talked and the ways they manage the talks influenced these different preferences.

Females tended to work with the same sex. Females find more comfortable to work with the same sex since their female counterparts allow them to speak freely without any hindering factors such as feeling ashamed, feeling reluctant, or not certain about their opinions. Nevertheless, they still considered to work together with different sex in order that they can take the advantage of it.

Males like to work with females since they saw the potential advantage of females who were sometimes diligent and therefore made them more communicative. Both of male and female students also considered mixed group as the best way to work in a group in order that they can be communicative and share to each other. In the mixed sex group, conversations between men and women tended to become hot discussion. Each of them was trying to take the floor for the conversations.

This study proves the existence of 'women's language' that had been observed by Lakoff (1976) and Tannen (1990). It had been observed that males and females have different styles of communication. This 'women's language' can affect the performance of English students in learning English. Studies also had revealed the influence of gender differences in communication in the field of English language teaching (Younger et al. 1999, Logan & Johnston 2009, Mahmud 2010, Nassab & Motlag 2017). The preferences of students in choosing the members of the group revealed in this study were mostly influenced by the notion of gender differences in communication, for examples, their topics for discussion tended to be different, female students were more diligent than men, etc.

In addition to these findings, there are some points to note regarding these differences. The passiveness of women as stated by Vanfossen (2001) may be reduced by putting them in groups. Women should be put with other women. In that way, they can interact well and overcome their reluctance to speak. Their intimacy will empower their activity in speaking. Men, on the other hand, should be put with females in order to break their "power". If they speak with the other males, their interaction will be limited. As stated by Stanton (2001), intimacy is the focus of women's conversation whereas for men, maintaining power is their crucial points. The grouping of the students based on their sexes as promoted in this study can become an alternative way to solve these communication problems between men and women.

The preference of respondents on the use of mixed sex grouping revealed in this study was in order that both male and females can interact and share each other. Therefore, teachers need to know the strategies in order that these differences are not interfering the learning process. By mixing the female and male students in the group, great influence in learning English may be acquired, especially in encouraging them to talk to each other. As shown in the results of this study, mixed group of female with male is good in encouraging them to speak. Female students, however, also demonstrated good interaction among their own group.

6 CONCLUSIONS AND LIMITATIONS

The result of the research shows that in speaking English, students' performance was affected by gender differences. Speaking with the same sex will encourage them to have good performance in English speaking. This case can be seen in the female single sex. When they were grouped together with all females, they could perform speaking well. For male students, the grouping with all males made them less active. Their speaking performance will be better if they interact with different sex. In the group mixing between male and female students, each member, female or male, was trying to dominate the floor of the conversation, which then made them active in discussion. Therefore, it can be stated that mixed sex group would be influential in encouraging the students in speak English.

In order to accommodate students' differences in the class, particularly differences caused by a gender factor, English teachers may need to a great atmosphere for learning. One of the important contributions of this study is about the benefit of grouping students either female single sex, male single sex, or mixed sex. This grouping can provide opportunities for students to learn conveniently and can minimize the different styles of learning caused by gender differences as revealed in this study.

REFERENCES

Biber, D. & Burges, J. 2000. Historical change in the language use of women and men: gender differences in dramatic dialogue. *Journal of English linguistics* 28(1): 21–37.
Eckert, P. 1998. Gender and sociolinguistic variation. In Jennifer Coates (ed.), *Language and Gender*. Massachusetts: Blackwell Publishers, Ltd.
Gray, J. 1992. *Men are from mars, women are from venus: A practical guide for improving communication and getting what you want in your relationship.* London: Thorsons.
Griffin, M.A., McGahee, D. & Slate, J. 1999. *Gender differences in nonverbal communication.* Valdosta: Valdosta State University.
Hassan, I.H. 2000. Language, gender, and power: Analysis of theme and topic management in Arabic conversational discourse. *The Humanities and Social Science* 61: 591.
Itakuro, H. & Tsui, A.B.M. 2004. Gender and conversation dominance in Japanese conversation. *Language in Society* 33: 223–248.
James, B. & Berger, J. 1996. Gender, status, and behavior in task situations. *Social Psychology Quarterly* 59(3): 273–283.
Jones, R.H. 2011. Data collection and transcription in discourse analysis. In K. Hyland & B. Paltridge (Eds.), *Bloomsbury companion to discourse analysis.* London: Bloomsbury.
Lakoff, R.T. 1976. *Language and woman's place.* New York: Octagon Books.

Logan, S. & Johnston, R. 2009. Gender differences in reading ability and attitude: Examining where these differences lie. *Journal of Research in Reading* 32(2): 129–214.

Mahmud, M. 2008. *Politeness in Bugis*. A Ph. D Thesis. Canberra: The Australian National University.

Mahmud, M. 2010. Language and gender in English language teaching. *TEFLIN Journal* 21(2): 172–184.

Mahmud, M. 2013. The roles of social status, age, gender, familiarity, and situation in being polite for Bugis society. *Asian Social Science* 9(5): 58–70.

Mahmud, M. 2017. Communicative styles of English students at the State University of Makassar. *GEMA online Journal of Language Studies* 17(1): 223–238.

Mellor, D. & Fung, S.W.T. 2012. Forgiveness, empathy, and gender: A Malaysian perspective. *Sex Roles* 67, 98–1–7.

Nasab, M.S.H. & Motlagh, S.F.P. 2017. Male and female students' narrative similarities and differences in the advance levels in line with advance organizers. *Communication and Linguistics Studies*. Special Issue: *Applied Linguistics in Line With TEFL* 3(1–1): 8–13. DOI: 10.11648/j.cls.s.2017030101.12.

Stanton, A. 2001. *Men and women in conversation: Finding a way to bridge the gap,* University of Massachusets. http://www.healthandage.com/public/health-center/28/article/1284/Men-and-Women-in-Conversation-Finding-a-Way.html. Accessed 10 July 2008.

Talbot, M.M. 2010. *Language and gender*. UK: Polity Press.

Tannen, D. 1990. *You just don't understand: Women and men in conversation*. New York: Harper Collins.

Tymson, C. 1998. *Gender games: Doing business with the opposite*. Australia: Tymson Communication.

Vanfossen, B. 2001. *Gender differences in communication*. ITROW's Women and Expression Conference.

Younger, M., Warrington, M. & Jacquita, W. 1999. The gender gap and classroom interactions: reality and rhetoric?. *British Journal of Socially of Education* 20(3): 325–341.

ELT in Asia in the Digital Era: Global Citizenship and Identity – Madya et al. (Eds)
© 2018 Taylor & Francis Group, London, ISBN 978-0-8153-7900-3

The relationship of English proficiency and socioeconomic status with the choice of language learning strategies among EFL students of Cenderawasih University Papua

R.D.B. Rambet
Indonesia University of Education, Indonesia

ABSTRACT: Language Learning Strategies (LLSs) refer to techniques used by learners for the purpose of regulating their own learning. Having plenty evidence about the effect of various factors on LLSs, the present study aimed at describing strategies students prefer to use in English language learning and find out whether the strategies have correlation to language proficiency. Moreover, Socio-Economic Status (SES) of parents was compared to find out whether it affected LLSs and the proficiency of a learner. The data of 32 university students taken from the Oxford's SILL test, English proficiency test, and parents' income were analyzed using the SPSS statistical software. The results showed that the participants were overall high strategy users and that strategies relating to understanding were most frequently used. Findings indicate only Metacognitive strategies that reveal to have significant correlation with the proficiency. Besides, SES does not significantly influence LLSs and English proficiency of a learner.

1 INTRODUCTION

1.1 *Language learning strategies in ESL/EFL context*

Language Learning Strategies (LLSs) have gained great importance in ESL/EFL learning context. They are among the main factors such as motivation, intelligence, aptitude, personality traits, context and so forth that help determine students' language learning. The correlation of those strategies employed by the students with other variables such as gender, proficiency level, belief, motivation, socioeconomic status, and course performance becomes the focus in the field of Second Language Acquisition research. Studies have shown the importance of LLSs in making language learning more efficient, producing a positive effect on learners' language use, and improving proficiency or achievement overall or in specific skill areas (Chamot & Kupper 1989, Oxford 2003).

Stewner-Manzanares et al. (in Oxford, 1986) define learning strategies, contrasted with teaching techniques or instructional strategies which are actions taken by the teacher to structure and present information in a way that will help students learn, as steps taken by the learner to facilitate the acquisition, storage, retrieval, or use of information. Language learning strategies refer to techniques used by language learners for the purpose of regulating their own learning.

Richard & Lockhart (1996) believe that language learners will be successful in the tasks due to use of an appropriate language learning strategy. According to Ellis (1994) type of learning strategies is related to language learners' achievement. Studies have shown a significant relationship at a general level between learners' age, gender, proficiency, motivation and cultural background and learners' choice of LLSs. In addition, external factors such as teaching approach and environment also influence the development and use of learning strategies of learners from different aspects.

The importance of learning strategies described by Wenden (1985) is as follows: (1) learning strategies are the key to learner autonomy; (2) one of the goals of L2 training should be to facilitate learner autonomy, although this facilitation might require overcoming the learner's belief that learning is classroom-dependent or teacher-dependent; (3) learning strategies are a source of insight into the difficulties of unsuccessful learners, whose learning problems are often related to not having an appropriate repertoire of learning strategies; and (4) teachers should become attuned to their students' learning strategies through observation and formal strategy assessment.

Oxford (1990) divides LLSs into direct learning strategies and indirect learning strategies. Direct strategies, including memory, cognitive and compensation strategies, involve the target language and require mental processing of the language. Memory strategies help students store and retrieve new information while cognitive strategies enable learners to understand and produce new language by many different means. Compensation strategies, on the other hand, allow learners to use the language despite their gaps in knowledge. In a different manner, language learning using indirect strategies has no involvement with the target language. They consist of metacognitive, affective, and social strategies. Metacognitive strategies allow learners to control their own cognition while affective ones help to manage emotions, motivations and attitudes of the learners. Furthermore, Social strategies support learners' interactive learning with others.

1.2 Studies of LLSs, English proficiency and SES

With respect to the relationship between LLSs and English proficiency of EFL learners, Park (1997) investigated 332 Korean university students and found that only Cognitive and Social Strategies had significant correlation to predict learners' scores of the Test of English as Foreign Language (TOEFL) than other strategy categories. This study has been cited by many second language researchers. Using ITP-TOEFL scores as proficiency indicator for listening and reading skills, while scores of speaking and writing skills were taken using other tests, the study of Setiyadi et al. (2016) found that the use of different learning strategies had significant correlation with the proficiency of listening, reading, speaking and writing skills of Indonesian EFL university students. Unlike the two studies mentioned earlier, Barrios (2015) used Oxford Placement Test to measure English proficiency. Barrios' research revealed that the participants, Spanish pre-service teachers of English, were medium-to-high learning strategies users. Metacognitive Strategies, along with, were most frequently used. In sum, studies have shown that the more proficient students use LLSs more frequently than the less proficient students.

With reference to effects of SES to LLSs students choose, Tam (2013) found that SES of Hong Kong university students' parents greatly influenced their use of Social Strategies. The research indicated that wealthier students could have more opportunities to practice their speaking skill with English-speaking speakers outside the classroom. In addition, Babikkoi & Razak (2014) found significant relationship between SES of parents of 559 Nigeria's secondary school students in the choice of Cognitive, Metacognitive, Affective, and Social Strategies. However, the results revealed no significance in the learner choice of Memory and Compensation Strategies.

In response to recommendation from the previous research, this present study provided empirical data on the unique or common patterns of EFL learners' LLSs preferences, proficiency, and SES in Indonesian context. Specifically, this investigation addresses the relationship between LLSs and proficiency among students majoring in EFL at Cenderawasih University, a state Indonesian university situated in Jayapura—the capital city of Papua Province, the most eastern part of the country.

2 RESEARCH METHOD

2.1 Research questions

The current study addresses the following research questions:

1. What are the relationships among six categories of LLSs (memory, cognitive, compensation, metacognitive, affective and social), total learning strategies, and English proficiency of EFL students of Cenderawasih University?

2. Which categories of learning strategies are predictive of (i.e., significantly correlated with) L2 proficiency?
3. Is there a difference in learning strategy preferences and proficiency by students from different SES?

2.2 *Method*

The participants of this study were 32 students of English Language Education program at Cenderawasih University, Jayapura. They consisted of 4 males and 28 females. The program annually admitted around 30 to 40 students. All participants were from the same admission year, the academic year of 2014/2015, and in the present study by the end of December 2016 they would have completed their fifth semester courses.

Among the participants, 21 of them representing 66 percent reported that their parents belong to middle level economic class and 11 participants representing 34 percent are within the lower level economic class; while no participants' parents is classified rich or the high level economic class.

The design used for this study is quantitative, correlational research. LLS preferences and English proficiency of the sample population were measured through the administration of the SILL and the Institutional Testing Program TOEFL (ITP-TOEFL).

The SILL Version 7.0, the ESL/EFL version of the test written in English, was used to measure learning strategy preferences. The SILL is a 50-item self-report, paper and-pencil survey designed to assess frequency and patterns of learning strategy use (Oxford 1990). The instrument consists of statements about strategies used by language learners, such as "I connect the sound of a new English word and an image or picture of the word to help me remember the word," and "I read English without looking up every new word." The 50-item questionnaire is distributed into six parts: Part A consists of 9 questions related to Memory Strategies; Part B involves 14 questions on Cognitive Strategies; Part C includes 6 questions about Compensation Strategies; Part D contains 9 questions about Metacognitive Strategies; Part E involves 6 questions on Affective Strategies; and Part F consists of 6 questions on Social Strategies.

Every participant responds to all items, based on his or her personal response, using a 5-point Likert scale ranged from 1-Never or almost true of me to 5-Always or almost true of me.

The instrument used in the present study, the Oxford's SILL version 7.0, has been confirmed reliable, valid and significantly related to language performance as indicated by grades, scores on other tests, self-ratings, and teacher ratings (Oxford 1990, Oxford & Burry-Stock 1995).

The ITP-TOEFL was used to measure English proficiency. Reliability of the TOEFL on a scale of .00 to .99 has been reported as .96, and high levels of validity have been reported in over 100 studies (Educational Testing Service 2006).

2.3 *Data collection procedures and data analysis*

To obtain the score indicating participants' English proficiency, the researcher collected the results of the ITP-TOEFL. The test was given in the end of the fourth semester of the academic year of 2015/2016. After collecting scores of proficiency, the researcher deployed the SILL.

The data, then, were analyzed using the SPSS statistical software version 16.0. for Windows. To examine the first research question: "What are the relationships among six categories of learning strategies (memory, cognitive, compensation, metacognitive, affective, and social), total learning strategies, and L2 proficiency?" the Pearson product–moment correlations were used.

The stepwise multiple regression was the method of data analysis for the second research question: "Which categories of learning strategies (memory, cognitive, compensation, metacognitive, affective, or social strategies), are predictive of (i.e., significantly correlated with) L2 proficiency?" Through this procedure, influence (or predictor) variables were used to predict the criterion variable of English proficiency. Multiple regression analysis was selected because it provides estimates of both the magnitude and statistical significance of relationships between variables (Malik & Hamied 2014).

Finally, multivariate analysis of variance (MANOVA) was conducted to answer the third research question—to determine whether there were significant differences in learning strategy scores and English proficiency scores by socio-economic status.

3 FINDINGS AND DISCUSSION

3.1 *LLSs and English proficiency*

Relationships among six categories of learning strategies, total learning strategies, and ITP-TOEFL score were examined using Pearson product–moment correlations. As argued by Malik & Hamied (2014), correlational techniques are used to answer three types of questions about two or more variables: the relationship between variables, the direction of relations, and the magnitude of relationship.

As presented in Table 1, results of a one-sample Kolmogorov–Smirnov test indicated approximately normal distribution of all variables, and the six categories of learning strategies were significantly correlated with one another and with the total learning strategies score. There were only two categories of learning strategies namely Metacognitive strategies and Social strategies, which showed significant correlation with ITP-TOEFL score.

3.2 *Predictive categories of LLSs toward English proficiency*

A stepwise multiple regression was generated to analyze variables of LLSs which cause the participants' scores of ITP-TOEFL. Particularly, in the present study, the regression analysis determined which LLSs were most strongly correlated with English proficiency. Six categories (Memory, Cognitive, Compensation, Metacognitive, Affective, and Social) were specified as predictor variables, with English proficiency as the criterion variable.

Table 1. Pearson *r* correlations among LLSs scores and ITP-TOEFL scores.

	A	B	C	D	E	F	TOTAL	TOEFL
Memory (A)	1	.796**	.383*	.467**	.649**	.581**	.807**	.184
Cognitive (B)	.796**	1	.478**	.602**	.792**	.564**	.876**	.240
Compensation (C)	.383*	.478**	1	.434*	.583**	.319	.657**	.316
Metacognitive (D)	.467**	.602**	.434*	1	.556**	.783**	.761**	.412*
Affective (E)	.649**	.792**	.583**	.556**	1	.611**	.872**	.165
Social (F)	.581**	.564**	.319	.783**	.611**	1	.743**	.406*
Total LLSs	.807**	.876**	.657**	.761**	.872**	.743**	1	.336
ITP-TOEFL	.184	.240	.316	.412*	.165	.406*	.336	1

*Correlation is significant at the .05 level (2-tailed).
**Correlation is significant at the .01 level (2-tailed).

Table 2. LLSs correlation.

Model	R	R^2	Adjusted R^2	Std. Error
1	.412a	.170	.142	29.872

	Change statistics				
Model	R^2 Ch.	F Ch.	df1	df2	Sig.F Ch.
1	.170	6.131	1	30	.019

a. Predictors: (Constant), METACOGNITIVE.
b. Dependent Variable: PROFICIENCY.

The regression model revealed that only one variable among six learning strategies—Metacognitive strategies was significantly correlated with the participants' English proficiency scores, $R^2 = .170$, $F = 6.131$, $p = .019$ (Table 2).

The metacognitive strategy variable entered the regression equation first (Table 3), with a standardized regression coefficient, $\beta = .412$ (Table 4).

The significance of the regression model was tested using Analysis of Variance (ANOVA) statistics generated as part of the regression procedure. Findings indicated that the predictor (i.e., learning strategy variables) included in the model were significantly associated with the dependent variable, ITP-TOEFL score, $F = 6.131$, $p = .019$ (Table 5).

3.3 LLSs and English proficiency toward SES

A one-way MANOVA was conducted to determine whether there were significant differences in LLSs scores or proficiency by SES. For this analysis, SES was configured as the independent variable, and on the other hand six LLSs, total learning strategies, and English proficiency scores (ITP-TOEFL) were configured as dependent variables (Tables 6 and 7).

Results of the MANOVA revealed no significant differences among low income parents and moderate income ones on any of the eight dependent variables, Wilks's $\Lambda = .799$, $F = .725$, $p = .668$.

Table 3.   Correlated variables.

Model	Variables entered	Variables removed	Method
1	METACOGNITIVE	.	Stepwise (Criteria: Probability-of-F-to-enter <= .050, Probability-of-F-to-remove >= .100).

a. Dependent Variable: PROFICIENCY.

Table 4.   Coefficients.

Model		Unstandardized coefficients		Standardized coefficients
		B	Std. Error	Beta
1	(Constant)	346.000	31.631	
	METACOGNITIVE	20.554	8.301	.412

Model		t		Sig.
1	(Constant)	10.939		.000
	METACOGNITIVE	2.476		.019

a. Dependent Variable: PROFICIENCY.

Table 5.   Regression.

Model		Sum of squares	df	Mean square	F	Sig.
1	Regression	5470.652	1	5470.652	6.131	.019a
	Residual	26770.816	30	892.361		
	Total	32241.469	31			

a. Predictors: (Constant), METACOGNITIVE.

b. Dependent Variable: PROFICIENCY.

Table 6. Description of LLSs, proficiency and SES.

SES	Memory		Cognitive		Compensation	
(N)	Mean	SD	Mean	SD	Mean	SD
Low (11)	3.16	.48	3.49	.51	3.62	.59
Moderate (21)	3.4	.6	3.81	.51	3.7	.62
Total (32)	3.32	.57	3.70	.52	3.67	.60

SES	Metacognitive		Affective		Social	
(N)	Mean	SD	Mean	SD	Mean	SD
Low (11)	3.62	.66	3.00	.61	3.12	.57
Moderate (21)	3.83	.64	3.28	.62	3.56	.7
Total (32)	3.76	.65	3.18	.61	3.38	.67

SES	LLSs total		Proficiency	
(N)	Mean	SD	Mean	SD
Low (11)	3.4	.47	412.1	26
Moderate (21)	3.61	.48	429.1	34.2
Total (32)	3.54	.48	423.2	32.3

Table 7. Multivariate test.

Effect		Value	F	Hypothesis df	Error df	Sig.
Intercept	Pillai's Trace	.995	5.781E2[a]	8.000	23.00	.000
	Wilks' Lambda	.005	5.781E2[a]	8.000	23.00	.000
	Roy's Largest Root	201.09	5.781E2[a]	8.000	23.00	.000
INCOME	Pillai's Trace	.201	.725[a]	8.000	23.00	.668
	Wilks' Lambda	.799	.725[a]	8.000	23.00	.668

The present study yielded three significant findings. First, Pearson r correlations revealed that two categories of language learning strategies namely Metacognitive Strategies and Social Strategies were significantly correlated with ITP-TOEFL score at the point .05 (two-tailed). Second, results of a multiple regression analysis indicated that only one variable—Metacognitive Strategies was significantly correlated with English proficiency. Finally, variations in language learning strategy scores and language proficiency score revealed that socio-economic status of parents was not influential.

Thus, results of the present research were not similar to Park's study (1997) that confirmed the role of Social and Cognitive Strategies in predicting TOEFL scores among Korean students. The other point revealed from the present study which confirms similar finding of other studies is the use of language learning strategies at a medium to high level.

Regarding participants' ITP-TEOFL scores which were lower than the average, it is in line with minimal correlation between learning strategies and proficiency found in the current study. In other words, learning strategies cannot predict language proficiency of the EFL learners. This finding might be due to:

1. the test, ITP-TOEFL, which was the first time-take test for all participants. The participants were not familiar with the models of the first section—Listening Comprehension that consists of 50 items divided into three different kinds of questions. The other two sections, Structure and Written Expression and Reading Comprehension showed similar challenges for participants. In fact, the participants of the present study were aware of

ITP-TOEFL as a worldwide test, however, this kind of test is to some extent different from other types of test they have had in their formal education. In addition, ITP-TOEFL does not cover all linguistic areas. Since the ITP-TOEFL does not measure speaking or writing, it might contribute to learning strategies that would correlate more strongly with other productive skills.

2. participants that used language strategies inappropriately. Vann and Abraham in Nisbet et al. (2005) reported that there were learners who actively used all learning strategies, yet they failed to manifest the strategies appropriately. As the result, English proficiency of EFL learners is predicted by the skillful application of strategies. The absence of LLSs exposure to the participants' prior knowledge may have more to do with proficiency.

3. other factors that influenced participants' language proficiency such as cognitive, affective, sociocultural, anxiety, motivation, and intelligence (Brown 2007).

4 CONCLUSIONS AND SUGGESTIONS

The pattern of strategy employment as revealed in the present study showed that, firstly, overall EFL learners in Papua generally use all language learning strategies, and the most frequently used strategies were Metacognitive, while the least used were Affective strategies. In addition, strategies a learner chooses are not predictive variables for determining his or her language proficiency in English. Eventually, with respect to socioeconomic status, LLSs a learner applies and English proficiency he or she possesses is not affected by socio-economic status of his or her parents. However, since the present study conducted only in a single university and limited in number of participants, this study cannot best represent the whole context of Indonesian students regarding SILL language learning strategies.

Based on the major findings of the present study, the researcher recommends for further researchers to conduct investigation into LLSs and English language proficiency of Indonesia university students with participants from regional parts such as eastern or western provinces of the country. The future researchers are also recommended to try complex variety of measures such as observation and think-aloud procedures. Moreover, ITP-TOEFL is not adequate to assess academic language proficiency, therefore researchers can combine it with or apply different test particularly ones that can measure linguistic aspect of productivity such as speaking and writing.

REFERENCES

Babikkoi, M.A. & Razak, N.Z.A. 2014. Implications of parents' socio-economic status in the choice of English learning strategies among Nigeria's secondary school students. *English Language Teaching* 7(8): 139–147.

Barrios, E. 2015. Spanish pre-service teachers of English perceived use of language learning strategies and its relationship with proficiency. *Revista Española de Lingüística Aplicada* 28(1): 48–72.

Brown, H.D. 2007. *Principles of language learning and teaching (5th ed.)*. Pearson Education, Inc.

Chamot, A.U. & Kupper, L. 1989. Learning strategies in foreign language instruction. *Foreign Language Annals* 22(1): 13–22.

Educational Testing Service (ETS). 2006. *TOEFL test and score data summary [Manual]*. Princeton, NJ: Author.

Ellis, R. 1994. *The Study of second language acquisition.* New York, NY: Oxford University Press.

Malik, R.S. & Hamied, F.A. 2014. *Research methods: A guide for first time researchers*. UPI Press.

Nisbet, D.L., et al. 2005. Language learning strategies and proficiency of Chinese university students. *Foreign Language Annals* 38(1): 100–107.

Oxford, R. 1986. Language learning strategies in a nutshell: Update and ESL suggestions. *TESOL Journal* 2(2): 18–22.

Oxford, R. 1990. *Language learning strategies: What every teacher should know.* New York, NY: Newbury House.

Oxford, R. 2003. Towards a more systematic model pf l2 learner autonomy. In P. Palfreyman, & R. Smith (eds), *Learner Autonomy across Cultures: Language Education Perspectives*: 75–91. Great Britain: Palgrave Macmillan.

Oxford, R. & Burry-Stock, J.A. 1995. Assessing the use of language learning strategies worldwide with ESL/EFL version of the strategy inventory for language learning (SILL). *System* 23(1): 1–23.

Park, G.P. 1997. Language learning strategies and English proficiency in Korean university students. *Foreign Language Annals* 30(2): 211–221.

Richards, J.C. & Lockhart, C. 1996. *Reflective teaching in second language classrooms*. Cambridge University Press.

Setiyadi, A.B. et al. 2016. How successful learners employ learning strategies in an EFL setting in the Indonesian context. *English Language Teaching* 9(8): 28–38.

Tam, K.C. 2013. A study on language learning strategies (LLSs) of university students in Hong Kong. *Taiwan Journal of Linguistics* 11(2): 1–42.

Wenden, A. 1985. Learner Strategies. *TESOL Newsletter* 19(5): 1–7.

ELT in Asia in the Digital Era: Global Citizenship and Identity – Madya et al. (Eds)
© 2018 Taylor & Francis Group, London, ISBN 978-0-8153-7900-3

Learners' native language interference in learning English pronunciation: A case study of Indonesian regional dialects

M.N. Jannah, K.H. Hidayati & S. Setiawan
Universitas Negeri Surabaya, Surabaya, Indonesia

ABSTRACT: English pronunciation is difficult for most Indonesian learners. Research shows that their native language is the most influential factor in this case. Therefore, this study aimed to find out learners' native language interference in learning English pronunciation by identifying the influence of two regional dialects (Madurese and Javanese). It also aimed to find out whether the English sounds lead to unintelligible pronunciation. The possible language contact related to Indonesian learners' pronunciation will be one of the analyses in this study by involving 12 Indonesian learners aged 14 to 18. They were asked to pronounce selected English words and read a given passage and these data were analyzed descriptively. The findings show that their pronunciation problems vary dealing with consonant and vowel sounds, some of which lead to unintelligibility. The conclusion was that the outcome of language contact that the learners' pronunciation is much interfered by their native language.

1 INTRODUCTION

Incorrect pronunciation not only often prevents the understanding of a message, but also can adversely affect the listeners' judgment. All too often bad pronunciation might be perceived as a lack of 'competence' since the way we speak immediately conveys something about ourselves to the people around us (Yates 2002). More importantly, Yates & Zielinski (2009) argue that learners with good pronunciation in English are more likely to be understood even if they make errors in other areas, whereas learners whose pronunciation is difficult to understand will not be understood, even if their grammar is perfect. It should be noted, though, that to become competent users of English, learners must focus on its various different aspects such as vocabulary, grammar and pronunciation.

However, foreign language learning tends to emphasize the importance of grammar and vocabulary, and this causes other aspects to be neglected (Harmer 2001, Backley 2015). Those being neglected are particularly the practical skills that allow learners to use the language for real communication (e.g. pronunciation). Therefore, it is common to find learners of English who have an extensive knowledge but lack the ability or confidence to use spoken English. Pronunciation is, therefore, is considered as one of complicated aspects for most EFL learners, Indonesian learners in particular (Menard 2010). Indeed, this is true that learning pronunciation does not aim to sound exactly like a native speaker of English, but it does aim to be intelligible, meaning that the pronunciation is clear enough to be understood. To some Indonesian learners some English sounds seem to be difficult to produce that sometimes lead to unintelligibility (Mathew 1997).

In response to pronunciation difficulties, some work has been conducted especially in countries in which people learn English as a foreign language (EFL). For instance, studies conducted to investigate problems with English pronunciation among Thai students and identify key reasons for the problems (Wei & Zhou 2002, Khamkhien 2010). They found that there are English consonants and vowels which appear to be problems for them; e.g. words with transcriptions ended with a consonant; consonant clusters; words with /ei/, usually pronounced as /e/; words with /r/, usually pronounced as /l/; words with /v/, usually pronounced as /f/; and words with /z/, usually pronounced as /s/ or voiceless, intonation and stress problems.

Moreover, the key reasons of the pronunciation problems are such as words directly borrowed from English into the Thai language are pronounced in Thai ways, the Romanization of the Thai language influences English pronunciation, and Thai intonations are applied into English pronunciations. This is to say that the native language is the most influential factor.

Moreover, studies on Indonesian learners' pronunciation have also been conducted. A study which was conducted towards English department students of Semarang State University, for instance, found out that most of them found it difficult to pronounce words with ED ending such as those found in regular past forms (Dewi 2009). In addition, pronunciation errors made by Indonesian learners in the province of Aceh, northern Sumatra, are not only in ED ending words, but any sounds which are largely limited to final stops and sibilants, and initial and final affricates and interdentals (Mathew 1997).

All in all, much has been written about EFL learners' pronunciation, indeed. However, most of the literature in the field is concerned with identifying pronunciation errors of learners in general and not many writers focus on identifying learners' native languages interference (i.e. by identifying the influence of different regional dialects) on their English pronunciation. More importantly, there have never been any studies considering the possible language contact related to Indonesian learners' pronunciation, which will be one of the analyses in this study.

Therefore, this study aims to find out native language interference in learning English pronunciation by identifying the influence of two different regional dialects of the learners. This is because native language is the most influential factor on one's pronunciation (Kenworthy 1987). More importantly, this study seeks to find out whether several English sounds interfered by the learners' native language leads to unintelligible pronunciation. Finally, to conclude the learners' pronunciation ability this study analyzes the possible influence of language contact. The result of the study would facilitate teachers to improve learners' pronunciation ability by recognizing the learners' native language sounds interference and emphasizing on the difficult sounds learners might encounter.

2 METHOD

This study used a qualitative research design. A qualitative research design is defined as documenting or portraying the everyday experience of individuals by observing or interviewing them (Fraenkel & Wallen 2006). It seeks to describe and analyze the data collected from the learners' pronouncing a list of English words and reading a given passage. It involved twelve (12) Indonesian learners who belong to Curahdami English Community (CEC). CEC is a study club of English learners from various levels of education in a village named Curahdami in Jember, East Java. The twelve learners were chosen randomly considering the length of learning English and having no difficulty recognizing English alphabets. They come from two different native languages and study in either public or private Junior and Senior High Schools. They were male and female of either Madurese or Javanese (i.e. two of many regional dialects in Indonesia). They are around fourteen (14) to eighteen (18) years old when involved in this study.

The data were collected from the above Indonesian EFL learners. They were asked to pronounce English words one by one. After all participants pronouncing the list of English words provided, they were assigned to read a passage. Before they read the passage, a video of the story on the passage was played once. This is to help them familiar with the words in the passage. The learners' pronouncing words and reading the passage were recorded. The researcher was the one assessing the learners' pronunciation. It is in fact proposed that in a qualitative research, the researcher was as a key instrument collecting the data (Krippendorf 1987). The assessment was adapted from Brown's pronunciation assessment (Brown 2004).

3 FINDINGS AND DISCUSSION

The findings are discussed into three main points in relation to the research questions, namely *English Sounds Produced by Madurese and Javanese learners, Unintelligible Pronunciation,* and *Language Contact.*

3.1 English sounds produced by Madurese and Javanese learners

As mentioned above, the twelve Indonesian learners were assigned to pronounce a list of English words and read an English passage. The twelve Madurese and Javanese learners erroneously pronounce several vowel sounds of both Monophthongs and diphthongs. The most Monophthongs erroneously pronounced were the sounds /æ/, /ɑ:/, /ɔ:/ and /u:/. The sound /æ/ in 'hat' was pronounced /e/ as in 'left', /ɑ:/ as in 'far' was pronounced /ʌ/ as in 'run', /ɔ:/ as in 'call' was pronounced similarly as /ɒ/ in 'dog', and /u:/ as in 'food' was like /ʊ/ in 'book'. Meanwhile, the diphthongs were /eə/ and /ʊə/. Learners whose native language is Madurese pronounced the sounds /eə/ as /e/ and /ʊə/ as /u:/, while Javanese pronounce them as /eɪ/ and /u:/. Thus, words like 'stairs' are pronounced with the vowel sound /e/ as in /pen/ by Madurese and pronounced /eɪ/ as in 'brain' by Javanese.

In addition, there are some other interesting differences between Madurese and Javanese learners. Learners whose native language is Madurese pronounce monophthong sounds /ɪ/ as in 'hit' and /i/ as in feel. Meanwhile, those whose native language is Javanese pronounced it correctly. Moreover, the diphthong vowel sounds erroneously pronounced by Madurese was /eɪ/ which was pronounced as monophthongs/e/. Thus, words like 'pain' and 'pen' are similarly pronounced with the sound /e/. The Javanese learners, however, erroneously pronounced diphthong /ɪə/ as in 'beer' as /i:/. Thus, the vowGoogle Search Google or type URL el sound in words like 'beer' and 'beat' are pronounced similarly by Javanese. For the Madurese, the diphthong /ɪə/ was pronounced correctly, since they find many Madurese words with the vowel /ɪə/.

Dealing with consonants, the Madurese and Javanese learners have mostly the same pronunciation errors. This can be seen as the errors of Indonesian learners in general, since Indonesian is their official language. Most of the learners found consonant sounds /θ/ and /ð/ difficult. Instead of pronouncing the consonant /θ/ as in 'thing' and /ð/ as in 'that', they pronounce /θ/ as /t/ and /ð/ as /d/. Moreover, other consonants they pronounced erroneously were the final /b/, final /d/ (by mostly Madurese), final/g/, /v/, /ʃ/ and /ʒ/. The final /b/ was erroneously pronounced as /p/, final/g/ as /k/, /v/ as /f/ and both /ʃ/ and /ʒ/ as /s/. For the Madurese and few Javanese, final /d/ was pronounced quite similarly as /t/.

3.2 Unintelligible pronunciation

As explained previously, the goal of learning pronunciation is not to sound like a native speaker, though it is good to be. Instead, learning pronunciation should aim to sound intelligible. Intelligible pronunciation is 'listener-friendly' pronunciation-one which listeners can understand without effort and which can be used to make meaningful conversation possible (Backley 2015). This is to say that when a listener (e.g. native or another speakers) hardly understands one's pronunciation, his/her pronunciation is unintelligible.

With regard to Madurese and Javanese learners' pronunciation of English, the errors found as a result of the two dialects' interference need to be analyzed in terms of the intelligibility. As the study had found that both Madurese and Javanese pronounced erroneously some vowels and consonants, the way to analyze the intelligibility was by identifying the errors as to whether their pronunciation errors were still 'understood' or 'unintelligible' already. The analysis was based on the result of the learners' pronouncing a list of words and reading a passage.

Regarding vowels, the researcher found some sounds pronounced by the learners unintelligibly. This was identified from a sentence (taken from the passage) like *the King wanted everyone to feel his pain*. Most of the learners pronounced the vowel sound in the word 'pain' as /e/ that makes it sound like 'pen'. Another example was in the sentence *Immediately, the King's servant put the hat on his head*. This is interesting since the word 'hat' and 'head' are pronounced exactly the same by either Madurese or Javanese. A more interesting finding was the word 'hate' appearing in the list and in some sentences of the passage, which was pronounced by most Madurese similarly as 'had', 'head' and even 'hat'. In some contexts, such pronunciation errors will lead to unintelligibility.

47

Regarding consonants, moreover, several sounds were also found intelligibly pronounced by the learners. They were mostly in the final consonant sounds such as the final /b/ and /p/ in the words 'cab' and 'cap'. However, the cases of unintelligibility in the vowels are more commonly found.

All in all, unintelligibility in the learners' pronunciation was found in some cases. Comparing to the intelligibility of the other sounds, however, the unintelligibility was very few encountered. In other words, their errors do not often lead to unintelligibility.

3.3 *Language contact*

One of the outcomes of language contact can be seen through phonology (sound systems) (Thomason, 2001). Phonology (sound system) is the one this study will analyze dealing with the learners' pronunciation. Phonological interference or transfer would appear likely that farther along in the contact history, in the process of acquiring bilingual competence, the version of the second language spoken by such people would still contain many phonological features derivable from their native language, i.e. substratum phonological influence (Sankoff 2001). Therefore, the case of language contact influence on the learners' pronunciations can be seen from several sounds which they pronounce erroneously as the interference from their native language.

4 CONCLUSION

To date, this study is the first to investigate Indonesian learners' native language interference by identifying two different regional dialects, namely Madurese and Javanese. Problems of pronunciation here were more sounds, than the unintelligible ones, which are still considered intelligible despite the two different dialects interference on the pronunciation. Finally, with regard to the result of the study, it concludes that it is the outcome of language contact that the learners' pronunciation is much interfered by their native language.

REFERENCES

Backley, P. 2015. Improving your English Pronunciation. *Pearson*: 125–137.
Brown, H.D. 2004. *Language assessment: Principles and classroom practices.* New York: Longman.
Dewi, A.K. 2009. *Pronunciation problems faced by the English department students in pronouncing—ed ending.*
Field, J. 2005. Intelligibility and the listener: The role of lexical stress. *TESOL Quarterly* 39(3): 399–423.
Fraenkel, J.R. & Wallen, N.E. 2006. *How to design and evaluate research in education.* New York: McGraw—Hill.
Harmer, J. 2001. *The practice of English language teaching* (3rd Ed.). Pearson Education Ltd.
Hickey, R. 2010. *Language contact and change.* Cambridge University Press.
Kelly, G. 2000. *How to teach pronunciation.* Edinburgh Gate: Pearson Education Limited.
Kenworthy, J. 1987. *Teaching English pronunciation.* Harlow: Longman.
Khamkhien, A. 2010. Thai learners' English pronunciation competence: Lesson learned from word stress assignment. *Journal of Language Teaching and Research* 1(6): 757–764.
Krippendorf, K. 1987. *Content analysis: An introduction to methodology.* London: Sage Publication Beverly Hills.
Mathew, I.B. 1997. Errors in pronunciation of consonants by Indonesian, Gayo and Acehnese learners of English as a foreign language. *Edith Cowan University Research Online.*
Matras, Y. 2009. *Language contact.* New York: Cambridge University Press.
Menard, R. 2010. Interference of Indonesian language in learning English. *Teaching English as a Second Language.*
Meng, J. 2009. The relationship between linguistics and laguage teaching. *Asian Social Science* 5(12): 84–86.
Sankoff, G. 2001. Linguistic outcomes of language contact. In P. Trudgill, J. Chambers & N. Schilling-Estes, *Handbook of Sociolinguistics* (pp. 638–668). Oxford: Basil Blackwell.
Thomason, S.G. 2001. *Language contact.* Edinburgh: University Press.
Wei, Y. & Zhou, Y. 2002. Insights into English pronunciation problems of Thai students. *Educational Resources Information Center (ERIC)*: 1–12.
Yates, L. 2002. *What is pronunciation?.* AMEP Research Centre.
Yates, L. & Zielinski, B. 2009. *Give it a go: Teaching pronunciation to adults.* Commonwealth of Australia.

ELT in Asia in the Digital Era: Global Citizenship and Identity – Madya et al. (Eds)
© *2018 Taylor & Francis Group, London, ISBN 978-0-8153-7900-3*

English Language Teaching (ELT) learners' communication strategies in exclusive and task-based learning

B. Kadaryanto, T.H. Febiani & D. Utaminingsih
University of Lampung, Lampung, Indonesia

ABSTRACT: This study is aimed at exploring communication strategies in a course called English Teaching (ET) Media where the participants were EFL sophomores in the English Education study program. One class was taught using an EXCLUSIVE learning model and another was given Task-based learning. The data from observation and a questionnaire were recorded, transcribed, and coded using Dornyei's Communication Strategies Taxonomy before being interpreted to see the distinction in difference between both classes. The results indicate that the EFL learners produced seven types of communication strategies such as Message Abandonment, Topic Avoidance, Use of All-Purpose Words, Non-Linguistic Signals, Code Switching, and Appeal for Help, and Time Gaining. However, their communication strategies occurred more frequently in the EXCLUSIVE learning model class. The EXCLUSIVE learning model stimulated 8.83% more of communication strategies than that of the Task-Based Learning class. The findings suggest an alternative learning model applicable in ELT classroom settings which may be applied in different classrooms.

1 INTRODUCTION

In English Language Teaching class context, it has been widely accepted that teaching speaking skills appears to be demanding for learners (Lazarton 2001, Gan 2012, Hughes & Reed 2016). The learners' ability to speak in the target language has become a major focus in defining the success of language learning classrooms (Nunan 1999, Gilakjani et al. 2012, Richards 2015). Meanwhile, most of Indonesian English as a Foreign Language (EFL) learners faced hesitations to speak in the language although they have been studying the language since junior high and some even since elementary schools. Learning a foreign language can be a particularly anxiety-provoking experience for several reasons. When learners are asked to express themselves using the foreign language in which they have limited competence, the task can be very threatening for them. In an oral discussion, for instance, shyness, nervousness, feeling afraid of making mistakes, and not knowing the way how to pronounce certain words were found to be the most potential problems for their speaking and hindered them to speak (Susilawati, 2007). However, when they happen to speak their native language beyond their consciousness, they often felt foolish and shy.

Furthermore, EFL learners frequently encounter problems when they attempt to speak the target language (Spolsky 1999, Cook 2013, Al Hosni 2014). Foreign language learners have troubles with certain syntactic constructions, find some sounds hard to pronounce, and are often faced with gaps in their knowledge of the second language vocabulary.

Since no individual's linguistic repertoire is perfect, most learners have experienced struggling to find the appropriate expressions or grammatical constructions when attempting to communicate their meaning. The steps taken by language learners in order to enhance the effectiveness of their communication are known as communication strategies (Rossiter 2003, Littlemore 2003, Kasper & Kellerman 2014). Communication strategies could keep speakers flexible, and confident, and make their communication more effective. Moreover, strategic competence serves as an important component of communicative competence in a language learning context. Communication strategies allow speakers to make up for a lack of mastery of the language and to make communication more effective. It is therefore clear to some extent that communication strategies have an important role in communication.

A number of communication strategies studies discussed in the literature have been adapted from Tarone (1977); Faerch & Kasper (1984) and Willems (1987); Sweeney & Hua (2010); Kasper & Kellerman (2014), among many others, where they can be classified into two types of strategies: reduction strategies and achievement strategies. Reduction strategies such as meaning replacement, message abandonment, and topic avoidance have been used for the purpose of giving up a fragment of the original communication goal while achievement strategies such as appeal, literal translation, code-switching, restructuring, word coinage, paraphrasing, and nonlinguistic strategies are used to maintain the original goal of the speakers in communication. Learning and using oral communication strategies can be beneficial for them in order for them to engage in effective conversations and to make them look good "at face value" (McDonough & Shaw 2003: 133).

In order to see how far communication strategies have been used by Indonesian EFL learners when they speak English, and specifically how learners use communication strategies in a subject-matter ELT Class at University of Lampung, a study on what types of communication strategies produced by students of ELT learning subject matter was undertaken through EXCLUSIVE (Kadaryanto & Santi 2014, Abdurrahman et al. 2012) and Task-Based Learning models. The research was particularly useful for exploring what and how communication strategies were produced in both classes. This would further be beneficial for teachers to be more aware of communication strategies the students employed as an effort to reduce their hesitation to achieve a better speaking performance.

An EXCLUSIVE learning model has been developed in five cycles of learning in a classroom. In the Exploring cycle, the students are driven to conduct apperception of the discussion, i.e. seeking for information related to the topic of the discussion. In the Clustering cycle, the students are grouped with a given topic of discussion. Then in the Simulating cycle, the students will do the simulation by understanding, realizing, and being aware of the given topic. Afterwards, in the Valuing cycle, the students will then internalize the values taken from the discussion and simulation and are often related to real life situations. At last, in the Evaluating cycle, the students together with the teacher will evaluate the knowledge and skills they have developed during the class.

Meanwhile in the Task-Based Learning model, learning is developed through performing a series of activities as steps towards successful task realization (Malihah 2010, Huang 2010, Willis & Willis 2013). By working towards task realization, the language is used immediately in the real-world context of the learner, making learning authentic. The task completion as the common way to approach Task-Based learning has been commonly classified into three sections: pre-task, task cycle, and language focus (Malihah 2010, Huang 2010, Willis & Willis 2013).

2 METHOD

This study was designed in a non-experimental descriptive study where a taxonomic analysis for analyzing the types of the communication strategies was adapted from Dornyei's Taxonomy (1995). The subjects of this study were ELT sophomores' students from the University of Lampung (UNILA here onwards). The students were expected to have both their spoken and written English skills enhanced to achieve the expected level of competence. When they are demanded to be active in a classroom discussion, they have to participate using the target language as well. Therefore, it would be interesting to find out about their speaking performance and whether they already utilize communication strategies when they speak in English, especially in subject matter classes.

The subject matter classes require the learners to communicate their ideas in English well. One of the subject matter classes in the ELT study program in UNILA is English Teaching Media (ET Media). This class is taught in 100 minutes per week. The lecturer taught them using two models of learning: EXCLUSIVE for A class and Task-Based Learning for B class. Some learners were assigned to perform in front of the class in a group while the rest listened to them and participated in the discussion. The audience was not allowed to interrupt or ask questions in the middle of the subjects' performance, except when they were already allowed to (i.e. when they were in question and answer session). The subjects had to come in front of the classroom in groups and presented their works.

Two types of data collecting techniques were used to elicit students' communication strategies, observation and questionnaires. Such a way of collecting data has been widely known as a triangulation method. A triangulation method is carried out in order to make the data more valid. The questionnaire used was mainly based on the Oral Communication Strategy Inventory (OCSI) designed by Nakatani (2006). The questionnaire consisted of 32 items of 8 factors for coping with speaking problems and 26 items of 7 factors for coping with listening problems experienced during the communicative task. On a five-point scale ranging from "never" to "always", participants circled the responses indicating how often they use the strategies.

The reliability of the 32 items addressing strategies for coping with speaking problems was re-examined by looking at the Cronbach's Alpha value, and the alpha for these 32 items was.86. This indicates a highly acceptable internal consistency for the questionnaire used. Besides, Nakatani's Inventory was originally designed for university students; in current study, EFL students of UNILA taking the subject matter course. In terms of validity, by using a hands-on questionnaire with Nakatani's Inventory, the validity was expected to be satisfactory in advance. Therefore, the used questionnaire was suitable to identify the frequency of certain communication strategies used by the participants when they communicate with others. All items in the questionnaire were written in English.

As for the observation technique, the class activities were recorded. The recorded data were then transcribed in details. This was aimed at getting to get more valid data about the participants' activities. It was further required to help the researcher to analyze the data from the class activities. The next step taken afterward was coding, which is categorizing the finding of communication strategies into Dornyei's taxonomy. After coding, the numbers and percentages of strategies occurring during EXCLUSIVE and Task-Based speaking activities were calculated. This was should be done to find out any significant differences of communication strategies in those two learning models.

In this study, a non-participant observer technique in the classroom discussions type of data collection was chosen. Therefore, there was no elicited but natural discourse data. Students' performance in both models of learning was recorded. Following the completion of their class performance, the students reported their communication strategies used by filling out the given questionnaire.

For the observation data validity, the observation activities were carried out by using a recording device. The recorded data then transcribed and identified in order to gather the communication strategies occurred in the class activities. The next step was analyzing the data to categorize the communication strategies types.

Different types of communication strategies identified in this study were coded into a matrix of twelve types of communication strategies based on Dornyei's taxonomy. The taxonomy was selected because the categories seemed clearly explained and a more recent as it was developed from previous communication strategies taxonomies from Tarone, Faerch, and Kasper. Frequency forms were designed to classify the communication strategies occurring during the classroom activities. Subsequently, qualitative descriptions about the data collected from both the observation technique and questionnaire were drawn to discuss communication strategies employed by the learners in the two models of learning applied.

3   FINDINGS AND DISCUSSION

The research was conducted in four meetings for each class, Task-Based Learning and EXCLUSIVE class. Each meeting was 100 minutes long. We observed and recorded the classroom interaction in three meetings per class. In the meetings, the lecturer applied two of learning models to lead the class discussions. The target of the recording was communication strategies occurring during the classroom discussion. In other words, the study was intended to find out under which models of learning that the communication strategies would occur more frequently.

The classroom teaching was set as follows. There was One group of five students presented their work. The rest of the students were assigned to ask questions and give feedbacks about the presented topics. The students were demanded to speak in English during the class, but they could switch to Bahasa Indonesia whenever necessary. Communication strategies occurring in the Task-Based Learning class is presented in Table 1 below.

From Table 1 above, it can be seen that there were seven communication strategies produced by the students in the Task-Based Learning class. The time-Gaining strategy was the most frequently used by them, (33%) or as many as 41 students. Meanwhile, the Non-Linguistic Signals strategy was the second strategy that were mostly used (20.16%), or as many as 25 students. The third most used strategy was Appeal for Help with the percentage of 17.7%, or as many as 22 students. Code switching strategies were 13.7% of total number of strategies employed, followed by Message Abandonment strategies, Use of All-Purpose Words, and Topic Avoidance strategies with the percentages of 7.25%, 6.45%, and 1,61% respectively.

The similar observation was held in class B that was taught by using the EXCLUSIVE learning model. Similar to class A which was taught by using Task-Based Learning, there were also seven strategies produced by the students in class B that was taught using the EXCLUSIVE learning model. The time-Gaining strategy was the most frequently strategy used by the students, with the percentage of 32.4%, or as many as 48 students. Meanwhile, Non-Linguistic Signals was the second strategy that was mostly used with the percentage of 22.29%, or as many as 33 students. However, unlike class A, the third most used strategy used in class B was Code Switching with the percentage of 16.8%, or as many as 25 students.

The Appeal for Help strategy was produced by 14.8% of total number of strategies employed, followed by other strategies such as the Use of All-Purpose Words, Message Abandonment, and Topic Avoidance respectively with the percentage of 6.75%, 5.4%, and 1,35%. From these figures, it can be safely concluded that there were some different communication strategies used in Task-Based Learning and EXCLUSIVE learning model activities. communication strategies used in the EXCLUSIVE learning activities were found more frequent than those in Task-Based learning activities. The spread of communication strategies produced by the students were different in frequencies as displayed in Table 2 below.

Given the tables of communication strategies in both classes, some examples of the produced expressions regarded as communication strategies need to be adequately elaborated. First of all, in the Message Abandonment strategy, the students left some incomplete messages or utterances due to language difficulties they may encountered. For instance, when a student said, "I mean, I want to know if we use games... How media such as games important to teaching?" This student failed to express the referred games and failed to connect what messages he actually wanted to deliver.

Table 1. Communication strategies in A class (task based learning).

Cycles	Types of communication strategies											
	MA	TA	C	APP	UW	WC	NS	LT	F	CS	AH	TG
Pre-Task	1	–	–	–	–	–	3	–	–	1	2	3
Task Cycle	8	2			8		18			15	20	37
Language Focus	–	–	–	–	–	–	4	–	–	1	–	1
Total	9	2	–	–	8	–	25	–	–	17	22	41
%	7.25	1.61	–	–	6.45	–	20.16	–	–	13.7	17.7	33

MA: Message Abandonment; TA: Topic Avoidance; C: Circumlocution; APP: Approximation; UW: Use of All-Purpose Words; WC: Word Coinage; NS: Non-Linguistic Signals; LT: Literal Translation; F: Foreignizing; CS: Code Switching; AH: Appeal for Help; TG: Time Gaining.

Table 2. Communication strategies in B class (EXCLUSIVE).

Cycles	Types of communication strategies											
	MA	TA	C	APP	UW	WC	NS	LT	F	CS	AH	TG
Exploring	–	–	–	–	–	–	–	–	–	–	–	–
Clustering	–	–	–	–	–	–	–	–	–	–	–	–
Simulating	7	2	–	–	9	–	23	–	–	19	19	38
Valuing	–	–	–	–	–	–	5	–	–	4	2	7
Evaluating	1	–	–	–	1	–	5	–	–	2	1	3
Total	8	2	–	–	10	–	33	–	–	25	22	48
%	5.4	1.35	–	–	6.75	–	22.29	–	–	16.8	14.8	32.4

MA: Message Abandonment; TA: Topic Avoidance; C: Circumlocution; APP: Approximation; UW: Use of All-Purpose Words; WC: Word Coinage; NS: Non-Linguistic Signals; LT: Literal Translation; F: Foreignizing; CS: Code Switching; AH: Appeal for Help; TG: Time Gaining.

In the Topic Avoidance case, the students avoided the topic areas or concepts that were very difficult for them such as, "Schemata is... Something we..." the student quit the speaking as the intended message or utterances were not able to be spoken well in the target language. In the strategy of Use of All-Purpose Words, this was identified by the use of a very general word instead of using a proper diction such as when they said, "When you begin to make lesson plan, you have to think that the learners lack of things." The word "Things" is too broad and they caused the audience to outguess the intended idea. In the Non-Linguistic Signals strategy, the speaker has a tendency to use mimes, gestures, facial expressions, or imitation. For example, one student said "Technology and media are important because they can (moving her hands to the front, making repetition), stimulate..." Here, such a learner used hand gestures which helped her or him to reexpress what she or he actually wanted to say.

In the Code Switching strategy, students produced and switched their native language with the target language during the class. For instance, a student said, "Please remember there are two rules. First one, the question should base on power point, not from is, eh, else... *Harus sesuai sama topik yang akan dibahas.*" The student switched between their native and target language.

In the Appeal for Help strategy, the students were trying to ask for assistance from the interlocutor either directly or indirectly as found in the following example, "So of the students interesting with something... like, like, *eh, apa ya ngomongnya?* What is it,..." Subsequently, the Time-Gaining strategy was used when the speaker used fillers or hesitation devices to fill pauses and to gain time to think. For example, "Schemata are the mental structure by each individual that per... um... (looking at the text) perceived from environment..."

From the results of the questionnaire, it was found that the students were aware of the strategies that they could apply when they were demanded to communicate with the target language as the medium in the subject matter classes. In addition, the questionnaire was given to see students' perception on how they used certain strategies to overcome problems when they had to speak in the target language. The questionnaire adopted for this study was Nakatani's OCSI consisting of 32 items related to factors for coping with speaking problem and 26 items related to factors for coping with listening problems. Each of the items was provided with answers number 1 to 5 or in a form of Likert scale. Based on the result of the questionnaire, the researcher analyzed the students' responses from 32 students of class A and 39 of class B. It was found that from the items related to factors for coping with both speaking and listening problems, students from classes A and mostly chose options 3 and 4 for most of the items. The detailed students' responses to the questionnaire is illustrated in Table 3.

It can be seen from Table 3 above that scale numbers 3 and 4 dominated the answers for the items in both categories: strategies for coping with speaking and listening problems. For strategies coping with speaking problems, 36.4% from 32 items were chosen with option 4 by students from classes A and B, or as many as 813 times. Option number 3 were chosen by

Table 3. Students' Responses to OCSI Questionnaire.

Class	Strategies for coping with speaking problems (32 items)					Strategies for coping with listening problems (26 items)				
	1	2	3	4	5	1	2	3	4	5
A	33	84	314	380	207	24	66	209	324	159
B	28	151	374	433	229	15	99	363	321	141
Total	61	235	688	813	436	39	165	572	645	300
			2233					1721		
%	2.7	10.5	30.8	36.4	19.5	2.3	9.6	33.2	37.5	17.4

30.8% or 688 times. Options 5, 2, and 1 were chosen respectively for 19.5%, 10.5%, and 2.7% or as many as 436, 235, and 61 times. Meanwhile, for the strategies of coping with listening problems, 37.5% from 26 items were chosen with option 4 by students from classes A and B, or as many as 645 times. Option 3 was chosen for 33.2% or 572 times. Options 5, 2, and 1 were chosen respectively for 17.4%, 9.6%, and 2.3% or as many as 300, 165, and 39 times.

In the meantime, the two top most used communication strategies in both models were found the same: the Time-Gaining and Non-Linguistic Signals. Both learning models were students-centered, which means that the students were expected to be active in participating in the discussion. However, the participation must be in English. Time-Gaining strategy by using fillers was mostly used by the students with the percentage of 33% in Task-Based class and 32,4% in EXCLUSIVE one. The aim of this strategy is to gain time to think while trying to make the oral task run smoothly at the same time, but in this strategy they have used was merely hesitation device such as *mmm* and *uh*.

The students might forget words or utterances they actually knew, or they could not concentrate well. It is acceptable because the discussion was held without any rehearsal between the presenters and the audience. In other words, the discussion was spontaneous. Therefore, the questions and answers, or the interaction were unexpected and some of the students might feel nervous while they were speaking in L2. Thus, time gaining was used to think an appropriate word, phrase, or even structures because they did not want to overcome mishap in the conversation. They also used non-linguistic means such as mime, gesture, facial expression, and imitations to help reminding the subjects certain words so they could keep speaking.

The third most-used communication strategies in Task Based Learning and EXCLUSIVE classes were different. In the Task Based class, it was the Appeal for Help, whilein the EXCLUSIVE, it was the Code Switching. The frequency of the occurrence of both types of communication strategies in both classes were the same, 22 in number. However, the Code Switching occurred more than the Appeal for Help in the EXCLUSIVE class. The Appeal for Help occurred often during TBL's Task Cycle and EXCLUSIVE's Simulating stage where the presentation and discussion sessions took place. The students used them mostly when the presenters were answering the questions from the audience and when the audience wanted to ask a question or argue the presenter's remarks. In this kind of situation, the Appeal for Help strategy was often used after the use of the Time-Gaining. After the students spent some time thinking about the exact word by using fillers and couldn't find any, they would consciously or unconsciously asked their friends about it, for example, using "what is it called?, "What is it?", "*apa*", or "*apa namanya*".

The Code Switching strategy was the third most used in EXCLUSIVE class. Students used this strategy when they gave up speaking in English and then switched to Indonesian. They avoided delivering difficult words or sentences owing to the shy feeling or being worried about making mistakes. This study suggests that Task-Based Learning (TBL) and EXCLUSIVE classes stimulate different communication strategies in terms of quantity.

However, all of the seven types of occurring communication strategies in both class were found to be the same. The similarity of code-switching types occurring in TBL and EXCLUSIVE classes could be caused by several factors like Wei (2011) stated: both classes A and B students are in the sophomore year; so they shared similar level of language proficiency and

English communicative experience. It could also be seen from the results of the questionnaire that the students from both classes gave similar answers. Most of them chose options 3 and 4 for most of the items, which means that they were actually aware of how to keep up English conversation using certain strategies. However, they did not always use them. This indicates their need of more communication strategies training.

On the other hand, the difference in terms of quantity can be related to Rodriguez & Roux's (2012) statement. They pointed out that learning activity type is one of the factors that influenced the communication strategies used. TBL has three cycles of learning while EXCLUSIVE has five. From the observation technique, the researchers noticed that class A was active during the Task Cycle and slightly more passive during the Language Focus. Meanwhile, class B students were active during the Simulating, Valuing, and Evaluating cycles. It can be assumed that class B students spoke up more than class A ones. Thus, more communication strategies occurred in the EXCLUSIVE class.

As discussed earlier, the students employed seven types of communication strategies in both classes: the one taught by using EXCLUSIVE learning model and the other Task-Based learning model. However, it was found out that the EXCLUSIVE class happened to stimulate more occurrence of communication strategies rather than the Task-Based Learning. This could be caused by the difference of cycles of learning between Task-Based and EXCLUSIVE models. EXCLUSIVE learning model has Valuing and Evaluating cycles where the students were asked to say what points could be taken from the topic discussed in the class and gave comments and suggestion towards their own or their friends' presentation. This led them to speak more and thus, the students had more chance and demanded to speak in English.

A training for communication strategies is important in learning speaking to help learners make up for the lack of mastery of the target language and to make communication more effective. In order to improve student speaking performance, communication strategies can be trained even in subject-matter classes such as those applied: the EXCLUSIVE learning and Task-Based Learning models.

4 CONCLUSIONS AND SUGGESTIONS

Seven types of communication strategies were produced by EFL students learning a subject matter class at UNILA: the Message Abandonment, Topic Avoidance, Use of All-Purpose Words, Non—Linguistic Signals, Code Switching, Appeal for Help, and Time Gaining. Communication strategies occurred more frequently under the EXCLUSIVE Learning. It stimulated 8.83% more of Code-switching than the class taught using the Task-Based Learning. Communication strategies were most used during the Task Cycle (in the Task-Based class) and the Simulation stage (in the EXCLUSIVE class) when they were demanded to perform in English.

Communication strategies were used in both models of learning when the students needed time to think of the correct L2 word (time-gaining), needed some device to make them remember (non—linguistics device), needed help from the interlocutors-whether it's really necessary or not (appeal for help), cold not remember the word, phrase, or even structure so they use general word (use of all purpose words), or even when they give up speaking in L2 (message abandonment, topic avoidance, code switching). This study investigated the use of communication strategies in a subject matter classes using Task Based and EXCLUSIVE models of learning. Future research could try to focus on investigating the use of communication strategies in different models and then relate them to other factors affecting the use of communication strategies.

REFERENCES

Abdurrahman, T.W. & Kadaryanto, B. 2012. Pengembangan model pembelajaran tematik berorientasi kemampuan metakognitif untuk membentuk karakter literate dan awareness bagi siswa sekolah dasar di wilayah rawan bencana. *Prosiding Seminar Nasional Pendidikan Sains (SPNS), November 3rd, 2012.* Surakarta: Sebelas Maret University.

Al Hosni, S. 2014. Speaking difficulties encountered by young EFL learners. *International Journal on Studies in English Language and Literature (IJSELL)* 2(6): 22–30.

Cook, V. 2013. *Second language learning and language teaching.* Routledge.

Dörnyei, Z. & Scott, M.. 1997. *Communication strategies in a second language.*

Dörnyei, Z. 1995. On the teachability of communication strategies. *TESOL Quarterly.*

Faerch, C. & Kasper, G. 1984. Two ways of defining communication strategies. *Language learning* 34(1): 45–63.

Gan, Z. 2012. Understanding L2 speaking problems: implications for ESL curriculum development in a teacher training institution in Hong Kong. *Australian Journal of Teacher Education* 37(1): 43–59.

Gilakjani, A., Lai-Mei, L. & Sabouri, N. 2012. A study on the role of motivation in foreign language learning and teaching. *International Journal of Modern Education and Computer Science* 4(7): 9.

Huang, J. 2010. Grammar instruction for adult English language learners: A task-based learning framework. *Journal of Adult Education* 39(1): 29–37.

Hughes, R. & Reed, B.S. (2016). *Teaching and researching speaking.* Taylor & Francis.

Kadaryanto, B. & Santi, S.A. 2014. Exclusive: Integrating student centered learning and metacognitive strategies in teaching speaking, *Prosiding CONEST 11: The Eleventh International Conference on English Studies.* Jakarta: Unika Atma Jaya.

Kasper, G. & Kellerman, E. 2014. *Communication strategies: Psycholinguistic and sociolinguistic perspectives.* Routledge.

Lazarton, A. 2001. *Teaching oral skills.* In Celce-MurciaM., (Ed.), *Teaching English as a second or foreign language: 103–116.* Boston: Heinle & Heinle.

Littlemore, J. 2003. 'The communicative effectiveness of different types of communication strategy. *System* 31: 331–347.

Malihah, N. 2010. The effectiveness of speaking instruction through task-based language teaching. *Register Journal* 3(1): 85–101.

McDonough, J. & Shaw, C. 2003. *Materials and methods in ELT: A teacher's guide.* Oxford: Blackwell Publishing Ltd.

Nakatani, Y. 2006. Developing an oral communication strategy inventory. *Modern Language Journal* 90: 151–168.

Nunan, D. 1999. *Second Language Teaching & Learning.* Boston: Heinle & Heinle Publishers.

Richards, J.C. 2015. The changing face of language learning: Learning beyond the classroom. *RELC Journal* 46(1): 5–22.

Rodríguez, C.C. & Roux, R.R. 2012. The use of communication strategies in the beginner EFL classroom. *Gist Education and Learning Research Journal* 6(1): 111–127.

Rossiter, M.J. 2003. It's like chicken but bigger: Effects of communication strategy in the ESL classroom, *Canadian Modern Language Review* 60: 105–121.

Spolsky, B. 1999. *Concise encyclopedia of educational linguistics.* Oxford: Elsevier Science Ltd.

Susilawati, A. 2007. *The effect of learning strategy training: socio affective strategy in improving speaking.* Bandar Lampung: University of Lampung, Unpublished Script.

Sweeney, E. & Hua, Z. 2010. Accommodating toward your audience: do native speakers of English know how to accommodate their communication strategies toward nonnative speakers of English?. *The Journal of Business Communication* 47(4): 477–504.

Tarone, E. 1977. Conscious communication strategies in interlanguage: A progress report. In H. D. Brown, C. A. Yorio & R. C. Crymes (eds.), *On TESOL* 77: 194–203.

Wei, L. 2011. *A Study of Chinese English Learner's Attitude and Reported Frequency of Communicative Strategies.* Sweden: Kristianstad University, Unpublished Script.

Willems, G. 1987. Communication strategies and their significance in foreign language teaching. *System* 15: 351–364.

Willis, J. & Willis, D. 2013. *Doing task-based teaching-oxford handbooks for language teachers.* Oxford University Press.

ELT in Asia in the Digital Era: Global Citizenship and Identity – Madya et al. (Eds)
© 2018 Taylor & Francis Group, London, ISBN 978-0-8153-7900-3

Exploring English lexical inferencing strategies performed by EFL university students

I. Hermagustiana
Mulawarman University, Samarinda, Indonesia

ABSTRACT: This study investigated two points: (1) Lexical inferencing strategies applied by the S2 students while inferring word meanings from an English research paper and (2) the problems the students deal with while inferring word meanings from an English research paper. An introspective method was employed since it investigated the set of strategies and sources of knowledge employed during reading. Six English EFL students participated in this study. It was found out that the learners basically employed 12 types of lexical inferencing strategies which were grouped into four major strategies, namely: form-focused strategy, meaning-focused strategy, evaluating strategy, and monitoring strategy. Moreover, there were five lexical problems when the learners inferred unknown word meanings from a reading text.

1   INTRODUCTION

1.1   *Background of the study*

Reading is the primary means by which the new words of a second language can be easily transferred (Sedita 2005). This statement shows that both reading and vocabulary are two integrated and unique components which mainly assist foreign or second language learners in their language proficiency. Learning vocabulary is typically identical with memorizing a new word along with its definition in learners' native language. The definition is frequently derived from looking it up a bilingual dictionary. In fact, regardless of how much learners acquire new vocabulary, they will always be coming across unfamiliar words in reading activities (Thornburry 2000).

One of the vocabulary learning strategies in reading is inferring words from context from which an unknown word can be guessed when there are other words surrounding that word usually showing up its meaning (Nassaji 2006). In this study, the vocabulary learning strategy through contextual cues is defined as inferring and identifying the meanings of unknown words by utilizing the familiar contexts (Nash & Snowling 2006). Furthermore, the context method provides learners with more information related to an unknown word (Nash & Snowling 2006). Learners could be strongly encouraged to guess the word meaning from context by creating a well-specified semantic representation or known as semantic mapping, working out the unfamiliar word's part of speech, searching the context for other words that will help them puzzle out the meaning of the new word, letting other words throw light on its meaning and finally checking it out whether it makes sense or not (Wang 2011).

Most research in L1 and L2 vocabulary learning indicate that learners can derive meaning of unknown words while reading by using the context in which they appear (Nassaji 2003, Hu & Nassaji 2014, Nash & Snowling 2006). Based on this indication, Nash & Snowling (2006) suggest that the context method is more effective for increasing vocabulary knowledge and improving reading comprehension than the definition method in children with poor existing vocabulary knowledge. They found out that when unknown words were derived by memorizing their definitions, that method was time consuming and costly.

Nash & Snowling's (2006) study has additionally echoed Li's (1988) study in which learners were given cue-adequate sentences and reported greater ease in word inference and score higher in inferring and remembering the contextual meanings of unfamiliar words. Hence, the higher the scores of word inference, the better the retention of the contextual meanings of the target words in the texts. Li's study finally confirmed these hypotheses which showed that learners who received sentences with adequate contextual cues reported greater ease in word inference than those receiving sentences with inadequate contextual cues.

Not only does the use of context apply to learning general language, but in the light of English for specific purposes (ESP), it also shows that context can greatly enhance learners' vocabulary knowledge and development. Pritchard & Nasr (2004) illustrate in their study that the effectiveness of mobilizing contextual clues in reading engineering texts among non-native students. The data showed that the experimental group who learned the word meanings from context achieved a higher performance than the control group for whom dictionary use was permitted.

Moreover, Nassaji (2003) examined the use of strategies and knowledge sources in L2 lexical inferencing and their relationship with inferential success. Analysis reveals that (a) overall, the rate of success was low even when learners used the strategies and knowledge sources they had at their disposal, (b) different strategies contributed differentially to inferencing success, and (c) success was related more to the quality rather than the quantity of the strategies used.

Last, a study from Hu & Nassaji (2014) investigated similar variables to those in Nassaji's (2003) study. Using think-aloud procedures with 11 Chinese ESL learners, this mixed-design study explored L2 learners' inferential strategies and the relationship with their success. Twelve types of inferential strategies were found to be used by all the learners, and two groups of learners were identified: successful and less successful inferencers. The results of both quantitative and qualitative analyses confirmed a number of differences between successful and less successful inferencers, which pertained to not only the degree to which they used certain strategies but also when and how to use them successfully.

1.2 *Research questions*

Based on a number of studies above, the researcher attempted to address the issue of students' lexical inferencing strategies through a reading text by formulating the following research questions:

1. What lexical inferencing strategies and knowledge sources do the S2 students apply while inferring word meanings from an English research article?
2. What inferencing problems do they deal with when inferring word meanings from an English research article?

2 METHODS

2.1 *Design*

This study applied an introspective method since it investigated the set of strategies and sources of knowledge employed during reading. As the main data of this study were the students' reading aloud transcriptions, a qualitative design was carried out.

2.2 *Participants*

This study involved six S2 students of the English Department, Faculty of Education, Universitas Mulawarman who were coded as P1 (1st participant), P2 (2nd participant), P3 (3rd participant), P4 (4th participant), P5 (5th participant), and P6 (6th participant). They were selected as the participants of this study after they had a vocabulary pre-test whose results categorized them into the high group. This group consisted of the students who scored above 50. In this study, the six participants were asked to infer some word meanings from a research article and verbalize their thoughts during reading process.

Table 1. Classification of lexical inferencing strategies.

Category	Strategy
Form-focused	Analyzing
	Associating
	Repeating
Meaning-focused	Using textual clues
	Using prior knowledge
	Paraphrasing
Evaluating	Making inquiry
	Confirming/disconfirming
	Commenting
Monitoring	Stating the failure/difficulty
	Suspending judgment
	Reattempting

2.3 *Instruments*

Two instruments were to help the researcher, as the key instrument, collect data in this study as follows:

1. Reading text: The researcher took a research article from a book chapter titled *Age of Second-Language Acquisition: Critical Periods and Social Concerns* written by David Birdsong and Jan Vanhove (2016) in *Bilingualism across the Lifespan: Factors Moderating Language Proficiency*. This is a 20-page research article; however, the researcher merely selected the first two pages with some considerations, such as time limit. 10 unfamiliar words were selected as the focus of the participants' thinking aloud activities.
2. Audio recorder: To record the students' verbalization of thoughts during reading, an audio recorder was employed. Each participant completed the think aloud procedure in 20–30 minutes.

2.4 *Data analysis*

The analysis of data began by transcribing the voice recording of students' think aloud during reading process. Following this, making codes for similar information from the transcripts was undertaken. Similar codes of information were applied to develop a small number of categories which were used to build main themes. The researcher based her data analysis on the categories developed by Hu & Nassaji (2014) on lexical inferencing strategies and sources of knowledge as seen in the following table (Table 1).

3 DISCUSSIONS

This section presents the answers of the questions of the research along with some relevant theories supporting them.

3.1 *What lexical inferencing strategies and knowledge sources do the S2 students apply while inferring word meanings from an English research article?*

Nassaji (2003) differentiate between strategies and appeals to knowledge sources. Strategies are defined as conscious cognitive or metacognitive activities that the learner used to gain control over or understand the problem without any explicit appeal to any knowledge source as assistance; while *knowledge sources are defined* as instances when the learner made an explicit reference to a particular source of knowledge, such as grammatical, morphological, discourse, world, or L1 knowledge (Nassaji 2003).

From the findings obtained, the learners applied all types of inferential strategies proposed by Hu & Nassaji (2014) in their word inferencing process. The strategies used included form-focused strategies, meaning-focused strategies, evaluating strategies, and monitoring strategies. Within Huckin & Bloch's (1993) model, the role of these strategies can be seen as examples of cognitive decision-making processes learners use while interacting with the text and formulating and testing their word meaning hypotheses. Among the lexical inferencing strategies, meaning-focused strategies were the most frequently employed strategies by the students. These strategies include using textual cues, using prior knowledge, and paraphrasing (Hu & Nassaji 2014). It demonstrates that the participants relied more intensely on the importance of the meanings of the words which were inferred through context rather than on the word forms.

Furthermore, all types of sources of knowledge as discovered in Nassaji's study (2003) were identified in this study. The knowledge sources which were discovered encompassed morphological, grammatical, L1, discourse, and world knowledge. The participants used discourse knowledge of the words as the source in inferring word meanings most frequently, indicating that they were very dependent on these kinds of knowledge when inferencing word meanings from context and that this knowledge provided an important knowledge base for their judgments. In contrast, world knowledge was the least used source of knowledge used in word inference which may imply that the participants lacked information beyond the context of the target words. The deficient use of world knowledge in this study is in contrast with Nassaji's (2003) study which discovered that world knowledge was the most frequently used knowledge in word inferencing strategy.

The data show that the use of lexical inferencing strategies does not predominantly determine the success of word inference. It means that the success of word inference does not depend on a particular strategy of a single source of knowledge, but it could come from various strategies, and could be influenced some other aspects.

3.2 What inferencing problems do they experience while inferring word meanings from an English research article?

From the data of successful and unsuccessful inferencing, it was found out that two participants (P1 and P4) were regarded as lexically skilled since they could infer 5 words or more out of 10 selected words, while four of them (P2, P3, P5, and P6) were considered less skilled for inferring fewer than 5 words. All of the participants applied all strategies with different levels of intensity and frequency. *Using textual cues* was the most frequently used strategy in both successful and unsuccessful word inference. The selection of strategy therefore did not determine the success of students' inference.

The unsuccessful inferencing lead to incorrect word meanings which resulted from a number of lexical inferencing problems. There are five inferencing problems identified from the students' attempts to infer word meanings from context as follows:

3.2.1 Misleading clues
The participants used the clues to infer word meanings from the text but the inference is not appropriate. There are three types of misleading clues identified in the findings:

1. Misleading root of a word
The participants mistakenly determine a root of a word which eventually affects the word inference.

Sample (P5):

> "Recurring...recur... One recurring critique is that nativelike performance on a small battery of L2 tasks ...recurring berarti perbaikan, memperbaiki kembali kali ya... kritik membangun mungkin...eemm... dari konteks kalimatnya ini ada kata kritik... eehh...kemudian ada cure yang meaningnya memperbaiki, eh cure menyembuhkan, sama re—berarti menyembuhkan kembali tapi kalau jadi kritik mungkin memperbaiki saya pikir"

The failure of word inferencing lies on learners' characteristics which are shown from some studies. Frantzen (2003) reveals learners' behaviour as one of the factors which affect the process of learning vocabulary from context. She illustrates various behaviours which support Huckin & Bloch's (1993) study reporting the errors made by their learners that could "be attributed largely to the subjects' failure to use context clues" (p. 160).

Learners often show inattention to the context. They frequently overlook when they make their guesses. As a result, misinterpretation occurs when they try to derive word meanings from context. This can be seen from the above sample where the learner did not really pay attention to the word being inferred. This inattentive behavior results in a wrong guess when inferring a novel English word.

2. Misleading word class

The participants mistakenly determine the word class of a word so it leads them to inappropriate inference.
Sample (P4):

> "Caveats... we illustrate how seemingly minor technical or statistical caveats... kalau ditembak dengan muncul bisa tidak ya... ini ditambah—s mungkin kata kerja, seperti appear gitu... karena ada minor technical, caveat disini mungkin kata kerja"

The learner's single focus on a particular word class diverted him to guess only one word class without analyzing the word more deeply. Moreover, this could result from the learner's lack of knowledge on other types of parts of speech and how he inappropriately beheld other surrounding words' word classes.

3. Misleading affix

The participants make a wrong inference due to prefix/suffix they thought they knew but it was wrong.
Sample (P2):

> "Their nonnativelikeness, nonnative berarti yang bukan native...might have been discerned...their nonnativelikeness, kemungkinan itu tidak... kalau dites terus kemungkinan, nonnativelikeness tidak terlihat, tidak nampak, atau bisa juga tidak apa ya... lawan kata dari tidak nampak...eh nampak ya...tidak nampak, lawan katanya tidak tampak, nampak, terlihat...discerned, tidak terlihat...yang lebih mendekati terlihat sih karena setelah tes tadi bahwa kemungkinan hilang karena berkali-kali dites, jadi mungkin tidak nampak, tidak terlihat"

In the above sample, the learner was distracted by the prefix *dis-* in discerned which he inferred into *tidak* in Indonesian. However, the prefix in that context does not explicitly nor implicitly involve a negative meaning as usually displayed by *tidak*. This tendency of using negation for the prefix dis—might come from the learner's familiarity with such words as disable, dislike, disapprove, etc, which possess negative meanings.

3.2.2 *Insufficient clues*

The participants tried to infer word meanings through contextual clues but the clues are not enough for them to achieve the correct inference, so they just guess most of the time and their guessing is often wrong.
Sample (P2):

> "apa ya....diverge...learners tend to diverge... menerka, memperoleh, memahami... from monolingual natives... mendengarkan... diverge from monolingual... I have no idea about this"

It cannot be taken for granted that clues are present in the text and need only to be discovered by the learners. They may be available there, or they may not. One cannot depend on contextual redundancy since there is no guarantee that a given context is redundant enough to provide clues to precisely those words that are unknown to the learners (Laufer 1997).

Furthermore, the contextual cue adequacy also determines whether the learners can successfully infer the meaning of a novel word. As Li (1988) found out that if the cues were sufficiently available in context, the learners easily inferred and recalled the target words. In other words, cue adequacy and availability facilitate both inferencing and retention.

Thus, the availability of contextual cues in a text becomes one of the main reasons why the learners can infer word meanings from context. When a text adequately provides some clues to the learners, it is very possible for them to understand the meanings of unfamiliar words. In contrast, as shown in the sample above, the insufficiency of clues leads the learners to the confusion.

3.2.3 *Inappropriate word association*
The participants associated a target word with either another English or an Indonesian word.

1. The participants associate a TW with another word which has similar sound or form but very different meaning (synforms)
   Sample (P5):

   "The last one, discerned…their nonnativelikness might have been discerned …sudah menjadi eehh masalah ya concern, perhatian kali…dari concerned"

This problem might be rooted from the phenomenon of synform as one of the types of deceptively transparent words which are defined as words which seem to provide clues to their meanings but they do not (Laufer 1989). The learners might have learnt one word of the pair/group, but since its representation in the memory is effective, a similar word which shares most of its formal features might look identical to it. Therefore, the synformic confusion takes place. In the above sample, the learner confused 'discerned' with 'concerned' due to the similar word parts.

2. The participants associate a TW with an Indonesian word which has similar sound or form but different meaning (word with multiple meanings).
   Sample (P3):

   "Conglomerate… it's like related to big…something like huge, rich…because of the Indonesian word. Although often referred to as the critical period hypothesis for L2 acquisition, the critical period hypothesis or second language acquisition is actually a conglomerate of partly overlapping, partly contradictory hypotheses … has a big position…has a big impact to something… must effect…huge effect"

Another problem with inappropriate word association above is the involvement of a word with more than one meaning (Laufer 1990). In the above sample, the learner seemed to be more familiar with one of the meanings of the word in Indonesian (learner's L1); therefore, he associated the more familiar meaning to the inferred word since he might know only that meaning.

3.2.4 *Lack of appropriate synonym/term*
The participants understand the concept but cannot manifest it in word representation.
   Sample (P6):

   "Berarti..eehhh to rehash… do not intend…tidak untuk di…rehash ini apa ya… saya ngerti tapi kata yang pas itu apa gitu…jadi inikan ada kata several recent overviews summarize studied insipired by ini and we don't intend to rehash…berarti kita tidak … emm…jangan memulai kembali survey tersebut"

One view on what goes wrong in this problem is that the learner's useful knowledge of words is not sufficient. Accordingly, in any given text there is a risk of comprehension failing because the processes that connect word meanings to text representations do not have enough high quality word representations with which to work. The lexical quality hypothesis (Perfetti 2007; Perfetti & Hart 2001) proposes that at least some comprehension problems originate in low lexical quality, defined as accessible knowledge of a word's form and meaning. It is shown in the above sample where the learner seemed to comprehend the overall meaning of the sentence. However, due to limited vocabulary representation both in English and Indonesian, or due to the fact that she has low lexical quality, she could not find an appropriate meaning for that word.

3.2.5 *Tendency of using "common term"*

The participants are familiar with the term and use it in their inference due to insufficient clues and limited vocabulary knowledge.

Sample (P3):

> *"Then another word... this chapter aims to provide readers with a technical toolkit to critically evaluate research on the divisive issue that is the critical period hypothesis or second language acquisition ... divisive issue, current maybe, current issue"*

In the above sample, it can be seen that the learner merely picked up a common term "current" as the synonym of the target word "divisive" to precede the word "issue". He made this inference when he was attempting to infer through the whole sentence where "divisive" is available. Since "issue" is the closest to the target word and the rest of the sentence did not really help him define the target word, "current" sounded better than other words to replace "divisive".

4   CONCLUSIONS AND SUGGESTIONS

The learners basically employed 12 types of lexical inferencing strategies which were grouped into four major strategies, namely: form-focused strategy, meaning-focused strategy, evaluating strategy, and monitoring strategy. Moreover, the learners attempted to infer word meanings through five identified sources of knowledge: morphological, grammatical, first language (L1), discourse, and world knowledge. Meaning-focused strategy was the most frequently applied strategy while discourse knowledge was the most used knowledge source when inferring word meanings. Moreover, there are five lexical problems when the learners inferred unknown word meanings from a reading text. The problems are misleading cues, insufficient cues, inappropriate word association, lack of appropriate term/synonym, and the tendency of using "common term".

However, this study needs some improvement due to some limitations identified. First, future researchers are suggested to use several reading texts with various fields of study in order that data comparison could be obtained. Second, future researchers are expected to employ more participants to get richer data about lexical inferencing strategies. The participants might have distinct levels of study to find out the tendency of using the strategies differently by different levels of students. Third, the strategies of word inferencing could be of benefit for English teachers who wish to improve their students' word inferencing technique and reading comprehension. Therefore, the teachers need to encourage the students to employ all inferential strategies, without merely focusing on one particular strategy. Last, in terms of sources of knowledge, it is expected that the teachers provide the students with general knowledge which eventually could help them understand assorted English texts along with the relevant vocabulary.

REFERENCES

Frantzen, D. 2003. Factors affecting how second language Spanish students derive meaning from context. *The Modern Language Journal* 87(2): 168–199.

Hu, H. M. & Nassaji. H. 2014. Lexical inferencing strategies: The case of successful versus less successful inferencers. *System* 45: 27–38.

Huckin, T., & Bloch, J. 1993. Strategies for inferring word-meanings in context: A cognitive model. In T. Huckin, M. Haynes, J. Coady (eds.), *Second language reading and vocabulary learning*: 153–176. Norwood: Ablex Publishing Corporation Norwood.

Laufer, B. 1989. A factor of difficulty in vocabulary learning: Deceptive transparency. In P. Nation & C. Carter (eds.), *Vocabulary acquisition: Issue 6 of the AILA review*. Amsterdam: Free University Press.

Laufer, B. 1990. Why are some words more difficult than others? Some intralexical factors that affect the learning of words. *IRAL* 28(4): 293–307.

Laufer, B. 1997. The lexical plight in second language reading: Words you don't know, words you think you know, and words you can't guess. In J. Coady & T. Huckin (eds.), *Second language vocabulary acquisition: A rationale for pedagogy*: 20–34. New York: Cambridge University Press.

Li, X. 1988. Effects of contextual cues on Inferring and remembering meanings of new words. *Applied Linguistics* 9(4): 402–413.

Nash, H., & Snowling, M. 2006. Teaching new words to children with poor existing vocabulary knowledge: A controlled evaluation of the definition and context methods. *International Journal of Language and Communication Disorders* 41(3): 335–354.

Nassaji, H. 2003. L2 vocabulary learning from context: strategies, knowledge sources, and their relationship with success in L2 lexical inferencing. *TESOL Quarterly* 37(4): 645–670.

Nassaji, H. 2006. The relationship between depth of vocabulary knowledge and L2 learners' lexical inferencing strategy use and success. *The Modern Language Journal* 90(3): 387–401.

Perfetti, C. A. 2007. Reading ability: Lexical quality to comprehension. *Scientific Studies of Reading* 11: 357–383.

Perfetti, C. A., & Hart, L. 2001. The lexical bases of comprehension skill. In D. Gorfien (ed.), *On the consequences of meaning selection*: 67–86. Washington, DC: American Psychological Association.

Pritchard, R., & Nasr, A. 2004. Improving reading performance among Egyptian engineering students: Principles and practice. *English for Specific Purposes* 23(4): 425–445.

Sedita, J. 2005. Effective vocabulary instruction. *Insights on Learning Disabilities* 2(1): 33–45.

Thornburry, S. 2000. *How to teach vocabulary*. England: Pearson Education Limited.

Wang, Q. 2011. Lexical inferencing strategies for dealing with unknown words in reading—A contrastive study between Filipino graduate students and Chinese graduate students. *Journal of Language Teaching and Research* 2(2): 302–313.

ELT in Asia in the Digital Era: Global Citizenship and Identity – Madya et al. (Eds)
© 2018 Taylor & Francis Group, London, ISBN 978-0-8153-7900-3

Digital collaboration and the impact on motivation and identity

S. Healy
Kyoto Institute of Technology, Kyoto, Japan

ABSTRACT: In common with most EFL students, Japanese university students have limited access to authentic and meaningful communication in English. To help to address this problem, Kyoto Institute of Technology (KIT) has been collaborating on a pilot classroom Skype project with an English conversation school based in the Philippines. Over the course of a semester, students worked in small groups on four presentations which they delivered on a monthly basis to the teachers in Cebu using Skype. It was found that the sessions, although limited in number, had a significant influence on the students which included a positive impact on their identities as language users and their levels of language anxiety, and even on their motivation to study English.

1 INTRODUCTION

The prevailing view of Japanese students' language abilities is largely negative, with a general belief amongst the public and academics that language education in Japan is ineffective (McVeigh 2002). In light of these opinions and the increased importance of globalization, the Japanese government has been encouraging students to develop higher-level skills to enable them to compete and cooperate internationally. For example, the recent Project for Promotion of Global Human Resource Development stated its aims were, "to foster human resources who can positively meet the challenges and succeed in the global field, as the basis for improving Japan's global competitiveness and enhancing the ties between nations" (MEXT 2012). To accomplish this, the government is promoting the development of language skills and advanced linguistic activities, such as debates and classroom presentations. This new focus on English as a Lingua Franca (ELF) increases the onus on the learner to engage practically with others, and in turn generates new challenges in motivation and the reduction of language-learning anxiety.

This study aims to show that students in Japan are able to enhance their language skills, especially in English, if they are enabled to adopt an 'international posture' (Yashima 2002) and participate in an international community which requires authentic communication. The findings also indicate that motivation to study is greatly improved if such real-world opportunities are provided. This is crucial at this time in Japan as it prepares to enter the global arena and is suffering from low ranking on world academic and communicative ability. It was placed 37th of 80 countries on the EF English Proficiency Index (2017) and 40th out of 48 countries on the Test of English for International Communication (TOEIC) in 2016. The results of this study of 4 sessions over a period of one semester have been analyzed qualitatively in four areas: perceived improvements of language skills; motivation; ambivalence; and 'international posture.'

2 LITERATURE REVIEW

Horwitz, Horwitz & Cope (1986) define foreign-language anxiety as, "a distinct complex of self-perceptions, beliefs, feelings and behaviors, related to classroom language learning, arising from the uniqueness of the language learning process." Anxiety may also be associated with Communication Apprehension (CA), fear leading to avoidance of interaction and anxiety about negative evaluation and opinions (McCrosky 1984). In addition, Horwitz et al. (1986) suggest that learners feel uncomfortable due to the gap between their high-level thinking skills and low-level linguistic skills. This disparity, along with the uncomfortable feelings it generates, may result in students' unwillingness to communicate and a serious lack of motivation. MacIntyre, Clement, Dornyei & Noels (1998: 546) defined 'willingness to communicate' (WTC) as "the probability of engaging in communication, when [an individual is] free to choose to do so."

In terms of motivation and identity in second-language acquisition, many studies have described both integrative and instrumental motivation. Gardner & Lambert (1972) characterize language learners with integrative motivation as being interested in the culture of the target language, wanting to 'fit in' with the target language group, and, in some cases because they have family members or significant others who live in the target language community. Instrumental motivation, on the other hand, is indicated by studying the target language to pass a test or get promoted at work. Perhaps it goes without saying that integrative motivation is considered more effective for language acquisition. Certainly, within the context of Japanese EFL (and ELF), students have so few opportunities to interact with international English speakers, and as such, it therefore may be difficult to develop integrative motivation.

Yashima (2002) believes that for Japanese students, English is a symbol of the surrounding world and a method of communication with people from other countries referring to this attitude as "international posture." This approach to motivation and identity, in the Japanese context, moves L2 learners away from trying to assimilate into a target-language community. The results of Yashima's 2002 study showed international posture to be a strong factor in both willingness to communicate and in galvanizing motivation.

Recent research on language-learning motivation has focused on the "ideal L2 self" and its impact on motivation. Dornyei (2013) describes the "ideal L2 self" as a powerful motivator, because most learners want to reduce discrepancies between their 'present self' and their "ideal L2 self." Dornyei in Yashima (2009) expands on this idea, saying students must develop a vivid idea of their L2 selves: "possible selves need to be something you can touch and feel, or that you are afraid of." (p.9) She also found a significant difference in levels of both international posture and willingness to communicate, when comparing students engaged in an actual L2 community—in this case, studying abroad—and students who were not.

3 METHOD

3.1 *Methods*

The online collaboration with Filipino teachers involved 40 first-year chemistry undergraduates at Kyoto Institute of Technology, a national university in Japan. There were two classes of twenty students, with only three female students and one student from either China or Malaysia enrolled in each class. The Skype teachers were all female from the Philippines. The teachers in Japan were from Britain and Japan respectively.

3.2 *Procedure*

The four synchronous, online, computer-mediated sessions occurred during the second semester of the academic year. Students and teachers in Japan had been working together since the beginning of the first semester so they knew each other well. Since Japanese academic semesters run for four months each, one session per month was scheduled in October, November, December, and January.

In October, students were given all the information regarding each session, including the topics to be covered. Then they were assigned randomly to groups which remained the same for all four of the Skype sessions. During the weekly class times, when students were preparing and practicing for the Skype sessions, they changed their Skype groups and worked with other people. The students didn't have the same teachers for each Skype session as the Filipino teachers changed for each session.

In the weeks prior to each Skype session, students reviewed the topic, brainstormed a theme, and shared ideas, each student choosing a different aspect of the topic to study. For the session on Japanese culture, the students used a package called 'Glocal Studies' (Kimura 2007) developed at Kyoto University to help Japanese students present aspects of Japanese culture in English. For example, when discussing Filipino life, one group of students chose the topic, "Industry in the Philippines," and different members of the group shared information they had researched concerning agriculture, fishing, electronics, shipping and tourism. As homework, they researched and prepared a presentation script, and the following week, practiced in groups, timing each other and critiquing their performances. Then, in the final week, they undertook the sessions in their designated Skype groups.

3.3   Data collection

MacIntyre & Gardner (1991) and MacIntyre, Burns & Jessome (2011) use the 'focused essay' technique to investigate students' willingness to communicate in an L2. This methodology is used as, "A qualitative analysis of these situations [which] provides a window into the thought processes of the students and highlights numerous interconnected and sometimes conflicted features of the learner, (and) the communication context." (p. 82). For the same reasons, the 'focused essay' technique was used in this study, participants being instructed to write an essay based on their experience of using Skype to communicate in English with Filipino teachers, describing what they liked and disliked about it and how they felt. The students had 30 minutes in class to write the essays in English.

These essays were analyzed initially using an open coding process adapted from Holton (2007), and the comments divided into 2 major categories, positive and negative. They were then re-examined in order to identify reoccurring themes and subsequently organized into relevant subordinate categories for analysis.

3.4   The sessions

The Skype sessions all took place using iPad minis to communicate with the teachers in the Philippines. When participating in the sessions, each student was assigned a role: presenter, timer and recorder, reporter, and questioner, with roles rotating each time the presenter changed.

The presenter spoke for five minutes; the timer kept time and recorded sessions on a second iPad mini; the reporter filled in a short questionnaire to give feedback to the presenter; and questioners were responsible for developing questions to direct at the presenter.

At the beginning of each session, students greeted the Filipino teacher, made small talk, and then began their five-minute presentations. Presenters used an informal presentation style, followed by two minutes of feedback and questions posed by the Filipino teacher, and two minutes of questions and discussion with other students, totaling nine minutes. Each group was allotted one hour, so there was usually adequate time for everyone to take a turn, and some remaining time for a group discussion with the teacher.

Session topics, in order, were:

1. Self-introduction, describing students' lives since entering university
2. Japanese culture
3. Filipino culture
4. Free topic

The choice of topics, by design, varied the role the students took. In the first two sessions, the students were given the role of "expert," but in the third, roles were reversed, since the teachers were "experts" on Filipino culture. The role of expert in the fourth session depended on the topic chosen. After each individual session, students were asked to complete reflection sheets concerning their performance, as well as that of others. The Filipino teachers gave immediate, verbal feedback to students following their presentations, commenting on positive aspects and advising on areas that needed further work. They also provided KIT teachers with written feedback on the sessions, describing problems encountered, positive results, and whether or not students were improving.

4 RESULTS AND DISCUSSION

Overall, students responded positively to the project. They were extremely nervous before the first session, and afterward, were exhausted; however, they were pleasantly surprised that they were able to make themselves understood in English.

A total of 43 essays were received and the analysis of the data revealed 6 significant themes as shown in Table 1.

To illustrate each focused essay theme, direct quotations (including spelling and grammar mistakes) from students' essays were selected.

Perceived improvement in English language skills

As mentioned, Japanese EFL students have few chances to engage in authentic communication in English and may be apprehensive of and lacking in confidence in communicating in English.

> *"I like Skype class. At first I didn't like it. But as I taked part in this class, I came to feel funny to talk with Phillipns teacher. Then I thought English isn't as difficult as I expected."*

> *"I thought English was hard and Filipn teacher not understand me, but I was surprised when she can."*

Here we can see evidence of apprehension at the start of the sessions which changed to feelings of enjoyment over time. The expectation that speaking in English would be very difficult was changed and accompanying this change there was a corresponding reduction in anxiety. Indeed, most studies of EFL learners show a reduction in anxiety about learning following positive learning experiences (Gardner et al. 1979, Tanaka & Ellis 2003, Tran & Moni 2015).

Further, many students remarked that they felt that their English had improved during the course.

> *"When I talked with them at last time I can speak fluently than for the first time."*

Self-evaluations of linguistic ability may be imprecise (Mochizuki 1999, Brantmeier 2006), but the salient factor is that the student believes that there has been an improvement and has re-positioned themselves as a successful language learner. MacIntyre & Gardener (1991) suggest that, "students taught to emphasize their own successful experiences in the second language would come to perceive themselves as more proficient language learners, increasing their self-confidence (p. 303)." Through their experiences of communicating with the Filipino teachers and writing the focused essays, students built up their confidence and altered their self-perceptions to form images of themselves as successful language learners.

Table 1. Themes from focused essays.

Theme	No. of entries
Perceived improvement in English language skills	25
Motivation to study English	20
Ambivalence about using English	17
Language user identity	11
International posture	8

Language user

> *"I studied a lot for tests in high school, but I did not speak. I had to use my English to talk on Skype."*

> *"It was hard to do Skype. I had to think myself contents and write it and speak it. I thought terrible, but I think now good and feel good."*

As is well-known, mainstream Japanese students have typically spent 6 years studying English for the most part using the grammar translation method in order to pass university entrance examinations (Nishino 2008). According to Ryan (2009) this situation is not compatible with the view that English is a system for communication between people in the flesh, not on paper, and has placed them in a passive role as a learner instead of an active role as a user of English. In addition, cultural beliefs concerning the use of English as an international language place Japanese students in the outer circle of language with little or no ownership of the language they are studying. In order to develop a stronger sense of ownership, Matsuda (2003) recommends interaction between non-native speakers. We can see that the Skype sessions with the Filipino teachers placed the students in an active role as users of English, and that, while they found this difficult, it was also satisfying.

This shift in identity from language learner to language user has consequences for the students' perceptions of their L2 selves moving towards an ideal self that includes someone who is a successful language user. This is undoubtedly a powerful motivator.

Motivation

> *"Before English was just for tests now I can use English another way. I am fun."*

> *"I only did English boring before from now I want to study more use English."*

Here students describe their previous experiences of studying English in junior and senior high schools where the emphasis was on testing to pass university entrance examinations, as uninteresting and limiting. The shift in focus in tertiary education in Japan to more communicative styles (Ryan op. cit.) is viewed positively here as an alternative and more interesting way to learn English. It may also express a movement from extrinsic motivation to intrinsic motivation, and from a tightly controlled environment to a less restricted one in which there is more individual autonomy and an emphasis on the social and communicative aspects of English.

A surge in motivation may also be found in student's relationships with each other.

> *"I listened other students English and I learned a lot of technics to communicate well, so I look forward to speak."*

In the above, the student shows increased motivation to speak English after working with other students. The support of other students has been shown (MacIntyre 2011) to create a positive atmosphere which leads to feelings of empowerment, which in turn generates feelings of increased confidence and motivation. The students in this present study clearly exhibit more eagerness to speak, and according to MacIntyre et al. (2011), they appear to "have met two major antecedents for L2 communication: having a feeling of self-confidence... and the desire to speak to a specific person for authentic communication."

In addition, students may feel increased confidence if they are able to compare themselves to other students in a favourable light.

> *"I listen to my friends and I thought I was same. I worried before, about my English. I thought good experience."*

Working in groups was perceived as beneficial and enjoyable by the students.

> *"I liked my group. They helped me a lot."*

> *"My group was fun and we learned a lot of things together. It was my precious experience."*

A supportive classroom culture is vital to successful language learning and the cooperative learning atmosphere created in the Skype activities provided this. Using Skype in the classroom encouraged varying interaction patterns and provided many opportunities for the students to use English meaningfully.

Ambivalence

'Ambivalence' refers to the situation in which learners hold both negative and positive feelings or attitudes at the same time. MacIntyre et al. (2009) observed that "ambivalence of the learner's psychological experience stems from several processes running simultaneously, often without the learner's explicit awareness" (p. 17).

> *I must speak English becus the Filipino teacher does not speak Japanese. It is tough for me. I don't like it, but it is good to practice.*

> *"About Skype, before I used Skype and talked with other country teachers, I didn't like to speak English. But I began to talk with them, more and more I like to speak English."*

> *"I liked it and I hated it. It was hard to do, my friends said too. But it was interesting."*

> *"Every time I didn't want to do it, but every time it was fun."*

> *I don't like English, but Skype was fun."*

The learners' conflicted attitudes are clearly apparent in their own words. We can see that learners want to communicate, but at the same time feel unwilling. This combination of willingness and unwillingness is often situation dependent, but may also be culturally or internally dependent. MacIntyre (2011) describes the duality many language learners experience and posits that willingness to communicate and unwillingness to communicate be conceptualized as "separate but interacting dimensions" (p. 93). This highlights the complicated psychological processes students are undergoing during L2 communication.

International posture

> *"I have not often talk with foreign people. It was so valuable experience."*

> *"I had never known interesting point about English before this class. But I can notice about talking with foreigner is very very interesting."*

> *"I didn't know about the Philippines but I think very interesting."*

> *"I want to go to Filippins now."*

Yashima's (2002) notion of 'international posture' was created to "capture a tendency to relate oneself to the international community rather than any specific L2 group, as a construct more pertinent to EFL contexts," (p. 2). She develops this further observing that in the Japanese EFL context learners are not interested in identifying with native speakers and that English is something that can be used to communicate with people all over the world. While using Skype with the Filipino teachers, the students were able to participate in an international community and generate English-using versions of selves. Furthermore, these L2 'selves' were real and as Dornyei (op cit) described "something you can touch and feel" (p. 9). Students felt that it was interesting to speak to people from other countries, which sparked an interest for them to explore other places in the world and to continue to improve their English in order to do this.

5 CONCLUSION

This educational initiative, although limited in its scope at this stage, appears to have had a positive influence on the participant's identities as language users, their levels of language anxiety and their motivation to study English. Importantly, it has enabled the students to create a positive image of themselves as successful L2 users rather than seeing themselves as failed native speakers (Cook 1999: 85). In addition, connecting with the Filipino teachers through Skype and so initiating their own international community has encouraged a more global outlook in which the participants could choose to be active users rather than passive learners of English, thus empowering them to make ownership claims.

It must be noted that there are several limitations to this study including the limited number of participants and the subjective nature of the focused essays. In the future, we would like to combine quantitative and qualitative data to form a more complete picture.

ACKNOWLEDGEMENTS

This work was supported by JSPS KAKENHI Grant Number 16K02882.

REFERENCES

Brantmeier, C. 2006. Advanced L2 learners and reading placement: self-assessment, computer based testing, and subsequent performance. *System* 34(1): 15–35.

Cook, V. 1999. Going Beyond the Native Speaker in Language Teaching. *TESOL Quarterly* 33(2): 185–209.

Dornyei, Z. & Ushioda, E. 2013. *Teaching and Researching: Motivation*. Routledge.

EF English Proficiency Index. 2017. Retrieved from https://www.ef.edu/epi/.

Gardner, R.C. & Lambert, W.E. 1972. *Attitudes and motivation in second language learning*. Rowley, MA: Newbury House.

Gardner, R.C., Smythe, P.C. & Clement, R. 1979. Intensive second language study in a bicultural milieu: An investigation of attitudes, motivation and language proficiency. *Language Learning* 29: 305–320.

Holton, J.A. 2007. The coding process and its challenges. In Bryant, A. & Charmaz, K. (eds.). *The Sage handbook of grounded theory: 265–289*. Thousand Oaks, CA: Sage.

Horwitz, E.K., Horwitz, M.B. & Cope, J. 1986. Foreign language classroom anxiety. *The Modern Language Journal* 70: 125–132.

Kimura, H. & Dantusji, M. (eds.) 2007. *Glocal Studies,* A collaborative creation by the Dantsuji laboratory at Kyoto University and Jonan-Ryoso High School.

MacIntyre, P.D. & Gardner, R.C. 1991. Investigating Language Class Anxiety Using the Focused Essay Technique. *The Modern Language Journal* 75: 296–304.

MacIntyre, P.D., Baker, S.C., Clement, R. & Donovan, L.A. 2003. Talking in order to learn: Willingness to communicate and intensive language programs. *Canadian Modern Language Review* 59: 587–605.

MacIntyre, P.D., Clement, R., Dornyei, Z. & Noels, K. 1998. Conceptualizing Willingness to Communicate in a L2: A Situational Model of L2 Confidence and Affiliation. *Modern Language Journal* 82: 545–562.

Matsuda, A. 2003. The ownership of English in Japanese secondary schools. *World Englishes* 22(4): 483–496.

McCroskey, J.C. 1984. Avoiding Communication: Shyness, Reticence, and Communication Apprehension. In Daly, J.A. & McCroskey, J.C. (eds.), *The Communication Apprehension Perspective*: 13–39. Beverly Hills, CA: Sage.

McVeigh, B. 2002. *Japanese Higher Education as Myth*. Armonk, NY: M.E. Sharpe.

Ministry of Education, Culture, Sports, Science and Technology—Japan 2012. *MEXT project for promotion of global human resource development*. Retrieved from: http://www.mext.go.jp/english/highered/1326713.htmhttp://www.mext.go.jp/english/highered/1326713.htm.

Mochizuki, A. 1999. Language Learning Strategies Used by Japanese University Students. *RELC Journal* 30(2): 101–113.

Nishino, T. 2008. Japanese Secondary School Teachers' Beliefs and Practices Regarding Communicative Language Teaching: An Exploratory Survey. *JALT Journal* 30(1).

Ryan, S. 2009. Self and identity in L2 motivation in Japan: The ideal L2 self of Japanese learners of English. In Z. Dornyei & E. Ushioda, *Multilingual Matters*. Bristol, UK.

Stefanova, M. 2010. Affect and Perceptions on a Multilingual Campus: Students' Perspectives on Second Language Use. *Ritsumeikan Journal of Asia Pacific Studies* 28. Retrieved from: http://www.apu.ac.jp/rcaps/uploads/fckeditor/publications/journal/RJAPS_V28_Marina.pdf.

Tanaka, K. & Ellis, R. 2003. Study abroad, language proficiency, and learner beliefs about language learning. *JALT Journal* 25: 63–85.

TOEIC 2016 Report on test takers worldwide. 2016. Retrieved from: https://www.ets.org/s/toeic/pdf/ww_data_report_unlweb.pdf.

Tran, T. & Moni, K. 2015. Management of foreign language anxiety: Insiders' awareness and experiences. *Cogent Education* 2: 992593 http://dx.doi.org/10.1080/2331186X.2014.992593.

Yashima, T. 2002. Willingness to communicate in a second language: The Japanese EFL context. *Modern Language Journal* 86: 54–66.

Yashima, T. 2009. International posture and the ideal L2 self in the Japanese EFL context. In Dörnyei, Z. & Ushioda, E. (eds.). *Motivation, language identity and the L2 self.* Bristol: Multilingual Matters.

Interpreting the demand of the curriculum creatively

A. Widyantoro
Yogyakarta State University, Yogyakarta, Indonesia

ABSTRACT: One of the most important factors in education is the curriculum. All educational levels base their activities in the teaching learning process on their curriculum. As science and technology develops, curricula change from time to time, often with certain time intervals. Facts from the field often show that teachers are generally worried about the curriculum change. They get upset when there is a new curriculum introduced by the government. They have been accustomed to a certain curriculum when suddenly the government changes the curriculum. In fact, they should not have to worry about the curriculum change as this is an inevitable condition. It is impossible for a school to have the same curriculum year after year without any changes. This paper tries to explore the reasons why curricula need to be changed, the reasons why teachers should not be worried about the change, and how to interpret the demand of the curriculum creatively. Being able to interpret the demand of the curriculum creatively is very important for teachers so that they will not get a lot of burden from the change of the curriculum.

1 INTRODUCTION

When someone talks about foreign language teaching or foreign language learning, there will be a lot of things to be discussed. There might be a discussion on how people learn a foreign language but there will be no definite answer to this topic. It is true that there are a lot of resources which can be used, which talk about various factors involved in the foreign language teaching and learning process. However, it may be difficult to find the most important factors which contribute the greatest on the students' success in mastering the foreign language.

One of the factors which can give great contribution to the success or failure in mastering a foreign language is the curriculum being implemented. This is because all the activities in the teaching learning process are based on the curriculum. A change in the curriculum may involve some changes in: the course book, the approach to teaching, the teaching techniques, and the assessment (Nation & Macalister 2010).

In Indonesia, there have been many curriculum changes since the 1950s. Of course, the government has expected that the curriculum change will result in the improvement of the educational achievement. However, experience shows that this does not always happen.

Changes introduced in relation to the curriculum may not be accepted by those involved in the educational system, like teachers, headmasters (Adamson & Davison 2008); (Goh & Yin 2008). Some teachers may be quite skeptical and some others may even not support the change.

The changes in the curriculum is not enough, especially when new things are introduced. Those involved in the educational process must also be aware about the changes. They need to change, too.

Teachers often see the change in the curriculum as something frightening. They will have to learn new things and they will also have to teach new things. Teachers often have difficulties in interpreting the demand of the curriculum.

2   WHY DOES A CURRICULUM NEED TO BE CHANGED?

Science and technology develops so fast. This means that those involved in the educational process must also realize this fast development of science and technology. However, it is not enough to have awareness of the fast development. The government, supervisors, school principals, teachers, and others must react in such a way so that they can catch up with the development of science and technology.

In the fast development of science and technology, new things will emerge and new challenges will be faced. It is the duty of those involved in the educational process to prepare the young generation to face such new challenges. This also means that there will be new learning needs, the needs which is not only related to individual needs, but also to the needs of the family, the community, the nation, or even the world. "The new world" will have "new needs" and this can be satisfied through education.

The development of technology has made some changes. One of them is related to the required competencies for different jobs. Some of the important competencies to be mastered are critical thinking, ICT competencies, decision-making, and communicating effectively (UNESCO 2002: 9). These new competencies and even other upcoming new competencies will have to be taught to students. Or, when students find these new competencies after they graduate from schools, they have to be taught or encouraged to develop their autonomous learning so that they will be ready to learn new competencies.

One of the solutions for the emerging problems or challenges is through changing the curriculum. With the development of science and technology, it is impossible for the curriculum not to be changed in accordance with the development. New things need to be taught to students and new skills need also to be learned. In the era of learning-centred, much attention has been paid to how well teachers satisfy the learning needs of their students (Price 2010: 101).

3   TEACHERS DO NOT NEED TO BE WORRIED ABOUT THE CHANGE

As curriculum change is an inevitable process, teachers do not need to be worried about the change. Of course, there will be problems in the implementation of the new curriculum. However, as professionals, teachers will have to face the reality that there can be problems. They have to be prepared to face the change. Nation and Macalister (2010) assure that curriculum change also involves the management of change. Teachers themselves need to change. They must not teach the same way they were taught as most people believe.

The goal of an educational system should be creating people who can do new things, who can solve new problems. They are not just the ones who will do the same as what their ancestors have done.

It is true that this will also depend on the change introduced. People believe that if the change is so drastic, students or teachers may have difficulty with the change. However, if the change is so drastic, teachers can try to make it manageable. They can start with the small thing and later to the greater thing. This is one way to manage the change.

Another possible problem is with the difference from the existing practices. Many teachers believe that if the change is very different from the existing practices, they will have difficulty. This is actually a problem of adaptation. When teachers have been accustomed to change, even if the change is very different from their existing practices, they will find it even challenging. They will have to believe that there is no ready-made recipe for any successful teaching. So, the change can be used as an alternative for possibly successful teaching. With this idea in their mind, they will not have to be worried about the change, even if it is very different from their existing practices.

It is necessary for teachers to obtain information related to the new curriculum. Teachers are encouraged to read the regulations related to the new curriculum, for example: the Decree of the Minister of Education and Culture No 22/2016 on the process standard, No 20/2016 on the competence of the graduates, No 21/2016 on the content standard.

It is also suggested that teachers obtain information about the approach or teaching methods as suggested by the new curriculum. From this information, teachers are expected to have sufficient information to make decisions about what to teach and how to teach.

Teachers are also suggested to develop their critical thinking. When a curriculum is introduced, there are at least three questions to be answered, i.e. questions related to the materials to be taught, the process of the teaching and learning, and the effectiveness of the teaching learning process (Breen & Candlin 2001: 9). Through their critical thinking, they can function better. They need to be able to function effectively as an analysis of the curriculum.

4 THE STRENGTH OF THE NEW CURRICULUM

As stated in the decree of the Minister of Education and Culture No 22, 2016, the teaching learning process should be carried out as such so that the students can become autonomous and creative people. Students are encouraged to be curious. This means that the new curriculum focuses not only in the aspect of the content, but it also focuses on the attitudes. This is good because the change in the attitudes, perceptions and actions is more fundamental (Law & Li 2013: 25).

It is also stated in the decree that the teaching learning process is not content-based but competence-based. In this 21st century, competence is considered as being more important than knowledge.

5 HOW TO INTERPRET THE DEMAND OF THE CURRICULUM CREATIVELY

The introduction of a new curriculum may mean that teachers need to learn something new. As stated before, this is actually a part of the teacher professional development. They need to catch up with the development of science and technology. However, the introduction of a new curriculum does mean that teachers will have to obey all the rules related to the curriculum. There is space for teachers to modify (Chapelle 2003: 40). There can be something that the teachers will "have to do" or will "have to obey", but there can also be a space for teachers to develop their own way or even their own materials.

What does that mean? Teachers will have to get enough information about the new curriculum and the characteristics of their subject. For example, in the 2013 curriculum in Indonesia, teachers of all subjects will have to use "the scientific approach" in their teaching. As analysts of the curriculum, they will have to think critically, and some questions may be put forward. "Is it a must for all teachers, including English teachers? What are the strengths and weaknesses of this approach? What is the basis of the introduction of this approach? Will this guarantee the success of teaching? Will students be able to use English in their communication if they are taught using this approach?"

These are some questions which can possibly be raised in relation to the introduction of the use of the scientific approach. Teachers have to keep in mind that in language learning, the purpose of the learning is that the students will be able to communicate using the language they learn. This can be the key factor to consider when teachers analyze the demand of the curriculum.

The approach introduced in a new curriculum may be appropriate for teaching certain school subjects but not for other subjects. In the case of the scientific approach, this approach may be appropriate for teaching science, chemistry, physics, or Biology. But, is it appropriate for teaching English? If the use of this approach may end in the failure of students to be able to communicate using English, then why do teachers have to use it? Again, teachers have the freedom to make decisions about their teaching. Although it is true that teachers will be supervised by supervisors, they have to convince that what they do is for the sake of the students' success (Bailey 2006: 81).

As Todd (2010: 1), teachers should respond to the learners' needs innovatively. A curriculum is often developed based on students' needs, their needs as individuals, as members of the society, as citizens of a country, or even as a member of the global world.

As good teachers, however, they have to try to find the benefit of using this approach. For example, in this approach, students are encouraged to develop their curiosity. This can be used in teaching English. Teachers can also develop their students' curiosity. However, of course, the curiosity developed in other subjects may be different from that developed in learning English. For example, in Physics students are encouraged to ask similar questions asked by Isaac Newton. "Why does an apple fall down to the earth?" This may not be appropriate for learning English. It is better for students to ask "What expression should I use if I want to say *Berdikit-dikit lama-lama menjadi bukit*?" It is good to think about what is said by Clay P. Bedford. He said, "You can teach a student a lesson for a day; but if you can teach him to learn by creating curiosity, he will continue the learning process as long as he lives."

Next, teachers need to analyze which activities will be needed by students to achieve in real life. It may be true that the materials as stated in the curriculum have been developed by experts but they are developed for general contexts and for students in general. Teachers may know the characteristics of their students and so they know what materials are appropriate for their students and which materials are not appropriate. Teachers may focus on the kind of learning called 'implicit learning' and 'explicit learning' (Ellis 2009: 3). In implicit learning, learners are not aware of the learning, but they then can feel the change in their behaviour. In explicit learning, the learners are aware that they have learned something.

It is also important for teachers to develop students' independence. Independent language learning can refer to a context or setting for language learning. In this context, the learners develop skills in the target language, although it is not always done individually. Independent learning can also be understood that the learners need to be trained to develop their independence in learning (White 2008: 5). Being independent also means developing the attitudes, beliefs, knowledge, and strategies for learning the language independently. This kind of teaching may not be found explicitly in the curriculum but as it is believed that it is important to develop students' independence, teachers will have to do this.

Another way of interpreting the demand of the curriculum is through analyzing the materials which are appropriate for developing students' communication ability. Findings of research in various fields, including linguistics, psycholinguistics, psychology, and socio-linguistics, have shown that communication is very crucial in language learning processes (Uso-Juan & Martinez-Flor 2006: 3). Further, they suggest that the degree of success achieved in the process depends on how meaning is negotiated in the communication process. If the materials do not support directly the development of the communication ability, then teachers need to be creative in developing their own materials based on the competence as suggested in the curriculum.

The materials as stated in the curriculum may be very general, not very specific. In order to make the materials meaningful to students, teachers need to think creatively. For example, they will have to think of the context in which the materials, say expressions, are really used in everyday life. Through this kind of consideration, teachers will not only be able to teach the materials as stated in the curriculum, but they can also adjust the level of the materials to their students' proficiency level. It is due to the fact that only by adjusting the materials to the students' proficiency level will the materials be meaingful to the students.

To be meaningful, the materials should also represent something or activities which really occur in the students' everyday life (Heller 2012: 96). Teachers should creatively find ways to make the materials really represent the students' experience. It should be kept in mind that students' learning does not only occur in the classroom (Tummons 2009: 69), but it also happens outside the classroom. Therefore, teachers will have to encourage the learning process outside the classroom by developing activities or materials which are useful for students' life.

When the materials represent the students' life, it will be possible for the students to learn indepedently. They can learn the materials any time and anywhere. This is sometimes referred to 'blended learning' (Shea & Stockford 2015:17).

Last but not the least, Teachers need to inspire their students to learn English well, although this may not be always easy. Teachers need strength, energy, and ability to be able to influence their students (Pachler & Redondo 2007: 4). William Arthur Ward says, "The mediocre teacher tells. The good teacher explains. The superior teacher demonstrates. The great teacher inspires." So, teachers need to be able to analyze which factors, aspects, materials, or approach taken from the curriculum will be able to be used for inspiring students to learn English.

6   CONCLUSIONS

From what has been discussed before, it can be concluded that the demand of a curriculum can be interpreted creatively in order to match the students' needs. This can be done by developing materials which match the students' level of proficiency. In order that students can learn English independently, teachers need to make the activities represent the students' daily life.

REFERENCES

Adamson, B. & Davison, C. 2008. English language teaching in Hong Kong primary schools: Innovation and resistence. In D.E. Murray (ed.). *Planning Change, Changing Plans: Innovation in Second Language Teaching.* Ann Arbor: University of Michigan Press.

Andrews, S. 2007. *Teacher language awareness.* Cambridge: Cambridge University Press.

Bailey, K.M. 2006. *Language teacher supervision: A case-based approach.* Cambridge: Cambridge University Press.

Breen, M.P. & Candlin, C.N. 2001. The Essentials of a Communicative Curriculum in Language Teaching. In Hall, D.R. & Hewings, A. 2001. *Innovation in English Language Teaching.* London: Routledge.

Chapelle, C.A. 2003. *English language learning and technology.* Amsterdam: John Benjamins Publishing Company.

Ellis, R., et al. 2009. *Implicit and Explicit Knowledge in Second Language Learning, Testing, and Teaching.* Bristol: Multilingual Matters.

Gage, N.L. 2009. *A Conception of Teaching.* Stanford: Springer.

Goh. C.C.M. & Yin, T.M. 2008. Implementing the English language syllabus 2001 in Singapore schools: Interpretations and Re-Interpretations. In D.E. Murray (ed.). *Planning Change, Changing Plans: Innovation in Second Language Teaching.* Ann Arbor: University of Michigan Press.

Hall, D.R. & Hewings, A. 2001. *Innovation in English language teaching.* London: Routledge.

Heller, D. 2012. *Curriculum on the edge of survival: How schools fail to prepare students for membership in a democracy.* 2nd ed. Lanham: Rowman & Littlefield Education.

Lau, J.Y.F. 2011. An Introduction to critical thinking and creativity: Think more, think better. New Jersey: A John Wiley & Sons, Inc., Publication.

Law, E.H. & Li, C. 2013. Curriculum innovations in changing societies: Chinese perspectives from Hong Kong, Taiwan and Mainland China. Rotterdam: Sense Publishers.

Nation, I.S.P. & Macalister, J. 2010. *Language curriculum design.* New York: Routledge.

National Research Council. 2007. Enhancing Professional development for teachers potential uses of information technology: Report of a Workshop: Washington: The National Academies Press.

Pagliaro, M.M. 2005. *Academic Success: Applying Learning Theory in the Classroom.* Lanham: Rowman & Littlefield Publishers, Inc.

Pachler, N. & Redondo, A. (Eds.). 2007. *A Practical Guide to Teaching Modern Foreign Languages in the Secondary School.* London: Routledge.

Price, L.R. 2010. Action research on e-learning essay unit at the Icesi University in Colombia. In Carmona, J.A. (2010). *Language Teaching and Learning in ESL Education.* Charlotte: Kona Publishing & Media Group.

Randall, M. 2007. *Memory, psychology, and second language learning.* Amsterdam: John Benjamins Publishing Company.

Shea, J. & Stockford, A. 2015. *Inspiring the Secondary Curriculum with Technology: Let the Students Do the Work.* London: Routledge.

Shehadeh, A. 2005. Task-based language learning and teaching: Theories and applications. In Edwards, C. & Willis, J. (Eds.). (2005). *Teachers Exploring Tasks in English Language Teaching.* New York: Palgrave Macmillan.

Todd, R.J. 2010. *Curriculum integration: Learning in a changing world.* Victoria: ACER Press.

UNESCO. 2002. *A curriculum for schools and programme of teacher development.* Paris: UNESCO.

Uso-Juan, E. & Martinez-Flor, A. 2006. *Approaches to language learning and teaching: Towards acquiring communicative competence through the four skills.* In Uso-Juan, E. & Martinez-Flor, A. (Eds.). (2006). *Current Trends in the Development and Teahcing of the Four Language Skills.* Berlin: Mouton de Gruyter.

White, C. 2008. Language learning strategies in independent language learning: An overview. In Hurd, S. & Lewis, T. (Eds.). (2008). Language Learning Strategies in Independent Settings. Bristol: Multilingual Matters.

ELT in Asia in the Digital Era: Global Citizenship and Identity – Madya et al. (Eds)
© *2018 Taylor & Francis Group, London, ISBN 978-0-8153-7900-3*

The effectiveness of an ELT model using Curriculum 13 to SMA students in Surakarta

Ngadiso
Sebelas Maret University, Surakarta, Indonesia

ABSTRACT: A model for teaching English using Curriculum 13 has been developed to overcome the weaknesses of the existing model. To make sure that the developed model is feasible, it had been tried out in three classes of three SMAs in Surakarta. To find out whether the developed model is more effective than the existing model, an experimental research was conducted. The research method used was Research and Development. The results of the first year research showed some weaknesses of the existing model, so the prototype was developed. In the second year, the prototype was tried out and revised. The result showed that the model was feasible for the teacher to teach, the students to study, and feasible for developing the students' four language skills, spiritual and social attitude. The result of the third year research showed that the developed model is more effective than the existing model.

1 INTRODUCTION

The fast-advancing world brings changes in many aspects of life including education. Thus, Ministry of education and culture of Indonesia through Ministry of Education Regulation No. 32 Year 2013 changed the previous curriculum, school-based curriculum (Kurikulum Tingkat Satuan Pendidikan – KTSP) to the next and latest curriculum named Curriculum 13. This curriculum requires every subject taught, including English, in elementary school up to senior high school to apply scientific approach. Consequently, this policy becomes controversial for English teachers as English teaching is different from science teaching. However, any opponent has to know that every curriculum made is always based on deep needs analysis conducted by the government trying to suit students' profile; it means that every school has to apply Curriculum 13.

Unfortunately, during the implementation of Curriculum 13, English teachers of SMA Surakarta still feel uncertain and unwilling to implement the newest curriculum in terms of developing the students' four English skill and social and spiritual attitude. This uncertainty results in the low quality of English teaching and learning process in SMA Surakarta. The teachers tend to focus only on one skill rather integrating them. They feel reluctant to connect the materials leading to the improvement of spiritual and social attitude. Therefore, it is necessary to design and develop an English teaching model using Curriculum 13.

The objective of the research is to design an English teaching model using Curriculum 13 which can develop skills and attitude simultaneously. In order to design and develop the apt teaching model using Curriculum 13, investigating the existing model is necessary to find out the weaknesses. During the investigation, it is also necessary to conduct a needs analysis to identify the needs of the students. Based on the weaknesses and needs analysis, a prototype of English teaching model is designed. The prototype is then tried out and observed to know its weaknesses by which revisions are made. Try out and revision are continually conducted until the model is feasible for learners to learn, teachers to teach, and researcher to develop the students' four English skills (listening, reading, speaking, and writing) and spiritual and social attitude.

To support the research, it is necessary to conduct literature review.

1.1 English teaching

Teaching is an action of assisting learners to learn how to do something, solve problem, and discover knowledge by optimizing their potential. Meanwhile, language teaching has additional goal to enable learners to communicate. In terms of objectives, teaching language has to enable learners to: a) understand spoken and written language, b) speak the language understandably, c) write the language accurately, and d) read the language with ease (Patel & Jain 2008).

In ELT, integrating four skills of English in class is vitally important. When learners are provided with integrated skills learning practice, continuity of learning will be met since activities conducted in the class are related and dependent on one to the others (Read 1991). By integrating four skills, learners can practice English within a steady and various real-life contexts which may improve their communicative competence (Byrne 1998, Mathews et al. 1991). Eventually, the quality of English class will be more flexible and effective.

In order to effectively improve the integrated skills, appropriate teaching model needs to be developed. Joyce et al. (2015) define model of teaching as "a way of nurturing and stimulating ecosystem within which the students learn by interacting with its components. Various models pull students into particular types of content (knowledge, values, and skills) and increase their competence to grow in the personal, social, and academic domains". Model of teaching touches not only the cognitive, behavioral, and affective aspects; but also the personal and social aspects of the students. Model of teaching can range from planning and using curricula, lessons, and units; developing instructional materials, to bringing up technology in the class.

There are several requirements in the development of good model of teaching as suggested by Joyce et al. (2015). The fulfillment of these requirements is used to make the developed model in a good quality.

Basically, model of teaching has to improve the quality of students' learning and help students to exceed their own limits and capacities. This improvement can be grasped if students know their responsibilities in learning and teachers are able to guide students to struggle with their emotions in order to overcome their own learning problems.

In order to monitor the quality of the students' learning and to identify different kinds of support needed, formative assessment has to be conducted. It is the assessment for learning which is generally designed to probe the progress and clarity (where learners are in their learning, where they are going to, and the steps needed to get there) of individual students during the teaching and learning process through observations and interaction analyses (Ahmed et al. 2011).

1.2 ELT model development

There are two types of teaching English models, English-only model and bilingual model (Moughamian et al. 2009). English-only model offers programs that involve the use of English in every instruction. Meanwhile, as reflected in its name, bilingual model offers the use of two languages in the class—the intensity and the length of time the second/foreign language is used can be varied.

The developed model adapts the notion of bilingual model—the classroom instruction is both in English and Bahasa. The use of Bahasa is to support the understandibility of the English material itself.

The development of the model is also based on the reference to the five views of English, which is popularly known as Cox models (Goodwyn & Branson 2005):

1. Personal Growth view, this view concentrates on the learners, centering on the relationship between language and learning happening in every individual as well as the role of literature in learners' imagination and aesthetic lives development.
2. Cross-curricular view, this view focuses on the school, centering on teachers' responsibilities to relate English with the other school subjects.

3. Adult Needs view, this view emphasises on the applicability of language as a means of communication since in order to face this fast- changing world, English is the primary need for every learner.
4. Cultural Heritage view, this view concentrates on the responsibilities of schools to guide learners to appreciate works of literature.
5. Cultural Analysis view, this view focuses on learners' awareness towards the role of English to make them able to blend in the world and the cultural environment in which they live.

Nevertheless, developing a model should be based on needs analysis (Kusumoto 2008, Brown 1995). Further, Brown (1995: 36) defines needs analysis as "the systematic collection and analysis of all subjective and objective information necessary to define and validate defensible curriculum purposes that satisfy the language learning requirements of students within the context of particular institutions that influence the learning and teaching situation."

1.3 *Previous study*

Several previous studies have shown some educational development resulting in the bigger effectiveness to the education itself. These prior studies also show usefulness of needs analysis.

Bosher and Smalkowski (2002) developed an English course to help nursery students to learn English as Second Language (ESL) effectively. The course named Speaking and Listening in a Health-Care Setting was implemented in health-care programs at a private college in Minneapolis, Minnesota. Through needs analysis, apt materials and methods could be grasped and hence the course can be very successful for the students to learn how to communicate in health-care settings.

Mastering English is seen as an important component for international industrial firm employees who need to communicate with foreign clients and suppliers. Therefore, Cowling (2007) conducted a needs analysis as a basic to design a syllabus for an intensive English language course. As a result of the needs analysis, notional- functional and content or task-based syllabi were designed.

English instruction quality becomes a major issue in Japan since improvements are hard to achieve. In order to improve the English instruction quality, Kusumoto (2008) conducted a study aiming at identifying the homeroom teachers' needs. In his study, it is found that homeroom teachers need adequate and proper training. Teacher training is seen as the finest solution to improve English instruction quality in Japan since teacher is the key of language education success. The result of this study is expected to suggest curriculum developer to develop teacher training programs in Japan.

1.4 *Curriculum 13*

In order for teachers to conduct teaching practices, a framework for guiding the classroom instructions called curriculum is vital. Curriculum is defined as all planned learning, what the teacher is going to teach and what the students are going to learn, for which the educational institution is responsible (Marsh 2009, Patesan & Bumbuc 2009). Richards (2013) states that curriculum is the overall plan for classroom instructions. This planned learning assists teachers to conduct effective teaching practices.

To create educational system improvements, curriculum development is required. Indonesian Ministry of Education and Culture recently developed a new curriculum known as Curriculum 13 as a response to overcome school-based curriculum weaknesses. As the result of curriculum change from school-based to Curriculum 13, there are several shifts in learning activities. There should be several learning activities shifts from 1) teacher to student-centered, 2) non-interactive to interactive, 3) classroom to any place, 4) passive to active, 5) individual to group-work, 6) single-media only to multimedia, 7) Individual differences, 8) mono-disciplinary to multi-disciplinary, and 9) passive to critical learning. In order to implement the shifts, scientific approach that comprises five main stages as observing, questioning, experimenting, associating, and communicating is chosen as a main approach of curriculum 2013 (Ministry of Education Regulation No. 69 year 2013). Curriculum 13 integrates character building covering attitude, knowledge, and skill. Attitude is further specified into spiritual and social attitude (Ahmad 2014).

2 RESEARCH METHOD

The research method used was Educational Research and Development. Educational Research and Development (Educational R&D) is a research used to create new or improved products. It is performed to test and refine products before it is used (Hall 2006). The term product is not only simply defined as materials object (textbooks, films, etc.), but also procedure and process (teaching methods) (Gall et al. 2003).

The researchers follow the three stages of R&D as suggested by Borg and Gall (1983) as follows: (1) exploration stage, (2) development stage, and (3) experiment stage. The stages are conducted in three successive years, a year for each. The first year, 2015, was used to do needs analysis and identify the weaknesses of the existing model used by teachers in SMA Surakarta as the basis to develop the prototype of the teaching model using Curriculum 13. In the second year, 2016, the prototype of the teaching model using Curriculum 13 was tried out until it became a feasible model. The last year, 2017, was used to compare the developed teaching model and the existing model in terms of the effectiveness of the two models.

The population of this research is senior high schools in Surakarta while the samples of this research are SMA N 1 Surakarta, SMA N 7 Surakarta, and SMA Batik 2 Surakarta. In this research, stratified cluster random sampling was used. It is a kind of sampling in which the samples were randomly selected from the population after the population was stratified. Based on the academic quality statistics, SMAs in Surakarta are divided into high, mid, and low. Stratified cluster random sampling is used because all clusters of the same class have similar characteristics so that extraneous variable can be controlled.

2.1 Data collection techniques

Observation and focus group discussion as the data collection methods employed in this research were used to know 1) the characteristics of the existing model, 2) the weaknesses of the existing model, and 3) the weaknesses of the developed prototype. Meanwhile, assessment is used to know the score of the students in experimental group and control group.

Observation was used to identify the weaknesses of the existing model (first stage) and the prototype (second stage). The researchers did the observation directly. In doing direct observation, any information found in the natural setting is written in the field notes (Tomal 2003). Direct observation allows the researchers to collect first-hand and more reliable information since collecting the data from the subjects or the third- party may not indicate the real-life situation (Tomal 2003).

Focus group discussion (FGD) is a dynamic group discussion used to collect information. As stated by Dzija et al. (2005), FGD is a-small group discussion led by a qualified leader. The discussion is conducted to study more about opinions on a chosen topic and then to guide further action. FGD is beneficial to collect in-depth information since the researchers have direct opportunity to ask about the problems under study. Besides providing direct opportunity to ask about the problems under study, FGD benefits researchers as it allows the participants to elaborate or explain their answers and to ask for clarification (Dzija et al. 2005). FGD was used to gather any opinions regarding the try out of the prototype from the researchers', students', and the English teachers' points of view. Based on the opinions, all of the FGD members drew the conclusion.

Besides observation and FGD, assessment which provides rich information regarding the students' progress in the form of score was conducted. Assessment is done by administering students' tests, portofolios, records, as well as directly observing students' skills and behaviors (Tomal 2003).

2.2 Data analysis technique

Experimental design was used in the last stage of this research to compare the effectiveness of the existing model (control) and the developed model (experiment). Sometimes, researchers can find a very clear-cut condition between the two conditions, but more often the difference between the two is not obvious. In this condition, the use of t-test is encouraged to know whether the difference between the two conditions is real, or it is because of the chance of oscillation from one time of testing to another (Tavakoli 2012).

3 FINDINGS AND DISCUSSION

The research was conducted in three sucessive years in three different schools (SMA 1, SMA 7, and SMA Batik 2). The similarity of the subjects in this school is that the teachers are all masters in ELT. Meanwhile, the differences are that the academic attitudes of the students and the facilities provided by the schools. SMA 1 has students with positive attitude and the best facilities, SMA 7 is in average, while SMA Batik 2 has the students with negative attitude and unsatisfactory facilities. However, the focus of the research is on the teaching model applied.

The research findings are divided into three stages: (1) exploration stage, (2) development stage, and (3) experiment stage. The research findings of the first stage are: (a) the existing model for teaching English in SMA Surakarta; (b) the weaknesses of the existing model for teaching English in SMA Surakarta; and (c) the prototype of teaching English using Curriculum 13.

The characteristics of the existing teaching model used by English teachers in SMA Surakarta can be sumarized as follows:

1. The meeting is opened by greeting, checking attendance, asking the students' conditions, reviewing materials, and stating the today's topic and its objectives.
2. The topic is explained by the teachers.
3. Examples are given to the students to make the materials clearer.
4. Drilling is given by the teachers while he students are imitating.
5. Answering questions related to listening recording is done by the students followed by making a conclusion based on the recording content.
6. Presenting the conclusion without clear explanation from the teacher.
7. Working on a worksheet becomes the last activity for the students.

Based on the identification of the characteristics of the existing model, there are several weaknesses:

1. The English teachers applied mixed methods in the class combining scientific and traditional approach, yet the latter was more dominant.
2. The development of the students' spiritual and social attitude was not found.
3. The lesson plan was not realized completely.
4. The students did not present the conclusion since they just read it.

The identification of the characteristics and weaknesses of the existing model becomes the basis of the development of the prototype. The prototype includes the steps suggested by Curriculum 13, namely:

1. Observing, the students investigate phenomenon to identify the problems that will be studied further.
2. Questioning, the students limit the problems and formulate questions based on their schemata and the phenomenon being observed.
3. Experimenting, the students utilize the questions and apt techniques to collect data relevant to the materials.
4. Associating, the students analyze the data and draw conclusion.
5. Communicating, the students report the conclusion.

Table 1. The significant difference between the developed
model and the existing model.

Schools	t_o	t_t
SMAN 1 Surakarta	(4.23)	(2.00)
SMAN 7 Surakarta	(6.79)	(2.00)
SMA Batik 2 Surakarta	(8.13)	(2.00)

Table 2. The effectiveness comparison between the developed model and the existing model.

Schools	Mean (experiment)	Mean (control)
SMAN 1 Surakarta	87.03	83.49
SMAN 7 Surakarta	85.4	79.87
SMA Batik 2 Surakarta	80.12	75.19

The second stage that was conducted in the second year showed that the prototype was feasible. The feasibility was obtained through several try-outs in three different SMAs in Surakarta and revisions. Firstly, the prototype was tried out in the English class of SMA 1 Surakarta on Saturday, October 8th 2016, during which observation was conducted and followed by FGD and revision. The first revision was then tried out again in the English class of SMA 7 Surakarta on Wednesday, October 12th 2016, and observed again with FGD and the second revision as the following steps. The second revision was then tried out and observed again for the last time in the English class of SMA Batik 2 Surakarta on Wednesday, October19th 2016, followed by FGD and final revision.

The third stage was conducted in the third year to compare the effectiveness of the existing model and the developed model. First of all, there is a significant difference between the developed model and the existing model to teach English since t_o (t-obtained) is higher than the t_t (t-table).

The data analysis shows that the developed model is more effective than the existing model to teach English to the students of SMA Surakarta.

4 CONCLUSION

Naturally, the implementation of new policy always divides people into proponents and opponents. It also happens to the implementation of Curriculum 13. The opponents argue that scientific approach is not suitable for English learning and teaching. On the other hand, the proponents say that curriculum is made through deep needs analysis over the entire students in Indonesia meaning Curriculum 13 is applicable for every school in Indonesia.

Unfortunately, many English teachers in Surakarta, Central Java, still feel dubious towards Curriculum 13. Instead, traditional approach still dominates their teaching. Therefore, the researchers develop a model using Curriculum 13 to help English teachers feel easy to implement it in terms of integrating the four English skills, and encourage the students' spiritual and social attitude; as well as to overcome the weaknesses of the existing model.

The result of the research shows that there is a significant difference between the developed model and the existing model to teach English. The developed model is more effective than the existing model to develop the students four English skills as well as spiritual and social attitude.

REFERENCES

Ahmad, D. 2014. Understanding the 2013 curriculum of English teaching. *International Journal of Enhanced Research in Educational Development* 2(4): 6–15.

Ahmed, N., Anwar, M.A. & Ameen, A.M.A. 2011. A database application for Bloom's taxonomy-driven assessment instruments development. *International journal of arts & sciences* 4(11): 1–9.

Borg, W.R. & Gall, M.D. 1983. *Educational research: An introduction.* Michigan: Longman.

Bosher, S. & Smalkoski, K. 2002. From needs analysis to curriculum development: Designing a course in health-care communication for immigrant students in the USA. *English forSpecific Purposes* 21: 59–79.

Brown J. 1995. *The elements of language curriculum: A systematic approach to program development.* Boston, MA: Heinle & Heinle.

Brown, D. 2001. *Teaching by principles, an interactive approach to language pedagogy.* New York: Pearson Education Ltd.

Byrne, D. 1988. *Teaching writing skills.* Singapore: Longman.

Cowling, J.D. 2007. Needs analysis: planning a syllabus for a series of intensive workplace courses at a leading Japanese company. *English for specific purposes* 26: 426–442.

Dzija, J., Foster, J., Hernandez, S., Nardi, S., Theriault, P. & Wynne, C. 2005. *How to conduct effective focus groups and surveys.*

Gall, M.D., Gall, Joyce P. & Borg, W.R. 2003. *Educational research.* Boston: Pearson Education, Inc.

Goodwyn, A. & Branson, J. 2005. *Teaching English.* London and New York: Routledge.

Hall, B.H. 2006. Research and development. *International encyclopedia of the social science* (2 ed.).

Joyce, B., Weil, M. & Calhoun, E. 2015. *Models of teaching.* New York: Pearson.

Kusumoto, Y. 2008. Needs analysis: developing a teacher training program for elementary school home-room teachers in Japan. *Second language studies* 26(2): 1–44.

Marsh, C.J. 2009. *Key concepts for understanding curriculum.* New York: Routledge.

Mathews, A., Spratt, M. & Dangerfield, L. 1991. *At the chalk face. practical techniques in language teaching.* Hongkong: Thomas Nelson and Sons Ltd.

Moore, K.D. 1998. *Middle and secondary school instructional methods.* New York: McGraw College.

Moughamian, A.C., Rivera, M.O. & Francis, D.J. 2009. *Instructional models and strategies for teaching English language learners.* Portsmouth, NH: RMC Research Corporation, Center on Instruction.

Patel, M.F. & Jain, P.M. 2008. *English language teaching: methods, tools, & techniques.* Jaipur: Sunrise.

Patesan, R. & Bumbuc, S. 2010. *A theoretical approach to the curriculum reform.*

Ministry of Education Regulation No. 19 Year 2013

Ministry of Education Regulation No. 32 Year 2013

Ministry of Education Regulation No. 69 Year 2013

Read, C. 1991. *Integrating the skills.*

Richards, J.C. 2013. Curriculum approaches in language teaching: forward, central, and backward design. *RELC Journal* 44(1): 5–33.

Tavakoli, H. 2012. *A dictionary of research methodology and statistics in applied linguistics.* Iran: Rahnama Press.

Tomal, D.R. 2003. *Action research for educators.* Maryland: Scarecrow Press, Inc.

ELT in Asia in the Digital Era: Global Citizenship and Identity – Madya et al. (Eds)
© 2018 Taylor & Francis Group, London, ISBN 978-0-8153-7900-3

Compromising between the general and specific skills in EAP syllabus development in Indonesian context

Jamilah
Yogyakarta State University, Yogyakarta, Indonesia

ABSTRACT: The quality of a language program is reflected in the syllabus used from which the aim, contents and belief about language instruction are revealed. Syllabuses for English for Academic Purposes in Indonesian universities have been developed, yet they are not quite satisfactory. This article is to explain how to develop a sound syllabus for EAP in Indonesian context, following the steps: context and needs analysis and syllabus planning. Data were collected through triangulated survey employing questionnaires, observation, document study and discussion. Research participants were students, English teachers, and management staff of YSU. Integrated, theme-based syllabus is proposed that includes study skills in higher education as the general theme, which is completed with specific themes related to students' disciplines. This way enables both general and specific skills of EAP to be included in a single syllabus.

1 INTRODUCTION

Efforts in developing English syllabuses for non-English major students in Indonesian context have produced various models of syllabuses. Mustadi (2011) developed competency-based model that focused more on grammar competence, Sholihah (2014) proposed learning outcome-based model, and Aini (2008) developed skill-based (Reading) syllabus. Those syllabuses are expected to be appropriate models to follow since they have undergone thorough theoretical as well as contextual consideration. However, it is not easy for other teachers to adopt those models due to the fact that every teacher has different point of view to the teaching of English in higher education. Furthermore, those syllabuses are not completely in compliance with the current theories of teaching English for higher education proposed by experts.

Jarvis (2001), Hyland (2006), Nation (2012), Grabe & Stoller (2011), Anderson (2012) & Brick (2012) state that the teaching of English in higher education is for preparing the students to better study their fields in English, and this is called English for Academic Purposes (EAP). Hyland (2006) classifies EAP into two categories, English for General Academic Purposes (EGAP) and English for Specific Academic Purposes (ESAP). EGAP is used by all students no matter what fields of study they get involved while ESAP deals with specific discourses used in certain fields, such as in medicine, law, and physics. Brick (2012) adds one more category to the EAP-study skills. Study skill approach focuses on the development of students' study skills common for all students of all fields. In this case, Hyland (2006) includes the study skills in the EGAP.

The choice between EGAP and ESAP as the focus of English teaching in higher education is much determined by the nature of disciplines and professions the students take. The more specific the disciplines (i.e., law, medicine, nurse) ESAP is preferred, and the more general the disciplines (i.e., education, social sciences, humanities), EGAP is taken (Brick 2012: 171). However, management policy of certain universities or faculties, and even certain departments may not conform to what Brick states, such as the case of Yogyakarta State University (YSU). The top management has determined to take EGAP as the focus of the English course and urged the Course Centre to develop a text book to be used by all students. They even proposed to develop an online examination for the course. However, some faculties and departments prefer ESAP for their students. As a result, there is no agreed sound syllabus for the English course for non-English majors, which, in Indonesian context, is included in the general course programs, coded as MKU6211. This paper explains an effort to solve the existing problem of syllabus development for English course for higher education. What English syllabus model most complies with the current theories of EAP and which kind of EAP, whether EGAP or ESAP should be adopted to suit the needs of the institution and students served?

Richards (2001) stated that a syllabus is a written document that shows the course contents and its sequence, and thus, syllabus development is a process of selecting, sequencing, and justifying the course contents. The course contents include the language to learn and learning experience the students should take. Syllabus development can be done after the environment and needs analysis, since a good syllabus is developed based on the needs of a certain institution and its students.

2 RESEARCH METHOD

To develop an English syllabus for higher education which complies with EAP theories and fulfills the institution and students needs, the study followed the following steps: 1) context and needs analysis, 2) planning the syllabus, 3) setting up the syllabus, and 4) evaluation

Step 1 is to identify general context and situation in which the students use the target language, and the communicative events in which the students get involved; Step 2 is to consider the aims and the contents of the course; Step 3 is to sequence and integrate all the elements in a table; Step 4 is to evaluate the product. Despite the 4 steps proposed, the paper focuses more on the second step, planning the syllabus, especially in considering the aims and contents.

Step 1 was done through triangulated survey. Data were collected by distributing questionnaires to students, interviewing the English teachers and management staff of YSU, and studying the available documents.

3 FINDINGS AND DISCUSSIONS

3.1 *Results of the context and needs analysis*

The result of context analysis showed that English in Indonesia higher education contexts is used as a foreign and additional language to the teaching and learning process besides Indonesian language. English is used in reading academic literature, including textbooks, references, and articles. The students have learned English at least for six years at high schools, and therefore are expected to be able to understand English texts. However, there are still a large number of students having not reached the thresh hold level to understand such texts, especially the academic ones (El-Furqaan 2014). Nation (2012) states that in order to understand academic texts in English, students should master at least 5000 word families. The facts show that the average numbers of vocabulary that Indonesian students master is less than 2000. The lack of vocabulary mastery is not the only problem the students face in understanding academic texts. Students surveyed also lack in grammar mastery, reading strategies, and reading practice to understand academic English.

Based on the needs analysis, the students surveyed confessed that they had many objectives in learning English, such as to be able to communicate with foreigners, to improve their TOEFL scores, to read books on their major, to read materials related to their major, and to use the Internet better. They realized that English was very important in their academic life. They used English for reading their learning materials and course books or references, listening to lectures, communicating with lecturers in English, writing their ideas in English, and presenting them in front of an audience. They wanted to achieve various objectives and therefore they needed a lot of learning hours and had to make enormous efforts to reach them. Unfortunately, they did not have intention to do so. Many of them did not like learning English. On the other hand, the course offered is so short. It is only a two-unit credit offered in one semester. Due to the time constraint, course aims and course contents should be carefully selected.

3.2 *Syllabus planning*

3.2.1 *Selecting the course aims*

It is almost impossible to transform students of under the threshhold level of English into competent users of academic English. What can be offered by a-two-credit-English course is very limited. However, students' learning autonomy may change the whole situation. Learning autonomy is an important principle in the communicative foreign language teaching (Nation & Macalister 2010, Kumaravadivelu 2008, and Brown 2007). Learning autonomy should be trained to students. Students with good learning autonomy can reach whatever objectives they want to pursue since they understand the purpose of their learning program, explicitly accept responsibility for their learning, take initiatives in planning and executing learning activities, and regularly review their learning and evaluate its effectiveness (Little 1991). Learning autonomy can only be trained to students, if the teachers or the tutors are also autonomous (Johnson, Pardesi, Paine 1990 as cited by Thanasoulas 2000). Autonomous teachers can train students the learning strategies in order to be autonomous learners. Oxford (1990) states that language learning strategies encourage greater autonomy for learners. Learning autonomy is particularly important for language learners because they will not always have the teacher around. With learning autonomy, students can actively develop their ability on their own without teacher supervision. Therefore, they need to be trained to be independent learners.

Learning strategies can be an appropriate choice to teach in a very short English course for higher education students in Indonesian context. English course books focusing on learning strategies can be found world-wide, yet it is quite hard to find English course syllabus focusing on the same things in Indonesian context. Relating this choice to the EAP teaching approaches, EGAP with study skills approach can be adopted. Study skills trainings are quite popular among university students worldwide, and they are easily found in the Internet, yet in Indonesia they have not been taken seriously. In general, students are not quite familiar with the academic rules and they do not know how to learn at university effectively. They need training on these skills. However, Wingate (2006) argues that enhancing students learning through separate study skills course is ineffective and counterproductive to learning. Therefore, learning to study effectively at university cannot be separated from subject content and the process of learning. The teaching of study skills can be integrated with the teaching of English, and it can be the content of the English course, besides the learning strategies and the language to understand the content. From this argument, students of higher education need to learn study skills integrated in the English course.

Communicative language teaching approach proposes that learning language means learning to communicate using the target language, and the language is in the form of texts together with the meanings and functions (Richards 2006). He further states that there are four frameworks in executing this approach. They are text-based, competency-based, task-based, and content-based language teaching. The first two models are included in product-based, while the second two models are the process-based models. Among the four, content-based instruction (CBI) is chosen for the teaching of EAP. EAP is a part of CBI, in which students learn certain content of their fields while at the same time they learn the language used to convey the content (Richards & Rogers 2001, Wesche & Skehan 2002, Krahnke in Richards 2006, Davis 2003, Nation & Webb 2012, as cited in Crandall 2012). EAP in CBI can be realized in three different instruction models—sheltered, adjunct, and theme-based instruction (Stoller & Grabe 1997). Among the three, theme-based instruction is the most suitable for Indonesian context, since the students mostly belong to the lower level of English competence. They don't use English as the only language for their study, and the course are mostly given by the language teachers, rather than the content teachers. This choice is supported by Davis (2003) who states that theme-based instruction is the most flexible model among the three and it is commonly found in the context where English is used as a foreign language.

In addition, theme-based language instruction is adopted due to the benefits it offers since it is a part of CBI. There are at least six advantages of the use of contents to the teaching of a foreign language. Firstly, contents facilitate comprehension; Secondly, they make linguistic forms more meaningful; Contents also serve as the best bases to teach the skills areas; they address students' needs, motivate learners, allow for integration of the four skills, and allow for use of authentic materials (Brinton, Snow & Wesche 1989, Richards 2001). Although theme-based instruction enables the integration of the four skills, due to the limited time, a skill should be chosen as the focus. Based on the needs assessment results, reading skill is mostly needed, since students have to read much in their study. Taking reading as the focus of EAP teaching is recommended by many scholars (Anderson 2012).

From these considerations, the aim of the English course for non-English major students of YSU should be to encourage students to practice reading academic texts in a way that facilitates autonomous learning to improve their English competence and to study their majors effectively. This general aim is then further developed into learning objectives that cover knowledge to master, skills to develop, and attitude to foster. Related to the knowledge, students are expected to get understanding of study skills needed to study at university, knowledge of academic reading strategies, linguistics knowledge to understand texts in English, and knowledge about their subject contents. Related to the skills, students are expected to develop the reading skills to learn at university, and for the attitude to foster is that students are expected to develop responsibility to learn autonomously.

3.2.2 *Selecting the course contents*

The first step in selecting contents for the theme-based language instruction syllabus is selecting the themes (Stoller & Grabe 1997). Considering the institution policy that the course is intended for students of all majors, general themes are preferred. Since the course is to make students autonomous in learning English, they should realize that English is really important for their academic life. This realization is expected to make them willing to improve their English competence without depending on their teachers. Besides, the course is also intended to make students able to learn their majors effectively; therefore they need study skills for studying in higher education. English as an International Language and Study skills at university are chosen as the general themes for the course. However, although general themes and EGAP seem quite reasonable for this course, some teachers from a number of study programs (i.e., Mathematics, Physics, Biology, and Chemistry) prefer to have ESAP or themes related to their majors. They argue that specific themes are what students really need. Students need to be familiar with specific terms and discourses of their fields. In addition, specific themes related to their majors would be much more interesting, and this in turn would motivate students more to learn.

Integrating general themes and specific ones and including many themes in the syllabus is justified as long as the allotted time permits it. However, as previously stated, this course is only a two-credit course. In Indonesian context, it means that there are only16 meetings times 100 minutes. Looking at the scope of the general themes, especially the second one, *Study Skills at University*, there are so many topics to cover. Referring to Allan (2010), for example, there are 14 topics to discuss. Topics of the general themes seem to have occupied all the provided time. On the other hand, when referring to Wingate (2006) that training study skills for university students should be integrated to the teaching of subject contents, specific themes related to students' majors cannot be skipped. There must be a way to include specific themes in the syllabus.

Designing the course that enables students to learn independently outside the class is a good idea to find space for the specific themes to be included. Learning materials for the general themes can be put in a module or be developed in an e-learning program so that students can learn autonomously outside the class anytime they want. Class time can be used to check students' work, clarify difficult concepts, and implement the learned skills and strategies in more meaningful activities. Besides maximizing the learning time, this way, at the same time, can foster students' independent learning.

General and specific themes together with the selected topics, then, can be put in a sequent order. Texts related to the topics, then, are selected. Academic texts taken from the Internet and textbooks used by university students are preferred. Based on the texts, learning tasks are developed, covering contents comprehension, reading strategy practices, and language items learning. The tasks are sequenced from the pre-reading, while-reading, and post-reading activities. Pre-reading tasks are meant to activate students' knowledge to understand the text, while-reading tasks are meant to train students to implement reading strategies needed in academic reading, and post-reading tasks are for relating what they have learned from the text with issues related to the topic. This can serve as transitions that link various tasks and topics. To link the three themes selected so that they have connection with one another to make the course coherent, a thread needs to be formulated. *Study skills training in English to encourage student's independent learning at university,* can be an alternative thread to link the three themes.

4 CONCLUSION

Theme-based syllabus is proposed as an alternative model for the teaching of English in Higher education in Indonesia. This model is supported by EAP teaching theories and suitable with the context in which English is used as an additional or foreign language.

The combination between EGAP and ESAP is proposed due to the needs of the students served. There are three themes selected for the EAP syllabus for non-English major students of Indonesian university. The first two themes are related to EGAP, *English as an International Language*, and *Study Skills at the University*, while the third theme is related to ESAP (the major the students take), such as *Learning Music* for students of Music Study Program. Two topics are selected for each theme to be discussed in the face-to-face meetings, while other topics of the second theme are presented on a module or an e-learning program for independent learning to give more reading practice, to encourage students' independent learning, and at the same time to save class time, so that students have sufficient time to deepening their understanding by applying the knowledge and skills they have learned to study their subject contents.

REFERENCES

Aini, C.H. 2008. *Rancangan Silabus Mata Kuliah Bahasa Inggris Semester Pertama: Sebuah Studi Kasus di Jurusan Budidaya Pertanian Universitas Malikussaleh.* Unpublished Thesis, Graduate Program of University of Indonesia, Jakarta.

Allan, B. 2010. *Study Skills Handbook.* Hull: Hull University Business School.

Anderson, N.J. 2012. Reading Instruction, in Burns & Richards (eds): *The Cambridge Guide to Pedagogy and Practice in Second Language Teaching.* Cambridge: Cambridge University Press.

Brick, J. 2012. Teaching English for Academic Purposes, in Burns & Richards (eds): *The Cambridge Guide to Pedagogy and Practice in Second Language Teaching.* Cambridge: Cambridge University Press.

Brinton, S. & Wesche. 1989. *Content-Based Language Instruction.* New York: Newbury House.

Brown, 2007. *Principles of Language Learning and Teaching.* New York: Longman.

Crandall, J. 2012. Content-based Instruction and Content Language Integrated Learning, in Burns & Richards (eds): *The Cambridge Guide to Pedagogy and Practice in Second Language Teaching.* Cambridge: Cambridge University Press.

Davis, S. 2003. Content Based Instruction in EFL Contexts, *The Internet TESL Journal February 2003* 9(2). Retrieved from: http://iteslj.org./downloaded on 9 October 2013 at 10.12.

El-Furqaan, Z. 2014. Blended Language Learning untuk Optimalisasi Pembelajaran Bahasa Inggris Tingkat Perguruan Tinggi di Universitas Indonesia, Universitas Indonesia: Jakarta.

Grabe & Stoller. 2001. *Teaching and Researching Reading,* 2nd edition, Harlow: Pearson Education Limited.

Hyland, K. 2006. *English for academic purposes, an advanced resource book*. London: Routledge.

Kumaravadivelu, B. 2008. *Understanding Language Teaching, from Method to Postmethod*. London: Lawrence Erlbaum Associates Publishers.

Little, D. 2000. Learner Autonomy: Why Foreign Fanguage should Occupy a Central Role in the Curriculum in S. Green (ed). *New Perspective on Teaching and Learning Modern Languages:* 24–45. Clevedon: Multilingual matters.

Mustadi, A. 2011. *Pengembangan Competency-task Based dalam Pembelajaran Bahasa Inggris Calon Guru SD*. Yogyakarta: Yogyakarta State University.

Nation, I.S.P. & Macalister, J. 2010. *Language Curriculum Development*. New York/London: Routledge.

Nation, I.S.P. 2012. *What should Every ESL Teacher Know?* Compass Publishing.

Oxford, R. 1990. *Language Learning Strategies, What Every Teacher Should know*. Boston: Heinle & Heinle Publishers.

Richards, J.C. 2001. *Curriculum Development in Language Teaching*. Cambridge: Cambridge University Press.

Richards, J.C. 2006. Communicative Language Teaching Today. Cambridge: Cambridge University Press.

Snow, M.A. 2001. Content-based and Immersion Models for Second and Foreign Language Teaching, in Celce-Murcia (ed): *Teaching English as a Second /Foreign Language*. New York: Heinle & Heinle Thomson Learning.

Solikhah, I. 2014. Silabus EAP Berbasis Learning Outcomes untuk Mahasiswa Jurusan Non-Bahasa Inggris di IAIN Surakarta. *Pedagogik* 8(1).

Stoller, F.L. & Grabe, W. 1997. *The 6 T's Approach to Content-based Instruction*. Longman.http://www.carla.umn.edu/cobaltt/modules/curriculum/stoller_grabe1997downloaded on 30 November 2013 at 3.19.

Thanasoulas, D. 2000. What is learner Autonomy and How can it be Fostered, *The internet TESL journal* 6(11). Retrieved from: http://iteslj.org/Articles/Thanasoulas-Autonomy.html, downloaded on 22 October 2014 at 15.4.

Wingate, U. 2006. Doing Away with Study Skills, in *Teaching in Higher Education* 11(4): 457–469.

ELT in Asia in the Digital Era: Global Citizenship and Identity – Madya et al. (Eds)
© 2018 Taylor & Francis Group, London, ISBN 978-0-8153-7900-3

Academic reading needs analysis: Preliminary study of Malaysian prospective higher education students

S.M. Damio & N.N. Rosli
Universiti Teknologi MARA, Malaysia

ABSTRACT: Academic reading (AR) is one of Academic Literacy (AL) competencies developed during students' earlier schooling prior to higher education. Nonetheless, there is a gap between AR demands in university and those in school. This article aims to look into Malaysian 2016 Sijil Pelajaran Malaysia (SPM) school leavers through a Needs Analysis (NA) study. Three varieties of NA namely Present Situation Analysis (PSA), Learning Needs Analysis (LNA) and Deficiency Analysis (DA) are explored using a questionnaire (quantitative method). A purposive sampling of ten participants is adopted to gather data which were then analysed and presented in descriptive statistics. The findings show that the participants have only a fair knowledge of AR and consider AR as vital for their success in higher education. The valuable insights and findings from this pilot study suggest that a full-scale study should be carried out to design an AR course to close the gap between AR in schools and higher education.

1 INTRODUCTION

This need analysis aims to investigate 2016 Sijil Pelajaran Malaysia (SPM) students' academic reading (AR) skills need. Benesch (1997) stated that needs assessment plays an essential role in all aspects of language education planning Individuals use different strategies while being engaged in reading tasks. AR strategies are deliberate, cognitive steps that learners can take to assist in acquiring, storing, and retrieving new information and thus can be assessed. These strategies will eventually become part of academic literacy (AL) skills.

2 LITERATURE REVIEW

There is a gap between academic literacy demands in university and those in school as students are exposed to limited academic literacy in school. According to Hirst (2002), there is an immediate need to look beyond the skills-based approach learners are equipped with, as a result of training for school literacy and the assumption that learners will be able to 'pick up tertiary literacy practices' and start thinking of how best to support learners in their engagement with tertiary literacy. Academic literacy has been established as an important enabling tool for tertiary learners as the ability to read, interpret and critically evaluate texts can help a learner participate effectively in the comprehending of academic texts and the writing of assignments (Nambiar 2007). Additionally, a successful learner normally is a successful reader, who employs the reading strategies judiciously. Reading actually empowers a learner and enhances the learning and thinking process.

Despite the importance of these skills for academic success, lecturers seldom teach them to the first-year undergraduates as they tend to assume that the students have already acquired these skills as part of their secondary education (Erikson et al. 2006). However, according to Hermida (2009), the reality is that most first-year undergraduates lack academic reading skills, especially because tertiary level reading demands greatly differ from reading skills taught in secondary school. Therefore, there is a need to analyze the 2016 SPM students' needs in their academic reading skill in preparing them for Higher Education.

The reviews of some literature related to 2016 SPM students' needs in reading skills. The review of the literature works is to understand the concept of English for Specific Purposes, Needs Analysis and Academic English Reading Skill. The resources of the materials collected such as journals, dissertations, articles, and previous research which are relevant to this needs analysis whether from Malaysia or international research have been quoted and featured according to the suitability to the topic of this needs analysis.

English for Specific Purposes (ESP) is English instruction based on actual and immediate needs of learners who have to successfully perform real-life tasks unrelated to merely passing an English class or exam. ESP is needs based and task oriented (Smoak, 2003)." According to Hutchinson and Waters (1987), ESP is an approach rather than a product, by which they mean that ESP does not involve a particular kind of language, teaching material or methodology. The absolute characteristics of ESP that have been defined by Strevens (1988) are that, ESP consists of English Language Teaching which is designed to meet specific needs of the learners; related in content to particular disciplines, occupations and activities; centered on language appropriate to those activities in syntax, lexis, discourse, semantics and so on, and analysis of the discourse; in contrast with 'General English'. He also stated the variable characteristics of ESP, in which ESP may be restricted as to the learning skills to be learned; and it may not be taught according to any pre-ordained methodology. Furthermore, Robinson (1991) stated that ESP is 'normally goal-directed', and ESP courses develop from a needs analysis, which aims to specify as closely as possible what exactly it is that students have to do through the medium of English.

Needs analysis (NA) is the procedures used to collect information about learners' needs. Iwai et al. (1999) defined needs analysis as the activities that are involved in collecting information that will serve as the basis for developing a curriculum that will meet the needs of a particular group of students. It is the first step in course design and provides validity and relevancy for all subsequent course design activities. Needs analysis aims to find out what language skills a learner needs in order to perform a particular role; to help determine if an existing course adequately addresses the needs of potential students; to determine which students from a group are most in need of training in particular language skills; and to collect information about a particular problem learners are experiencing.

Besides, there are several approaches to needs analysis, which are the Target Situation Analysis, Present Situation Analysis, Pedagogic Needs Analysis, Deficiency Analysis, Strategy Analysis or Learning Needs Analysis, Means Analysis, Register Analysis, Discourse Analysis, and Genre Analysis. This study focuses on the Present Situation Analysis, Learning Needs Analysis, and Deficiency Analysis. Present Situation Analysis tries to identify the expectations of the learners at the beginning of needs analysis; estimates strengths and weaknesses in language, skills, and learning experiences; and can be carried out using established placement tests. Learning Needs Analysis involves the strategies that learners employ in order to learn another language as it tries to establish how the learners wish to learn rather than what they need to learn. Deficiency Analysis conform the basis of the language syllabus as it should provide data about both the gap between present and target extra-linguistic knowledge, mastery of general English, language skills and learning strategies.

Reading Skills for Academic Purposes or Academic Reading (AR) skills is one of the branches of English for Specific Purposes. Reading is a crucial element in the study of an undergraduate in higher education since it is likely to take up most of the time the student devotes to his university work. Reading for pleasure is in many ways quite different from academic reading. Often the ability to read, which is, to decode the text on a page into understandable language, is taken as being all that need to have accomplished. Nonetheless, decoding is one element of the process, but understanding what you have decoded, and being able to do this in a highly effective manner, is a vital element of the complete skill of reading, especially in advanced educational settings.

In the Malaysian ESL secondary school classroom, the learners have to read a text for the purpose of answering comprehension questions. Ponniah (1993) claimed that the teaching of reading in schools focuses on literal comprehension skills such as word or sentence recognition. It is unlikely to have learners go beyond the information in the text and relate new information to background knowledge to have a holistic understanding of the text. They also do not have the skill of questioning what they read in order to have a better understanding of the text. However, the undergraduates are demanded to read, interpret, and critically evaluate an academic text and process that information in a written or spoken form. According to Spack (1997), tertiary literacy is a process of actively engaging with what is read, finding information and understanding this by thinking through it and lastly interpreting the content to suit prototypical academic writing tasks like summarizing, presentations and discussions. Hence, students, who are planning to pursue their studies into higher education, should be prepared with academic reading skills in order to have a smooth and enjoyable experience in learning.

Therefore, the objective of this needs analysis is to investigate the needs of 2016 SPM students AR skills, particularly related to Present Situation Analysis (PSA), Learning Needs Analysis (LNA) and Deficiency Analysis (DA).

3 METHOD

The aim of this section is to set out the methodological approach employed to discover the current SPM leavers' needs in AR skills in preparation for their Higher Education. This section presents the methodological approach implemented in this pilot study. It also presents the samples which were selected and sets out the method used of data collection along with the process of data analysis.

A purposive sampling is seen as the most appropriate method for this study. Dolores & Tongco's steps in purposive sampling are used as guidelines in deciding the participants as this pilot study is looking into "the sampling of unique or special cases" (Tedlie & Fen Yu 2007: 78). Students who were sitting for SPM examination and more likely to further their studies into higher education is the main criterion of the participants. The population was 2016 SPM students of SMK Bukit. Only ten were purposively selected through personal contacts of the researcher. The students' English AR skills can be said as in need of enhancement. Therefore, this AR skills NA pilot study is aptly timed.

A questionnaire was used in which it asked the participants for the following information: demographic information, Present Situation Analysis, Learning Needs Analysis, and Deficiency Analysis. The decision to self-devise the NA was driven by the researchers' knowledge of the context and participants of the study. The questionnaire was checked and approved by a content expert prior to distribution on 27th October 2016.

The needs analysis consists of four sections, which are personal background, Present Situation Analysis, Learning Needs Analysis, and Deficiency Analysis.

3.1 *Personal background*

Section A covers the participants' personal background by enquiring the participants' gender, age, school, class and year of SPM examination. These information are needed as they reflect the criterions that are needed from the participants of this needs analysis.

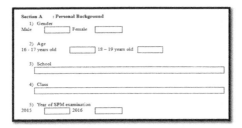

This needs analysis asks about the gender of the participants in order to ensure that there is no bias towards certain gender in collecting the data. The age of the participants and their year of SPM examination are also needed to make sure they are current SPM students, who are sitting for the examination in November 2016. This is because the objective of this needs analysis is to investigate the current SPM leavers' needs in reading skill. Hence, the participants, who are going to graduate from secondary school this year, seem to be fit for this needs analysis. The items of the participants' school and class deem to be essential in this section as to find out their school, the location and background of the school, as well as the students' academic performance. These are vital informationational points to the researcher as those inform the researcher about the students' potential in pursuing their studies into higher education. The Reading Skill Course that the researcher is going to develop would not benefit those who are not planning to further their studies into higher education.

3.2 *Present situation analysis*

Section B encompasses the Present Situation Analysis of the participants.

Present Situation Analysis tries to identify the expectations of the learners at the beginning of needs analysis; estimates strengths and weaknesses in language, skills, and learning experiences; and can be carried out using established placement tests. Hence, this section wants to study the participants' interest in taking an English reading skill Course; present rate of English reading skill; feelings on improving English reading skill; as well as their favorite reading materials. The first item aims to identify the participants' interest to take part in the English Reading Skill Course that would be developed later on based on the findings of this needs analysis. Then, the researcher is able to determine the participants' present rate of English reading skill in the second item of this section. They need to be at least fair in this skill since ESP is intended for participants who are intermediate and above in term of their proficiency. Next, it is also vital to identify the participants' views on improving their English reading skill in order to know the importance of providing the course to them. Also, the researcher wants to find out the participants' preferences of the reading materials as to identify the suitable reading materials should be utilized in the course later on.

The fifth item of this section covers the participants' perceptions of their ability to accomplish the English Reading Skills listed above. A Likert Scale has been used to collect the participants' opinions. According to Bertram (2007), Likert Scale is a psychometric response scale primarily used in the questionnaire to obtain participants' preferences or degree of agreement with a statement or set of statements. The statements above are the college reading skills that have been adopted from the chapters in a book entitled 'Exercise Your College Reading Skills: Developing More Powerful Comprehension' written by Janet Elder. The researcher chose this particular book as the students of the Foundation of TESL use it in one of their course in order to enhance their academic reading skills. Thus, it is fair to give the SPM leavers the luxury to learn and enhance their academic reading skills as well, before pursuing their studies in various courses in the higher education later on.

5) Read the statements below thoroughly and tick the respective boxes according to your views.

Statements	Strongly Disagree	Disagree	Neutral	Agree	Strongly Agree
I am able to skim the reading material					
I am able to scan the reading material					
I am able to determine the meaning of an unfamiliar word through context					
I am able to determine the topic of a paragraph					
I am able to identify the stated main idea sentence of a paragraph					
I am able to identify the supporting details of a paragraph					
I am able to distinguish facts from opinions					
I am able to make inferences and draw conclusion					
I am able to draw conclusion					
I am able to find a word in an English dictionary					
I am able to find the meaning of a word in an English dictionary					
I am able to use the pronunciation information in an English dictionary					
I am able to use the contents page of a book					
I am able to use the index of a book					

3.3 *Learning needs analysis*

Additionally, Section C incorporates the participants' Learning Needs Analysis, which covers the participants' preferences in learning styles.

Learning Needs Analysis involves the strategies that learners employ in order to learn another language as it tries to establish how the learners wish to learn rather than what they need to learn. This section seeks to identify whether the participants prefer to learn the English reading skill individually, by group work, or both. The findings can be the basis for the researcher to develop the preferable activities in the course afterward.

3.4 *Deficiency learning needs*

Section D looks into the Deficiency Analysis, which analyzes the participants' experiences in learning English Reading Skill.

Section D: Deficiency Needs Analysis

Please tick your answers in the respective boxes.

8) I have learnt English Reading Skill in English classes before.
Yes [   ]   No [   ]

If you tick 'Yes', please answer Question 9 and Question 10. If you tick 'No', please answer Question 11.

9) If yes, how useful was the English Reading Skill classes?
Not useful [   ]   Somewhat Useful [   ]   Useful [   ]

Please state your reasons.
_____
_____
_____

10) What would you like to improve on the English Reading Skill classes?
_____
_____
_____

11) If no, how do you want the English Reading Skill classes to be?
_____
_____
_____

It explores whether the participants actual wish was being incorporated when they were in the class; as well as their wants in the English Reading Skill Course. According to West (1994), Deficiency Analysis can be considered as learners' present needs or wants. Therefore, the researcher asks whether the participants have had English Reading Skill in their English classes beforehand, and examine their needs and wants through the open-ended questions. The open-ended questions in the questionnaire were intended to encourage a full and meaningful answer from the participants' own knowledge and opinions.

4   DISCUSSION

The discussions focus on the findings of Present Situation Analysis, Learning Needs Analysis, and Deficiency Analysis.

Based on the data collected for Present Situation Analysis, all of the participants are interested in taking an English Reading Skill Course. The majority of them believe that they have fair knowledge on the English reading skill and feel that it is essential for them to improve their English reading skills (Figure 1). This is supported by Smoak (2003) in his article that instructions are needed to improve skills.

Some of their favorite reading materials, as shown in Figure 2 are magazines, comics, fiction book, newspapers, poetry, encyclopedia, recipes, catalogs, dictionaries, brochures, and a nonfiction book.

Besides, the participants seem to be able to skim, scan, determine the meaning of an unfamiliar word through context, identify the supporting details of a paragraph, make inferences, use the pronunciation information in an English dictionary, use the contents page of a book, and use the index of a book. Even though they agreed on having these abilities, there are still areas to be improved and polished to ensure they are strongly able to apply those English reading skills (Nambiar, 2007).

Furthermore, the participants appear to be indifferent about their ability in skimming, determining the meaning of an unfamiliar word through context, determining the topic of a paragraph, identifying the stated main idea sentence in a paragraph, distinguishing facts from opinions, making inferences, and drawing a conclusion. These are exemplified in the

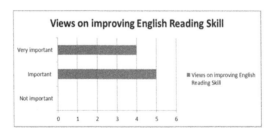

Figure 1.   Interest in taking an English reading skill course.

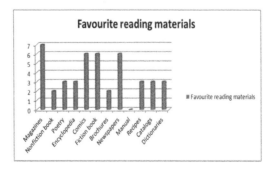

Figure 2.   Favourite reading materials.

following figures (Figure 3, 4, 5, 6). The figures show that participants chose to only disagree, neutral or agree) while only 10% in "the ability to determine the meaning of an unfamiliar word through context" put it as strongly disagree. It appears that they could not decide whether they have the ability or not on those English reading skills.

Therefore, it is recommended to equip them with those skills in the English Reading Skill Course to ensure their smooth journey in gaining knowledge in the tertiary level afterward.

Learning Needs Analysis findings show that the participants prefer to learn English reading skill in a group work better than individually as shown in Figure 7. The reasons for favoring this style of learning is because they want to learn from the other friends; they want to exchange opinions; they feel that they can detect their mistakes easily from their friends; and they are able to ask questions in a group work activity (Table 1). Hence, the course designer should consider more group activities as compared to individual tasks in order to engage the participants to the teaching and learning session.

The reasons for choosing to learn AR skills in groups are as stated in the following table. These are answers taken from the open-ended questions in the questionnaire.

Findings of the deficiency analysis in the questionnaire reveal that most participants have not learned English reading skill (extensively) in English classes before (Figure 8).

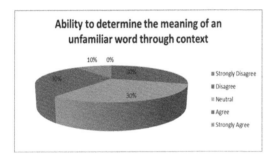

Figure 3.   Ability to determine the meaning of an unfamiliar word through context.

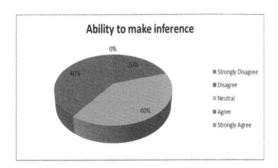

Figure 4.   Ability to make inferences.

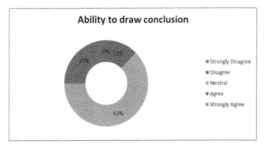

Figure 5.   Ability to draw conclusion.

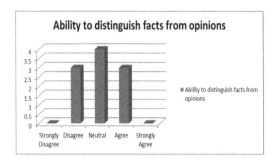

Figure 6.   Ability to distinguish facts from opinions.

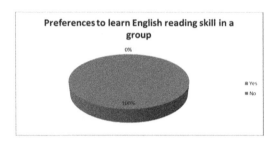

Figure 7.   Preferences to learn English reading skill in a group.

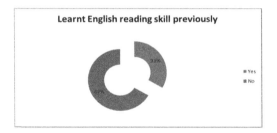

Figure 8.   Learnt English reading skill previously.

Table 1.   Reasons of choosing 'Yes'.

	Reasons
1	Because we can change the idea in a group and can understand the English grammar better.
2	I will know my fault on the spot because the group members will teach me.
3	Because I can learn new thing and new words from the others.
4	Because I can learn from other students.
5	Because I would get new vocabulary from my friend.
6	Because I can talk and ask about something that I do not understand about English.
7	Because I can talk and ask about something that I do not understand about English.
8	We can exchange our opinion.
9	Because I can learn from other friends.

Thus, they suggest their needs on the English reading skill classes that they want to participate. Some of the suggestions are that they want to learn in a group about the unfamiliar words, English, and reading skill; they want to have classes in a computer lab to read using the internet; they want to have outdoor activities; as well as they want to learn the reading skill using interesting materials. However, there are still several participants that have learned English reading skill in English classes beforehand and they think that the English reading skill learned was useful. In their opinion, it is useful as it is easier for them to get information while reading books, newspapers, and magazines. When asked about what they want to improve on the English reading skill classes that they have attended, they want a class that allows them to practice the English reading skills; they want the teacher to use materials with pictures and diagrams; and they want the class to be interactive and fun.

Figure 9 shows the participants' perspectives on the usefulness of attending English reading classes. 33% cited it as 'Useful' 67% of the samples selected 'Somewhat useful' as their views on the usefulness of the attended English reading skill classes. The reasons for selecting 'useful' are presented in Table 2 while Table 3 shows the reasons for selecting 'somewhat useful'.

When asked on suggestions to improve the English reading classes, the participants suggested the following (Table 4):

To the issues of their wants in an English reading skills class, the cited reasons are as follow (Table 5).

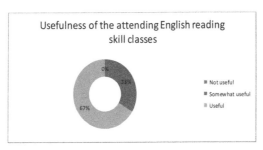

Figure 9.   Usefulness of the attending English reading skill classes.

Table 2.   Reasons for choosing 'Useful'.

	Reasons
2	Because we are in a modern world and every single thing we do need us to communicate in English and it is also useful when we are going to attend an interview to have a job.
6	Because it is easier for me to get information while reading books, newspapers and magazines.

Table 3.   Reason for choosing 'Somewhat useful'.

	Reason
7	Because I rarely use my knowledge in reading skill.

Table 4.   Ideas on what can be improved in the English reading skill classes attended.

	Ideas on what can be improved in the English reading skill classes
2	I will always practice English reading skills.
6	I prefer my teachers to use materials which have pictures and diagrams in reading classes.
7	I would like to have an interactive and fun class.

Table 5.   Wants on the English reading skill classes.

	Wants on the English reading skill classes
1	No comment.
3	I want to study with English teacher and ask friends about the words I do not understand.
4	I want to study with teachers and friends about English or reading book.
5	I want my teacher to bring me to the computer lab to read using the internet.
8	It would be interesting to have classes outside our classroom.
9	I do not have a lot of time to study. So, I want my teacher to teach me how to read properly using interesting materials.

5 CONCLUSION

To conclude, it is recommended that the English Reading Skill Course, that will be developed, considers the participants' needed skills in English reading, preferred learning style, preferred reading materials, and preferred environment of the classes. Based on the findings, an interactive, fun activities using either magazines; newspapers; comics; or fiction books are most favorable by the participants. Hence, the course designer should include more group activities and all of the skills asked in item five of the Present Situation Analysis into the English Reading Skill Course along with preparing a conducive learning environment for the learners Last but not least, it is proven that the participants desire to participate in the English Reading Skill Course is high as they feel the need to learn and improve their present English reading skill. Hence, it seems essential to design an English Reading Skill Course for the current SPM leavers as there are a lot of English reading skills that needed to be taught, refined, and polished in order to ensure their readiness to pursue higher education. The course would benefit various stakeholders especially the students and lecturers in the higher education for the reason that reading is an essential skill used in the tertiary level of education.

REFERENCES

Benesch, S. 1996. Needs analysis and curriculum development in EAP: An example of a critical approach. *Tesol Quarterly* 723–738.

Bertram, D. 2007. Likert scales. Retrieved November, 2, 2013.

Dolores, C. & Tongco. 2007. Purposive sampling as a tool for informant selection. Downloaded from file:///C:/Users/User/Downloads/126-454-1-PB.pdf on 30 May 2017.

Elder, J. 2004. Exercise your college reading skills: Developing more powerful comprehension. McGraw-Hill.

Erickson, B.L., Peters, C.B. & Strommer, D.W. 2006. *Teaching first-year college students.* San Francisco, CA: Jossey-Bass.

Hermida, D. 2009. The importance of teaching academic reading skills in first-year university courses. The importance of teaching academic reading skills in first-year university courses (June 14, 2009).

Hirst, E.W. 2002. Engaging heterogeneity: Tertiary literacy in new times.

Hutchinson, T. & Waters, A. 1987. *English for specific purposes.* Cambridge University Press.

Iwai, T., Kondo, K., Lim, D.S., Ray, G., Shimizu, H. & Brown, J.D. 1999. Japanese language needs analysis 1998–1999.

Nambiar, R.M. 2007. Enhancing academic literacy among tertiary learners: A Malaysian experience. 3 L; Language, Linguistics and Literature, *The Southeast Asian Journal of English Language Studies* 13: 77–94.

Ponniah, K.S. 1993. Improving academic reading ability of EFL students at tertiary level. Unpublished Doctoral Dissertation. University of Malaya, Kuala Lumpur.

Robinson, P.C. 1991. ESP today: A practitioner's guide. Hemel Hempstead: Prentice Hall.

Smoak, R. 2003. What is English for specific purposes. *In English teaching forum* 41(2): 22–27.

Spack, R. 1988. Initiating ESL students into the academic discourse community: How far should we go? *TESOL quarterly* 22(1): 29–51.

Strevens, P. 1988. The learner and teacher of ESP. *ESP in the classroom: Practice and evaluation* 39–44.

Teddlie, C. & Fen Y. 2007. Mixed methods sampling: A Typology with examples journal of mixed methods research 2007; 1; 77. Downloaded from http://mmr.sagepub.com/cgi/content/abstract/1/1/77 on 30 May 2017.

West, R. 1994. Needs analysis in language teaching. *Language teaching* 27(01): 1–19.

ELT in Asia in the Digital Era: Global Citizenship and Identity – Madya et al. (Eds)
© *2018 Taylor & Francis Group, London, ISBN 978-0-8153-7900-3*

Using multi techniques to improve reading fluency in ESL classrooms

D.B. Devi
R.E.A.L. Kids, Selangor, Malaysia

M. Dhamotharan
SEGi University, Selangor, Malaysia

ABSTRACT: Teachers are particularly concerned with the development of reading skills in English. Fluent reading skills help to stir the minds of readers and incontrovertibly contribute to the conscious and unconscious thinking processes. Conventional methods suggest that teachers make little difference in improving pupils' reading fluency unless through remedial classes. Research also shows teachers can make a noticeable difference by intervention to produce positive results. This paper creates an awareness of the potential of multi approaches to improve reading fluency in a selected primary school classroom in Selangor, Malaysia.

1 INTRODUCTION

According to Anderson, Hiebert, Scott, & Wilkinson (1985), reading is a basic life skill and is a cornerstone for a child's success in school and throughout life as a lifelong skill. It is common knowledge that without the ability to read well, opportunities for personal fulfilment and job success are inevitably lost. The ever-increasing demand for high levels of literacy in our technological society makes this problem even more pressing (Snow, Burns, & Griffin, 1998).

Reading is one of the most challenging areas in the education system as reading skills are fundamental in order to function in today's society. They develop the mind, creativity and imagination. Teaching young children to understand the written word helps them develop their language skills, learn to listen attentively and build self-confidence.

In order to succeed academically, effective and fluent reading is essential as fluent reading skills help stir the minds of readers and incontrovertibly contribute to the conscious and unconscious thinking process (Mikulecky 1990:1).

2 AREA OF CONCERN

This paper focuses on improving reading fluency using multi approaches with a selected Year Two class in a National School in Selangor, Malaysia. The Year Two English Language curriculum requires pupils to learn thematic topics; long vowel; and diagraph sounds. However, this Year Two class pupils' reading skills fall far below par as most are not able to read their textbooks or sound the letters correctly. Classroom observation showed that the teacher used Bahasa Malaysia during instructions and had not practised differentiated teaching to enable the learning process.

3 FACTORS INFLUENCING READING LEVELS

3.1 *Pupils background*

The pupils in this selected Year Two class come from immigrant parents with low SES and most of them only speak Bahasa Malaysia. Most of their parents do not see the need or are not able to send their children for tuition and extra English classes. Therefore, whatever the pupils learn in school is all they get.

3.2 *Preschool experience*

Half the pupils in this Year Two class have been to preschool and half of them have only been to a Malay-medium preschool or *tadika* where the emphasis is on Bahasa Malaysia.

3.3 *Culture and motivation*

Another issue is the culture of the parents and pupils who view English as a foreign language as irrelevant. This attributes to the way pupils process in Bahasa Malaysia and translate into English which affects their fluency, intonation, pronunciation, spelling, tense, reading, and writing.

The perception of English as irrelevant influences mind-sets leading to a lack of interest and focus. The learning becomes mundane without being meaningful and purposeful. The teaching is too teacher-centred without activities to stimulate pupils' minds.

4 READING AND CURRICULUM

The development of reading fluency is an important component for advanced reading comprehension skills (Gorsuch & Taguchi 2008, Grabe 2009, Klauda & Guthrie 2008, Taguchi et al. 2012). Grabe & Stoller (2011, 2014) suggested that the goal for reading should be viewed and instructed on a general level, which is to incorporate key component skills and knowledge into a reading curriculum in a principled and consistent way so that it complements pupils, teachers, school management and curriculum. According to Grabe & Stoller (2011, 2014), these principles should include a curricular framework, reading resources, additional student-centred activities for pre-reading, during-reading, and post-reading sessions, word recognition skills, vocabulary building, extensive reading, and motivation.

5 THEORIES OF READING

There are three main theories which explain the nature of learning to read. The first is the traditional theory, or bottom up processing, which focuses on the printed form of a text. It suggests that learning is based upon habit formation, brought about by the repeated association of a stimulus with a response (Nunan 1991). In recent times, the main method associated with the bottom-up approach to reading is known as phonics or phonemic awareness which requires the learner to match letters with sounds in a defined sequence.

The second is the cognitive view, or top-down processing which enhances the role of background knowledge. A meaningful learning method, where new information is presented in a relevant context and is related to what the learner already knows, so that it can be easily integrated into one's existing cognitive structure (Nunan 1991).

Third is the metacognitive view, which is based on the control and manipulation that readers can have on comprehending text, which emphasizes the involvement of the readers thinking about what they are doing while reading (Block1992). In the context of reading, meta-cognition involves thinking about what one is doing while reading.

5.1 Types of reading

According to Brown (1989), there are several types of reading. Oral Silent Intensive—specific reading skills (a) linguistic (b) content; Extensive—large quantities of materials (1) scanning (2) skimming (3) global

6 DIFFERENTIATED LEARNING

Tomlinson (2000) suggested that differentiated instruction means tailoring instruction to meet individual needs. When teachers use differentiated content pupils need to learn to access the information, process the activities in which they engage in order to make sense of the content, to rehearse, apply, and extend what they have learned. The learning environment and use of on-going assessment and flexible grouping makes this a successful approach for instruction and provides a platform for pupils to show evidence of their learning.

7 USING MULTI APPROACHES

Providing pupils with multiple ways to access content improves their learning (Hattie 2011). Using multiple ways to demonstrate knowledge and skills increases engagement and learning and provides teachers with more accurate understanding of pupils' learning (Darling-Hammond 2010).

8 METHODOLOGY

The Kemmis and McTaggart Model (1986) of cyclic action was followed to provide interventions through the use of songs or rhymes, realia, flashcards, and games to improve reading. The procedures comprised: planning to initiate change; implementing the changes and observing the process of implementation and consequences; reflecting on processes of change and re-planning; acting and observing; and reflecting.

8.1 Data collection

Prior to the introduction of the multi approaches, pupils were interviewed with a structured questionnaire using close and open-ended questions to collect feedback regarding reading habits, interests, support and strategies used, which provided useful information. The data were collected from pupils, observations, teacher's journal, and recordings.

8.2 Data analysis and discussion

There were 21 Year Two pupils in the class. The data for their reading performance level were collected from the school exam department for the 2015 standardized exam (Table 1) as well as the March 2016standardized reading skills assessment (Table 2). In addition, the data from their Literacy and Numeracy Screening (LINUS) from the Ministry of Education were also taken to observe their performance (Table 3). These data sources helped to gain some insights into the pupils' reading proficiency level and decide on multi approaches to help improve their reading fluency.

Table 1. Reading assessment results for 2015.

Weak readers	Average readers	Good readers	Proficient readers
0.5 points	3 points	4 points	5 points
12 Pupils	6 Pupils	2 Pupils	1 Pupil

Table 2. Reading assessment results for March 2016.

Weak readers	Average readers	Good readers	Proficient readers
0.5 points	3 points	4 points	5 points
7 Pupils	11 Pupils	2 Pupils	1 Pupil

Table 3. Literacy and numeracy screening results (LINUS) 2016.

Weak readers	Average readers	Good readers	Proficient readers
0–9 points	10–19 points	20–29 points	30–40 points
5 Pupils	12 Pupils	2 Pupils	2 Pupils

8.3 Cycle 1: Songs

Research shows that use of music and songs, activates more parts of the brain and increases test scores as it enhances motivation and engagement especially in phonemic awareness, fluency, vocabulary, and comprehension. Songs can also be used to focus on smallest sound units from which words are formed and categorized as vowels and consonants. Songs are authentic and easily accessible. Many songs are packed with alliteration and rhyme. An awareness of sounds within a word and noticing the same sounds in different words help with word recognition when reading. Songs can be used to focus on words that help learners to associate the syllables and stress on these words with rhythm.

Repetition is the key to fluency and music makes repeated practice enjoyable. Pupils are able to experiment with grammatical rules rhyming through songs. Singing songs helps reading by stressing on correct pronunciation. Songs also focus on connecting speech. Connecting speech is the natural way we speak, linking together and emphasizing certain words, rather than each word standing alone. Songs provide lively oral language experience. Pupils repeatedly hear higher-level vocabulary with simple melodies and rhymes. Many of the reading strategies like re-telling, visualizing, and questioning can be practiced with songs.

The Audio-Lingual Method by Kind (1980) uses familiar songs to teach English which helps learners overcome fear and resistance to the unknown. Kind's (1980), Audio-Lingual Method has been developed and tested at Harvard University and other European schools. According to Kind (1980: 49), "It has been found that foreign languages can be taught more rapidly, more effectively and with greater recall through the use of song, rather than the mechanical classroom drills". Cooley (1961) showed varying degrees of correlation, all positive, between language reading ability and music ability.

The Multidimensional Fluency Scale rates reader fluency in the areas of expression and volume, phrasing, smoothness, pace, and miscues. Scores below 10 indicate that fluency may be a concern. The results from the observations for Cycle 1 are shown in Figure 1.

The use of songs did show improvement in pronunciation of certain specific words through repetitions and singing. Singing songs created a low-anxiety environment and interaction to the otherwise extremely quiet class. It also benefitted this age group as they were able to move about in class and interact with their friends (Schunk 2009). There was evidence that most of the pupils benefitted from songs, however, there were some pupils who did not manage to benefit from this approach and are struggling readers in dire need of help to overcome their difficulties.

8.4 Cycle 2: Realia

Realia helps to make English lessons memorable by creating a link between the objects and the word or phrase they represent. This stimulates the mind and encourages creativity by involving the senses which gives rise to comprehension and fluency. Using realia saves time, reduces lengthy explanations and creates a conducive atmosphere. According to McCarthy

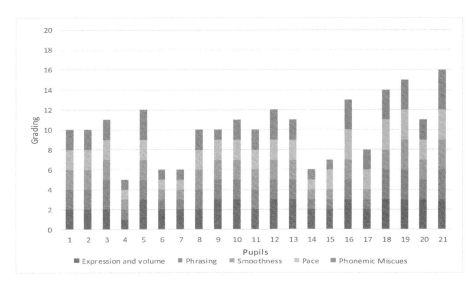

Figure 1. Observation results from reading skills in cycle 1.

(1990: 12), we concentrate on the vocabulary presentation in the classroom from the teacher's point of view, but success in vocabulary lessons crucially depend on the interaction between teacher and learners, and on the work the learners themselves put into the assimilation and use of new words.

Teachers should have certain techniques of presenting new words to weak learners through concrete objects (Schunk 2009). Scott & Yterberg (1990), suggested that teachers should not rely on the spoken word only and that activities for weaker learners should include movement and the senses, which encourages the use of objects and pictures to work with, and to make full use of the school and surroundings.

According to Harmer (1991) using realia improves classroom instruction. Realia according to him brings life, reality, and context to the learning while improving comprehension and reading fluency.

The pupils were introduced to new vocabulary and sentences using realia and the reading observations for Cycle 2 are shown Figure 2. The results showed there were some positive improvements especially among the weak readers. The overall results indicated that 17 pupils improved in their reading fluency and there were still 4 weak readers.

Although two thirds of the class managed to read and meet the criteria, it was not good enough as there were still some pupils who were borderline achievers. Data showed there were 4 weak readers and 17 average to good readers. These 4 weak readers did not show improvement with the use of songs and realia although both the approaches did benefit them in other aspects. The conclusion from the data suggested that their intensive reading needed to be brushed up specifically in reading and decoding of words.

8.5 Cycle 3: Flashcards

Researchers and educationists showed positive evidence for flashcards to decode and read words fluently, to benefit visual, audio, and tactile learners (Schunk 2009). Flashcards have been used for years in classroom instruction by language teachers for teaching as well as displaying items.

Gardner's (2006) multiple intelligences theory suggests that there are many types of learners within any one class and teachers should aim to appeal to all the learner types and learning styles at some point during the course of the lesson. Flashcards appeal to a wide range of learning styles as they are bright, colourful, and versatile, often an underexploited resource although it promotes autonomous learning (Kohyama & Shimada 2005).

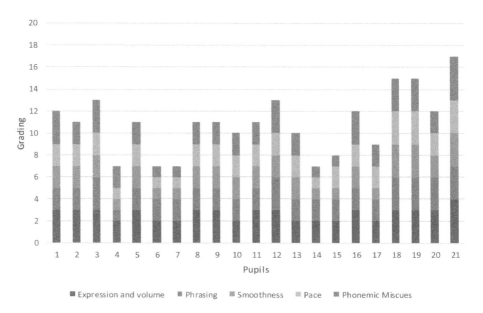

Figure 2.   Observation results from reading skills in cycle 2.

Flashcards may improve autonomy in three ways: words selection, instructing pupils how to select words, and information selection for vocabulary to facilitate memorization by repetition. Nunan (1997: 192–203) divided levels of implementing autonomy into five categories: awareness, involvement, intervention, creation, and transcendence. At awareness level, pupils are made aware of the goals and contents of the materials. At involvement level pupils are encouraged to make choices of activities from a range of alternatives. Intervention level requires pupils to modify the tasks or goals of the course according to their needs and interests and are required to do more reflective thinking. At creation level pupils create their own objectives and tasks and finally at transcendence level pupils become teachers beyond classrooms, do project work, and teach each other.

This way, pupils may become motivated to learn and manage their own learning, and make concerted efforts to the best of their abilities. This may build a foundation for the promotion and implementation of self-access language learning, which is learning a language through the use of a self-established learning environment with readily accessible materials (Chung 2013).

Results for Cycle 3 reading observation can be seen in Figure 3. The results showed that the flashcards approach had very positive and fruitful effect. Most of the pupils showed improvement in their reading fluency with good scores. The remarkable performance was by the weak pupils who reached the improving fluency stage of 10 points while some pupils remained at the same score without declining. The use of flashcards proved to be successful as a resource. There was evidence of learning to decode words by the pupils.

8.6   Cycle 4: Games

Since the use of flashcards proved successful, it was retained and improvised to facilitate the tactile and kinaesthetic learners through games. There was ample evidence that showed games benefit and create proficient and fluent readers.

Well selected games are invaluable as these allow pupils to practise language skills through cooperative, challenging, and entertaining activities.

Lee (1979) said that most language games make learners use the language instead of thinking about learning the correct forms which should be treated as central to and not peripheral to language teaching.

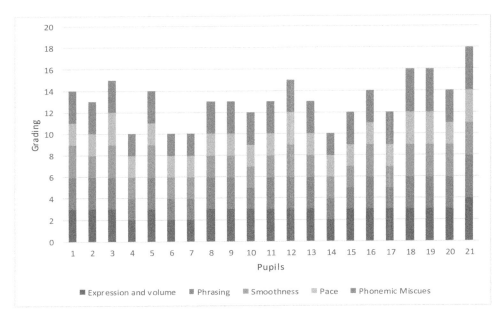

Figure 3.   Observation results from the reading skills in cycle 3.

A similar opinion is expressed by Richard-Amato (1988) who believes games to be fun but warns against overlooking their pedagogical value, particularly in language teaching. Games are known to lower anxiety, thus making the acquisition of input more likely. They are highly motivating and entertaining, and they can give shy pupils more opportunity to express their opinions and feelings (Hansen 1994: p. 118).

Richard-Amato (1988) suggested that they add diversion to the regular classroom activities. A relaxed atmosphere helps pupils remember things faster and better (Wierus & Wierus 1994: 218). It is also believed that teachers are enthusiastic about using games as a teaching device as mere time-fillers, such as a break from the monotony of drilling or frivolous activities. Games according to Lee (1979), ought to be at the heart of teaching languages as they can be productive. Games can be used at all stages of the lesson, provided that they are suitable and carefully chosen.

Games are fun and pupils like to play them. Through games pupils experiment, discover, and interact with their environment (Lewis 1999). Games add variation to a lesson and increase motivation by providing a plausible incentive to use the target language. Games can provide this stimulus and bring the target language to life (Lewis 1999).

The effects of using games as an approach in the reading observation for Cycle 4 are shown in Figure 4. The results showed that games proved positive and effective. All the results showed that the approach benefitted and fulfilled the learning needs of the pupils. It proved to be most successful compared to all of the other approaches. Using flashcards as the material and incorporating the games strategy proved to be the element of success these Year Two pupils needed. The most successful group was the weak group where there was a full turn around in the results compared to the first approach. The healthy competition and points awarded in the games proved successful as the pupils learnt to push themselves to their full potential through extrinsic and intrinsic motivation (Schunk 2009).

The incorporation of games all through the lessons made the lessons interesting, fun, and the learning criteria were met because there was a relaxed atmosphere that promoted less anxiety (Schunk 2009). These games allowed all the pupils to participate and perform individually, and as a group, reinforcing teamwork and team spirit. The safe, supportive, and conducive environment created for the pupils became the bedrock for successful learning (Schunk 2009). On the whole, games and classroom activities promoted self-regulated learning.

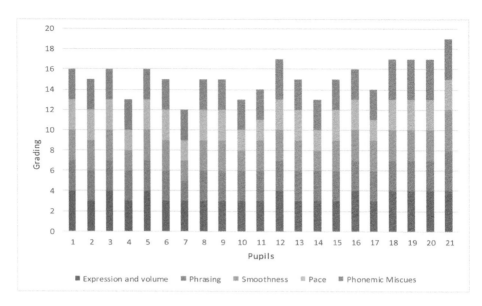

Figure 4.   Observation results from the reading skills in cycle 4.

The learning process involved the use of flashcards in games that allowed the brain to process whole and parts simultaneously. The differentiated learning activity through the recall of different words helped and motivated to build confidence and self-esteem amongst the weak readers.

9   CONCLUSIONS AND RECOMMENDATIONS

The research showed that there were differences in the results with each approach used as it helped pupils in different ways. The data and information collected through each of the four approaches demonstrated pupils' responsiveness and growth in their reading fluency at varying degrees. The best results in this multi approaches were through using flashcards and games, as these helped enhance reading fluency.

As each pupil is an individual, it was crucial that the teacher took time to study and understand their development and the use of appropriate intervention to enable every pupil to grow intellectually, emotionally, socially, psychologically, and physically. The class-based action study showed that understanding and including appropriate theories in varying situations helped reading fluency. Teachers need to consider using principled eclecticism of various teaching styles in a discriminating manner as required by learner needs and styles to enhance pupils' potential (Principled Eclecticism 2017).

The use of songs, music, and rhythm helped pupils with pronunciation of words through repetitions and learning in a fun way creating an environment of low-anxiety without coercion. The activities conducted in a low anxiety environment promoted safety which in turn made learning fun and yielded productivity.

The use of realia showed evidence of comprehension of subject matter and made learning purposeful and meaningful. It catered to pupils' use of their schema to assimilate and accommodate learning which motivated them to become self-regulated leaners. This approach would be appropriate for beginners who are learning English.

The use of flashcards enabled pupils with verbal linguistic intelligence to read and learn better. The exercise of drilling, repetitions, memorizing letter sounds, and rote learning saw pupils display their skills of decoding graphemes and converting them into phonemes. Drilling and rote-learning benefitted pupils who were weak readers as it provided them with the decoding method and enabled them to read correctly and fluently.

Games and flashcards proved to be most successful as these were embedded with elements of fun, safety, and subconscious learning. The use of games promoted healthy competition, self- regulated learning, intrinsic and extrinsic motivation. Schema was used to connect and analyse information. In addition, learning and playing games in teams sparked the use of peripheral learning as learning is enhanced by challenging activities. Flashcards in games allowed the brain to process whole and parts simultaneously. Playing these specific games also helped the audio, visual and tactile learners to read fluently.

The teacher's method of using differentiated learning and creating a conducive reading environment proved positive in creating a supportive environment while building confidence and self-esteem. The teacher role-modelled the correct pronunciation.

Teachers could include all the approaches in a single lesson plan which can be directed to different stages in the lesson plan such as the, set induction, pre-learning, while-learning, and post-learning stages. This would invigorate the lesson and activities as it is of vital importance that the pupils read with correct pronunciation; comprehension; able to decode words; and have meaningful and fun lessons.

Teachers should know the pupils to understand their learning needs so that the appropriate approach could be applied one at a time to bring out the best results from specific groups of pupils as every class has its own learning needs. Teachers need to give enough opportunities for pupils to practice these strategies inside and out of the classroom. Modelling and guided practice are extremely important when teaching, as teachers should never assume that pupils already know the information. There is also a need for research to understand the long-term effects of reading strategies on achievement, to understand pupils' strengths and weaknesses.

In conclusion, teachers and teacher trainers should be aware that language evolves and that both the teachers and pupils should be ready to receive and accept changes. As English is an international language, needed academically, or in trade, and communication, teachers should equip themselves with the latest pedagogical knowledge and information that they can pass on to the learners. Teachers therefore not only educate a class of pupils but they also empower the mindsets of future generations.

REFERENCES

Anderson, R., Hiebert, E., Scott, J. & Wilkinson, I. 1985. Becoming a nation of readers: The report of the commission on reading. Washington, DC: National Institute of Education and the Centre for the Study of Reading. Block, C. & Israel, S. (2005).

Block, E.L. 1992. How they read: Comprehension Monitoring of L1 and L2 Readers, *TESOL Quarterly* 26(2).

Brown, D. 1989. *Teaching by principles: An interactive approach to language pedagogy.* Upper Saddle River, Prentice Hall Regents.

Bygrave, P.L. 1995. Development of receptive vocabulary skills through exposure to music, Bulletin of the *Council for Research in Music Education* 127: 28–34.

Cooley, J.C. 1961. A study of the relation between certain mental and personality traits and ratings of musical abilities, *Journal of Research in Music Education* 9: 108–117.

Darling-Hammond, L. 2010. Performance counts: Assessment systems that support high quality learning. Washington, DC: Council of Chief State School Officers.

Gorsuch, G, & Taguchi, E. 2008. Repeated reading for developing reading fluency and reading comprehension: *The case of EFL learners in Vietnam. System* 36: 253–278.

Grabe, W. & Stoller, F. 2011. *Teaching and researching reading* (2nd ed.). Harlow, UK: Pearson Longman.

Grabe, W. & Stoller, F. 2014. Teaching reading for academic purposes. In M. Celce-Murcia, D. Brinton & M. Snow (Eds.) Teaching English as a second or foreign language (4th ed.) Boston, MA: National Geographic Learning, 189–205.

Grabe, W. 2009. *Reading in a second language: Moving from theory to practice.* New York: Cambridge University Press.

Hansen, M. 1994. Vol 36 No 1, Jan - Mar 1998 Page 20. Dosfan.lib.uic.edu. Retrieved 24 April 2017, from http://dosfan.lib.uic.edu/usia/E-USIA/forum/vols/vol36/no1/p20.htm

Harmer, J. 1991. *The practice of English language teaching.* New York: Longman.

Hattie, J. 2011. *Visible learning for teachers: Maximizing Impact on learning.* New York, NY: Routledge.

Kemmis, S. & McTaggart, R. 1986. *The action research planner,* (3rd ed.). Geelong, Victoria: Deakon University Press.

Kind, U. 1980. *Tune in to English,* 49. New York: Regents Publishing Company.

Klauda, S., & Guthrie, J. 2008. Relationships of three components of reading fluency to reading comprehension, *Journal of Educational Psychology* 100: 310–321.

Kohyama, M., & Shimada, M. 2005. Curriculum: Entering the courtyard of freedom: Facilitating autonomy for young learners. In K. Bradford-Watts, C. Ikeguchi, & M. Swanson (Eds.). JALT2004 Conference Proceedings. Tokyo, Japan: JALT. Retrieved from http://jaltpublications.org/archive/proceedings/2004/E75.pdf.

Lee, W.R. 1979. *Language teaching games and contests.* Oxford: Oxford University Press.

Lewis, G., & Bedson, G. 1999. *Games for children.* Oxford: Oxford University Press.

McCarthy, M. 1990. *Vocabulary* (1st ed.). New York: Oxford University Press.

Mikulecky, B.S. 1990. *A short course in teaching reading skills.* UK: Longman Publications.

Nunan, D. 1991. *Language teaching methodology.* Hertfordshire: Prentice Hall International.

Nunan, D. 1997. Designing and adapting materials to encourage learner autonomy. In P. Benson & P. Voller (Eds.). Autonomy and independence in language learning. New York, NY: Addison Wesley Longman 192–203.

Principled Eclecticism. 2017. Retrieved 4 April, 2017, from http://www.thoughtco.com/what-is-principled-eclecticism-1210501.

Rasinski, T., & Zutell, J. 1991. *Assessing reading fluency* (1st ed.). Hawaii: Pacific Resources for Education and Learning.

Richard-Amato, P.A. 1988. *Making it happen: Interaction in the second language classroom from theory to practice.* New York: Longman.

Schunk, D.H. 2009. *Learning theories: An educational Perspective* (5th ed). Upper Saddle River, New Jersey: Pearson Prentice Hall.

Scott, W.A. and Yterberg, L.H. 1990. *Teaching English to children.* Harlow: Longman.

Snow, C.E., Burns, M.S. & Griffin, P. (Eds.) 1998. *Preventing reading difficulties in young children.* Washington, DC: National Academy Press.

Stanovich, K.E. 1980. Toward an interactive-compensatory model of individual differences in the development of reading fluency, *Research Reading Quarterly* 16(1): 32–71.

Taguchi, E., Gorsuch, G., Takayasu-Maass, M. & Snipp, K. 2012. Assisted repeated reading with an advanced-level Japanese EFL reader: A longitudinal diary study, *Reading in a Foreign Language* 24: 30–55.

Tomlinson, C.A. 2000. Differentiation of Instruction in the Elementary Grades. *ERIC Digest.,* (1), 3. http://dx.doi.org/ED443572.

Tomlinson, C.A. 2014. *The differentiated classroom: Responding to the needs of all learners.* Alexandria, VA: ASCD.

Wierus, B., & Wierus, A. 1994. Games in learner based teaching. *American International Journal of Contemporary Research* 4(9): 218–222.

ELT in Asia in the Digital Era: Global Citizenship and Identity – Madya et al. (Eds)
© *2018 Taylor & Francis Group, London, ISBN 978-0-8153-7900-3*

Collaborative summary writing as an activity to comprehend reading texts

L.A. Mauludin
Universitas Airlangga, Indonesia

ABSTRACT: Reading and writing are interrelated skills that should be mastered by EFL students. The ability to write is highly influenced by reading skills. Thus, those two skills need to be mastered simultaneously. This study investigates the role of collaborative summary writing to improve their ability in understanding reading texts. The emphasis of writing summaries collaboratively is significant since it helps the students to master the skills with the guidance of a teacher and peers as the primary stage before the students master the skills independently. Thirty university students participated in the present study for about two months. The students were assigned to read some texts during the study. Then, they wrote the summary of the text in pairs and in groups. The students were asked to show their comprehension of the text by writing the important points from the text. The results of the summary writing were compared and discussed with other groups. The students then reflected their results of summary writing through a questionnaire. The data were analyzed through descriptive analysis. The results showed that collaborative summary writing helps the students to understand the text better. The activity helped them to achieve the goal of communication in reading texts.

1   INTRODUCTION

Reading and writing are interrelated skills that should be mastered by English as a Foreign Language (EFL) students. The relation between reading and writing is considered to be essential. In this case, sources of reading are beneficial in providing information and materials to create a text (Hirvela & Du, 2013). Some studies mention the important connection between reading and writing in an English Language teaching and learning environment (Burgin & Hughes, 2009; Gebril, 2010; Wang, 2012; Williams & Larkin, 2013; Yoshimura, 2009; Chan, Inoue, & Taylor, 2015; Zsigmond, 2015). Integrated skills of reading and writing are considered to be beneficial in improving high creative performance (Wang, 2012). Students who employ their time on reading and writing are considered to have higher creative thinking. Reading and writing also assists students to recognize genre (Yoshimura, 2009). In this case, writing helps students to understand the scheme and the organization of the text, meanwhile reading supports them by offering valuable information during the writing process. In terms of metacognitive strategy, specific writing instruction stimulates the metacognitive strategy in reading comprehension (Zsigmond, 2015). Therefore, the ability of reading and writing respectively influences each other.

To comprehend a text, it is important that the students have the ability to absorb the meaning and recognize the pattern of information. In this case, the students need an objective. Therefore, specific instruction is needed to set the objectives of reading. With the positive correlation between reading and writing, it is important to insert the process of writing in comprehending the text. Summary writing is one of the alternatives of the goal of reading. Summarizing can be defined as a process of reading to write (Marzec-stawiarska, 2016). Reading to write can be observed from two kinds of perspectives (Fitzgerald & Shanahan, 2000). The first one is pedagogical. In this perspective, reading to write refers to the combination of reading and writing to create specific instructional tasks in different educational purposes. One example is the use of summary writing as a learning tool. The second perspective is theoretical. The theoretical perspective is related with the fundamental skills that learners possessed when performing the tasks.

In reading comprehension, reading to write encompasses reading to learn and reading to integrate information (Delaney, 2008). The learners select the information from the source text and identify the content. This process enables them to create the elaborate model of the text structure. Therefore, they can evaluate and integrate the text structure into a composition/writing. The process of reading to write is also influenced by the skills and objectives of an individual (Grabe, 2001). The basic knowledge and ability of an individual in literacy skills highly affect the process of reading to write. Furthermore, the skills of reading to write are different from the skills of writing without using text (Delaney, 2008). The connection between reading to write emphasizes the content of information, organization of the text, and the connection between the available information with the readers' previous knowledge. Therefore, writing independently without reading sources will eliminate one or perhaps all the above aspects. The important of writing with sources is the accuracy of information, organization, and the goal of the reading itself. It can be said that by comprehending texts well, a good text can be created.

In relation with summarization, reading to summary writing needs specific active procedures that aim to formulate a specific text (Marzec-stawiarska, 2016). Reading to summarize encompasses the aspects of recognizing the content of information and restructure it in a different form. This procedure is considered to be challenging because the readers need to keep all the important information from the text. Furthermore, this activity is complex because it requires students to perform paraphrasing and reorganizing the text (Hassani, Nor, Tengku, & Maasum, 2012). Especially in a foreign language context, the process of transferring the information from the first into the target language needs specific understanding of the text sources. In summary, there are three strategies that should be conducted; deletion, generalization, and construction (Kintsch and Van Dijk, 1978). In deletion, the information that is considered to be trivial and unnecessary should be eliminated. Then, in generalization, the available information is generalized. The specific topic is blended with other similar topics. Finally, in construction, the implicit information should be discovered by analyzing the main idea of each paragraphs.

Some studies investigate the importantance of summary writing in comprehending texts (Hassani, Nor, Tengku, & Maasum, 2012; Sajedi, 2014; Marzec-stawiarska, 2016). Marzec-Stawiarska (2016) studied the influence of summary writing on the development of EFL students' reading skills. Eighty university students participated in the study for about six months. It was found out that summary writing is highly advantageous to the development of reading skills especially for the weaker readers. In the study, the students who performed summary writing achieved high results in a reading test. Furthermore, the process of summarizing also has high pedagogic value. It is concluded from the study that the development of reading skills is affected by the depth of the text processing that the students' face while summarizing.

Hassani, Nor, Tengku, & Maasum (2012) examined the impact of two test formats summary writing and open-ended questions on students' reading performance and its relationship to students' English language proficiency. They used two test formats in the form of an expository paragraph. Thirty-five postgraduate students participated in this study. The study compared the results of reading comprehension between summarization and open-ended questions. The results showed that the test takers performed better in summarization than in the open-ended questions. Thus, it can be concluded that summary writing has positive influence on students' reading performance.

Furthermore, the ability to comprehend the text is not merely influenced by a certain method of teaching. One important factor that influences the ability of learners in the teaching and learning process is environment. Therefore, a supportive teaching condition is needed to support this objective. Vygotsky's Zone of Proximal Development Theory suggests that in the teaching and learning process, before the learners are able to solve the problem individually, they need guidance by peers or teachers. Therefore, cooperative or collaborative learning is essential in supporting this condition. Collaborative learning suggests that the learners assist and encourage each other during the learning process. In this case, they can share ideas and support each other efforts to solve the problem. The learners are less intimidated when they are working in pairs or in groups. It is also important to note that less stress and anxiety are claimed to be the benefits of collaborative learning. In addition, there are two advantages of the participation of students working in groups (Cohen, 1994). First, it can be an alternative way of a traditional teaching method. Second, it can be an activity that fosters active communication to develop the use the learners' target language. In his study, Sajedi (2014) investigated the effectiveness of collaborative summary writing on university students' second language development. The study examined eighty-six university students. The results show that the students' writing skills improved significantly in terms of content, organization, and vocabulary.

Based on the literature review, it can be concluded that reading and summarizing have significant connections especially in the development of reading comprehension. Furthermore, it is also noted that collaborative learning also plays an important role in the teaching and learning process. Therefore, this study aims to find out the role of collaborative summary writing to improve the students' ability in comprehending texts.

2 METHODOLOGY

The method of this study is qualitative research. Thirty students of the English Diploma Program of a public university participated in the study. They were all in their third year of their study. The study was conducted in the class of Reading III. This course taught them to read high intermediate reading texts. To be able to attend Reading III, the students need to pass Reading II. Their reading skills are varied but most of them are at the intermediate level. The reason to choose this class is because the writer is the teacher of this class. Therefore, it is easier for the writer to conduct the study effectively and efficiently.

The study was conducted through four meetings in two months in the second term of their study. Actually, reading class has one meeting per week, however, due to some national holidays, there were only four meetings available.

The data were gathered through classroom observation and a questionnaire. During the classroom observation, the writer wrote journals to record the activity during teaching and learning process. The questionnaire was given in the last meeting. There were 11 questions on the questionnaire.

In the first meeting, the students were asked to read two kinds of text. In the first text, the students read and analyzed the text independently. After a short discussion of the first text, the activity for the second text began. The students were assigned in a group of four. They read and discussed the text in a group. Then, they wrote a summary within the group. After that, all the groups were assigned to write a summary in front of the class. Each representative of the group came in front of the class and wrote two or three sentences with a computer connected to a LCD projector about the text. Each representative took turns to write the sentences. The first student was given the freedom to write anything he wanted from the text. The following student could write the information to complete the previous information. It could be information before or after the stated information. After the whole summary was written, the students discussed the results and clarified any wrong information or misunderstanding. Finnaly, they performed the tasks to answer the questions available in the textbook about the reading.

In the second meeting, again, two kinds of text were presented. In the first text, the students read it individually. For the second text, the activity of summary writing began. In this activity, the students were assigned in pairs. After reading, analyzing, and creating a summary in pairs, one of the students within the group were to write the summary in two sentences in front of the class. The activity was similar with the previous activity when they took turn to write the sentences until the whole summary was completed. After that, they had a discussion and clarification session. For the third meeting, the activity was similar with the second meeting's activity. The difference is in this meeting each student needed to come to write their sentences instead of only one representative in each group. Therefore, all of the students in the classroom took turns to write sentences to compose a summary.

Finally, in the fourth meeting, the students read the text individually without group or pair activity. After reading and analyzing independently, they took turns writing the summary one by one. Each student was assigned to write one sentence only. After finishing the summary, they discussed and clarified the results of the summary. Finally, the students were given the questionnaire to reflect their experience during the four meetings of writing colloaborative summary.

The results of the questionnaire then were tabulated in form of percentages and described to analyze their opinion about the activity. The journal of the observation was used to support the results of the questionnaire.

3   RESULTS AND DISCUSSION

Based on the data analysis, it can be seen in general that the students have positive responses on the use of collaborative summary writing in a reading class activity. Most of the students are favorable to use the method since it is considered to be effective. During the observation, the students showed a highly motivated spirit when being assigned to do summary writing in groups. During the class group summary writing, they also showed high interest which means that this activity built their motivation in comprehending the text. Mostly, reading class is considered to be a boring class since the students need to read many kinds of texts. Furthermore, the literacy interest among the students vary. Most of the students usually are not avid readers, therefore, specific instruction to improve their motivation was needed. The results of the students' responses toward the activity can be seen in Table 1.

According to the Table 1, it can be seen that 50% of the students think that the activity helps them to improve their ability to understand a text with another 35% of the students mention that it really helps them to understand the text. In this activity, the students were given the opportunity to share their ideas and opinions in groups as well as clarifying the information. In the process of clarifying, the students can discuss their difficulty with their friends. This peer activity helps them to overcome their anxiety during the learning process. This is in line with the purpose of the ZPD theory as one of the purposes is to reduce the

Table 1.   Results of the self-assessment of the use of collaborative summary writing.

Items	Strongly agree	Agree	Neutral	Disagree	Strongly disagree
The functions of the activity are easy to use.	35	50	15	0	0
This activity is helpful to understand reading text.	35	50	15	0	0
The activity is helpful to enhance my reading ability.	30	45	25	0	0
Using this activity, I can reach the goal of communication.	0	60	35	5	0
I have a positive evaluation of this activity.	30	45	25	0	0
I am interested in using this activity to facilitate understanding reading text.	50	20	30	0	0
I will continue using this activity in the future.	15	50	35	0	0
I will recommend this activity to others.	5	65	30	0	0
I am satisfied with the result of summary writing from the reading text.	10	50	35	5	0
I like language learning activities in which students work together in pairs or small groups.	15	40	35	10	0
I prefer to work by myself in this language class, not with other students.	5	15	50	25	5

*The number is in form of percentage.

anxiety of the students during the learning process. This supporting environment positively contributed to their development.

Furthermore, this result also proves that the activity of summary writing is effective to enhance students' reading skill. In the process of summary writing, the students need to analyze the content and the organization of the text. Thus, their pedagogic skills in comprehending texts is forced. In producing an accurate summary, the students need to understand the content deeply. Their skills in analyzing the depth of the text are a challenge in this case. This is in line with Marzec-Stawiarska's (2016) study that mentions the improvement of reading skills is influenced by the depth of the text processing that the students face while summarizing. The goal of summarizing stimulates the students' motivation to fully understand the text. This aspect supports the development of the students' skill in comprehending the text. Based on the observation, in the discussion process after the summarization in class, the students tended to analyze their peers' works. When they thought that the information was different with their understanding, they tried to clarify it. Several opinions came up during the discussion. This process strengthened the students' analytical skills when using integrated skills. Their understanding in reading was clarified by looking at the results of the summary. Therefore, they can realize that the more accurate their understanding the text, the more accurate the result of the summary. This supports the study that emphasizes that reading comprehension plays an important role in the integrated skills of reading to writing (Plakans, 2009).

Another important point is the aspect of communication during the collaborative summary activity. It is shown that 60% of the students feel that this activity assists them to reach the goal of communication. It is known that the peer or group activity gives the opportunity for the students to speak more in their target language (McDonough, 2014). This opportunity enriches their skills in communicating with others. In the process of discussion, the students conveyed their opinion and their understanding about the text. This peer discussion stimulated their critical thinking that enforced them to use a variety of vocabulary and expressions so that they can reach the target of communication.

In response to the collaborative learning itself, 40% of the students feel that they like the method, meanwhile 15% of them really like the method. About 35% of the students feel neutral about it. It can be said that more than half of the students enjoy the process of collaborative learning. However, there is about 10% of the students who do not like working in groups or pairs. It is observed that the students that like to work in groups were more active in engaging in the process of discussion, meanwhile a few students passively contributed to the discussion. On the other hand, an interesting finding is found in the last response. 50% of the students actually feel neutral when they have the choice to work in grousp or individually. It is assumed that if the students like to work in groups or in pairs, they will prefer to work in groups or in pairs.

However, this result shows that, although, they enjoy collaborative learning, they do not think that collaborative learning is better than individual learning. Presumably, most students are actually flexible in using a collaborative learning activity or individual activity. In short, the results show that in general the students enjoy their collaborative learning activity, even 65% of the students suggest that they will recommend this method to the others. Although there is small number of students that feel neutral to the activity, that does not mean that they have little interest in this activity, it only means that they like both the collaborative and individual activity.

4 CONCLUSION

Based on the results and data analysis, some important points can be drawn. Firstly, collaborative summary writing is actually helpful for the students to comprehend the text better. By collaboratively working on the summarization process, the goal of understanding the text was achieved better. Then, by comprehending the text, the students can improve their reading skills. This refers to the level of accuracy of the meaning of the text when it compares to the results of the summary writing. By comparing what they understand individually and in groups, they can test their level of understanding about the text. Thirdly, the activity improves the students' communication skills. This includes their ability to have a discussion and convey their opinion about the content and the meaning of the text. By discussing and clarifying the content of the text, the students have more opportunity to exchange information using their target language. Finally, collaborative learning has a positive influence on the students' skills since it provides opportunity for them to share ideas to solve a problem.

There are some limitations of this study. The number of participants in this study is quite small, and they were in a specific classroom condition, therefore the results of this study cannot be broadly generalized in a different setting. The data gathered in this study is only through observation and a questionnaire, so proof in terms of statistical results have not been presented. Therefore, further studies should be conducted to prove the effectiveness of collaborative summary writing to help the students' understanding in comprehending reading texts.

REFERENCES

Burgin, J. & Hughes, G.D. 2009. Credibly assessing reading and writing abilities for both elementary student and program assessment. *Assessing Writing* 14: 25–37. https://doi.org/10.1016/j.asw.2008.12.001.

Chan, S., Inoue, C. & Taylor, L. 2015. Assessing writing developing rubrics to assess the reading-into-writing skills : A case study. *Assessing Writing* 26: 20–37. https://doi.org/10.1016/j.asw.2015.07.004.

Delaney, Y.A. 2008. Investigating the reading-to-write construct. *Journal of English for Academic Purposes* 7: 140–150. https://doi.org/10.1016/j.jeap.2008.04.001.

Fitzgerald, J. & Shanahan, T. 2000. Reading and writing relations and their development. *Educational Psychologist* 35: 39–50.

Gebril, A. 2010. Bringing reading-to-write and writing-only assessment tasks together : A generalizability analysis. *Assessing Writing* 15(2): 100–117. https://doi.org/10.1016/j.asw.2010.05.002.

Grabe, W. 2001. Reading-writing relations: theoretical perspectives and instructional practices. In D. Belcher, & A. Hirvela (eds.), *Linking literacies: Perspectives on L2 reading-writing connections*: 15–47. Ann Arbor: University of Michigan Press.

Hassani, L., Nor, T., Tengku, R. & Maasum, M. 2012. International Conference on Education and Educational Psychology (ICEEPSY 2012) A Study of Students ' Reading Performance in Two Test Formats of Summary Writing and Open-ended Questions. *Procedia - Social and Behavioral Sciences* 69: 915–923. https://doi.org/10.1016/j.sbspro.2012.12.016.

Hirvela, A. & Du, Q. 2013. Why am I paraphrasing ? : Undergraduate ESL writers' engagement with source-based academic writing and reading. *Journal of English for Academic Purposes* 12(2): 87–98. https://doi.org/10.1016/j.jeap.2012.11.005.

Kintsch, W. & van Dijk, T.A. 1978. Toward a model of text comprehension and production. *Psychological Review* 85(5): 363e394.

Marzec-stawiarska, M. 2016. The influence of summary writing on the development of reading skills in a foreign language. *System* 59: 90–99. https://doi.org/10.1016/j.system.2016.04.006.

McDonough, K. 2004. Learner-learner interaction during pair and small group activities in a Thai EFL context. *System* 32: 207–224.

Plakans, L. 2009. The role of reading strategies in integrated L2 writing tasks. *Journal of English for Academic Purposes* 8(4): 252–266. https://doi.org/10.1016/j.jeap.2009.05.001.

Sajedi, S.P. 2014. Collaborative Summary Writing and EFL Students ' L2 Development. *Procedia – Social and Behavioral Sciences* 98: 1650–1657. https://doi.org/10.1016/j.sbspro.2014.03.589.

Wang, A.Y. 2012. Exploring the relationship of creative thinking to reading and writing. *Thinking Skills and Creativity* 7(1): 38–47. https://doi.org/10.1016/j.tsc.2011.09.001.

Williams, G.J. & Larkin, R.F. 2013. Narrative writing, reading and cognitive processes in middle childhood : What are the links ? *Learning and Individual Differences* 28: 142–150. https://doi.org/10.1016/j.lindif.2012.08.003.

Yoshimura, F. 2009. Effects of connecting reading and writing and a checklist to guide the reading process on EFL learners ' learning about English writing. *Procedia - Social and Behavioral Sciences* 1(1): 1871–1883. https://doi.org/10.1016/j.sbspro.2009.01.330.

Zsigmond, I. 2015. Writing Strategies for Fostering Reading Comprehension. *Procedia – Social and Behavioral Sciences* 180 (November 2014): 1698–1703. https://doi.org/10.1016/j.sbspro.2015.05.073.

ELT in Asia in the Digital Era: Global Citizenship and Identity – Madya et al. (Eds)
© 2018 Taylor & Francis Group, London, ISBN 978-0-8153-7900-3

Integrating CEFR, thematic contents, and intensive instruction in developing speaking materials for first-year English language teacher trainees

C.A. Korompot
Universitas Negeri Makassar, Makassar, Indonesia

ABSTRACT: Speaking skills are compulsory for students at Initial English Teacher Education (IETE) institutions in Indonesia. Over the decades, speaking courses have been offered at
the introductory, basic, intermediate, and advanced levels. A main drawback observed in the
current curriculum and materials for the courses, however, was a lack of oversight in the proficiency standards, contents, and instructional approach. This paper reports a study on developing English speaking materials for the Basic Speaking course for second semester freshmen.
Using three elements, i.e. the Common European Framework of Reference for Languages, thematic approach to materials development, and "intensive speaking" instructional approach, as
well as Four-D Model of materials development process, the study resulted in a set of materials
consisting of a syllabus, lesson plans, and a series of 13 weekly modules. The study offers new
insights on the application of the three elements in teaching IETE trainees in the EFL context.

1 INTRODUCTION

The study reported in this paper is expected to fill the knowledge and praxis gaps in three
different yet interconnected aspects. Firstly, despite the adoption of the Common European
Framework of Reference for Languages (CEFR) as proficiency standards by many language
education institutions (including publishing companies) in Europe and the rest of the world
(Ayala Zárate & Álvarez V. 2005), very little is known about the implementation of the CEFR
in developing the English proficiency of initial English teacher education (IETE) trainees.

Secondly, the proliferation of commercial English language (EL) course books has led to
IETE instructors' excessive use of and reliance on ready-made EL materials (Charalambous
2011) to teach their trainees. As a result, many instructors lack the experience of developing their own English speaking materials with their own trainees in mind, in the spirit of
Paulo Freire's thematic approach to materials development (Cantú & Farines 2007), which
is referred to as TAMD in this paper. In the Indonesian context, no previous studies have
considered this issue before.

Thirdly, the present study argues for what the author terms "intensive speaking" instructional approach (ISIA) to enable first-year IETE trainees to speak English fluently, com-
prehensibly, and accurately. This is an oppositional extension of the "extensive reading"
(Renandya et al. 2009) and "extensive listening" (Widodo & Rozak 2016) scholarships in
English language teaching (ELT).

1.1 *Background*

The present study was conducted at the English Department of Universitas Negeri Makassar
(UNM), located in Makassar, South Sulawesi, Indonesia. This IETE institution—referred to
as ED-UNM in this article—prepares undergraduate students to become EL teachers at junior
and senior high schools. At ED-UNM, English skills (listening, speaking, reading, and writing)
have for decades been taught and labeled as separated skills courses, e.g. Speaking I, Speaking

II, Speaking III, and Speaking IV respectively. The author has been teaching these courses, among other things, since taking up teaching position at ED-UNM over a decade ago.

However, the nation-wide trend of applying the "integrated skills" and "systemic functional" approaches to IETE curriculum has prompted ED-UNM to revise its curricula. Thus, in the recently-revised curriculum, Speaking I is now treated as the speaking component in the Intensive Integrated English Course offered in the first semester; Speaking II is now referred to as Basic Speaking (in the 2nd semester), which is the focus of this study; Speaking III has now become Intermediate Speaking (3rd semester); and Speaking IV is now called Advanced Speaking (4th semester).

Despite the revisions, however, some fundamental components of the courses remained the same. One case in point is the course books for speaking. The lecturers assigned to teach speaking skills courses, the author included, had always used and relied on ready-made, English speaking skills materials in commercial ELT course books issued by well-known international publishing houses. In recent years, these course books have included features such as the CEFR, which is used as proficiency standards, and up-to-date materials (including pictorials, audio-video recordings, and online access) which may appeal to the contemporary audience—students and teachers alike. Perhaps due to their being developed in English-speaking countries, the main drawback of these course books, however, is a lack of oversight in the contents and instructional approach.

Having used such course books at ED-UNM since the year 2005, the author arrived at the conclusion that a research study on English speaking materials development was necessary in order to address at least three issues. First, there needed to be English speaking skills course books which complied with some international standards of competencies (i.e. the CEFR) in order to reveal the competency levels expected of the students. Second, the materials in the course books should be based on or relevant to students' real lives, which means that they should be developed using the TAMD. Finally, in teaching the course books, a specific instructional approach should be adopted. It was decided that the introductory, basic, and intermediate speaking courses should be taught using an "intensive speaking" instructional approach (ISIA) which prioritizes speaking accuracy and comprehensibility over fluency, while the advanced speaking course may be done using the extensive speaking approach which prioritizes fluency and comprehensibility over accuracy.

It was also decided that this research and development (R&D) study would be conducted in three consecutive years and began with the Basic Speaking course. To date, no previous research has integrated the CEFR, TAMD, and ISIA in developing English speaking skills materials for teacher trainees in the Indonesian IETE context.

1.2 *Literature review*

The present study is concerned with integrating three elements, namely the CEFR, TAMD, and ISIA, in developing Basic Speaking course materials for teacher trainees in the Indonesian EFL context using the Four-D Model (Thiagarajan et al. 1974). To that end, this section will review literature in the three elements and the Four-D Model.

1.2.1 *CEFR*

CEFR stands for "the Common European Framework of Reference for Languages: Learning, Teaching, Assessment" (Figueras 2012: 477). It is a descriptive scheme for analysing learners' needs, specifying second language (L2) goals, guiding L2 materials and activities development, and assessing L2 learning outcomes (Little 2006: 167), as well as for reflecting (on teaching and learning) (North 2011: 228). It was first published in 2001, and has since had "an immediate and significant impact" in the areas of L2 curricula, assessment of L2 proficiency, and L2 teaching and learning in many European countries and other countries outside of Europe (Little 2006, Valax 2011). The CEFR is almost always associated with its six levels of communicative proficiency (A1, A2, B1, B2, C1, C2). These levels elaborate three bands of proficiency (Basic User, Independent User, Proficient User), each of which, as shown in Table 1, comes with its own description.

Table 1.   Bands and levels of proficiency in the CEFR (adapted from Little 2006).

Proficient user

C2:   Can understand with ease virtually everything heard or shared. .... Can express him/herself spontaneously, very fluently and precisely, differentiating finer shades of meaning even in more complex situations.

C1:   Can understand a wide range of demanding, longer texts, and recognize implicit meaning. .... Can produce clear, well-structured, detailed text on complex subjects, showing controlled use of organizational patterns, connectors and cohesive devices.

Independent user

B2:   Can understand the main ideas of complex text on both concrete and abstract topics, including technical discussions with him/her field of specification. .... Can produce clear, detailed text on a wide range of subjects and explain a viewpoint on a topical issue giving the advantages and disadvantages of various options.

B1:   Can understand the main points of clear standard input on familiar matters regularly encountered in work, school, leisure, etc. .... Can describe experiences and events, dreams, hopes and ambitions and briefly give reasons and explanations for opinions and plans.

Basic user

A2:   Can understand sentences and frequently used expressions related to areas of most immediate relevance (e.g. very basic personal and family information, shopping, local geography, employment). .... Can describe in simple terms aspects of his/her background, immediate environment and matters in areas of immediate need.

A1:   Can understand and use familiar everyday expressions and very basic phrases aimed at the satisfaction of needs of a concrete type. .... Can interact in a simple way provided the other person talks slowly and clearly and is prepared to help.

Since its publication, the use of CEFR has had positive impacts on L2 teaching and learning in a number of ways. Figueras (2012) notes that the good influence of the CEFR has been felt at least in the following situations: (1) teaching and assessment practices; (2) research network and teacher training; and (3) reference level descriptors producing outcomes.

Besides the above, however, Figueras (2012) also notes that the CEFR poses at least three main challenges, namely: (1) there are insufficient definitions, gaps, and terminological incoherencies; (2) the level descriptors are not based on SLA development; and (3) the level descriptors do not cater for learning diversity along the proficiency continuum. Still according to Figueras (2012), the CEFR has also been misused by some people. For example, (1) it has been used at all levels of education; (2) it has been used to teach first language (L1); and (3) it has been used to teach language for specific purposes.

As stated earlier, one of the uses of the CEFR is guiding the development of L2 materials and activities. In recent years, the CEFR is increasingly being used internationally as language proficiency standards for commercial ELT books published by major publishing houses such as Oxford University Press and Cambridge University Press.

In the Indonesian context, there is a small growing body of literature about the use of CEFR in L2 materials development. However, apart from Yuniarti (2017) who developed CEFR-based materials for developing the English speaking skills of a vaguely identified group of students, most of the relevant previous studies (Dewi n.d. Saddhono 2016, Susilo 2016) were on developing CEFR-based materials for teaching Indonesian as a foreign language. Therefore, the implementation and impacts of the CEFR in the Indonesian context are still largely unknown. This is particularly the case with the use of the CEFR in developing ELT materials in the university setting and for the purpose of training future EL teachers' English speaking skills. The present study will shed some light on these gaps in our current understanding.

1.2.2 *TAMD*

The TAMD was introduced by Paulo Freire in 1986 with the notion that "learning activities must be developed around generative themes that are part of the students' cultural environment" (Cantú & Farines 2007). It is believed that such themes:

increase the students' motivation and allow them to extend their knowledge about the subject, including social and political factors that can contribute in producing complete professional and citizens with innovative and critical minds. (Cantú & Farines 2007)

In the present study, thematic approach means that the materials developed for the course are based on what the students are familiar with. These include English speaking themes relevant to the students' social, cultural, economic, and educational backgrounds, and their future career. It is expected that the students will be interested in and enthusiastic about discussing them, thus improving both their world view and spoken English skills.

To date, however, there is a very small body of literature available that looks at the use of thematic approach in instructional/L2 materials development. The present study will contribute to and expand that body of knowledge.

1.2.3 *ISIA*

The notion of "intensive speaking" as an instructional approach (ISIA) has been almost unheard of, if not under researched, until now. In a nutshell, intensive speaking is the speaking version of "intensive reading" which is often contrasted from "extensive reading"—a reading instructional approach that involves "independent reading of a large quantity of material for both information and pleasure" (Renandya et al. 2009), and that lets students decide what, when, where, how much, and how they should read in L2. The lack of literature on intensive speaking in this case makes it necessary to bring intensive reading into perspective when discussing intensive speaking.

According to Bamford & Day (1997), intensive reading engages students in "careful reading...of shorter, more difficult foreign language texts with the goal of complete and detailed understanding." In other words, intensive reading is the traditional way of teaching reading. It is characterized by the employment of reading materials chosen by the teacher, reading and related activities as well as grammar and vocabulary exercises led by the teacher within the confines of the classroom, comprehension-questions, and assessment done by the teacher (see also Al-Homoud & Schmitt 2009).

Extending the above definition and applying the intensive reading principles to EL speaking instruction, intensive speaking in the context of this research is understood as an approach that engages students in intensive, teacher-led/teacher-assisted activities to develop proficiencies in the spoken EL skills with the goal of complete mastery of EL proficiencies. Students practice the oral component skills and elements by pronouncing segmental sounds, suprasegmental sounds, and complete utterances; reading aloud or performing oral discourse and communicative tasks; and using listening, reading, and writing skills in their speaking activities, etc. Therefore, the teacher "runs the show" as he or she plans and chooses the materials, guides and manages the classroom activities and exercises, gives corrective feedback, and carries out the assessment. These characteristics have a lot in common with the "other-regulation" approach (Thornbury 2005: 41–88) in teaching speaking skills which aims at promoting awareness-raising activities and appropriation activities.

The introduction of intensive speaking as an instructional approach in teaching EL speaking (ISIA) is a significant contribution made by this research.

1.2.4 *Four-D model*

Although a number of instructional development models have been used all over the world, the "Four-D Model" (Thiagarajan et al. 1974), which has been adopted and adapted in this research, is perhaps the most popular one used in Indonesia so far.

The Four-D Model is essentially a "systems-approach" that divides the instructional development process into four stages, namely "Define, Design, Develop, and Disseminate" (Thiagarajan et al. 1974: 5, emphases in original). A brief description of the model's stages and steps is given in Table 2.

Table 2. The Four-D Model's stages and steps* (adapted from Thiagarajan et al. 1974).

Stages	Steps
Define	Front-end Analysis (FEA); Learner Analysis (LA); Task Analysis (TA); Concept Analysis (CA); Specifying Instructional Objectives (IOs)
Design	Criterion-referenced Tests (CRT); Media Selection (MS); Format Selection (FS); Initial Design (ID)
Develop	Expert Appraisa (EA); Developmental Testing (DT)
Disseminate	Validation Testing (VT); Packaging (Pk); Diffusion and Adoption (D&A)

*The abbreviations introduced here will be used in the other sections.

The Four-D Model has been used by many Indonesian academics, practitioners, and researchers for designing curriculums, instructional activities, and developing materials in various areas of education. Not many of these works, however, are visible in reputable, international scholarly publications.

For example, in the field of language teaching, the Four-D Model was used for (1) developing Indonesian language materials with national character values for junior high school students in regional South Sulawesi (Saleh & Sultan 2016); (2) developing language games to teaching EL speaking to high school students joining an extra-curricular program in Gresik, East Java (Amrullah 2015); and (3) developing writing learning materials for teaching high school students in Batu, East Java, how to write explanation texts in Indonesian language (Istiqomah 2016).

Despite the popularity of the Four-D Model and body of literature on its application, however, none of the previous studies that used the Four-D Model, in the Indonesian context at least, has considered integrating the CEFR, TAMD, and ISIA in developing EL speaking materials for first-year IETE trainees. The present study intends to fill this gap in the literature and offer practical solution to the problems associated with the teaching of the Basic Speaking course at ED-UNM.

2   RESEARCH METHOD

2.1   The study

As described earlier, this paper reports a study on developing materials using the Common European Framework of Reference for Languages (CEFR), TAMD, and ISIA in teaching the Basic Speaking course at ED-UNM.

The study was conducted at ED-UNM between February and June 2017. It involved 71 freshmen attending their second semester at the IETE institution. While the whole study employed Thiagarajan's Four-D stages (Thiagarajan et al. 1974), this paper focuses only on the outcomes of the Define and Design stages. The Develop and Disseminate stages are still underway and will be reported on another occasion.

2.2   Research problem

Given the background of the study and a critical review of the related literature, the research problem is formulated as follows: Can the CEFR, TAMD, and ISIA be integrated to develop spoken English materials to teach second semester freshmen at ED-UNM?

2.3   The define stage

As prescribed by Thiagarajan et al. (1974), the Define steps undertaken in this research included FEA, LA, TA, CA, and IOs (see Table 2). Their outcomes are described in Table 3.

Table 3. The Define steps taken and their results (adapted from Thiagarajan et al. 1974: 6).

Steps	Description
FEA	(1) The basic problem facing the lecturer was to lay a solid foundation of spoken English skills in ED-UNM's freshmen; (2) Alternative materials for teaching the Basic Speaking course be developed using the CEFR, TAMD, and ISIA
LA	(1) The students' English proficiency was between the upper beginner and pre-intermediate level; (2) The students had no or little previous exposure to the application of the CEFR, TAMD, and ISIA, esp. in their spoken English courses
TA	The main skill required by the freshmen was spoken English at the basic/pre-intermediate level
CA	The major concepts were spoken English themes (1) aligned to the CEFR's A1 and A2 levels; (2) relevant to the students' backgrounds; (3) delivered in an "intensive speaking" fashion
IOs	The main objective was to enable the ED-UNM fresh-men to speak English actively at the basic/pre-intermediate level using materials that conform to the CEFR's A1 and A2 levels, are relevant to their personal, social, cultural, educational backgrounds and future prospects, and are delivered in an "intensive speaking"

Table 4. The Design steps taken and their results (adapted from Thiagarajan et al., 1974, p. 7).

Steps	Description
CRTs	An oral, criterion-referenced test developed based on the IOs (see Table 3) was administered at the commencement of the course (20 February 2017). The average score obtained from the two classes was 7.61 on a 0 to 10 scale. This means that the freshmen had the language required to speak English at A1 and A2 levels, yet they needed more practice to improve, consolidate and reinforce their spoken English skills at this level.
MS	The appropriate medium for use would be a Basic Speaking course book.
FS	The course book would consist of 13 units, each of which revolving around a theme in line with the CEFR's A1 and A2 levels.
ID	Each of the unit would be developed and taught weekly over a 16-week period from February to June, 2017. Each unit would comprise a number of sections and subsections spread over 4–5 pages. Photocopies would be made for all students before each lesson began.

2.4 *The design stage*

The Design stage of this research included the steps referred to as CRTs, MS, FS, and ID (Thiagarajan et al., 1974, p. 7) (see Table 2). These steps and their results are shown in Table 4.

3 FINDINGS AND DISCUSSION

The study revealed that the answer to the research question was affirmative. That is, the CEFR, TAMD, and ISIA could be successfully integrated to develop spoken English materials to teach second semester freshmen at ED-UNM.

3.1 *Findings*

The major findings of the study are organized in the ensuing sections according to the three elements of materials development considered in this study, namely CEFR, TAMD, and ISIA.

3.1.1 *CEFR*
It was found that the CEFR's A1 and A2 proficiency levels and descriptions were applicable to the materials development in two ways. First, they were applicable to teaching the IETE

freshmen. This is of high importance given (a) the overall proficiency of the students based on the results of the oral, criterion-referenced test administered at the commencement of the course, which averaged 7.61 on a 0–10 scale, and (b) the EL proficiency standards required of the students as individuals, members of the local and wider communities, regional and global citizens, Indonesians, and future EL teachers. Second, they were applicable to developing suitable Basic Speaking materials for the IETE freshmen. For the researcher as the materials developer, this was of technical importance as the CEFR served as guidelines for constructing the Basic Speaking materials, which was done on a weekly basis during the first two stages of the project.

3.1.2 *TAMD*

The research data and outcomes show that the TAMD was a very useful approach to developing materials that take into account (a) the CEFR proficiency levels; (b) the students' social, cultural, economic, and educational backgrounds, and (c) the students' career choice as future EL teachers. Table 5 shows the syllabus of the Basic Speaking course as it is informed by the CEFR and TAMD.

Note that the above syllabus comes with a detailed lesson plan for each of the units.

3.1.3 *ISIA*

A generic structure was created to organize and order the materials in the Basic Speaking course. This structure was applied as much as possible to all the 13 units (see Table 6).

Table 5.   The syllabus for basic speaking course at ED-UNM.

Week	Unit	Topic
1	N/A	Introduction to the Course
2	1	Myself
3	2	My Family
4	3	My Relatives
5	4	My Friends
6	5	My Teachers
7	6	My Neighbors
8	7	My Hobbies and Interests
9	N/A	Mid-semester Test
10	8	My Home
11	9	My School
12	10	My University
13	11	My Hometown/Village
14	12	My Place of Origin
15	13	My Country (Indonesia)
16	N/A	Final Semester Test

Table 6.   The basic speaking syllabus at ED-UNM.

Section	Content/topics
A	Getting Started (Look at the picture; Write down your ideas.)
B	Q & A (Answer the following questions. Write your answers next to the question. Work on your own.)
C	Talk to a Friend (With a classmate, ask and answer the above questions.)
D	Talk to Other Friends (Interview two other classmates; ask them the above questions. Write their information in the chart below.)
E	Talk to the Class (Introduce/Talk to the class about one of the two classmates you interviewed. Use he or she.)
F	Task (Make a poster etc.)

Each of the activities above is carried out in ways which prioritize speaking accuracy and comprehensibility over fluency. This is done in order to apply the "intensive speaking" principles (see subsection c. ISIA in the literature review section).

3.2 *Discussion*

As the study findings have shown, the CEFR, TAMD, and ISIA can be integrated to develop speaking materials for first-year IETE trainees. This was made possible by at least four contributing factors: relevance, urgency, novelty, and feasibility.

First, relevance was noteworthy because the three elements (CEFR, TAMD, ISIA) and the Four-D Model combined were applicable to developing English speaking materials for IETE freshmen at the upper beginner and pre-intermediate levels in the Indonesian context. Second, urgency was one the driving forces behind the decision to create the Basic Speaking materials literally from scratch—similar to Saleh and Sultan's (2016) rationale for developing their Indonesian language materials. As described earlier, this was prompted by the lack of Basic Speaking materials that are based on recognized proficiency standards—hence "putting the CEFR to good use" (North 2011); relevant to students' backgrounds and future prospects (TAMD)—a Freirean approach (Cantú & Farines 2007); and taught in ways that prioritize accuracy and comprehensibility over fluency (ISIA)—hence the emphasis on "other-regulated" instruction (Thornbury 2005). Third, novelty was a significant contribution of this research as it has filled the absence of Basic Speaking materials—at least in the ED-UNM context—that conform to the three elements and are developed using the popular Four-D Model. The same rationale was put forward by Saleh and Sultan (2016) for their Indonesian language project. Finally, feasibility of the project is ensured due to the study's relevance, urgency, and novelty, the researcher's experience in ELT, curriculum-and-materials development (CMD), IETE programs, and access to research facilities.

4 CONCLUSIONS AND FOLLOW UP

Using three elements (CEFR, TAMD, ISIA) and employing the Four-D Model's Define and Design principles, the study succeeded in producing a syllabus, lesson plans, and a series of 13 weekly modules for teaching first year undergraduate ELT students the Basic Speaking course. Having completed these, the project will continue with and complete the Four-D Model's Develop and Disseminate stages to try out and further refine the materials, examine their effectiveness, and make them applicable to future Basic Speaking classes at ED UNM or equivalent courses at other institutions.

The study has shed light on three issues germane to the research. First, it reveals that the CEFR is applicable to curriculum and materials development at IETE institutions particularly in the EFL context. Second, it shows the need to incorporate the CEFR with specific materials development and instructional approaches so that the results would be suitable for the students and teachers in the context which adopts it. Third, it provides evidence that when it comes to teaching undergraduate ELT students in the EFL context an essential EL skill such as speaking, an "intensive" approach is required in the first year before an "extensive" approach may be introduced in the forthcoming years.

REFERENCES

Al-Homoud, F. & Schmitt, N. 2009. Extensive reading in a challenging environment: a comarison of extensive and intensive reading approaches in Saudi Arabia. *Language Teaching Research* 13(4): 383–401. https://doi.org/10.1177/1362168809341508.

Amrullah, A.Z. 2015. Developing language games to teach speaking skill for indonesian senior high school learners. *JEELS* 2(2).

Ayala Zárate, J. & Álvarez V.J.A. 2005. A perspective of the implications of the Common European Framework implementation in the Colombian socio-cultural context. *Colombian Applied Linguistics Journal* 7: 7–26.

Bamford, J. & Day, R.R. 1997. Extensive reading: What is it? Why bother?. *Language Teacher-Kyoto-JALT* 21: 6–8.

Cantú, E. & Farines, J.M. 2007. Applying educational models in technological education. *Education and Information Technologies* 12(3): 111–122. https://doi.org/10.1007/s10639-007-9038-4.

Charalambous, A.C. 2011. The role and use of course books in EFL. *Online Submission*.

Dewi, R.P. n.d. *Pengembangan buku ajar pemula bahasa Indonesia bagi penutur asing berbasis CEFR*.

Figueras, N. 2012. The impact of the CEFR. *ELT Journal* 66(4): 477–485. https://doi.org/10.1093/elt/ccs037.

Istiqomah, S.P. 2016. The development of learning material: explanation text based on multimodal by using sway app in 11 th grade of SMAN 1 Batu. *International Journal of Education and Research* 4(9): 313–322.

Little, D. 2006. The Common European Framework of Reference for Languages: Content, purpose, origin, reception and impact. *Language Teaching* 39(3): 167–190.

North, B. 2011. Putting the Common European Framework of Reference to good use. *Language Teaching*: 1–22. https://doi.org/10.1017/S0261444811000206.

Renandya, W.A., Rajan, B.R.S. & Jacobs, G.M. 2009. *Extensive reading with adult ESL learners of English as a second language*. https://doi.org/10.1177/003368829903000103.

Saddhono, K. 2016. *Teaching Indonesian as foreign language in Indonesia: Impact of professional managerial on process and student outcomes*.

Saleh, M. & Sultan, S. 2016. Pengembangan bahan ajar bahasa Indonesia berbasis kurikulum 2013 yang mengintegrasikan nilai karakter bangsa di SMP. *Jurnal Pendidikan Dan Pembelajaran (JPP)* 22(2): 117–129.

Susilo, J. 2016. Pengembangan kurikulum bahasa Indonesia bagi penutur asing. *Deiksis Jurnal Pendidikan Bahasa Dan Sastra Indonesia* 3(1).

Thiagarajan, S., Semmel, D.S. & Semmel, M.I. 1974. *Instructional development for training teachers of exceptional children: A sourcebook*.

Thornbury, S. 2005. *How to teach speaking*. Longman.

Valax, P. 2011. *The Common European Framework of Reference for Languages: A critical analysis of its impact on a sample of teachers and curricula within and beyond Europe*. University of Waikato.

Widodo, H.P. & Rozak, R.R. 2016. Engaging student teachers in collaborative and reflective online video-assisted extensive listening in an Indonesian initial teacher education (ITE) context. *Electronic Journal of Foreign Language Teaching* 13(2): 229–244.

Yuniarti, Y. 2017. Developing speaking materials based on the Common European Framework (CEFR) for increasing the students' speaking skill. *Pedagogy Journal* 4(2): 143–156.

ELT in Asia in the Digital Era: Global Citizenship and Identity – Madya et al. (Eds)
© *2018 Taylor & Francis Group, London, ISBN 978-0-8153-7900-3*

Developing public speaking materials based on communicative language teaching for EFL learners in Indonesia

M.A.R. Hakim & M.J.Z. Abidin
Universiti Sains Malaysia, Penang, Malaysia

ABSTRACT: Public Speaking is a main subject in the English Departments to be mastered by EFL learners. However, its supporting materials are insufficient and causing problems for the learners in mastering the skills. Therefore, education administrators need to develop and design the relevant curriculum. This study is a Research and Development beginning with information collection consisting of identifying the problem, choosing the means of solving the problem, theoretical study, selecting and assembling materials consisting of technique, the processing teaching and learning, scriptwriting consisting of material development, experts validation to get feedback, revising of material revision based on experts' verification, evaluation consisting of trial, revision and finishing. This paper explains the development of public speaking materials based on communicative language teaching as a solution to the problems faced by the learners. The results of the study are supplementary materials consisting of five chapters which help the improvement the learners' public speaking skills.

1 INTRODUCTION

Public speaking is not as easy as what people generally think. Pan (2010) states that standing and doing speech in front of the public such as speaking in front a large number of audiences in particular occassions are the biggest fears for many people. Public Speaking is one form of communication that can make a big difference in someone's ability to influence decisions in public and private sectors (Hakim 2015). In public speaking, people have the opportunity to convey a message without being reproached by a few individuals or millions of people. Public speaking has many similarities in common with other types of communication. However, it also differs from them for some aspects. The first aspect is the speakers as the main component in speaking, as the source of the message. The second aspect is the audience because the speaker should analyse the audience first to decide how to present his/her ideas. The third aspect is the plot, which refers to the way we convey the message that consists of movement, target, tone of voice and words to communicate. The fourth aspect is the message that will be conveyed to the audience, and the last one is the feedback that will relate about the information received by the speaker from the audience about the presentation and the speaker's response to audience reaction.

Regarding the statement above, Revola (2016) states that speakers usually think about: first, the audience, second, the arguments and evidence. Then, they begin to gather the evidence and put it into some patterns, which are arranged. They give some opinions about the language they use, both before and during a speech, and of course in the delivery of the speech.

The study conducted by Brown (2001) reveals that, the problems faced by students in using English or delivering English speech are anxiety, pride and motivation. Anxiety to speech is not a new thing—it has been happening as people have been talking to each other. Most of speakers who have experienced anxiety during a speech know the importance of calmness and confidence when speaking. According to Hornby (2010), anxiety is a state where one feels nervous or worried that something bad will happen. Further, anxiety is worry and fear, especially about what might happen (Manser in Revola 2016). Some people feel nervous while others remain calm and relaxed when speaking. Factors that cause anxiety to the speech must be different between one another. However, those factors are generally applicable to all of us. On the other hand, problems with high level speaking anxiety, as stated by Jane (2006), are that people with high level speaking anxiety often avoid communication. They are rarely considered as a leader, other people may have a negative perception of them as they would look unfriendly, but people with high levels of anxiety can be taught how to regulate their anxiety (Jane 2006).

According to Ayres & Miller (1994), during a speech anxiety, fear associated with delivering a speech, is an important issue for many people. Associated with pride and self-restraint, the concept of anxiety plays an essentially important role in an effective English language acquisition. Even though all students know what anxiety is and all students have the experience of anxiety, anxiety is still not easy to define in simple sentences. Scovel in Brown (2001) suggests that anxiety is associated with feelings of worry, frustration, self-doubt, fear, or concern.

In line with previous expert literature review, the researchers attempts to find out other factors related to problems faced by the EFL learners in *public speaking* by observing and analising teaching and learning process *Public Speaking class* at the State Islamic Institute of Bengkulu. The results indicated that the main obstacles are teaching materials, which are not qualified enough with the subject. Based on the evidence above, the researcher feels it is better to develop teaching materials for public speaking class to improve students' ability by applying appropriate teaching materials with specific learning approaches or theories. According to Richard & Rodger (1999), the elements that underlie the theory of learning can be seen in some practices of CLT. However, one of these elements can be described as the principle of communication: activities that involve real communication that develop learning. The second element is the principle of duty: activity in which the language is used to carry out the tasks which means developing learning. The third element is the principle of meaningfulness: language, which means supporting the learning process for students. Learning activities are therefore selected according to how well they engage students in the use of language that is meaningful and real (not just machines that practice on language patterns). According to this theory, the acquisition of communicative competence in the language is the example of development skills that involves both cognitive and behavioural aspects. The cognitive aspect involves the internalization of a plan to make the appropriate behavior. To the use of a language, this plan comes mainly from the language system. They include the rules of grammar, the procedures for selecting vocabulary, and social tradition and customs about speaking. Behavioral aspects involve the automation of these plans so that they can be converted into a smooth performance in a real time. This happens mainly through practice in converting plans into performance (Littlewood 2002). In this theory, there is an encouragement and an emphasis on practice as a way to develop communicative skills. To understand the communicative teaching model in detail, the researcher described how teaching model should do. This picture is adapted from Patel in Efrizal (2012) with few modifications.

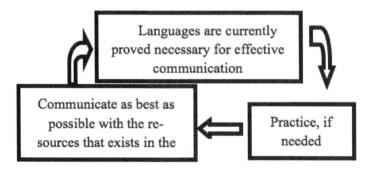

Figure 1.   The illustration of communicative language teaching model.

2 RESEARCH DESIGN

2.1 *Research and development*

This study was a Research and Development. According to Latief (2012), Educational Research and Development is a design study to develop educational products such as curriculum, syllabus, textbooks, instructional media, modules, instruments, and others. In this study, the researcher took the model of development procedures a Gall, Gall & Walter (2005), which starts from obtaining information consisting of identifying the problem, choosing the means of solving the problem and the study of theory, selecting and assembling materials consisting of technique, the processing teaching and learning, scriptwriting consisting of material development, experts validation to get feedback, revising of material revision based on experts' verification, evaluation consisting of trial, revision, and validation based on feedback during the learning process and finishing final product development of public speaking teaching materials.

2.2 *Need analysis*

The researchers gave need analysis to the students and lecturers to find out the instructional public speaking material needed by the students, the students opinion about public speaking class, students' activities and interest in public speaking class and the importance of developing material, the existing materials.

3 FINDINGS

3.1 *Development result*

The results of needs assessment discussed the data gathered from questionnaires, interviews, and syllabus. Those are used to find out information related to English teaching and learning process, particularly in Public Speaking subject at English Department of IAIN Bengkulu. Based on the results of students' needs analysis, they need supplementary teaching materials that focus on public speaking skills to help them to overcome their problems in learning public speaking which is based on communicative language teaching approach which is matched with the syllabus at the English Education Study Program of IAIN Bengkulu.

The supplementary teaching materials are designed in the form of five chapters: preparing speaking publicly, speech outlining, overcoming fears and building confidence, presenting public speaking, and types of speeches. Those chapters are completed with brainstorming, theories concerned with teaching materials to be studied so that the students were able to determine the structure of Public Speaking they learned, provided authentic language to directing the students on how to construct a sentence correctly and at the end of the matter is the reflection. This reflection must be submitted by students with oral language and becomes part of the reinforcement material.

3.2 *Expert validation*

In this step, firstly the researchers made a draft and consulted it to the experts to be evaluated to ensure that the supplementary materials were applicable to be applied to the students. The results are in the form of comments and suggestions as a basis to create a better draft. The first expert approved that the material was very well developed and appropriate to be applied in the teaching and learning process in Public Speaking class for second-year students at English Department IAIN Bengkulu by the curriculum and syllabus that are being used. However, they suggested creating the contents of the materials with more authentic or contextual with the students real life. Also, the expert validator advised the researcher to be more specific about the procedures in delivering Public Speaking which is right and relevant to the students' needs in the fifth unit.

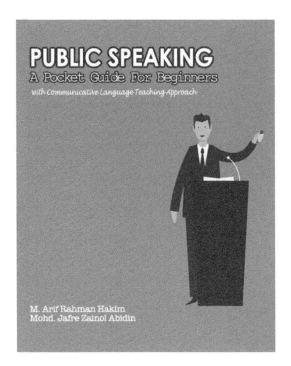

Picture 1. The cover of developed teaching materials.

The second expert commented on teaching strategies, and conformity with the principles of communicative teaching materials developed. He agreed that it was systematic and could motivate students to be more active in public speaking. The delivery of materials made the students' construction frame clear and easy to follow so that the teaching strategies presented will make students enthusiastic in his Public Speaking practice properly and regularly. Moreover, he also commented on the aspect of communicative principle, and he firmly insisted that the materials developed were very communicative in accordance with communicative principles. However, he suggested that the researchers add activities that motivate students to be more active in public speaking.

3.3 *Teaching materials revision*

After validation done by the experts, the researchers revised the product based on the corrections and suggestions from the experts. The revision is about the text and content change that was not based on their needs, typos, misspelling of words and punctuation. All the materials that had been revised were validated for the second time to the experts in order to make the material more comprehensively developed and qualified. Therefore, the researcher consulted with the experts about the quality of the content, language, teaching strategies, and conformity with the principle of communicative.

All pieces of advice from both experts for material developments were helpful in making the material developed for the better. All aspects concerning the weakness in the developed supplementary teaching materials had been redesigned based on feedback and had been validated by two experts. Later, the materials were improved and ready to be tested.

3.4 *Try-out result*

To determine the application of developed teaching materials, it was necessary to apply the product in a real field in which the move was made to get some information related to the materials that need to be improved to determine the suitability of materials developed for the students. Therefore, the researcher tried-out the materials to the second-year students at the English Department. During the trial the researchers acted as collaborators of a Public Speaking class, and the lecturer of the course served as a teacher applying teaching materials developed during the learning process in the try-out process. In this case, the researchers observed the effectiveness of teaching materials developed based on the activities and responses, students interest toward the material, the students' opinion about the materials developed. The results showed that the students were very enthusiastic during the teaching and learning process of Public Speaking class. Moreover, during the trial researchers wrote several important aspects based on the situation that occurred through the field when the lecturer was teaching using the developed materials. Based on the try-out process, data were collected using questionnaires for students who focused on five points representing the opinions of students about the Public Speaking material already developed. The five points were on appeal in substance, complexity, operational measures, the usefulness of the materials in favour of the practice of Public Speaking, and aspects of practicality.

Based on data collected from 33 students, it was found that 45% students insisted that the appeal of the developed materials was very good. Further, 42% of them said that the appeal of the developed materials was good. They claimed that the appeal of the material motivated them to be better, and 12% or 4 students said that the appeal of the developed material was sufficient. None of the students said that the teaching materials that had been developed were less attractive.

In the aspect of materials difficulty level, 81% of students or 27 students stated that the teaching materials were less difficult. The teaching materials could be adequately understood in order to increase their skills in public speaking, especially during practice in class, and 18, 18% or 6 students said that the material was quite difficult to understand. When the researcher explained what difficulties they encountered, the students said that some words were new to them. But there was no student who said that the developed material was difficult or very difficult to understand or practice.

In the aspect of operational procedures, 36% of them or 12 students said that the operational procedures in the material were very well developed. The materials were arranged a logical order that was good. In addition, 45% of them or 15 students claimed that the operational procedures in the developed materials were good, and 18% or 6 students said that the operational procedures in the material were quite well developed. None of the students said that the operational procedures were less good.

In aspects of the use of developed materials to support the practice of English language, 60% of them, or 20 students said that the aspects of the used materials were very well developed. Besides that 39% of them, or 13 students stated that the aspects of the use of developed materials were good.

The last aspect represented students' opinion about the material that was developed after the try-out is the aspect of practicality. In the aspect of practicality, 75% of students or 25 students said that the practicality aspect of the developed materials was very good, and 24% of them or 8 students stated that the practicality aspect of the materials developed was good. Moreover, none of the students said that the practicality aspect of the materials was less good or good enough.

3.5 Revision after try-out

In line with the results collected from the try-out, the researchers revised the shortcomings and weaknesses of the developed materials involves the difficult vocabulary from idioms, types, spelling mistakes, and long texts or sentences. After that, they were consulted with the experts to be revised, so as the material became more ideal and qualified for the students' needs in learning public speaking.

4 CONCLUSSION

The final product of this study was the developed teaching materials in the form of supplementary teaching materials which complete and cover the shortfall of the main book of public speaking subjects. It was developed based on communicative language teaching appraoch to assisting lecturers in teaching Public Speaking in their courses. It is also used to help students by providing more opportunities to practice their public speaking as a solution of the problems faced by the students at *IAIN* Bengkulu, and the results indicated that the material was effective in achieving the goal of public speaking class. However, the materials have weaknesses, it is only designed for the students in English education study program and on the other hand, the material has strength, it covers the shortcomings of major books used by lecturers which the instructional materials cannot meet the needs of the students maximumly in teaching Public Speaking. Through this study, the researchers recommended lecturers should use developed materials in accordance with lesson plans to meet the students' needs in Public Speaking by considering their needs, conditions, and time. However, since these materials were only as supplementary teaching materials, the researcher also suggested that lecturers of Public Speaking combine the developed materials with a major book or other sources. In addition, the researchers suggested that the students use developed teaching materials effectively by practicing the material content that is not only in the classroom, but also outside the classroom. By practising effectively, the researcher believes that their problems in Public Speaking will be addressed well.

REFERENCES

Ayres, J & Milleer, J. 1994. *Effective public speaking* (Fourth Edition). McGraw-Hill Humanities: New York.

Brown, H.D. 2001. *Teaching by principles: An interactive approach to language pedagogy*. New York: Logman.

Efrizal, D. 2012. Improving students' speaking skill through communicative language teaching. *International Journal of Humanities and Social Science* 2(20): 127–134.

Gall, J.P., Gall, M.D & Walter, R.B. 2005. *Applying educational research: A practical guide*. London: Pearson.

Hakim, M.A.R. 2015. Experienced EFL teachers' challenges and strategies in teaching speaking for introvert students. *European Journal of Social Sciences* 48(4): 437–446.

Latief, M.A. 2012. *Research method on language learning: An introduction*. Malang: UM Press.

Littlewood, W. 2002. *Communicative language teaching*. Cambridge: Cambridge University Press.

Miller, J. & Weinert, R. 1998. *Spontaneous spoken language*. Oxford: Clarendon Press.

Pan, L. 2010. A study of public speaking in Korean education for Chinese students. *Journal of Language Teaching and Research* 1(6): 922–925.

Revola, Y. 2016. The analysis of tertiary EFL students' on English speech. *Proceedings of the Fourth International Seminar on English Language and Teaching* 4 (2): 458–467.

Richards, J.C. & Rodgers, T.S 2001. *Approaches and methods in language teaching,* United Kingdom: Cambridge University Press.

ELT in Asia in the Digital Era: Global Citizenship and Identity – Madya et al. (Eds)
© *2018 Taylor & Francis Group, London, ISBN 978-0-8153-7900-3*

Improving learners' vocabulary mastery through the use of scaffolding strategies while storytelling in an EFL multiethnic classroom

Istiqamah
IAIN Pontianak, West Kalimantan, Indonesia

ABSTRACT: This research aimed to improve multiethnic learners' vocabulary mastery while storytelling in an English Foreign Language setting. This was a two cycle classroom action research. The BUdata were collected through oral tests, observations, and learner's self-checklists. Then, the data were analyzed using descriptive statistics, a rubric and Miles & Huberman's framework. This research found that after cycle one 3 out of 22 participants failed to improve their vocabulay mastery because they failed to meet the criterion of minimum completeness. After cycle two, all participants improved their vocabulary mastery because all met the criterion. It was also found that participants selected scaffolding strategies such as gestures, visuals, and modelling while storytelling. Then, across ethnic background they encountered problems in past tense and verb formation while storytelling. Concerning an EFL context, native languages interfered their vocabulary mastery.

1   INTRODUCTION

Storytelling was one of the speaking skills that had to be accompanied by the mastery of vocabulary in large numbers. Therefore, storytelling was hampered because learners were lack of vocabulary mastery. One solution to problems in vocabulary mastery was the implementation of scaffolding strategies that were assumed to offer advantages such as allowing the use of the mother tongue, building creativity and initiatives through the use of teaching aids, promoting background knowledge, and giving rooms to learners' independency.

This research seeked for evidences that the practices of scaffolding strategies during storytelling indeed improved vocabulary mastery. Furthermore, since learners in this study came from several ethnics such as Malay, Sundanese, Javanese, Maduranese, and Bugeese and learned English as a Foreign Language (hereafter EFL), this research studied the role of ethnic backgrounds and EFL in an attempt to master vocabulary during storytelling applying scaffolding strategies.

1.1   Research objectives

The aim of this research was to improve learners' insufficient vocabulary mastery during storytelling. It was assumed that scaffolding strategies would be a solution to the problem. Thus, the study objectives were as follows.

1. To improve multiethnic learners' vocabulary mastery while storytelling in an EFL setting
2. To improve multietnic learner' scaffolding strategies while storytelling in their attempt to master vocabulary in an EFL setting

1.2   Related studies

The following studies stated the use of storytelling in vocabulary mastery in relation to abilities in speaking, writing, and reading. First, Salman and Shaaban (2015) found that three types of storytelling techniques such as storytelling accompanied by reading, storytelling performed digitally, and conventional storytelling improved abilities to compose English paragraphs. Second, Cubukeu (2014) found that storytelling through Total Physical Response, known as TPRs, improved vocabulary mastery. Third, Abasi & Saori (2014) found that knowledge about vocabulary influenced language skills. Fourth, Soleimani (2013) found that storytelling influences vocabulary mastery of six years old children. Fifth, a study by Akhyak & Indramawan (2013) found that storytelling improved the ability to speak in English in the areas of fluency, grammar, pronunciation, and vocabulary development. Sixth, Jeong & Unkyoung (2012) also found that storytelling and storytelling accompanied by reading influenced negatively to reading comprehension. Seventh, Van de Pol, Volman, & Beishuizen (2010) found three types of scaffolding strategies such as contigency, fading, and transfer of responsibility.

1.3 *Literature review*

1.3.1 *Vocabulary*
Vocabulary is crucial because it is essential to build communication. One cannot listen, speak, read, or speak adequately with limited vocabulary. Therefore, vocabulary mastery should be prioritized before grammar and pronunciation.

Vocabulary is defined as a collection of words available in a language (Cambridge Advanced Dictionary 2009). Words mean parts of speech. Thus, vocabulary mastery is about mastering parts of speech (Frank 1972). Frank (1972) states that parts of speech from one language to another differ in forms and depend on contexts in use. Learning parts of speech in a context of a university should utilize strategy development (Nation & Newton 2009). The reason relies on the nature of the university learning that is characterized by independent or autonomous learning. Being independent helps build creativity in producing utterances either in written or oral form.

1.3.2 *Storytelling*
Storytelling has long been known as oral telling serving as a cultural preservation to a number of stories from generation to generation. Storytelling requires two main components: a story and a teller. Stories in the context of storytelling refers to naratives from fables, fairy-tales, legends, to myths. To be able to perform skillfully in storytelling, the teller should adequately comprehend the story. To do so, he has to have adequate vocabulary classified *high frequency words*, a terminology by Nation & Newton (2009). Furthermore, Nation & Newton (2009) mention approximately 2000–3000 word families considered as high frequency words. Mastering high frequecy words can be accomplished by developing strategies that encourage a learner's autonomy. This autonomy found their ways through the use of scaffolding strategies.

1.3.3 *Scaffolding strategies*
Scaffolding is believed to play an important role in language learning (Pawan 2008, Kim 2010). The important role means that it assists learners to achieve two goals: stronger understanding and greater independence (edglossary.org). To do so, scaffolding strategies centers on the practices of the first language, reading aloud, modelling or gestures, intentional small group/partner group, sentence structures/starters, background knowledge, graphic organizers, visuals and realia (www. mshouser.com/teaching-tips/8-strategies-for-scaffolding-instruction). Similarly, Brush and Sage in Pawan (2008) states that scaffolding varies from the use of a multitude tools and guides to resources.

Scaffolding strategies are commonly practiced by teachers. However, with the changing in classroom practices from teacher-centered to learner-centered and inspired by strategies-based instruction (hereafter SBI), a terminlogy by Brown (2007), they are possibly used by learners for self-help. The use of scaffolding strategies under SBI benefit learners' vocabulary mastery. It promotes learners to be aware of and to take control of their own learning process. In other words, it promotes independent learning that motivate learners' investment to their own learning. It is believed that it leads to high achievement in vocabulary mastery.

1.3.4 *Learning English as a foreign language*

Learners in a foreign language setting need to cope with limited exposures that stem from the characteristics of EFL learning that is formality, a short duration of learning, and a native language as a language for interaction in a classroom, and learning strategies as an important thing. The first three characteristics slow down the learning process. The following is explanation on these three.

Formality means that English is learned, but not acquired. Ellis (1994) states foreign language learning takes place in settings where language plays no role in the community and is primarily learnt only in the classroom. English is a subject matter in a classroom in which materials are selected based on certain standards or qualifications

The second characteristic is that classroom interaction happens in a short duration. In Indonesia, junior high school students spend approximately 160 minutes in a week to learn English but senior high school students spend approximately 160 minutes in a week. University students spend 1–3 semesters to learn English. All these levels of education are invested to learn English for Academic purposes. The third characteristic is that language for commmunication in class dominantly uses Indonesian. The dominat use of Indonesian affects the degree to which inputs that learners should get from the teacher's talk. This unfortunate condition strongly affect advanced English learners who need to expose themselves in a large number of English input.

1.3.5 *Learning English vocabulary in a multiethnic classroom*

Learners come to class with their mother tongues (hereafter L1) that can either facilitate or impede the learning of English (hereafter L2) vocabulary. L1 benefits L2 in away that they indicate similarities in vocabulary building so that it assists the learning. Example, an Indonesian student whose native language is Malay uses his background knowledge ye to understand *yes*. L1 impede L2 because of differences in vocabulary building. Example, an Indonesian student who is Maduranese fails to understand *blue* because no word to present it in Madura language. Above all, taking a side that L1 can facilitate vocabulary learning, L1 can possibly be used to beginners. As time goes on, the use of L1 is gradually reduced.

The use of L1 in class affects the selection of teaching methods and strategies. Methods such as Grammar-Translation and Community Language Learning support the use of L1. As to teaching strategies, scaffolding strategies support the use of L1.

2 RESEARCH METHOD

This was a classroom action research (hereafter CAR) with two cycles (Cresswell 2008, Ferrance 2000, Koshy 2005). This CAR adopted Kurt Lewin's design. Each cycle consisted of stages such as planning, acting, observing, and reflecting.

2.1 *Participants*

Participants were 22 second semester students whose ages were approximately 19 years old. They were registered at the Faculty of Tarbiya and Teacher's Training majoring at the Department of Elementary School Teacher Education. The participants came from five ethnic backgrounds such as Malay, Sundanese, Javanese, Maduranese, and Bugeese.

2.2 *Instruments, data collection, and data analysis*

Data were gathered using oral tests, observation, and learner's checklist. The former used a scoring guidance to evaluate students' performances during storytelling, The latter used field notes to record descriptions of the event and self-checklists to identify participants' ethnic backgrounds and the selection of the scaffolding strategies. The oral tests required participants to storytell a fable containing approximately 200 words. The storytelling lasted in 5 minutes. It was evaluated by two raters.

Table 1.   The rubric to analyze a number of words produced during storytelling.

No	Number of words developed after treatments	Levels
1	000–100	1
2	101–200	2
3	201–300	3
4	301–400	4
5	401–500	5
6	501–600	6

Table 2.   The rubric to decide Leaners' Minimum Mastery Criterion Higher Education at the Faculty of Tarbiya & Teacher's Training IAIN Pontianak.

Predicates	Scores
Passed	5 or 6
Passed	4
Passed	3
Passed	2
Failed	1

The data collection took quantitive and qualitative forms. The quantitative data were analyzed using a rubric.

The rubric was interpreted using Adams dan Frith in Hughes (2003: 131).

1: vocabulary inadequate for even the simplest conversation
2: vocabulary limited to basic personal and survival areas (time, food, transportation, family, etc)
3: choice of words sometime inaccurate, limitations of vocabulary prevent discussion of some common professional and social topics,
4: professional vocabulary adequate to discuss special interests; general vocabulary permits discussion of any non-technical subject with some circumlocation
5: professional vocabulary broad and precise; general vocabulary adequate to cope with complex practical problems and varied social situations
6: vocabulary apparently as accurate and extensive as that of an educated native speaker

In addition, the quantitative data were analyzed using a rubric of the Minimum Mastery Criterion that was the criteria of success as follows.

It was expected that the participants could 100% passed the criteria.

The qualitiative data taking forms of field notes were analyzed applying descriptive analysis by Miles and Huberman (1994). The analysis requires three steps: data reduction, data display, and conclusion/verification. Data from filed notes were verified by the learners' self checklists.

3   FINDINGS AND DISCUSSIONS

3.1   *Findings*

3.1.1   *Findings from cycles one and two*
This research found as follows. Cycle one consisted of the following activities. Planning consisted of activities such as designing lesson plans and a scoring system, identifying participants' ethnic background, selecting a story, and carrying out interrater reliability and readability tests. Planning also determined the criteria of success that is 100% participants achieved the Minimum Mastery Criterion.

Acting consisted of two meetings. The first meeting took place on Wednesday June 8, 2016 from 08.00–08.50. The class started by explaining the concepts of storytelling and scaffolding strategies. The second meeting took place on Wednesday, June 8, 2016 from 08.50–11.00. It was the storytelling time and also consisted of the activity in which two raters who were the researcher and her collaborator scored the participants' performances based on audio-visual recording.

Observing gave evidences that on the first meeting one participant selected one scaffolding strategy. On the second meeting five participants failed to finish their storylines.

Reflection was a stage in which data from learners' self checklists, field notes and scoring sheets were analyzed. It was revealed that the majority of the participants applied one scaffolding strategy. Moroever, five participants had to improve their vocabulary mastery because they failed to pass the Minimum Mastery Criterion. It was concluded that on the second cycle the participants had to select more than one scaffolding strategies to improve their vocabulary mastery while storytelling.

Cycle two consisted of activities as follows. Planning consisted of designing lesson plans, reviewed explanations on storytelling and scaffolding strategies, and assisted the participants to select more than one scaffolding strategies.

Acting consisted of two meetings. The first meeting took place on Friday June 10, 2016 from 13.30–1420. The class reviewed scaffolding strategies and assisted the participants to select at least two scaffolding strategies. The second meeting was on Friday, June 10, 2016 from 14.30–16.30. The class consisted of the storytelling activity and the recording of the activity. Two raters who were the researcher and her collaborator scored participants' performances based on audio-visual recording.

Observing gave evidences that on the first meeting the participants encounterd problems to decide scaffolding strategies that could support the vocabulary mastery while storytelling. On the second meeting, they could accomplish telling the stories.

Reflection studied field notes and scoring sheets. It was revealed that the one participant failed to meet the Minimum Mastery Criterion.

3.1.2 *The average scores of the participants storytelling skill in cycles one and two*

No	Name (Initials)	Cycle one	Cycle two
1	A1	3.00	3.50
2	A2	1.50	2.50
3	A3	0.00	2.50
4	A4	0.00	1.50
5	A5	3.00	3.50
6	D1	2.00	2.50
7	D2	1.00	2.50
8	F	3.00	3.50
9	H1	3.00	3.00
10	H2	2.25	3.25
11	L	3.00	3.25
12	M1	2.75	3.25
13	M2	3.50	3.50
14	M3	2.50	3.50
15	N1	2.50	2.50
16	N2	3.00	3.25
17	N3	2.50	3.00
18	N4	2.50	2.50
19	P1	2.50	3.50
20	P2	3.00	3.50
21	S1	0.00	2.50
22	S2	2.50	2.50
	Average scores	2.23	2.70

3.1.3 *The description of participants' scaffolding strategies to help improve their vobulary mastery while storytelling*

Table 3. The description of participants' choices of the scaffolding strategies.

No	Scaffolding strategies	
	Cycle one	Cycle two
1	Visuals	Visuals
	1. Pictures	1. Pictures
	2. Puppets	2. Puppets
2	Gestures	Gestures
3	Modelling	Modelling
	1. Voice imitation	1. Repetition
	2. Intonation manipulation	2. Intonation manipulation
		3. Silent way

3.1.4 *The description of participants' utterances based on ethnic backgrounds as follows*

Table 4. Ethnic backgrounds and participants' utterances.

Ethnic Backgrounds	Utterances
Javanese	I will storytelling about... .
	As soon as, receive the river bank... .As soon as they reach ... .
	He has to eat my heart of the monkey.
	I will the storytelling
	Today, I want the storytelling about... .
Bugeese	The crocodille swim down the river...
	I want to talk about the story.
Malay	He tell the monkey that her father is very sick
	He have a good idea.
	I want to storytelling about ... The crocodille jump of the crocodille's back.
	The monkey to jump on ... .
Sundanese	One day, he want to cross the river.
Maduranese	The crocodile agree and told the monkey to jump on his back.
Javanese, Maduranese, Dayaknese, Bugeese, Malay	Unluckily, the crocodile was very angry.
Javanese, Bugeese, Malay	He stop in the middle of the river.
Javanese, Bugeese, Sundanese Javanese, Malay	

3.1.5 *The contributions of the EFL setting on vocabulary mastery was described in the following table*

Table 5. EFL and vocabulary mastery.

Utterances
I will storytelling about... .
As soon as, receive the river bank... .
As soon as they reach ... .
He has to eat my heart of the monkey.

(Continued)

140

Table 5. *(Continued)*.

Utterances
I will the storytelling
Today, I want the storytelling about... .
The crocodille swim down the river... .
I want to talk about the story.
He tell the monkey that her father is very sick
He have a good idea.
I want to storytelling about ... .
The crocodille jump of the crocodille's back.
The monkey to jump on ... .
One day, he want to cross the river.
The crocodile agree and told the monkey to jump on his back.
Unluckily, the crocodile was very angry.
He stop in the middle of the river.

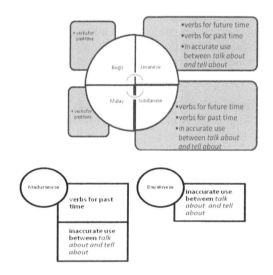

Figure 1.   The description of problems in verb formation based on ethnic backgrounds.

3.2 *Discussion*

1. After cycle one the use of scaffolding strategies while storytelling by multiethnic participants in a class of EFL indicated that their vocabulary mastery was between levels 1 and 3. However, it was found that most participants vocabulary mastery was in level 2 indicating that their vocabulary mastery was from 101 to 200 words. Adam and Frith in Hughes (2003: 131) described that level 2 can be interpreted that vocabulary was limited to basic personal and survival areas (time, food, transportation, family, etc).

2. After cycle two the use of scaffolding strategies while storytelling by multiethnic participants in a class of EFL indicated that their vocabulary mastery was between levels 1 and 3. However, it was found that most participants vocabulary mastery was in level 3 indicating that their vocabulary mastery was from 201–300. Adam and Frith in Hughes (2003: 131) described that level 3 can be interpreted that choice of words sometime inaccurate, limitations of vocabulary prevent discussion of some common professional and social topics.

3. Table 3 showed that verbal and nonverbal scaffolding strategies were the participants' learning approach to assist them to master vocabulary while storytelling. The verbal scaffolding strategies were telling stories by integrating voice imitation and intonation manipulation. The nonverbal ones were telling stories with pictures, puppets, and gestrues.

4. Table 4 indicated that in order to master vocabulary participants in a multiethnic class encountered problems in parts of speech. Specifically, they had a problem in the selection of verb formation. Figure 1 provided specific descriptions of their problems in verbs.
5. Table 5 described that in the EFL class participants experienced interlanguage. It was specifically identified as interferences.

4 CONCLUSION

This research concluded that the use of scaffolding strategies such as visuals, gestures, and modelling assisted participatns to improve their vocabulary mastery while storytelling.

In an attempt to master the vocabularies, Javanese and Sundanese had problems with verbs for past and future times. It also indicated that Malay, Maduranese, Dayaknese, and Bugis had problems with verbs for past time. Furthermore, Javanese, Maduranese, and Malay produced utterances containing inaccurate use of *tell about* and *talk about*. The finding also indicated that English parts of speech became a problem. Participants failed to differentiate between English and Indonesian parts of speech. Evidences from samples of utterances provide participants' lack of understanding in this area.

For future instructions, it was recommede to teach English parts of speech either explicitly or implicitly. It was assumed that accurate and appropriate understanding on the parts of speech assisted in producing correct English sentences. In an attempt to teach parts of speech, it was strongly recommended to discuss grammar because they were like two sides of one coin.

In addition, it was recommended that the teaching of English vocabulary adopted learner-centered vocabulary learning. It prioritized vocabulary learning in isolation emphasizing on leaners' autonomy or independency.

REFERENCES

Abasi, M. & Soori, A. 2014. Is storytelling effective in improving the English vocabulary learning among iranian children in kindergarten? *Journal of Education & Literary Studies* 2(3). available online at http://dx.doi.org/10.7575/aiac.ijels.2n.3p.7.

Akhyak & Indramawan, A. 2013. Improving the students' English competence through storytelling. *Journal of Language and Literature* 1(2). available online www. ijll-net.com.

Brown, H.D. 2007. *Teaching by principles*. New York: Pearson Education.

Cresswell, J. 2008. *Educational research*. New Jersey: Upper Saddle River.

Cubukcu, F. 2014. A Synergy between storytelling and vocabulary teaching through TPRS. *ELT Research Journal* 3(2): 84–90. available online at www.udead.org.tr/journal.

Ellis, R. 1994. *The study of second language acquisition*. New York: Oxford Univ. Press.

Ferrance, E. 2000. *Action research*, USA: Brown University.

Frank, M. 1972. *Modern English: a pratical references guide*. New Jersey: Prentice Hall.

Hughes, A. 2003. *Testing for language teacher*. New York: Cambridge Univ. Press.

Jeong In, Moon & Unkyoung, M. 2012. *The effects of storytelling & storysinging on L2 reading comprehension in primary English education* 18(2): 389–404. available online at www.kapee.or.kr.

Kim, Y. 2010. Scaffolding through questions in upper elementary ELL learning. *Litracy Teaching & Learning*, 15 (1&2): 109–137.

Koshy, V. 2005, *Action reserach for improving practice*, California: SAGE.

Nation, I.S.P & Newton, J. 2009. *Teaching ESL/EFL Listening and Speaking*. New York: Routledge.

Pawan, F. 2008. Content area teachers and scaffolded instruction for English language learners. *Teaching & Teacher Education* 24: 1450–1462. available online at www.sciencedirect.com.

Salman, S. & Abou, S. 2015. The effect of digital storytelling, storytelling, and stroyreading on enhancing Palestinian ninth graders paragraph writing skills. *Journal of Education Studies* 7 (1). available online at www. ozelacademy.com.

Soleimani, H. & Mahkamah, A. 2013. *The effect of storytelling on children's learning English vocabulary: A case in Iran. Journal of Applied and Basic Sciences* 5(1): 104–113 /2013, ISSN 2251–838x. available on line www.irjabs.com.

www.mshouser.com/teaching-tips/8-strategies-for-scaffolding-instruction.

The effect of school origins on the grammatical competence of university students

C.H. Karjo
Bina Nusantara University, Jakarta, Indonesia

R. Djohan
Gunadarma University, Jakarta, Indonesia

ABSTRACT: This study addressed the issue of whether students' school origins (Jakarta and non-Jakarta) affect their grammatical competence in the university. The participants for this study were 250 first semester students of Faculty of Economy of a private university who graduated from various high schools. They were given a TOEFL style grammar test consisting of 30 questions of various grammatical items. The students' answers were analyzed quantitatively using independent sample T-test and Analysis of Variance (Anova) and the answers were also analyzed qualitatively to find out the types of grammatical items that are problematic for the students. The results showed that in general, students from Jakarta performed better in the grammar test including, some of the problematic areas such as subject-verb agreement and participle adjectives. Further implications on teaching and materials development are discussed.

1 INTRODUCTION

Academic achievements of students in higher education (university) are influenced by many factors, namely academic, psychosocial, cognitive, and demographic (McKenzie & Schweitzer 2001). All of these factors have been extensively explored and examined by previous research. Among the academic factors, for example, McKenzie & Schweitzer (2001) and McKenzie et al. (2004) study the effect of prior academic achievement on academic performance at higher levels.

Prior academic achievements of university students can be obtained from the scores they gained in high school exams. In Indonesia, high school students take a national examination as an obligatory requirement to graduate from high school. In 2017, 1.8 million students from 9661 high schools all over Indonesia took the national exams (http://un.kemdikbud. go.id/un-2017/). Yet, not all the students passed their national exams. The passing rate of high school students differs from one province to another. High schools in Jakarta, as the capital city of Indonesia, usually yield more graduates than high schools in other provinces. Many schools in Jakarta have 100% passing rate, although some high schools in remote areas have a 0% passing rate.

Five course subjects are tested in the national examination; one of the subjects is English. English has become a test subject because it is the acknowledged first foreign language based on Law 2 of 1989 on the National Education System, which makes it one of the compulsory subjects to be taught and tested at the secondary level (Komaria 1998, Lauder 2008). However, the English scores obtained in the national examination raises several questions, such as: are the students' results in the national exam reflective of their actual English competence? What kinds of English competence are measured by the national exam? Do their high schools affect the students' achievement in the exam? And finally, do the students' high schools give sufficient preparation for studying (English) in higher level?

This study attempts to answer such questions. Different high schools offer different kinds of materials, use different teaching methods, have different quality teachers, have various school facilities, etc. These differences might explain why high school graduates from different high schools exhibit different levels of English competence even though they obtained similar scores in the national examination. For example, if two students from two different schools get an English score of 80 on the national examination, it may not necessarily mean that those students have similar competence in English. Several studies have confirmed the existence of a such relationship between the school quality and the students' academic achievement (Eide & Showalter 1998a).

To overcome the discrepancy of previous academic achievement of high school graduates, universities usually hold an admission test, of which the results will be used as the basis for the admitting candidates. The admission test can be categorized as a criterion reference test (CRT). Richards et al. (1985) define CRT as a test which measures a student's performance according i a particular standard or criterion which has been agreed upon. The students must reach a certain level of performance to pass the test, in order to be admitted to a university.

To test the English ability of the candidates, a TOEFL—like test is widely used in many universities in Jakarta, such as in Binus University, Atmajaya University and Gunadharma University. TOEFL is, "arguably the most well-known and widely used large-scale language assessment in the world" (Kunnan 2008: 140). TOEFL was first developed in the United States to help in the assessment of the language competence of non-native speakers. It is a standardized test of English proficiency administered by the Educational Testing Service, Princeton. Up to now, TOEFL has widely been recognized as a model test and a have-to-take test for students, graduate and post graduate, as well as for teachers and researchers in universities who wish to develop their potentials.

The TOEFL-like test given to the new university students functions as a diagnostic test. This test is used to diagnose particular linguistic aspects that they already learnt from the previous level of education (high schools). Ideally, the diagnostic tests are designed to assess students "linguistic knowledge (knowledge of and about language) and language skills (listening, speaking, reading and writing) before a course is initiated (Benmostefa 2008). However, due to the limitation of time and resources, only some linguistic knowledge are tested to the new students. The most common tests provided are reading and grammar tests. In this study, therefore, the linguistic skill that will be discussed is only the grammatical knowledge.

Why is grammatical knowledge important? Soepriyatna (2012) claimed that the mastery of English grammar is the basic requirement for the students to communicate in acceptable English. Moreover, Ranjbar (2012) said that knowledge of grammar helps vocabulary acquisition and grammar can help learners as a tool to self-correct and self-edit the utterances they produce in daily life. Moreover, Ellis (1991) says that grammar knowledge help learners to understand meaning of a discourse. Knowledge of grammar can also improve learners' writing (Ellis 2008) In short, grammatical knowledge is the basic requirement to be able to perform well in the other language skills (listening, speaking, reading and writing) (Martirosyan 2015). Without grammatical knowledge, a learner would not be able to produce well-formed sentences, either spoken or written. Thus, testing the grammatical knowledge for first year university students is necessary to get a broad picture of the students' English competence. Such a test will also become an important input in designing the course materials for the teaching of English in the university level (Kamimura & Ellis 2012).

Moreover, since the new university students come from various high schools in Indonesia, the results of this test can also be used to assume the quality of the students' previous high schools, in particular in the teaching of English. The results of the test can also reveal the extent of the students' grammatical knowledge.

Considering the above issues, the present study attempts to find the relationship between the students' grammar test scores with their English mastery gained in their previous high schools. The dependent variable in this study is the origins of the high schools. This study wants to find out whether the school origins affect the students' performance in the English grammar test.

Thus, there are three research questions which were investigated in this study.

1. What is the correlation between the school origins and the participants' scores?
2. Which groups of students perform better in TOEFL-like grammar test?
3. Which grammatical items are problematic for the students?

2 RESEARCH METHODOLOGY

2.1 *Participants*

The participants for this study were 250 first semester students of Faculty of Economy and Business, Atma Jaya University. They consist of 143 students from high schools in Jakarta and 107 students from high schools outside Jakarta. They participated in this study as part of the requirements for the English subject in the university.

2.2 *Instrument*

The instrument used was a TOEFL-like test taken from Longman's *Introductory Course for the TOEFL test: The Paper Test* by Deborah Phillips. The test consists of 30 multiple choice questions. These 30 items represent the majority of grammatical items discussed in the book.

2.3 *Data collection procedure*

Before starting the new semester, all students of Faculty of Economy and Business, Atma Jaya University, who take the English subject for that semester, should take the entry test. The function of the entry test is to measure the students' English competence. Since students come from many different schools from all over Indonesia, the test results can also be used to determine the English level of their school origins.

Thus, an entry test in TOEFL format was administered to the students at the first meeting. The results were calculated and scores were given. The scores were then processed using statistical program SPSS to find out the correlation between the participants' school origins and their present TOEFL test scores. The statistical results were also used to discover which group of students performed better in terms of grammatical knowledge. Further analysis discussed the grammatical items which were problematic for the students, i.e. the grammatical items that caused a lot of incorrect answers. The discussions were based on the researchers' experience as teachers and results of interviewing some of the students.

3 RESULTS AND DISCUSSION

3.1 *Results*

The results displayed below consist of correlation between school origins and students' scores, comparison of means and independent sample t-test. The statistical results are presented to answer the first and second research questions; while the third research question is discussed in separate section.

3.1.1 *Correlation between school origins and students' scores*

The first research question asked: What is the correlation between the school origins and the participants' scores? The table below shows the Pearson correlation coefficient between the school origins and the students' scores.

The above table shows that the correlation coefficient is $r = -0.165$ and the p-value $= 0.009$, which is smaller than $\alpha = 0.05$. Thus the hypothesis H0: $p = 0$ is rejected. The conclusion is that there is a linear significant relation between the school origin and the TOEFL scores. In other words, the school origins affect the amount of scores obtained by the students.

Table 1. Correlations.

		school	score
School	Pearson Correlation	1	−.165**
	Sig (2-tailed)		.009
	N	250	250
Score	Pearson Correlation	−.165**	1
	Sig (2-tailed)	.009	
	N	250	250

**Correlation is significant at the 0.01 level (2-tailed).

Table 2. Comparison of means.

	School	N	Mean	StD	St.Error Mean
Score	Jakarta	143	20.34	4.662	.390
	Non Jakarta	107	18.74	4.875	.471

Table 3. Independent sample T-test.

	F	Sig.	Sig.(2-tailed)	Mean difference
Score	112	.738	.009	1.604

3.1.2 *Comparison of means*

The second research question asked: which students perform better in the TOEFL test? As the correlation table showed, there was a significant difference between the scores of students from Jakarta and from outside Jakarta. However, the correlation coefficient obtained has not indicated which group of students performed better in grammar test. The results can be seen in the following table, in which the mean scores of both groups of students were compared.

Table 2 shows that the students from Jakarta achieved better mean score compared to students from outside Jakarta. Jakarta students obtained the score of 20.34, which means they can answer around 67.80% of all the test items correctly. On the other hand, the students from outside Jakarta only gained the mean score of 18.74, or they can give 62.46% correct answers.

3.1.3 *Independent sample T-test*

Aside from comparing the means of the two groups of participants, further analysis using Independent Sample T-Test was done to find out whether the difference of means between the two groups was significant or not. The result can be seen in Table 3 below.

From the results shown in Table 3, the assumption that both variances are equal are fulfilled based on the hypothesis: *H0:* $\sigma 1 = \sigma 2$ (in which $\sigma 1$ = variance of Jakarta group and $\sigma 2$ = variance of non-Jakarta group). This is because the *p-value* = 0.738 which is bigger than $\alpha = 0.05$ for equal variance assumed, thus *H0:* $\sigma 1 = \sigma 2$ cannot be rejected. That means that both groups have equal variance. Meanwhile t-test for hypothesis *H0:* $\mu 1 = \mu 2$ gives a *p-value* = 0.009. Because *p-value* = 0.000 is smaller than $\alpha = 0.05$, then *H0:* $\mu 1 = \mu 2$ is rejected. When the H0 is rejected, that means that there is a significant difference between the scores of students from Jakarta and from outside Jakarta.

3.2 Discussion of results

Generally, the results of this study show that students' academic achievements are highly correlated with the quality of schools from which they graduated. In other words, schools from Jakarta and schools from outside Jakarta offer have dissimilar quality. The fact that school quality affect the academic achievement of the students seems to corroborate previous studies (Ayers & Peters 1977; Eide & Showalter 1998; Ehrenberg & Brewer 1995; Hanushek 1996).

The findings of this study suggest that students from Jakarta schools had better English grammar knowledge compared to students from outside Jakarta. In input-output theory as stated by Hanushek (2005), if all the educational inputs have been fulfilled (in this case the supply of teaching materials and equipment, school facilities and qualified teachers), then automatically schools can yield expected qualified graduates. Thus, when the findings of this study indicate that the students from Jakarta get higher grammar scores, it can be assumed that they got better inputs (such as better English lessons or better teachers) from their previous high schools.

A report from the World Bank (*siteresources. worldbank.org/INTINDONESIA/...education.pdf*)
also mentions that there are some discrepancies between schools in Jakarta and other areas. For example, several schools in Central Java and NTT were in a very dismaying condition without sufficient teaching learning equipment. Besides, schools in remote areas have limited number of teachers and inadequate quality of teachers. Another big problem for the schools outside Jakarta is dissimilar school funding. Without sufficient funding, schools cannot provide facilities such as libraries, teaching materials, internet access, etc. Moreover, there are barely little opportunities for teachers to increase their knowledge by participating in seminars, conferences, training, and so on.

However, as a whole the results show that both groups of students, either from Jakarta and non-Jakarta gained the scores ranging from 62.46–67.80. These scores were quite below expectation. The finding suggests that students were not familiar with either the material or the format of the test. In high schools, the main emphasis was on the reading comprehension. So, discussion of grammar was embedded in the reading materials. Thus, when students had to analyze which sentences were grammatical and which were not, they would be in trouble. Moreover, the format of the test was a little bit confusing for them. Even though the TOEFL—like test use the familiar Multiple Choice type, the second part that they have to find the incorrect words, instead of the correct ones, was still causing many mistakes.

The low scores also indicate that there is a discrepancy between what students have learnt in high schools and what their actual grammatical competence is. Moreover, the results also bring about another crucial question, whether TOEFL should be taught in the university or not. TOEFL may be an effective test instrument in ESL learning context where English is used as a medium of instruction (Al-Ansari & Al-Musawi 1999) where students have linguistic and cultural background to pursue their studies through English. Yet, in Indonesia, English is considered as the foreign language and not all the students want to continue their education in English speaking countries.

3.3 Problematic grammatical items

The last research question was: which grammatical items are problematic for the students?

It turned out that the students, either from Jakarta or outside Jakarta have the same problems regarding the grammatical items which caused many wrong answers. From the 30 items, there are five items which got less than 50% correct responses.

The question that triggered the most incorrect response was the one relating to agreement after expression of quantity. Let's see the question.

Question 17: Some <u>of the</u> District of Columbia

               A

<u>are</u> <u>on</u> low-lying, <u>marshy</u> ground.

B C   D

The wrong choice for this question is B. *are*, it should be changed into *is*. However, for this question, 172 persons (68.8%) (98 from Jakarta, 74 from outside Jakarta) made mistakes, while 78 persons (31.2%) answered correctly. The problem occurs because the subject of the quantifier can be singular or plural, thus, the verb must agree with the subject. In this sentence, *some* is used for mass noun *District of Columbia*, so it should be considered as singular noun which need *is,* instead of *are.* When asked why they made mistakes in this sentence, some students said that they made wrong judgment because of the expression of quantity *some.* Naturally *some* indicates plurality, so they did not choose B(are) as the incorrect item.

The next problematic item is the question regarding participial or verbal adjective.

Question 10: The sound produced by an object.......in a periodic way involves more than the simple sine wave.

A. It vibrates

B. Vibrating

C. is vibrating

D. vibrates

For this question, 170 persons (68%) made mistakes (98 Jakarta, 72 non-Jakarta). In a complex sentence where several verb-like words occur (produced, vibrate, involves); we have to differentiate which one is the predicate of the sentence and which are not. There should be only one predicate in the sentence, and the others should be changed into verbal adjectives (verb+ed/ing which function as adjective). Thus, the correct answer for question 10 is B *vibrating.* The students interviewed for this question said that they did not know that verbs can function as adjectives. They have never learnt this construction at high school and they never used verbs for any other function. Verbs must function as verbs. So, for them, verb+ing indicates continuous tense and verb+ed indicates past tense.

Another issue is the question regarding the object of preposition as can be seen in the following example.

Question 13: The use of shorthand died out in the Middle Ages because of...with witchcraft.

A. The association was imagined

B. Associate the imagination

C. imagined the association

D. the imagined association

The correct answer for this question is D *the imagined association.* This sentence needs a noun phrase as the object of preposition. Again, the noun phrase *the imagined association* contained the verbal adjective *imagined.* As previously discussed, most of the students did not know that a verb can be changed into an adjective. They still stuck to the notion that verbs should be used as verbs. Another misconception was relating to the structure after *because* and *because of. Because* needs a clause, while *because of* is followed by a noun phrase. That is why, 142 students (78 from Jakarta and 64 from outside Jakarta) still made mistakes for this question. Some of them reasoned that they did not know the difference between *because* and *because of.* For them, both words mean *'karena'.*

The following issue is subject-verb agreement. Let's see the question below.

Question 25:

In <u>many languages,</u> the forms of a word <u>varies</u> to ex

      A   B

press <u>such</u> contrast as number, gender, and <u>tense</u>.

     C   D

Surprisingly, for this question, 132 students (52.8%) made the wrong choice of answer. They failed to notice that the subject of this sentence is *the forms of a word*, which headword *the forms* is in plural form. Thus, it requires a plural verb *vary*, instead of *varies*. The students said that they were distracted by the word *a word* which is adjacent to the verb *varies*. They thought that *a word* is the subject of the sentence which requires a singular verb. Therefore, they did not regard choice B as the answer to this question.

The final problematic question is question no. 30 which also poses the issue of subject-verb agreement.

Question 30:

No one <u>who</u> has studied the Battle of Little Bighorn

       A

<u>know</u> the exact route that Custer and <u>his</u> detachment

  B   C

<u>took</u>.

  D

This question triggered 119 incorrect answers (47.6%). The problem is similar with the previous question. Students were unable to identify the complete subject of the sentence which is *No one who has studied the Battle of Little Bighorn. No one* is considered as a singular noun, so it requires singular verb, which is *knows,* instead of *know.* In a complex sentence which contains several subordinate clauses, it is sometimes difficult to identify the subject and predicate of the sentence. When asked about this question, students admitted that they rarely encountered complex sentences in their high school textbook.

4 CONCLUSION

This study showed that there was a significant difference of grammatical knowledge between the students from high schools in Jakarta and those from outside Jakarta. From this study, we can conclude that schools in Jakarta provide better English lesson than school outside Jakarta, thus students from Jakarta were more prepared to learn English in university level. However, regarding the grammatical items that causes difficulty, both Jakarta and non-Jakarta students had trouble regarding the subject verb agreement, verbal adjectives, and object of preposition.

Besides determining the English level of the students, the findings of this study can also be used to prepare learning materials for English in the university. For further research, the data from the entry test can be compared with the post test result to discover whether the teaching method is applicable and effective in teaching English to university students.

REFERENCES

Al-Ansari, S.H. & Al-Musawi, N.M. 1999. Test of English as a Foreign Language and First Certi ® cate of English tests as predictors of academic success for undergraduate students at the University of Bahrain. *System* 27: 389–399.

Ayers, J.B. & Peters, R.M. 1977. Predictive validity of the Test of English as a Foreign Language for Asian graduate students in engineering, chemistry, or mathematics. *Educational and psychological measurement* 37(2): 461–463.

Benmostefa, N. 2008. *Types of language tests*, Chetouane, Algeria.

Ehrenberg, R.G., Brewer, D.J. 1995. Did teachers' verbal ability and race matter in the 1960s? Coleman revisited. Economics of Education Review 14: 1–21.

Eide, E.R. & Showalter, M.H. 1998b. The effect of school quality on student performance: A quantile regression approach. *Economics Letters* 58(3): 345–350.

Ellis, R. 1991. Grammar teaching– practice or consciousness-raising. In R. Ellis (eds), Second language acquisition and second language pedagogy. Clevedon: Multilingual Matters.

Ellis, R. 2008. Investigating grammatical difficulty in second language learning : Implications for second language acquisition research and language testing 18(1).

Hanushek, E. 1996. School resources and students performance. In: Burtless, G. (ed.) Does Money Matter? The Effect of School Resources on Student Achievement and Adult Success. Brookings Institution, Washington D.C. 43–73.

Hanushek, E.A. 2005. Economic outcomes and school quality, *Education Policy Series* 4, IEA, Paris.

Jaedun, A. 2011. Benchmarking standar mutu pendidikan. In Bogor: Pusat Penilaian Pendidikan Kemendikbud 1–27.

Kamimura, T. & Ellis, R. 2012. An investigation of the developmental pattern of Japanese EFL students ' grammatical competence 1 18(1): 65–88.

Komaria, O. 1998. The history of English teaching in Indonesia. Unpublished thesis submitted for the degree of M.A. Applied Linguistics (English Language). Atma Jaya Catholic University, Jakarta.

Kunnan, A. J. 2008. Large scale language assessments. In *Encyclopedia of language and education,* 2275–2295. Springer US.

Lauder, A. 2008. The status and function of English in Indonesia: A review of key factors. *Makara, Sosial Humaniora* 12(1): 9–20.

Martirosyan, N.M. 2015. Impact of English proficiency on academic performance of international students 5(1): 60–71.

McKenzie, K., Gow, K. & Schweitzer, R. 2004. Exploring first year academic achievement through structural equation modelling. Higher Education Research and Development 23: 95–112.

McKenzie, K. & Schweitzer, R. 2001. Who succeeds at university? Factors predicting academic performance in the first year Australian university students. Higher Education Research and Development 20: 21–33.

Ranjbar, M. 2012. The relationship between grammatical knowledge and the ability to guess word meaning: The case of Iranian EFL learners with upper intermediate level of proficiency 2(6): 1305–1315.

Richards, J.C. 1985. The context of language teaching. *New York: Cambridge.*

Soepriyatna. 2012. Investigating and assessing competence of high school teachers of English in Indonesia. *Malaysian Journal of ELT Research.*

Part II: Exploring the relationship between the knowledge-based era and TEFL development

ELT in Asia in the Digital Era: Global Citizenship and Identity – Madya et al. (Eds)
© *2018 Taylor & Francis Group, London, ISBN 978-0-8153-7900-3*

When ELF meets BELF: Building business communication into ELF-informed curriculum

Y.J. Yujobo
Tamagawa University, Tokyo, Japan

ABSTRACT: What are the disparities between the rapidly evolving use of English and English taught in Japanese universities? EFL ideology upheld native-speaker (NS) standards for non-NS learner's repertoire by focusing on errors and deficiencies in classroom pedagogy. Emerging out of the realization that most Japanese students will have greater opportunities to interact with other NNS, English as a lingua franca (ELF) -informed pedagogy focuses on communicative and strategic competence without adherence to NS norms. According to Räisänen's trajectory framework, EFL and ELF are still a part of the buildup toward successful communicative effectiveness and intercultural competence in English as a business lingua franca (BELF) (Räisänen 2013, Ehrenreich 2016). This paper argues for inclusion of BELF into ELF-informed curriculum and prepare students with key global competence skills in business English and in deeper learning skills, 21st century skills and communication strategies prior to entering the professional world and produce competent BELF communicators.

1 INTRODUCTION

1.1 *Japan's current dichotomy: EFL vs ELF*

Japanese higher English education presents serious questions on the development of future global human resources. The challenges of the young generations' inwardness and unsuccessful levels of communicative competence traces back to heavily based orthodox assumptions that Anglo-American native speaker (NS) were the only standard model for EFL. However, unnatural use and unattainable NS norms in Japanese university classrooms have developed graduates without any skills. No, success is measured by achieving goals through their "own version of English by cooperatively co-constructing meaning among themselves" (Murata 2016). Smit (2010) defines this version as English as a lingua franca (ELF) and used among outer and expanding circle countries, and inner circle countries as the only choice for common language.

When a Japanese practitioners' choses the road of departure from NS attachment, classes will shift from a literacy-based of EFL focused approach, to a competency based or knowledge-based era due to IT advances and the rapid speed of globalization and mobility of global human resources.

English was once taught with the focus on deficiencies and errors, but now it focuses on adequacies of the interlocutors.

1.2 *Reality of ELF use in Japan*

ELF is used daily in the realistic field of business needs include communicating with others from different language backgrounds (NNS and NS) in a variety of situations, ranging from virtual to actual, which are phenomena very likely to be encountered in the business world (Seidlhofer in Terauchi & Araki 2016). With many manufacturing companies set up in Southeast Asia regions, Murata (2016) reminds educators of the rapidly changing situations of global mobility and diversity of its workforce also in Japan. ELF is not used only outside of Japan but within everyday work as more companies are adopting English as a corporate language especially for written documents and for meetings.

1.3 *Japanese students' inwardness*

Kubota (2016) mentions the implications for education and policy to include a need to critically reflect on the promise of English to seek beyond linguistic accuracy and fluency, and develop dispositional and strategic competence. The reason for this can be linked back to the beginning of the lost decade marking a significant decrease in the popularity of studying abroad by Japanese students and young professionals. Japan experienced a sense of unprecedented stagnation during the lost two decades with the end of bubble economy and not only pushed the country to be inward, but the mindset of the young also became closed (Iino & Murata 2016). Ota (2013) concluded factors of economic recession and reduced expenditures on education per capita, declining birth rate, obstacles to Japanese university entrances and problems of transferring credits, difficulties in joining job hunting interviews, issues of safety, and the inability to successfully utilize their new acquired English skills to get ahead in old-school Japanese corporations.

Data from a survey of newly hired employees show how detrimental these inward notions have hurt Japan's development of global human resources. Yonezawa states that 80% of Japanese companies that have already penetrated in overseas markets are facing a lack of young Japanese global personnel and even more alarming is that in 2013, 58.7% of surveyed newly employed workers (ages 18–26) stated that they preferred to not work overseas. This was an increase from 28.4% taken in the 2004 initial survey. Reasons put forth were the attractiveness of stable domestic labor market and lack of confidence in language ability (65.2%). Also, reasons included uncertainty of overseas life (50.4%) and non-attraction to life in foreign countries (35.5%) among other responses (2014, p. 46).

According to data compiled by the Japanese MEXT (2015) - Ministry of Education, Culture, Science and Technology—Japan placed fifty-fourth out of sixty nations and lingered near the bottom of all Asian nations in the study in terms of language skills not meeting the needs of the enterprises. In the same data, declining numbers of student-aged mobility outbound raised further red flags. Japan had placed forty-first in data which looked at national tertiary-level students studying abroad per 1000 inhabitants.

2 INTRODUCING BELF AND LITERATURE

The term BELF was coined by Louhiala-Salminen and her colleagues (2005) to distinguish business communication via ELF. Consequently, whether or not BELF communication is either success or not is unrelated to the approximation of NS competence. But it is on whether or not they possess high levels of flexibility and strategic competence for coping with global business interactions including communicative challenges (Ehrenreich 2016).

The study of BELF also includes the understanding of the role of L1 and also the learning of the local language of multinational workers as also important to relationship and rapport building. The use of mother tongue, ELF, and local languages of host country are interwoven to build intercultural BELF competencies where bilingual, multilingual or plurilingual speakers accommodate with one another to reach the same goal of successful communication.

The transformation and development from EFL to ELF are only a part of a trajectory framework moving toward integrated and mutual goals for successful communicative effectiveness and intercultural competence in English as a business lingua franca (BELF). The major trajectory of repertoire construction framework describes the moving of the point of reference along a scale from left to right.

On the far left is occupied by EFL and NS point of references of learner repertoire. This idea is summarized by linguistic resources and deficiencies which effect school success. The trajectory then develops into the second point of reference of ELF learners and NNS. This idea includes the ELF user repertoire for interactional resources and language as meaning, and adequacies and not on precision nor grammatical accuracy. Finally, the trajectory on the far right shows the combining of both EFL, ELF communicators toward a BELF point of reference for professional communicative repertoire. This is based communicative abilities, communicative resources, and success in working life (Räisänen in Ehrenreich, 2016).

2.1 Use of BELF in multinational corporations

Research in ELF business settings is still quite a new and limited field. Pioneering work from Louhiala-Saliminen & Kankaaranta (2011, as cited in K. Murata, ed. 2016) analyzed communication research and the role of BELF in global operations in Finland based multinational corporations (MNCs) and German based MNCs observed BELF use as an intercultural hybrid by being dependent with the BELF speakers' linguacultural backgrounds. Thus, "BELF is highly dynamic communicative mode and in a constant state of flux" (Ehrenreich 2013).

Kubota (2016) described an investigation into the role of English and other languages in international business setting. Specifically, Japanese expats working in China, South Korea and Thailand were interviewed and data was collected qualitatively on which language was used for communicating with local staff and customers in meetings. Findings discussed a dispositional dimension of communication that resulted in a range of various affective and attitudinal factors and dependent on the situation.

The role of the L1 or the local language was chosen in small talk, outside formal business talks, as a way to build rapport and create a feeling of togetherness rather than opting to use English which was neither owned by the interlocutors. BELF users in global business communities created a new culture focusing on the genre knowledge of their own specific field of expertise, and the need for shared understanding of communicative knowhow with the mutual goal to get the job done, build relationships, and accommodate to each other.

2.2 Problems in multinational corporations

It is important to acknowledge that not all BELF communication is successful. Several Japanese companies adopted English as the new corporate language, (i.e. First Retailing, Rakuten, and Bridgestone) and board meetings shifting to held in English (i.e. Honda, Nissan, and Toshiba) out of need to diversify the homogeneous workforce, intensify global competition, increase global marketing strategies for its diverse customers around the world, and to globalize the production strategies (Murata 2016). Although this shift is welcomed in multinational corporations, the reality is quite different.

In a large survey of over seven thousand Japanese businesspersons conducted by Terauchi and Araki (2016), findings revealed that their ability to work sufficiently in a foreign country by using English or the local language to communicate with local staff and customers in meetings. Overall, 40.5 percent of the Japanese multinational businesspersons answered that they could use English successfully. Percentages ranged by area and finding found over 90 percent had reported that they were able to work successfully and those who reported somewhat sufficiently in Europe and North America. However, in regions such as Southeast Asia and China, only 76.2 percent and 54.7 percent respectively reported that they were able to use English sufficiently in meetings. This means that a large percentage reported that they were not able to use English at all or had significant difficulty in the region.

What can tertiary education do to better prepare and increase ELF interactions with Asian varieties? This question calls for the very reason why NS based materials are not properly developing global human resources in NNS countries, especially Southeast Asia regions and China.

2.3 MEXT revisions

In Japan, positive pro-active revisions have been more recently set out by The Japanese Ministry of Education, Culture, Science and Technology (MEXT). In the *Course of Study Guidelines for Senior High School,* it states the "need to enhance students' abilities to evaluate facts, opinions from multiple perspectives and communicate through reasoning and a range of expressions, while fostering a positive attitude toward communication through the English language" (MEXT 2009).

Also, MEXT announced another additional revision for elementary school, junior high, and high school to focus on soft skills or three pillars of individual communication skills, thinking skills and expression, and intercultural awareness and development (MEXT 2014). Students require global competence and deeper learning skills in order to confidently maneuver the unforeseen future in ten years from now will include jobs that have not yet been invented. MEXT realizes the need to improve language input from NNS varieties and have launched internship programs and study abroad programs to give Japanese students a chance to work and study in Asia. At the same time, an increase in English as a medium of instruction programs attract Asian students to study in Japanese universities.

3 BUILDING DEEPER LEARNING SKILLS INTO BELF-INFORMED PEDAGOGY

The gap between what is being taught in higher education and what employers want from new hires cause a concern for employability. Success is now valued in the ability to apply one's ability to reach levels of using academic knowledge and transfer it to the real world through problem solving and answering complex questions (Buck Institute of Education 2015).

3.1 Communication strategies

Communication strategies (CSs) are often employed by ELF learners in order to deal with non-understanding, breakdown of communication, and to increase clarity and confirmation of their understanding. Kaur (2014) suggests that teachers should encourage students to pursue understanding through the use of CSs. Some of the examples include collaborative completion of utterances, repetition, paraphrasing, seeking for clarification, checking for understanding, and replacing general terms with more specific terms.

ELF research focuses on the importance of CSs because they are often used to accommodate the other speaker and co-construct meaning for the same goal of successful communication.

In the classroom, students can be pre-taught the CSs and practice them in class. Data by Dimoski and colleagues suggest that the explicit teaching of CSs enabled students to consciously repair non-understanding more effectively and resulted in a positive influence on the perceived ability to use CSs effectively (Dimoski et al. 2016). BELF and ELF speakers and learners find these CSs useful and transferable to real-world because of its intentions of understanding the message.

3.2 Higher order cognitive skills

Suarez-Orozco and Qin-Hilliard claim that "an education for globalization should nurture the higher-order cognitive and interpersonal skills required for problem finding, problem solving, articulating arguments, and deploying verifiable facts or artifacts to substantiate claims (2004)". This can be said for not only for language learners, but also for BELF users.

English language programs especially in Japan need to include deeper cognitive based curricula not at their L2 level of competency by using simplified and non-authentic materials that have been altered by the NS for the NNS. However, students' L1 ability to cognitively relate to the topic is far greater. Too often, EFL materials are set at cognitive levels of their L2, and usually at the expense of passing up a chance to involve the student in interesting, timely, and relevant cognitive challenging materials. However, in a BELF situation, business materials will be authentic and uses non-simplified materials for a L2 businessperson. Thus, the BELF learner is responsible for not only understanding the written English, but to also utilize deeper learning skills and higher order critical thinking skills in order to extract necessary and important information and other BELF related competencies for business success.

In the same way, students should interact with authentic materials and timely materials. In a classroom, these materials (news, journals, and Internet sources) can be pre-taught for vocabulary or read by chunking. However, by giving students a shortened version of an authentic text, will be of further value than an extrapolated EFL simplified classroom English version. Treating students as the young adults and young entrepreneurs that they soon will become will give added value to an English class. Language is not the only skill being taught in the classroom in the 21st Century. All deeper learning and 21st century skills need to be practiced and reflected on as deep learners and as mindful practitioners.

3.3 *Deeper learning skills*

Wagner (2008) reveals deeper learning dispositions address the gaps between what students are learning in classrooms, and what employers expect of them after graduation. Seven of these dispositions are mentioned as the Seven Survival Skills from the Global Achievement Gap which includes critical thinking and problem solving, collaboration across networks, agility and adaptability, initiative and entrepreneurialism, effective oral and written communication, assessing and analyzing information, and curiosity and imagination. These skills are needed by all students whether they are language learners or language acquirers, skills beyond textbook knowledge are necessary skills for work, learning, and citizenship in the 21st century and BELF situations.

3.4 *Other gaps to fill*

Many educators have probably heard of synonymous movements across the United States and abroad with a focus on filling in the missing gaps. Global Achievement Gap (Wagner 2008), 4Cs of 21st century skills (Partnership for 21st Century Skills), Deeper learning beyond 21st century skills (Bellanca 2015), success skills, employability skills, or career and readiness skills are just a few from lengthy list but all point to the need for proactive learning. Not surprisingly, employers commented that all they wanted was newly hired employees who can "just go figure it out"-employees who can be creative problem solvers or innovators (Wagner 2015).

BELF speakers need to be proactive learners and proactive listeners. In a classroom, proactive listening activities can be used to give students a chance to actively negotiate and construct meaning. Proactive comprehension is an approach that transforms traditional forms of listening comprehension activities into dialogic events more reflective of real-world processes (Dimoski et al. 2016).

4 21ST CENTURY SKILLS INTO BELF INFORMED PEDAGOGY

In Japan, the 21st Century Skills have been quickly accepted into many secondary schools to answer the shift in MEXT's policies for communicative curriculum and changes to the National Center Entrance Exam for all public universities and some private colleges and universities. Success is now valued in the ability to apply one's ability to reach levels of using academic knowledge and transfer it to the real world through problem solving and answering complex questions (Buck Institute of Education 2015).

The history of 21st Century Skills begins in 2002 in the United States when a coalition of business leaders and policymakers founded The Partnership for 21st Century Skills to list the skills that were needed for college and career success. The coalition developed a framework to position 21st century readiness skills to better prepare students to be college and career-ready. Executive director of Partnership for 21st Century Skills, Soule (2014) stated that it is easy to see that the standard of excellence cannot be achieved without the 4Cs (critical thinking and problem solving, communication, collaboration, and creativity and innovation.

In Japan, 21st century Skills is becoming synonymous with active learning and project based learning activities. Both project based learning (PBL) and active learning (AL) promised a move away from the stagnant teacher-centered education away from note-taking and memorization of regurgitated facts and brought the students to the center of the classroom. Teachers on board with 21st century skills have transformed their craft of teaching to empower students with applied skills to succeed in jobs that have not yet been created, technologies not yet invented, and problems not yet known (Schleicher 2010).

4.1 *Project based learning and active learning*

PBL is a teaching model that focuses on projects which require students to collaborate, think deeply through critical reasoning and inquiry in response to a relevant real-life challenge and prepares a final presentation on a solution or on a creation of a new idea. This method ends with a presentation and through the process, it employed all of the 21st century skills through collaborative group work and creative and critical problem solving. Eight essential components are necessary for it to be called a PBL. First, it must have a driving question that does not have an immediate answer. It needs to nurture curiosity for sustained inquiry, and be authentic. Students use real resources to go about their research. Student voices and choice are respected. And a reflection and revision are part of the final steps prior to the final recommendations or solutions. It mimics the steps of a real-life challenge used in daily global business.

BELF learners especially in Japan find this as one of the most challenging areas. Problem solving tasks which include many facets and positions can help students to practice and understand the array of different levels in critical thinking.

Active learning and 21st Century Skills must work hand in hand. Without one, the other does not work. Active learning is a methodology to focus on giving students engaging activities and requires deeper thinking about what they are doing. In a task as reading, writing, discussing, or problem solving, there is a level that promotes analysis, synthesis and evaluation of class content (Bonwell & Eison 1991). The main problem with active learning is that students are not ready if they have not been exposed to the 21st century skills.

4.2 *Critical thinking and creativity*

The National Education Association (NEA) (n.d.) states that Americans used to perceive creativity and innovation as secondary, but creativity and innovation are key drivers in the global economy today. Creative thinking according to Partnership for 21st Century Skills (n.d.) is defined with the skills to think creatively, work creatively with others, and the ability to implement innovation.

4.3 *Collaboration and communication*

Collaboration is essential in all academic and business setting in order to improve the ability to work effectively, respectively with diverse teams and to exercise flexibility, willingness, and shared responsibility. The NEA (n.d.) explains how people use 'wisdom of crowds' in the new economy and under the right circumstances, groups are remarkably intelligent, and are often smarter than the smartest people in them.

Communication has measurable indicators and several modes such as receptive communication, written communication (formal essay, formal, informal), and through spoken communication of monologic types such as presentations and dialogic types such as interviews, pair talk, debates, and discussions.

In an ELF-informed pedagogy, Kaur (2014), finds collaborative class work can provide realistic and valuable opportunities for students to practice several different communication strategies. For BELF, this teamwork aspect is also vital. Teamwork is necessary in all aspects of a BELF communicator as all communication is dialogic and monologic events do not give the speaker a chance to use communication strategies as used in real-communication between interlocutors. BELF communication includes all modes of communication in the real world from informal to formal writing, speaking. Students need to know how to choose the appropriate mode and formality when ELF and BELF is being used among the interlocutors.

4.4   *The other Cs*

Trilling and Fadel (2009), categorized the 7Cs by including computer literacy skills, cross-cultural understanding, and career and learning self-reliance. These three extra Cs are valuable to all ELF users, but perhaps most critical is cross-cultural understanding for BELF users.

From a BELF user perspective, cross cultural competence is foremost important when interacting with people from other countries. Cross-cultural competence developed as a concept of analyzing skills and attitudes toward mutual intercultural understanding. Some of the key attitudes for having reached an intercultural competence as a model global human resource would not judge quickly on cultural differences but show interest and take flexible action. Also, that person would be aware of the existence of different values and communication methods on the basis of diversified backgrounds. Finally, the BELF user should recognize the strengths of diverse people with cultural differences as a strength for creating new values through synergetic effect (METI 2010).

5   CONCLUSION

Huitt (1998) claims that we are now in the information age requiring students to focus on 'good thinking' as an important element of life success. Also, this generation no longer can place old standards of simply being able to score well on a standardized test of basic skills, or even university entrance exams. Why? Because knowledge based skills cannot be the sole means by which we judge the academic success or failure of our students. Competency based and employability are how we judge the success of the graduates. In Japan, the English language program is still an English language program teaching components of language. But there is a strong wind of support toward a more practical and communicative pedagogy with an ELF-informed curriculum. Japan's ELF-informed curriculum though needs to meet with the components of what BELF users actually use language for. When ELF meets BELF, a new and ELF-Reformed curriculum will be the next steps in preparing university students to become ELF competent users, and also as BELF competent young employees. It is with hope that the BELF-informed ELF reformed curriculum will begin to build bridges between EFL and ELF and cross over to BELF.

Visions for a more active learning classroom using PBL and critical thinking skills and 21st century skills will provide a more dynamic classroom environment similar to the real challenges. Overall, students will come to an English class for college credit, but will finish the course with mastery in skills of flexibility, tolerance, and intercultural experience and transform from ELF and BELF learners to successful and competent ELF and BELF users.

REFERENCES

Bellanca, J.A. 2015. *DeeperlLearning: Beyond 21st century skills*. Indiana:Solution Tree Press.
Bonwell, C. & Eison, J. 1991. *Active learning: creating excitement in the classroom.*
Buck Institute of Education. 2015. *Research summary: PBL and 21st century competencies.*
business contexts: Key issues and future perspectives. In K. Murata (ed.), *Exploring ELF in Japanese academic and business contexts*: 135–155. London: Routledge.
Dimoski, B., Yujobo, Y.J., & Imai, M. 2016. Exploring the effectiveness of communication strategies though pro-active listening in ELF-informed pedagogy. *Language Education in Asia* 7 (2): 67–87.
Ehrenreich, S. 2016. English as a lingua franca in international
Huitt, W. 1998. Critical thinking: an overview. *Educational Psychology Interactive*. Georgia: Valdosta State University.
Iino, M. & Murata, K. 2016. Dynamics of English communication in an English-medium academic context in Japan: from EFL learners to ELF users. In K. Murata (ed.), *Exploring ELF in Japanese academic and business contexts*: 111–132. London: Routledge.
Kaur, J. 2014. Teaching the effective use of ELF: Insights from research into ELF pragmatics. *WASEDA Working Papers in ELF* 3: 158–168.

Kubota, R. 2016. Language is only a tool: Japanese expatriates working in China and implications for language teaching. In K. Murata (ed.), *Exploring ELF in japanese academic and business contexts*: 156–179. London: Routledge.

Louhiala-Saliminen, L. Charles, L.M. & Kankaaranta, A. 2005. English as a lingua franca in Nordic corporate mergers: Two case companies. *English for Specific Purposes* 24(4): 401–421.

METI. 2010. Global human resource development committee of the industry-academia partnership for human resource development. *Ministry of Economy, Trade and Industry website.* http://www.meti.go.jp/policy/economy/jinzai/san_gaku_ps/global_jinzai.htm.

MEXT. 2009. Koutougakkou gakushuu shidou yoryo (Translation: Study of course guideline for foreign languages in senior high schools) http://www.mext.go.jp/a_menu/shotou/new_cs/youryou/eiyaku/__icsFiles/afieldfile/2012/10/24/1298353_3.pdf.

MEXT. 2014. Gurobaruka ni taioushita eigokyouiku kaikakuno itsutsu no teigen (Translation: 5 points of improvement for Global innovation of English education). *Ministry of Education, Culture, Sports, Science and Technology website.* http://www.mext.go.jpb_menu/shingi/chousa/shotou/102/houkoku/attach/1352464.htm.

MEXT. 2015. The number of japanese nationals studying overseas and the annual survey of international students in Japan. *Ministry of Education, Culture, Sports, Science and Technology website.* www.mext.go.jp/en/news/topics/detail/1372624.htm.

Murata,K. 2016. Introduction: Researching ELF in academic and business contexts. In K. Murata (ed.), *Exploring ELF in Japanese academic and business contexts*: 1–13. London: Routledge.

NEA- National Education Association. n.d. *Preparing 21st century students for a global society: An educator's guide to the four Cs.* http://www.nea.org/assets/docs/A-Guide-to-Four-Cs.pdf.

Ota, H. 2013. Reflection of internal preferences by Japanese students. In M. Yokota & A. Kobayashi (eds), *Daigaku no okusaika to nighongngakusi no osaishiosei: 67–93.* Tokyo: Gakubunsha.

Partnership for 21st Century Skills. n.d. Framework for 21st century learning. http://www.p21.org/our-work/p21-framework.

Räisänen, T. 2013. Professional communicative repertoires and trajectories of socialization into global working life. PhD dissertation: University of Jyväskyla. In K. Murata (ed.), *Exploring ELF in Japanese academic and business contexts*: 1–13. London: Routledge.

Schleicher, A. 2010. The case for 21st century learning. *OECD website.* http://www.oecd.org/general/thecasefor21st-centurylearning.htm.

Seidelhofer, B. 2001. Closing a conceptual gap: The case for a description for English as a lingua franca. *International Journal of Applied Linguistics.*

Seidelhofer, B. 2011. *Understanding English as a lingua franca.* Oxford: Oxford University Press.

Smit, U. 2010. Conceptualizing English as a lingua franca (ELF) as a tertiary classroom language. *Stellenbosch Papers in Linguistics* 39: 59–74.

Soule, H. (2014). The power of the four Cs: The foundation for creating the gold standard in project based learning. *Buck Institute of Education.* https://www.bie.org/blog/the_ power_of_the_4cs_the_foundation_for_creating_a_gold_sta ndard_for_projec.

Suarez-Orozco, M. & Qin-Hilliard, D. 2004. *Globalization: Culture and education in the new millennium.* Los Angeles: University of California Press.

Terauchi, H. and Araki, T. 2016. English language skills that companies need. In K. Murata (ed.), *Exploring ELF in Japanese academic and business contexts*: 180–193. London: Routledge.

Trilling, B. & Fadel, C. 2009. *21st century skills: Learning for life in our times.* San Francisco: Jossey-Bass.

Wagner, T. & Compton, R.A. 2015. *Creating innovators: The making of young people that will change the world.* New York: Scribner Publishing.

Wagner, T. 2008. *The global achievement gap: Why even our best schools don't teach the new survival skills our children need—and what we can do about it.* New York: Basic Books.

Wen, Q. 2012. English as a lingua franca: a pedagogical perspective. *Journal of English as a Lingua Franca* 1(2): 371–376.

Widdowson, H.G. 2016. Competence and capability: Rethinking the subject English. *Exploring ELF in Japanese academic and business contexts*: 213–223. London: Routledge.

Yonezawa, A. 2014. Japan's challenge of fostering "global human resources": Policy debates and practices. *Japan Labor Review* 11(2): 37–52.

ELT in Asia in the Digital Era: Global Citizenship and Identity – Madya et al. (Eds)
© 2018 Taylor & Francis Group, London, ISBN 978-0-8153-7900-3

Indonesian English as a foreign language teachers' instructional curriculum design: Revealing patterns of needs analysis

A. Triastuti
Yogyakarta State University, Yogyakarta, Indonesia

M. Riazi
Macquarie University, Australia

ABSTRACT: Needs analysis in school contexts has not been much researched despite the strategic role of needs analysis in providing essential curriculum development-related information (Brown 1995, Richards 1990, 2001). The present study intended to examine Indonesian English as a Foreign Language (EFL) teachers' patterns of conceptualizations in analyzing student needs. Such patterns were portrayed within a larger study on teachers' conceptualizations of Pedagogical Content Knowledge (PCK) as represented in their instructional curriculum design. A qualitative multiple-case study involving purposive within- and cross-case sampling techniques (Miles et al. 2014, Stake 2006, Yin 2014) was employed to select three experienced and three inexperienced EFL teachers of public junior high schools in the Yogyakarta Province, Indonesia. Sources of data included instructional curriculum design assessments and pre-lesson semi-structured interviews were conducted. The cross-case comparisons revealed that the teachers' patterns of conceptualizations in analyzing needs were characterized by the form and sources of needs analysis.

1 INTRODUCTION

In academic contexts, studies of needs analysis have commonly been conducted within English for Specific Purposes (ESP) and English for Academic Purposes (EAP) programs and predominantly at tertiary level. Research on needs analysis in universities show that needs analysis is conducted along with other strategies for the purpose of refining the design of the ESP/EAP programs (see, e.g., Aliakbari & Boghayeri 2014, Atay & Shoja 2011, Cabinda 2013, Hoang Oanh 2007). The practice of needs analysis at the tertiary level is done more formally and systematically as part of the overall systematic needs assessment commonly in practice at this level. At the school level, however, small-scale needs analysis is done by school teachers through ongoing classroom activities (Tarone & Yule 1989, Richards 2001). Recent studies highlight strategies or procedures and the impact of teachers' analysis on their student needs in the school context (e.g. Hite & Evans 2006, Li 2013, Yoon 2007). Needs analysis in the school context by teachers for instructional purposes is, therefore, limited. Little is known how teachers view and generate their conceptualization of student needs to inform and improve their instruction.

This paper is to present part of a larger study exploring Indonesian EFL teachers' conceptualizations of pedagogical content knowledge (PCK) (Shulman 1987) as represented in their dynamic and multifaceted instructional curriculum development (Graves 2000, 2008). The presented part in this paper elaborates on teachers' conceptualizations in analyzing their student needs for planning their instruction. Graves's (2000) dynamic framework for course development processes was used as the analytic framework to guide the exploration of teachers' conceptualizations of PCK in their instructional curriculum design. The framework, originally consisting of eight course development processes, was adapted and used with five processes: (1) analyzing needs, (2) formulating learning objectives and competence achievement indicators, (3) conceptualizing content and organizing the instruction, (4) developing instructional materials, and (5) assessing student learning. Hence, both Shulman's (1987) conception of PCK and Graves's (2000) framework of course development processes were used to explore teachers' conceptualizations of PCK as applied to analyzing students' needs. Accordingly, teachers' conceptualization of PCK refers to teachers' understanding of content and their transformations of content into particular pedagogical forms or strategies related to their student needs for planning their instruction more effectively.

2 LITERATURE REVIEW

2.1 *Pedagogical Content Knowledge (PCK) and English instructional curriculum development*

Rooted in the general education research, pedagogical content knowledge (PCK) was introduced by Shulman (1987) to illuminate the crucial relationship between content and pedagogy. PCK is viewed as a knowledge category that bridges pedagogical knowledge (PK) and content knowledge (CK). Shulman (1987) advanced the definition of PCK as follows:

> It represents the blending of content and pedagogy into an understanding of how particular topics, problems, or issues are organized, represented, and adapted to the diverse interests and abilities of learners, and presented for instruction. (p. 8)

The intersection of content and pedagogy as stated in Shulman's definition signifies teachers' capability in changing the complex subject matter into "new ways, activities and emotions, metaphors and exercises, examples and demonstrations" (Shulman 1987 13) that are understandable to students.

Along with teachers' growing interest in PCK, research on PCK both in general education and in English Language Teaching (ELT) have expanded. In line with research on PCK in general education, research on PCK in ELT not only examines the development of PCK in classroom practices (e.g. Howey & Grossman 1989, Irvine-Niakaris & Kiely 2014, Liu 2013, Richards et al. 1995, Sanchez & Borg 2014) but also those aspects contributing to the development of PCK as teaching experience (e.g. Asl et al. 2014, Atay et al. 2010, Komur 2010), and teachers' professional development activities (e.g. Huang 2007, Smith & Anagnostopoulos 2008, Walker 2012).

In regard to the interconnection between PCK and English instructional curriculum development, a number of studies on PCK have addressed teachers' development of PCK in classroom practices for teaching such content as grammar (e.g. Johnston & Goettsch 2000, Sanchez & Borg 2014), reading (e.g. Irvine-Niakaris & Kiely 2014), and literature (e.g. Howey & Grossman 1989, Richards et al. 1995). Despite this research, teachers' development of PCK in classroom practices is not yet portrayed within a complex and dynamic instructional curriculum development in which the interconnection between teachers' instructional curriculum development and their knowledge base for teaching is explored. As argued by Deng (2007), "transforming the subject matter" must be done within "a complex curricular endeavour" (p. 290), as explored in the present study on teachers' conceptualizations of PCK within the dynamic and multifaceted instructional curriculum development. The present study, therefore, contributes to the exploration of teachers' transformation of subject matter as they work on their instructional curriculum design.

2.2 *Classification of needs analysis*

Needs analysis began with the works of the Council of Europe (Richterich 1983) and Munby's communicative needs analysis model (Munby 1978) as a formal process for exploring students' needs. Needs are interpreted as "felt needs" and "perceived needs" (Berwick 1989: 55). The former is viewed from the perspectives of learners, and the latter is seen from the perspectives of teachers, schools, and other stakeholders. Berwick (1989) further argued that this classification of felt needs and perceived needs is useful since it locates the source of needs. From another perspective, needs are defined as "necessities", "lacks", and "wants" (Hutchinson & Waters 1987: 55–57). From this perspective, felt needs are realized into students' wants, whereas perceived needs refer to teachers' perceptions or interpretations on students' necessities and lacks. In addition, learner-centered inputs are described as 'subjective needs', while teacher-centered inputs are labeled as 'objective needs' (Richterich 1980 cited in Berwick, 1989: 56, & in West 1994: 4).

On the other hand, Brindley (1989) defined needs as necessities or demands (objective, product-oriented or perceived needs), learners' wants (subjective or felt needs), and the methods for linking the gaps between these two (process-oriented needs). As regards the classification of 'needs' in the current study, we adopted Berwick's (1989: 55) "felt needs" and "perceived needs" as we believe this classification is suitable for describing teachers' patterns of needs analysis in school context. Accordingly, teachers' analysis of student needs will be presented in terms of the forms and sources of needs analysis.

3 METHODS

This study employed a multiple-case study method that involved within- and cross-case study design (Miles, Huberman, & Saldana 2014, Stake 2006, Yin 2014). Details of the study are presented in the next sections.

3.1 *Participants and sampling strategy*

A purposive sampling technique was adopted to select six teachers of public junior high schools (PJHS) in the Yogyakarta Province, Indonesia. The six teachers were drawn from the target population of EFL teachers of PJHS in four regions within the province. These regions comprised three regencies of Kulonprogo, Bantul, Gunungkidul, and one municipality of Yogyakarta.

Three teachers represented experienced and three represented inexperienced EFL teachers of PJHS in the province. The experienced teachers were characterized as certified teachers who had gained teaching experience for a minimum of five years and more, and had passed the National Teacher Certification Program (NTCP). The inexperienced teachers were selected from among uncertified teachers who had less than five years of classroom teaching experience, and were not yet entitled to take the NTCP. Table 1 provides information about the teacher participants, in which their names are pseudonyms.

Table 1.   The profile of the teacher participants.

Teachers	Years of Experience (Counted up to December 2013)	Certification status
Experienced Teachers		
Meri	16 years 10 months	Certified in 2010
Susan	16 years 11 months	Certified in 2009
Sisilia	24 years 9 months	Certified in 2009
Inexperienced Teachers		
Etta	3 years 11 months	Non-certified
Nuri	2 years 11 months	Non-certified
Tria	1 year 5 months	Non-certified

3.2 *Data collection instruments and data collection procedures*

The teachers' conceptualizations of PCK for the process of analyzing needs in this study were assessed by examining their transformations in using their knowledge of students by gathering information about the students' characteristics (e.g. sociocultural background, their level of language proficiency, their interests, and their preferences for particular types of learning activities) and about their future aspirations (e.g. expectations, communicative skills and tasks, target topics and content of texts) from a variety of sources when planning their lessons.

In order to investigate the teachers' patterns of analyzing their student needs, we used instructional curriculum design assessment forms and pre-lesson semi-structured interviews. The instructional curriculum design assessment sheet and the pre-lesson semi-structured interview guidelines were adapted from Graves's (2000) framework of course development processes. The assessment form contained the scale and the descriptors of teachers' conceptualization of PCK in the five processes of instructional curriculum design, including the process of analyzing needs. The semi-structured interviews consisted of thirteen questions to collect teachers' recollections of planning their instruction.

The instructional curriculum design assessments were done by the researcher on the provision of the teachers' lesson plans and the supporting teaching aid. The teaching aid consisted of teaching materials for the lessons either in the form of loose worksheets or systematically designed units, and the media used such as cards, pictures, and samples of additional texts.

The pre-lesson semi-structured interviews were conducted in a mixed mode, in which the teacher participants were free to code-switch between *Bahasa Indonesia* and English. Each interview lasted for 45–60 minutes. The interviews were reasonably similar in length across the six cases, and elicited similar amounts of information from all the participants for the purposes of within- and cross-case comparisons (Cohen et al. 2007). All the interviews were audiotaped and fully transcribed. The interview segments in *Bahasa Indonesia* were translated by the researcher. The accuracy of the translation for the selected interview data segments was verified by the teacher participants. The average pre-lesson interviews were about 3,262 words for the experienced group and 3,658 words for the inexperienced group. Overall, the average of the interviews was 3,460 words.

3.3 *Data analysis*

Data analysis on the assessments was performed by developing matrices including the evidence provided by the teachers for their conceptualizations of analyzing student needs for designing their instruction. The data obtained from the pre-lesson interviews were constantly compared with those gathered from the researcher's assessments of the teachers' lesson plans and the supporting materials they made prior to their teaching sessions. Emerging patterns of the teachers' conceptualizations were identified. Shared and merged findings of the within- and cross-case comparisons of the teachers' patterns of conceptualization were, therefore, generated from the matrices (Stake 2006).

The pre-lesson interview data analysis was done by employing three processes of data analysis. Firstly, the NVivo 10 program was used for coding the data. This was done by segmenting and labeling particular units of meaning in the interview transcripts that were related to the process of analyzing needs (Miles et al. 2014). Inter-coding data checking was done to verify the accuracy of the thematic analysis and the data coding of the pre-lesson interviews. The inter-coding checking by another researcher showed a similarity in which similar codes were attached to the selected data segments of the pre-lesson interviews for the process of analyzing needs. Secondly, the manual content analysis was carried out for extracting the relevant codes and putting them in the matrices (Patton 2002, Saldana 2013, Stake 2006, Yin 2014). The theme-based assertions from the within- and cross-case patterns of conceptualization were then identified. Finally, summative data analysis was undertaken in regards to each participant within the same group of teachers (within-case analysis) and across the two different groups of teachers (cross-case analysis) (Creswell 2013).

4 FINDINGS

4.1 *Within- and cross-case patterns of needs analysis*

Within the process of analyzing needs, the teachers' PCK conceptualizations of their student needs yielded the teachers' perceived student needs and the sources of needs analysis as shown in the following table.

The following sub-sections present the analysis of the teachers' conceptualizations of PCK in perceiving their student needs when designing their instruction based on the 2006 SBC.

4.1.1 *The case of experienced teachers*

The teachers' perceived student needs, inferred from the 2006 SBC, were frequently stated by the three experienced teachers in their pre-lesson interviews (LIs) (Meri, Pre-LI Process 1, Meetings 2–4; Susan, Pre-LI Process 1, Meeting 3; and Sisilia, Pre-LI Process 1, Meetings 1, 3, 4). Their assessment of what their students needed to learn, as required by the curriculum, was reflected in their decision to plan their lessons around the target text types and skills, as stated in the SC and the BC. For example, in the first teaching session, Sisilia planned to explain the use of simple past tense and to provide the examples of sentences in simple past tense, so as to ease her students' understanding of the recount genre. Another example was shown in Susan's plan for her first three teaching sessions. She realized, when she decided to develop the students' speaking skill, that she had to plan the lessons in a way to provide her students with the experience of using the target language expressions:

> So, today I'm going to have assessment on speaking utterances on offering, accepting, and declining things, and also how to ask, to give or to reject things. And I'm going to have students in group presentation. (Susan, Pre-LI Process 1, 3c-d)

Table 2. Within- and cross-case patterns of needs analysis.

Experienced teachers		Inexperienced teachers	
Perceived student needs	Source of needs analysis	Perceived student needs	Source of needs analysis
Learning text types, macro and micro English skills as stated in the standard of competence (SC) and basic competence (BC) of the 2006 School-based Curriculum (SBC)	The 2006 SBC	Having the continuation of the past lessons	Reflections on past teaching experience
Being exposed to relevant learning activities and topics of interest, and having students' learning expectations fulfilled.	Reflections on past teaching experience	Being presented with relevant instructional materials that fit the students' background and life experiences	Teachers' observations
Having the instruction in accordance with the students' background knowledge and their socio-economic background	Teachers' observations	Having clear instructions about classroom learning activities and experiencing activities that helped the students gain more confidence and a sense of learning achievement.	Reflections on past teaching experience
Having the instruction in accordance with the students' level of competence as informed by the students' average school entry scores and their mixed language ability	Teachers' observations		

165

The second shared pattern of the teachers' perceived student needs was having been exposed to relevant learning activities and topics of interest, and having students' learning expectations fulfilled. This pattern derived from the teachers' observation and reflection on their own past instruction (Meri, Pre-LI Process 1, Meeting 3; Susan, Pre-LI Process 1, Meeting 4; Sisilia, Pre-LI Process 1, Meetings 2 & 4). Susan and Meri, for instance, planned more relevant learning activities to embrace their students' learning needs after reflecting back on their past teaching experiences. Reflecting on a writing class that she previously taught, Susan took into account students' constraints in learning writing, which were in lacking confidence and being worried about making mistakes. Therefore, in the fourth teaching session, she planned to assign the students a writing practice task in groups so that the students had a chance to share their ideas and to collaboratively construct meaning on the given topic. In the same manner, Meri prepared a fun activity, i.e. a game, for her students in her third teaching session, as she reflected that the activity of identifying implied information of the text in the second session was hard for the students. The second pattern shared by the experienced teachers is as exemplified in the following interview excerpt:

> So, I make the activities in group first, in pairs actually, and then in groups of four, and then finally they have individual practice. So, in writing sometimes they are stuck on an idea, they don't know what to write, they don't have any idea about what to write, but when I have the activity in groups they will share the idea. (Susan, Pre-LI Process 1, 4e)

Reflecting on her past experience of collecting materials for last year's class, Sisilia found that students were likely to be interested in the topic of 'football'. In her second teaching session, she, therefore, related her previous students' general interest in football to her current teaching of recounts:

> Because I know that some of my students like football. So, I take the material(s) which are essential for their interest. We know that last year I teach (taught) this material also for my students. They said to me that "*Wah kalau pelajaran bahasa Inggris seperti ini mudah sekali*" ("Wow, if the English lesson is like this, it's so easy") (laughing)... they said like that... "*enak*" ("easy"), *mereka senang ya* (they were happy yeah). (Sisilia, Pre-LI Process 1, 2b-c)

Relying on her reflection on the unfulfilled expectations of her students' past learning in her third teaching session, Sisilia decided to continue teaching the listening skill and narrative in the fourth teaching session. She found that her students' learning expectation in the third teaching session was not sufficiently fulfilled because of the time limitation and poor quality of audio recordings.

Having the instruction in accordance with the students' background knowledge and their socio-economic background is the third major pattern shared by the experienced teachers (Susan, Pre-LI Process 1, Meetings 3–4; Sisilia, Pre-LI Process 1, Meeting 4). In the third teaching session, Susan included the students' background knowledge about restaurants in Yogyakarta to support the students' speaking practice:

> *Ya* (Yes), this is on the theme, the context is on the restaurant, but different purpose on the intended text. (Susan, Pre-LI Process 1, 3a-b)

Susan also used the students' background (prior) knowledge of restaurants, constructed in the third teaching session, as the foundation for facilitating the students' learning process in the fourth teaching session. Perceiving the students' needs to learn more oral language (listening and speaking skills) due to their life circumstance of living in a village and getting no English exposure from their parents, Sisilia decided to add more hours to teach the listening skill:

> Yeah, I hope my students will accustom to hear English words. I am sure they almost never hear English at home. They never speak with their parents in English because they never hear English at home. (Sisilia, Pre-LI Process 1, 4a)

Planning instruction based on the students' level of language competence and mixed language ability was made by Meri in her first teaching session and Susan in her second teaching session (Meri, Pre-LI Process 1, Meeting 1; Susan, Pre-LI Process 1, Meeting 2). Meri adjusted her selection of learning materials based on the students' average entry level of competence, as reflected in their entry test scores, in her first teaching session. Whereas, Susan considered the heterogeneity of her students' speaking skills when organizing the student group performances in her second teaching session. She planned to mix the students with less, average, and good speaking skills in one group.

> I think today I will use heterogen in grouping so I hope that students will cooperate the one who has good speaking skill with the one who are not. (Susan, Pre-LI Process 1, 2a-b)

4.1.2 *The case of inexperienced teachers*
The pre-lesson interviews showed that the inexperienced teachers felt each lesson should have been built on and continued from the previous lessons. This was shown from the three inexperienced teachers' reflection-on-action. Reflecting on her first teaching session, Etta perceived her students' need to learn the writing skill in her second teaching session, after they were previously taught the reading skill. In the same manner, Nuri perceived that her students needed to continue learning a different example of recount text, i.e. biography, in her first teaching session. Nuri's perception was informed by her general observation that, in the previous semester, her students had learnt about someone's past experience along with learning particular skills. Nuri continuously used her reflection-on-action to provide other particular linguistic features of recount, such as conjunctions and expressions used in spoken monologue recount, for her third teaching session. She realized that her students had learnt past tense as the main linguistic feature of recount in her second teaching session. Finally, in the case of Tria, she perceived the need for her students to learn the writing skill, and a birthday invitation text in her fourth teaching session. This perceived student need was grounded on Tria's consideration that, in their previous class, the students had learnt the reading skill and the same text type. The three inexperienced teachers' reflection-on-action for perceiving their student needs was as exemplified below:

> I use my previous teaching experience to this students in which I know that they already learn about recount text, so that we can continue it. I already told them or the students already learn about past tense. So, here I did not talk more about past tense, but directly here today I move to the use of conjunction and also some expressions used in oral expression. (Nuri, Pre-LI Process 1, 3a-b)

Attempting to accommodate the students' life experiences, Etta integrated their perceived life experience of going camping into a particular model text for teaching recount in her fourth teaching session. She also accommodated the students' background knowledge on such famous tourism destinations as Yogyakarta and Bali in the model texts, for teaching the same text type in her third teaching session (Etta, Pre-LI Process 1, Meetings 3–4). Whereas, to relate the students' sociocultural background and their life experience to the instruction, Nuri planned to present some pictures of local tourism spots in Yogyakarta in her second teaching session, and a series of pictures of going camping for teaching recount in her fourth teaching session (Nuri, Pre-LI Process 1, Meetings 2–4). In order to accommodate students' daily life experiences, Tria integrated topics on healthy habits, such as eating fruit, washing their hands, or brushing their teeth, and going to a birthday party, into the model texts (Tria, Pre-LI Process 1, Meetings 1–3).

> Yes, uumm... I relate this topic, this healthy habits with our daily routines, I mean uumm... at school or at home, the students must be aware of their health about being healthy and umm... I believe that most of them eemm... are diligent to washing their hand to wash their hands to do the... to brush their teeth or to comb their hair or change their clothes. So, uumm... I have related this topic with their daily routines, their daily activities. (Tria, Pre-LI Process 1, 2a-b)

Meanwhile, concerning providing clear instructions, by reflecting on her first teaching session, Etta realized that the students did not actively participate in the class discussion she managed. She predicted that her instructions were probably not clear enough, so she planned to provide clear instructions in managing a group activity for her second teaching session. Resulting from her reflection on her first and third teaching sessions, Nuri perceived that her students needed to obtain more confidence in their learning. Therefore, for her second and fourth teaching sessions, she prepared such interactive activities as a role play and a chain story for her students to better express themselves in practicing monologue recount. Activating her reflection on her students' difficulty in completing the given activity in her third teaching session, Tria perceived the need for her students to develop a sense of learning achievement, providing another doable activity, to explore the generic structure of birthday invitations in her writing class for her fourth teaching session. Tria considered that the activity of choosing suitable details for completing the parts of a birthday invitation was more easily completed by her students in her fourth teaching session. The teachers' attempts to accommodate such students' perceived needs were as reflected in the sample of the interview statement below.

> ... and today, I want my students to be able to write, the skill is on writing. I relate my today's lesson plan with the previous one because I still bring the same and maybe some other new examples of invitation cards. And I will still remind them about main parts of invitation texts and the language focus is still the same. Looking back to my experience, today I will bring a filling-in blank (paragraph) activity because choosing words, choosing some suitable words are easier for my students in my own opinion... (Tria, Pre-LI Process 1, 4b)

5 DISCUSSION

As the findings of the study revealed, both the experienced and inexperienced teachers drew on three sources to conceptualize "student perceived needs" (Berwick, 1989, p. 55). These sources included:

1. the 2006 SBC,
2. the teachers' reflections on their past teaching experience, and
3. their observations of their students' socio-educational context

As related to the 2006 SBC, the experienced teachers explicitly stated their intention, in their pre-lesson interviews, to accommodate the students' learning needs to learn text types and develop macro and micro English language skills as indicated in the SC and BC of the 2006 SBC. In the case of the inexperienced teachers, although such intention was not explicitly stated in their interviews, the inexperienced teachers' instructional curriculum design referred to the SC and BC of the 2006 SBC. The experienced and inexperienced teachers' intention to refer to the 2006 SBC was also shown when they observed and attended to the aspects of their students' social, economic, and cultural background, and incorporated such aspects into their instructional curriculum design.

Both the experienced and inexperienced teachers were found to reflect on their past teaching experience in order to perceive their students "felt needs." Their reflections-on-action (Schon 1983, Gebhard & Oprandi 1999) led them to make necessary changes and adjustments in their instructional curriculum design, based on the students' learning needs they perceived. However, the evidence on the teachers' conceptualizations of student needs analysis showed that, compared to the experienced teachers, the inexperienced teachers were more consistent in drawing perceived student needs from their previous classroom practices as the primary sources that provided "immediate perceptions" (Richards 2001: 53) about their student needs. The inexperienced teachers' reflections were, therefore, concerned with providing what their students needed in their future instruction, such as the continuation of the lessons, the relevance of the materials, activities and procedure, to best facilitate student learning. For this reason, the inexperienced teachers' perceived student needs were more informed and validated, in being captured from their ongoing classroom activities as their primary source of needs analysis (Graves 2000, Richards 2001). In the case of the experienced teachers, their reflections were occasionally anchored in their past teaching experiences as related to their teaching of the same grade in the previous semester or year. This is exemplified by Sisilia's reflection-on-action for her second teaching session, when she decided to present the topic of 'football' for her students to teach the recount text (Sisilia, Pre-LI Process 1, Meeting 2), and is as shown when in her fourth teaching session, Susan channeled her reflection-on-action to students' common constraints in learning writing (Susan, Pre-LI Process 1, Meeting 4) in her past writing class.

Relating the findings to English language teaching in the Indonesian EFL context, the experienced teachers' tendency to solely perceive their student needs from the SC and BC of the 2006 SBC indicates their strong adherence to the learning needs as formulated in the national EFL curriculum. Such strong attachment is triggered by the tension brought by the National Examination (NE), as also confirmed by the findings of the experienced teachers' conceptualizations in the other processes of instructional curriculum design, which are not reported in this paper.

The contrasting conceptualizations demonstrated by the experienced and inexperienced teachers in this present study also depict two major insights. First, Yogyakarta experienced teachers who had passed the National Teacher Certification Program have not necessarily gained knowledge and skills to conduct their student needs analysis to design effective instruction. Second, Yogyakarta early career teachers are feasibly more capable of perceiving their students' felt needs from their own current classroom activities by developing the sense of being reflective teachers and of incorporating such needs in planning their instruction.

6 CONCLUSION

The present study aimed to explore how school teachers conceptualize their student needs analysis for designing effective instruction. The exploration in this present study is deemed important to contribute to a handful of research on needs analysis in school contexts for instructional purposes. The findings of this present study showed the patterns of the teachers' conceptualizations of student needs analysis, as derived from the form or type of needs analysis and the sources the teachers used in their needs analysis. The cross-case comparisons revealed that the teachers' patterns of conceptualization in analyzing needs were characterized by the following characteristics: 1) the teachers from both groups shared a commonality in terms of drawing "student perceived needs" (Berwick 1989: 55); 2) the student perceived needs were mainly derived from three main sources comprising the national EFL curriculum called the 2006 School-based Curriculum, the teachers' reflections on their past teaching experience, and their observations of their students' socio-educational context; and 3) the teachers' reflections-on-action (Schon 1983, Gebhard & Oprandi 1999) to perceive their student needs differed from the extent to which the teachers' needs analysis was informed by their own ongoing classroom practices, as the primary sources, to accommodate their students' "felt needs" (Berwick 1989: 55, Brindley 1989: 65).

The patterns of the teachers' conceptualizations in analyzing their student needs to inform and improve their instruction, as explored in this present study, raise important concerns that teachers need to make use of other, varied primary sources to gain immediate perceptions about their student needs (Richards 2001). Teacher training programs need to equip teachers with knowledge of, and in particular skills in, the variety of small-scale needs analysis by means of their classroom activities (Richards 2001), and how they can be an effective catalyst for accommodating their student needs by taking into account students' felt needs as well as students' perceived needs (Hite & Evans 2006, Li 2013, Nunan 1988, Richards 2001, Yoon 2007). Referring to the sources of needs analysis that the teachers in the present study used, the teachers were mostly able to perform reflection-on-action or reflection-in-practice (Schön 1983). Therefore, it is important for pre—and in-service teachers in Indonesia to be trained to operate their reflection-on-action, and in particular their reflection-in-action, as effective ways to gather information about their student needs from their ongoing classroom activities. By systematically employing formal or informal techniques of needs analysis, and complementing the adopted techniques with a reflective attitude that involves contextual constraints, teachers, therefore, enable themselves to turn their needs analysis into more comprehensive needs analysis, called needs assessment (Graves 2001).

REFERENCES

Aliakbari, M. & Boghayeri, M. 2014. A needs analysis approach to ESP design in Iranian context. *Procedia—Social and Behavioral Sciences* 98: 175–181.

Asl, E. S., Asl, N. S. & Asl, A. S. 2014. The erosion of EFL teachers' content and pedagogical content knowledge throughout the years of teaching experience. *Social and Behavioral Sciences* 98: 1599–1605.

Atay, D., Karlioglu, O. & Kurt, G. 2010. The pedagogical content knowledge development of prospective teachers through an experiential task. *Social and Behavioral Sciences* 2: 1421–1425.

Atay, M. R., & Shoja, L. 2011. A Triangulated study of academic language needs of Iranian students of computer engineering: Are the courses on track? *RELC Journal* 42(3): 305–323.

Berwick, R. 1989. Needs assessment in language programming: From theory to practice. In R. K. Johnson (Ed.), *The second language curriculum* (pp. 48–62). Cambridge, UK: Cambridge University Press.

Brindley, G. 1989. The role of needs analysis in adult ESL programme design. In R. K. Johnson (Ed.), *The second language curriculum* (pp. 63–78). Cambridge: Cambridge University Press.

Brown, J. D. 1995. *The elements of language curriculum.* New York: Heinle & Heinle.

Cabinda, M. 2013. The need for a needs analysis at UEM: Aspects of and attitudes towards change. *Linguistics and Education* 24: 415–427.

Cohen, L., Manion, L. & Morrison, K. 2007. *Research methods in Education* (6th ed.). NY: Routledge.

Creswell, J. W. 2013. *Qualitative inquiry and research design: Choosing among five approaches* (3rd ed.). CA: Sage Publications, Inc.

Deng, Z. 2007. Transforming the subject matter: Examining the intellectual roots of pedagogical content knowledge. *Curriculum Inquiry* 37(3): 279–295.

Gebhard, J. G. & Oprandy, R. 1999. *Language teaching awareness: A guide to exploring beliefs and practices.* Cambridge: Cambridge University Press.

Graves, K. 2000. *Designing a language course.* Boston: Heinle & Heinle Publishers.

Graves, K. 2001. A framework of course development processes. In D. R. Hall & A. Hewings (Ed.), *Innovation in English Language Teaching* (pp. 27–45). London: Routledge.

Hite, C. E. & Evans, L. S. 2006. Mainstream first-grade teachers' understanding of strategies for accommodating the needs of English language learners. *Teacher Education Quarterly* 89–110.

Hoang Oanh, Duong Thi. 2007. Meeting students' needs in two EAP programmes in Vietnam and New Zealand. *RELC Journal* 38(3): 324–349.

Howey, K. R. & Grossman, P. L. 1989. A study in contrast: Sources of pedagogical content knowledge for secondary English. *Journal of Teacher Education* 40: 24–31.

Huang, Yi-Ching. 2007. How teachers develop their professional knowledge in English study group in Taiwan. *Educational Research & Review* 2(3): 036–045.

Hutchinson, T. & Waters, A. 1987. *English for specific purposes.* Cambridge: Cambridge University Press.

Irvine-Niakaris, C. & Kiely, R. 2014. Reading comprehension test preparation classes: An analysis of teachers' pedagogical content knowledge in TESOL. *TESOL Quarterly* 0(0): 1–24.

Johnston, B. & Goettsch, K. 2000. In search of the knowledge base of language teaching: Explanations by experienced teachers. *Canadian Modern Language Review* 56(3): 437–468.

Komur, S. 2010. Teaching knowledge and teacher competencies: A case study of Turkish pre—service English teachers. *Teaching Education* 21(3): 279–296.

Li, N. 2013. Seeking best practices and meeting the needs of the English language learners: Using second language theories and integrating technology in teaching. *Journal of International Education Research* 9(3): 217–222.

Liu, S. 2013. Pedagogical content knowledge: A case study of ESL teacher educator. *English Language Teaching* 6(7): 128–138.

Marshall, C. & Rossman, G. B. 2011. *Designing qualitative research* (5th ed.). CA: Sage Publications, Inc.

Miles, M. B., Huberman, A. M. & Saldana, J. 2014. *Qualitative data analysis: A methods sourcebook* (3rd. ed.). CA: Sage Publications, Inc.

Munby, J. 1978. *Communicative syllabus design*. Cambridge: Cambridge University Press.

Nunan, D. 1988. *The learner-centered curriculum*. Cambridge: Cambridge University Press.

Patton, M. Q. 2002. *Qualitative research & evaluation methods* (3rd ed.). CA: Sage Publications, Inc.

Richards, J. C. 1990. *The language teaching matrix*. Cambridge: Cambridge University Press.

Richards, J. C. 2001. *Curriculum development in language teaching*. Cambridge: Cambridge University Press.

Richards, J. C., Li, B. & Tang, A. 1995. A comparison of pedagogical reasoning skills in novice and experienced ESL teachers. *RELC Journal* 26(1): 1–24.

Richterich, R. 1983. *Case studies in identifying language needs*. Oxford: Pergamon.

Saldana, J. 2013. The coding manual for qualitative researchers. London: Sage Publications, Inc.

Sanchez, H. S. & Borg, S. 2014. Insights into L2 teachers' pedagogical content knowledge: A cognitive perspective on their grammar explanations. *System* 44: 45–53.

Schon, D. A. 1983. *The reflective practitioner*. London: Basic Books.

Smith, E. R. & Anagnostopoulos, D. 2008. Developing pedagogical content knowledge for literature-based discussions in a cross-institutional network. *English Education* 41(1): 39–65.

Stake, R. E. 2006. *Multiple case study analysis*. NY: the Guilford Press.

Tarone, E. & Yule, G. 1989. *Focus on the language learner: Approaches to identifying and meeting the needs of second language learners*. Oxford: Oxford University Press.

Walker, E. 2012. Literacy-oriented pedagogy in the advice of experienced language teachers as prospective practicum assessors. *Pedagogies: An International Journal* 7(2): 182–198.

West, R. 1994. Needs analysis in language teaching. *Language Teaching* 27(01): 1–19.

Yin, R. K. 2014. *Case study research: Design and methods* (5th ed.). CA: Sage Publications, Inc.

Yoon, B. 2007. Classroom teachers' understanding of the needs of English-language learners and the influence on the students' identities. *The New Educator* 3(3): 221–240.

ELT in Asia in the Digital Era: Global Citizenship and Identity – Madya et al. (Eds)
© 2018 Taylor & Francis Group, London, ISBN 978-0-8153-7900-3

Need analysis of English needs of midwifery students in Indonesia

F. Fahriany & N. Nuraeni
Syarif Hidayatullah State Islamic University of Jakarta, Jakarta, Indonesia

ABSTRACT: The emergence of English for Specific Purposes (ESP) teaching approach has been in response to be English language needs of learners in accordance with their profession or job description. This paper focuses on the importance of considering students' needs and objectives from the ESP courses of the midwifery students in Indonesia. Some graduates of the ESP program are willing to work at the international hospitals and will be required to communicate in English for being a midwifery. This paper reports on the process of identifying the target needs of ESP for midwifery students. The finding shows that the lecturer is enabled to choose those kinds appropriate techniques and methods in teaching ESP for midwifery students.

1 INTRODUCTION

English for Specific Purposes (ESP) is understood as preparing learners to use English within academic, professional, or workplace environments. Furthermore, the first step in an ESP course design is a need analysis. It is also known as needs assessment. On the other hand, it has a vital role in the process of designing and carrying out any language course, whether it is English for Specific Purposes (ESP) or general English course. Sifakis (2003) argues that "If we had to state in practical terms the irreducible minimum of an ESP approach to course design, it would be needs analysis".

The key stage in ESP (English for Specific Purposes) is needs analysis. Needs analysis is the corner stone of ESP and leads to varied focused course (Mazdayasna 2008). According to Tzotzou (2014), "needs analysis is generally regarded as critical to ESP, although ESP is by no means the only educational enterprise which makes use of it". Sifakis (2003) argue that any language course should be based on needs analysis. Needs analysis is fundamental to an ESP/EAP approach to course design (Basturkmen 2013).

It is obvious that needs analysis is a very crucial first step on designing and developing a language course, producing materials for teaching and learning, and developing language test. Harwood (2005) states that language needs analysis is essentially a pragmatic activity focused on specific situations, although grounded in general theories, such as the nature of language and curriculum. Therefore, in the ESP context, needs analysis is crucial in determining the aspects of language that are important for a particular area of teaching.

Needs Analysis is very important before designing teaching materials for English for Specific Purposes. This study is aimed to explore the learning needs of midwifery students. Needs Analysis in this study is categorized as Target situation Analysis, Present Situation Analysis, Deficiency Analysis, Strategy Analysis, Constraint Analysis, Pedagogic Need Analysis, and Subjective Need Analysis (David 2013).

This study will have differences among the previous studies. Although this study will focus on needs analysis, it will use a comprehensive concept of needs analysis which is proposed by Brindley (2009), to gain the information about learners' needs in order to develop a tentative syllabus and speaking materials for midwifery students.

2 METHOD

This research was classified into a qualitative research. Then, a case study design was employed to conduct this research. The case is based on the general assumption that English language teaching at university level is considered as ESP and needs analysis is a crucial part but it seems to be neglected. The research was conducted at the *Sekolah Tinggi Ilmu Kesehatan*: Higher Education of Health Widya Dharma Husada South Tangerang Jakarta, Indonesia.

The subject of the research is the first-semester students of midwifery program at the *Sekolah Tinggi Ilmu Kesehatan*: Higher Education of Health Widya Dharma Husada Indonesia, the alumni, the English lecturers and the head of midwifery program. To collect the data of this research, the writer took thirty midwifery students who were given question-naires about their needs and wants in learning English. Then, five alumni who were inter-viewed to know what language skills they needed in their workplaces.

In addition, several techniques were employed in collecting the data as follows: (a) inter-view, (b) questionnaire, and (c) documentation. It was in line with Cresswell, stating that we can see the varied nature of qualitative forms of data when they are placed into the follow-ing categories: observations, interviews and questionnaires, documents and audio materials (Cresswell 2012: 212).

3 RESULT

3.1 *Method of teaching English for midwifery*

Based on the interview with the English lecturers and students, they assumed that the meth-ods were repeated. The lecturers often applied the drilling technique in presenting English materials before practicing the conversation on hand out. Then, the students were encour-aged to read the dialogues and then performing in front of the class one by one. The lecturers asked the students to translate, to do exercise given and read dialogues. Besides, the teacher seemed to be the central in teaching and learning process and the students only received what the lecturers taught. The midwifery students assumed that they needed an appropriate method that used in teaching and learning process, the method that encouraged them to be more active and to be the centered of learning process.

3.2 *Personal information about the learners*

Many factors that could influence the students' way in learning such as wants, means, and subjective needs. In this section, the researcher gave the questionnaires to the students. In addition, the other factors were about the personal information about the learners included their background information, their purposes of learning English, their learning preferences, their attitude towards the English language. Thus, the students' responses in both quantitative and qualitative descriptions. The personal information of students presented some aspects,

Table 1. Students' personal information.

Age	16–18	23.30%
	19–21	76.70%
	22–24	0%
Studied English previously	Yes	100%
	No	0%
Make an effort to improve English	Yes	80%
	No	20%
Frequency of Practicing English outside schools	Not at all	23.30%
	1–2 hours	76.70%
	3–5 hours	0%

Table 2. Students' attitude towards the English language.

Subject	Very important	Important	Less important	Unimportant	Very Unimportant
English	76.70%	23.30%	0%	0%	0%

for instance, age, previous English competencies, making an effort to improve English, frequency of practicing English outside schools). The data would be presented on the Table 1:

Based on Table 1 above, it indicated that the category of midwifery students' age was divided into three categories and the dominant percentages of students' ages was on the category of 19–21 years old, totally 76.70%. Most of them were the fresh graduates from senior high schools who continued their study in midwifery academy. Then, all of the midwifery students had studied English before, as long as they graduated from senior high schools. They learned English in their schools. While the frequency of practicing English outside the school was around 76.70% at 1–2 hours, here some students took an English course, watched movies and listened to the English songs.

3.3 *Students attitude towards English*

The student's attitude towards the English language presented in the Table 2:

Based on Table 2, the students were asked about their consideration of the English subject. Most of students regarded English as the most important (76.70%) and important (23.30%). It showed that the students had given weight to the English subject. Based on the interview of some students, they stated that there were several reasons about the importance of English. Firstly, they considered that English as the international language. Secondly, they needed to learn English to compete after their graduation. It is in line with the interview results of the head of midwifery program and English lecturers. Finally, they intended to work in International Hospital.

3.4 *Students' English proficiency*

The students' opinion about their English proficiency can be seen clearly in the Chart 1:

The students were also asked to evaluate their own English ability. Based on the chart above, it illustrated that the midwifery students had a lower belief in their English ability. Most of them had leveled themselves that they were satisfactory (66.70%), poor (26.70%) and good (6.70%) ability of English. It was in line with the interview conducted with English lecturers who said the English proficiency of midwifery students were varied. It ranged from good, satisfactory and poor. He assumed that the proficiency variety was caused by the differences of the high school graduation. Some of students came from good schools but some others came from various senior high schools in remote areas.

3.5 *Purpose of learning English*

The purposes of learning English may vary with different people. The researched midwifery students were found to have different purposes of learning English, which include include for studying on other subjects, interacting with other people, preparing for a future career, and reading medical articles. The data are presented in the Table 3:

The students were also asked their preferred situations of learning English. It could be seen that the students preferred to learn English and use the language for their future careers. Based on the interview, some students were going to work at the international hospital. Therefore, English is very important to be mastered. Hence, they needed to be more familiar with English in midwifery terms. The lecturers assumed that he always gave such motivation to the students in order to learning English well as the basic aspect for them to use in their future careers.

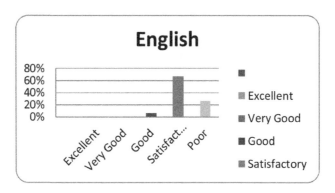

English

Chart 1. Students' English proficiency.

Table 3. Purpose of learning English.

Study other subject	13%
Interact with people	13%
Use in my future career	67%
Read medical article	7%

3.6 *Weaknesses in learning English*

The weaknesses in learning English could be explained by the students' lower skills in the grammar mastery, vocabularies building, pronunciation, speaking skill, listening skill, reading skill, and writing skill. Those problems became the weaknesses in learning English for midwifery students. Moreover, the comparison for each skill could be identified clearly in the chart below:

Based on the chart, the highest percentage of students who thought English less difficult than others showed about 46.7% in the use of English grammar. Furthermore, most of the midwifery students thought be difficult in learning English showed about by 46.7% in the vocabularies mastery. On the other hand, The midwifery students thought difficult in English pronunciation showed as well by 43.3%. From the chart above, it can be concluded that 60% students had low ability in speaking skill and it caused the difficulties in communicate in English. Finally, pronunciation skill, vocabularies building, and shyness could be referred to the reasons that caused the midwifery students difficult in learning English.

Also, some students found many unfamiliar vocabularies in English, especially in midwifery terms. Some respondents felt difficult to pronounce the words and sentences because English has different forms about how to pronounce and how to write the words or sentences. The second reason was about vocabulary mastery. The students were difficult to learn English because lack of vocabularies. It was argued that vocabularies being one of English micro skills that was very important for all of the English skills. The last reason was about the shyness. The respondents feel shy to speak English. Therefore, they were hesitate in giving their opinion or ideas. In this case, some students considered that they needed to have high confidence and much practices to increase their speaking ability.

3.7 *Needed skill in learning English for midwifery students*

The needed skills in English required four English basic language skills such as speaking, listening, reading and writing. Those skills became the most important skill to learn in English for midwifery students. The data about the needed skills in learning English for midwifery students were presented in the Table 4:

Referring to the Table 4, it could be concluded that the needed skill is speaking. The midwifery students needed to learn speaking skill while the reasons are varied. However, it was

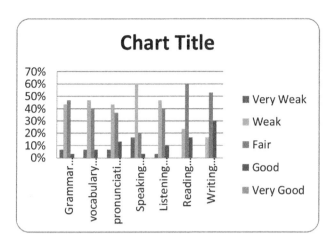

Chart 2. The students' weaknesses in learning English.

Table 4. Needed skill in learning English for midwifery students.

Skills	Very important	Important	Less important	Unimportant	Very Unimportant
Speaking	43.3%	53.3%	3.3%	0%	0%
Listening	10%	36.6%	53.3%	0%	0%
Reading	0%	36.6%	53.3%	0%	0%
Writing	3.3%	30%	53.3%	10%	3.3%

classified into three dominant reasons. Firstly, speaking was very important for the students and they were willing to be able to speak English naturally. The respondents stated that the benchmark of English mastery was speaking skill. Secondly, the students were willing to speak English naturally. Because some of midwifery students wanted to work in international hospital, it meant that they needed to be able to communicate English naturally. Therefore, speaking skill helps them to socialize in their workplace. Therefore, it was in line with the result of alumni interview.

3.8 *Activities needed in the classroom*

Based on the writers' observation, there were five activities that needed in the classroom. For instances, pair work, whole class, group work, individual, and out of the class. Those activities could become the expected activities in the class for midwifery students. Here are the attractive and communicative activities that could be implemented in the classroom activities. The data were presented in the Table 5:

It could be demonstrated from the table above that the midwifery students strongly agreed in doing pair work activities (56.60%). The activities could be modified to stimulate the midwifery students in learning English while role play activities should be varied. Those activities were needed by the midwifery students in order to adapting the hospital or maternity clinic situations.

3.9 *Materials needed*

Referring to the interview, the midwifery students would get the appropriate material based on their field. Therefore, the midwifery topics were more valuable. Then, vocabularies building were also more specific. There were some midwifery terms should be mastered by the

Table 5. Needed activities in the class.

Activities	Strongly agree	Agree	Neutral	Disagree	Strongly disagree
Pair work	56.60%	33.30%	10%	0%	0%
Whole Class	30%	43.30%	26.60%	0%	0%
Group Work	3.30%	13.30%	30%	40%	0%
Individual	6.60%	23.30%	33.30%	20%	0%
Out of the Class	13.30%	43.30%	40%	3.30%	0%

Table 6. Needed materials.

Topics	Strongly agree	Agree	Neutral	Disagree	Strongly disagree
Greeting and introducing	46.6%	36.60%	16.60%	0%	0%
Midwife's Schedule	26.6%	46.60%	26.5%	0%	0%
Parts of the Human Body and Health Problem	3.30%	73.30%	23.3%	0%	0%
Asking and Giving Direction in Hospital	26.60%	46.60%	26.60%	0%	0%
Admission in Maternity Clinic	16.60%	40%	36.60%	6.60%	0%
Sign and Symptoms of Pregnancy	16.60%	63.30%	20%	0%	0%
Personal Hygiene during Pregnancy	10%	70%	20%	0%	0%
Balanced Diet during pregnancy	20%	50%	26.60%	3.30%	0%
Checking Vital Sign	20%	50%	30%	0%	0%
Component of Labor	43.30%	40%	16.60%	0%	0%
Stages of Labor	10%	66.60%	23.30%	0%	0%
Post-Partum	23.30%	43.30%	26.60%	6.60%	0%
Newborn Baby Care	43.30%	40%	16.6%	0%	0%
Family Planning and Reproductive Health Counseling	36.60%	36.60%	20%	6.60%	0%

students to support their career as a midwife or to continue their study in post graduate. Furthermore, the materials also provided the grammar and pronunciation. Then, the topics were chosen concerning the pregnancy and elaborating them with the skills, which should be achieved with grammar and vocabulary focus. The data were presented in the Table 6:

4 DISCUSSION

As the objective of this research, it is designed to fulfill the specific needs of the learners (Tomlinson 2011). It is originated to fulfill the demand by many learners around the world who needed to learn English to have access to science, technology and economical resources. A needs analysis is also known as needs assessment. Furthermore, it has a vital role in the process of designing and carrying out any language course, whether it is English for Specific Purposes (ESP) or general English course. "Needs analysis is the process of establishing the "what and how" of a course". From the findings above, it can be summed up that the midwifery students at STIKES Widya Dharma Husada Pamulang Indonesia needs. Firstly, the standard facilities for learning process and some of midwifery students hope language laboratory will be available to improve their English ability and avoid boredom in using one classroom. Then, the creative lecturer is needed to teach them, not only experience in teaching ESP but also the teacher who consider about students need. the lecturer should provide the appropriate methods for them, considering the main objective of the course is to develop the students' abilities in using English for communicative purposes and their future professional needs. Therefore, a key question for the teacher is finding materials and methodologies which are effective for a particular class. A good method can help the students in comprehending and mastering the lesson. One of the teaching failures is caused by an unsuitable method. As Harmer (2007) stated that "The method used has often been said to be the cause of success or failure in language; for it is ultimately the method that determines the what and the how of language interaction". Then, the objectives of midwifery students to learn English is for the sake of their future career; they have decided their own purpose to learn the language. Therefore, ESP is suitable for them, especially English for midwifery. It is in line with Tomlinson (2011) who points out that English for Specific Purposes (ESP) is an umbrella term that refers to the teaching of English to students who are learning the language for a particular work or study-related reason. As long as they have an ambition to work in international hospitals, so, interacting with patients using English is inenvitable, but they still find difficulty in speaking English. The questionnaire gave information that the students have weaknesses among skills (grammar, vocabulary, pronunciation, speaking, listening, reading and writing) in English.

In addition, all four language skills, which are speaking, listening, reading and writing, are needed in ESP context according to the needs of particular group of learners in the specialized area. One of these skills is sometimes more emphasized than the others. These depend on the objectives of the language course, method of teaching and need of learners. So, English course for midwifery students at STIKES Widya Dharma Husada Indonesia, based on the need analysis profile findings, the skills is emphasized on speaking skill.

Furthermore, they need varied activities such as role play, discussion etc. it is in line with Harmer (2007) states six classroom speaking activities. They are acting from script, communication games, discussion, prepared talks, questionnaires, simulation and role play.

5 CONCLUSION AND RECOMMENDATION

Based on the findings of this study, needs analysis is considered to be the corner stone of English for Specific Purposes (ESP). The concept of need analysis has been different along decades. At the initial stages of ESP (the 1960s and early 1970s), needs analysis consisted in assessing the communicative needs of the learners and the techniques of achieving specific teaching objectives. Nowadays the role of needs analysis is much more complex; it aims at collecting information about the learners and at defining the target situation and environment of studying ESP.

ACKNOWLEDGMENT

We would like to thank the principal, lecturers and all of the first-semester midwifery students from STIKES Widya Dharma Husada, Indonesia for their gracious help in admitting the research. Also, we would like to thank to one of the lecturers of English Education Department at Syarif Hidayatullah Jakarta State Islamic University who has given her suggestions and critics.

REFERENCES

Ahmad, D.J. 2012. Theoretical framework & growing demands of ESP in Saudi Arabia. *Arts and Humanities* 5(5): 114–120.
Alharby, M. 2005. ESP Target situation needs analysis: The English language communicative needs as perceived by health professional in the Riyadh area, (Unpublished doctoral dissertation). Athens, GA: University Georgia.
Ananyeva, M. 2014. A learning curriculum: Toward student driven pedagogy in the context of adult English for Academic Purposes English for Specific Purposes, and Workplace English Programs. *TESOL Journal* 5(1): 8–31.
Basturkmen, H. 2013. *Need analysis and syllabus design for language for specific purposes* in. CA. Chapelle (Ed) The Encyclopedia of Applied Linguistics, Blackwell, Unpaginated.

Brindley, G. 2009. The role of need analysis in adult ESL program design. In R.K. Johnson (ed), The Second Language Curriculum. New York: Cambridge University Press.

Chien, Ching-Ning. 2011. Needs-based analysis of freshman English courses in Taiwan University, *International Journal of Humanities and Social Science* 1(11): 121–224.

Creswell & John, W. 2012. *Qualitative inquiry & research design: Choosing among five approaches.* Singapore: Sage.

Edwards, N. 2000. Language for business: Effective needs assessment, syllabus design and materials preparation in a practical ESP case study. *English for Specifics Purposes* 19: 241–296.

Eslani, Z.R. 2010. Teachers' voice vs students' voice: A needs approach to English for Academic Purposes (EAP) in Iran. *English Language teaching* 3(1): 311.

David, R. hall (ed). 2013. *Need analysis for language course design: A holistic approach to ESP.* Cambridge: Cambridge University Press.

Flowerdew, J. & M. Pencock 2001. *Research perspectives on English for Academic Purposes.* Cambridge: CUP

Gass, J. 2012. Need analysis and situational analysis designing ESP curriculum for Thai nurses. *English for Specific Purposes World* 36 (12).

Hamied, F.A. 2012. *English in multicultural and multilingual Indonesian education, a book chapter.* German: Springer.

Harmer, J. 2007. *How to teach English.* Malaysia: Longman.

Harwood, N. 2005. What do we want EAP teaching for? *Journal of English for Academic Purposes* 149–161.

Huhta, M.K. Vogt, E. Johnson & H. Tulkei 2013. *Needs analysis for language course design: A holistic approach to ESP.* Cambridge: Cambridge University Press.

Hutchinson & Waters. 2007. *English for Specific Purposes.* New York: Cambridge University Press.

Jordan, R.R. 2007. *English for Academic Purposes.* CUP.

McDonough, J. 2004. *ESP in perspective: A practical guide.* London: Jo McDonough.

Mazdayasna, G. 2008. Developing a profile of the ESP needs of Iranian students: The case of students of nursing and midwifery. *English for academic purposes* 7: 277–289.

Sifakis, N.C. 2003. Applying the adult education framework to ESP curriculum development: An integrative model. *English for Specific Purposes* 22: 195–211.

Tomlinson, B. 2011. *Materials development in language teaching* (2nd Ed). Cambridge: Cambridge University Press.

Tzotzou, M.D. 2014. Designing and administering a needs analysis survey to primary school learners about EFL learning: A case study. *Laboratory of Pedagogical Research & Applications* 2(1): 59–82. doi: dx.doi.org/10.12681 /ppej.62.

ELT in Asia in the Digital Era: Global Citizenship and Identity – Madya et al. (Eds)
© 2018 Taylor & Francis Group, London, ISBN 978-0-8153-7900-3

Teachers' accountability in the post-method era: Balancing freedom and responsibility

Sugirin
Universitas Negeri Yogyakarta, Yogyakarta, Indonesia

ABSTRACT: This paper aims to formulate a way of coupling the post-method teachers' freedom with the responsibility it entails. As Kumaravadivelu (2006) claims, educational change is a systemic change involving both challenges and opportunities. The post-method concept allows teachers freedom to take whichever teaching path as long as they are responsible for the achievement of the students' learning outcomes. However, Akbari (2008) re-minds us that the application of the concept is not plausible by novice teachers. Even experienced teachers are not all prepared to accept the concept—to base their teaching on the honest reflection of what aspects have made their teaching effective or unsuccessful. Youssef and Dahmani (2008) even see that institutional policy may hold up teachers' freedom. This paper proposes that English language teachers implement the post-method pedagogic parameters with caution to ensure that their decisions and actions suit the stakeholders' expectations (Levitt, Janta & Wegrich 2008).

1 INTRODUCTION

Within the history the English language teaching methods, from the Grammar Translation Method (GTM) to the Audio-Lingual Method (ALM), the teacher has full control over classroom instruction. The teacher is an authorized instructor who determines what will happen in the classroom, how it will happen, and what the desired outcome will be like. The advent of the Communicative Approach to Language Teaching (CALT) and the Designer Nonmethods (Kumaradivelu 2006) recognizes that learners are human beings, not robots, so that humanizing them is a must. Learners have the right to enjoy services fully in line with their individual interests, values, abilities, and their learning needs, which are certainly diverse. The post-method era allows the teacher freedom to decide what is best to do to achieve the instructional objectives.

This poses a challenge for the teacher who has been accustomed to following the neatly prescribed classroom procedures of the method era. Despite the freedom allowed, as Madya (2013) suggests, changes in teaching methodology or a paradigm shift in language pedagogy do not alter the demand for language instruction. The teacher must be responsible for the achievement of the instructional objectives. This is in line with Nilufer's (2009) claim that when teachers should decide on their own way of teaching, it does not mean that they are completely free in their decision. They have to consider salient principles in carrying out effective lessons. However, Baker (2017) warns us that balancing freedom and responsibility is not easy. One can easily get caught up in freedom and forget the responsibilities attached.

This paper attempts to elaborate the challenges in balancing the teachers' post-method pedagogic freedom with responsibilities it entails to ensure their accountability. This attempt is urgent to avoid misunderstanding of the post-method pedagogic concepts and to provide a guide for their implementations.

2 METHOD

To achieve the aim of the study, the paper presents the shifts of approaches in English language teaching approaches, the concepts of post-method pedagogy with their related challenges, and teachers' accountability as a proposed solution.

3   THE SHIFT OF APPROACHES IN ELT INSTRUCTION

The history of methods in English language teaching (ELT) has shown that the shift from one method to another did not happen by chance. As Brown (2001) neatly elaborates, the Direct Method (DM) succeeded the Grammar Translation Method (GTM) due to the demand for the learners' ability to communicate with people speaking the target language. The DM which emphasized communication in the target language better fitted the need of the learners who wanted to benefit directly from the booming industry which entailed more opportunities in international trade and travel. The DM soon enjoyed popularity in Europe, but it did not gain the same period of support from public education in the US. The Coleman Report published in 1929 concluded that focusing on oral foreign language mastery was considered irrelevant. What the US public school graduates needed was the ability to comprehend reading passages through silent reading and discuss the passages in English. This was the basis for the so-called Reading Method. However, with the advent of the World War, this method did not meet the needs of US soldiers and other related parties who urgently demanded speaking proficiency in the language of their enemies and allies. Hence, they developed a language training program which was later known as the Army Method. After the World War, support from Structural linguists and the Behaviorist psychologists made the method (e.g., pattern drills) theoretically sound—the patterns were based on the work of the Structuralists while the drills (aiming at habit formation) were based on stimulus-response of the Behaviorists. Under the name of the Audio-Lingual Method (ALM), this method gained world-wide acceptance. However, the ALM then received strong criticism from a notable cognitivist, Chomsky.

Chomsky (1965), as reiterated by Nordquist (2017), believed that grammar has recursive rules allowing one to generate grammatically correct sentences over and over. Our brain has a mechanism which can create language by following the language principles and grammar. Hence, language learning is not merely a process of habit formation.

However, Hymes (1972) asserts that communicative competence is not only a matter of generating grammatically correct sentences but also as the ability to use those correct sentences in a variety of communicative situations. Hence, this brings Hymes' sociolinguistic perspective into Chomsky's linguistic view of competence (Bagaric 2007). Within the method history, the teacher' roles have been rigidly prescribed. In the GTM the teacher is an authorized instructor providing texts, glossary and grammar rules, translation practice, and functions as a translation assessor. In the DM the teacher serves as the director of class activities, motivator, error corrector, and learner's partner. In the Reading Method (Blair, Rupley & Nichols 2007) the teacher acts as a reading expert and a reading coach who strategically, in a variety of ways, helps learners to comprehend the texts. In the ALM, one of the teacher's major roles is that of a model of the target language and of an error corrector (Larsen-Freeman, 2000). In the Communicative Approach to Language Teaching (CALT) the teacher's major role is of a facilitator enabling the learners to use the language in the real-world communication. In all these methods, the teacher's roles have been prescribed so that his/her task is making an effort to understand and implement them in the teaching acts. The shift from the GTM, DM and ALM to the CALT is part of the struggle based on the myths of the method concept.

Related to these concerns, Kumaravadivelu (2006) sees the concept of method carrying the myths that (1) there is a best method out there ready and waiting to be discovered; (2) method constitutes the organizing principle for language teaching; (3) method has a universal and a historical value; (4) theorists conceive knowledge, and teachers consume knowledge; and (5) method is neutral, and has no ideological motivation. Richards (2001) already predicted that the quest for the best method would remain a preoccupation of language teaching for the next twenty years. However, in reality there has never been any best method. Hence, Allwright's (1991) contentious talk has slowly but surely and ultimately been applauded, followed by a shift from method to the post-method era.

Pennycook (1989) argues that methods represent interested knowledge and they serve the dominant power structures in society, leading to "a de-skilling of the role of teacher, and greater institutional control over classroom practice." No wonder that Allwright (1991: 1) deliberately gave his plenary paper a contentious title "The Death of the Method" to emphasize "the relative unhelpfulness of the existence of methods".

Rivers (1991) had already pointed out that the different methods listed previously were merely variants of the existing methods with considerable overlap in their theory and practice. What became her concern was the myth surrounding the concept of method. The concern turns more serious when method is defined as "a fixed set of classroom practices that serve as a prescription and therefore do not allow variation" (Bell 2003).

4.1 *Method versus post-method*

It is important to have a clear understanding of the distinction between the concept of method and post-method. While method is defined to "consist of a single set of theoretical principles derived from feeder disciplines and a single set of classroom procedures directed at classroom teachers" (Kumaravadivelu 1994), post-method can be defined as the construction of classroom procedures and principles by the teacher himself/herself based on his/her prior and experiential knowledge and/or certain strategies. In other words, the concept of method involves theorizers constructing "knowledge-oriented" theories of pedagogy and post-method involves practitioners constructing "classroom-oriented" theories of practice (Kumaravadivelu 1994). Therefore, post-method is totally different from the existing methods, emerging as a result of the limitations of the methods and, thus, another method cannot aim to overcome the limitations of the concept of method. Hence, the concept of post-method comes into existence. One of the characteristics of the post-method era is the teachers' autonomy, freedom with attached responsibility.

4.2 *Teachers' autonomy*

While method-based pedagogy relies on *the professional theories*, post-method pedagogy allows freedom for teachers to decide what best to do based on the reflection of their prior knowledge, their experience as teachers as well as their experience as learners. This reflection will allow them to analyze what has made their own learning and their teaching acts successful or fail. As McIntosh (2010) claims, reflection can be used to create depth of knowledge and meaning, both for self and for those practiced upon.

The ability to make reflections will enable them to initiate changes in their teaching, to monitor the effects of the changes made, and to decide what to do next. In other words, post-method teachers are required to generate their *personal theories* of pedagogy, making a decision on what works best to achieve the ultimate goals of the teaching and learning process. Citing Little's (1995) words, Smith (2000) describes teacher autonomy as having a strong sense of personal responsibility for their teaching, exercising via continuous reflection and analysis the highest possible degree of affective and cognitive control of the teaching process, and exploring the freedom that this confers.

However, as Madya (2013) suggests, despite changes in teaching methodology or paradigm shifts in language pedagogy, the demand for language instruction—the achievement of the instructional objectives remains the same and that becomes the teacher's responsibility. However, in achieving the instructional objectives the teacher should no longer rely on top-down teaching prescriptions of the past, the method. He/she has to reflect honestly on what aspects have made the teaching successful or fail Teachers are asked to honestly theorize their practice and implement their theories into practice. This is the core of the post-method concept that has stirred reactions from some authors.

4.3 *Reactions towards the post-method concepts*

A number of authors have argued that lay teachers are not prepared for theorizing their practice and practicing the theory conceived as it is not a simple undertaking. Reiterating Akbari's claim (2008), Masouleh (2012) holds that in the concept of theorizing practice of post-method perspectives, the whole system must be touched upon, not just a teacher as the key feature of post-method. And if it is said there should be an attempt to find an alternative to method, not an alternative method, it is really illogical to imagine that even a novice teacher must seek for it. Responding to this objection, Richards & Rodgers (2001) suggest that applying procedures and techniques developed by others should be an essential starting point for inexperienced teachers. However, as teachers gain more experience, they had better try to develop an individual approach, reflecting their beliefs, principles and experiences. This kind of transition is not only allowed but suggested in the spirit of the post-method pedagogy.

4.4 *The post-method pedagogic parameters*

What is needed in entering this post-method era is the construction of the post-method pedagogy (Kumaravadivelu 2006). For this purpose, he proposed three pedagogic parameters: particularity, practicality, and possibility.

The parameter of *particularity* claims that a meaningful pedagogy must be constructed with a holistic interpretation of particular situations, particular teachers, particular learners, particular learning objectives, etc. A teaching innovation that works well for a particular group of learners in a particular situation may not work for another group of learners in a different situation. A study by Özbilgin & Tannacito (2011) shows the need to encourage teaching sensitive to the particularities of aim, student, and milieu.

The parameter of *practicality* suggests the shift of the teaching foundation from top-down professional theories to bottom-up personal theories which demands teachers to develop their own theories gained from theorizing their own teaching practice and learning experience. They are required to reflect on their practice and using their insights and intuition to act on what is considered to best serve the achievement of the instructional goals. McIntosh (2010) claims that reflection and reflexivity through recognizing their inherent qualities is central to becoming a practitioner-researcher. In this regard, Richards & Rodgers (2001) suggest that applying procedures and techniques developed by others should be an essential starting point for inexperienced teachers. However, as teachers gain more experience, they had better try to develop an individual approach, reflecting their beliefs, principles and experiences. In other words, they need to develop their own theories of successful instruction. These theories are needed as theoretical perspectives can provide consistency in their efforts (Lafortune et al. 2009). Lafortune & Deaudelin (2001) suggest that in order to bring about change, the persons involved should work in collaboration so that each can contribute to developing the collective model. This will build the sense of ownership so that each will adapt it to his or her own way of achieving the instructional goals.

The parameter of *possibility* demands the understanding of what is possible from both the internal and external factors of the teachers and the learners. This parameter recognizes how the teachers and learners are brought up, which social, economic, and political environment they are in. Teachers' ideal conception of teaching must consider whether the environment allows them to practice what they conceive. Teachers are required to be creative but they must also be sensitive towards the existing situations so that their creativity is acceptable. However, in the 1960s when English language teaching meant to consider learners' motivation, the atmosphere had not allowed so that teachers still focused on how learners learned (Richards 2001). This illustrates how teachers' accountability is being tested.

5 SEARCHING FOR A SOLUTION THROUGH THE DEVELOPMENT OF TEACHERS' ACCOUNTABILITY

Following Bovens (2005), Levitt, Janta & Wegrich (2008) define accountability as the methods by which the actor may render an account (i.e. justify their actions and decisions) to the stakeholders and by which the stakeholders may hold the actor to account (i.e. impose sanctions or grant permissions). Hence, teachers must insure that their actions and decisions suit the expectations of the stakeholders (those with a particular interest in the work of the teachers, including the teachers' conduct, perceptions, attitudes and the outcomes of their activities) and by which the stakeholders may impose sanctions if the teachers do not meet their expectations.

5.1 *Types of accountability*

Accountability can be classified into five types: organizational, political, legal, professional, and moral/ethical (Ferlie, Lynn & Pollitt 2005). In the educational context, organisational accountability defines the relationship between schools' organisational characteristics and teachers' empowerment, measured as the experience of individual teachers. Teachers are professionals so that they must be professionally accountable, in the sense that they have to conform to standards and codes of conduct checked by professional peers, through their institutions. As teachers do not only teach but also educate, they have an ethical obligation and moral responsibilities. In addition, they have to comply with government regulations, especially those pertaining to education policy.

As Levitt, Janta & Wegrich (2008) claim, a key challenge for public services in general and professionals working in schools in particular is how to combine two imperatives: (a) a performance orientation (in the sense of measurable performance against published targets) that satisfies the principal stakeholders, and (b) maintenance or revival of broader professional values. Doing their best to ensure that the students pass the national exam satisfies the school principals and the parents. However, helping the students to develop the skills excluded from the national exam but which are paramount in the job market, such as speaking skill, is a value worthy of appreciation though not many teachers may be interested in doing so. Levitt, Janta & Wegrich (2008) further state the levels of teachers' autonomy or control by the public in any given situation usually reflect the level of trust the public has on the teachers. If the trust is low, the public control will be strong but when the trust is high, teachers' autonomy will most probably be strong.

However, Youssef & Dahmani (2008) find there are contradictory results in the empirical literature due to the lack of organisational change which holds up teachers' autonomy. In countries such as Australia where Action Research Planner (McTaggart 1979) was written, implementing Kumaradivelu's (2006) parameter of *possibility* sounds easier as the country has long empowered teachers' autonomy by encouraging them to make reflections on their teaching and learning activities. In countries where education is still centrally controlled by the government, the condition is different. Teachers who are used to following a top-down policy in their day-to-day job description find it difficult to work the other way round. For example, the 2013 Indonesian school curriculum, known as the 2013 Curriculum, demands that in order to promote learners' creativity every teaching and learning process should use the scientific approach, following the steps of *observing – questioning – experimenting – associating – networking* (*Wakil Menteri Pendidikan dan Kebudayaan R.I. Bidang Pendidikan,* 2014). It is prescriptive in nature and may not always suit the teaching learning process of every aspect of language. This demand may discourage English language teachers from developing their initiative to draw up theories from what is successful and unsuccessful in their instructional practice as suggested for the post-method teachers (Kumaravadivelu 2006).

However, as learners' creativity, one of the goals of the 2013 Curriculum, is in line with autonomy allowed for the post-method learners, it is the teachers' creativity that plays an important role in responding to the *parameter of possibility*. As Madya (2013) suggests, rather than complaining about the change, teachers should try their best to adapt to the change as 21st century teachers are those who are effective adaptors to the changing world. The approach prescribed by the 2013 Curriculum should be treated as a guideline so that teachers' autonomy in deciding the best way to achieve the instructional goals matches the learners' autonomy in achieving their learning goals.

5.2 *Learners' autonomy*

Though learners' autonomy was commonly seen in terms of strategies for independent and individual learning (Borg & Al-Busaidi 2012), it includes capacity and willingness of learners to take responsibility for their own learning (Sinclair 2000). In a similar spirit Benson (2011) defines learner autonomy as the capacity to take charge of one's own learning, a natural product of the practice of self-directed learning in which the objectives, progress and evaluation of learning are determined by the learners themselves. While the narrow view of learners' autonomy treats learning to learn a language as an end in itself, the broad view treats learning to learn a language as a means to an end, the end being learning to liberate. The former stands for academic autonomy, and the latter stands for liberatory autonomy. The *academic autonomy* enables learners to be effective learners and *liberatory autonomy* empowers learners to be critical thinkers (Kumaradivelu 2006).

While teachers' autonomy earns centrality in the post-method pedagogy, educating post-method learners becomes the responsibility of the post-method teachers. What does it mean? As Little (2000) claims, teachers can only develop learner autonomy if they themselves are autonomous. This means that they must be able to autonomously reflect on their own self-managed learning processes and apply them in helping the learners to manage their own learning, to build their learning autonomy. The teacher has a commitment to empowering his/her learners by creating appropriate learning spaces and developing their capacity for autonomy. La Ganza (2008) admits that learner autonomy is constantly being negotiated within the teacher-learner relationship which depends upon the capacity of the teacher and the learner to develop and maintain a condition in which the teacher holds back from influencing the learner, and the learner holds back from seeking the teacher's influence.

6 CONCLUSION

It has been pointed out that throughout the method history there has never been any best method. The post-method teachers do not seek an alternative method but an alternative to method. As Richards & Rodgers (2001) suggest, applying procedures and techniques developed by others should be an essential starting point for inexperienced teachers. However, as teachers gain more experience, they need to develop their own experience-based approach, reflecting their beliefs, principles and practices as teachers and as learners. They have to reflect on what has made their teaching a success or a failure, and decide what is best to do in their own classroom independently but responsibly. Other than managing to achieve the students' learning outcomes, they have to ensure that the learners' achievement comes from their own effort to take charge of their own learning. It is the teachers' reflection-based creativity in designing tasks or generating a conducive atmosphere that will help learners to be responsible for their own learning. To maintain the sustainability of the success, the teachers should make collaborative efforts in constructing a collective instructional approach which allows each teacher to contribute to the development of the approach. This way, each has the sense of belonging which will insure the sustainability of its implementation.

REFERENCES

Akbari, R. 2008. Postmethod discourse practice. *TESOL Quarterly* 42(4).
Allwright, R.L. *The death of method* (Working Paper #10). Lancaster: The Exploratory Practice Centre, The University of Lancaster.
Baker, Q. 2017. Balancing freedom and responsibility at school. *The Ontarion.* Accessed 12/10/2017 from https://www.theontarion.com/2017/09/balancing-freedom-and-responsibility-at-school/ Bell, D. M. 2003. Method and postmethod: Are they really so incompatible. *TESOL Quarterly* 37(2): 325–336.
Benson, P. 2011. *Teaching and researching autonomy* (2nd Ed.). London and New York: Routledge Taylor & Francis Group.

Blair, T.R., Rupley, W.H. & Nichols, W.D. 2007. The effective teacher of reading: Considering the "what" and "how" of instruction. *International Reading Association*: 432–438. doi:10.1598/ RT.60.5.3.

Brown, H.D. 2001. Teaching by principles: An interactive approach to language pedagogy (2nd Ed.). New York: Pearson Education.

Chomsky, N. 1965. *Aspects of the theory of syntax*. Cambridge, Massachusetts: The M.I.T. Press.

Coleman, A. 1929. *The teaching of modern foreign languages in the United States: A report prepared for the modern language study*. New York: Macmillan.

Ferlie, E., Lynn, L.E. & C. Pollitt. 2005. *The Oxford handbook of public management*. Oxford: Oxford University Press.

Kumaravadivelu, B. 2006. *Understanding language teaching: from method to postmethod*. Mahwah, New Jersey: Lawrence Erlbaum.

Kumaravadivelu, B. 1994. The postmethod condition: (E)merging strategies for second/foreign language teaching. *TESOL Quarterly* 28(1): 27–48.

Kumaravadivelu, B. 2001. Toward a postmethod pedagogy. *TESOL Quarterly* 35: 537–560.

La Ganza, W. 2008. Learner autonomy—teacher autonomy: Interrelating and the will to empower. In Jiménez Raya, M., Lamb, T.E. & Vieira, F. 2007. *Pedagogy for autonomy in language education in Europe: towards a framework for learner and teacher development*. Dublin: Authentik.

Lafortune, L. & Deaudelin, C. 2001. *Accompagnement socioconstructiviste. Pour s'appropier une reforme en education*. Quebec City: Presses de l'Universite du Quebec.

Lafortune, L., Lapage, C., Persechino, S. & Aitken, A. 2009. *Professional competencies for accompanying change: A frame of reference*. Quebec: Presses de l'Universite du Quebec.

Levitt, R., Janta, B, & Wegrich, K. 2008. *Accountability of teachers: Literature review*. Cambridge: Rand.

Little, D. (2000). We're all in it together: exploring the interdependence of teacher and learner autonomy. In *All together now, papers from the 7th Nordic conference and workshop on autonomous language learning, Helsinki, September 2000*, L. Karlsson, F. Kjisik & J. Nordlund (eds), 45–56. Helsinki: University of Helsinki Language Centre.

Madya, S. 2013. *Metodologi pengajaran bahasa dari era prametode sampai era pascametode* (Language teaching methodology from premethod era to postmethod era). Yogyakarta: UNY Press.

Masouleh, N.S. 2012. From method to post method: A panacea! *English Language Teaching* 5(4). Accessed 12 April 2017 from *www.ccsenet.org/elt*.

McIntosh, P. 2010. *Action research and reflective practice*. London & New York: Routledge.

Nilüfer, C. 2009. Post-method pedagogy: Teacher growth behind walls. *Proceedings of the 10th METU ELT Convention,* 22–23 May.

Nordquist, R. 2017. *Transformational grammar (tg) definition and examples*. Accessed on 25/06/2017 from https://www.thoughtco. com/ transformational-grammar-1692557.

Özbilgin, A. & Tannacito, D.J. The parameter of particularity: A critical analysis of a supervisory observation of an EFL teachers's classroom in Turkey. Accessed 12/09/2017 from https://www. academia. edu/4173068/The_Parameter_of_ Particularity_A_Critical_Analysisof_a_SupervisoryObservation_ of_an_EFL_Teacherss_Classroom _in_Turkey?auto=download.

Pennycook, A. 1989. The concept of method, interested knowledge, and the politics of language teaching. *TESOL Quarterly* 23(4): 589–618.

Richards, J.C. & Rodgers, T.S. 2001. *Approaches and methods in language teaching*. Cambridge: CUP.

Richards, J.C. 2001. *Curriculum development in language teaching*. Cambridge: CUP.

Rivers, W.M. 1991. Mental representations and language in action. *The Canadian Modern language Review* 47: 249–265.

Smith, R.C. 2000. Starting with ourselves: teacher-learner autonomy in language learning. In Sinclair, B., McGrath, I., & Lamb, T. (eds.). *Learner autonomy, teacher autonomy: Future directions*. Harlow: Longman.

Wakil Menteri Pendidikan dan Kebudayaan R.I. Bidang Pendidikan (Vice Minister of Education and Culture of the Republic of Indonesia). 2014. *Konsep dan implementasi kurikulum 2013 (Concept and implementation of the 2013 curriculum)*. Accessed 20-09-2015 from https:// kemdikbud.go.id/kemdik-bud/dokumen/Paparan/ Paparan%20Wamendik.pdf.

Youssef, A. B. & Dahmani, M. 2008. The impact of ICT on student performance in higher education: direct effects, indirect effects and organisational change. *RUSC* 5(1) (2008) ISSN 1698-580X.

ELT in Asia in the Digital Era: Global Citizenship and Identity – Madya et al. (Eds)
© *2018 Taylor & Francis Group, London, ISBN 978-0-8153-7900-3*

Pre-service teachers' self-reflection on their pedagogical competences upon joining the *SM-3T* program

N.A. Nurichsania & S. Rachmajanti
State University of Malang, Malang, Indonesia

ABSTRACT: Considering that growing professionally is of great importance for teachers in Indonesia, the government has established an one-year program for pre-service teachers to improve their professional skills in teaching, known as *Sarjana Mendidik di daerah Terdepan, Terluar, dan Tertinggal* or *SM-3T* (bachelor graduates teaching in underprivileged areas). This study explores the implication of the *SM-3T* program for pre-service teachers' professional development, particularly referring to pedagogical competence, and factors affecting the pre-service teachers' professional development through their self-reflection. A case study with retrospective pretest method was employed encompassing a self-evaluation sheet and a semi-structured interview to elicit the data. High and low achiever teachers in the 2nd batch of the program in the year of 2012 were opted for the study. The findings revealed that the low achiever's pedagogical competences differed significantly, while the high achiever teacher merely made a slight advancement after completing one-year teaching practices in the underprivileged schools.

1 INTRODUCTION

Indonesia has been fronting insuperable educational problems for decades, especially in the frontier, outlying, and underdeveloped areas, the so-called *3T* areas. In the attempt to improve the educational quality in Indonesia, the government made endeavors to enhance the quality of its teachers since teachers hold a prominent key in educating students. By means of improving teacher quality in Indonesia, the government expects students to receive a quality education. Hence, in 2011, the Ministry of Culture and Elementary and Secondary Education through the Directorate General of Higher Education established a program, namely *Sarjana Mendidik di daerah Terdepan, Terluar, dan Tertinggal (SM-3T)*. This program recruits recent graduates (in the latest four years of recruitment processes) of undergraduate program from accredited teaching departments who are willing to teach in impoverished areas across Indonesia for a year. After finishing one-year teaching practices in the assigned *3T* schools, teacher candidates were granted a scholarship of teaching training program and certification for pre-service teachers, namely *Program Pendidikan Profesi Guru (PPG)*.

According to *Direktorat Jenderal Pendidikan Tinggi* (2012), to be a part of the program, the teacher candidates must meet the requirements and pass a series of recruitment procedure. Particularly, the program is in a quest to find candidates who comprehend their education-related major in line with the required subjects in this program, have at least GPA of 3.0, and have to be physically healthy with a medical certificate. They also must show a proof of Indonesian citizenship and good behavior from a police department, and agree not to have any marital status until the completion of the program. In addition, the *SM-3T* program will value more pre-service teachers who experienced in students association activities. For those who meet the criteria, they had to pass selections in a national and a selected teacher training institution level. The pre-service teachers who passed the selections are considered as part of the program. Afterwards, they were obliged to join the *SM-3T* training comprising of academic and non-academic training before teaching in the *3T* areas (Direktorat Jenderal Pendidikan Tinggi 2012).

Through the *SM-3T* program, a good quality of education is expected to be achieved by elevating the competences of pre-service teachers to the brink of professional teachers. One of indispensable competences to be prospective professional teachers is pedagogical competences. The Ministry of Education and Culture and Elementary and Secondary Education Regulation No. 16 Year 2007 about Standards of Academic Qualifications and Teacher Competences specifically outlines core competences in pedagogical domain for professional teachers. Those competences consist of teachers' ability to comprehend students' traits, educational theories and the principles of its implementation, the development of syllabus and lesson plans, the implementation of instructional activities, the deployment of Information and Communication Technology (ICT), the ways to develop students' ability and aptitude, the interpersonal communication strategy, the learning assessment and evaluation, the use of evaluation results, as well as the reflective teaching (Departemen Pendidikan Nasional 2007).

Understanding the pre-service teachers' practices in pedagogical domain is acutely significant because pedagogical competence is one of pivotal factors contributing to an effective teaching (Syahruddin, et al. 2013). Thus, the area of pedagogical domain is vital to be scrutinized. A previous study by Sadilia (2014) aiming at appraising 14 pre-service teachers' pedagogical competences in the first batch of the *SM-3T* program who taught in the eastern part of Indonesia discovered that all pre-service teachers own most of all pedagogical competence criteria assessed. She examined pre-service teachers' pedagogical levels of planning, applying, and evaluating teaching practices by administering a self-designed test instrument in the form of multiple-choice test. Nonetheless, after learning the test items deployed in the Sadilia's test instrument, the items actually did not cover all detailed components of pedagogical competence standards stipulated in the Ministry of Education and Culture and Elementary and Secondary Education Regulation. Therefore, the researchers intended to conduct a study on this area in a broader scope. In this current study, the researchers adopted and adapted teacher standards from the undermentioned government regulation and Teaching Knowledge Test (TKT) to create teacher standard components and utilize them as the basis to construct instruments applied in this study.

Due to the fact that the *SM-3T* program was a newly-established program, it surely needs pre-evaluation as well as insights from research to probe its tenets and self-proclaimed merits in order to optimize the accomplishment of the program aims. Teachers, as human agents, would bring rich experiences and narratives to expound the *SM-3T* program. With that notion, this present study endeavored to pre-evaluate the program implementation and investigate its efficacy of elevating pre-service teachers' pedagogical competence through pre-service teachers' self-reflection on their teaching practices before and after enrolling at the program. By understanding the quality of pre-service teachers' competence, it certainly gives evidence of the program accomplishment in achieving its aims. The attempt to delve into such rich descriptions based on pre-service teachers' one-year field experiences, then reveal them into a set of thorough report is of great significant to arrive at the role of research, which is to better understand the reality of the *SM-3T* program.

2 RESEARCH METHOD

This qualitative design deployed a case study with a retrospective pretest method to allow pre-service teachers to look back on what they have done in prior teaching experiences before enrolling for the *SM-3T* program and compare it to teaching performances after completing the program (Drennan & Hyde 2008). There were two participants majoring in English Language Teaching (ELT) involved in this study to represent high and low achiever teachers in the 2nd batch of the program who had done one year of teaching in the selected *3T* areas. To obtain all data, the researchers employed two instruments which were a self-evaluation sheet and interview guide. The analysis of data gathered from those instruments were supported by schools' curriculum and pre-service teachers' English syllabus as well as lesson plans implemented in the *3T* schools.

Table 1. The scoring categorization of pre-service teachers' pedagogical competences.

Scale	Description	Interpretation
5	Strongly Competent	Teachers are categorized as strongly competent when they fulfill 85–100% criteria of teacher competence
4	Competent	Teachers are categorized as competent when they fulfill 69–84% teacher competence criteria
3	Fairly competent	Teachers are categorized as fairly competent when they fulfill 53–68% criteria of teacher competence
2	Incompetent	Teachers are categorized as incompetent when they fulfill 36–52% teacher competence criteria
1	Strongly incompetent	Teachers are categorized as strongly incompetent when they only fulfill 20–35% criteria of teacher competence

The self-evaluation sheet was developed based on two standards. The first standard was from the Ministry of Culture and Elementary and Secondary Education Regulation No. 16 Year 2007 about the standards of competencies and academic qualification of teachers in Indonesia. Meanwhile, the second standard was Teaching Knowledge Test (TKT), a test for English language teachers produced by University of Cambridge ESOL Examination. The two participants were requested to fill in the self-evaluation sheet for the purpose of self-evaluating whether or not there was a change on their pedagogical competence upon joining the program. The self-evaluation sheet used a five-point Likert scale ranging from strongly incompetent (one), incompetent (two), fairly competent (three), competent (four), and strongly competent (five). The data elicited from the self-evaluation sheet were analyzed utilizing Microsoft Excel to ascertain if there were any competence changes or not after the program. The analysis was under five variables of teachers' pedagogical competence standards conveying teachers' ability to understand students' characteristics, to plan teaching and learning activities, to deliver instructional activities, to do evaluation in teaching, and to do teaching reflection. The results of the data analysis were in the form of percentages. The percentages were then interpreted by a scoring categorization which is displayed in Table 1.

Afterwards, the researchers interviewed all the participants using an interview guide functioning to explore factors affecting pre-service teachers' competence changes (or lack thereof) upon embarking on the *SM-3T* program. The data were subsequently transcribed and coded under the same variables as the self-evaluation sheet. Then, the researchers interpreted the data to divulge factors affecting pre-service teachers' competence changes (or lack thereof). At last, the researchers collected pre-service teachers' documents, such as schools' curriculum, syllabi, and lesson plans to support data analysis.

3   FINDINGS AND DISCUSSION

The findings are elaborated with the related theories and previous studies under the five teacher standards of pedagogical competences. It was discovered that, firstly, pertaining to pre-service teachers' ability in understanding students' characteristics, the principle results of the study disclosed that both HAT and LAT developed their ability after enrolling at the *SM-3T* program. Even so, in self-evaluating themselves, HAT showed a higher level of competence than LAT prior to and at the end of the program. This situation endorses a research finding by Gnanaguru and Kumar (2007) stating that a high achiever teacher tends to show more positive attitude toward teaching performance than a low achiever teacher. In specific, prior to entering the program, HAT's ability in understanding students' characteristics was categorized as competent for he attained 80% criteria of teachers' pedagogical competence, whereas LAT was categorized as strongly incompetent since he only got 22.2% of the criteria. After teaching in the assigned place, HAT's ability increased one level to strongly competent since he fulfilled 100% of the criteria. Besides, LAT's competence improved two levels to fairly competent as he owned 55.5% of teacher competence criteria. However, LAT made more progress than HAT. LAT advanced his competence two levels from strongly incompetent to fairly competent and made 33% progress while HAT merely enhanced his competence into one level from competent to strongly competent with 20% progress.

The changes of their competence were influenced by four factors, which were pre-service teachers' perceptions toward students' traits, the knowledge from prior teacher education, teaching span in the *3T* area, and efforts to understand students' traits as well as decision making to solve the associated problems. In accordance with the matter, HAT added that there were two more factors leading to his competence changes, which were prior teaching experience and information about students' traits in the *3T* area during the *SM-3T* trainings. However, LAT did not have the same perspectives with HAT. It was because LAT had poor prior teaching practices and the program did not provide information of students' conditions in Nunukan. In response to the occurrence, it is suggested that the program committee delivers complete information in regard to prospective schools' and students' conditions in each regency of the *3T* areas during the training for the purpose of equipping all pre-service teachers with equal understanding of their future students so they could plan teaching better. In addition, LAT presumed that a minor factor hindering his competence change in understanding students' traits was the prevailing tradition held by the local people in the *3T* area prohibiting newcomers to do or say something that might hurt the feeling of native students. Thereby, it affected LAT to be a passive teacher to solve problems in relation to the native students. For this matter, the *SM-3T* program should discuss the local tradition with the locals and make a deal of a satisfactory solution for both locals and newcomers.

Secondly, the next aspect to be examined in the pedagogical competence is the ability to plan classroom activities. From the scoring categorization, HAT appraised his own ability in planning teaching and learning activities higher than LAT prior to and after enrolling at the *SM-3T* program. HAT achieved 80% of teacher competence criteria before joining the program and 83.3% of teacher competence criteria after teaching in the *3T* school. Thus, he could be categorized as competent before and after the program. On the contrary, LAT owned 28.3% of teacher competence criteria before joining the program so he could be categorized as strongly incompetent. Then, after doing teaching obligation in the *3T* school, LAT attained 65% of teacher competence criteria so his ability could be categorized as fairly competent. Although LAT valued himself lower than HAT, LAT succeeded in making more advancement than HAT. After finishing the teaching practices in the *3T* schools, LAT boosted his ability two levels from strongly incompetent to fairly competent. In contrast, HAT did not make any development in his ability for the fact that he was categorized as competent before and after one-year teaching experience. Additionally, based on the percentage, LAT's ability increased 36.7%, whereas HAT merely made 3.3% progression of his ability in planning teaching documents.

In line with the changes of pre-service teachers' competence in their ability to plan teaching and learning activities, there were two factors affecting them, which were the availability of lesson plan development guidebooks in the *3T* schools and pre-service teachers' efforts to develop lesson plans to match students' and schools' conditions in *3T* areas as well as decision-making toward the developing situation. Besides, HAT perceived that a factor influencing the lack of his competence changes was the same lesson planning between teaching practices in the *3T* area, in his prior teacher education, and in prior teaching experiences before the *SM-3T* program. In addition, there were two factors hindering pre-service teachers' competence changes. The first factor was the shortage of facilities to support teaching in the *3T* schools. The finding attests what Ntim and Korletey (2015) investigate pertaining to teachers in Ghana. They reveal that facilities shortages in Ghana greatly hinder the teachers from performing at their best in planning and delivering teaching activities. The second factor was insufficient information regarding lesson plan development appropriate for the conditions in the *3T* area during the program training. Hence, it is recommended that it is a must for the *SM-3T* program to train pre-service teachers to plan teaching activities suitable with students' needs in the *3T* area so that they could better improve their ability to plan teaching activities.

Thirdly, similar to previous findings, HAT self-assessed his ability of delivering teaching activities higher than LAT. HAT categorized himself as competent before and after experiencing teaching in the *3T* school for the fact that he had fulfilled 82.2% criteria of teacher competence before the teaching practices and 84.4% of teacher competence criteria after teaching practices in the *3T* area. Nevertheless, LAT categorized himself as strongly incompetent before teaching in the *3T* area due he owned 31.1% of teacher competence criteria. After teaching obligation in the *3T* area, his competence developed to fairly competent since he was able to attain 60% criteria of teacher competence. In spite of HAT's perceptions on assessing himself higher than LAT, LAT made much more progression. LAT could advance his ability two levels with 28.9% advancement. Conversely, HAT did not progress his ability in categorization at all, but he made progression in percentage, which was 2.2%.

The changes of pre-service teachers' pedagogical competences was influenced by their efforts to deal with problems appearing in the *3T* area and decision-making to cope with the problems. LAT himself perceived that teaching evaluation program in the *3T* school was a factor changing his competence. Further, factors affecting the lack of pre-service competence changes were the same teaching implementation between prior teaching experiences and teaching practices in the *3T* area as well as the facility shortage to support teaching in the *3T* schools.

LAT also thought that his lack of knowledge and ability to implement creative learning activities and media apt to the school's and students' conditions in the *3T* area had impact on his lack of competence changes. The findings from the interviews discovered that LAT only deployed an English module as the lesson plans and reaped the benefit of the materials in the module during teaching *3T* students. LAT's practices in which he relied on the module in his teaching were in line with Richard's finding (2011) arguing that teachers who have low level of proficiency are likely to be more dependent on textbook to be able to teach effectively. The next factor that influence LAT's limitation in progressing his competence were his lack of ability in classroom management and the school tradition prevailing score manipulation in the *3T* school. Based on the interviews, LAT declared that the practice of score manipulation in the *3T* school diminished native students' learning motivation as they knew that it was meaningless to put efforts in learning for they would gain good scores and pass the standards. In order to increase students' motivation in learning, LAT applied some games in learning activities. However, the class was in the state of utter chaos. LAT could not manage the classroom consisting of 35 students well. Later on, LAT gave up on creative learning activities and only used lecturing method in most of his teaching. Commenting on this issue, LAT should make endeavors to elevate his teaching performance quality, specifically in classroom management and improvisational teaching with the intention that he could minimize factors hindering his competence development in delivering instructional activities.

Fourthly, regarding to the ability to do evaluation, HAT mentioned that he did not make any competence changes since the data showed that his ability was 76.6% before and after teaching practices in the *3T* area. On the contrary, LAT advanced his competence in doing evaluation during classroom activities with 23.3% advancement after completing teaching practices in the *3T* area from 33.3% to 56.6%. Based on scoring categorization, LAT could be categorized as strongly incompetent since he fulfilled 33.3% criteria of teacher competence before the program and be categorized as fairly competence as he owned 56.6% teacher competence criteria, whereas HAT was categorized as competent for his achievement remained the same, 76.6% before and after the program. To conclude, HAT's ability was higher that LAT but LAT made more progress than HAT after the teaching practices in the *3T* area.

There were two factor affecting LAT's changes of pedagogical competence. They were efforts in developing and implementing assessment and evaluation instruments as well as the existence of teaching evaluation program that obliged all teachers to report the results of students' learning evaluations to the headmaster and the head of curriculum department in the *3T* school. Aside from that, there was a reason hindering LAT's development of the competence. It was the practice of score manipulation in the *3T* school. The school obliged all teachers in the school to pass students who could not accomplish the standards in tests. In return, the students' parents should donate facilities to support the school. There were no teachers in the school chastising such a practice. Thus, as a newcomer teacher at the school, LAT just followed this obstructive regulation. In response to the case, the stakeholders of the *SM-3T* program should take action to deal with the problem. They should warn or give punishment to schools committing such a fraudulent practice.

Furthermore, there were two factors halting HAT's ability progress. First factor was the same planning and implementation of evaluation administered in the *3T* area and in HAT's previous teaching experiences. The second factor was the shortage of learning media and materials to support assessment and evaluation in the *3T* school. Concerning to assessment and evaluation processes in the *3T* schools, HAT verily had willingness to administer various kinds of assessment in the course of his teaching practices. Regrettably, he gave up on doing so since the *3T* schools underwent the shortage of school facilities. The same condition is also found in an ethnographic study by Earthman (2002) unravelling the correlation between the facility shortage and teachers' motivation. He identified that the lack of school facilities gave a negative impact on teachers' motivation in teaching. In relation to the HAT's practice, it is suggested that HAT should find out more about possible innovative assessment, aside from he had already known, that could be done in the disadvantaged schools before going to the assigned *3T* school. This is so, for assessment is inextricably linked with systematic attempts intended to monitor the students' learning progress.

Ultimately, the results of the self-evaluation sheet disclosed that HAT considered his ability in doing reflection higher than LAT before and after teaching in the underprivileged area. HAT was categorized as competent prior to and after the teaching practices, while LAT was categorized as strongly incompetent before the program and was categorized as incompetent after teaching practices in the *3T* schools. Despite the fact that HAT perceived his ability higher than LAT, LAT made more improvement than HAT. Based on the percentage data, it showed that LAT increased his ability 20%, from 30% to 50%. On the opposite, HAT could not make any progress in his ability, as he merely attained 80% of teachers' competence criteria. In conclusion, LAT succeeded in advancing one level of his ability while HAT could not boost his ability in doing teaching reflection.

A factor affecting the changes of LAT's ability in administering reflection was his efforts in reflecting his past teaching and decision making of the related problems arousing during classroom practices. On the contrary, HAT's stagnant progress was influenced by the less frequency and opportunities to conduct reflection in the assigned school compared to his previous teaching practices as he felt that there was no problem in the midst of his classroom activities. Without the continuous practices of teaching reflection, HAT was surely not able to enhance his ability in reflection. Employing the finding as the basis, the researchers suggest HAT to reflect his teaching practices prudently since teaching experience itself is not enough, but pre-service teachers should also do teaching reflection to develop their competence (Richard, 2008).

Meanwhile, it was found that there were two factors impeding the development of pre-service teachers' ability in doing reflection, which were no request from the program to report the practice of CAR and the obligation to teach lessons other than English. Based on the interviews with both pre-service teachers, they approved that they did CAR, but were not able to produce scientific product of writing because of no request from the program and there was no time doing so since they were obliged to teach lessons other than English. For that issue, the *SM-3T* program should oblige all pre-service teachers to make products of CAR during their teaching practices in the *3T* schools and strictly punish *3T* schools who requested pre-service teachers to teach other subjects than English.

4   CONCLUSIONS AND SUGGESTIONS

According to the foregoing findings in this study, it could be concluded that the *SM-3T* program successfully accomplished one of its objectives, which was to improve pre-service teachers' pedagogical competences to the brink of being prospective professional teachers, especially for a low achiever teacher. The results of the self-evaluation sheet exposed that LAT succeeded in making more advancement of pedagogical competence criteria than HAT, while HAT just made a slight progression after teaching practices in the *3T* school.

Based on the interview, pre-service teachers' changes of the pedagogical competence were prejudiced by several factors, which were their perceptions toward the prospective schools' and students' conditions in the *3T* area, the knowledge of theories related to teaching from prior teacher education, the intensive teaching practices in the *3T* area, pre-service teachers' efforts and decision-making toward the associated problems appearing during teaching practices in the *3T* schools, and the availability of lesson plan development guidebooks in the *3T* schools. In addition to those five aforementioned factors, HAT predominantly believed that his good prior teaching experiences and information about the condition of the prospective school in the *3T* area during the program training led to the changes of his competence. Further, LAT added that teaching evaluation program in the *3T* school was one of factors contributing to his competence changes.

Apart from factors affecting the changes, the researchers found four factors influencing pre-service teachers' lack of pedagogical competence changes which were insufficient information regarding teaching instruments as well as its implementation suitable for the conditions in the *3T* area, the shortage of school facilities to support teaching, the same teaching practices demonstrated in prior teaching experiences and teaching practices at the *3T* area, and the obligation to teach lessons other than English. Additionally, HAT affirmed that the same lesson planning during teaching practices in the *3T* area, in teacher education, and in prior teaching experiences caused the lack of his pedagogical changes. LAT then specified that there were five factors influencing his lack of pedagogical competence changes, which were poor prior teaching experiences, the scarcity of information related to LAT's prospective school's conditions in the *3T* area during the program training, the lack of teaching knowledge, and the prevailing tradition as well as the score manipulation practice in the *3T* school.

In the endeavour to maximize the improvement of pre-service teachers' pedagogical competence as well as the attainment of the program aims, the researchers propose some recommendations. Firstly, for English pre-service teachers in the *SM-3T* program, especially low achiever teachers, they should be acutely aware of pedagogical competence standards that a teacher should own in order to be a professional teacher and make attempts to achieve the standards. Secondly, for the stakeholders of the *SM-3T* program, they should provide information of all prospective *3T* areas during the program training, without exception and the program should equip pre-service teachers with adequate pedagogical content knowledge of planning and implementing teaching instruments suitably corresponding with the conditions in the *3T* areas before sending the pre-service teachers to the assigned teaching sites. The *SM-3T* program should also oblige pre-service teachers to conduct and report CAR during their teaching practices in the *3T* areas. Not only that, the program should provide coaching and monitoring during pre-service teaching practices to confirm that pre-service teachers only teach their subject mastery and the teaching objectives were effectively accomplished. The program should also build a good communication with the headmasters of *3T* schools to ensure a good practice for education in the areas. Intended for *3T* schools who commit score manipulation, the *SM-3T* program should give a verbal warning. However, when it does not work, the program should mete out punishments to the schools.

Additionally, the Indonesian government should enhance the quality of institutions operating teacher education throughout Indonesia, thus, the student teachers will own the expected output standards due to the fact that the success of the program is interrelated with the quality of the prospective *SM-3T* pre-service teachers. As the government announced that the *SM-3T* program would be reviewed and possibly be reformed into a new program with similar objectives, it is recommended to the government to go through the standards and regulation of the teacher input, the process, and the teacher output in the *SM-3T* program, and subsequently, utilize them as the benchmark in formulating standards in the forthcoming new program replacing the *SM-3T* program. Lastly, for other researchers interested in this topic, it is suggested that they elicit data about pre-service teachers' actual teaching performances in the *3T* schools and validate the match as well as the mismatch between their perceptions of pedagogical competences and their teaching performances.

REFERENCES

Departmen Pendidikan Nasional. 2007. *Peraturan Menteri Pendidikan Nasional No. 16 Tahun 2007 tentang Standar Kualifikasi Akademik dan Kompetensi Guru* (the Ministry of National Education Regulation No. 16 Year 2007 about Standards of Academic Qualifications and Teacher Competences). Jakarta: Badan Standar Nasional Pendidikan.

Drennan, J. & Hyde, A. 2008. Controlling response shift bias: the use of the retrospective pre-test design in the evaluation of a master's programme. *Assessment & Evaluation in Higher Education* 33 (6): 699–709. Retrieved from http://www.researchrepository.ucd.ie/bitstream/handle/10197/4097/Controlling_response_shift_bias_2008.pdf.

Direktorat Jenderal Pendidikan Tinggi. 2012. *pedoman pelaksanaan program sarjana mendidik di daerah terdepan, terluar, dan tertinggal* (Guidelines on the implementation of the *SM-3T* Program). Jakarta: Direktorat Jenderal Pendidikan Tinggi.

Earthmen, G. 2002. *School facility condition and student academic achievement. Institute for Democracy, Education and Access (IDEA)*. Berkeley: University of California. Retrieved from http://escholarship.org/uc/item/5sw56439.

Gnanaguru, S. A. & Kumar, S. 2007. Attitude of under normal and overachievers towards teaching profession and their home environment. *Journal of All India Association for Educational Research* 19(3): 36–37.

Ntim, C.K. & Korletey, J.T. 2015. The impact of educational facilities on teaching and learning drawing: what it means to visua arts education in Ghana. *International Journal of Innovative Research and Development* 4(6). Retrieved from http://www.ijird.com/index.php/ijird/article/download/71519/56403.

Richards, J.C. 2008. Toward reflective teaching. *The Teacher Trainer Journal* 33. Retrieved from http://www.tttjournal.co.uk.

Richards, J.C. 2011. *Competence and performance in langage teaching*. New York: Cambridge University Press.

Sadilia, S. 2014. *Pedagogical competence of the english teachers of SM-3T program*. Unpublished Thesis. Graduate Program in English Language Teaching. Malang: State University of Malang.

Syahruddin, et.al. 2013. Teachers' Pedagogical Competence in School-Based Management. *Journal of Education and Learning* 7(4): 213–218. Retrieved from http://www.journal.uad.ac.id/index.php/EduLearn/article/view/195/pdf_12.

ELT in Asia in the Digital Era: Global Citizenship and Identity – Madya et al. (Eds)
© *2018 Taylor & Francis Group, London, ISBN 978-0-8153-7900-3*

Exploring types and levels of motivation of Indonesian EFL learners

A. Budiman
Sebelas Maret University, Surakarta, Indonesia

ABSTRACT: This survey study was aimed at exploring types and levels of motivation of learners in an Indonesian private university. It used a descriptive method and involved 151 third semester learners of non-English majors of Faculty of Education and Teacher Training in academic year of 2015/2016 as respondents. A questionnaire was administered to these learners to find out types and levels of their motivation. The results revealed that (1) types of motivation of the learners were more integrative (M = 3.72) than instrumental (M = 3.70). Furthermore, (2) the learners were moderately motivated (M = 3.71). This indicated that the learners learnt English to communicate in English and they would learn English even if it were not obliged by the university. These results imply several suggestions: (1) in TEFL practice, lecturers should provide the learners with appropriate instructional materials, (2) teaching learning process should be stimulating, and (3) assessment techniques must stimulate and sustain learners' motivation.

1 INTRODUCTION

Many factors can influence learners in mastering English; one of them is motivation. To do with this, Harmer (2007) says that motivation is an important factor in English language learning, but it seems to be neglected in the teaching learning process. The root of motivation is from the Latin verb, "movere" which means to move (Ushioda 2007, as cited in Griffiths 2008). Dornyei (1998) says that motivation refers to an internal power in humans, which arouses, directs and controls their interest and behavior. So, motivation to learn English as a foreign language is an internal power in learners that arouses effort which moves or drives them to learn English.

Furthermore, there are two types of motivation; integrative and instrumental (Gardner & Lambert 1972, as cited in Gardner 1985). Integrative motivation is built by the learners' desire to identify with or to integrate with the target culture. On the other hand, instrumental motivation is connected to the prospects of their school or career growth (Gardner & Lambert 1972, as cited in Gardner 1985).

Several researches have been conducted to find out learners' types of motivation in learning language. One of the researchers is Lamb (2004) who conducted a series of research indicated that motivation of learners in secondary level both instrumental and integrative motivation in relation to learning English as a global language is moderate. Indonesian secondary learners have more integrative motivation, considering English as a global language, rather than instrumental motivation (Liando et al. 2005, as cited in Astuti 2013).

In spite of its undeniable importance, it is widely acknowledged that Indonesian EFL learners in the secondary level generally have characteristics of low motivation (Astuti 2013). One of the causes is the large classroom size (Bradford 2007, as cited in Astuti 2013).

It is explained that the types of motivation of the learners in secondary level in Indonesia tend to be more integrative motivation. In addition, the levels of motivation of the learners in secondary level in Indonesia are considered between low and moderate. However, research dealing with the types and levels of motivation of learners in university in Indonesia is still rarely found. Besides, no matter how good the curriculum is designed, the material is structured, and the model is implemented, if the learners are not motivated to learn, the teaching and learning process will be meaningless (Alrabai 2014, Ryan & Deci 2000).

Regarding this issue, it is very important to figure out types and levels of motivation of the learners in university in Indonesia. By recognizing the types and levels of motivation quantitatively, it is expected that English lecturers or teachers gain better understanding on how to design curricula, syllabuses and pedagogical practices to stimulate and maintain learners' motivation. It can, of course, be done through an understanding of the types and levels of motivation of learners in university in Indonesia.

1.1 Definition of motivation

Motivation has been widely accepted as one of the key factors that influence the success of foreign language (FL) or second language (L2) learning. Although it is a term frequently used in both educational and research contexts, there is little agreement as to the exact meaning of this concept (Dwinalida 2015). The following are some definitions quoted from different researchers.

Motivation refers to the choices people make as to what experiences or goals they will approach or avoid, and the degree of effort they will exert in that respect (Keller 1983, as cited in Crookes & Schmidt 1985). When people make certain choice and use effort to attain it, they are motivated.

Motivation can be defined as a direction of attentional effort, the proportion of total attentional effort directed to the task (intensity), and the extent to which attentional effort toward the task is maintained over time (persistence) (Kanfer & Ackerman 1989, as cited in Dornyei 1998). Motivation deals with effort, proportion, and the maintenance of the effort.

Researchers view motivation as the driver of human action for a special purpose. In addition, motivation is thought to be responsible for why people decide to do something, how long they are willing to sustain the activity and how hard they are going to pursue it (Dornyei 2001).

Therefore, this research draws a conclusion that motivation is responsible for:

1. why people decide to learn a language (here in this means English as a foreign language);
2. how hard they are going to pursue this study;
3. how long they are willing to sustain the activity.

1.2 Types of motivation

There is a speculation saying that learners' underlying attitudes to the target language culture and people will have a significant influence on their motivation and thus their success in learning the language. This speculation gives rise to the now classic distinction between integrative and instrumental motivation, the former reflecting a sincere and personal interest in the target language, people, and culture and the latter its practical value and advantages (Gardner & Lambert 1972, as cited in Lamb 2007).

In addition, Crookes & Schmidt (1985) state that when an individual is driven to learn a foreign language because he or she is genuinely interested in the culture of the language, it is referred to as integrative motivation. Besides, when learners are driven to learn English because they believe learning it will benefit them in certain, specific ways (meeting other people, getting a job, and social pressure), this is referred to as instrumental motivation because the foreign language (English, in this case) is learned so that it can be used as a tool to improve the learners' lives.

1.3 Levels of motivation

Highly motivated individual enjoys striving for a goal and makes use of strategies in reaching that goal (Gardner 2001, as cited in Cheng & Dornyei 2007). Motivation to learn a foreign language is often triggered when the language is seen as valuable to the learner in view of the amount of effort that will be required to be put into learning it. With the proper level of motivation, language learners may become active investigators of the nature of the language they are studying.

In an EFL setting, for example, in a country like Indonesia, English is a compulsory subject, so learners definitely have no choice but take the course. Without effort, persistence will make little sense and motivation will be greatly weakened (Hsu 2010, Kassing 2011, Skehan 1989).

Indonesian EFL learners are regarded as having low motivation. One of the causes is the large classroom size (Astuti 2013). This is supported by Lamb (2007) stating that Indonesian high school learners are initially motivated to learn but their experience of learning English at school decreases their motivation over time. In general, Indonesian learners, like other Southeast Asian learners, tend to be passive and nonverbal in class.

On the contrary, some researches have been conducted to find out the learners' motivation in learning language. One of the researchers is Lamb (2004) who conducted a series of research by looking at 11–12 years old children's English learning motivation in the Indonesian context. They are junior high school learners and most of them start learning English for the first time. In elementary school, English is not a compulsory subject. Lamb used open and closed questionnaire items followed by class observation and interviews. His findings indicated that learners' motivation both integrative and instrumental in relation to learning English as a global language is moderate.

2 RESEARCH METHODOLOGY

This research used survey study to find out and explore types and levels of motivation of EFL learners at Faculty of Education and Teacher Training of an Indonesian private university. Third semester EFL learners of Faculty of Education and Teacher Training in academic year of 2015/2016 were chosen as the population in this research except English Education Department learners. English Education Department learners were excluded because learners coming from that department have different English materials in the classroom and they study English in every semester. Additionally, eight departments of Faculty of Education and Teacher Training were chosen with the number of third semester learners of each department namely Indonesian Education Department, Mathematics Education Department, Biology Education Department, History Education Department, Civics Education Department, Geography Education Department, Elementary Education Department (PGSD), Early Childhood Education Department (PG PAUD). The total numbers of third semester EFL learners of eight departments of Faculty of Education and Teacher Training in academic year 2015/2016 are 605 learners in this research. This research used probability sampling, specifically simple random sampling to take samples from the population.

To collect the data, this research administered questionnaire to know the learners' types and levels of motivation. The questionnaire in this research was "closed" questionnaire (Arikunto 2010, Creswell 2013, Sugiyono 2012). It consisted of two types of motivation namely integrative motivation and instrumental motivation. This research followed Gardner's types of motivation. There are 26 items on the questionnaire and they were rated on a five-point Likert scale ranging from "Strongly disagree" to "Strongly agree". Several items of questionnaire were taken and adapted from relevant research (e.g., Alrabai 2014, Dornyei 1994, Dwinalida et al. 2015, Gardner 1985). The questionnaire was administered in Bahasa Indonesia, the learners' native language, to eliminate the risk that limited English competence of some respondents would affect their ability to respond all questions/statements.

This research used grille and indicators to obtain validity of the instrument. In addition, consultation to the experts was also done as well to obtain a really steady research instrument. To acquire the reliability of the instrument, this research administered the instrument twice to the part of population (N = 20) which were, of course, not the samples within two weeks as the gap. It was done after the validity of the instrument was acquired. Having administered the instrument twice, it was revealed that the mean scores of each item of the instrument from the first administration and the second administration were relatively the same. Thus, the instrument was considered reliable.

This research used percentage and descriptive analysis including mean and standard deviation to analyze the data. To make the calculation of percentage, mean and standard deviation easier, Microsoft Excel 2016 was used. Microsoft Excel is one of Microsoft Office applications which has function to number processing.

To measure the levels of motivation, the data interpretation which was in the form of mean was used based on the following guide:

1.0 – 3.0 = lowly motivated
3.1 – 4.0 = moderately motivated
4.1 – 5.0 = highly motivated

(adapted from Alrabai 2014, Dornyei 1994)

3 FINDING AND DISCUSSION

3.1 *Types of motivation*

Based on the results of the questionnaire, respondents were more integrative (M = 3.72) than instrumental (M = 3.70). However, the difference was not significant so that the learners actually possessed almost balanced motivation. As in the case of learners who are motivated by both instrumental and integrative motivation, this is not always true that these two motivational factors may be seen as being in opposition to each other (Crookes & Schmidt 1985).

In addition, when results showed that learners had more integrative motivation, it meant that they had desire to learn a foreign language because they were genuinely interested in the culture of the language. Additionally, the primary reasons why the learners were more integrative than instrumental were that actually they felt proud if they could speak English (M = 4.21), they wanted to be able to interact more easily with speakers of English (M = 4.13), and they felt their own satisfaction if they could learn English more than what they expected (M = 4.11). As Crookes & Schmidt (1985) state that one is integratively motivated if he or she desires to learn a foreign language simply because they find the target language culture, group, or the language itself to be attractive.

Furthermore, this research also found that the learners were also instrumentally motivated. Their primary reasons why they were instrumentally motivated were that they learnt English in order to search for information and materials in English easily (M = 4.37), they also learnt English in order to help them find a good job (M = 4.27), they learnt English to help them when they continue studying in the future in English-speaking countries (M = 4.21), and they learnt English in order to achieve good score in English subject (M = 4). As Crookes and Schmidt (1985: 471) state that when learners are driven to learn English because they believe learning it will benefit them in certain, specific ways (meeting other people, getting a job, and social pressure), this is referred to as instrumental motivation because the foreign language (English, in this case) is learned so that it can be used as a tool to improve the learners' lives.

The findings of this research were in line with the research conducted by Nichols (2014) in the elementary and secondary level. The findings stated that Indonesian EFL learners were more integrative. The primary reason why the learners were more integrative emphasized on the admission that Indonesians do express a desire to befriend native English speakers.

In addition, other research conducted in Indonesia by Lamb (2004) found that Indonesian high schools were more integrative than instrumental in studying English as a foreign language. The primary reason for studying English in those research contexts was to be able to have opportunities in a conversation with English speaking people, rather than pragmatic goals like in assisting in the pursuit of a career.

The findings of the above researches were in line with this research which found that Indonesian university learners were more integrative, but it had different primary reasons. The primary reasons why the learners were more integrative than instrumental were actually they wanted to be able to interact more easily with speakers of English, they felt proud if they could speak English, and they felt their own satisfaction if they could learn English more than what they expected.

However, In case of EFL learners, the findings of this research showing that Indonesian university EFL learners had more integrative motivation were not in line with the findings of the research done by Ma & Ma (2012) in Chinese learners. It was found that in a Chinese cultural setting, learners were more instrumently motivated. Ma & Ma (2012) attributed this tendency to the fact that Chinese learners learning English did so because of the important international role that English holds, as well as the government requirements.

3.2 Levels of motivation

According to the results of the questionnaire, it was revealed that the level of motivation of EFL learners in one of Indonesian private universities was 3.71. So, the level of motivation of the learners was moderate. It meant they were willing to learning English.

This above research finding was in line with the research conducted by Lamb (2004) in junior high school learners. It was found that learners' motivation both integrative and instrumental in relation to learning English as a global language was moderate.

Table 1. Descriptive statistics for each type of motivation.

Integrative motivation

M = 3.72 SD = 0.82	Mean	SD
I learn English because I will be able to interact more easily with speakers of English.	4.13	0.74
I learn English because I will be able to know the life of the English-speaking nations	3.50	0.92
I learn English because it will allow me to have English-speaker friends.	3.53	0.86
I learn English because it will allow me to appreciate English art and literature.	3.56	0.80
I will keep learning English even if I have graduated from university.	3.83	0.96
I would learn English even if it were not required by this university.	3.65	0.82
I want to be a part of English-speaking group.	3.27	0.96
I want to participate in the cultural activities of English-speaking group.	3.23	0.89
I feel happy when learning English.	3.64	0.87
I feel proud if I can speak English.	4.21	0.83
I learn English to enrich my knowledge.	4.35	0.56
It is my own satisfaction if I can learn English more than what I expected.	4.11	0.79
I want to integrate with English-speaking group.	3.34	0.79

Instrumental motivation

M = 3.70 SD = 0.87	Mean	SD
I learn English because it will be useful in getting a good job.	4.21	0.71
I learn English because I need it to pass English exams and graduate from the university.	4.02	0.90
I learn English because I will be able to search for information and materials in English.	4.37	0.67
I learn English because I like to travel to countries where English is used.	3.01	1.01
I learn English because it will help me when I continue studying.	4.21	0.76
I learn English to have a better salary later on.	3.35	1.03
I learn English because it will help me improve my competence in my career.	3.98	0.77
I learn English to have better life later on.	3.63	0.87
I learn English in order to achieve good score in English subject.	4	0.87
I learn English in order that people respect me more because I can speak English	2.88	1.07
I learn English because jobs require good English ability.	3.79	0.84
I learn English because I want to understand films, videos, and programs in English easily.	3.88	0.81
I learn English because my parents will give me reward if I master it.	2.70	1.04

On the contrary, in the context of Indonesian learners, this research finding was not in line with the finding of previous research conducted by Astuti (2013). It was stated that Indonesian EFL learners had low motivation. However, Astuti (2013) conducted the research in secondary level whereas this research was conducted in university level. In addition, other previous researches also stated that Indonesian high school learners are initially motivated to learn but their experience of learning English at school decreases their motivation over time (Lamb 2007).

In line with the level of motivation, cognitive skills in the target language do not guarantee that a learner can successfully master a foreign language. In fact, in many cases, learners with greater level of motivation of second/foreign language learning motivation receive better grades and achieve better proficiency in the target language (Brown 2000). In addition, high levels of motivation can make up for considerable deficiencies both in learners' language aptitude and learning context (Dornyei 2001). Without motivation, even the most intelligent learner can fail to learn the language. Additionally, motivated learners can master their target language regardless of their aptitude or other cognitive characteristics.

4 CONCLUSION AND SUGGESTION

Based on results and discussion, it could be concluded that types of motivation of EFL learners in one of Indonesian private universities were more integrative than instrumental motivation. This could reflect that the learners were actually sincere and had personal interest in the target language, people, and culture. It could be seen from the reasons why they actually learnt English such as learners really enjoyed learning English as they wanted to interact with English-speaking group easily and they would learn English even if it were not required by the university. They also felt proud if they could speak English and eventually they would be satisfied if they could learn English more than what they expected. In addition, the level of was 3.71. It indicated that they were willing to learning English and they believed that learning English is important.

This research implies a number of suggestions for EFL lecturers, EFL learners, and EFL curriculum designers. This research suggests that EFL lecturers should care for their learners' motivation by demonstrating proper personal and teaching behaviors in the classroom. Lecturers have to pay special attention to instructional media and the way they assess their learners in order to stimulate and maintain learners' motivation as well as raise learners' levels of motivation. In addition, lecturers should support their learners rather than be controlling or demanding. Moreover, lecturers must go beyond the fixed curriculum and the traditional methods of EFL teaching, and involve as many motivational techniques as possible in their teaching. Lecturers have to consider the types of motivation of their learners as well in order to choose appropriate instructional media and teaching learning process. For example, in the integrative motivation, in this research, the highest indicator was the learners learn English in order to interact with natives easily, as a consequence, lecturers should provide them with natives in once a month or more so that they can enjoy learning English and keep motivated. Then, in the instrumental motivation, the highest indicator was learning English in order to search for information and materials in English easily; in consequence, lecturers should provide them with materials in English so that they have to understand the language by learning English. Besides, lecturers should explain the benefits of learning English to their learners as well.

This research advises that Indonesian EFL learners be aware of the feelings and beliefs they experience when learning English. In this regard, learners have to recognize their irrational beliefs, fears, and feelings in order to interpret them in more realistic ways. They have to talk openly to their lectures about the nature of these feelings and beliefs in order to be known what types of motivation to learn English they actually possess.

This research recommends that curriculum designers of university are to design the EFL curriculum in ways that allow for the utilization of motivational techniques done by lecturers in order to stimulate and maintain learners' motivation as well as raise learners' levels of motivation. EFL curriculum content should be built on what learners see as important, not what designers think is important. In this regard, there should be clear and effective ways to connect the content of learning tasks to learners' interests, needs, goals, experiences, daily life activities, and real-world situation. In addition, learning tasks should contain novel and attractive elements that arouse learners' curiosity to learn and enhance their motivation too. The learning tasks should contain balanced content between integrative and instrumental motivation so that learners will not get doctrine toward a certain type of motivation. Finally, the quality rather than the quantity of the curriculum content should be cared for when designing the curriculum.

REFERENCES

Alrabai, F. 2014. Motivational practices in English as a foreign language classes in Saudi Arabia: Teachers beliefs and learners perceptions. *Arab World English Journal* 5(1): 224–246.

Arikunto, S. 2010. *Manajemen penelitian.* Jakarta: Rineka Cipta.

Astuti, S.P. 2013. Teachers' and students' perceptions of motivational teaching strategies in an Indonesian high school context. *TEFLIN journal* 24(1): 14–31.

Brown, H.D. 2000. *Teaching by principles: An interactive approach to language pedagogy.* California: Longman.

Cheng, H. & Dornyei, Z. 2007. The use of motivational strategies in language instruction: the case of EFL teaching in Taiwan. *Innovation in language learning and teaching* 1(1): 153–174.

Creswell, J.W. 2013. *Research design: Qualitative, quantitative, and mixed method approaches (3rd ed.).* California: SAGE Publications.

Crookes, G. & Schmidt, R. W. 1985. Motivation: Reopening the research agenda. *Language Learning* 41(4): 469–512.

Dornyei, Z. 1994. Motivation and motivating in the foreign language classroom. *Modern Language Journal* 78(3): 273–284.

Dornyei, Z. 1998. Motivation in second and foreign language learning. *Language Teaching* 31(3): 117–135.

Dornyei, Z. 2001. New themes and approaches in second language motivation research. *Annual Review of Applied Linguistics* 21(1): 43–59.

Dwinalida, et al. 2015. The relationship between students' motivation and English learning achievement in senior high school students. *Proceeding of International Conference of Teaching English as a Foreign Language* 7: 385–392.

Gardner, R.C. 1985. *Social psychology and second language learning: The role of attitudes and motivation.* London: Arnold.

Griffiths, C. 2008. *Lessons from good language learners* (ed.). New York: Cambridge University Press.

Harmer, J. 2007. *The practice of English language teaching.* Cambridge: Ashford Color Press.

Hsu, L. 2010. The impact of perceived teachers "nonverbal immediacy" on students' motivation for learning English. *Asian EFL Journal* 12(4): 188–204.

Kassing, R.B. 2011. *Perceptions of motivational teaching strategies in an EFL classroom: The case of a class in a private university in Indonesia.* (Published Thesis). Victoria University of Wellington.

Lamb, M. 2004. Integrative motivation in a globalizing world. *System* 32(1): 3–19.

Lamb, M. 2007. The impact of school on EFL learning motivation: An indonesian case study. *TESOL Quarterly* 41(4): 757–780.

Ma, Z & Ma, R. 2012. Motivating Chinese students by fostering learner autonomy in language learning. *Theory and Practice in Language Studies* 2(4): 838–842.

Nichols, R. 2014. *Motivating English language learners: An indonesian case study. Master of Education Program Theses.* (Published Thesis). University of Texas, Arlington.

Ryan, R & Deci, E. 2000. Intrinsic and extrinsic motivations: classic definitions and new directions. *Contemporary Educational Psychology* 25(2): 54–67.

Skehan. P. 1989. Individual Differences in Second-Language Learning. *Issues in Applied Linguistics* 2(1):168.

Sugiyono. 2012. *Metode penelitian pendidikan: Pendekatan kuantitatif, kualitatif, dan R & D.* Bandung: Alfabeta.

ELT in Asia in the Digital Era: Global Citizenship and Identity – Madya et al. (Eds)
© 2018 Taylor & Francis Group, London, ISBN 978-0-8153-7900-3

Influence of motivation and language learning environment on the successful EFL learning

Masyhur
FKIP Riau University, Riau, Indonesia

ABSTRACT: The research seeks to investigate successful learners' motivational changes and learning histories from the first time they studied English until the achievement of high proficiency in the foreign language. The central research questions are to reveal (1) what motivational changes and learning histories these learners display and (2) how they have sustained their learning motivation while studying in EFL environments. This is a case study involving both holistic and specifically focused analyses of six adult participant's learning history is collected through individual interviews. The research reports each participant's learning history resulting in the idea that sustained motivation is not always present in successful foreign language learning. What make these six successful EFL learners different from other learners are their perseverance and intensively-prioritized EFL learning or they develop a more intentional psychological force, known as commitment. The results provide new, engaging, and important information to what extent commitment to learn determines foreign language proficiency.

1   INTRODUCTION

These are the conditions found in many provincial areas of Indonesia. Government and international donors have long complained of inadequate levels of English among university graduates (for example, Sinclair & Webb 1985, Priyadi & Ismuadi 1998). Data from some universities in Sumatra indicate that about 75 per cent of students enter university with no more than 'elementary' level proficiency even after six years of English at school (Lamb 2000). Universities themselves rarely provide more than four credits (64 hours maximum) of English instruction for non-English majors, with the result that students are unable to read the English language textbooks in their subject areas, are thereby denied access to further language learning opportunities (as well as contemporary subject knowledge), and finally enter the labor market without the economically valuable asset of English proficiency.

Despite all the facts mentioned above, researchers have revealed many EFL learners who have been successful in the histories of their English Language learning. (see for example, Stevick 1989). These learners, despite the odds, have succeeded in achieving a degree of communicative competence in English. This similar situation has also occurred in the EFL Indonesian context e.g., in Riau Province. Although few in number, there are successful EFL learners in the province who have managed to become competent in the English language.

Researchers attribute the learners' success mostly to motivation. As a result, there has been an increase in research interest for the past four decades on language learning and has important implications on EFL learning success in both classroom and naturalistic learning environments. Recent work such as Csizer et al. (2010) emphasizes the dynamic nature of motivation. "Motivation not only changes through the different phases of language learning, but it can also fluctuate within a relatively short time interval due to the influence of external and internal factors" (Csizer et al. 2010: 473). While many studies have examined motivation as a learner trait at one point in time (e.g. Chen et al. 2005, Bernaus & Gardner 2008, Dörnyei & Kormos 2000), few studies (e.g. Dörnyei & Csizer 2002 & Gao 2008) have examined changes in motivation over time. The present research, therefore, aimed at examining in depth the motivation changes of the few EFL successful language learners in Riau Province Indonesia. The emergence, source, ways, order and time of motivation of their English language learning histories were examined in depth. If it can be discovered what enabled these few individuals to transcend the contextual constraints, we may be able to better help the majority who fail to do so, and who carry the burden of their failure with them throughout their working live.

The objectives of the present research firstly seek to display successful learners' dynamic motivational changes and their learning histories from the first time they studied English until the achievement of highly proficiency. Secondly, it also aims to examine how these learners have sustained their learning motivation while studying in EFL environments. While the two research objectives guide the overall study, several associated specific objectives were pursued the objectives are associated with when the most intensive learning took place, what learning strategies were employed, why intensive learning took place during those particular period(s), and other relevant issues that might have influenced their learning such as their family environment, influential people, and their interest other than English.

2   LITERATURE REVIEW

A study of foreign adults learning Norwegian was carried out by Svanes (1987) in Norway. She found that European and American students were more integratively motivated than the Middle Eastern, African and Asian students who were found to be more instrumentally motivated. Swanes reflects that westerners can have "luxury motives for coming to Norway to study", whereas for students from developing countries their motivation is "to get an education". In Swanes' study there was also a significant difference in the grades recorded, with Europeans having the best and Asian students the poorest scores. According to Swanes, and corresponding to Dörnyei's findings, this indicates that integrative motivation rather than instrumental motivation may lead to better proficiency. He points out that familiarity with the culture and the language will make it easy to communicate and learn the language. She maintains that such a closeness in culture develops an integrative motivation towards the target language culture which fits in with Schumann's (1978) theory that the social distance an L2 learner has with the TL community is a major factor in language learning. Asian women were found to be significantly less instrumentally motivated than Asian men but no such differences were found among the other groups. Such a low instrumental motivation could be due to lack of opportunities for women at least until recent times. No survey has been done which looks at his factor in the Japanese context in particular but there is a good chance that this difference may exist here also.

In a recent study, Schmidt, Boraie & Kassabgy (1996) investigated learners of English in an adult EFL setting in Cairo. Egypt would be representative of the developing countries which Swanes talked about in his research, the difference being that these learners were "on home turf." The authors were interested in finding out what "spurs thousands of Egyptians to exert the effort required and pay the fees for private instruction in English". Schmidt found a significant instrumental motivation which compares to Dörnyei's study (1990). Schmidt argues that instrumental factors are important for adults who have chosen to study English privately in contrast with young learners who take English as a school subject and who are not yet faced with career choices or the need to be concerned with making a living.

The remaining studies deal with younger learners—at the secondary and university level. Clement, Dörnyei & Noels (1994) looked at secondary level Hungarian students. They found that although these learners viewed English as an ordinary school subject with few chances for communication with the target culture on a personal level, they did think that contact with English was possible through the media and technology and English was widely recognized as the lingua franca of international communication. They found an instrumental orientation based on the acquisition of knowledge, rather than on the achievement of pragmatic outcomes and an integrative one based on expected foreign friendships through travel and an interest n English culture. This anticipated contact in the study resembles that of the adult learners in Dörnyei's previously cited study, indicating that adults and younger learners in an EFL context share similar integrative orientations.

The authors included the instrumental-knowledge orientation in the integrative motive, putting an end to what they and Oxford (1996) consider the "misleading use of a simplistic integrative-instrumental dichotomy". They also found two other motivation components-linguistic self-confidence and classroom group dynamics. They argue that group dynamics in the classroom setting have particular relevance to L2 instruction since communicative methodologies stress interaction between learners. Oxford (1996b) has stressed the need for longitudinal studies in order to monitor developmental changes in learners' motivation. Two studies, one by Teweles (1996) and the other by Berwick & Ross (1989) are longitudinal in nature. However, although Teweles claims his study to be part of a longitudinal study, he fails to point out any changes that occurred during the period of the study and indeed doesn't mention how long the study itself was. Teweles found differences between Chinese and Japanese university students, with the Japanese showing more of an integrative motivation than the Chinese who showed more of an instrumental motivation. This difference in motivations between the Japanese and Chinese learners is partly explained by the fact that English assumes a very specialized role in the Chinese context, with courses offered in connection with special needs such as 'Business English', but it could also have something to do with the difference Swanes (1996) found, as Japanese learners are way more affluent than their Chinese counterparts and perhaps also feel less of a social distance with the west. Teweles quotes Berwick & Ross' comment that there is a considerable decline in "instrumental interest" once the college entrance exams are over, as the reason Japanese students tended to score higher in integrative motivation.

Berwick & Ross (1989) assessed the motivation of university students at the beginning and end of their freshmen year. Their analysis indicated a limited development of an orientation towards personal growth through widening of their horizons and a desire to study abroad. While they support the idea that it is difficult to bring students back from the boredom of exam fever they also maintain that the curriculum is at fault, by not being relevant to learners' needs and motives for language study. They contrast this 'motivational vacuum' with the extraordinary interest in language learning among adults in Japan and emphasize that universities must do much more to motivate students in this direction.

Greer (1996) claims that a motivation survey of Japanese female junior college students he teaches is a useful tool in curriculum development. By understanding why students learn English, he uses the results to shape the course of classes he teaches especially when choosing textbooks or deciding how much conversation practice to do. He has found that integratively motivated students respond better to texts weighted towards conversation and more instruction. The majority $N \leq 68$ of students he surveyed were integratively motivated.

In a comparative study, Okada, Oxford & Abo (1996) found that the motivation of American learners of Japanese was far greater than that of learners of Spanish and concluded that motivation must be higher when one tries to learn a more difficult language because greater persistence and determination are needed to cope with the stress of a difficult situation. Conversely one might assume that for EFL learners in Japan, English is a difficult language to learn and so, such persistence and determination must also be present in order for language learning to be successful.

However this is rarely the case and unlike the U.S.A. where generally the motivated and able students choose to study Japanese, in Japan everyone has to learn English so teachers have to search for ways to motivate these less able students. It could be argued that one way to motivate these less able students is to offer incentives. Gardner & MacIntyre (1991) studied the effects of both instrumental and integrative motivation among university students. Results showed that both types of motivation facilitated learning but that those who were instrumentally motivated studied longer than those who were integratively motivated. They offered financial incentives for high performance on vocabulary tests and found that when the incentive was removed, students stopped applying more effort. Gardner & McIntryre stress this as being the major disadvantage of such instrumental motivation, but add that if the goal is continuous, instrumental motivation would continue to be effective.

Dörnyei (1994) stresses that the question of how to motivate students is an area on which L2 motivation has not placed sufficient emphasis in the past. He points to the lack of research into extrinsic motives such as grades and praise. Financial incentives such as those offered by Gardner & Lambert (1991) are not often feasible but other types of incentives such as certificates may work well especially with younger learners. Access to the Internet and other media such as newspapers and magazines in schools may take advantage of the "acquisition of knowledge" factor which Dörnyei (1994) found to be important for the students in his study. Such knowledge can be seen as 'intrinsic motivation' or motivation brought about by the stimulating or interesting presentation of the subject of study itself, an area where the teacher has the most influence and is therefore of paramount importance. However, as Ellis (1994) noted, there has been very little systematic research of the effects which pedagogic procedures have on motivation.

This lack of focus on intrinsic motivation has been borne out by the studies in this section. Intrinsic factors have been touched on but have not been the focus of research. As it has been found by Chihara & Oller, Schmidt, Teweles, Berwick & Ross that intended contact of some nature with the target culture plays an important role in motivation, a combination of strategies to motivate learners integratively and intrinsically is probably the key to enhancing language performance. Indeed, Berwick & Ross (1989) maintain that motivation to learn a language can be expanded by offering programs that offer attainable short-term goals, exchange programs with foreign colleges, short-term homestay programs overseas and programs with foreign students in Japan. These would seem to be a combination of intrinsic and integrative factors.

Oxford (1996b) contends that intrinsic motivation in the form of the classroom experience can be a big determiner in motivating power and with Okada et al. (1996) maintains that it is desirable to use activities in the classroom that "engage and enhance the learners' motivation." They consider that learners are not just interested in language but also in culture. Therefore motivation might be stimulated by weaving culture into classes more effectively in the form of "content of conversations, tapes, readings ....sociolinguistic aspects, cultural elements in games, simulations, and role plays which also reduce anxiety."

Dörnyei (1994) recommends 30 different ways to promote motivation among students. These serve as a very practical checklist for teachers, covering areas related to language, learner and learning situation plus teacher-specific and group-specific motivational components. As teachers in the foreign language classroom we have to be aware of the kinds of motivations our students bring with them but we also have to be aware of our own power to enhance those motivations and/or introduce different kinds which will further develop language learning.

3 METHODOLOGY

This study employed a multiple case study as suggested by Yin (2009). To this end, presenting a comprehensive case study protocol is crucial in this case. A case study protocol is applied in order to describe the process which was followed throughout the study; this includes aspects of the study that were added and altered as the study proceeded. Specifically, information concerning the case study design, participants, instrumentation, interviews, follow-up e-mail messages, case study questions, analyses, and case study report, are presented in the protocol.

The participants were the following six persons using pseudonyms, which were used based on those participants' requests: Dinda, Athalla, Pathia, Ratna, Indra, and Putri. They are highly proficient in English proved by their TOEFL/TOEIC scores and estimated written receptive vocabulary sizes. Table 1 presents the backgrounds of the six participants.

All the participants are native speakers of Bahasa Indonesia who were English instructors working in the same English faculty in a state university located in Riau Province. Some of them are lecturers, and others are part-time university instructors in more than one educational institution. A salient characteristic of the six participants was their advanced English speaking ability. Some university English instructors in Riau are unable to speak English well even though they are able to teach English (e.g., grammar and reading), but this was not the case with the English faculty in the department. This occurred because of the head of the department had extensive experience teaching English in a number of language schools before

Table 1. Participants' backgrounds.

Name	Gender	Age of starting to learn English	Total time studying English	Highest TOEFL Score	Highest TOEIC Score	Estimated Written Receptive Vocabulary Size
Dinda	Female	12	26 years	630	NA	12,700
Athalla	Male	12	33 years	NA	950	12,700
Pathia	Female	13	13 years	NA	920	11,500
Ratna	Female	13	39 years	270 (CBT)	990	13,200
Indra	Male	13	40 years	NA	NA	13,200
Putri	Female	10	19 years	283 (CBT)	980	10,000

becoming a university lecturer, and he recruited most of the new instructors utilizing his own personal network when he was put in charge of creating a new faculty, not through publicly posting the positions. As a consequence of this unique recruiting process, the new faculty members had advanced English-speaking proficiency. Furthermore, they came from a variety of backgrounds, which was another advantage of choosing research participants from this group.

4 RESULTS AND DISCUSSIONS

There are three issues discussed. The issues emerged from the collective analyses of the six case studies of the participants' English learning histories. First, fundamental issues concerning the characteristics of the participants are emphasized, their motivational development, and their learning. Second, the exploration focuses on seven motivational sources salient in the participants' English learning histories. Third, there is an examination of the initial proposition 1 concerning the participants' sustained motivation and discuss a new concept, commitment to learning.

4.1 Fundamental issues

The six case studies revealed that the participants were not special learners who were destined to consistently possess high levels of learning motivation and become highly proficient in English. Rather, at the onset of their English study, they were indistinguishable from many students found in English classrooms across Indonesia: They were from middle class families, their parents were not proficient in English, and they did not visit or live in an English-speaking country in their childhood. Most of them began studying English as a school subject at age 13 in a junior high school, and they studied to pass entrance examinations in their final years in junior high school and high school.

Academically, they were generally not exceptional students who were the top of their class in elementary and secondary school. English was not their only interest; they were involved in many other activities, such as playing music and sports, watching movies, painting, reading, writing, studying science and Japanese, and spending time with their friends. The participants' broad interests indicate that English learning represented just one of their interests. Despite the impression that they were unexceptional in most respects, the participants became exceptional English learners. Why was this possible? Did this happen partially because of the participants' innate traits and partially something they learned from the environment? Though the issue concerning the ratio between the inherited and the learned is hard to speculate and beyond the scope of this study, research on the development of expertise provides a clue to the answer to the question; a number of researchers have reported that an extended number of years of intensive practice of an activity is essential to achieve expertise in a field (Bloom 1985, Erricsson et al. 1993). This was true with the participants in this study; they prioritized acquiring English and they studied intensively for an extended period of time, both of which differentiated them from most other English foreign learners. The participants' perseverance was a primary reason for their exceptional achievement.

4.2 Salient motivational sources

In this section, seven salient motivational sources in the six participants' learning histories are discussed. Salient means: (a) the motivational source appeared in four or more of the six case studies, or (b) fewer than four but the issue was important to those participants. Five of these motivational sources, personal disposition, key people, internally emergent motivation, external goals, and authentic communicative experiences using English, played generally positive roles. In contrast, the final two motivational sources, *national examinations and classroom experience*, influenced the participants generally negatively.

4.3 The key to success in foreign language learning

In this section, the key to successful foreign language learning is discussed. In the first half, the initial underlying proposition of this study – successful learners have experienced motivational declines at least once, but they overcome such setbacks – is examined over the six case studies. After reconsidering the notion of sustained motivation, a new assumption concerning the key to successful foreign language learning is presented. In the charts presented in this section, the dotted line indicates the times of motivational decline and the solid lines indicate the times when motivational resurgence took place in the participants.

4.3.1 Dinda
Dinda stated that her motivation repeatedly increased and decreased, and that high levels of motivation were not sustained for longer than three years (See Figure 1). The primary pattern she displayed in her English study was based on goal achievement: she experienced a sharp motivational increase before achieving the goals and a sharp decline after attaining them. Dinda stated that she never particularly liked English, but she believed that English was a necessary tool in her quest to achieve other goals: enrolling in a good public high school, studying for the university entrance examinations, and enrolling in and academically succeeding in her undergraduate program and graduate program in the United States. She studied English with great intensity in order to achieve these goals. Therefore, her English learning motivation inevitably rose when she targeted a goal that required English skills and diminished when she achieved the goal.

4.3.2 Athalla
Athalla's major motivational increase and decrease happened at ages 24 and 26 (See Figure 2). The first motivational decrease took place at age 24 after he graduated from his

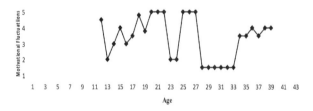

Figure 1. Dinda's motivational fluctuations.

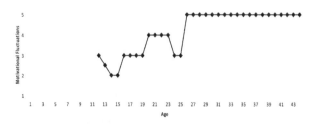

Figure 2. Athalla's motivational fluctuations.

university. He abandoned his hope to become a professional musician, but he did not have a specific alternative in mind for a while. As he was not serious about a future profession, he worked as a telex operator for two years after graduating from the university. At age 26, his motivation resurged when he ended his moratorium period and decided to become a fully engaged in mainstream society. When considering a possible professional goal, he selected an English-related profession and reentered the university to study English literature. Because his academic and professional pursues were related to English, he was motivated to improve his English skills.

4.3.3 *Pathia*

Pathia's motivation noticeably declined at age 18 and began a resurgence at age 20 (See Figure 3). Before this largest fluctuation occurred, her motivation increased to all time high at age 17 when she participated in a two week study abroad program in the United States. Because of the impact from that study abroad program, she wished to study English intensively to become a good English speaker after enrolling in the university she wanted to attend; however, she temporarily postponed her desire because she had to study for the university entrance examinations for the entire next year. Her motivational decline happened because of the negative washback of the university entrance examinations. After being free from the intensive studying for the entrance examinations, she allowed herself to enjoy a more relaxed life as a university student. As a result, her English learning motivation was weakened and she did not seriously study English for the next two years. At age 20, visiting Australia triggered her learning motivation again.

Using English communicatively in an English-speaking country led her to regret the past two years during which her English did not improve at all; however, it also promoted her to recall her desire to become a good English speaker. This experience provided her with a strong impetus to study English, and she once again began to pursue her goal to become a good English communicator.

4.3.4 *Ratna*

Ratna's motivational decrease took place at 18 and her motivational resurgence occurred when she was 29 (See Figure 4). The decrease occurred when she enrolled in the Japanese literature department in her university. Even though English was her favorite subject and she liked and was enthusiastic to study it in high school, it was merely one of many school subjects to her. After completing the university entrance examinations, English became nearly irrelevant in her life, a situation that continued for the next 10 years. After finishing her undergraduate studies, she worked at the city office for eight and a half years but was never satisfied with the job. While searching for a more interesting and challenging career, she

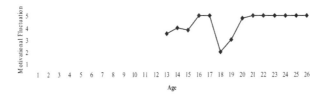

Figure 3.   Pathia's motivational fluctuation.

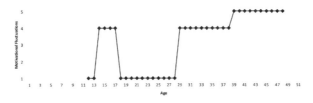

Figure 4.   Ratna's motivational fluctuation.

encountered English again and her motivation to study was revived. English once again captured her interest and provided her with a new profession, teaching English. Since that time, she has been motivated to improve her English skills for the sake of her profession.

4.3.5 *Indra*
Similar to Dinda, Indra stated that his learning motivation rose and fell periodically. His motivation to study English emerged primarily internally and was based on his interest in English, learning English, and English related activities. Figure 5 illustrates his motivational fluctuations, which moved in accordance with the changes of his interest. Although his motivation temporarily decreased at age 16 after failing the high school entrance examinations and at 18 after failing the university entrance examinations, his motivation resurged when he engaged in English-related activities that captured his interest, for example, studying English, especially memorizing a great deal of vocabulary in high school, speaking English and forming the English club at 20, acting as a tour guide and interpreter and leading the student tour guide interpreter club at the age of 21, passing the tour guide test and teaching English at a language school at 22, and studying linguistics in graduate school at 33. Each case clearly shows that every participant experienced at least one motivation decline followed by a subsequent resurgence in motivation. Thus, initial proposition 1 was supported by all six case studies. The participants potentially could have lost their learning motivation and not experienced its resurgence; consequently, they would not have achieved a high level of English proficiency, as is the case with the majority of English learners in Japan. This suggests that successful learners' advanced proficiency is a consequence of conquering motivational challenges that occurred in their long-term learning histories. The path to advanced proficiency in a foreign language is rough and winding, rather than smooth and straight.

4.3.6 *Putri*
Putri's brief motivational fluctuation took place between the ages of 17 and 18 (See Figure 6). Her motivation has been constantly high because her interest in English had never dwindled and she had selected an English-related career goal at age 15 by choosing to focus on English rather than the piano; however, a motivational decrease occurred because of the disappointing classroom experience she had in her university. At age 18 when she became a univer-

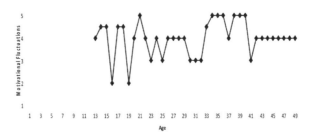

Figure 5.   Indra's motivational fluctuation.

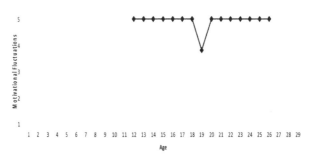

Figure 6.   Putri's motivational fluctuation.

212

sity freshman, she had to take a general English course with relatively unmotivated and lower proficiency students. Even though she had had a long term English goal and had been motivated to study English in high school, her motivation was affected negatively when facing the demotivating class atmosphere. She felt that studying hard was neither encouraged nor appreciated in the class where few students tried to study hard. If she had experienced the same kind of course next year, her motivation might have been jeopardized further. However, her motivation resurged to its highest level the next year because she obtained the qualification to take the intensive English course in the university. The class atmosphere was entirely different from the course she took the previous year: The students were highly motivated, and a number of them aimed to study abroad. The course instructors were also enthusiastic, and hard work was rewarded and valued. In addition, taking the course was an important step in applying to the study abroad program in her junior year. Therefore, her English learning motivation returned to its previous high level.

4.4 *Applying the motivation-commitment model to the participants*

Finally, let us reexamine the participants' English learning histories, this time applying the motivation-commitment interaction model. The primary focus is on: (a) the important motivational sources that underlie the formation and emergence of commitment and, (b) when English became important to the participants, as this provides a clue to the emergence of commitment. In addition, the participants' investment in activities involving studying English, prioritizing these activities over other alternatives, and the challenges they faced are also discussed. Because the concept of commitment emerged in the final phase of the data analyses, I have never asked the participants about their commitment to learning. Thus, the following discussions are based on my interpretation of their learning histories as viewed through the lens of the motivation-commitment interaction model. In the figures below, the arrows schematize the formation and emergence of commitment in the participants. The motivational source(s) in bold are directly and immediately involved in the moment when English became important to each participant.

4.4.1 *Dinda*

Studying English became important for Dinda when she studied abroad at ages 17, 20, and 25. Her primary motivation was instrumental, as English was a tool for her to achieve her other goals that always required advanced English proficiency because she was competing with native speakers of English. When necessary, she exerted a tremendous effort and studied intensively to "win the game," or to succeed in the academic programs in which she was enrolled. In particular, in the first one-year study abroad experience at age 17 and the second one when she attended the undergraduate program in the United Stated to study journalism at age 20, English was a crucial requirement, given that she would not have been able to participate in and complete these programs successfully without achieving advanced English abilities. In the beginning of both study abroad experiences, she faced linguistic, academic, and

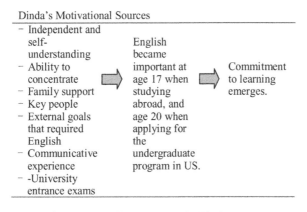

Figure 7.   The formation and emergence of commitment in Dinda.

213

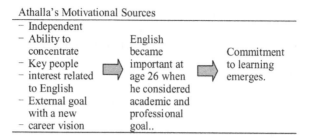

Athalla's Motivational Sources

– Independent
– Ability to
  concentrate
– Key people
– interest related
  to English
– External goal
  with a new
– career vision
	English
	became
	important at
	age 26 when
	he considered
	academic and
	professional
	goal..
		Commitment
		to learning
		emerges.

Figure 8. The formation and emergence of commitment in Athalla.

cultural challenges, which she overcame with unexceptional hard work. She prioritized achieving her goals to a degree that resulted in serious health problems. Although her commitment might not necessarily have been to learning English, I believe that commitment to achieving her goals likely formed and emerged during these periods of studying abroad (Figure 7).

4.4.2 Athalla

English became important for Athalla at age 26 when he considered what academic and professional career he wanted to pursue. At the age of 26, he decided to return to his university to study English literature. Until that time, he had not considered his long-term goals realistically. He had valued English to a certain degree since he was a high school student, as he frequently read English novels and watched western movies, and he was inspired by his reading teacher in the university, but he studied English primarily to satisfy his own interest. In contrast, the decision he made at age 26 was more serious and associated with a professional goal, and he has continuously made an effort to improve his English skills. I believe that his commitment to learning emerged with this decision (See Figure 8).

4.4.3 Pathia

English attained a special value for Pathia when she met and communicated with the American high school students at age 17 when studying abroad for the first time. Though she had liked English as a school subject in junior high school and she enrolled in the English course in high school, the impact she received from the experience in the study abroad program changed her perception toward learning English. Because her English communicative ability had not developed yet, participating in the communicative activities with the American students was great deal of challenging experience for her. After this experience, the American students became role models whom she perceived in an idealistic way, and acquiring a high degree of English proficiency became the goal that she most wanted to achieve.

This goal was set autonomously and consciously by Pathia and was not based on encouragement from other people, such as her parents or teacher. Although it took Pathia several years to begin seriously pursuing her goal and investing a great deal of time and energy in English study due to the powerful negative washback from the university entrance examinations, her commitment to learning likely started sometime around this event (see Figure 9).

4.4.4 Ratna

English became important to Ratna at around age 29 when she resumed studying English at the end of her prolonged period of job searching. She had had a stable job she was not satisfied with and wished to quit for eight years. Working in the unsatisfying and frustrating situation, her psychological challenges gradually developed into physical health problems. She encountered English at this time again. Though her initial motivation was merely instrumental—she thought that passing the second level of the English test might help her find a new job, English soon became interesting and important to her. Unlike her high school period, English was not just one of her favorite school subjects; acquiring English became an important goal that provided her with an interesting and challenging career. The intensive study, effort, and investment she made afterward to improve her English skills and develop her English teaching career indicate that her commitment to learning emerged at this time (see Figure 10).

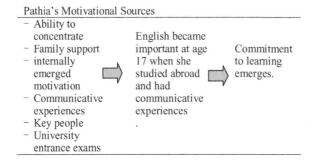

Figure 9.   The formation and emergence of commitment in Pathia.

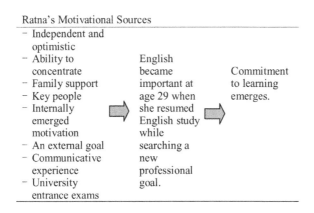

Figure 10.   The formation and emergence of commitment in Ratna.

4.4.5   *Indra*

English became special for Indra at age 19 when he began speaking English for the first time in his university course. Having only studied reading, grammar, and vocabulary in high school, speaking English was novel and fascinating to him. Even though he was a fundamentally science-oriented person and his favorite subject had been physics, speaking English captured his interest, and he made an extraordinary effort to improve his speaking skills. It was a starting point for him to participate in a variety of English-related activities in which he used and improved his English speaking skills to establish the ESS club, become a tour guide interpreter, teach English, publish English textbooks, and study linguistics. His exceptional effort to improve his English skills has not stopped since then. Thus, his commitment to learning might have begun to form at this time (see Figure 11).

4.4.6   *Putri*

English became special for Putri at age 15 when she decided that her future career options related to English were more practical and achievable than the career as a professional pianist, though she had enjoyed and enthusiastically engaged in both activities since she was an elementary school student. Because of her family environment and her parents' support, she had been exposed to and had liked English since she was a child; however, her decision at age 15 to select an English-focused high school course increased the importance of English for her. While playing the piano became a hobby, increasing her English proficiency became a serious and concrete goal for her. After prioritizing English over the piano, Putri has invested a great deal of time and energy in developing her English skills. Thus, it is possible that her commitment to learning emerged after this event (see Figure 33). The entrance examinations, her commitment to learning likely started sometime around this event (see Figure 12).

215

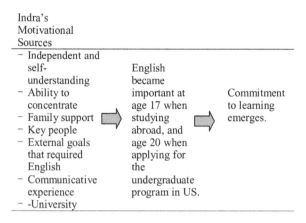

Figure 11.   The formation and emergence of commitment in Indra.

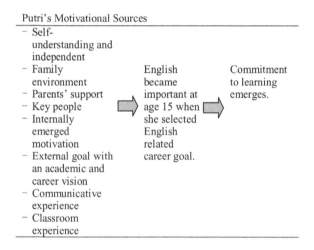

Figure 12.   The formation and emergence of commitment in Putri.

4.5   *Applying the motivation-commitment model to English learners in Riau*

The motivation-commitment interaction model allows us to perceive motivational development in foreign language learning from a new angle, which can help us better understand learners' motivational development and their eventual successes and failures in foreign language learning. For instance, important questions, such as why only a limited number of foreign language learners become proficient in English in spite of the fact that a large number of young learners are motivated to study the language, or why negative washback from taking the entrance examination occurs frequently in university students, can be explained by the model. Conventional wisdom suggests that these results occur because the learners' learning motivation is too weak, but the model provides an alternative explanation: For the majority of English learners in Riau, English is not important in any realistic sense—they can carry on their lives without using English, and commitment to learning it is unlikely emerge in that context. Even if they are motivated to study English when they begin their formal education in the language or they think that English is important when studying for the entrance examinations while in middle school, they have not been intentional and autonomous about their learning to a degree that allows them to prioritize studying English over other important activities, to persist in their efforts to develop their English skills further, and to overcome the challenges they inevitably encounter. The motivation-commitment interaction model implies that acquiring a foreign language in an EFL context is not necessarily a task that "motivated" learners can achieve.

216

5 CONCLUSIONS

This multiple case study was an investigation of six highly proficient learners' motivational changes and their learning histories. The results illuminate the complex and dynamic development of the participants' motivational fluctuation in the long-term process of foreign language learning. Each participant's learning history vividly shows that each individual's motivational development and learning history was fundamentally unique because a number of motivational sources interacted with one another at different times, in different orders, and in different contexts. Second, the six case studies allowed me to confirm an underlying proposition concerning successful learners' foreign language learning motivation I made at the onset of the study: Successful learners have experienced one or more motivational declines but have overcome such experiences. This indicates that the path to acquiring high proficiency in a foreign language is a dynamic and challenging one in which motivational fluctuations are a common occurrence. Third, searching for the keys to the participants' sustained motivation revealed seven salient motivational sources in their learning histories: the learners' personal dispositions, their family environment, internal factors, especially interest, external goals, their communicative experiences, especially those that occurred while studying abroad, the entrance examinations, and their classroom experiences.

Finally, exploring the participants' learning histories collectively led to the emergence of two new related findings regarding the key to successful foreign language learning. First, sustained motivation is not always a prerequisite for achieving high levels of proficiency and in some cases is insufficient. Second, the emergence of commitment, which is an intentional, enduring psychological force, is more important in the long term than what has been called motivation and is perhaps necessary in some learning contexts, such as those in which access to linguistic input and communicative opportunities are limited. The data gathered in this study suggest that one key to success in foreign language learning is commitment to learning, a cognitive change that emerged at some point in each of the participants' learning histories through the interaction of several motivational sources. This change always occurred after the participants perceived that English was important to them and sometimes involved challenges they had faced previously and wanted to overcome. Commitment is conceptualized as a key element in the motivation-commitment interaction model, and the participants' learning histories were reexamined using the model. I propose that the model plausibly explains the tremendous effort and extraordinary achievements the participants made in their acquisition of English; motivation alone failed to completely explain these achievements. Centering the analysis on the learners' voices and their stories made these new insights possible.

REFERENCES

Beglar, D. 2010. A Rasch-based validation of the vocabulary size test. *Language Testing* 27(1): 101–118.

Benson, P. 2004. (Auto) biography and learner diversity. In P. Benson & D. Nunan (Eds.), *Learners' stories: Difference and diversity in language learning* (pp. 4–21). Cambridge: Cambridge University Press.

Benson, P. 2006. Autonomy in language teaching and learning. *Language Teaching* 40: 21–40.

Bjork, C. 2004. Decentralization in education in Indonesia. *International Review of Education* 50: 245–262.

Brown, H.D. 2000. *Principles of language learning and teaching* (4th ed.). NY: Addison Wesley Longman, Inc.

Brown, J.D. 2005. *Testing in language programs: A comprehensive guide to English language assessment.* New York: McGraw-Hill.

Chen, J.F., Warden, C.A. & Cheng, H. 2005. Running head: Motivators that do not motivate. *TESOL Quarterly* 39(4): 609–633.

Coon, D. 2001. *Introduction to psychology: Gateways to mind and behavior* (9th ed.). Belmont, CA: Wordsworth.

Creswell, J.W. 2007. *Qualitative inquiry and research design: Choosing among five approaches.* Thousand Oaks, CA: Sage.

Deci, E.L. & Ryan, R.M. 2000. The "What" and "Why" of goal pursuits: Human needs and the self-determination of behavior. *Psychological Inquiry* 11(4): 227–268.

Donitsa-Schmidt, S., Inbar, O. & Shohamy, E. 2004. The effects of teaching spoken Arabic on students' attitudes and motivation in Israel. *Modern Language Journal* 88(2): 217–28.

Dornyei, Z. & Schmidt, R. (Eds.) 2001, *Motivation and second language acquisition*. Honolulu, HI: University of Hawaii Press.

Dornyei, Z. 2000. Motivation in action: Towards a process-oriented conceptualization of student motivation. *British Journal of Educational Psychology* 70: 519–538.

Dörnyei, Z. 2001. *Teaching and researching motivation*. Harlow: Longman.

Dornyei, Z. 2003. Attitudes, orientations, and motivations in language learning: Advances in theory, research and applications. *Language Learning* 53(1): 3–32.

Dornyei, Z. 2003b. Introduction. In Z. Dornyei (Ed.) *Attitudes, orientations, and motivations in language learning: Advances in theory, research and applications*. Blackwell Publishing.

Dörnyei, Z. 2005. *The psychology of the language learner: Individual differences in second language acquisition*. Mahwah, NJ: Erlbaum.

Dörnyei, Z. & Ushioda, E. 2011. *Teaching and researching motivation* (2nd ed.). Harlow: Longman.

Dörnyei, Z., Csizér, K. & Németh, N. 2006. *Motivation, language attitudes and globalisation: A Hungarian perspective*. Clevedon: Multilingual Matters.

Duff, P.A. 2008. *Case study research in applied linguistics*. Mahwah, NJ: Lawrence Erlbaum.

Falout, J. & Maruyama, M. 2004. A Comparative Study of Proficiency and Learner Demotivation. *The Language Teacher* 28(8): 3–9.

Gable, S.L. & Haidt, J. 2005. What (and why) is positive psychology? *Review of General Psychology* 9(2): 103–110.

Gao, Y., Li, Y. & Li, W. 2002. EFL learning and self-identity construction: three cases of Chinese College English Majors. *Asian Journal of English Language Teaching* 12(2): 95–119.

Gardner, R.C. 2001. Integrative motivation: Past, present and future. *Distinguished Lecturer Serious*. Temple University Japan, Tokyo, February 17, 2001. Retrieved October 10, 2003 from http://publish.uwo.ca/~gardner/GardnerPublicLecture1.pdf.

Gardner, H. 2006. *Multiple intelligences: New horizons*. New York: Basic Books. Gardner, R.C. (1985). *Social psychology and second language learning*. London: Edward Arnold.

Gardner, R.C., Masgoret, A.-M., Tennant, J., & Mihic, L. 2004. Integrative motivation: Changes during a year-long intermediate-level language. *Language Learning* 54(1): 1–34.

Gershenson, C. 2002. Contextuality: A Philosophical Paradigm, with Applications to Philosophy of Cognitive Science. [Departmental Technical Report] (Unpublished document). Retrieved 30.05.08 from http://cogprints.org/2621/.

Harmer, J. 2003. *The practice of English language teaching*. Harlow, England: Pearson Education Limited.

Hayashi, H. 2005. Identifying different motivational transitions of Japanese ESL learners using cluster analysis: Self-determination perspectives. *JACET Bulletin* 41: 1–17.

Heckhausen, J., & Heckhausen, J. (Eds.). 2008. *Motivation and action*. New York: Cambridge University Press.

Hidi, S., Renninger, K.A. & Krapp, A. 2004. Interest, a motivational variable that combines affective and cognitive functioning. In D.Y. Dai & R.J. Sternberg (Eds.), *Motivation, emotion, and cognition* (pp. 89–115). Mahwah, NJ: Erlbaum.

Horwitz, E.H. 2000. Teachers and students, students and teachers: An ever-evolving partnership. *The Modern Language Journal* 84(4): 523–535.

Inbar, O., Donitsa-Schmidt, S & Shohamy, E. 2001. Students' motivation as a function of language learning: The teaching of Arabic in Israel. In Z. Dornyei & R. Schmidt (Eds.) *Motivation and second language acquisition* (Technical Report #23, pp. 297–311). Honolulu: University of Hawai'i, Second Language Teaching and Curriculum Center.

Janssens, S. & Mettewie, L. 2004. Cross-sectional and longitudinal view of attitudes and motivations to SLL. Paper presented at the 15th Sociolinguistics Symposium. Newcastle, April 2004. Retrieved 3.05.2008 from http://www.ncl.ac.uk/ss15/papers/paper_details.php?id=176.

Kanno, Y. 2003. *Negotiating bilingual and bicultural identities: Japanese returnees betwixt two worlds*. Mahwah, NJ: Erlbaum.

Lamb, M. & Coleman, H. 2002. Literacy in English and the transformation of self and society in Post-Suharto Indonesia. *International Journal of Bilingual Education and Bilingualism*.

Lamb, M. 2002. Explaining successful language learning in difficult circumstances. Prospect: *.4n4 ustralian Journal of TESOL* 17(2): 35–52.

Lamb, M. 2004. Integrative motivation in a globalizing world. *System* 32(1): 3–19.

Lamb, M. 2005. "It depends on the students themselves": Independent language learning at an Indonesian state school. *Language, Culture, and Curriculum* 17(3): 229–245.

ldrus, N. 2000, 26th September. Education: Sad facts in Indonesia. *The Jakarta Post*, 4.

Lim, H.-Y. 2002. The interaction of motivation, perception, and environment: One EFL learner's experience. *Hong Kong Journal of Applied Linguistics* 7(2): 91–106.

Little, D. 2007. Language learner autonomy: Some fundamental considerations revisited. *Innovation in Language Learning and Teaching* 1(1): 14–29.

Locke, E. & Latham, J. 2002. Building a practically useful theory of goal setting and task motivation: A 35-year odyssey. *American Psychologist* 57(90): 705–717.

Masgoret, A.M. & Gardner, R.C. 2003. Attitudes, motivations, and second language learning: A meta-analysis of studies conducted by Gardner and associates. *Language Learning* 53(1): 123–163.

McGroarty, M. 2001. Situating second language motivation. In Z. Dornyei & R. Schmidt (Eds.) Motivation and second language acquisition (Technical Report #23, pp. 69–92). Honolulu: University of Hawai'i, Second Language Teaching and Curriculum Center.

McIntosh, C.N. & Kimberly N.A. 2004. Self-determined motivation for language learning: The role of need for cognition and language learning strategies. Zeitschrift fur Interkulturellen Fremdsprachenunterricht [Online], 9(2). Retrieved July 14, 2004 from http://www.ualberta.ca/~german/ejournal/Mcintosh2.htm.

Mistar, J. 2001. Maximizing learning strategy to promote learner autonomy. *TEFLIN* 12(1).

Miura, T. 2007a. *Success after failure: An introspective case study of L2 motivation.* Paper presented at the 2007 Applied Linguistics Colloquium, Temple University Japan.

Miura, T. 2007b. Vocabulary development in relation to motivational trajectory: Retrospective case studies of high proficiency learners. Unpublished manuscript. Temple University Japan.

Miura, T. 2010. The changes of L2 learning motivation. *JALT Journal* 32: 29–53.

Morita, N. 2004. Negotiating participation and identity in second language academic communities. *TESOL Quarterly* 38(4): 573–603.

Nairne, J.S. 2000. *Psychology: The adaptive mind.* Belmont, CA: Wordsworth.

Nakata, Y. 2006. Motivation and experience in foreign language learning. Bern, Switzerland: Peter Lang.

Nation, I.S.P. 2001. *Learning vocabulary in another language.* Cambridge: Cambridge University Press.

Nation, I.S.P. 2007. The vocabulary size test [Electronic Version]. Retrieved February 27, 2007 from http://www.vuw.ac.nz/lals/staff/paulnation/ nation.aspx.

Nikolov, M. 2001. A study of unsuccessful language learners. In Z. Dörnyei & R. Schmidt (Eds.), *Motivation and second language acquisition* (pp. 149–169). Honolulu, HI: University of Hawaii at Manoa. Second Language Teaching and Curriculum Center.

Nisbet, D.L., Tindall, E.V. & Arroyo, A.A. 2005. Language learning strategies and English proficiency of Chinese university students. *Foreign Language Annual* 38(10): 100.

Noels, K. 2001. New orientations in language learning motivation: Towards a model of intrinsic, extrinsic, and integrative orientations and motivation. In Z. Dörnyei & R. Schmidt (Eds.), *Motivation and second language acquisition* (pp. 44–68). Honolulu: University of Hawai'i.

Noels, K.A. 2001. Learning Spanish as a second language: learners' orientations and perceptions of their teachers' communication style. Language Learning 51(1): 107–144.

Noels, K.A., Pelletier, L.G., Clement, R. & Vallerand, R.J. 2000. Why are you learning a second language? Motivational orientations and self-determination theory. *Language Learning* 50(1): 57–85.

Noels, K., Pelletier, L.G., Clement, R. & Vallerand, R.J. 2000. Why are you learning a second language? Motivational orientations and selfdetermination theory. *Language Learning* 50(1): 57–58.

Ortega, L. 2009. *Understanding second language acquisition.* London, UK: Hodder Education.

Oxford, R. 2001. "The bleached bones of a story": learners' constructions of language teachers. In M. Breen (Ed.), *Learner Contributions to Language Learning*

Oxford, R.L. 1990. *Language learning strategies: What every teacher should know.* Boston: Heinle & Heinle Publishers. languages (pp. 167–172). Cambridge: Cambridge University Press.

Pagliaro, A. 2002. Motivation and its implications in tertiary Italian studies. Proceedings of Innovations in Italian teaching workshop (pp. 16–25). Italy: Griffith University. Retrieved 25.10.03 fromwww.gu.edu.au/centre/italian/pdf/2_pag.pdf.

Pajares, F. 2001. Toward a positive psychology of academic motivation. *The Journal of Educational Research* 95(1): 27–35.

Peterson, C. 2000. The future of optimism. *American Psychologist* 55(1): 44–55.

Richards, J.C. & Lockhart, C. 2004. *Reflective teaching in second language classroom.* Cambridge: Cambridge University Press.

Ryan, S. 2009. Self and identity in L2 motivation in Japan: The ideal L2 self and Japanese learners of English. In Z. Dörnyei & E. Ushioda (Eds.), *Motivation, language identity and the L2 self* (pp. 120–143). Bristol: Multilingual Matters.

Sawir, E. 2005. Language difficulties of international students in Australia: The effects of prior learning experience. *International Education Journal* 6(5): 567–580.

Sawyer, M. 2007. Motivation to learning foreign language: Where does it come from, where does it go? *Gengo to Bunka* 10: 33–42.

Schumann, J.H. 2001. Appraisal psychology, neurobiology, and language. *Annual Review of Applied Linguistics* 21: 23–42.

Schwarz, A. 2000. A Nation in Mailing: Indonesia's search for stability. Boulder, CO: Westview Press.

Seidman, I. 2006. *Interviewing as qualitative research: A guide for researchers in education and the social sciences* (3rd ed.). New York: Teachers College Press.

Seligman, M.E.P. & Csikszentmihalyi, M. 2000. Positive psychology. *American Psychologist* 55(1): 5–14.

Setiyadi, B. 2001. Language learning strategies: Classification & pedagogical implication. *TEFLIN* 12(1).

Shoaib, A. & Dörnyei, Z. 2004. Affect in lifelong learning: Exploring L2 motivation as a dynamic process. In P. Benson & D. Nunan (Eds.), *Learners' stories: Difference and diversity in language learning* (22–41). Cambridge: Cambridge University Press.

Snyder, C.R. (Ed.). 2000. *Handbook of hope: Theory, measures, and applications*. San Diego, CA: Academic Press.

Spolsky, B. 2000. Anniversary article: Language motivation revisited. *Applied Linguistics* 21(2): 157–169.

Spolsky, B. 2000. Language motivation revised. *Applied Linguistics* 21(2): 157–169.

Squires, T. & Kawaguchi, Y. 2004. *Construction of subjectivity in learners' motivation narratives.* Paper presented at the JALT 2004 Nara: Language Learning for Life, Nara, Japan.

Sternberg, R.J. 2006. A duplex theory of love. In R.J. Sternberg & K. Weis (Eds.), *The new psychology of love* (pp. 184–199). New Haven: Yale University Press.

Takeuchi, O. 2003. What can we learn from good foreign language learners? A qualitative study in the Japanese foreign language context. *System* 31: 385–392.

Tse, L. 2000. Student perceptions of foreign language study: A qualitative analysis of foreign language autobiographies. *Modern Language Journal* 84: 69–84.

Ushioda, E. 2001. Language learning at university: Exploring the role of motivational thinking. In Z. Dörnyei & S. Richard (Eds.), *Motivation and second language acquisition* (pp. 93–125). Honolulu, HI: University of Hawaii at Manoa. Second Language Teaching and Curriculum Center.

Ushioda, E. 2007. Motivation, autonomy and sociocultural theory. In P. Benson (Ed.), *Learner autonomy 8: Teacher and learner perspectives* (pp. 5–24). Dublin, Ireland: Authentik.

Ushioda, E. 2008. Motivation and good language learners. In C. Griffiths (Ed.), *Lessons from good language learners* (pp. 19–34). Cambridge: Cambridge University Press.

Ushioda, E. 2009. A person-in-context relational view of Emergent Motivation, self and identity. In Z. Dörnyei & E. Ushioda (Eds.), *Motivation, language identity and the L2 self* (pp. 215–228). Bristol: Multilingual Matters.

Vandergrift, L. 2005. Relationships among motivation orientations, metacognitive awareness and proficiency in L2 listening. *Applied Linguistics* 26(1): 70–89.

Verhoeven, L. & Vermeer, A. 2002. Communicative competence and personality dimensions in first and second language learners. *Applied Psycholinguistics* 23: 361–374.

Vohs. K., Baumeister, B., Jean M. Twenge, J., Nelson, N. & Tice, D. 2008. Making choices impairs subsequent self-control: A limitedresource account of decision making, self-Regulation, and active initiative. *Journal of Personality and Social Psychology* 94(5): 883–898.

Watkins, D., McInerney, D.M., Lee, C., Akande, A. & Regmi, M. 2002. Motivation and learning strategies. A cross-cultural perspective. In D.M. McInerney & S. Van Etten (eds.), *Research on Sociocultural Influences on Motivation and Learning* 2. Greenwich, CT: Information Age.

Webb, V. 2002. English as a second language in South Africa's tertiary institutions. *World Englishes* 21(1): 63–81.

Werf, G.v.d., Creemers, B. & Guldemond, H. 2001. Improving parental involvement in primary education in Indonesia: Implementation, effects and costs. *School Effectiveness and School Improvement* 12: 447.

Widiastono, T. 2006. Pelajaran bahasa asing di sekolah: Adakah yang salah? *KOMPAS*. Jakarta, Indonesia. Available at http://www.kompas.com/kompas-cetak/ 0407/08/PendlN/11 36711.htm [accessed 29.01.07]

Yashima, T. 2002. Willingness to communicate in a second language: The Japanese EFL context. *Modern Language Journal* 86: 54–66.

Yashima, T. & Zenuk-Nishide, L. 2008. The impact of learning contexts on proficiency, attitudes, and L2 communication: Creating an imagined international community. *System* 36(4): 566–585.

Yin, R.K. 2006. Case study methods. In J.L. Green, G. Camilli & P.B. Elmore (Eds.), *Handbook of complementary methods in education research* (pp. 111–122). Mahwah, NJ: Erlbaum.

Yin, R.K. 2009. *Case study research: Design and methods* (4th ed.). Thousand Oaks, CA: Sage.

ELT in Asia in the Digital Era: Global Citizenship and Identity – Madya et al. (Eds)
© *2018 Taylor & Francis Group, London, ISBN 978-0-8153-7900-3*

L2 learning motivation from the perspective of self-determination theory: A qualitative case study of hospitality and tourism students in Taiwan

H.T. Hsu
National Taiwan Normal University, Taipei, Taiwan

ABSTRACT: This study adopted the Self-Determination Theory (SDT) (Deci & Ryan 1985) to examine EFL hospitality and tourism students' L2 learning motivation. By analyzing interview data obtained from four EFL hospitality and tourism students, this study focuses on their English learning motivation from the SDT perspect. These students were sophomores and studied in the University Hospitality and Tourism in Taiwan. The findings reveal that the learning environment and teachers' teaching style can facilitate or undermine learners' English learning motivation. Besides, the learners can gain satisfaction from intrinsically motivated task engagement. The learners also become self-determined because they see the English learning relevance to their future job based on the concept of identified regulation. Finally, participants think it is right and suitable for them to be members of the English-speaking community according to integrated regulation. The study provides pedagogical implications on how to enhance non-English major students' motivation to learn English.

1 INTRODUCTION

Over the past decades, the importance of motivation for successful second language (L2) learning has been recognized by researchers in social psychology and education (Gardner 1985, Gardner & Clement 1990). Dörnyei (2001) indicated that motivation is regarded as a key role in every learning. Without this factor, it seems very hard to learn or teach. Dö rnyei & Ryan (2015: 72) also mentioned that motivation can provide "the primary impetus to initiate L2 learning and later the driving force to sustain the long, often tedious learning process". Besides, motivation is a key factor which determines "the amount of effort a learner is ready to put into language learning (Nunan 1991: 131). Dörnyei (2001) states that a learner with enough motivation is likely to gain an acceptable knowledge of an L2. Masgoret & Gardner (2003) indicate that a motivated learner expands endeavor, is determined and attentive to the task, has goals and desires, enjoys the activity, experiences reinforcement from success and disappointment from failure and makes use of strategies to assist in attaining aims. Richard & Schmidt (2002) mentioned that motivation is a driving force that triggers someone to make decisions and those decisions are influenced intrinsically and extrinsically by social context when individual is exposed to society. Therefore, motivation is one of the most significant factors in L2 learning. In order to investigate L2 learning motivation, the Self-Determination Theory (SDT) was adopted in this study. The strong connection between the SDT concept of learner autonomy or self-determination and success in L2 learning has been a focus of considerable research interest (Benson 2001, Dickinson 1995, Ehrman & Dörnyei 1998). As learners become more autonomous, "they not only become better language learners, but they also develop into more responsible and critical members of the communities in which they live" (Benson 2001: 1). Moreover, learning has to be initiated and completed by the learner. Therefore, "teaching cannot cause or force learning; at best it can encourage and guide learning. The impetus for learning must come from the learner, who must want to learn" (van Lier 1996: 12). However, much research on L2 learning motivation has not offered answers to two main questions. First of all, based on SDT, what changes learners' L2 learning motivation has been somewhat ignored. Finally, most studies related to L2 learning motivation from the SDT perspective were conducted in general English (GE) context. Very little empirical research has investigated how learners in English learning as Specific Purpose (ESP) context form L2 learning motivation from the SDT perspective. The purpose of the study is to answer the two above questions. This study is concerned with the understanding of L2 learning motivation in the hospitality and tourism context from the SDT perspective.

2 LITERATURE REVIEW

2.1 Self-determination theory

Deci & Ryan (1985) presented a self-determination theory (SDT) which is useful in exploring educational motivation in the L2 context. Human motivation in the theory can be seen to exist on a six-point continuum, ranging from amotivation on the left, through four categories of extrinsic motivation (EM), to intrinsic motivation (IM) on the right. The four categories of extrinsic motivation (external regulation, introjected regulation, identified regulation and integrated regulation) are listed in order of their degree of internalization and self-regulation.

Intrinsic motivation generally refers to motivation to engage in an activity because that activity is enjoyable and satisfying to do. IM arises out of three psychological needs (self-autonomy, competence and relatedness). Self-autonomy also regarded as self-regulation or self-determination is defined as the degree to which learners regard their activity as being self-initiated and not controlled by others (Deci & Ryan 2002). The need for competence involves being able to see oneself as fully capable to produce desired outcomes and, at the same time, to avoid negative results (Deci & Ryan 1985). The need to strive for a feeling of relatedness is related to a feeling of being "securely connected to the social world and to see oneself as worthy of love and respect" (Jacobs & Eccles 2000: 413).

Extrinsically motivated behaviors as those behaviors that are performed not because of inherent interest in the activity, but in order to arrive at some instrumental end, such that the source of regulation is external to the activity per se (Deci & Ryan 2000). EM has four subtypes depending on its degree of self-determination. Firstly, external regulation is the least autonomous form of EM. Learners are motivated by external reward or punishment as operant reinforcement. Secondly, introjected regulation is a degree of internalization of external regulation, but it is not integrated within the self. These behaviors are performed to avoid shame and guilt, or to attain feelings of esteem or self-worth. Thirdly, identified regulation is a more self-determined form of motivation as there is a conscious acceptance of the behavior as personally important. Finally, integrated regulation is the most self-determined form of EM. It is internalized and entirely integrated within the self and brought into congruence with needs and values that already become part of the self.

Amotivation means that there is no incentive or motivation to engage in any activity at all on the part of the learner. "Students with this motivational style would be very unmotivated for school due to the low value, efficacy, and internal control they feel for school activities" (Brown 2002: 262). When amotivated, learners either do not engage at all in the activity, or they act passively, going through the motions to carry out an activity that makes no sense to them until they can escape it (Dörnyei & Ushioda 2009).

2.2 Studies of second language learning from the SDT perspective

Several studies have suggested that IM and EM may be useful constructs for understanding L2 motivation (Brown 1994, Dickinson 1995, Dörnyei 1994, Schmidt et al. 1996, Ushioda 1996). Besides, Ramage (1990) found that continuing students were more intrinsically motivated than discontinuing students who were more extrinsically motivated.

Furthermore, Tachibana, et al. (1996) found that Japanese students' interest in English was pertinent to increased intrinsic motivation, more determination to achieve better English scores, and a greater likelihood of achieving high scores. SDT is importantly mentioned by authors writing it as the subject of educational motivation in general (Brown 2002, Pintrich & Schunk 2002, Stipek 2002). Rogers (1985) suggested that positive feedback should be seen by the students as informational. If praise is perceived by the students as being manipulative, the controlling aspect will become salient and result in a decrease in motivation. According to the results from McDonald (1982), those students receiving verbal praise for their competence reported significantly higher task interest than those in the other groups. Verbal praise for competence was highly effective in sustaining intrinsic interest in the task.

Absence of any motivation is the state of amotivation. Some studies have showed that students who are amotivated feel that what happens to them is independent of how they behave. Such an experience is suggested to be similar to "learned helplessness" (Abramson et al. 1978, Seligman 1975). Amotivated learners feel a lack of competence or control over their external environments, a feeling of helplessness caused by lack of contingency between behaviors and outcomes (Vallerand & Ratelle 2002). They "go through the motions with no sense of intending to do what they are doing" until they quit the activity (Ryan & Deci 2002: 17).

2.3   *The present study*

As mentioned previously, there have been a number of studies regarding the relationship between the L2 learning and SDT. However, little research focuses on how learners in ESP context form L2 learning motivation from SDT perspective. Therefore, the aim of this study is to investigate what may influence and change students' L2 learning motivation from the SDT perspective in the hospitality and tourism context. Two research questions will be addressed as below:

1. What may change students' L2 learning motivation in the hospitality and tourism context from the SDT perspective?
2. What are L2 learning motivational patterns which hospitality and tourism students form from the SDT perspective?

3   METHOD

3.1   *A qualitative case study approach*

To gain an in-depth understanding (Merriam 1998, Stake 1995) of learners' L2 learning motivation in the hospitality and tourism context, I aimed for thick descriptions (Greetz 1973) of the individual cases and attempted to identify some general phenomenon and significant patterns among them. Both member checking and summary offered for the participants before the study was written were used to reduce effect of investigator bias. The study documented the participants' process of L2 learning motivation formation from their past L2 learning experiences to current L2 learning experiences, uncovering their varying L2 learning motivation formations and transformations.

3.2   *Context and participants*

Four primary participants from English Listening and Speaking (3) are two sophomores majoring in Hotel Management and the other two sophomores majoring in Applied Japanese in the hospitality and tourism field. All had agreed to participate in this study by signing the consent form.

3.3   *Data collection*

Two sets of formal interviews were conducted with the four participants (8 interviews; average 1 hour). Member checking was devised to ask the participants whether I "got it right." I offered the participants summaries before writing up my study and asked for their reactions, corrections, and further insights (Marshall & Rossman 2011).

3.4 *Data analysis*

The data analysis is primarily inductive. Categories and themes emerged mainly from the collected data. Interview transcripts were reviewed multiple times throughout the study. Salient themes and categories were generated based on SDT. Comparison and contrast were produced during the data analysis phase.

3.5 *The researcher and the researched*

In many ways, I was an insider to them. Firstly, we all spoke Mandarin. Secondly, we are teacher-student relationship. Thirdly, they study and I teach in the same university. Finally, I am the instructor for their two professional English presentation competitions. These helped me to better understand their needs and perspectives, develop rapport and create opportunities for highly interactive and dialogic research. At the same time, we occupied different institutional positions such as teacher versus students, which also shaped our relationships. For instance, to them all, I was a friendly and senior with more English teaching and learning experiences.

4 FINDINGS

To address each of the questions, Table One shows the summary of the overall findings, and then this part highlights the four students' past and current motivation changes from the perspective of SDT. Because space is limited, however, I present only one case study example for each type of motivation changes.

4.1 *Participants' past motivation changes*

4.1.1 *Positive motivation changes*

> *I have started learning English since I studied in a bilingual kindergarten and kept learning English in EFL cram schools; therefore, I had many opportunities to learn English with good English teachers and I was motivated to learn English a lot.*
>
> (Student A)

Students A and C were motivated to learn English due to the fact that they met good teachers with good teaching styles and good learning environment.

4.1.2 *Negative motivation changes*

> *I have started learning English since I studied in an English cram school, but I gradually lost my motivation to learn English when I studied in high schools because the teachers' teaching styles were old school and they offered me with less opportunities to speak English in class. For me, studying English was only for tests.*
>
> (Student D)

Participants B and D were not motivated to learn English because they met teachers without good teaching styles and they did not have good learning environment.

4.1.3 *Amotivation*

> *I had had no interest in learning English since I studied in a kindergarten. I did not encounter good English teachers and had no relevant English learning environment. When I studied in senior vocational school, I just focused on my major studies, so I totally lost motivation to learn English. I did not have patience and was fed up with learning English.*
>
> (Student B)

Table 1. Past and current motivation changes.

Past motivation changes

	IM	EM	AM	Factors
A		*		1. Learning Environment.
B		*	*	2. Teacher's Teaching Styles.
C		*		
D		*		

Current motivation changes

	IM	EM	AM	Factors
A	*	*		1. Future Job. 2. Language Certificates. 3. Presentation Competition Attendance.
B	*	*		1. Desire to have English Edge. 2. Desire to know differentforeigners' thoughts via English. 3. Future Jobs. 4. Presentation Competition Attendance.
C	*	*		1. Desire to be a person speaking English very fluently. 2. Future Jobs. 3. Presentation Competition Attendance.
D	*	*		1. Language Graduation Threshold. 2. Language Certificates. 3. Future Jobs. 4. Presentation Competition.Attendance.

Note. Intrinsic Motivation (IM), Extrinsic Motivation (EM), Amotivation (AM).

Participant B lost her motivation to learn English during her high schools since she did not have relevant English learning environment and meet good English teachers.

4.2 Participants' current motivation changes

4.2.1 Positive motivation changes

> *In order to successfully find a good future job, I regard English learning as a priority. Besides, I am still studying English hard to get the best scores for my New TOEIC test.*
> (Student A)

Identified regulation of EM was shown in the findings of the four participants. They are motivated to learn English because of their future job and English certificates (importance of learning English).

> *Right now, one factor motivates me to keep learning English is English Graduation Threshold Policy in my university. I have to pass New TOEIC 550 Score, so I can successfully get my bachelor degree.*
> (Student D)

External regulation of EM was discovered from the findings of Student D because he is also motivated to learn English because of the language graduation threshold which means students have to get an English certificate with the certain score (New TOEIC Score: 550) for their graduation.

> *I would like to be part of English-speaking community because I want to directly know native speakers' thoughts and experience their cultures in person without someone' translation assistance. Therefore, I desire to have the English edge.*
> (Student B)

Integrated regulation of EM was unveiled from the findings of Students B and C. They are being motivated to learn English in that they desire to be part of English community and to have great English proficiency like native speakers.

> *Due to the second place for the first competition, my partners and I are very active and confident to attend the second competition to obtain the first place in the competition. Besides, I want to show that I have the ability to fluently present professional knowledge in English.*

(Student C)

Intrinsic motivation occurred in the findings of the four participants' L2 learning process. They were designated by their English teacher to attend the first professional English presentation competition based on their best performance in their midterm oral presentation. They got the second place, so they obtained the much confidence and great sense of achievement from their first competition. Therefore, due to their great confidence and sense of achievement, they become self-determined and self-initiated to attend their second professional English presentation competition.

5 DISCUSSION

In this study, I have explored learners' motivation changes and what caused their motivation to be changed from a SDT perspective by focusing on their description and explanation in their past and current L2 learning processes, and I provided an in-depth examination of learners' inner voices concerning their L2 motivation changes across their past and current L2 learning processes. Their focal inner voices clearly answered the two research questions.

5.1 Research question one

The first research question asked what may change students' L2 learning motivation in the hospitality and tourism context from the SDT perspective. From the findings of the in-depth interviews, some factors give rise to learners' positive and negative motivation changes. On the one hand, teachers' teaching styles and learning environments may positively enhance or negatively undermine learners' L2 learning motivation and further affect their future ongoing English learning. Take Students A and C as examples, both of them met English teachers with good teaching styles and had good English learning environments in the past; therefore, the two factors positively influence their future English learning performance. They have good performance on their current NEW TOEIC scores (775 and 570). Currently, they have more impetus to learn English. On the contrary, Students B and D met English teachers without good teaching styles and learned English in bad learning environments. Those indeed negatively undermine their L2 learning motivation and future ongoing English performance. Although the four students are sophomores, Students B and D have worse performance on their current New TOEIC scores (465 and 450) than Students A's and C's. On the other hand, some current factors (future jobs, English certificates, English graduation threshold, English edge gain and confidence and satisfaction the English competitions brought) positively change their L2 learning motivation. These factors make them have more incentives and impetus to learn English.

5.2 Research question two

The second question asked what L2 learning motivational patterns which hospitality and tourism students form from a SDT perspective are. From the findings, five patterns obviously appear in their L2 learning process. The first pattern is amotivation. Take Student B as an example, she did not have relevant and positive English learning environment and meet English teachers with good teaching styles. Therefore, she lost her motivation to learn English during her vocational high school period. Secondly, external regulation of EM also influenced learners to make a decision to learn English. It is the least autonomous. Due to school regulation (Language Graduation Threshold) as operant reinforcement, Student D was motivated to study English. Thirdly, identified regulation of EM was found in the findings because future jobs and English certificates are very important for the four learners. Those two motivated them to decide to learn English. This pattern is more self-determined. Fourthly, integrated regulation of EM was also discovered from the findings. It is the most self-determined form of EM. Students B and C stated that they desired to be part of English community to have great English proficiency like native speakers. Hence, this is the most self-determined form of EM. Finally, intrinsic motivation could be found based on the findings. Due to their much confidence and great sense of achievement, the four learners initiated to attend their second professional English presentation competition one year after they had attended their first professional English presentation competition. Therefore, their behavior could clearly be self-initiated and self-autonomy. Self-autonomy also regarded as self-regulation or self-determination is defined as the degree to which learners regard their activity as being self-initiated and not controlled by others (Deci & Ryan 2002).

6 CONCLUSION

The present study investigated learners' L2 learning motivation in the hospitality and tourism context from Self-Determination Theory. To summarize, learners' English learning motivation can be enhanced or undermined by learning environment and teachers' teaching style. Learners can be satisfied because of intrinsically motivated task engagement (two professional English presentation matches). Based on the concept of identified regulation, learners become self-determined because English learning is relevant to their future jobs and they want to meet job market demands to find a good job. According to integrated regulation, some learners think it is right and suitable for them to be a member in English-speaking community. This study also offers the support for pedagogical implications for how to enhance non-English major students' motivation in English language learning. Firstly, it can help teachers to realize what factors cause students' motivational changes and to avoid undermining students' English learning motivation. Secondly, it can also benefit learners to know how to enhance their English learning motivation or to be autonomous to learn English.

Although the findings offer practical and beneficial suggestions to teachers and learners, the present study is subject to two certain limitations, time and additional data-collection ways. Time for interviewing the four learners can last longer to obtain more in-depth results. Finally, in order to make the study be more triangulated, observation should be taken into consideration. The benefits of learners' L2 learning motivation in the hospitality and tourism context found in the present study highlight various directions for future studies. The future study can replicate this study in different fields such as medical field and engineer field. Maybe results will be similar or different. Besides, the future research may investigate what teaching styles and learning environments may positively or negatively influence learners' L2 learning motivation. Finally, evidence for how learners' L2 learning motivation is changed needs deeply exploring and discovering.

REFERENCES

Abramson, L.Y. Seligman, M.E.P. & Teasdale, J.D. 1978. Learned helplessness in humans: Critique and reformulation. *Journal of Abnormal Psychology* 87: 49–74.
Benson, P. 2001. *Teaching and researching autonomy in language learning.* New York: Longman.
Brown, H.D. 1994. *Teaching by principles.* Englewood Cliffs, NJ: Prentice Hall.
Brown, H.D. 2002. *Strategies for success: a practical guide to learning English.* New York: Longman.
Deci, E.L. & Ryan, R. 1985. *Intrinsic motivation and self-determination in human behavior.* New York: Plenum.
Deci, E.L. & Ryan, R. (Eds.), 2002. *Handbook of self-determination research.* Rochester, NY: The University of Rochester Press.
Dickinson, L. 1995. Autonomy and motivation: A literature review. *System* 23:165–174.
Dörnyei, Z. 1994. Motivation and motivating in the foreign language classroom. *Modern Language Journal* 78: 273–284.

Dörnyei, Z. 2001. *Teaching and researching motivation*. New York: Longman.

Dörnyei, Z. & Ushioda, E. 2009. *Motivation, language identity and the L2 self*. Bristol: Multilingual Matters.

Dörnyei, Z. & Ryan, S. 2015. *The psychology of the language learner revisited*. New York: Routledge

Ehrman, M.E. & Dörnyei, Z. 1998. *Interpersonal dynamics in second language*. Thousand Oaks, CA: Sage Publications.

Gardner, R.C. 1985. social psychology and second language learning. London: Arnold.

Gardner, R.C. & Clement, R. 1990. Social psychological perspectives on second language acquisition. In H. Giles and W.P. Robinson (Eds.), *Handbook of social psychology* (pp. 495–517). Chichester, UK: John Wiley & Sons.

Geertz, C. 1973. *The interpretation of culture*. New York: Basic Books.

Jacobs, J.A. & Eccles, J. 2000. Parents, task values, and real-life achievement-related choices. In C. Sansone & J. Harackiewicz (Eds.), *Intrinsic and extrinsic motivation: The search for optimal motivation and performance* (pp. 405–439). San Diego, CA: Academic Press.

Marshall, C. & Rossman, G.B. 2011. Designing qualitative research (5th Edition). Thousand Oaks, CA: Sage

Masgoret, A.M. & Gardner, R.C. 2003. Attitudes, motivation, and second language learning: A meta-analysis of studies conducted by Gardner and associates. *Language Learning* 53: 123–163.

McDonald, C.H. 1982. *A validation of cognitive evaluation theory*. Paper presented at the Annual Meeting of the Midwestern Psychological Association, Minneapolis, MI., May 6–8, 1982.

Merriam, S.B. 1998. *Qualitative research and case study applications in education*. San Francisco: Jossey-Bass.

Nunan, D. 1991. *Language teaching methodology*. Hertford shire: Prentice Hall International.

Pintrich, P. & Schunk, D. 2002. *Motivation in education: Theory, research and application* (2nd Edition). Upper Saddle River, NJ: Merrill Prentice Hall.

Ramage, K. 1990. Motivational factors and persistence in foreign language study. *Language Learning* 40: 189–219.

Richard, J.C. & Schmidt, R. (Eds.), 2002. Longman dictionary of language teaching and applied linguistics (3rd ed.). London: Longman.

Rogers, B.T. 1985. Cognitive evaluation theory: The effects of external rewards on intrinsic motivation of gifted students. *Roeper Review* 7(4): 257–260.

Ryan, R.M. & Deci, E.L. 2000. Intrinsic and extrinsic motivations: Classic definitions and new directions. *Contemporary Educational Psychology*, 25: 54–67.

Ryan, R.M. & Deci, E.L. 2002. Overview of self-determination theory: an organismic dialectical perspective. In: Deci, E. L, Ryan, R.M. (Eds.), Handbook of Self-determination Research. University of Rochester Press, Rochester, NY, 3–33.

Schmidt, R. Boraie, D. & Kassabgy, O. 1996. Foreign language motivation: Internal structure and external connections. In R.L. Oxford (Ed.), *Langauge learning motivation: Pathways to the new century* (pp. 14–87). Honolulu, HI: The University of Honolulu Press.

Seligman, M.E.P. 1975. *A series of books in psychology. Helplessness: On depression, development, and death*. New York: W H Freeman/Times Books/ Henry Holt & Co.

Stake, R.E. 1995. *The art of case study research*. Thousand Oaks, CA: Sage.

Stipek, D. 2002. *Motivation to learn: Integrating theory and practice* (4th Edition). Boston, MA: Ally & Bacon.

Tachibana, Y. Matsukawa, R. & Zhong, Q.X. 1996. Attitudes and motivation for learning English: A cross-national comparison of Japanese and Chinese high school students. *Psychological Reports* 79: 691–700.

Ushioda, E. 1996. *Learner autonomy*. Dublin, Ireland: Authentik.

Vallerand, R.J. & Ratelle, C.F. 2002. Intrinsic and extrinsic motivation: A hierarchical model. In E.L. Deci, & R.M. Ryan (Eds.), *Handbook of self-determination research* (pp. 37–63). Rochester, New York: Rochester University Press.

van Lier, L. 1996. *Interaction in the language classroom*. New York: Longman.

ELT in Asia in the Digital Era: Global Citizenship and Identity – Madya et al. (Eds)
© 2018 Taylor & Francis Group, London, ISBN 978-0-8153-7900-3

A comparison of gender disparity in East Asian EFL textbooks

N. Suezawa
Kobe University, Kobe, Japan

ABSTRACT: English textbooks play an important role not only in learning the English language but also in conveying the image of English usage in this global society. This study comprises a comparative corpus analysis of contemporary EFL high school textbooks in China, Korea, and Japan, with the aim of exploring gender representations therein. The objects of analysis included male-to-female ratios, attributions of gender-marked nouns, and common types of activity associated with men and women. The results demonstrated a great disparity between the number of male and female characters depicted in Chinese and Japanese textbooks. Furthermore, while female characters predominate in Korean textbooks, male-oriented stories and stereotypical descriptions are widely found. Despite international awareness and efforts for gender equality, male supremacy, female invisibility, and stereotypical descriptions continue to predominate in the EFL textbooks examined.

1   INTRODUCTION

Gender does not comprise a biologically determined sex but is, rather, a socially, culturally, and historically established concept that strongly influences our current conceptions, recognition, disciplines, and social values (Odhiambo 2012). From the international declaration of Elimination of All Forms of Discrimination against Women (CEDAW) in 1979 to the Sustainable Development Goals (SDGs) in 2015, international bodies, governments, NGOs, and educational institutions have been making a great effort to achieve gender equality and equity in this global society, in all spheres of socio-cultural activity and educational opportunity. Furthermore, international gender equality awareness, the global spread of English as an international language, and English textbooks all play an important role not only in allowing students to acquire English communication skills but also in displaying historical, racial, and multicultural contents that foster international understanding. According to the Global Gender Gap Index issued by the World Economic Forum, China, Korea, and Japan rank 99th, 116th, and 111th respectively out of 144 countries despite their economic and social development. This index ranks countries according to the gap between men and women in four fundamental categories: Economic participation and opportunity, educational attainment, health and survival, and political empowerment.

Cheng (2014) points out that in these countries, there remains a patriarchal political and socioeconomic system where female inferiority is regarded in terms of traditional virtue. Therefore, it is important to examine current English textbooks in these three countries from the gender perspective. Furthermore, the lack of international comparative textbook studies among these EFL countries should also be emphasized.

2   LITERATURE REVIEW

Since the 1970s, much attention has been paid to gender-representation in ESL/EFL materials, amid the second women's liberation movement in the USA, and scholars have examined various types of gender manifestation in textbooks (Hartman & Judd 1978, Porecca 1984, Graci 1989, Sakita1995, Jessey 1997, Matsuno 2002, Lee & Collins 2008, 2009, Mustapha 2014). The prominent features of gender representation are as follows: 1) female invisibility,

2) gender stereotyping, 3) gender-biased language, 4) asymmetrical female titles, and 5) male firstness. Female invisibility means that females appear less often in textbooks or pictures than males. Gender stereotyping represents the typical traditional social roles and characters of men and women (e.g., while males are engaged in various occupations, females are described as housewives and mothers. Boys are depicted as active, adventurous, and ambitious, while girls are passive, following, and supportive). The appearance of gender-biased language has recently been decreasing with the rise of gender-neutral awareness (e.g., person instead of human, businessperson instead of businessman). Asymmetrical female address titles refer to the fact that a woman's marital status is revealed from the honorific titles of Mrs. versus Miss, while the male title Mr. does not reveal a man's marital status. In order to redress this inequality, the neutral title Ms. was introduced as a substitution for Mrs. and Miss. Male Firstness refers to the fact that typical mating expressions (e.g., Mr. and Mrs., he or she, and men and women) put men first, while females seldom come first (e.g., ladies and gentlemen, beauty and the beast).

Most previous studies employing textbook analysis have used manual methods and, as pointed out by Carrol and Kowitz (1994), it is relatively difficult to detect subtle gender biases in context using such methods. Regarding computational corpus analysis, there has recently been some research (Jasmani et al. 2011, Yang 2012, Lee 2014). Regarding the advantage of corpus linguistic techniques, Yang (2012: 34) mentioned that they are helpful for researchers to investigate collocations because they provide information about the absolute frequency of each collocation. By applying corpus techniques to textbook research, in addition to finding male dominance, they found a detailed classification of verb usage, which differs between males and females based on their gender roles, and stereotypical activities. For example, verbs tend to portray men as engaging in physical activities, while women are engaged in care-taking or housework. One notable finding by Lee (2014) was that the "saying" verbs of insist, speak, tell, order, shout, and talk are associated with the pronoun "he" in a Japanese EFL textbook.

3   METHOD

To add to the manual methods adopted by many previous studies, to ensure validity and in-depth investigation, this study has applied a corpus linguistic technique, which involves a collection of texts of written or spoken language in electronic form, and the computer concordance program AntConc (Anthony 2012). For the content analysis, the gender orientation of each reading passage was classified manually based on the story and the number of male and female characters in the text. This study focused on a corpus of reading sections from three popular senior high school EFL textbooks published in the 2010s in China, Korea, and Japan. The detailed information is as follows: the Chinese textbook, *New Senior English for China Students book 1*, comprises 11 reading units with 13,997 words. The Korean textbook, *High School Basic English,* comprises eight units of listening, reading, speaking, and writing with 6,780 words. In this research, only the reading sections from each unit were retrieved to ensure alignment between the materials from China and Japan. The Japanese textbook, *Crown*, contains 10 reading units comprising 25,438 words. The corpus data include all the reading texts in each unit, but exclude glossaries, picture captions, and supplementary chapters at the end of the books.

The research questions were as follows: 1) What is the ratio of male and female appearances? 2) What are the common adjectives used to depict men and women? 3) Are men more associated with "saying" verbs than women?

4   DISCUSSION

RQ 1: What is the ratio of male and female appearances?

Table 1 shows the total number of male and female characters in all textbooks.

Tables 2, 3, and 4 show the gender orientation of each reading passage based on the content analysis.

As seen in Table 5, which summarizes Tables 2, 3, and 4, all countries display male-oriented topics, while few chapters portray females.

Table 6 shows the result of analysis of masculine and feminine pronouns.

The results replicate the findings with regard to the number of male and female characters: Considerably more masculine than feminine pronouns were used, with a male to female ratio of 2.39:1 for China, 2.35:1 for Korea, and 4.39:1 for Japan, indicating that female invisibility is most ostensible in the Japanese textbook. In order to compare between countries, a chi-squared analysis in R was applied with a significance level of $p \leq 0.05$ and a degree of freedom of one. No significant difference was found between the Chinese and Korean textbooks ($X^2 = 0.0034$, $p = 0.953$), but a significant difference was found between the Korean and Japanese textbooks ($X^2 = 7.574$, $p = 0.005$) and also between the Japanese and Chinese textbooks ($X^2 = 9.346$, $p = 0.002$).

RQ 2: What are the common adjectives used to depict men and women?

Table 7 shows the personal adjectives collocating with he/she, man/woman, men/women, and boy(s)/girls(s).

One of the noteworthy results was that adjectives recalling traditional gender stereotype roles between men and women appear in China and Korea, and this tendency is particularly

Table 1. Total ratio of male to female characters in textbooks.

	CHINA	KOREA	JAPAN
MALE: FEMALE	11:6	8:11	17:10

Table 2. Reading topic and gender orientation in China.

	TITLE	Gender orientation	M	F
1	Anne's best friend	F-only	0	2
2	The road to modern English	equal share	0	0
3	Journey down the Mekong	equal share	1	1
4	A night the earth didn't sleep	equal share	0	0
5	Elia's story	M-only	1	0
6	In search of the amber room	M-dominated	1	1
7	An Interview	F-dominated	2	1
8	Who am I?	M-only	1	0
9	How Daisy learned to help the world	Equal share	1	1
10	Festivals and celebrations	M-only	2	0
11	Come and eat here	M-dominated	2	0

Table 3. Reading topic and gender orientation in Korea.

	TITLE	Gender orientation	M	F
1	Boost your self esteem	M-only	1	0
2	My Chinese mom	M-dominated	2	1
3	Senses sell	Equal-share	1	1
4	Climate change	Equal-share	0	0
5	Korea seen through western eyes	Equal-share	1	1
6	Ski jumping	M-dominated	1	1
7	A lucky day	M-only	2	0
8	Hairspray	F-only	0	7

231

Table 4. Reading topic and gender orientation in Japan.

	TITLE	Gender orientation	M	F
1	Going into space	Males-only	1	0
2	A forest in the sea	M-dominated	2	1
3	Writers without borders	F-only	0	3
4	Playing by ear	Male-dominated	3	2
5	Food bank	Male-only	1	0
6	Roots & shoots	F-dominated	1	1
7	Diving into history	Equal share	1	1
8	Not so long Ago	Equal share	1	1
9	Paddling a log	Male-only	4	0
10	Good ol' Charlie Brown	Male-dominated	3	1

Table 5. Summary of gender orientation.

	M-Only	M-Dominated	F-Only	F-Dominated	Equal share
China	3	2	1	1	4
Korea	2	2	1	0	3
Japan	3	3	1	1	2

Table 6. Masculine and feminine pronouns.

	Nominative		Accusative/Genitive		Total	
	He	She	his/him	her	masculine	feminine
China	112 (71.8)	44 (28.2)	74 (68.5)	34 (31.5)	186 (70.5)	78 (29.5)
Korea	66 (75.0)	22 (25.0)	47 (63.0)	26 (37.0)	113 (70.2)	48 (29.8)
Japan	126 (78.7)	34 (21.3)	123 (84.2)	23 (15.8)	249 (81.4)	57 (18.6)

Note: The figures in brackets show percentage terms.

Table 7. Personal adjectives collocating with he/she, man/woman, men/women, boy(s)/girl(s).

	Gender	Adjectives
China	Masculine	young (2), old (2), better (1), business (1), quiet (1), rich (1), brave (1)
	feminine	weaving (1)
Korea	Masculine	reliant (1)
	feminine	blind (3), aged (1), teenage (1)
Japan	Masculine	little (2), small (1)
	feminine	little (4), young (1)

high in China where males were depicted with physical and mental strength, success, and wealth (better, business, quiet, rich, brave, reliant). Regarding female depictions in Korea, they were often associated with age and appearance (aged, young, teenage, little). This result reveals that there remains a gender imbalance and gender stereotyping associated with adjectives, as described in previous textbook research.

Table 8.

	Gender	Verbs	Total
China	he	say (8), ask (3), tell (4)	15
	she	say (12), speak (2), ask (6), tell (3)	23
Korea	he	say (8), talk (2)	10
	she	say (1), speak (2), ask (1), tell (4)	8
Japan	he	say (14), speak (2), ask (6), tell (3)	25
	she	say (14), talk (6), answer (3), ask (3), tell (2)	28

RQ 3: Are men more associated with "saying" verbs than women?

To investigate the association of "saying" verbs, including say, talk, speak, ask, answer, and tell (including the *-ed* and *-ing* forms), with the pronouns "he" or "she," the collocates of he and she in a span length from 5 L (5 words left from he/she) to 5R (5 words right from he/she) were analyzed. Table 8 shows that, contrary to Lee's (2014) research, Japan and China show a higher frequency of the pronoun "she" with "saying" verbs.

5 CONCLUSION

To enhance the reliability of textbook studies, this study applied corpus and computer software techniques. In the textbooks examined, it was found that gender disparities against women still prevail in current English textbooks in China, Korea, and Japan. A common feature of the results was notable female invisibility and gender stereotyping. This implies that women are portrayed as having a less important existence and as being less qualified than men. The collocational analysis also suggests that the traditional stereotypical image of men and women remains prevalent: While males are associated with business, economic success, and strength, females are associated with their age and appearance. This gender disparity and female underrepresentation in textbooks may reinforce learners' gender identity, gender bias, and stereotypes as a dominant assumption. To eliminate gender inequality in this global society, textbooks play an important role in social change. Therefore, textbook writers, publishers, and teachers should be more sensitive in providing educational materials that aim at 1) balanced representation of men and women, and 2) characters who challenge traditional gender stereotyping with regard to their roles, activities, and displays.

6 STUDY LIMITATIONS

1) This study comprised an exploratory analysis of textbooks in three countries and it may be difficult to generalize the results to other textbooks. Therefore, a large-scale study based on a larger corpus of textbooks for different levels of students would provide more reliable data and increase understanding. 2) Since this research comprised a quantitative analysis based on corpus and concordance computational software, qualitative discourse analysis, focusing on characters' behavior and interactions, was omitted due to the page restrictions. A combination of qualitative and quantitative analysis should thus be further investigated.

REFERENCES

Anthony, L. 2012. *AntConc.* Retrieved from http://www.antlab.sci.waseda.ac.jp/software.html.
Carroll, D. & Kowitz, J. 1994. Using concordancing techniques to study gender stereotyping in ELT textbooks. In J. Sunderland (ed.). *Exploring gender: Questions and implications for English language education*: 73–82. New York: Prentice Hall.
Graci, J.P. 1989. Are foreign language textbooks sexist? An exploration of modes of evaluation. *Foreign Language Annall* 22(5): 477–486.

Huang, M. et al. 2014. Paternalistic Leadership in Four East Asian Societies: Generalizability and Cultural Differences of the Triad Model. *Journal of Cross-Cultural Psychology* 45(1): 82–90.

Jasmani, M.F.I. et al. 2011. Verbs and gender: The hidden agenda of a multicultural society (Special issue). *Southeast Asian Journal of English Language Studies* 17: 61–73.

Jassey, I.A. 1997. Gender representation in Japanese elementary school textbooks (unpublished EdD dissertation). Columbia University.

Hartman, P.L. & Judd, E.L. 1978. Sexism and TESOL materials. *TESOL Quarterly* 12(4): 383–393.

Lee, J.F.K. & Collins, P. 2009. Australian English-language textbooks: The gender issues. *Gender and Education* 21(4): 353–370.

Lee, J.F.K. 2014. A hidden curriculum in Japanese EFL textbooks: Gender representation.

Lee, J.F.K. & Collins, P. 2010. Construction of gender: A comparison of Australian and Hong Kong English language textbooks. *Journal of Gender Studies* 19(2): 121–137.

mMbo, C. 2012. The name game: Using insults to illustrate the social construction of gender. *College Teaching* 60(1): 25–30.

Matsuda, A. 2002. Representation of users and uses of English in beginning Japanese EFL textbooks. *JALT Journal* 24(2): 182–200.

Matsuno, S. 2002. Sexism in Japanese radio business English program. *JALT Journal* 24(1): 83–97.

Mustapha, A.S. 2014. Dynamics of gender representations in learning materials, GÉNEROS. *Multidisciplinary Journal of Gender Studies* 1(3): 243–270.

OdhiaLee, J.F.K. & Collins, P. 2008. Gender voices in Hong Kong English textbooks – Some past and current practices. *Sex Roles* 59(1/2): 127–137.

Porreca, K.L. 1984. Sexism in current ESL textbooks. *TESOL Quarterly* 18(4): 705–724.

Sakita, T.I. 1995. Sexism in Japanese English education: A survey of EFL texts. *Women and Language* 18(2): 5–12.

World Economic Forum. 2016. *The global Gender Gap Report 2016*. Retrieved from: http://reports.weforum.org/global-gender-gap-report-2016/.

Yang, C.C.R. 2012. Is gender stereotyping still an issue? An analysis of a Hong Kong primary English textbook series. *Hong Kong Journal of Applied Linguistics* 13(2): 33–49.

ELT in Asia in the Digital Era: Global Citizenship and Identity – Madya et al. (Eds)
© *2018 Taylor & Francis Group, London, ISBN 978-0-8153-7900-3*

EFL students' perception on the role of target-language culture in CCU class

N. Hidayati, Sumardi & S.S. Tarjana
Sebelas Maret University, Surakarta, Indonesia

ABSTRACT: Students and lecturer have their own perceptions of what works best in the classroom process; thus, listening to students' perceptions can be a salient way in exploring the best environment in teaching and learning process. This paper aimed to find out the students' perception on the role of target-language culture in cross-cultural understanding class viewed from students' judgment and prediction. This study utilized qualitative research in the form of the case study as the research method. The subjects of the research were students of fourth semesters in Mataram University who take CCU course. The data were collected through observation, interview and document analysis then analyzed using interactive model (data reduction, data display, and drawing conclusion or verification). The results show that: 1). Students' judge the role of target-language culture as interesting, 2). Students predict that learning target-language culture can facilitate them to go abroad someday.

1 INTRODUCTION

In regard to the more modern era, English becomes more powerful as the lingua franca around the world including in Indonesia. It is a widely known that English language subject becomes one of the obligatory subjects in the national curriculum of Indonesia. However, the grammatical pressure is indeed dominance. Students are tied keenly by the grammatical material to be learned whereas in the real context, grammar is no longer needed since the students know the cultural context how and where to use the language. This is in line with Alptekin (2005) who states that language and culture cannot be separated; language could only be fully understood if it is connected to its culture.

In addition, teacher/lecturer usually has the authority of how the class run, thus, the students' role usually just as the follower, not as the creator. On the other hand, both teacher/lecturer and the students have their own perception of what works best in the process of learning. Therefore, listening to students' perceptions on the role of target-language culture in foreign language learning can be a pledge solution because there is no one knows the best for learners but they are. Students' perceptions need to be considered for both teacher and students bring with their own perceptions of what constitutes language teaching, language learning, learning the outcome, and their own prescriptions about their classroom roles ought to be (Kumaravadivelu 1991). Therefore, this paper aims to explore the EFL students' perception on the role of target language culture in cross-cultural understanding class in Mataram University. Theoretical insight was drawn from Barkhuizen's (1998) concept of 'perception' which involves students in making the judgment, and prediction.

Based on Adaskou, et al. (1990), the reason for involving culture in foreign language learning is to facilitate the learners in their future to visit the foreign country where they concerned or contacts with people with totally different. It is also to integrate the language course in an interdisciplinary and thematic curriculum. The insertion of cultural aspect in language teaching can be very meaningful for students' future since the world becomes more modern.

Besides, Alptekin (1993) states that culture plays a major role in cognition. It is certainly flourishing to relate culture in the process of foreign language teaching and learning. The processes of teaching and learning language are also considered as cognition process. Further, Alptekin (1993) gives an example in reading comprehension of the conflict where target-language culture unmatched with the native culture. It happens because the different prior knowledge and the current knowledge when one learns a foreign language. This explanation emphasizes on how important the target-language culture be included in EFL teaching for students' cognition process.

In addition, Abdollahi-Guilani et al. (2012) state that "learners should be exposed to other countries' cultural perspectives, so that, their preventive obstacles can be softened to welcome the new language more cordially". The emergence of inserting culture in foreign language learning becomes more crucial if it is related to the use of culture in its proper context. In addition, since culture is custom, the cross-cultural understanding class can be called the culture of learning.

Some previous works are considered relevant to this current study, among others; Lai (2014) in Taiwan explored the EFL learners' perceptions of the ownership of English and acquire cultural knowledge. The results reveal that: students reveal negative perception toward the notion that English is belonging to a specific country in this world; it belongs to who are willing to study and use it. Moreover, students also have a willingness to explore the culture worldwide by using English as the international language. This study has similarity to the current study in the form of knowing the students' perception in regards to the culture.

Another relevant study conducted by Mansourzadeh et al. (2014) in Iran to find out what are the roles of foreign language culture in classrooms in the Iranian context. The result reveals that the attitude between the participant and the cultural frameworks are correlating each other. At the end, the writer suggests that culture is something important to consider in foreign language classroom. The current study and this previous study have the same aims in gaining the result about target-language culture. However, what makes them different is the method of collecting the data. The SPSS is used in the previous study to analyze the result of questionnaire while this current study will use the interview as the data collection method and will be analyzed using interactive model.

Another relevant study might be relevant conducted by Brooks-Lewis (2014) in Turkey to find out learner-participants' perceptions of their experience of target-culture in EFL context. The result revealed that the breadth and depth of participants' responses to explicitly learn about culture in the foreign language classroom are incisive and sometimes astonishing. In addition, it is surprising how many made reference to how learning about another culture had helped learners to become aware of their native culture. This study is similar to the current study in term of revealing students' judgment of the target culture.

In 2015, Fichtner conducted a study in Germany to explore the advantages do students describe with regard to the use of English and German during culture instruction. The finding reveals that the students emphasize the use of English helped them relate the German language and culture to American English and their own culture as well as to better understand the relationship between the German language and German-speaking culture. This study is somehow different to the current study in term of the perception but similar in term of the setting; EFL class and learning the target culture. Those are some theories and previous related studies to this current research, below is the method of the study.

2 RESEARCH METHOD

The current research was conducted at Mataram University in Lombok Island, West Nusa Tenggara Province, in Cross-Cultural Understanding Class of English Department. Cross-Cultural Understanding subject is offered to students of fourth semesters.

This research utilized qualitative research in the form of case study. It is a study of an issue explored by one or more cases by using a bounded system (Creswell 2007). In addition, Yin (2015) defines case study as "a contemporary phenomenon (the "case") in depth and within its real-world context, especially when the boundaries between phenomenon and context may not be clearly evident. It was used to collect the information about the students' perceptions of cultural engagement in EFL classroom.

The data sources were divided into three parts; respondents, events, and documents. The respondents of the research were the class A students of the fourth semester who take Cross-Cultural Understanding Class in academic year 2016/2017. They are assumed to have more exposed to target-language culture in CCU class since they are in time taking CCU class. Besides, the events are the processes of Cross-Cultural Understanding course in the classroom. In addition, the documents chosen are the syllabus, materials used by the lecturer, and students' textbook. Those material were analysed to explore the role of the target-langugae culture which then linked to the result of observation and interview.

In gathering the data, observation, interview and document analysis were used. The results from those three data gathering were linked each other to see whether the data able to answer the questions or not. In addition, to validate the data, the triangulation, rich and thick description, and clarifying biases were used. This stage helped to clarify the results of the research. At the end, the model adopted for analyzing the data was an interactive model from Miles and Huberman (1984) which it components consists of data reduction, data display, and conclusion; drawing or verification.

3 FINDINGS AND DISCUSSIONS

There are two ways to explore students' perception based on the adaptation of Barkhuizen's (1998) concept of 'perception'. Those two ways are the process involving learners in making a judgment and making a prediction. Based on the research findings, students judge target-language culture in CCU class as interesting. Besides, they predict that learning target-language culture is a good means of preparation for their future. Those judgments and predictions require students to think about the class they have just joined regarding its roles for themselves.

The first students' perception is drawn from judgment. The students' judge learning target-language culture in CCU class is interesting as stated by one of the student's statements below:

> St 2: it's kinda interesting to learn the new culture, from that we can familiar with the foreign culture when we go abroad or welcome the guests/people from abroad, we will have no problem to blend it.
> (Interview, March 7th, 2017)

Similar to the respond of student 2 above, the result of classroom observation also shows that the students are interested during learning process proven by their enthusiastic by asking some question regarding the topic they learn. They learn target-language culture using the aesthetic sense or capital C culture which includes the media, the cinema, music, and literature of the foreign culture (Adaskou et al. (1990). Based on the result of interview and questionnaire, lecturer suggests students learn from various media and as many as references. Students also mention some capital C culture that they use in learning target-language cultures such as foreign movies and songs. The characters, settings and the actions on the movies can be a good reference to learn the target-langue culture. Besides, students also exposed to some expressions in songs they are listening to.

Moreover, based on Brooks-Lewis (2014) research finding in Turkey about learners' perceptions of the significance of culture in foreign language teaching and learning, there is a surprising finding. The utilization of many made references to how learning about another culture had helped learners to became aware of their native culture. The judgment of students might be based not only on their own private feeling but influenced by the resources they use when learning whether from foreign movies or songs, the internet, or other printed books. At the end, the students not only realize the foreign culture but also their native culture.

The second perception was drawn from students' prediction. It is stated from the student's statement below:

> St 2: what I can predict from the role of target-language culture is that easy to get along with the society. It means that when we visit England to continue our studies, for example, we don't have to think and overreact to face the habit of Englishmen, we will

let it flow because we have already known their culture and how to apply it. I think this is one of the important things besides the mastery of English language.

(Interview, March 7th, 2017)

By having exposed to target-language culture, student 2 predicted that it will not be difficult to live his life in a new society. He predicted that he can live his life in a harmony toward the actions and habits of Englishmen because he already knows it before living there. It can facilitate his future that there will be no longer misunderstanding when living in a new place because he has studied it in CCU class. There will be no a longer culture shock because of the living in the totally different environment and cultures.

Related to the above prediction, it is in line with the statement of Alptekin (1993) who states that culture plays a major role in cognition. The cognition links to the knowledge of culture and the other skills related to the culture being learned such as speaking or reading. The students' prediction relates to their accomplished knowledge they get in CCU class so that they are willing to apply their cognition in the real English-speaking countries. Besides, Adaskou et al. (1990) also support the above-mentioned willingness by stating that learning target-language culture gives them supplies to visit English-speaking countries after finishing their study. Based on the thinking of their own future, the students can predict that the class that they attend will be useful one day after they finish their study.

Furthermore, students also have dreams to go abroad whether to continue their study or to look for the job. They predict that someday, the target culture they learn in CCU class will facilitate them to live in the wider context. They will have a good preparation to be applied in their future. Related to this prediction, the statement by Abdollahi-Guilani et al. (2012) might be relevant that learners should be exposed to other countries' cultural perspectives so that their preventive obstacles can be softened when involving in that culture. By having a cross-cultural understanding class, aware or not, the students already prepared to face their future in the more global world.

In conclusion, students' perceptions need to be seriously considered. Both teacher and students bring with their own perceptions of what constitutes language teaching, language learning, learning the outcome, and their own prescriptions about their classroom roles ought to be (Kumaravadivelu 1991).

4   CONCLUSION AND SUGGESTION

After looking deeply into the students' perception on the role of target-language culture in cross-cultural understanding class, a conclusion can be drawn as follows: 1). The students' judgment regarding the role of target-language culture in CCU class is as interesting class since it provides their future preparation in the wider world. 2). Students predict that learning target-language culture can facilitate them to go abroad in the future.

By considering the students' perceptions, the lecturer can prepare the best material which is useful for students' future in cross-cultural understanding class. The lecturer can also design the class as interesting as possible in order to provide the best classroom environment for the students.

REFERENCES

Abdollahi-Guilani, M. Mohamad S.M.Y., Tan, K.H. & Khadijeh, A. 2012. Culture-integrated teaching for the enhancement of EFL learner tolerance. *Asian Social Science* 8(6).
Adaskou, K,D. Britten., B. Fahsi. 1990. Design decisions on the cultural content of a secondary English course for morocco. *ELT Journal Volume* 44(1): 3–10.
Alptekin, C. 1993. Target-language culture in EFL materials. *ELT Journal* 47(2): 136–143.
Alptekin, C. & Margaret, A. 1984. The question of culture: EFL teaching in non-English speaking countries. *ELT Journal Volume* 38(1): 14–20.
Alptekin, Cem. (2005). Dual language instruction: Multiculturalism through a lingua franca. *TESOL Symposium on Dual Language Education: Teaching and Learning Two Languages in the EFL Setting. Teachers of English to Speakers of Other Languages, Inc*: 1–8.

Barkhuizen, G. 1998. 'Discovering learners'. perceptions of ESL classroom teaching/learning activities in a South African context'. *TESOL Quarterly* 32(1): 85–108.

Brooks, L. & Kimberly, A. 2014. Adult learners' perceptions of the significance of culture in foreign language teaching and learning. *Journal of Education and Training Studies* 2(2): 9–19. doi:10.11114/jets.v2i2.250.

Creswell, J.W. 2007. *Qualitative inquiry and research design, choosing among five approaches* (2nd Ed.). London: Sage Publications.

Fichtner, F. 2015. Learning culture in the target language: the students' perspectives. *A Journal of American Association of Teachers of German*: 229–243.

Kramsch, C. 2013. Culture in foreign language teaching. *Iranian Journal of Language Teaching Research* 1(1): 57–78.

Kumaravadivelu, B. 1991. Language-learning tasks: Teacher intention and learner interpretation. *ELT Journal* 45: 98–107.

Lai, Hsuan-Yau Tony. 2014. Learning English as an international language: EFL learners' perceptions of cultural knowledge acquisition in the English classroom. *Asian Social Science Journal* 10(1): 1–11.

Mansourzadeh, N., Esa P., Yavar H., & Akramalsadat. 2014. Culture: Its manifestations in the classrooms. *Journal of Elementary Education* 24(2): 65–80.

Miles, M.B. & A. Michael Huberman. 1984. *Qualitative data analysis: A sourcebook of methods*. London: Sage Publications.

Papa, I. 2015. Culture and language as factors related in the process of learning and education. *European Journal of Language and Literature Studies*. 1(1): 16–19.

Yin, R.K. 2015. *Case study research: Design and methods* (5th Ed.). Los Angeles: SAGE Publication, Inc.

ELT in Asia in the Digital Era: Global Citizenship and Identity – Madya et al. (Eds)
© 2018 Taylor & Francis Group, London, ISBN 978-0-8153-7900-3

Sundanese local content integration in English for young learners' classroom

I.A. Alwasilah
Semesta Learning Evolution, Bandung, Indonesia

ABSTRACT: A number of English teaching practitioners have affirmed that English learning activities should embed to the learners' cultural background. This assumption raises based on the consideration that localized teaching materials can be used as a means to strengthen local genius, in order to address the diversity and richness of the English used today. This study investigated the implementation of Sundanese local content integration in English for Young Learners (EYL) Classroom, which was conducted in one of the classes in English for Young Learner course in Bandung. A case-study design was employed and the data were collected from classroom observation, teacher and students interview, and document analysis. The results show that this technique can be utilized as a proposed strategy to promote cultural literacy skills. Correspondingly, in classroom context, it can address the difficulties in providing culturally appropriate English materials for students in West Java.

1 INTRODUCTION

Many English teachers in Indonesia are overwhelmed in using Western-culture-based English textbooks (Sudartini 2009), which is usually inappropriate with Indonesian local culture. This cultural barrier is a product of curriculum that pays less attention to the needs and local context of the learners (Freire 1997, in Larson 2014).

To address this issue, a locally appropriate English teaching material is needed as an effort to provide more student and teacher-friendly material. This is considered important since English teaching cannot be effectively carried out without giving understanding of accompanying culture (Sudartini 2009).

In relation to above issue, the intertwined nature of language and culture shows that English language teaching cannot be separated from the learner's cultural background. It is in line with an argument that an effective education practitioner has to study not only the methods of education practiced in that society, but also its cultural bases (Buchori 2001).

This notion emerges based on constructivism theory, proposed by Piaget and Bruner, that students learn best when the materials are associated with their cultural prior knowledge and experience (Lynn 2001, Pinter 2006). In response to this, some practitioners have acknowledged that English teachers should (a) develop a localized English teaching (McKay in Sukarno 2013, McKay in Huang & Wang 2008); (b) use cultural content and authentic materials (Kilickaya 2004); and (c) help students to develop their positive self-concept and cultural identity (Biles 1994).

As the second largest local culture in Indonesia (45 million people in 2015), Sundanese culture capital has potential to be developed as a medium of English teaching in West Java. Its content can be used as an encouraging device to bridge English learning activities associated with students' cultural background and experience. This can be considered as the product of ethnopedagogy proposed by Alwasilah, Suryadi, Karyono (2009), which is a local wisdom-based educational practice. This ethnopedagogy practice is expected to address the issue that Indonesia needs a more flexible English teaching approach that takes classroom diversity into account (Larson 2014).

A study conducted by LoCastro (1996 in Larson 2014) found that that the developed language teaching approach is not effective for sociocultural context of Japan. Similarly, Sonaiya's (2002 in Larson 2014) study found a mismatch between English teaching methodology and culture of the Yoruba people of Sub-Saharan Africa. These previous studies focus on classroom teaching method in general and show that localized English teaching material is important.

Based on the aforementioned issues, this study has conducted a more in-depth investigation by focusing on one specific classroom practice to certain level of students. Young learner is prioritized to be involved in this study as Regmi (2011) suggests that the use of local content should give more priority in the earlier stage of English language learning.

Furthermore, this study seeks to address the lack of research on local culture integration in English teaching as a response to multicultural nature of Indonesia. In a broader scope, it has intention to revitalize Sundanese culture and to promote localized English learning, in order to fulfill the needs of cultural literacy skills, which 21st century generation has to possess (World Economic Forum 2015).

2 LITERATURE REVIEW

2.1 Embedding culture into local content

Local content is an expression of local knowledge and experience that is relevant to community's situation (Khan in Uzuegbu 2012). In specific, it can be used as the medium to transmit culture through teaching language, as Kilickaya (2004) affirms that using content is a key to effective teaching and learning a language.

Tomalin & Stempleski (1993) state that using local culture in English teaching and learning activity is beneficial since it promotes effective language use and language skills acquisition, and encourages integrative project. Hence, its implementation can cultivate effective learning atmosphere when being tailored to suit particular community needs (Regmi 2011). The needs of young English learners has to be taken into account since they should be given opportunities to learn their own culture as it promotes cultural pride and self-understanding, and helps children see themselves as cultural beings (Ford 2006).

2.2 Embedding culture into local content for young learners classroom

In embedding culture into language learning, Peck (1991) suggests that the teacher should: (1) learn all about the students' culture, and use it as subject matter; and (2) plan activities that will be interesting, and slightly novel. This can be done by using song, drawings, artifacts, stories, making contact with real people, and projects or topics (Brewster 2003).

The specific techniques used in integrating Sundanese local content in English learning can be done by employing content-based instruction. It is a method that emphasizes the learning about something, rather than learning the language (Davies 2003), where the students simultaneously acquire subject matter expertise and greater proficiency in English (Raphan & Moser in Quincannon & Naves 2000).

Content-based instruction has been known to provide some benefits in language learning, namely: (1) Making language learning more interesting and motivating and widening students' knowledge (Peachey 2003); and (2) Intrinsically interesting and cognitively engaging (Teddick et al. 2001).

Thus, in choosing appropriate Sundanese content that fits young learners' characteristics, the Sundanese traditional games like *jeblag panto, babandringan* and *bebentengan* can be used as warming-up activity to prepare the students to learn and to introduce the target language.

Besides that, some Sundanese traditional songs like *oray-orayan, trang-trang kolentrang,* and *tokecang,* can be modified to meet the criteria of lesson plan objectives. In addition, some Sundanese toys (as authentic media and artifacts) can also be used to support the classroom activities. Those toys are *egrang, kelom batok, gatrik, gasing,* and *bedil jepret.*

3 RESEARCH METHOD

3.1 *Research design*

This study employs a qualitative case-study design, since it was done in one single classroom, as Ary et al. (2010) point out that case-study research focuses in a single unit, such as one individual, one group, one organization, or one program. Cohen & Manion (1990) state that the purpose of case study design is to deeply and intensively examine the multifarious phenomena in order to establish generalization of wider population. Based on the above definition, this study has examined deeply the integration of Sundanese local content in one EYL class in Bandung, in order to establish generalization of wider population.

3.2 *Research site and participants*

One of English for Young Learner Courses in Bandung was chosen as the research site based on the following consideration: (a) The selected class consisted of students with Sundanese cultural background; and (b) The teacher of selected class was willing to be trained and conduct an English learning using Sundanese local content.

The class consisted of three participants (with Sundanese background) aged 9–10 years old and who were in their 3rd and 4th grade of primary school. They were in Starters 2 Level of the EYL course.

The teacher was a master student of English Education study, who was born as Sundanese and speaks Sundanese in daily basis. She had been teaching English in this course for about four years and had expertise in English teaching to young learners.

3.3 *Research instruments*

To ensure the internal validity, several methods of data collection should be used for triangulation purposes (Yin 2003). Therefore, this study used observation, interview and document analysis as the research instruments.

The classroom observations were conducted eight times, in order to investigate the lesson plan implementation. Next, the interview was done to the teacher to gain information about her experience, feeling and responses towards the integration of Sundanese local content in her classroom; and to the students to know their responses about their English learning through Sundanese content. Lastly, the document analysis is a collection of written data instruments that consists of lesson plans, classroom observation sheets, classroom observation transcripts, interview transcripts, teacher's reflective journal, students' works' and parents survey.

This study has ensured its validity and reliability done by using triangulation and inter-rater reliability test, as Fraenkel & Wallen (2009) point out that in a qualitative study, ensuring validity and reliability can be done by cross-checking sources of information between peers and triangulation that involves multiple data sources. The recurring patterns from multiple sources and the results of inter-rater reliability test showed the data is valid and reliable.

4 FINDINGS AND DISCUSSION

4.1 *Findings*

4.1.1 *The preparation*
A syllabus was developed to meet the objective of this study, which then divided into eight meetings or lesson plans. This syllabus was formulated based on the categories proposed by Tomalin & Stempleski (1993), namely: (1) recognizing cultural images and symbols; and (2) working with cultural products. These categories were depicted into the following syllabus.

The general outcome of this syllabus is to provide an English learning atmosphere that has cultural familiarity to the teacher and students. In specific, it is expected that the students are able to describe something about their culture in English. This in accordance the notion

Table 1. The developed syllabus.

Meeting	Topic	Language focus
1–2	Sundanese clothes and accessories	I am wearing *kebaya*. He is wearing *beubeur*. They are wearing *beskap*.
3–4	Free-time activities	I like cooking *cuhcur*. She likes practicing *Jaipong* Dance. He likes playing *Jeblag Panto*
5–6	Tourism places in West Java	In Kampung Jelekong, we can buy paintings and meet many *dalang*. In Saung Angklung Udjo, we can watch angklung art performance and buy some bamboo souvenirs.
7	Review	(all of the above) Done in form of activities.
8	Booklet making	(all of the above) Done in form of activities.

that the teacher should develop teaching-learning materials contents that are generally based on the pedagogical and curricular guideline, yet the teaching-learning activities are based on students' cultural background (Mohani 2010).

The next preparation stage was teacher training. It was intended to make the teacher well-prepared to implement this technique. The training consisted of: (1) researcher presentation of syllabus, lesson plans, and expected outcomes; (2) lesson-plan reading by the teacher; (3) lesson-plan, teaching aids and reflective journal explanation by the researcher; (4) researcher and teacher discussion; and (5) teacher's microteaching (if needed).

The lesson plans were the main documents that provided the comprehensive information about the lesson date, level of students, lesson/chapter, time allocation, language skill/grammar focus, media, vocabularies, objectives, and teaching and learning stages. Purgason (1991) defines that lesson plan is a chronicle for a teacher to be well-prepared about the content, media, material, activities, and teaching pace. They were developed based on three-phase teaching cycle, namely: pre-activities, whilst-activities, and post-activities.

In the pre-activities, the activities were used to attract students' attention (by using song and Sundanese traditional game), to review the previous materials, and to provide learning context for the students. Next, the whilst-activities consisted of some activities that were used to reach the lesson objectives and to make the students able to use the language focus and target vocabulary. Lastly, the post-activities consisted of closing activities that were used to review the lesson, ask students' favorite activity, and reflect the richness of Sundanese culture.

4.1.2 *The implementation*

In general, the implementation of Sundanese local content was done in five stages: (1) Puppets introduction; (2) Warming up-activities; (3) Main performance and its aid; (4) Product making; (5) Cultural reflection; and (6) Exhibition.

The puppet introduction stage was done in the first meeting, where the teacher introduced two puppets, named Neneng and Ujang. These puppets were used as teacher's avatars, where teacher talked to students through them. They were utilized as the medium to teach a new song, to ask students some question, to check students' understanding, and to do role-play. Similarly, the students created their own puppet and its Sundanese identity. The students used their puppets as the medium to perform role play, to read aloud their writing products, and to do presentation.

Student 1 named his puppet 'Asep'. His puppet wears a red *beskap*, Batik *sinjang*, *bendo*, and *selop*. Next, Student 2 named her puppet 'Cucu'. The puppet wears a pink *kebaya*, Batik *sinjang*, earrings, *kembang goyang*, and *selop*. Lastly, Student 3 named her puppet 'Ceuceu'. The puppet wears green *kebaya*, batik *sinjang*, earrings, *kembang goyang*, and *selop*. All of the puppets have Sundanese names and wear Sundanese traditional clothes.

Student 1's puppet   Student 2's puppet   Student 3's puppet

Figure 1.   Students' puppets.

In the warming-up stage, the teacher used Sundanese song and traditional game that had the intention to make the students ready to learn. The song was a nursery rhymes that had its lyric modified, so it contained English and Sundanese vocabularies. Meanwhile, *Babandringan* and *Jeblag Panto* games were utilized to introduce the target vocabularies.

Next, in the main performance and its aid stage, the teacher asked students to do discussion, role-play, crafting, drilling, imitating writing, games, vocabulary game and reading aloud to facilitate the their learning performance in using the target language. The aids used were flash cards, puppets and their boxes, picture and its description, song, booklet, Power Point slides, traditional games tools, and the map of West Java

In the product making stage, the students were asked to create learning products as records of their learning achievement, which consisted of puppet description, dialogue, mind-map, writing, and reading aloud. Then, the students should present their products in front of the class or in a form of role-play using their puppets.

The cultural reflection stage was done in the end of every lesson. Before closing the session, the teacher had reflection time with the students. The students were involved in a short discussion where they shared their feeling or attitude towards their own culture.

Lastly, in the exhibition stage, all the learned learning materials (meeting 1–6) were reviewed in the seventh meeting. In this meeting, the students exhibited their prior learning in forms of structured activities. After that, in the last meeting (day 8), the students made a booklet as their final project of Sundanese culture-based English learning. This is in line with Tomalin & Stempleski (1993) that local culture in English learning encourages integrative project.

4.1.3 *Output*
Generally, the integration of Sundanese local content was considered beneficial in English learning, as it supported teacher and students' prior experiences and knowledge. The teacher concurred that the integration of Sundanese local content was a new engaging and innovative way to teach English to young learners in West Java since both teacher and students' culture are valued.

During the teaching and learning processes, the teacher had chance to share her childhood memories of playing certain Sundanese traditional games and knowledge of her hometown city. Similarly, the students could also share their prior knowledge and experience of using Sundanese traditional clothes in Bandung's *Rebo Nyunda* campaign that has been executed in their school. It is a Bandung's government weekly campaign that is performed every Wednesday, where the members of all institution and school in Bandung are suggested to wear *Kebaya* (female) and *Pangsi* (male) and the people are suggested to speak Sundanese. This cultural familiarity supported teacher to provide appropriate context for the students.

Regarding the media used in the classroom, the teacher stated that puppet and traditional game were considered as the best media to use in the classroom. This puppet attracted longer attention span from the students, while the game was engaging since they students had not played that traditional game before.

4.2 Discussion

4.2.1 The suitability and compatibility with learning climate

This integration of local culture in English learning was considered novel by the teacher. Its newness required adaptation as the teacher had to be knowledgeable and well-prepared before delivering the materials to the students. However, this issue could be solved as she was benefitted from the study. She discovered that the learning was engaging and she had the chances to learn the culture from the children's eyes. It is in accordance with Peck's (1991) idea who states that by attending to culture, a teacher can comprehend the way the students see themselves.

It can be said that this technique is suitable and compatible to be implemented in EYL classroom because: (1) it is a tool to know the students better, since the teacher has chance to take a deeper look into students' cultural background; (2) it becomes a place where students share mutual understanding of their own culture, resulted in better students' engagement; (3) it makes the students feel that they are closer to their native culture; (4) it is an proposed strategy to simultaneously preserve Sundanese culture and teach English; and (5) the Sundanese contents are used to reach English learning objectives. To ensure that these benefits are gained, a teacher training needs to be conducted in order to achieve the desired learning objectives.

4.2.2 The availability of teaching resources

In regards to preparing teaching materials, finding reliable data about Sundanese people was not easy to do. Most printed books do not provide the real picture of Sundanese people and the online literature only provides superficial information of Sundanese culture. It is consistent with UNESCO's (2003) findings that one of the problems in using local culture as a medium of instruction is the shortage of education materials.

This barrier was in line with the teacher who experienced such problems in using English textbooks for young learners. For example, topics like seasons and celebration cannot be used in her classroom due to their inappropriateness in Indonesian or Sundanese contexts. Besides that, the teacher should also adapt the difficulties and complexity of the textbooks. She stated that an English textbook (published by an international publisher) was designed for a certain level of students, which can only be used in lower level students in Indonesia.

4.2.3 The outgoing processes and final outcomes

The integration of Sundanese local content in EYL classroom was equipped with several aids to expand students' attention span. Most aids, especially puppet and Sundanese traditional games, successfully kept students engaged as Peck (1991) believes that cultural background is a natural source of subject matter. They like to share their prior experience and knowledge about their own culture.

Seen from teacher's perspective, the outgoing process was challenging in the beginning, but she found out that her adjustment had helped her to reach the desired learning goals, to improve her teaching performance, and to prevent inappropriate contents delivered to the students.

Seen from students' point of view, the outgoing process was considered exciting because they had chance to share their own prior knowledge and experience of Sundanese culture in an English class. This finding is in line with the theory proposed by Peck (1991), which states that children often enjoy studying aspects of life in their native culture because they fondly remember their time there and because it is something they can collectively explain to the teacher.

5 CONCLUSION

This study found out that the integration of Sundanese local content is promising and viable to be implemented in English classes due to many advantages gained in the learning processes.

However, the main foundation of a successful implementation of using local content relies on teacher's preparation. It is essential since the teacher should be knowledgeable about the culture and ready to deliver the cultural content in an appropriate pedagogical manner.

Seen from classroom practices aspect, the integration of Sundanese local content in English classroom is a proposed strategy to simultaneously preserve the culture and teach English. Its familiarity encourages the teacher and students to fondly share their cultural knowledge and experience in a structured English lesson. This also can address the difficulty in providing culturally appropriate materials for students in West Java.

Although the teacher needed a lot of adaptation and content preparation in the beginning, it is believed that this English teaching technique can be used as a means of Sundanese culture revitalization to make the students more engaged and interested in the English learning activities, to build students' feeling of participation in preserving the culture, and to promote cultural literacy skills.

REFERENCES

Alwasilah, A.C. Suryadi, K.. & Karyono, T. 2009. *Etnopedagogi: Landasan praktek pendidikan dan pendidikan guru.* Bandung: Kiblat Buku Utama.

Ary, D., Jacobs L.C., Sorensen, C.K., Razavieh, A. 2010. *Introduction to research in education (8th ed.).* California: Wadsworth Cengage Learning.

Biles, B. 1994. Activities that promote racial and cultural awareness. *Family Child Care Connections* 4(3): 1–4.

Brewster, J., Ellis, G. & Girard, D. 2003. *The primary English teacher's guide (New Edition).* London: Penguin Longman Publishing.

Buchori, M. 1994. Cultural transformation and educational reform. In Buchori, M (Ed)., *Sketches of Indonesian Society: A look from within.* Jakarta, Indonesia: IKIP Muhammadiyah & The Jakarta Post.

Cohen, L. & Manion, L. 1990. *Research methods in education (3rd ed.).* London and New York: Routledge.

Davies, S. 2003. *Content based Instruction in EFL Contexts.* Retrieved from http://iteslj.org/Articles/Davies-CBI.html

Ford, D.Y. 2006. *Raising culturally and responsible children.* Retrieved from http://tip.duke.edu/node/634.

Fraenkel, J.R. & Wallen, N.E. 2009. *How to design and evaluate research in education (7th ed.).* New York: McGraw-Hill Publishing Company.

Huang C. & Wang, B.T. 2008. A task-based cultural activity for EFL students: The dragon boat festival and rice rumplings. *The Internet TESL Journal* 14(6). Retrieved from http://iteslj.org/Lessons/Huang-CulturalActivity.html

Kilickaya, F. 2004. Authentic materials and cultural content in EFL classrooms. *The Internet TESL Journal* 10(7). Retrieved from http://iteslj.org/Techniques/Kilickaya-AuthenticMaterial.html

Larson, K.R. 2014. Critical pedagogy(ies) for ELT in Indonesia. *TEFLIN Journal* 25(1).

Lynne, C. 2001. *Teaching languages to young learners.* Cambridge: Cambridge University Press.

Mohani, T. 2010. Raising teacher consciousness of cultural sensitivities in the classroom. *The 4th International Conference on Teacher Education: Teacher Education in Developing National Characters and Cultures.* Conference conducted at the meeting of Student Executive Organization, of Indonesia University of Education, Bandung.

Peachey, N. 2003. *Content-based instruction.* Retrieved from http://www.teachingenglish.org.uk/article/content-based-instruction.

Peck, S. 1991. Recognizing and meeting the needs of ESL students. In Celce-Muria, Marianne (Ed), *Teaching English as a second or foreign language (second language).* Massachusetts: Heinle & Heinle.

Pinter, A. 2006. *Teaching young language learners.* England: Oxford University Press.

Purgason, K.B. 1991. Planning lessons and unit. In Celce-Muria, Marianne (Eds), *Teaching English as a second or foreign language (second language).* Massachusetts: Heinle & Heinle Publishers.

Quincannon., N. 2000. *Naves' grid of Content-based Instruction (USA) and CLIC (Content and Language Integrated Classroom) (Europe).* Retrieved from http://www.ub.edu/filoan/CLIL/CLILby-Naves.htm.

Regmi, M. 2011. *The role of local culture in English language teaching.* Retrieved from http://neltachoutari. wordpress.com/2011/04/01/the-role-of-local-culture-and-context-in-english-language-teaching.

Sudartini, S. 2009. Issues of cultural content in English language teaching. *The First International Graduate Students Conference on Indonesia: "(Re) Considering Contemporary Indonesia: Striving for Democracy, Sustainability and Prosperity.* Conference conducted at the meeting of Academy Professorship Indonesia in Social Sciences & Humanities & The Graduate School of Gadjah Mada University with the support of The Royal Netherlands Academy of Arts and Sciences (KNAW).

Sukarno. 2013. Promoting Blended Culture in TEIL. *Conference Proceeding of 3rd International Conference on Foreign Language Learning and Teaching* (pp 437–446). Language Institute of Thammasat University, Bangkok – Thailand.

Teddick, D.J., Jorgensen, K. & Geffert, T. 2001. *Content-based language instruction: The foundation of language immersion education in the bridge: From research to practice.* ACIE Newsletter.

Tomalin, B. & Stempleski, S. 1993. *Cultural awareness.* England: Oxford University Press.

UNESCO. 2003. *Education in a multilingual world.* Paris: UNESCO.

Uzuegbu, C.P. 2012. *The role of university libraries in enhancing local content availability in the Nigerian community.* Library Philosophy and Practice (e-Journal).

World Economic Forum. 2015. *New vision for Education: unlocking the potential of technology.* Geneva: World Economic Forum.

Yin, R.K. 2003. *Case study research design and methods.* California: Sage Publications.

ELT in Asia in the Digital Era: Global Citizenship and Identity – Madya et al. (Eds)
© *2018 Taylor & Francis Group, London, ISBN 978-0-8153-7900-3*

Written corrective feedback in a writing skill development program

S. Hidayati, A. Ashadi & S. Mukminatun
Yogyakarta State University, Yogyakarta, Indonesia

ABSTRACT: This article is aimed to (1) analyze learners' perspectives on Written Corrective Feedback, (2) identify the types of feedback preferred by the learners, and (3) discover how learners make use of the feedback to improve their writing skills. This study adopted a case study design with qualitative approach to gain in-depth information from 16 adult learners of English proficiency improvement program in a teachers' college. Data comprised observation results, learners' writing portfolio, interview transcripts, and questionnaire tabulation. The results indicated that learners viewed feedback positively as a means of the teacher to improve their writing. In terms of feedback types, most learners preferred to have direct and unfocused feedback for their writing. Further results showed that learners benefited from the feedback as a source of grammar learning to be discussed with classmates, source of motivation, self-correction and self-reminder. Subsequent implications of the teaching of writing are discussed.

1 INTRODUCTION

The ability to write in English is academically necessary for those interested in pursuing the study in universities using English as the medium of instruction. Such ability should, in fact, be mastered before the study because English proficiency test scores are normally used as one of the admission requirements. English as a Foreign Language (EFL) learners often find difficulties in meeting style and standard in academic writing due to various reasons.

The difficulties in writing different types of texts stem from the fact that English as a Foreign Language (EFL) learners should understand the language features of various types of text (Hyland 2003). In addition to understanding these linguistic features, EFL learners are confronted with a more serious challenge, which is the capacity to cohesively write based on the specific conventions of the text (Flowerdew 2002).

Indirectness strategies and markers have frequently been spotted in Non-native speakers' written dis-course including Indonesians. In fact, in native speaker's academic writing practice, explicit expressions and direct sentences are much expected. Hinkel (1997) found that Asian NNS, including 30 Indonesians used more rhetorical questions and tags, vague and ambiguous pronouns, repetition, and passive voice more often than native speakers did. These potentially become problems in proficiency writing test when the examiners/raters are native speakers who rarely get along with the culture of in-directness.

In responding to the problems, Written Corrective Feedback (WCF) is usually given to the learners writing every time they finished working on a writing task. The provision of WCF serves several objectives, namely: (1) raising learners' awareness of their weaknesses and strengths in writing in the target language; (2) providing opportunities for participants to improve their writing skills by reflecting on errors in writing; and (3) training learners to identify common errors that might have been made at the time of writing and correcting those errors.

Based on the problems identified above, the current study focused on analyzing learners' perspectives on Written Corrective Feedback to improve their writing skills. The problem is formulated as follows:

1. How do the participants view the importance of WCF for their writing activities?
2. What types of feedback do the participants perceive as effective for their writing improvement?
3. How do the participants use WCF to improve their writing skills?

2 WRITTEN CORRECTIVE FEEDBACK

Feedback has a vital role in the development of writing skills in second/foreign language. Hyland & Hyland (2006) explain that the benefits of feedback can at least be explored in three different aspects. First, in classes that focus on the process and not on the learner, feedback plays a role in improving the capability of learners to be able to build self-expression. Second, feedback serves to build learners' response to form a unity of meaning in an interactionist perspective. Third, feedback becomes a scaffolding vehicle for teachers on genre-based learning to provide a source of literacy and increase learner's confidence to use his skills in the context of real communication.

Feedback provided by teachers varies depending on the function and medium used. Also, the feedback provided also depends on the learner's level of proficiency and their needs in the learning process. Hyland & Hyland (2006) divide the types of feedback into four types that include teacher written feedback, teacher conferencing and oral feedback, peer feedback, and computer-mediated feedback. Furthermore, Ellis (2009) provides feedback typology as Direct, Indirect, Metalinguistic, Focus, and Electronic.

In this study, written corrective feedback is given in the form of direct and unfocused pointers. Direct feedback allows the learner to see firsthand the type of error made and the correct version of the error because in providing direct feedback, according to Hendrickson (1980), the teacher not only gives a mark on learning errors but also provides the correct form of the error. Therefore, direct feedback is considered more useful for learners because this type of feedback offers clear information about the structure of the target language (Bitchener & Knoch 2010). Meanwhile, in unfocused feedback, teachers provide corrections that cover all types of mistakes made by the learner (Ellis et al. 2008, Ellis 2009). The type of unfocused feedback is given because this type of feedback allows the learner to get corrections for all types of errors in writing (grammar, organizational text, and written mechanics), and a training time of only three months is not enough if the feedback is focused on one type of error.

Some studies of learner preferences on WCF show that the views on WCF vary. Results from several studies (Ferris 1995, Lee 2005) suggest that learners required different types of WCF regardless of the types of errors. Zamel (1985) and Woroniecka (1998) show that learners expected WCF in the form of comments on the content and the ideas rather than the grammar and surface errors that include punctuation, spelling, and word selection. In contrast, the results of research by Ashwell (2000), Leki (1991), and Ziv (1984) suggest that learners wanted WCF not only in the form of comments on the content and ideas but also the grammar and the surface errors that include punctuation, spelling, and word selection. Meanwhile, a study conducted by Lee (2005) shows that learners preferred a comprehensive WCF that covered a lot of things to WCF that was limited to only certain aspects. Also, the learner expected corrections and comments both directly and clearly, or indirectly as just marking (coding). With the mixed results of research in WCF from different settings, the current study attempts to examine their perspectives on the WCF, identify their preferred types of feedback, describe how they make use of the feedback.

3 METHOD

3.1 *Research setting and design*

This research adopted a case study design with a qualitative approach to obtain a thick description of the WCF phenomena. A total number of 20 participants including four

Table 1. Perspectives towards the use of written corrective feedback in writing.

No.	Item	SA	A	D	SD
1	I find written corrective feedback is beneficial in writing	15	1	–	–
2	Writing an essay by using the result of written corrective feedback is more effective	13	2	–	–
3	I expect to receive feedback every time I write.	14	2	–	–
4	My ability in writing increases because of written corrective feedback.	11	5	–	–
5	Written corrective feedback is the best way to give correction in writing.	9	7	–	–

lecturers were engaged in the data gathering processes. With the unit analysis in the form of feedback to learners' writing products in the Preparation Program, the case study attempts to uncover the phenomenon within certain limits (Yin 2009). Further, Stake (2006) adds that from studying these cases we can study the larger phenomenon.

3.2 *Research instruments*

Research instruments to collect data were observation guides, test materials, field notes guides, interviews and questionnaires. The data obtained were observation records, field notes, written texts produced by participants, interview transcripts and tabulation of questionnaires.

3.3 *Data collection and analysis*

Preliminary data were obtained from classroom observations to see the teaching situation and the interaction between participants and instructors documented in the observation sheets and field notes. Questionnaires were given closer to the final stages of the program to see progress and if there was a change in the views of the participants. Interviews were conducted after the program completed to verify their views on corrective feedback and as a method of triangulation (Cohen & Manion 2013).

After the initial observation, the observation notes were paired with the questionnaire to classify what important themes emerged and to compare them continuously with the results of the observations. According to Miles, Huberman & Saldana (2013), this constant comparison leads to the emergent themes and significant categories in this study.

The categories were displayed in tables and matrices to facilitate further analysis. Interviews were then conducted, and the results were coded to confirm with tables and matrices. Withdrawal of conclusions was held inductively based on the data and deductively by comparing to the literature in line with the formulated questions.

4 FINDINGS AND DISCUSSION

Based on the results of the questionnaire analysis, all participants considered that WCF was useful in the learning process. Different views were only found at the level of agree and strongly agree. This is shown by quantitative data (Table 2) that out of the 16 participants, 15 of them strongly agreed and 1 participant agreed.

In relation to the expected types of feedback, the participants expected the type of direct feedback because they thought that if a correction comes without the correct form, it will not tell the errors and cannot be utilized as a source of learning.

Table 2. Perspectives on the types of written corrective feedback.

No.	Item	SA	A	D	SD
1	I like to be provided with error correction on my essay	10	3	2	–
2	I like to be provided with error correction plus comment on my essay	14	2	–	–
3	I like to be provided with error correction without comment on my essay	1	3	9	2
4	I like to be provided with overt correction by the lecturer on my essay	8	4	1	1
5	I like to be provided with no error correction at all	2	1	4	8

Table 3. Perspectives towards different types of errors.

No.	Item	SA	A	D	SD
1	I am in favour of receiving feedback on organizational aspects (*Example: Paragraph structure, sentence order*)	13	3	–	–
2	I am in favour of receiving feedback on grammatical errors (*Example: Tense, sentence structure*)	14	1	–	–
3	I am in favour of receiving feedback on punctuation errors (*Example:,. ? !*)	9	5	1	–
4	I am in favour of receiving feedback on capitalization errors	8	6	1	–
5	I am in favour of receiving feedback on vocabulary errors (*Example: Wrong vocabulary choice*)	12	3	–	–
6	I am in favour of receiving feedback on ideas development aspect (*Example: The ideas are not fully developed*)	12	2	1	–
7	I am in favour of receiving feedback on spelling errors	10	5	–	–

In addition to direct feedback, participants also opted for the type of unfocused feedback because participants expected corrections in all aspects (unfocused). It is also noted that participants expected feedback ranging from grammatical aspects to paragraph organization, idea development, vocabulary, spelling and punctuation.

All of the participants in the current study preferred feedback provided with a comment from the teacher, which Ellis (2008) categorizes as direct feedback, i.e. the teacher includes the correct form of an incorrect expression in giving feedback. Direct feedback was seen as facilitating them to explain and correct their mistakes. Otherwise, they would be confronted with uncertainty about how to correct errors, as reflected in the following interview results:

(Crossing mistakes out)…. is not enough to help us because we still need to look for (the mistakes).. it means I still find the point of error that I can not correct (cannot)… (I/Cathy)

Yes.. should be explained.. the error is here. If it is not too clear where the mistake is, I sometimes feel it is fine. That's something that I frequently don't know. (I/Raina).

More specifically, the participants expected teacher's error corrections on aspects such as organization, grammar, vocabulary, and spelling. In other words, the participants required the provision of unfocused feedback, which allowed the teacher to see all the errors in all the elements required in writing, as recorded in the following interviews:

...because if you write, it is inevitable that you must care for punctuation, and spelling as well as grammar. So I think all the feedback given should be comprehensive to all aspects. (I/Ann).

The current study also shows that WCF was made use by participants to improve writing skills as a source of grammar learning, discussion materials with colleagues, learning motivation, self-correction (while editing), and self-reminder (when writing).

Another interesting point is the participants' views on how to give feedback, i.e. the participants require the feedback to be given gradually. The intended stages are from a specific aspect, such as grammar, gaining more attention at the beginning of the training, and more detailed feedback at the beginning of the training and then progressively reduced as the participants' writing skills increase.

The use of WCF in promoting learning has been examined in different research settings. Relevant studies have shown that WCF is likely to affect improved understanding and use of the targeted structures (Bitchener 2012). The current study can confirm the usefulness of WCF as a source of learning. Han and Hyland (2015) also point out that WCF can increase learner engagement when teachers have a comprehensive understanding of the student's background and beliefs. In this way, teachers can plan appropriate WCF strategies to engage the learners. The participants' backgrounds and purpose to learn writing are well shared among instructors in the examined program. These may lead to the level of agreement expressed by the participants as most instructors always provide different types of feed-backs on their work.

The participants' positive perceptions on the WCF is further followed by the preference on unfocused feedback. There is a sense that this type of feedback is at the top of the other due to the nature of the training for the proficiency test. Moini & Salami (2013) suggested that unfocused WCF reflects better teacher's objective as it views writing correction as a whole skill rather than as a way of practicing grammar. The instructors in the studied program tried to avoid the perception that the writing improvement program is almost similar to a grammar class. In a rather different setting, Park, Song & Shin (2016) showed that learners were able to self-correct more than 30% of their errors and that the non-native language learners were significantly better at perceiving their errors on mechanics. Similar to the current study, they also found that the higher proficiency language learners were better in self-correcting their errors. Therefore, it implies the importance of considering learner's factors, such as their prior L2-learning experience, when providing written corrective feedback.

With most of the participants preferred to be given feedback on the sentence level and organization of ideas strongly confirms Russel and Spada's research (2006) on the effectiveness of WCF on L2 grammar learning. Concerning this preference, Shintani, Ellis & Suzuki (2014) argue that when form-focused written feedback addresses at saliency and complexity, learners are likely to pay attention to the structure that contributes more to the whole textual meaning. Noticing, in line with, L2 acquisition theory will enable the effectiveness of learning process (Ortega 2009). Their research also indicates that directly correcting the errors learners make concerning a complex syntactical structure proves to be more beneficial than giving them a metalinguistic explanation.

5 CONCLUSIONS

This study has shown that all participants perceive that WCF is useful for improving their writing skills. They consider that WCF can effectively facilitate them in learning and provide the constructive guidance needed in their learning to-write process.

The type of feedback mostly expected by the participants is direct and unfocused. The former is considered useful because corrections without providing the correct form will not show the errors and cannot be used as a source of learning. Unfocused feedback is required because participants want corrections in all aspects of their writing such as paragraph organization, idea development, vocabulary, spelling, and punctuation (mechanics). This study confirms that that certain types of WCF provide different benefits for improving writing skills, as a source of particular aspects of language learning, discussion materials with colleagues, learning motivation, self-correction, and self-reminder.

The result of this study also indicates that: 1) the provision of WCF is seen as an opportunity to learn grammar simultaneously, and 2) feedback can be a map for participants to allow the description of their writing development profile. They will be able to reflect their weaknesses and strengths so that strategies for improving writing results can be formulated. Further, in terms of instructional practice, different student profiles and course settings may require different feedback treatment. Therefore, teachers need to consider the different settings in which they work to implement the types of written corrective feedback appropriate for certain students.

REFERENCES

Ashwell, T. 2000. Patterns of teacher response to student writing in a multiple-draft composition classroom: Is content feedback followed by form feedback the best method? *Journal of Second Language Writing* 9: 227–257.

Bitchener, J. & Knoch, U. 2010. The contribution of written corrective feedback to language development: A ten month investigation. *Applied Linguistics* 31: 193–214.

Bitchener, J. 2012. Written corrective feedback for L2 development: Current knowledge and future research. *TESOL Quarterly* 46(4): 855–860. http://doi.org/10.1002/tesq.62.

Cohen, L., Manion, L. & Morrison, K. 2013. *Research methods in education. (7th ed)*. London: Routledge.

Creswell, J.W. 2012. Qualitative inquiry and research design: choosing among five approaches. Thousand Oaks: Sage.

Ellis, R. 2009. A typology of written corrective feedback types. *ELT journal* 63(2): 97–107.

Ellis, R., Sheen, Y., Murakami, M. & Takashima, H. 2008. The effects of focused and unfocused written corrective feedback in an English as a foreign language context. *System* 36(3): 353–371.

Ferris, D.R. 1995. Student reactions to teacher response in multiple draft composition classrooms. *TESOL Quarterly,* 29: 33–53.

Flowerdew, J. 2002. Genre in classroom: A linguistic approach. In A. M. Johns (ed), *Genre in classroom: Multiple perspective*. Marwah: Routledge.

Han, Y. & Hyland, F. 2015. Exploring learner engagement with written corrective feedback in a Chinese tertiary EFL classroom. *Journal of Second Language Writing* 30: 31–44. http://doi.org/10.1016/j.jslw.2015.08.002.

Hendrickson, J.M. 1980. The treatment of error in written work. *Modern Language Journal* 64: 216–221.

Hinkel, E. 1997. Indirectness in L1 and L2 academic writing. *Journal of pragmatics* 27(3): 361–386.

Hyland, K. 2003. *Second language writing*. Cambridge: Cambridge university press.

Hyland, K. & Hyland, F. 2006. Feedback on second language students' writing. *Language Teaching* (39): 83–101.

Lee, I. 2005. Error correction in the L2 classroom: What do students think? *TESL Canada Journal* 22: 1–16.

Leki, I. 1991. The preferences of ESL students for error correction in college level writing classes. *Foreign Language Annals* 24: 203–218.

Miles, M.B., Huberman, A. M. & Saldana, J. 2013. *Qualitative data analysis: A methods sourcebook*. SAGE Publications, Incorporated.

Moini, M.R. & Salami, M. 2013. The impact of indirect focused and unfocused corrective feedback on written accuracy. *International Journal of Foreign Language Teaching and Research* 2(4): 32–41.

Ortega, L. 2009. Understanding second language acquisition. Routledge: New York.

Russell, J. & Spada, N. 2006. The effectiveness of corrective feedback for the acquisition of L2 grammar. *Synthesizing Research on Language Learning and Teaching:* 133–164. http://doi.org/10.1075/lllt.13.

Shintani, N., Ellis, R. & Suzuki, W. 2014. Effects of written feedback and revision on learners' accuracy in using two English grammatical structures. *Language Learning* 64(1): 103–131. http://doi.org/10.1111/lang.12029.

Stake, R. E. 2013. *Multiple case study analysis*. Guilford Press.

Woroniecka, I. 1998. A *nonnative student's reactions to instructors' feedback on hispapers: A case study of an undergraduate history student*(Master's thesis).University of Toronto: Department of Curriculum, Teaching, and Learning: Ontario Institute for Studies in Education of the University of Toronto. Retrieved from http://www.nlcbnc.ca/obj/s4/f2/dsk1/tape11/PQDD_0004/MQ40680.pdf.

Yin, R.K. 2009. Case study research: Design and methods, 4th. *Thousand Oaks*.

Zamel, V. 1985. Responding to student writing. *TESOL Quarterly* 19: 79–101.

Ziv, N.D. 1984. The effect of teacher comments on the writing of four college freshmen. In R. Bach and L. S. Bridwell (eds.), *New directions in compositionresearch* (pp. 362–280). New York: Guilford Press.

ELT in Asia in the Digital Era: Global Citizenship and Identity – Madya et al. (Eds)
© 2018 Taylor & Francis Group, London, ISBN 978-0-8153-7900-3

Contact with the nature: Field trip strategy in enhancing writing descriptive text

Rugaiyah
Islamic University of Riau, Pekanbaru, Indonesia

ABSTRACT: Field trips are recognized as important moments in learning; a shared social experience that provides the opportunity for students to encounter and explore novel things in an authentic setting. This paper is focused on analyzing the effectiveness of field trips on students' writing descriptive text for a group of 30 students of second semester of FKIP UIR Pekanbaru, Indonesia in the academic year 2016/2017 who were selected by using random sampling. The data were collected by giving tests (pre-test and post-test). This study used experimental research, through the Mann-Whitney U t-test. The normality of the test was analyzed through Kolmogorov-Smirnova. The results indicated that the asymptotic significance of less than 0.05 ($p = 0.00 < 0.05$) means the students' ability in writing descriptive text increased significantly after learning through field trips.

1 INTRODUCTION

Teaching English as a second or foreign language has been a constant challenge due to the interference of the first language. Efforts to motivate learners must first look into the teaching methods, as implementing the conventional way of teaching English was found to be unmotivating. Especially when they are restricted to classroom learning which would expose them to a limited scope of knowledge, the situation does not reflect a positive trend in teaching and learning English.

One of the core subjects taught at schools up to universities in Indonesia is the English language. The Curriculum Specifications prescribed by the Ministry of Education specify the four skills which need to be mastered by the learners, namely listening, speaking, reading and writing. Writing is one of the skills which needs to be mastered by the learners. Students learn different genres of writing like descriptive, expository, recount narrative, and others based on the prescribed syllabus of the Ministry of Education. Writing is generally considered to be one of the most difficult skills for foreign language students. Even native speakers have difficulty in showing a good command of writing (Johnstone et al. 2002).

Considering the fact that writing is often a challenge for EFL learners as it is considered to be the most painstaking and challenging language skill, the researcher, with several years of experience of teaching EFL in Indonesia, has been witness to this challenging task. It has been a challenging task for EFL teachers because students, as observed in their writing samples do not take much interest in writing either for academic, professional or personal purposes. Moreover, writing requires an in-depth understanding of the target language. On the other hand, they also have difficulty to explore their ideas as well into written form. Those problems cause the students to be bored in the classroom. They could not explore their ideas as well to write although the theme has been already clearly determined. In relation, Raimes (1983) thinks that: When students complain about how difficult it is to write in a second language, they are talking not only about the difficulty of finding the right words and using the correct grammar but also about the difficulty of finding and expressing ideas in a new language".

Moreover, the importance of teaching how to write focused on descriptive paragraphs can be analyzed from the viewpoints: inside the classroom and outside the classroom. The freshmen are faced with the need of describing events, experiences, areas, and objects inside the language classroom. No matter what the level is, students always ask about what they did during vacation. They are also requested to provide a physical description of themselves and others. Outside the classroom, most freshmen are supposed to put into practice all the knowledge that they have acquired in their English lessons. Nowadays, knowing how to write in English has become a transcendental feature of a 21st century citizen. Students have to express themselves in English in writing to establish relationships with foreigners and people outside the country. Most of the time, students have to describe events, experiences and so forth in their writing. Therefore, in writing that text, students need to observe things, places, and animals in their natural habitats.

From the explanation above, this research aims to find innovative ways to write descriptive text for students who have difficulty in creative writing class. Most students sometimes feel restricted when they have to write in a classroom. It happens because somehow they cannot get any ideas when they have to complete their writing tasks, so it makes them hate writing class.

Therefore, the need to develop an effective environmental education program ranks as one of the major challenges facing education in the next decade. Learning can take place anywhere. Not only in the classroom or in school environment. This is not just talking about a particular type of education, it could be any type, formal, informal or non-formal education, it is all about learning in general. Furthermore, in order to create an efficient learning ambience, language teachers need to focus on the core principles of the learning community which includes the integration of curriculum, active learning, and student engagement in field-based learning, all of which have been used to generate student interest, enhance student learning, and help them acquire hands-on experience. Though mostly used in education, field-based learning, primarily field trips, can be useful in undergraduate and graduate education where students connect the textbook and classroom learning with the real world.

Therefore, giving students and involving them in experiential learning experiences in a real world experience makes learning more meaningful and memorable. As a result, students will have more of a concept on the topic as they have learnt through their hand-on experiences. It allows students to have a real-world experience. For example, a textbook lesson on domestic animals can be enhanced by a trip to a local farm where the students can clearly see the domestic animals.

2 REVIEW OF RELATED LITEATURE

2.1 *Field trips*

Many researchers have investigated knowledge gain and learning that occurred during field trips; (Tal & Morag 2009, Stainfield at al. 2000). It provides students with an opportunity to see and experience what they have been taught in the classroom. Field trips provide real world settings in which students are challenged to apply knowledge learned in the classroom. Many students enjoy the less formal setting in which the learning takes place (Falk 1983, Flexer & Borun 1984, Braund & Reiss 2006). As a result, these students may become more excited about their school subjects (Michie 1998, Storsdieck 2001). Field trips have great potential to positively affect students' learning (MacKenzie & White 1982, Flexer & Borun 1984, Lisowski & Disinger 1991, Farmer, Knapp & Benton 2007) and students' attitudes towards their education (Wendling & Wuensch 1985, Price & Hein 1991, Michie 1998, Hannon & Randolph 1999). Students who directly participate during a field experience generate a more positive attitude about the subject. (Behrendt & Franklin 2014) Fuller at al. (2003) conclude in their study that students perceived field work to be beneficial not only to their learning which develops the subject knowledge and the technical and the transferable skills, but also some concomitant values like social interaction with their lecturers and peers. The value of a field trip lies particularly in providing students with a better sense of the real world and direct experience with concrete phenomena.

Mayer et al. (2009) consider the reason why nature can be beneficial to creation. In all three of their studies they discovered that exposure to the natural world enhanced the positive emotions of the participant as well as increased their attention, motivation and the way they meditate and problem-solve. Alawad (2012) examined natural sound and whether this could be of benefit to the art classroom environment. She considered whether natural sound could foster creativity. This study found that natural sound in the art classroom enhanced students' creativity and raised students' marks in their art tasks (Alawad 2012). Therefore, looking to the natural locations for field trips, such as a desert and outside space could stimulate a student's creativity and thirst for knowledge. This study will explore the role of field trips within the English curriculum. In particular, it will consider if field trips positively affect students' creative thinking and practices in writing descriptive text. As the aim of this research is to observe the subject in its natural state and possibly collect samples.

Field trips offer opportunities to students that they may not have known existed, and expose them to learning experiences that cannot be duplicated inside the classroom. These "out-of-school" experiences have been a tradition since the earliest schools were founded. The outdoor field experience has traditionally been an important component in curricula. Students do seem to benefit from the learning experiences that occur outside the classroom according to another key researcher into the area of field trips. Patrick (2010) proposed that field trips should be weaved into the teaching schedule as this will provide an opportunity for students to view information for themselves and use their own senses to touch, or feel materials that they had previously only heard about (Patrick 2010). This immediacy and accessibility is a key feature of field trips and one of its redeeming features. Leaving the school premises is a social experience and one, which provides a change of tempo and scenery for students which will allow them to learn through their experiences and reflections. The fact that everything and every event of life provides information for education, justify teacher's effort to take students outside the four walsl of the classroom for effective learning. This could be better explained in the values that educators attached to the relevance of field trips in the teaching and learning process. The traditional practice of field trip as an instructional strategy takes the students outside of the school environment. Thus field trips become a form of community contact instructional strategy adopted in the formal school system for the purpose of education.

Field trips are recognized as important moments in learning; a shared social experience that provides the opportunity for students to encounter and explore novel things in an authentic setting. Krepel and Durrall (1981) describe field trips as a school or class trip with an educational intent, in which students interact with the setting, displays, and exhibits to gain an experiential connection to the ideas, concepts, and subject matter. Futher. Oloyede et al. (2006) inferred that field trips are the act of taking pupils out of the classroom into the community for the purpose of learning. Nabors et al. (2009) share the same view as the prementioned authors that field trips are a type of experiential learning that gets children away from the traditional classroom setting and into a new mode of learning. Tal and Morag (2009) have different opinions from those of other scholars, they describe field trips as student experiences outside of the classroom at interactive locations designed for educational purposes. This view is that the general perception of people as regards field trips are any teaching and learning process carried out by a group of people outside of the classroom environment.

The purpose of the trip is usually observation for education to provide students with experiences outside their everyday activities, such as going on the trip with the teacher and their classmates. Field trips are also used to produce civilized young men and women who appreciate culture and the arts. It is seen that more-advantaged children may have already experienced cultural institutions outside of school, and field trips provide a common ground with more-advantaged and less-advantaged children to have some of the same cultural experiences in writing descriptive text.

Field trips cannot replace school-based education but they should not have to compete to demonstrate their pedagogical worth. In formal education, learning outcomes are customarily pre-decided independently of the learner, for example through curricula and defined standards. In field trips, learners are invited to drive their own learning outcomes. Notwithstanding, the learning outcomes a field trip can impart are conditioned by the structure of the field trip, the personal context of children, the social context of the visit, the novelty of the physical context, teacher agendas and actions during the field trip, and the quality of preparations and follow-up experiences.

During the field trip it is possible that teachers divide learners into groups and assign them team tasks. When groups work together throughout a field trip, it improves learner communication with peers. Educational trips offer interaction and cooperation among students, teachers, other administrative staff and representatives at the field trip destination who offer guided tours and conduct question-and-answer sessions. The allows learners to expand their educational networks through interacting with others during field trips (Arduini, 2012). This social training also provides for the learners who come from different social-cultural backgrounds an opportunity to behave and control emotion in different situations (Shakil et al. 2011).

2.2 *Features of field trips*

1. Facilitate the learning of abstract concepts. Taking students on a field trip makes learning more effective as they will be able to gain vast ideas on the topic.
2. Motivate students through increased interest and curiosity. Field trips can add variety to the regular classroom instructional program and they tend to be special and enjoyable learning experiences. As a result, students will develop positive attitudes in students toward related classroom activities.
3. Increase student-student and student-teacher social interaction. Field trips provide an opportunity to involve students, parents, and the teachers in the instructional program. Students can select the place to be visited, developing questions to ask, writing reports or thank you letters after the trip, or evaluating the experiences.
4. Develops social awareness. Field trips make students aware of learning activities in everyday life.

2.3 *Purpose of field trip*

From the previous research, it can be drawn that the purposes of field trip are as follows:

1. Experiential learning experiences. Involvement in a real world experience makes learning more meaningful and memorable. As a result, the students will have more concept of the topic as they have learnt through their hands-on experiences.
2. Concrete skills such as note taking. Students have to develop questions to be asked, write reports or thank you letters after the trip, or evaluate their experiences. By doing such activities, students will develop various skills such as note taking skills, speaking skills, and writing skills will enhance.
3. Addional variety to the regular instructional program; they tend to be special and enjoyable learning experiences, ones which develop positive attitudes in students toward related classroom activities. Field trips are rich in educational possibilities because students learn from actual firsthand experiences, rather than by simply reading or hearing about something.

Moreover, field trips help the students appreciate the relevance and importance of what they learn in the classroom. Furthermore, field trips are rich in educational possibilities as students learn from actual hands-on experiences, rather than by simply reading or hearing about something. Therefore, involvement in a real world experience makes learning more meaningful and memorable compared to regular classroom instructional programs.

2.4 *The procedures of field trips*

Myers and Jones (2009) describe that educational field trips should be designed around specific educational objectives. If a field trip is not planned well in advance it will end in confusion and will be a waste of time and money. So field trips should be planned as a cooperative activity involving full pupil participation under the teacher's supervision. When planning and organizing a successful field trip, three important stages should be included i.e. the pre-trip stage of a field trip involves two major components: administration and instruction. The second stage of a successful field trip is the trip itself. It also has two components: the role of the student and the role of the teacher. The third and final stage of a successful field trip is the post-trip stage which also consists of two components: debriefing and culminating activity. The objective of this study is to know if there is a significant effect of field trips on students' writing descriptive text.

3 RESEARCH HYPOTHESES

From the aforementioned objective the following are the research hypotheses;

(H0): There is no significant effect of field trip on students' writing dscriptive text.
(H1): There is a significant effect of field trips on students' writing descriptive text.

4 METHODOLOGY

The population of this study was 180 second-year English major students in the second semester of the academic year 2016/2017 at Islamic University of Riau Pekanbaru Indonesia. The study sample consisted of two classes each consisting of 30 students selected by simple random sampling from seven classes. Therefore, the researcher took the experimental group on two separate field trips to the zoo and a museum. The field trips were each a day in length. The students in this group were given writing materials (explaining all components of writing) and supplementary material prior to each trip. While, the control group of students (30 students) were also given the same writing material, this group was not taken on these trips.

Data were collected from the students' scores of the pre-test and post-test of writing descriptive text. The data obtained from this method of teaching in the study was analyzed and interpreted through quantitative analysis. Quantitative data includes the data obtained from the pre-test and the post-test. The t-test was to compare the students' writing descriptive text.

4.1 *Procedure of research*

Before the experiment, the writing test and the rating rubric were designed. Then, the test validity and reliability were identified. the objectives of teaching writing and the writing topics were formulated. Next, the Teacher's Manual was designed to provide step-by-step procedures for teaching writing using field trips. It included how to help learners apply the suggested three stages of the field trip strategy. The experiment began on the second week of the first term of the academic year 2016–2017. At the beginning, out of seven classes, the participants were randomly assigned to the control group (Class A, N = 30) or the experimental group (Class C, N = 30). Then, they were introduced to the purposes of the study. The writing test was administered to both groups as a pre-test. Afterwards, the control group was taught writing descriptive text through a traditional method. The teacher demonstrated the process of writing by giving a sample of good writing while showing students photographs or posters of the object being discussed. Next, the students were asked to write descriptive text based on the topic given. Finally, the teacher and students together discussed the results of students' writing. While the experimental group was taught writing by using the field trip strategy which included three stages. At the end of the experiment, both groups were post-tested using the same writing test. Field trips are recognized as important moments in learning; a shared social experience that provides the opportunity for students to encounter and explore novel things in an authentic setting. It is important to recognize that learning outcomes from field trips can range from cognitive to affective outcomes (Heath 2012).

4.2 *The procedures of field trip based on this research*

4.2.1 *Before the field trip*

The teacher visited the sites (museum and zoo) prior to the field trip to gather information about them. In the classroom, the teacher demonstrated the process of writing. Teacher and students discussed the focus and purpose of the field trip together, while showing photographs and posters of the sites. After a while, the teacher organized all of the administration and instruction. Then the teacher asked for permission from the dean. Afterwards, the teacher explained about the location and checked all the details about the trip. Further, the teacher set a standard conduct code and discussed money usage, lunch plans, dress code and other necessary things and then, discussed how to ask good questions and make a list of the open-ended observation questions to gather information. Thereafter, the teacher checked an overview the field trip schedule. Likewise, Pace (2004) and Myers and Jones (2009) state that one needs to prepare a conceptual foundation on which the students may connect their experiences before the trip. In brief, the teacher gave instructions by explaining the rules in the pre-trip session. Finally, the teacher checked the students' preparation such as required documentation.

4.2.2 *During the field trip*

When the field trip began, the teacher divided learners into groups and assigned them team tasks. When groups work together throughout a field trip, it improves learner communication with peers. The teacher may need to help some students become comfortable in the new environment. Then, the teacher asked students to apply field trip strategy by giving the topic while connecting the students' experiences on the trip with concepts and lessons taught in the classroom. Next, the teacher kept the students engaged and used worksheets to help students focus on exploring and learning the targeted concepts. Afterwards, the teacher let students do excursions to locations selected for educational purposes, during which students interacted with exhibits, facilities, and surroundings in their functional settings to gain an experiential connection to ideas, materials, or phenomena they study (from afar) in the classroom. Furthermore, the teacher gave students extended opportunities and encouragement to engage in discussion with their peers/ group. Finally, the teacher asked students to explore their ideas into writing descriptive text.

4.2.3 *Post trip*

The students' experiences need to be reinforced through discussion, activities, reading, a television show or movie (Falk & Dierking 2000, Kisiel 2006a, Orion & Hofstein 1994, Pace & Tesi 2004, Tal & Steiner 2006). At the beginning, teacher helped students to connect new classroom concepts to the students' field trip experiences. Thereafter, the teacher started each topic by exploring it with the students through class discussion and through sharing her own ideas and her writing. The students shared their observations and reactions to field trip experiences. Furthermore, they were asked to create a classroom bulletin board displaying material collected while on the field trip. Therefore, this served to demonstrate the process of writing in order to give the students the experience of being good writers, to help them get the sense that this was a collaborative endeavour to provide examples of good writing. Furthermore, the teacher corrected students' writing, these pieces were revised and "published" in booklets which were put on display in class, and students were encouraged to read and write comments on each other's writing in their free time. In relation to this finding, Moffett (1968) suggests that the topics started with the students' concrete experiences and moved towards more abstract concepts. Consequently, this aimed at making the writing tasks more relevant to students by introducing topics related to their experience and social world and by providing a real audience and a real purpose for writing.

5 FINDINGS AND DISCUSSION

This research project was aimed at establishing the effectiveness of field trips on students' writing descriptive text in a group of 30 students. Based on the analysis of the data and the findings the researcher states that students showed an improvement in their writing descriptive text. As a result of the implementation of Process writing can be shown in the following table.

Table 1 shows that only the data of the experimental class is normally distributed 0.117 > 0.05. Therefore, to determine whether the hypothesis should be rejected or not. This was tested at 0.05 level of significance. The decision role is such that the null hypothesis (H0) is rejected if the value of sig. (2-sided) is less that 0.05. the essence of the hypothesis is to determine the effectiveness of field trips on students' writing descriptive text.

Table 2 shows the statistical description of the pre and post test results of the two types of instructional strategies on the students' writing descriptive text with conventional strategy pre-test Mean of 52.333, field trip strategy pre-test Mean of 55.5000, and conventional strategy post-test Mean of 64.1667, field trips strategy post-test Mean of 76.1667. To determine if the observed effectiveness is significant at the 0.05 level, the Mann-Whitney T test was used and the summary of the analysis is presented in Table 3.

Table 3 shows the results from the pre- and post-trip students, respectively. The asymptotic, two-tailed significance (also known as the –p‖ value) generated from the Mann-Whitney U test. The asymptotic, two-tailed significance is an indication of probability that the – null hypothesis‖ cannot be rejected. The null hypothesis here is that the data from the independent samples come from the same population; in other words, the samples are not different from each other. Thus, a low value of the significance indicates that the null hypothesis can be rejected and the two samples are different from each other. The statements with the asymptotic significance of less than 0.05 ($p = 0.00 < 0.05$).

From Table 3 the results show that there is a significant effect of the field trip strategy on students' writing descriptive text with $0.00 < 0.05$. This means that the null hypothesis (H0) is

Table 1. The normality of the test.

	Kolmogorov-smirnova			Shapiro-wilk		
	Statistic	df	Sig.	Statistic	df	Sig.
Experimental class	0.144	30	0.117	0.945	30	0.126
Control class	0.173	30	0.022	0.935	30	0.065
Experimental class	0.174	30	0.022	0.921	30	0.028
Control class	0.219	30	0.001	0.888	30	0.004

a. Lilliefors significance correction.

Table 2. Statistical description of field trips and conventional strategies on students' writing descriptive text.

	N	Minimum	Maximum	Mean	Std. Deviation
Pre-test of experimental class	30	40.00	70.00	55.5000	8.64531
Pre control class	30	40.00	70.00	52.3333	8.48257
Post experimental class	30	60.00	90.00	76.1667	8.87493
Post control class	30	55.00	75.00	64.1667	4.56435

Valid N (list wise) 30.

Table 3. Mann-whitney u test for the descriptive writing text test.

	Score
Mann-Whitney U	170.500
Wilcoxon W	635.500
Z	–4.208
Asymp. Sig. (2-tailed)	0.000

a. Grouping Variable: class.

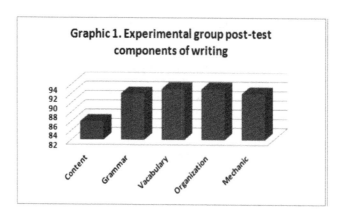

Graphic 1. Experimental group post-test components of writing

Figure 1. Illustrates the experimental group's post-test evidence that the highest component scores of writing were for vocabulary and organization (93), while the lowest was for content (86).

rejected and (H1) is accepted. Furthermore, field trips enhance learners mental development through observation and offer opportunities to students to explore their ideas based on their own experience. In other research Mhgoub M Yassir (2014) agreed that field trips to natural and industrial locations were a beneficial learning aid and a means of fostering students' creativity and practices in art education. Obadiro (2016) found that virtual field trips and real field trips are effective strategies in enhancing students' knowledge in Social Studies. Haw-Jan "John" Wu (2009) stated that field trips do increase student interest in OM among other positive feelings of the students. When students have an interest, they tend to learn the subject materials better.

6 CONCLUSION

In conclusion, field trips applied to the Process approach were a suitable strategy for EFL students from the first grade at Islamic University of Riau Pekanbaru, Indonesia to increase their writing descriptive text. In addition, this type of resource was a means for increasing students' motivation to improve and practice their descriptive writing text. Even though they attained, the results of this study reveal that subjects who went on field trips out performed students from the control group who used the conventional strategy of writing. Moreover, it should also be noted that having students experience real-world activities outside of the classroom may have positive results not measured in this or any similar short-term study. The majority of the related literature deals with the more general sphere of informal science education, which covers natural—or social—science-based learning activities such as short-term visits (hours to a day) to natural areas and more structured settings such as museums and zoos, aquaria, or gardens. In addition, the study found that students learn quite a lot. In particular, enriching field trips contribute to the development of students into civilized young men and women who possess more knowledge about art, have stronger critical-thinking skills, exhibit increased historical empathy, display higher levels of tolerance. Here, the researcher reviews the informal science education literature with a focus on the effectiveness of informal science learning experiences on the students' writing descriptive text.

REFERENCES

Alawad, A. 2012. Can we bring the natural environment into the art classroom? Can natural sound foster cretivity?" *Educational Research and Review* 7(28): 627–631.
Arduini, J. 2012. The Significance of Field Trips in Education. eHow online article retrieved on 21/01/2013 from http://www.ehow.com /about_5439078_virtual-vs-physical-field-trips.html#ixzz2IbvuLj2U.

Behrendt, M. & Franklin, T. 2014. A Review of research on school field trips and their value in educa-tion. *International Journal of Environmental & Science educa-tion* 9: 235–245.

Behrendt, M. & Franklin, T. 2014. A review of research on school field trips and their value in educa-tion. *International Journal of Environmental and Science Education* 9(3): 235–245.

Braund, M. & Reiss, M. 2006. Towards a more authentic science curriculum: The contribution of out-of-school learning. *International Journal of Science Education* 28 (12): 1373–1388.

Falk, J.H. & Dierking, L.D. 2000. Learning from museums: Visitor experiences and the making of meaning. New York: Altamira Press.

Falk, J.H. 1983. Field trips: A look at environmental effects on learning. *Journal of Biological Education* 17(2): 137–142.

Farmer, D., Knapp, D. & Benton, G.M. 2007. An elementary school environmental education field trip: Long-term effects on ecological and environmental knowledge and attitude development. *Journal of Environmental Education*, 38(3): 33–42.

Flexer, B.K. & Borun, M. 1984. The impact of a class visit to a participatory science museum exhibit and a classroom science lesson. *Journal of Research in Science Teaching* 21(9): 863–873.

Fuller, I.C., Gaskin, S. & Scott, I. 2003. *Student perceptions of geography and environmental science fieldwork* in the light of restricted access to the *field*, caused by foot and mouth disease in the UK in 2001. *Journal* of *Geography in Higher Education* 27(1): 79–102.

Hannon, K. & Randolph, A. 1999. Collaborations between museum educators and classroom teachers: Partnerships, curricula and student understanding. Retrieved from Eric Document Reproduction Service (EDRS) database. (ED 448 133).

Haw-Jan, W. 2009. Using field trips to enhance students learning in operations management: *Literature Review and Field Observations.* California State University San Bernardino, CA. California Journal of Operations Management © 2009 CSU-POM.

Heath, D. 2012. The Significance of Field Trips for Students. *eHow online article.* Retrieved on 21/01/2016 from http://www.ehow.com.

Johnstone, K.M., Ashbaugh, H. & Warfield, T.D. 2002. Effects of repeated practice and contextual-writing experiences on college students' writing skills. *Journal of Educational Psychology* 94(2): 305.

Kisiel, J. 2006a. More than lions and tigers and bears–Creating meaningful field trip lessons. *Science Activities* 43(2): 7–10.

Krepel, W.J. & Durral, C.R. 1981. Field trips: *A guideline for planning and conducting educational experi-ences.* Washington, DC: National Science Teachers Association.

Lisowski, M. & Disinger, J.F. 1991. The effect of field-based instruction on student understanding of ecological concepts. *Journal of Environmental Education* 23(11): 19–23.

MacKenzie, A.A. & White, R.T. 1982. Fieldwork in geography and long-term memory structures. American Educational Research Journal 19(4): 623–232.

Mahgoub M.Y. 2014. The Impact of Field Trips on Students' Creative Thinking And Practices In Arts Education: King Faisal University, Faculty of Education, Department of Art Education. Cited from http://www.jofamericanscience.org.

Mayer, S F., Frantz C.M., Bruehlman, E. & Dolliver, K. 2009. "Why Is Nature Beneficial? The Role of Connectedness to Nature Environment and Behavior". Volume 41, Number 5.

Michie, M. 1998. Factors influencing secondary science teachers to organize and conduct field trips. *Australian Science Teacher's Journal* 44(4): 43–50.

Moffett, J. 1968. *Teaching the universe of discourse.* Portsmouth: Boynton/Cook.

Nabors, M.L. Edwards, L.C. Murray, R. & Kent. 2009. Making the Case for Field Trips: What Research Tells Us and What Siie Coordinator Have to Say Education 129(4): 661–667 Sum.

Nabors, M.L., Edwards, L.C. & Murray, R.K. 2009. Making the case for field trips:What research tells us and what site coordinators have to say. *Education* 129(4): 661–667.

O J. Dibu-ojerinde, O.O.and Ajibade, Y.A. *Curriculum and the teaching process.* Ghana, Dama Educa-tional Services Ltd.

Obadiora A.J. 2016. Comparative Effectiveness of Virtual Field Trip and Real Field Trip on Students' Academic Perfomance in Social Studies in Osun State Secondary Schools: *Mediterranean Journal of Social Sciences MCSER* Publishing, Rome-Italy 7(1 January 2016)

Oloyede, E.O., Ajibade, Y.A. & Bamidele, E.F. 2006. *Choice and effective use of teaching methods.* In Ehindero,

Orion, N. & Hofstein, A. 1994. Factors that influence learning during a scientific field trip in a natu-ralenvironment. *Journal of Research in Science Teaching* 31: 1097–1119.

Pace, S. & Tesi, R. 2004. Adult's perception of field trips taken within grades K-12: Eight case studies in the New York metropolitan area. *Education* 125(1): 30–40.

Pace, S. & Tesi, R. 2004. Adult's perception of field trips taken within grades K-12: Eight case studies in the New York metropolitan area. *Education* 125(1): 30–40.

Patrick, O.A. 2010. "Effects of Field Studies on Learning Outcome in Biology", *J Hum Ecol* 31 (3): 171–177.

Price, S. & Hein, G.E. 1991. More than a field trip: Science programmes for elementary school groups at museums. *In-ternational Journal of Science Education* 13(5): 505–519

Shakil, A.F., Faizi, W.N. & Hafeez 2012. The need and importance of field trips at high level in Kirachi, Pakistan. *International Journal of Academic Research in Business and Social Sciences* 2(1).

Stainfield, J., Fisher, P., *Ford,* B. & Solem, M. 2000. *International virtual field trips: A new direc-tion? Journal of Geography in Higher Education* 24(2): 255–262.

Storksdieck, M. 2001. Differences in teachers' and students' museum field-trip experiences. *Visitor Studies Today* 4(1): 8–12.

Tal, T. & Steiner, L. 2006. Patterns of teacher–museum staff relationships: School visits to theeducational center of a sci-ence museum. *Canadian Journal of Science, Mathematics and Technology Education* 6: 25–46.

Wendling, R.C. & Wuensch, K.L. 1985. A fifth-grade out-door education program: expectations and effects. *Journal of Interpretation* 10(1): 11–20.

ELT in Asia in the Digital Era: Global Citizenship and Identity – Madya et al. (Eds)
© *2018 Taylor & Francis Group, London, ISBN 978-0-8153-7900-3*

Inquiring language awareness of TEFL master students in advanced grammar course

M.D.A. Rizqan
Sebelas Maret University, Solo, Central Java, Indonesia

ABSTRACT: The knowledge-based Era demands scholars to be experts in their fields. Language Awareness (LA) is L2 explicit knowledge about language. Its presence as one of the expertise qualifications for foreign language learners is inevitable. This study aims to describe the extent of LA within the qualitative case study approach. Eight TEFL master students were chosen as the subjects. The researcher collected the data from exams and interviews. The general findings showed that the students have 'adequate' LA. In a closer look, their analyzed knowledge was better than metalinguistic knowledge; it was a relatively normal condition since analyzed knowledge requires simpler cognitive process rather than metalinguistic knowledge. Additionally, it seemed that the multiple choices in the exams enlighten the cognitive process within analyzed knowledge. However, their metalinguistic knowledge had a problem with grammatical terminologies. In sum, both knowledge are vital but metalinguistic knowledge deserves more priority to be improved.

1 INTRODUCTION

Language Awareness (LA) is *explicit* knowledge about language (ALA 2016); explicit means that the users of LA are consciously aware of their knowledge. Bolitho, et al. (2003) define it as a mental attribute which develops through language in use to gradually gain insights how language works. Meanwhile, Carter (2003) sees it as the development of consciousness of and sensitivity to the forms and functions of language which also stresses the cognitive advantages of reflecting upon language. In short, LA is a form of knowledge within learners' consciousness.

Explicit knowledge, in its complete definition, is "Declarative and often anomalous knowledge of the phonological, lexical, grammatical, pragmatic, and socio-critical features of an L2 with the metalanguage for labeling this knowledge (Ellis 2004)". Although it covers many areas, most studies select grammar as the most iconic area which represents explicit knowledge. Ellis (2004, 2005, 2006) believes that explicit knowledge is comprised of two independent knowledge. First, analyzed knowledge is knowledge of structures that can be verbalized on demand. Second, metalinguistic knowledge is knowledge of the metalanguage for labeling the structures; metalanguage is *language* (words or phrases) that is used to explain about language such as grammatical terms (Berry 2010).

The similarities between LA and explicit knowledge in cognitive, consciousness, and form/function of language areas imply that these terms can be used interchangeably.

Some recent studies within the grammar area of LA show interesting reports. Based on the test of language awareness, Tsang (2011) found that 20 Chinese English teachers achieved a higher score in the recognition and the production tasks than in the correction and the explanation tasks. It seemed that they had a partial understanding of metalanguage and little knowledge of the sub-categories of the grammatical forms. However, there was no significant difference for less experienced (6 years) and more experienced (> 6 years) teachers. Meanwhile, Mirzaei et al. (2011) proved that the students' explicit knowledge in two different types of tests showed similar results. There was a strong relationship based on their scores in the Untimed

Grammaticality Judgment Test/ UGJT (a type of short answers test) and TOEFL (a type of multiple choices test). Particularly, the students' explicit knowledge strongly correlated to their general L2 proficiency. On the contrary, their implicit knowledge did not correlate to their L2 proficiency. Then, Gutierrez (2016) tried to find out a clearer relationship between analyzed knowledge, metalinguistic knowledge, and second language proficiency from 51 Spanish students. The results showed that the students demonstrated a rather low level of analyzed knowledge than metalinguistic knowledge. Although both knowledge were important components of L2 proficiency, analyzed knowledge played a major role related to target grammatical accuracy. Moreover, this knowledge was a better predictor of L2 proficiency than metalinguistic knowledge. These previous studies concluded that explicit knowledge, either analyzed or metalinguistic knowledge, was the best predictor of general proficiency in the EFL contexts.

Advanced Grammar Course is one of the major lectures which conducted by TEFL Master Program of Semar University during 6 months. According to the lecturer, its purpose is the students are not only learning how to know the (in)correct form of sentences but also to understand the reasons or the explanations behind it; it means that this course prioritizes metalinguistic knowledge rather than analyzed knowledge.

This present study focuses on describing the extent of students' LA in Advanced Grammar Course based on two different types of tests.

2 RESEARCH METHOD

The researcher used the qualitative case study which was supported with the data from the results of each exam and the interviews. 8 students of Advanced Grammar Course were taken randomly as the subjects. All students' names were pseudonyms.

As the assessment, this course employs two exams. First, the mid-term exam is a type of short-answer test which is adapted based on TOEFL Book II; the guidance book which was used as the primary sources in Advanced Grammar Course. This exam consists of 2 Sections. Section 1 is the identification and correction tasks which contain 15 (un)grammatical sentences. The students are instructed to identify ungrammatical sentences and give the correct form. Meanwhile, Section 2 is the explanation task which contains 10 ungrammatical sentences. In this Section, the students are instructed to explain the reasons why those sentences are ungrammatical. Second, the final term exam is a type of multiple choices test which is adopted based on TOEFL Model Examinations (structure and written expression). This exam consists of 2 Sections. Section 1 was the completion task which contained 15 incomplete sentences. Section 2 is the identification task which consisted of 25 ungrammatical sentences. In this Section, surprisingly, the lecturer gives an additional instruction to explain what the error for each sentence is.

The interval period between the mid- and the final-term exam was 2 months. Both exams are marked by the lecturer himself. The lecturer gives 1 point for the correct answer and ½ for the partially correct answer.

Table 1. The score conversion.

Score	Letter	Level
> 90	A	very good
80–89	A–	
75–79	B+	good
70–74	B	
67–69	B–	
64–66	C+	adequate
60–63	C	
50–59	D	poor
< 50	E	very poor

To analyze the data, the researcher calculated the mean score for each exam and its section then converted it into a letter.

For the short answers, the researcher compared the similarities between the lecturer's answers and the students' answers. The interpretation of the interviews was used to explain the reasons related to the exams' results.

3 FINDINGS AND DISCUSSIONS

Based on mean scores from both exams, the students had 'adequate' LA. Table 2 showed that the students achieved better in the final exam rather than the mid exam. Even though there was a slight improvement of their LA, however, the lecturer said that these results were less ideal (B or higher). The factor which affected these results was the type of the exams; the short answer and the multiple choices.

The multiple choice test (i.e. the final exam) was easier than the short answer test (i.e. the mid exam). All students agreed that the multiple choice test was easier to be done than another test according to the interviews. The multiple choice test required less cognitive process than the short answer test because any multiple choice tests had been provided by its possible answers. The provided or possible answers were narrowing others possible answers which are thought by the students; it also meant that the provided answers reduced the probability of error. Additionally, the majority of the students were more familiar with the multiple choice test rather than short answer test in any grammar exams in their undergraduate degree. "I'm not used to doing TOEFL exam with reasons, because beforehand ... nor the real TOEFL did not ask for reasons" (Farel/ Interview04/ February 2017). "In my experiences, doing grammar or structure exams, we choose the right or the wrong answer, or making sentences based on the patterns, without explaining why it is wrong ... So, it is something new for me" (Atep/ Interview03/ January 2017). The familiarity towards the type of the test made them more comfortable than unfamiliar ones because they felt a bit nervous. In sum, the type and the familiarity towards the exam became the influential factors of these results.

3.1 Analyzed knowledge

The students' analyzed knowledge was categorized as 'good'. Table 3 showed that the students performed better in Section 1 of the final exam than the mid exam.

Analyzed knowledge was used differently in the mid and final exam. On the one hand, analyzed knowledge which used to complete the mid exam required more complex processes than the final exam. In the mid exam, analyzed knowledge was used to judge whether the sentences

Table 2. The results of the exams.

	Score (%)	Letter
Mid-exam (n = 25)	63,5	C+
Final-exam (n = 40)	67,7	B–
Mean	65,6	C+

*n = total items in the exam.

Table 3. The results of section 1.

	Score (%)	Letter
Mid-exam (n = 15)	65,7	C+
Final-exam (n = 15)	78,3	B+
Mean	72	B

*n = number of items.

are grammatically correct or not. If it was ungrammatical, analyzed knowledge should revise it with appropriate features to make it grammatically correct. For instance, on item number 5 should be done by a tiny correction-omitting the commas after 'winter' and 'unit'.

Item 5, the mid-exam, identification and correction

– In the cold winter, the wall heating unit, would not turn on
  Answer key
– In the cold winter the wall heating unit would not turn on
  Examples of the students' answers
– In the cold winter, the wall heating unit would not turn on. (Partial correct)
– The electrical *mechine, the wall heating unit, would not turn on. (Correct judgment, incorrect answer)

These answers indicated the students' analyzed knowledge was able to judge that item number 5 as the ungrammatical sentence. Unfortunately, many of them omitted only one of the commas and it made them only got half point. Meanwhile, the others failed to analyze what the ungrammatical feature is. *One of them even made the unrelated answer with incorrect spelling (mechine-machine) by replacing 'in the cold winter' with 'the electrical mechine'; it seemed they forgot the instruction of the exam. This error of unrelated answer only can be found in the short answer test because there is no choice that can be selected.

On the other hand, in the final exam, analyzed knowledge was only used to select multiple choices (parts of speech) in completing the sentences. As mentioned earlier, the multiple choices not only prevent unnecessary or unrelated answers which possibly produced by the students but also 'enlighten' the cognitive 'burden' of analyzed knowledge. The students perceived that they just needed to select the answers, not to search it. "Multiple choices [is easier than short answer] because we only need to choose it" (Rulo/ Interview04/ February 2017). It meant that they did not have to retrieve their (cognitive) memory. A multiple choices item seemed less challenging than the short answer item.

At a glance, the students' analyzed knowledge may be similar with implicit knowledge because the quick judgment in deciding the grammaticality of sentences or the appropriateness of missing features of incomplete sentences could be done in seconds. However, it had been proved that this judgment has no relationship with implicit knowledge (Mirzaei et al. 2011). Besides, studies (Ellis 2005, Han & Ellis 1998, Mirzaei et al. 2011) so far reported that the evidence of implicit knowledge only can be validated if the tests are in a type of TRUE/ FALSE test which must be done in less than 10 seconds/item. Clearly, analyzed knowledge and implicit knowledge are two different things.

3.2 *Metalinguistic knowledge*

The students' metalinguistic knowledge was categorized as 'adequate'. Below, Table 4 showed that metalinguistic knowledge in the mid and final exam achieved same results.

Different from the use of analyzed knowledge, the use of metalinguistic knowledge in the mid and final exam was quite similar. Both exams required the use of metalanguage to explain what the grammatical error in each sentence. In the mid exam, there were many students failed to achieve full point because their answers were incomplete. "Because although the answer is correct, but the rules or reasons are too long, it would be wrong, so ... there is no point in it" (Ivan/ Interview03/ January 2017). For instance, on the item number 8, the full correct answer used grammatical terms such as inverted, subject, and verb. Meanwhile, the partial correct answer replaced subject and verb with I and believed. Indeed, 'I' and subject were interchangeable but it seemed that the use of grammatical terms was preferable in the lecturer's judgment.

Item 8, the mid-exam, explanation

– Never in the world I believed that this would be happened
  Answer key

– Problem with inverted subject verb after negative

Table 4. The results of section 2.

	Score (%)	Letter
Mid-exam (n = 10)	60	C
Final-exam (n = 25)	60	C
Mean	60	C

*n = number of items.

Examples of the students' answers

– Inverted subject and verb after negative is incorrect. (Full correct)
– There is no inversion of "I" and "believed". (Partial correct)

From the interviews, some students said that *the problem with inversion* was relatively new for them. It was not one of the topics that included in their Advanced Grammar Course when they were undergraduate students. Also, half of them even felt less confidence/ uncertain to state that rule as their judgment for explaining the ungrammatical sentences.

The final exam gave some advantages which did not provide by the mid exam. (1) Since the final exam was the multiple choices test, the ungrammatical features could be selected from the choices. This advantage raised the possibility of correct answers (fully correct/1 points) and the score. For instance, the students selected the correct choices but they produced incorrect grammatical rules to explain the errors then it would be considered as partially correct (½ points). (2) Metalanguage which were used in the final exam were simpler/shorter (e.g. comparative rather than comparative degree) than in the mid exam. This made the students' and the lecturer's answers were quite similar. Unfortunately, according to the students' interviews, some grammatical rules such as multiple number and subjunctive have not been taught in their course. "So when the grammar final exam turns out, there is a material that is not loaded in our guidebook as for example it is subjunctive ... that's where I make a lot of mistakes" (Atep/ Interview03/ January 2017). "As in the guidebook we studied, there is no subjunctive, but in the exam, there is subjunctive" (Ivan/ Interview04/ February 2017). "But at that time, there is no subject matter about subjunctive" (Uzy/ Interview06/ February 2017). None of the students gave accurate rules to answer item number 28 and 33 (see Table 5).

Providing the same grammatical rules such the lecturer's expectation was very difficult and the researcher believed that it was not the purpose of examining metalinguistic knowledge. "I don't understand what kinds of answers that wanted by him [the lecturer]. The answer is short but ... [specific]" (Rizuki/ Interview07/ February 2017). As far as the rules contained the essential feature of its complete rule (e.g. parallel in parallel structure) then it should be considered as the correct answer.

In his interview, the lecturer explained some rationales why he asked the students to produce metalanguage as the answers. First, metalanguage in form of grammatical rules could be used as the representative of the error of ungrammatical sentences. Second, it saved time to be written (Berry 2010); metalanguage can take form in word or phrase but non-metalanguage should take form in clauses or sentences. The explanation of ungrammatical sentences become less—and even un-focused if it does not involve the use of grammatical terminologies.

These entire results, on the surface, were similar with Tsang's (2011) study. The explanation task (Section II of the mid and the final exam) received lower scores than the identification task (Section 1 of the mid and the final exam). It implied that metalinguistic knowledge is a type of explicit knowledge which is difficult to be mastered by many language scholars; whether they are the TEFL master students or even the experienced English teachers. However, these results contradicted with Gutierrez's (2016) study where the students performed better in metalinguistic knowledge than analyzed knowledge. Possibly, it was caused by the different instrument which used to measure the analyzed knowledge. Furthermore, he argued that determining the grammaticality of a sentence and then identifying the error and correcting it in the ungrammatical sentences demanded a higher level of analyzed knowledge than

Table 5. Section II final-exam (Explanation).

Item	Answers key		The students' answers
17	A	Condition	Agreement of modal in conditional sentences
19	A	The form of verb	Problem with form of the verb
20	B	Parallel	Parallel structure agreement
21	A	Noun	Should be noun "capability"
22	B	Preposition	Prepositional use
24	A	Repetitive/double	Double adverb
28	A	Subjunctive	(none)
29	B	Subject/verb agreement	Agreement subject & verb
30	A	Relative pronoun	Relative pronoun
33	B	Multiple number	(none)
34	B	Adverb	Should be adverb "broadly"
36	C	Comparative	Comparative degree
38	C	To infinitive	To + infinitive

identifying and correcting error when all sentences were ungrammatical and the errors have already be identified.

These findings also implied that there were several difficulties related to the students' metalinguistic knowledge. The familiarity of the exams, the complexity of rules, and the material (i.e. *subjunctive*) of the exam were some factors which closely affected their knowledge. These factors were in line with Graus & Coppen (2015) which investigated the students' difficulty with grammar. This case was commonly known as *subjective* difficulty which defined as the ratio of the rule's difficulty inherent linguistic complexity to the students' ability to handle such rule (DeKeyser 2003). To be precise, it was the major impact of metalanguage in the grammar exams.

Indeed, this study contained some weaknesses. First, the definition of analyzed knowledge that the researcher used in this study required stronger notions from another expert. Unfortunately, so far, the researcher have not found related articles which provided this issue besides Ellis's serial works (Ellis 2004, 2005, 2006, Han & Ellis 1998). Second, the results of both exams could not be considered as the real outcome because neither reliability nor validity has not been statistically measured by the lecturer. The purpose of these exams is purely reducing subjective judgment of the lecturer in measuring the students' LA. Third, the metalanguage which were used as the answer keys of both exams were not the real grammatical rules such as mentioned in grammar books. In fact, these were the subtopics' names (e.g. be careful of appositives, invert the subject and verb after negatives, use parallel structure with comparisons, make articles agree with nouns, etc.) of *TOEFL Book II*. The researcher labeled it as grammatical rules because these were quite similar to the real ones; in some grammar books, grammatical rules are addressed by other names such as grammatical categories, syntactic categories, syntactic rules etc. The researcher hoped these weaknesses did not make any confusion for other scholars.

4   CONCLUSIONS AND SUGGESTIONS

The findings of this study describe how the students' LA is and how it works. Analyzed and metalinguistic knowledge are the essential feature for the TEFL master students, nevertheless, their metalinguistic knowledge still needs much more improvement.

The lecturer should be more focus on adapting/designing types of the short answer (not the multiple choices one) test which is able to explore and examine the students' metalinguistic knowledge. Also, the researcher believe that it would be much better if there are some suggested correct answers in any grammar exam to reduce the diversity of answers which possibly arise from the students (see Tsang 2011). Moreover, in order to reduce subjective judgment and enhance precise results, such a rating scale for multilingual comments can be adapted as an alternative to the scoring method (see Ellis 2004). The aim of test should be decided carefully before designing a test so that the students not only understand their own knowledge but also receive the benefits of the test they were taken.

REFERENCES

ALA. 2016. *Association for language awareness.* Retrieved June, 2016, from http://www.languageaware-ness.org/.

Berry, R. 2010. *Terminology in English language teaching: Nature and use* (Vol. 93). Bern: Peter Lang.

Bolitho, R., Carter, R., Hughes, R., Ivanic, R., Masuhara, H. & Tomlinson, B. 2003. Ten questions about language awareness. *ELT Journal* 57(3).

Carter, R. 2003. Language awareness. *ELT Journal* 57(1): 64–65.

DeKeyser, R. 2003. Implicit and explicit learning. In C. J. Doughty & M. H. Long (Eds.), *The handbook of second language acquisition*:313–348. Oxford: Blackwell.

Ellis, R. 2004. The definition and measurement of 12 explicit knowledge. *Language Learning* 54(2): 227–275.

Ellis, R. 2005. Measuring implicit and explicit knowledge of a second language: a psychometric study. *SSLA* 27: 141–172.

Ellis, R. 2006. Modelling learning difficulty and second language proficiency: The differential contributions of implicit and explicit knowledge. *Applied Linguistic* 27(3): 431–463.

Graus, J. & Coppen, P.A. 2015. Defining grammatical difficulty: A student teacher perpective. *Language Awareness* 24(2): 101–122.

Gutierrez, X. 2016. Analyzed knowledge, metalanguage and second language proficiency. *System* 60: 42–54.

Han, Y. & Ellis, R. 1998. Implicit knowledge, explicit knowledge and general language proficiency. *Language Teaching Research* 2(1): 1–23.

Mirzaei, A., Rahimi, M. & Shakerian, Z. 2011. Differential accessibility of implicit and explicit grammatical knowledge to EFL learners' language proficiency. *Iranian Journal of Applied Linguistics* 14(2): 111–143.

Tsang, W.L. 2011. English metalanguage awareness among primary school teacher in Hong Kong. *Journal of Language Studies* 11(1): 1–16.

Part III: Exploring and understanding today's demands for foreign languages: Going beyond English language competencies

ELT in Asia in the Digital Era: Global Citizenship and Identity – Madya et al. (Eds)
© 2018 Taylor & Francis Group, London, ISBN 978-0-8153-7900-3

Developing fluency

I.S.P. Nation
Victoria University of Wellington, Wellington, New Zealand

ABSTRACT: This paper looks at fluency development for learners of English as a foreign language. It describes the nature of fluency and a range of activities for developing fluency across the four skills, and looks at linked skills activities in detail. It describes the conditions needed for fluency development and the evidence that fluency activities work. It also suggests focuses for further research in this area.

1   WHAT IS FLUENCY?

In general, fluency means making the best use of what is already known. Fillmore (1979) described several senses of the word fluency of which one was "the ability to fill time with talk" (p.93). If we apply this sense to a wider range of skills than speaking, then fluency can be described as the ability to process language receptively and productively at a reasonable speed. In this paper, this is the definition that I want to use, noting that it is primarily a quantity-based definition rather than one that considers quality of production. Lennon (1990) investigated several measures of fluency in speaking using such a quantitative definition.

2   HOW SHOULD FLUENCY FIT INTO A LANGUAGE COURSE?

Fluency development is one of the four strands of a well-balanced language course. The strands include meaning-focused input, meaning-focused output, language-focused learning, and fluency development (Nation 2007a). Each of these four strands should get roughly equal time in a course, so one quarter of the total time in a language course should be spent on fluency activities. However, the other three strands also contribute to fluency. The language-focused learning strand may involve the deliberate learning of multiword units, which as Palmer (1925) has noted, can be the basis for early fluency in speaking – "*Memorize perfectly the largest number of common and useful word groups!*" (p. 187). The language-focused learning strand may also be where learners practice fluency in accessing individual words. The meaning-focused input and meaning-focused output strands are also likely to provide opportunities for fluency development if the burden of unknown words is not too heavy in activities in the strands. These, however, are not substitutes for the fluency strand, and it is important that there is a fluency strand in the course from the very first day of learning. Even with a very small amount of language knowledge, learners should be able to use this knowledge in fluent ways. This is most clearly seen in courses with very limited goals, such as a course on survival English. The survival vocabulary for foreign travel (Nation & Crabbe 1991) contains around 120 items which are very useful for a traveller spending a few days or weeks in another country. These include items like *Thank you very much, How much does it cost?, It's delicious, Goodbye.* It may take just a few hours to memorise these 120 items, but it is important that they are not only memorised and pronounced correctly, but that they are also practised so that they are fluently available for both reception and production under real time pressure

It is important that each of the four skills of listening, speaking, reading, and writing has its own fluency development focus. As yet, there is no research looking at the effect of fluency development in one skill, for example reading, on another skill, for example writing. It is likely that there is some transfer between skills but it is clearly most efficient to give skill-based fluency practice. In the following section we look at some of the most useful fluency development activities across the four skills.

3   WHAT ARE THE MOST USEFUL FLUENCY ACTIVITIES?

Fluency is important in the receptive skills of listening and reading as well as in the productive skills of speaking and writing. Although we tend to think of fluency as relating to speaking, people read at different speeds and write at different speeds. While learners need to read at different speeds with different kinds of material, they also need to be able to be flexible in their reading so that they can adjust their speed when they need to. Similarly, in listening, listeners have only small degrees of control over what they listen to and so need to be able to adjust to the speed of the speaker.

In line with a skills-based approach to fluency development, the following activities are divided up into the skills of listening, speaking, reading and writing.

3.1   *Listening fluency*

3.1.1   *Listening to easy stories*
The teacher reads an interesting graded reader aloud to the learners as a serial, reading a few pages each day. As the learners get used to the story the teacher gradually speeds up the reading. Lists of prize-winning graded readers can be found on the Extensive Reading Foundation website http://www.erfoundation.org/erf/.

3.1.2   *Repeated listening to CDs*
The learners listen to CDs that come with graded readers. They listen to the same story several times over several days until it is easy to listen to. One of the most exciting recent developments with the potential for improving listening fluency is the availability of digital recorders where the playback speed can be adjusted to be either slower or faster without distorting the pitch of the playback. This allows learners to listen slowly, and to increase the speed of their listening as they listen again to the same material or as their proficiency develops.

3.1.3   *Focused repeated listening*
The teacher writes the items to be learned, for example the numbers from 1 to 10, on the board and then says them quickly in a random order while a learner points to them. Then the learners do this in pairs. The activity continues for several minutes until the learners are starting to get faster at recognizing the numbers.

3.2   *Speaking fluency*

4/3/2
The learners work in pairs. Learner A talks to learner B on a very familiar topic for four minutes. At the end of four minutes the teacher stops them and tells them to change partners. Then learner A gives exactly the same talk to their new partner for three minutes. They change partners once again and learner A for the third time gives exactly the same talk to their new partner for two minutes. Then it is learner B's turn (Maurice 1983).

3.2.1   *The best recording*
The learner makes a recording of a short text. Then she listens to it and then re-records it until she is satisfied that this is her best recording of it.

3.3 Reading fluency

3.3.1 A speed reading course
The learners read very easy passages which are all the same length and record their speed on a graph. They answer multiple-choice questions and record their comprehension score on a graph. For speed reading courses in a controlled vocabulary see Nation & Malarcher (2007), Paul Nation's website (for a free 1000 word level speed reading course), and Sonia Millett's website (for free 1000, 2000, and 2000 plus Academic Word List reading courses) http://www.victoria.ac.nz/lals/staff/sonia-millett.aspx.

A speed reading course takes around 10 minutes per session. It should run for around 20 sessions which could be somewhere between seven and ten weeks. It requires no real work from the teacher. It brings about substantial increases for most learners. This small time investment brings large benefits.

3.3.2 Easy extensive reading
The learners quickly read lots of easy graded readers that are way below their level. Working with very easy material means that it can be processed at a speed that is faster than learners' normal reading. This practice increases learners' speed of access to these very common and useful words and phrases.

3.3.3 Repeated reading
Each learner reads the same short text three times in immediate succession. This activity can be done silently or reading aloud.

3.4 Writing fluency

3.4.1 10 minute writing
The learners write for exactly 10 minutes on a very familiar topic. They count the number of words they wrote and put the number on a graph. The teacher does NOT correct their work but praises them for quantity of writing and responds positively to the content of the writing. The learners do this kind of writing two or three times a week. Their goal is to write as much as they can within the ten minutes.

4   LINKED SKILLS

The learners work on the same material through three successive skills, for example (1) they read the material, (2) then they listen to it, and (3) then they write about it. There are many such combinations. The last activity in each series becomes a fluency development activity because of the previous practice in the other two skills. We look more closely at linked skills activities later in this chapter.

All these activities share common features that make them fluency development activities. In the following section we look at these common features.

5   WHAT CHARACTERIZES FLUENCY ACTIVITIES?

The fluency strand only exists if certain conditions are present.

1. The learners' focus is on receiving or conveying meaning.
2. All of what the learners are listening to, reading, speaking or writing is largely familiar to them. That is, there is no unfamiliar language, and there are largely familiar content and discourse features.
3. There is some pressure or encouragement to perform at a faster than usual speed.
4. There is a large amount of input or output.

You can decide if an activity is a fluency development activity by seeing how well it involves these four conditions. For example, the 4/3/2 activity is message focused because the speaker has to deliver the talk to a listener. The listener changes for each delivery so that the task remains message focused even though the talk is repeated. The task is easy because the speaker speaks on a very familiar topic, and repeats the talk. There is pressure to go faster because the time reduces for each delivery (from 4 minutes to 3 to 2), and there is quantity of practice because each learner speaks for a total of 9 minutes (4 + 3 + 2). The 4/3/2 activity thus meets all the conditions needed for a fluency activity. Not all fluency activities meet all of these conditions, but at the very least they should meet the easy material condition.

Easy extensive reading, for example, does not meet the pressure-to-go-faster condition, but it meets the conditions of message focus, easy material and quantity of practice, and is thus a very useful fluency development activity. Reading unsimplified text is not a fluency development activity for most learners and thus, as Hunt and Beglar (in press) have shown, is not an effective fluency development activity.

It is a useful teacher development activity to analyse potential fluency activities to see how well they meet the four conditions. This analysis has the benefits of developing awareness of the conditions, emphasizing the idea that it is the conditions that make an activity a fluency activity, and suggesting ways in which activities can be turned into fluency activities.

6   HOW CAN TEACHERS DESIGN THEIR OWN FLUENCY ACTIVITIES?

The essence to designing new fluency activities is to make sure that the conditions of a message focus, easy material, pressure to go faster and quantity of practice are designed into the activities. Of these four conditions, easy material is the most important. It is hard to become fluent when working with material that is too difficult. There are many ways of making sure that the material the learners will use is easy for them. For example, learners can practice fluent writing by:

1. Writing about what they have read (in English or the first language)
2. Writing about what they have written before
3. Writing on a series of closely related topics
4. Writing about what they already know a lot about
5. Writing about what they have just experience
6. Writing where the language has been pre-taught
7. Writing about what they have just discussed.

Note that all of the above writing tasks are easy because the learners bring a lot of previous knowledge to them, either through past experience, or pre-teaching.

We have looked at linked skills activities briefly above. Let us now look at them again in more detail because they provide a very effective and flexible way of creating fluency development activities.

7   LINKED SKILLS ACTIVITIES

Linked skills activities have many benefits, and these benefits are typical of those where a single topic or subject is focused on for a considerable period of time, as in content-based learning. One of the major benefits for a teacher is that they generally require very little work to prepare and organize, but they get a lot of work from the students. They can also provide very useful conditions for language and content learning. Let us look first at how linked skills activities can be made, and how to judge whether a linked skills activity has been well made or not.

7.1   *Designing linked skills activities*

Let us take a typical piece of material which may be used when making linked skills activities—a reading passage with accompanying questions. The example I have used in class when training teachers is from the series *Timed Readings* (Spargo 1989). The particular text is on food handling safety in order to avoid food poisoning.

The activities are described in Table 1 which should be read horizontally. It contains five sets of linked skills activities. Each row is one linked skills series of three activities. The item on the left is the first activity in the series, which is then followed by the one in the middle, and then by the one on the right. Theoretically, there are twenty-four possible linked skills sequences (four choices from listening, speaking, reading and writing for the first activity, a choice from three for the second activity, and a choice for two for the third activity) if no skills are repeated in the series. Note however that there can also be a lot of variety in the nature of actual activity. That is there are many kinds of speaking activities for example, so twenty-four is clearly an underestimate.

So, in the first linked skills series, learners read the questions by themselves and try to choose the correct multiple-choice answers. Then they hear the text being read to them by the teacher while they look at the questions and their answers, correcting them when necessary. In the third step, they talk to a partner about their guesses and the correct answers and report orally to the whole class on the most difficult questions. The last activity in the series is a fluency activity because the previous work has made this final activity easy.

Note in the fifth linked skills series that the sequence is Speak-Read-Speak. In the last step the learners work in pairs, one learner delivering talk 1 about food storage and the other student giving talk 2 about dangers. Linked skills activities need not use three different skills but can repeat a skill aiming for a higher performance in the second use of the same skill.

Note that it is possible to mix and match some of the individual activities in Table 1 to make a new series.

How can we judge which series of activities is likely to be the most effective? We will look at this from the perspective of vocabulary learning, and also from the perspective of the relative difficulty of the activities in the series.

1. Ideally, all three activities in the series should draw very strongly on the same piece of content material. This will ensure that the activities become easier as learners proceed through the series and that the same vocabulary and grammatical structures are repeated during the series.
2. Essentially, the three activities should make use of the same language items, particularly vocabulary and multiword units. The recurrence of the vocabulary will help learning through the opportunity for repeated retrieval and hopefully creative use of the vocabulary.

Table 1. Five sets of linked skills activities.

First activity	Second activity	Third activity
1 Read the questions without seeing the text and try to guess the answers (Read)	Listen to the text and check and correct your answers (Listen)	Talk about the differences between your guesses and the right answers (Speak)
2 Read the text (Read)	Listen to the questions and write answers to them (Listen/Write)	Write guidelines for storing food safely (Write)
3 Write guidelines for storing food safely using your own experience and background knowledge (Write)	Talk about your guidelines with another student (Speak)	Read the text and answer the questions (Read)
4 Listen to the text being read to you by the teacher taking notes if you wish (Listen)	Write what you can remember about the text (Write)	Do a 4/3/2 activity on the content of the passage (Speak)
5 Talk to a partner about what you know about good food storage procedures (Speak)	Read the text and answer the questions (Read)	Either prepare and deliver a talk to your partner about (1) good food storage procedures OR (2) the danger of not handling food carefully (Speak)

3. Typically, the last activity in a series of three is highly likely to be a fluency development activity, because at this point the material that learners are working with is very easy because they have now worked with it at least two times. That is, they should be well in control of the content of the material and of the language used to express this content. The challenge to them is to use this now familiar content and language through a skill (listening, speaking, reading, or writing) which has previously been unpractised with this material. If the teacher does have a fluency goal for this final activity in the series of three, or wants the activity to be done particularly well, the teacher should look at the final activity to see if it is a receptive skill (listening or reading) or a productive skill (speak ing or writing). If it is a productive skill, then it is probably important that one of the two preceding activities in the series also involves productive use of the language. So if the final activity is a writing activity, it may be useful to make sure that one of the two preceding activities is a speaking activity, or vice versa. This is because productive skills (speaking and writing) are usually much more challenging than receptive skills, particularly from a vocabulary perspective. Having practised the material with a productive skill once makes it much easier to use it again productively in the next or later activity in the series. Thus, in Table 1 above, the fifth linked skills series beginning with speaking is likely to be very effective in preparing for the final activity in the series. Similarly series 4, where the productive skill of writing is followed by the productive skill of speaking, is likely to enable better performance of the speaking activeity than if both of the preceding activities had been receptive activities.

7.2   *Monitoring linked skills activities*

The following things are worth looking for when linked skills activities are being used. They relate closely to the three design features just described above.

1. Are the learners coping well with the activities, especially in the last two steps of the series?
2. Do the same language items keep recurring in each of the three activities?
3. Are the learners retrieving the target vocabulary in activities 2 and 3 in the series rather than repeating them from the input sheet?
4. Do activities 2 and 3 involve generative use of the vocabulary from activity 1?
5. Are the learners handling the content of the activety more confidently in the later steps?

The activities which are the last two steps in linked skill series are highly likely to be experience tasks (Nation 1990, 2007b). That is, they are activities where learners bring a lot of background knowledge to the activity. The early steps of the series of linked skills activities can create and strengthen this knowledge. Because of this, typically the last activities in a linked skill series are likely to have many of the features of a fluency development task. That is, the task is very easy to do and learners can do it at a faster than usual speed. For this reason, it is important that it is not just used as a throwaway activity (for example, for homework write ...), but is given the time and attention that it deserves.

7.3   *Procedures*

In many ways procedures share many of the possible helpful learning conditions found in linked skills activities. A procedure is a way of breaking down an activity into steps, partly to make sure that the learners do not shorten the activity but not doing all that is required and partly to improve conditions for language learning during the activity (Nation 1989). Here are some common procedures:

1. The pyramid procedure (Jordan 1990), where learners do a task such as a ranking activity, individually, then do it again in pairs, then in a group.
2. The expert-groups/family-groups procedure (Nation & Newton 2009, pp. 70–71), where learners split up into groups with each group preparing for a different part of a subsequent

task. They then reform their groups so that one person from each of the specialist groups is in each reformed group. They then combine their specialist knowledge to do the whole task.

3. Reporting back. After learners complete a problem-solving or ranking task, they report back to the class on the solution they reached.

4. Do and be tested. After doing a task, learners form different groups test learners from the other groups on the task.

Many common classroom activities such as ranking activities, reading, presenting a talk, or listening to a talk can be adapted to have a fluency goal. For example, a ranking exercise can be done as a pyramid activity starting with individual ranking, then ranking in pairs, groups of four, and then the whole class.

All true fluency tasks are experience tasks (Nation 2007b). That is, they are tasks where the learner brings a lot of previous knowledge to the task and the only major aspect of knowledge outside the learner's knowledge is fluency. This means that the language features (vocabulary, collocations, grammar, discourse) and the ideas involved in the activity are all largely within the learner's previous experience.

There are two major paths to fluency—through repetition (the well-beaten path) and through meeting the same items in a variety of contexts (the rich and varied map). Activities like 4/3/2 and repeated reading are repetition type activities. The learners deal with the same material several times. Activities like reading graded readers, speed reading courses, and listening to easy stories are rich and varied map activities. The learners meet the same language items in a variety of different contexts.

8   HOW CAN WE INCREASE THE EFFECTIVENESS OF FLUENCY DEVELOPMENT ACTIVITIES?

Most fluency development activities are effective, but their effectiveness can be enhanced in several ways. Firstly, learners should understand why there is a fluency development strand to a course and they should understand the nature of the strand, namely that it involves working with easy material to reach a higher level of performance. When they do a fluency activity they should be aware that it is a fluency activity and should appreciate its purpose.

Secondly, learners should have opportunities to reflect on the value of fluency development activities. Through discussion and reflection they should consider the value of being able to process and produce language at a reasonably fluent speed. This of course is particularly important where learners have to sit timed tests and examinations, but fluency also has more widely applicable advantages, such as when having to read to use language under normal time constraints in daily language use.

Thirdly, the teacher should make sure that wherever possible, fluency development activities involve clear markers of progress. With speed reading for example, the graph tracking reading speed and the graph tracking comprehension level are very clear indicators of progress. 4/3/2 activities do not involve such an obvious marker of progress, but with some thought a teacher may be able to include occasional measures which will allow learners to see that their spoken fluency is progressing through the use of such activities.

Fourthly, we can monitor and counsel learners who are not making progress in a range of fluency development activities. There is evidence from an unpublished study of a speed reading course that learners who were not initially making progress in the course all made progress as a result of one-to-one counselling with the teacher running the course. Speaking to learners individually may increase their commitment to the learning program.

Fifthly, the teacher should make sure that fluency development activities are done regularly and that commitment to the program does not tail off towards the end of the program.

Fluency development is a very important strand of a course, and thus it is important to make sure that it is properly done.

9   WHAT EVIDENCE IS THERE THAT FLUENCY DEVELOPMENT ACTIVITIES WORK?

Fluency development in the learning of English as a second or foreign language is a largely unresearched area with regard to the effectiveness of classroom-based activities (Rossiter et al. 2010). This is particularly striking when we compare the amount of research done on fluency with the amount of research done on the other three strands of meaning-focused input, meaning-focused output, and language-focused learning. Within the area of fluency, most research has been done on speed reading courses, although quite a lot of corpus-based investigation has been done on spoken English (Kirk & Carter 2010).

Many of the studies of speed reading have not involved a control group, although some of the earlier studies involved a comparison of first language and second language increases, presumably as a result of transfer of training (Bismoko & Nation 1974, Cramer 1975, West 1941). In general, research has found reliable increases of a substantial nature in speed reading courses. Hunt and Beglar (in press) have shown reading speed increases from extensive reading, especially extensive reading using simplified texts.

Research on the 4/3/2 activity (Arevart & Nation 1991, Nation 1989) has shown an increase in speed during the activity, but there is no research evidence to show that it affects speaking outside the activity.

10   WHAT RESEARCH NEEDS TO BE DONE ON FLUENCY DEVELOPMENT?

There is clear evidence from research on speed reading courses and the 4/3/2 speaking activity that fluency improves during the activity. Research is needed however to show that these increases in fluency transfer outside of the activity itself. Even within the activities however there is evidence of transfer of fluency from one part of the activity to the other. For example, in speed reading courses we typically see a gradual increase in speed from one passage to the other, showing that increases made in the previous passages transferred to the next passage read. A student project as part of an MA course (Wright, 2010) showed that when the learner did the 4/3/2 activity on a different passage each day, the speed on the first delivery of the day was greater than the speed on the first delivery of a different passage of the preceding day. That is, fluency gains from previous uses of the activity on different texts transferred to the following texts. More convincing evidence however would be of transfer to different kinds of activities, such as transfer from a speed reading course using hard copy materials to a reading text of a different nature read on a computer, or to reading for pleasure.

A problem in interpreting these kinds of studies is what is bringing about the increase in fluency. Clearly, there will be an element of task familiarity. For example, in a speed reading course the learners need to get used to the activity which involves reading a text, recording the time, answering the questions, and entering the scores on a graph. This is why, in the Chung & Nation (2006) study, when measuring fluency increases in the speed reading course, it seemed best to take the average of the speed of reading the first three passages and compare this with the average of the last three passages. However, the effect of task familiarity should disappear quite early into a sustained fluency development course.

It is interesting to speculate about what changes in the brain when fluency develops (Schmidt 1992, Segalowitz 2010). One possible change is at the level of vocabulary. As a result of doing fluency activities, the fluency of access to individual words could be increased. This certainly happens, but we know that the majority of different word forms in a typical speed reading course occur only once or twice. It is likely that only the most frequent words get enough practice in such a course to increase fluency of access to them as a result of repeated meetings with those words. It could be that the increase in fluency of these most frequent words is enough to bring about the speed increases that we see resulting from a speed reading course.

It may be that at least the initial effects of fluency development are at a lower level than this, in that a speed reading course for example at first develops fluency in recognising individual letters and combinations of letters. As learners become more advanced in their knowledge of the language, then fluency development courses could be developing not only fluency of access to word forms but also to multiword units. It is likely that fluency develops in two related ways; (1) by increasing speed and automaticity, and (2) by increasing the size of the language unit being worked with.

We know from research on the 4/3/2 speaking activity that fluency development not only results in changes in speed but also results in changes in accuracy and complexity. It would be useful to see if a comparable range of changes accompany fluency increases in writing. For example, do learners doing the ten minute writing activity produce better writing at the end of the course in terms of amount written, quality of organization of the writing, number of grammatical errors, number of more complex sentences, sentence length, number of more complex noun groups, average length of noun groups, lexical richness, and quality of information content. In such a study it would be essential to have a control group that did not do the 10 minute writing activity but did writing tasks without a fluency focus.

It could be more challenging but equally rewarding to measure other changes that accompany increases in listening and speaking fluency. Such measures could include memory span, comprehension (see Chang 2010), and skill in comprehending more complex sentences.

Research in second and foreign language fluency development is still in its infancy, but it promises to be a very rewarding area of research which is likely to support the idea that a substantial part of any well-balanced course is a fluency development component in each of the four skills of listening, speaking, reading, writing.

REFERENCES

Arevart, S. & Nation, P. 1991. Fluency improvement in a second language. *RELC Journal* 22(1): 84–94.

Bismoko, J. & Nation, I. S. P. 1974. English reading speed and the mother-tongue or national language. *RELC Journal* 5(1): 86–89.

Chang, A. C-S. 2010. The effect of a timed reading activity on EFL learners: Speed, comprehension, and perceptions. *Reading in a Foreign Language* 22(2): 284–303.

Chung, M. & Nation, I. S. P. 2006. The effect of a speed reading course. *English Teaching*, 61(4): 181–204.

Cramer, S. 1975. Increasing reading speed in English or in the national language. *RELC Journal* 6(2): 19–23.

Fillmore, C. J. 1979. On fluency. In C. J. Fillmore, D. Kempler, and W. S-J. Wang (eds.) *Individual Differences in Language Ability and Language Behavior*: 85–101. New York: Academic Press.

Hunt, A. & Beglar, D. In press. The effect of pleasure reading on Japanese university EFL learners' reading rates. *Language Learning*.

Kirk, S. & Carter, R. 2010. Fluency and spoken English. In M. Moreno Jaen, F. Serrano Valverde, and M. Calzada Perez (eds.) *Exploring new Paths in Language Pedagogy: Lexis and Corpus-Based Language Teaching*: 25–28. London: Equinox.

Jordan, R. R. 1990. Pyramid discussions. *ELT Journal* 44(1): 46–54.

Lennon, P. 1990. Investigating fluency in EFL: a quantitative approach. *Language Learning* 40(3): 387–417.

Maurice, K. 1983. The fluency workshop. *TESOL Newsletter* 17(4): 29.

Nation, I. S. P. 1989. Improving speaking fluency. *System* 17(3): 377–384.

Nation, I. S. P. 1990. A system of tasks for language learning. In S. Anivan (ed.) *Language Teaching Methodology for the Nineties*. RELC Anthology Series 24: 51–63.

Nation, I. S. P. 2007a. The four strands. *Innovation in Language Learning and Teaching* 1(1): 1–12.

Nation, I. S. P. 2007b. Vocabulary learning through experience tasks. *Language Forum* 33(2): 33–43.

Nation, I. S. P. 2009. *Teaching ESL/EFL Reading and Writing*. New York: Routledge.

Nation, P. & Crabbe, D. 1991. A survival language learning syllabus for foreign travel. *System* 19(3): 191–201.

Nation, P. & Malarcher, C. (2007). *Reading for Speed and Fluency, Books 1, 2, 3 & 4* Seoul: Compass Publishing.

Nation, I. S. P. & Newton, J. 2009. *Teaching ESL/EFL Speaking and Reading*. New York: Routledge.

Palmer, H. 1925. Conversation. In R.C. Smith (ed.) (1999). *The Writings of Harold E. Palmer: An Overview*: 185–191. Tokyo: Hon-no-Tomosha.

Rossiter, M. J., Derwing, T. M., Manimtim, L. G. & Thomson, R. I. 2010. Oral fluency: the neglected component in the communicative language classroom. *Canadian Modern Language Review* 66(4): 583–606.

Schmidt, R. W. 1992. Psychological mechanisms underlying second language fluency. *Studies in Second Language Acquisition* 14: 357–385.

Segalowitz, N. 2010. *The Cognitive Bases of Second Language Fluency.* New York: Routledge.

Spargo, E. 1989. *Timed Readings: Fifty 400-Word Passages with Questions for Building Reading Speed* (3rd ed.). Illinois: Jamestown Publishers.

West, M. 1941. *Learning to Read a Foreign Language.* London: Longmans.

Wright, A. 2010. Unpublished MEd course assignment on fluency development. Temple University Japan.

Paul Nation's website: http://www.victoria.ac.nz/lals/staff/paul-nation.aspx (*Vocabulary Resource Booklet*, publications, speed reading course, Vocabulary Size Test) Sonia Millett's website: http://www.victoria.ac.nz/lals/staff/sonia-millett.aspx (Free 1000, 2000, and 2000 plus Academic Word List reading courses).

The Extensive Reading Foundation: http://www.erfoundation.org/erf/.

Foregrounding global citizenship in EFL using UNESCO's category of core values

Masulah
Universitas Muhammadiyah Surabaya, Jawa Timur, Indonesia

ABSTRACT: With the changes of English curriculum across the world, one thing remains: that teaching English deals with more than just language competencies. Teachers can teach English while at the same time addressing essential values. Scholarly discussion on the nature of literary text and literary teaching emphasizes that adressing value in teaching is feasible and demandable within the EFL classroom. However, inspite of the realization about the importance of addressing value aspects in literature teaching, studies on this subject have been insufficient. This paper discusses how values related to the issue of global citizenship can be addressed in English classrooms, especially in literature classes. It uses UNESCO's core values category focusing on *National Unity and Global Solidarity* and its related values: love of country, democracy, active and responsible citizenship, interdependence, international understanding, global peace, and unity and diversity.

1   INTRODUCTION

Teaching any subject is values-laden and teachers are inevitably responsible for bringing up values in their teaching. The function of Indonesian National Education is to develop students' potentials in order to become a faithful and devoted man to the One God, noble, healthy, well knowledged, skillful, creative, independent, and become democratic and responsible citizens (DIKNAS 2003). Education is defined with emphasis on a deeper goal than just superficial achievement. This goal of National education is in line with the views of Ki Hajar Dewantara, the most celebrated pioneer of Indonesian education. During the Dutch occupation in Indonesia, he made all efforts to provide equal education for natives Indonesians. He argues that education should be based on the values of common humanity and human freedom. He views that education is cultural efforts intended to give guidance for the growth of students' physical and spiritual progress towards civilized humanity achievement within their personal nature and the influence of environment (Ki Hajar Dewantara 2011). UNESCO's concept of holistic education shares the same view, that education must contribute to the total development of the whole person and should focus on the full development of human person's capabilities, "physical, intellectual, aesthetic, ethical, economic, socio-cultural, political, and spiritual as they interact one another in the family, community, nation, region, and the world" (UNESCO 2002).

The increasing concern for the value aspects in literature teaching necessitates literature teachers to begin reflecting that the essential goal of literature teaching is helping students develop their full potential in order to become successful members of a global society. With such a goal, literature teaching should not be done simply for the sake of academic and occupational needs. Rather, it gives space for the exploration of human core values through "various problems of the world and "man's unconquerable mind with its humanizing influence and the revelation of the significance of everyday life" revealed in literary works (Cox 2002).

It is within this context that this paper discusses Global citizenship values that can be addressed overtly or covertly in literature teaching.

2   THEORIES OF VALUES

Literature of values provides explanations on how values may be understood and categorized. Value is something good, thought to be good, and has good connotation, loved and desired representing moral judgments upon which one bases his actions. Value is one element of culture, together acquired through learning and influenced by society (Benninga 1991, Bertens 2000, Graeber 2001, McLaughlin 1965). The notion that values engage moral considerations is important for the present study. The broad characterization of values as "anything desired or desirable" will imply the importance of "values in education". Furthermore, values are identified as the deepest layer of culture and thus are relatively stable in time. They can only be observed indirectly through rituals, heroes and symbols as the outer layers of culture. Furthermore, values are culturally determined and more or less stable within a person's life (Inglehart 2008, Hofstede 2008, Rokeach 1973). However, Rokeach (1973) believes that values can be dogmatically taught in deliberate fashion whereas Hofstede (2008) and Inglehart (2008) emphasize more on cultural values and see values as a part of an environment.

Values are categorized variably by theorists. Rockeach believes that values are distinguished into 2 types, namely instrumental and end-values. Examples of the first are true friendship, mature love, self-respect, equality, freedom, pleasure or social recognition and examples of the second are ambition, cleanliness, self-control, honesty, imagination or obedience. (Rokeach 1973). Another category of values are based on cultural dimensions like, "Power distance, individualism and collectivism, Femininity versus masculinity, Uncertainty avoidance, and long-term versus short-term orientation" (Hofstede 2008) or traditionalism versus secularism, rationalism and self-expression versus survivalist (Inglehart 2008). They deal with such pairs as "evil versus good, dirty versus clean, dangerous versus safe, forbidden versus permitted, decent versus indecent, moral versus immoral, ugly versus beautiful, unnatural versus natural, abnormal versus normal, paradoxical versus logical, irrational versus rational."

UNESCO believes that education should foster the full development of human's capacities residing in values category called eight core values: "Health and Harmony with Nature, Truth and Wisdom, Love and Compassion, Creativity and Appreciation for Beauty, Peace and Justice, Sustainable Human Development, National Unity and Global Solidarity, and Global Spirituality". The National Unity and Global Solidarity values correspond to the values of "Love of Country, Democracy, Active & Responsible Citizenship, Interdependence, International Understanding, Global Peace, and Unity in diversity" (UNESCO 2002).

3   VALUES EDUCATION

The concepts of education as stated by UU Sisdiknas No. 22, 2003, Ki Hajar Dewantara and UNESCO emphasize the aspect of value in the curriculum formation in all educational levels, including higher education. One of the key components within the ecosystem of higher education is teachers, or lecturers. As educators, lecturers are expected to ensure that value education takes place in their instruction, whether they decide to state values explicitly and formally in their teaching and teaching practice or train it implicitly within the hidden curriculum of the school (Narvaez & Lapsley in Cubukcu 2014). Halstead (2000) suggests that there should be conscious efforts to bring up value issues in the classroom in order that students develop values (Halstead 1996). Whereas Straughan (1998) argues that values are implicitly present. Experienced teachers who are aware of the school's role in the formation of the students' values tend to teach values more consciously, while the less experienced ones will approach value teaching more implicitly by relying on transmission and the hidden curriculum. Either way, the general principle is that value-related issues should become a concern and be dealt with in the curriculum (Al-Hooli 2009).

Coming to terms with the primary goal of education as conceptualized by National Education System, Ki Hajar Dewantara and UNESCO, teaching literature in higher education is supposed to take into account the value aspect. In fact, it is a subject which requires serious consideration (Beach 2011), that the construct of literature as a value-oriented subject. So far, a large number of scholarly discussions have suggested that literature teaching has been directed towards value-related goals through an approach known as "cultural understanding," "personal involvement, "or "content knowledge" (Barrette et al. 2010, Plastina 2000). The ways literature can be treated as value education and give space for value exploration have also been discussed through the "Personal Growth Approach" and "dialogic model" (Lazar 1993, Carter & Long 1991). Basically, literature teaching has been established as a field loaded with cultural values and all students should be taught about it. (Cox 2011).

The point of scholarly discussion about literature teaching is that it is inherently value bound. However, little attention has been given to the value aspects in the teaching and learning of literature in ESL classrooms (Basthomi 2003). Goodwyn (2012) warns that, treated improperly, the literature teaching curriculum has covered a much deeper issue and the essential goal of literary teaching has been drastically diminished.

Scholars discuss values education in different perspectives. For example, Halstead (1996) and Morrison (2000) argue that values should be explicitly taught and stated in the curriculum, whereas Straughan (1998) suggests that values are implicitly present within the hidden curriculum of the institution. However, all believe that education always brings about values in its practice. In this context, lecturers are faced with the choice between practicing values education implicitly within the covert values of the school and explicitly as part of the designed curriculum (Narvaez & Lapsley in Cubukcu, 2014)

4 MODELS OF VALUE TEACHING

To discuss the central question to this study, how values related to the issue of global citizenship can be addressed in the literature classroom, a brief description of various models of value teaching is necessary. Basically, values occurrence in teaching can be categorized into four models: value transmission, value neutrality, values clarification, and values across the curriculum (Straughan 1998). The underlying notion of these four models are conscious and unconscious with value transmission and value neutrality belonging to the first notion and values clarification and values across the curriculum belonging to the second one.

Values transmission refers to the view that teaching and learning activities in a classroom are inevitably value-laden and that teachers cannot avoid transmitting values to the students without planning it. In this case, the teacher relies on the hidden curriculum of the institution (Straughan 1998). Straughan describes this transmission strategy as "transitory" in the sense that teachers usually employ it temporarily before they move to a more deliberate approach to teaching values. In the values neutrality model, the teacher offers topics for the students to discuss and debate. The teacher plays a neutral leader role in the class discussion and avoids taking sides on any views expressed by the students. They respect differences rather than push the students to come to an agreement. Values clarification model tries to equip the students with the capacity to reflect consciously on value-related issues. The emphasis of this model is the process of valuing, that is understanding and internalizing values students should experience. The strategies of this model include discussions, games, and role playing in its practice in order that students have a clear idea of their values (Straughan 1998).

Values across the curriculum adopt the strategy of both value transmission and value clarification. In one way, like value transmission it is based on the idea that everybody by nature contains moral value dimensions. In another way, similar to value clarification, it suggests conscious efforts to ensure that the students realize the moral dimension in their nature and encourage them to develop their values through reflection and the discussion of values issues (Straughan 1998).

5 GLOBAL CITIZENSHIP IN LITERATURE TEACHING IN THE EFL CONTEXT

In the context of EFL, literature teaching has been claimed to bring not only advantages such as language skills, sociolinguistic/pragmatic knowledge, emotional intelligence (EQ) and critical thinking (Dewi 2007, Karasik 2015), but also the cultivation cultural/intercultural and global awareness values (Karasik & Pomortseva 2015). Karasik and Pomortseva's assertion about intercultural and global awareness values literature teaching can bring up rightly responds to the demands of the global challenges students are faced with nowadays (Perez 2013). In this context, teaching literature for English learners in their bachelor's degree needs careful considerations in terms of value education (Beach 2011). Global awareness is indeed one crucial value in the teaching and studying of literature for as Tony Wagner (2008) asserts, it is a value that underlies a person's ability to adjust himself in a different cultural situation and context in order to survive in the 21st century.

Foregrounding global citizenship values in literature teaching requires a teaching which makes literature meaningful for the students and leaves a constructive effect upon the learners' cultural knowledge. In other words, literature should be taught meaningfully (Collie & Slater 1987). Louse Rosenblatt's transactional theories could be a proper reference to ensure meaningful literature teaching for it gives much space to the reader's background knowledge in deriving the meaning of a text. Rosenblatt argues that reader's "emotional disposition, thought, and memories "contribute to a literary text. Reader's personal experience and background are crucial to the interpretative process (Bellour 2012). The process should not become an interpretive process outside the reader's personal experience since meaning is constructed in relation to the reader's personal experience and background. Reading literary text this way might deepen students' understanding of the text's socio-cultural context and help foreground global citizenship values.

The descriptions of the four models of values education in this section can be described briefly as follows. Among the four models, value transmission is the approach which needs neither teacher's planning nor deliberate practice in the classroom. As Straughan (1998) emphasizes, it completely relies on the institution's hidden curriculum. Supporting Straughan's assertion, Hansen (2003) states that values are embedded in teaching rituals such as classroom beginnings, teachers' style and in the curriculum design. Through the rituals, values of global citizenship can be transmitted covertly to the institution's community (teachers and students are included). The emphasis of particular values related to global citizenship can be different from one institution to another since morals and values in a society are bound to the so-called "moral universalism and relativism" implying that the formation of values depends on individual teaching styles and philosophies of the teachers. However, there has been a belief that some values are universal, shared by everyone regardless of the differences in cultures, religions or social groups. These kinds of values are identified as "core values" or "consensus values" (Hofstede 2010).

In the value transmission approach, teachers can strengthen the global citizenship values by having students involved in various activities the institution designed as a means of value transmission. Although a valuing project is not stated in the teacher's lesson plan, students should be equipped with general guidelines to ensure that the activities they participate in cultivate the values of global citizenship. The activities should aim to facilitate students with: (1) The opportunity to reflect on the values global citizenship: love of country, democracy, active & responsible citizenship, interdependence, international understanding, global peace, and unity in diversity. (2) The development of insight into global citizenship values. (3) The development of personal attributes required for active proponent of global citizenship values. At particular times during the course of the semester, students could write an essay or make a class presentation on global citizenship values they reflect on and advocate in the activities they participate in.

In the values neutrality model, the teacher uses discussion as the main teaching strategy. He has controversial issues for the students to reflect on, discuss and debate related to global citizenship values. Instead of entering into the discussion with his own views, the teacher only leads the students to come to a common ground among themselves about a certain issue. Beach's (2016) model of engaging students with literature and its underlying values is adapted as a model of values neutrality in literature teaching and is examined below. It consists of:

Step 1. Value Exposure: opinion survey
Teacher presents some value-related statement that students feel particularly strongly about and respond why their experience of the world leads them to feel so strongly about the state-

ment. For example: 1. Love for country overpasses anything else including family or religion. 2. Love for country means never betraying the country regardless of the president. 3. It is better to live in a more prosperous country for everyone in today's world to be a global citizen 4. There should be no country boundaries geographically, politically and culturally.

Step 2. Think-aloud before Reading (Setting Purposes, Activating Background Knowledge; Building High Expectations)

In this step the teacher asks the students to anticipate what the text is about by looking at the title, headings, and skimming through the text. For example, the teacher can ask: (1) Tell me what you think this text is about (2) talk about the values you expect to emerge from this text (and how it might relate to our essential question of values (3) Talk about why you think the text might be useful to read related to the values we discuss, and so on.

Step 3. Think-aloud during reading

The focus in this step is the reader's understanding about the text and the contained values in it. The teacher might ask such questions: (1) what parts of the text are particularly important or relevant to the discussed values? (2) Talk about what values you can think of as you read the text, (3) Talk about what values you most agree or oppose as you read. (4) Articulate personal connections as you read to controversial values you know in the world, and so on.

Step 4. Think-aloud after reading

In this step, the teacher monitors the students' "Metacognitive awareness and Self-monitoring". Teacher might ask the following questions: (1) what value realize as you read? (2) Do you understand the text you read or the values in it, (3) how do the issues in the text connect to your prior experiences and interests? (4) How are the value issues in the text helpful or harmful for your or other people's lives? And so on.

Values clarification model is a variation of values neutrality. In this model, students are deliberately led to valuing process and made conscious about particular values issues emerging in the teaching learning activities. The strategies that can be used to promote values in this model are discussions, games and simulation. A suggested model for values clarification adapted from Bohlin (2005) is demonstrated below. The model describes the process of mapping out an essential valuing process leading to values clarification through characters in a literary work.

With some adjustments, the table can be applied to explore values through other literary elements in other literary genres.

Values across the curriculum necessitates the incorporation of values in teaching instruments and practices explicitly. One of the models adapted from Mishan (2005) is suggested as follows.

Table 1. Value clarification model.

Character		Clarified values	
Mapping essential points	Definition	Illustration	Value judgment
Moral starting points, habits, disposition and context	What we know about the character's behavior, attitudes, dispositions as well as initial aspirations and goals		
1st essential value point	Shake-up, realization that character is not pursuing the most possible value		
2nd essential value point	Leap in self-knowledge, clearer perspective on a worthy judgment		
Challenge point	Meets a challenge that imposes stress or pressure; value becomes clear but it is difficult to pursue. The character chooses a course of action and exercises practical wisdom in achieving that goal		
Value clarification			

Table 2. Value across the curriculum model.

Literary text	e.g. Short story
Targeted value	e.g. Love of country
Valuing purpose	Engaging
Authentic task type	Reaction, response
Aim	To react to value occurrence input

In this model, students have the following learning experiences:

Step 1. Preparation: Teachers choose a literary work which gives the best chance for value discussion in literary elements.

Step 2. Distribute roles or list of characters or events in the work among learners (for large classes: a group can all play the same character or act out the same events. For small classes: one learner can play multiple roles).

Step 3. Teacher reads certain parts of the work and learners act out and reflect on it as it is read

Step 4. Group acting recommended in which better students can 'lead' the slower ones either in understanding the work or in reflecting on the contained values.

6 CONCLUSIONS

To sum up this paper, value is an enduring belief that informs one's mode of conduct. They are references that guide a person in making judgments about life, and on which he bases his actions consistently and repeatedly. Values are implicit, stable, and invisible and associated with motives, emotions, and taboos, therefore sharply differentiated from practices.

It is unlikely to teach without values content. Value education might be taught consciously or unconsciously. The conscious approach such as in the cases of value clarification and values across the curriculum is practiced by integrating values in the teaching or curriculum design. It might be stated explicitly in the teaching instruments or practiced deliberately in the classroom activities. On the contrary, the unconscious approach is done in an unplanned fashion as a part of hidden curriculum. Value transmission and value neutrality belong to this approach. The first approach is more common in tertiary education, especially universities, whereas the second one generally occurs in primary and secondary levels of education. Either approach, the general consensus is that values should be concerns of the curriculum (Al-Hooli 2009).

In spite of the strong suggestions that literature teaching is loaded with the issues of value, attention for values complexities in literature teaching concerning teachers, students, literary works and classroom experiences has been insufficient. There is still a relative lack of research into literature teaching associated with core values, in English departments. Insufficient attention for values in literature teaching overlooks the possibility that values-based literature reading can be used as sources of inspiration for achieving the fundamental goal of literature teaching, namely broadening reader's insight about human beings as creatures with both physical and spiritual dimensions.

Therefore, studies or discussions on how core values, especially those related to global citizenship, contained in literary works can be identified, negotiated, and revealed in literature are worth doing. The findings or recommendations of such study and discussion can be useful references for the university's policy maker to identify and plan a model of classroom-based values education. Finally, the integration of value education into literature teaching can offer teachers a way to engage students with core values and teach them life-lessons that can lead them towards reaching life wisdom.

REFERENCES

Al-Hooli, A. & Shammari, Z.A. 2009. Teaching and Learning Moral Values through Kindergarten Curriculum. *Education 129(3): 382.* Alabama: Project Innovation. Retrievedfrom:https://www.researchgate.net/profile/Zaid_AlShammari2/publication/234671665_Teaching_and_Learning_Moral_Values_through_Kindergarten_Curriculum/links/54fc31460cf2c3f524227d82.pdf.

Barrette, C.M., Paesani, K. & Vinall, K. 2010. Toward an integrated curriculum: Maximizing the use of target language literature. *Foreign Language Annals 43*(2): 216–230. Retrieved from: http://e-resources.perpusnas.go.id:2156/ContentServer.asp?T=P&P=AN&K=62187274&S=R&D=eh h&EbscoContent=dGJyMNHX8kSep7Q4wtvhOLCmr0%2Bep69Ssa%2B4TbKWxWXS&Content Customer=dGJyMOzprkixr69MuePfgeyx44Dt6fIA.

Beach, R., Appleman, D., Fecho, B., & Simon, R. 2016. *Teaching literature to adolescents.* Routledge.

Benninga, J.S., Berkowitz, M.W., Kuehn, P. & Smith, K. 2006. Character and academics: What good schools do? *Phi Delta Kappa 87*(6): 448–452.

Bellour, L. 2012. The Literary Text Wants Readers, not Reading: The Implications of Louis Rosenblatt's Transaction Theory in the Literature Class. *Arab World English Journal 3(3): 58–105.* Retrieved from: http://awej.org/images/AllIssues/Volume3/VolumeeNumber3September2012/6.pdf.

Bertens in Taneri, A. P. D. P. O., Gao, P. S. J., & Johnson, P. S. R. 2016. *Reasons for the deterioration of moral values: cross-cultural comparative analysis.* Retrieved from:https://scholar.google.com/schola r?q=Bertens%2C+2000.+%E2%80%9CValue%E2%80%9D+refers+to+what+is+valued%2C+judged+ to+have+value%2C&btnG=&hl=en&as_sdt=0%2C5.

Bohlin, K.E. 2005. Teaching character education through literature. New York: Routledge.

Collie, J. & Stephen, S. 2002. *Literature in the language classroom.* New York: Cambridge University Press.

Cox, A. (ed). 2011 *Teaching the short story.* London: Palgrave Macmillan Palgrave Macmillan.

Cubukcu, F. 2014. Values Education through Literature in English Classes. *Procedia-Social and Behavioral Sciences 116: 265–269.* Retrieved from: http://libgen.io/scimag/ads.php?doi=10.1016%2Fj.sbsp ro.2014.01.206&downloadname=.

Diknas, UU RI No.20 Tahun 2003 Tentang Sistem Pendidikan Nasional, (Jakarta: Sinar Grafika, 2003)

Hofstede, et al. 2010. *Cultures and organizations.* New York: Mcgraw-Hill Companies.

Halstead, M. 1996. *Values in education and education in values.* London Washington, D.C: Falmer Press.

Inglehart, R. 2008. Changing values among western publics from 1970 to 2006. *West European Politics* 31(1–2): 130–146. Retrieved from: https://www.researchgate. net/profile/Inglehart_Ron-ald/publication/253550249_Changing_Values_Among_Western_Publics_from_1970_to_2006/ links/56dccd7308aee1aa5f8746b3.pdf.

Karasik, O. & Pomortseva, N. 2015. Multicultural challenges: teaching contemporary American literature for Russian philological Students." *Procedia-Social and Behavioral Sciences* 684–688. Retrieved from: http://ac.els-cdn.com/S1877042815046170/1-s2.0-S1877042815046170-main. pdf?_tid=dee2e1f2-272c-11e7-995600000aacb35d&acdnat=1492846113_8ba0e2148f754ee89db07b 586c7ce9cb.

Ki Hadjar Dewantara. 1977. *Bagian pertama: Pendidikan.* Yogyakarta: Majelis Luhur Persatuan Taman Siswa.

Mishan, F. 2005. *Designing authenticity into language learning materials.* Intellect Books.

Morrison, T. 2002. How can values be taught in the university? *Peer Review: Emerging trends and key debates in undergraduate education.* Retrieved from: http://e-resources.perpusnas.go.id:2156/ContentServer. asp?T=P&P=AN&K=7498656&S=R&D=ehh&EbscoContent=dGJyMNHX8kSeqLA4v%2BbwOLCm r0%2BeprBSsKm4S7CWxWXS&ContentCustomer=dGJyMOzprkixr69MuePfgeyx44Dt6Fi.

Perez, J. 2013. *Global issues in the teaching of language, literature and linguistics.* Bern: Peter Lang AG, International Academic Publishers.

Rokeach, M. 1973. T*he nature of human values.* New York: The Free Press Collier MacMillan.

Rosenblatt, L.M. 1988. *Writing and reading: The transactional theory.* Reader, 20, 7.Retrieved from: https://scholar.google.com/scholar?q=Rosenblatt+theory%2C+&btnG=&hl=en&as_sdt=0%2C5.

Straughan, R. 1988. *Can we teach children to be good? basic issues in moral, personal, and social education* (Vol. 157). UK: McGraw-Hill Education.

UNESCO. 2002. *Learning to be: a holistic and integrated approach to values education for human develop-ment: core values and the valuing process for developing innovative practices for values education toward international understanding and a culture of peace.* Bangkok: UNESCO Asia and Pacific Regional Bureau for Education.

Wagner, T. 2008. *The global achievement gap.* New York: Basic Books.

ELT in Asia in the Digital Era: Global Citizenship and Identity – Madya et al. (Eds)
© 2018 Taylor & Francis Group, London, ISBN 978-0-8153-7900-3

Pedagogical movements in teaching English in the emerging issues of World Englishes

N. Mukminatien
Universitas Negeri Malang, Malang, Indonesia

ABSTRACT: This paper aims to examine the status of English with its varieties. This leads to a possible pedagogical movement into non-inner circle Englishes in the teaching of English to Indonesian learners. It makes changes in the areas of a new "place" of NNS teachers, English varieties to be exposed to the learners, in relation to which standard to adopt, and the production models and the production target for communication. NNS teachers will no longer be marginalized by NS teachers in the hiring of English teachers. Which English varieties to learn depends on the purpose of learning English while the standard to adopt would remain one of the inner-circle Englishes. In terms of models for production and production target, they may vary depending on the target community the learners will communicate in English.

1 INTRODUCTION

The spread of modern technology has made English spread globally and so there are many Englishes in the world exposed to non-native speakers (NNS) of English. The new varieties of English, called World Englishes (WEs) are basically "new Englishes" in the expanding circle different from the inner circle and outer circle ones. The new Englishes are those used by NNS and belong to everyone who speaks the language, but they are nobody's mother tongue (Rajagopalan 2004). Referring to Kachru's (2005) classification of English, three terms are known as Inner Circle (USA, UK, Canada, Australia, New Zealand), Outer Circle (Bangladesh, India, Ghana, Kenya, Nigeria, Malaysia, Pakistan, The Philippines, Singapore, Sri Lanka, Tanzania, and Zambia), and Expanding Circle (China Egypt, Indonesia, Israel, Japan, Korea, Nepal, Saudi Arabia, Taiwan, Russia, Zimbabwe, South Africa, and Caribbean Islands. Due to its spread, English in the context of language teaching can be classified into three terms (Kirkpatrick 2007): English as a native language (ENL), English as a second language (ESL), and English as a foreign language (EFL). The expanding circle is growing larger in number due to communicative, educational, and professional demand in the global world. This phenomenon has been discussed in relation to its implications where ELT practices should accommodate WEs in the teaching of English in the expanding circle (Mukminatien 2012a). It is evident that English now has achieved its global status because it plays a new role that is recognized in almost all expanding countries (MacKay 2009), especially in the form of a policy that makes English an important foreign language of the country. New terms then emerge to add the list, such as English as an international language (EIL) English as a Global Language (EGL), and English as a lingua franca (ELF) in addition to the previously known terms ESL (English as a second Language, EFL (English as a Foreign Language, and ENL (English as Native Language).

Concerning its status as EIL, the definition and its elaboration makes a number of assumptions in terms of the relationship between EIL and culture. McKay (2009) quotes Smith's idea (1976) concerning its implications in ELT. First, the learners do not need to internalize the cultural norms of the native speakers of that language. Second, the ownership of international language becomes 'de-nationalized.' (McKay uses the term 're-nationalized'). Lastly, the educational goal of learning EIL is to enable learners to communicate their ideas and culture to others. As a result, EIL users, whether in global or local sense, and do not need to internalize the Inner Circle's cultural norms. In the case of ELT in Indonesia, the facts show that learners learn English in their native culture, (Indonesian culture), and they will more likely use English in the context of EGL or ELF. It rarely happens that they have to communicate with the native speakers of English), unless they go to an overseas university in an English-speaking country. So, the previously stated goal of learning English in the communicative approach for developing communicative skills with the native speakers of English needs to be reconsidered (Mukminatien, 2012a).

2 THE PLACE OF NON-NATIVE SPEAKERS (NNS)

I would like to highlight that the teaching of English in Indonesia would likely be different compared to its status decades ago. Both the teachers and the learners share similar characteristics in that both are NNS of English, living in an expanding circle (EFL) countries who share the same first national language and holding the same culture. These would make the differences in ELT practices. In such a status as EIL, EGL, or ELF, the teaching of English in Indonesia would have special characteristics. I would like to start with suggestions made by McKay (2009) in relation to the possible revisions concerning EIL and culture as follows. Due to its EIL status, English is used both in a global sense and its local sense. In a global sense, it is used for international communication between countries whose people do not speak English as their native or second language. It is also used in a local sense as a language of a wider communication within multilingual societies. So, the use of English is no longer connected to the culture of the Inner Circle countries, but it becomes embedded in the culture of the country in which it is learned and used. In addition, in a global sense, one of its primary goal of learning and using English is to enable speakers to share with others their ideas and culture. So, expecting learners to achieve a native-like proficiency is not always relevant because most of them, in fact, communicate in English with other NNS.

Before discussing the rising status of NNS English teachers, it is better to look back at the status of NS/NNS English teachers viewed by Braine (2010:9) as the following.

> ...., the NS/NNS distinction is not as simple as that. The term "native speaker" undoubtedly has positive connotations: it denotes a birthright, fluency, cultural affinity, and sociolinguistic competence. In contrast, the term "non-native speaker" carries the burden of the minority, of marginalization and stigmatization, with resulting discrimination in the job market and in professional advancement.

The belief about the differences between NS and NNS speakers (teachers and students) seem no longer valid. In terms of population, the number of NNS people who speak English (for different reasons and situation) outnumber the NS (Kachru 2005). In addition, in this current booming of NNS who have a lot of opportunities to go abroad and graduate from overseas universities, NNS English teachers are no longer considered "less qualified" among NS English teachers for several reasons. The first and most important reason is that NNS have shown their equal and competing knowledge and skill as NS do. They have overseas experiences with relevant and sufficient pedagogical background, and strong professionalism. It is true that NS English teachers outperform fluency, and naturalness, and sociolinguistic competence but it does not mean that NNS have less and inadequate professional capital. They have shown their professional competence in pedagogy, methods of language teaching as shown by their publications both in national and international journals written in English. So, questioning the quality of NNS teachers are irrelevant before examining their real performance.

One of the causes that makes NNS English teachers equal in status and quality with NS English teachers is the role and significant contribution of information and technology (IT) in language teaching. Utilizing technology in the form of teaching innovation in the areas of teaching method/techniques and material development are now common practices of NNS English teachers. For example, a lot of innovation and materials development have been made by Indonesian scholars and teachers in ELT practices. Take for example, listening materials developed by Yaniafari (2012a, 2014b), reading materials by Tungka and Mukminatien (2012), and web-based writing media by Silcha (2016). Yaniafari (2012) developed multimedia-based listening materials for vocational high school students, and the second is listening materials for university students. Tungka and Mukminatien (2016) developed reading comprehension materials in the form of multimodal English medium texts, and Silcha developed a web-based writing media for feedback. These indicates that NNS English teachers are innovative teachers; they can make use of technology to support their teaching to make it more qualified and innovative.

These indicate the important roles NNS teachers play in their practices to give the best services for quality teaching. Those materials have been implemented in the blended learning platform, a combination between online learning and face-to-face format in language teaching (Thorne 2003). Moreover, because access in technology is getting easier and cheaper, IT-based materials and innovation have become the trends in the final year projects made by the English Department students of *Universitas Negeri Malang*. The phenomenon is evidence of the increasing quality of NNS English teachers and students who can take their roles as materials developers for English classes relevant to their students' need. In short, they are no longer considered as "second rate" as stated by Braine (2010). This is the evidence of the phenomena of non-native speaker movement where local English teachers, as NNS, are able to show their professional competence equal to NS. These characteristics of qualified teachers are valuable asset in ELT. With the help of technology advancement, NNS English teachers are capable of preparing for their teaching in a more updated way, and therefore, they no longer depend on NS-made English materials. This is about the importance of having capability in addition to competence. Hargreaves & Fullan (2012) state that developing teachers' professionalism needs a combination between competence and capability. Competence refers to the teacher's ability to act in their expertise, while capability means having not only competence but also an ability to accomplish their responsibility that needs supporting competence to respond to any possible changes of life.

3 ENGLISH VARIETIES AND STANDARD TO CHOOSE.

Many English varieties exposed to learners and a question about which standard to choose in ELT are two different aspects to pay attention to because the first is the fact while the second is a decision or a policy to make. Concerning the purpose of ELT, Melchers & Shaw (2003) has given three questions to answer: (a) what exposure do we give the learners, (2) what production model should we choose, and (3) what production target should we aim for. Exposure means what the English learners listen to or read; usually learners are exposed to predominantly American and British English through the media both print (newspaper, magazines, brochures, advertisements) and non-print (TV series, movies, video, and web-based texts). The model is the teacher's usage, spoken and written materials, while the production target means the aim for learners to learn. They also state that in the expanding circle, learners need English to communicate with anyone in the global community. Seeing that in this context the aim is learning English as an international language (EIL), learners should be able to understand as many accents and varieties as possible. In communicating with other speakers, either NS or NNS, they should avoid culturally specific and pragmatic behaviors. The language they produce should be comprehensible to speakers of different varieties.

3.1 *English varieties*

In reference to the existing varieties of English as sociolinguistic reality (Hudson 2007), it is necessary to seek the implications of Kachru's classification of the spread of English. The classification of English varieties suggests that there are many varieties or models, and consequently, there are many Englishes to choose. ELT practitioners, are faced with many models and norms all of which are characterized by internal variations. According to Kirkpatrik

(2007), "in the context of ASEAN, the role of English is de-facto lingua franca". According to him, in ASEAN context, learners need an English language teaching curriculum that teaches them about cultures of the people they are most likely to use English with. The most factual example is the annually held RELC (Regional English Language Center) International Conference, a reputable forum where teachers of English in ASEAN countries and some English-speaking countries share ideas in ELT practices in the forms of paper presentation, workshops, and posters. In this forum, English is used as ELF for ASEAN people in their academic forum, where it is also a place to compare, relate and present their own culture and ideas to others. In summary, the teaching of English in ASEAN countries should accommodate the varieties that are mostly used by the people in the ASEAN countries. As a matter of fact, learners are not only exposed the Inner Circle varieties of English but also many expanding circle varieties of English. It is obvious that Indonesian learners are exposed to many varieties of English through many different kinds of media and sources, such as those from TV, the internet, books, magazines, newspapers. Rich in exposure to different varieties, Indonesian learners are given a lot of knowledge of different kinds of English worth studying. So, giving as many varieties of English as possible is good for comprehension, while for production it depends on the purpose of learning English, whether it is for studying in the ENL country or just for learning another language for communication among NNS.

So far, however, English language teaching in Indonesian schools has been oriented to the American and British, and some Australian for listening and literature reading materials (Mukminatien, 2012a). English textbooks and other spoken models used in language laboratory are mostly American and some British and Australian varieties. In the English Department of *Universitas Negeri Malang* (UM), for example, a lot of materials for language skills such as listening, reading, speaking, and writing) and grammar are mostly American. In communication practices, either written or spoken, most of the characters in the dialogs are among native speakers (NSs-NSs) of English and little, if any, between (NNS) and NS. Dialogs between NNS are rarely found. In short, the standard of competence in ELT has been oriented to the ultimate goal of achieving the competence close to native speaker's proficiency. The teaching of Inner Circle English only is also reported in Japan (Matsuda 2003). It is obvious that using Inner Circle English only might bring problem because Inner Circle orientation to ELT may be appropriate for ESL program, but not for EFL. For EIL orientation, Inner Circle English variety is not suitable either because EIL learners will use English mostly among themselves rather than to NS of American or British.

3.2 *The standard to adopt*

Adopting merely Inner Circle English is inadequate because the emerging WEs lead ELT practitioners to reconsider relevant materials to teach. Kirpatrick (2005) gives an inspiring example of intelligibility in ASEAN Englishes in developing oral proficiency (Mukminatien 2012b). He asserts that ASEAN provides settings where intelligibility is crucial when English functions as lingua franca. So, in this case, I am of the opinion that teaching English in Indonesia should also concern with intelligibility among target speakers rather than just native speaker's proficiency as its ultimate goal. In other words, in oral communication, learners do not need to always adopt RP (Received Pronunciation) in England when they communicate with other EFL speakers; rather, they should focus on making their pronunciation intelligible. For that purpose, Matsuda (2003) highlights that it is necessary to accept multiple varieties of English, and therefore, ELT should be matched with pedagogical approaches for relevant teaching goal.

As it has been discussed earlier, teaching English using an Inner Circle native speaker model only is not adequate. This is because adopting Inner-Circle linguistic and pragmatic norms and inner circle cultures is not appropriate since many learners of English live and study English in their home country, non-Inner Circle countries (Kirkpatrik 2005a, 2007b). So, a question concerning which standard to adopt, might be answered with "it depends." The answer deals with the purpose of the ELT Program. If the ELT program is designed for learners who wish to continue their study in one of the Inner Circle countries, then the standard should be the norms of the Inner Circle Country (Mukminatien 2012b).

4 THE PRODUCTION MODEL AND TARGET FOR COMMUNICATION.

In developing communicative competence, which model to learn is necessary to consider, and it is appropriate to use one of the Inner Circle models such as American and/or British. This is because EFL learners are mostly exposed to predominantly American and British variety. Melchers & Shaw (2003) highlight the fact that even though we expose learners to a number of language varieties, it does not mean that those varieties are selected for learners to learn. It is necessary to consider the goal of teaching English in the Expanding Circle countries. The standard model would be one of the ENL's if this program uses examination where NS norms are used. However, if the ELT program is a subject in schools in the expanding circle, ELF or EGL are necessary to accommodate, and English competence is measured for intelligibility among speakers whose native language is not English, or among NNS. What norms are used is also in question whether there is any good and suitable model of ELF or EGL. After all, accommodating the existing ELF and EGL means accepting variations which are not for "native-like proficiency" but for intelligibility. In short, if ELT practitioners acknowledge and accept WEs, they need to think the most suitable approach to ELT. So, ELT practices need to be reviewed to accommodate WEs.

Seeing that English language teaching in Indonesian schools has been oriented to the American and British, and English textbooks and other spoken models are mostly American and some British and Australian varieties, ELT practitioners should design the ELT program by paying attention to the purpose of teaching English so that they can provide suitable materials and approaches. The emerging WEs suggest that ELT practitioners reconsider approaches in developing students' communicative competence. So, the most crucial factor in developing communicative competence is not "near native proficiency" but intelligibility among speakers or users of English. It is necessary to accept multiple varieties of English, and therefore, ELT should be matched with pedagogical approaches.

5 CONCLUSION

Due to the spread of English globally, as one of sociolinguistic realities, NNS learners are exposed to WEs as new varieties of English. NNS English teachers might be as qualified as NS teachers depending on the context and goals of teaching English, whether to prepare learners for pursuing their study in an English-speaking country or just to help them communicate among NNS or comprehend academic sources written in English as a foreign language (EFL) for searching information in their native country. In other words, ELT practices should be adapted to the learning context. Learning EFL for communicative purposes requires the learners to be able to use English for effective communication. However, achieving native-like proficiency should be considered in terms of the target production. In this case, the success of oral communication is not measured against a native speaker of the Inner Circle because the most important thing is intelligibility. Their production should be comprehensible among speakers of different varieties since English is the language spoken around the world by people of different mother tongue. Exposure for comprehension can be from many WEs, but production target should be relevant to which target community they would likely be involved. Concerning norms, it would be suitable to choose those from one of the Inner Circle Countries which has a dominant status and which provides internationally recognized standard.

REFERENCES

Braine, G. 2010. *Nonnative speaker English teachers. Research, pedagogy, and professional growth.* New York: Routledge Taylor and Francis Group.

Hargreaves, A. & Fullan, M. 2012. *Professional capital. transforming teaching in every school.* New York: Teachers College Press.

Hudson, R.A. 2007. *Sociolinguistics.* Cambridge: Cambridge University Press.

Kachru, B.B. 2005. *World Englishes.* Power Point Presentation

Kirkpatrick, A. 2005. *Oral communication and intelligibility among Asian speakers of English.* A Paper presented at 40th RELC International Conference, 18–20 April, 2005.

Kirkpatrick, A. 2007. *World Englishes: Implications for international communication and English language teaching.* Cambridge: Cambridge University Press.

Matsuda, A. 2003. Incorporating world Englishes in teaching English as an international language. *TESOL QUARTERLY.* 37(4): 712–729.

McKay, S.L. 2009. *Teaching English as an international language. rethinking goals and approaches.* Oxford: Oxford University Press.

Melchers, G. & Shaw, P. 2003. *World Englishes.* New York.: Oxford University Press.

Mukminatien, N. 2012a. *Providing multiple media form experiences in a reading comprehension class.* A Paper Presented at 47th RELC International Conference, Singapore.

Mukminatien, N. 2012b. Accommodating world englishes in developing EFL learners' oral communication. *TEFLIN Journal* 23(2): 222–232

Pakir, A. 2000. The development of English as a "global" language: New Concerns in the old saga of language teaching. In Ward, C. & Ho, W.K. 2000 (eds). *Language in the global context: implications for the language classroom* (Anthology Series 41). Singapore: SEAMEO Regional Language Centre.

Rajagopalan, K. 2004. The concepts of world englishes and its implications for ELT. *ELT Journal* 58(2): 111–117.

Silcha, W.N. 2016. *Developing a web-based argumentative writing media for English department students.* Universitas Negeri Malang: Unpublished Thesis for Master's Degree.

Thorne, K.V. 2003. Blended learning: how to integrate online and traditional learning. London: Kogan Page.

Tungka, N.V & Mukminatien, N. 2016. *The investigation of EFL students' experiences, skills, and preferences in comprehending multimodal English medium Texts.* A Paper presented at TESOL Indonesia International Conference, August 11–13, 2016 at the University of Mataram in Lombok, Indonesia.

Yaniafari, R.P. 2012. *Multimedia based listening materials for 1st grade students of SMK.* Universitas Negeri Malang: Unpublished Bachelor Thesis.

Yaniafari, R.P. 2014. *Developing listening courseware as supplementary listening materials.* Online Article, Fakultas Sastra.

Considering English varieties in Indonesia's EFL teaching and learning

E. Andriyanti
Yogyakarta State University, Yogyakarta, Indonesia

V. Rieschild
Macquarie University, Sydney, Australia

ABSTRACT: The perceived significance of English as a global language in Indonesia can be seen mostly in its educational context, with its prominent position culminating in the National Examinations. Despite numerous efforts and actions taken, English learning at schools in Indonesia has been less successful to produce learners with communicative competence. This paper highlights the current emphasis on Standard English and correct grammar during the learning process, which does not likely provide sufficient time and supporting environment for most learners to speak English frequently and in a relaxed way. This mixed-methods study collected its data through survey, interview and observation. The findings indicate that as an 'expanding circle' country, Indonesia also needs to consider a non-native English variety in its school contexts. This study proposes two phases of EFL teaching and learning: early years focusing on general English and oral competence and later years on academic or other specific purposes and reading competence.

1   INTRODUCTION

The position of English as a global language relates to its functions as a lingua franca. Different from other international languages such as Arabic, French and Spanish which are less predominant, English is recognised as a means of global or inter-lingual communication (Ammon 2010: 102, Crystal 2003: 3, Majhanovich 2014: 168–169, Mufwene 2010: 42–43, Ricento 2010: 127). This global language has dual sides: a part of educational system and knowledge economy (Majhanovich 2014). The first side appears as, for example, the most globally taught language, academic and professional requirements in educational settings, and the most expected language to be used in scientific publication. The second relates to its being as one of "global literacy skills", which is needed in business and global markets and as a "saleable product" (Block 2010: 295 & 300, Coulmas 2009).

The global use of English involves its variation in space, that is, the notion of a range of "Englishes". Kachru (1983, 1988, 1997) broadly locates the varieties in three circles, with native English in the inner circle, non-native English as a second language in the outer circle and non-native English as a foreign language in the expanding circle. These circles are similar to native, official and priority foreign Englishes proposed by Nunan (2003: 590). Mufwene (2010: 43) recognises another variety spoken in the Caribbean and the Pacific islands as creole/pidgin English.

English in Indonesia belongs to the expanding circle as a priority foreign language. Although it is not a second language, its wide use in various sectors has made it an "additional language" (Lowenberg 1991: 136). The perceived significance of English in Indonesia can be seen, for example, in the country's acceptance of English as ASEAN's lingua franca (Kirkpatrick 2012: 331); in educational contexts it culminates in its being a language tested in the National Examinations.

The long history of English as a foreign language (EFL) teaching and learning in Indonesia dates back to the pre-colonialism of Dutch (Lauder 2008: 9, Lowenberg 1991: 128). The impetus to improve English learners' competence is evident in the dynamics of school curricula and their methodologies, which from 1984 have applied the communicative approach (Dardjowidjojo 2000: 25–26, Latief 2014, Lie 2007: 4, Reg. No. 160, 2014, Puspitasari 2016, Sahiruddin 2013: 568–570, Yulia 2014: 15–17). Despite decades of serious attempts at change made by the Indonesian government, language policy makers, educators as well as assistance from Anglophone countries, an assured success of English language teaching (ELT) in Indonesia is still elusive. Challenges related to language policy, class sizes, quality of teachers, students' motivation, and teaching strategies have been reported in a large number of research for almost three decades (Hamied 2012, Lengkanawati 2004, 2005, Lie 2007, Lowenberg 1991, Madya 2002, Marcellino 2008, Musthafa 2001, Panggabean 2015, Sahiruddin 2013, Smith 1991, Yulia 2014).

This study proposes a different perspective on making Indonesian ELT more successful in achieving its main goal. In addition to continuing to address challenges mentioned in prior research, this study examines the importance of considering English varieties in Indonesian education as a way of enhancing the success of Indonesia's ELT.

2 RESEARCH METHOD

All relevant data in this paper form a small portion of data for a large-scale educational sociolinguistic study on multilingualism of young people in Yogyakarta, Indonesia. Mixed-methods approach was applied, with student and teacher surveys, interviews with school authorities and in and out of class observations as methods of collecting data.

Data were collected from ten high schools: five junior and five senior high schools. The research participants included 1,039 students, 34 language teachers: 9 of them were English teachers, and 11 school authorities: 9 principals, 1 vice-principal, and 1 language teacher coordinator.

SPSS 21 and its newer version of SPSS 22 were used to deal with statistical data analyses. NVivo 10 was used for qualitative data analyses.

3 FINDINGS AND DISCUSSION

3.1 *Discrepancy between the communicative approach and Indonesia's ELT*

The communicative approach stresses that a language is basically a communication system and therefore language teaching and learning must be oriented towards learners' ability to communicate in the given language or in a particular socio-cultural group (Breen & Candlin 2001: 10, Celce-Murcia 2001: 6, Richards 2006: 1–2 & 22, Savignon 2007: 208–209). Agustien et al. (2004: 47) recommend the application of communicative competence model—with discourse competence as the core—proposed by Celce-Murcia et al. (1995) in Indonesia's EFL teaching and learning; and remind that linguistic knowledge is important but needs to be conditioned in language environment to become ready-for-use competence (p. 53).

The students' survey results, the reports of eight principals and the observations revealed that in the general school context or even within English classes, English was not used daily between pupils or between teachers and pupils. The survey data on how often they used English show the mean score of 2.37 out of 1–5 Likert scales, implying this language was still part of their multilingualism. Positioned between the scales of 2 and 3 for frequency of language use, this figure indexed the range between 'Rarely' and 'Frequently enough'. Findings on their English competence show a number of facts. Regarding their academic achievements, they reported that their competence in English was much lower than that in Bahasa Indonesia and similar to their local language. Considering the four main language skills, they self-rated their speaking skills lower than they rated their other skills. These findings support the claim that most high school graduates cannot communicate intelligibly in English (Dardjowidjojo 2000: 27, Lie 2007: 1, Sahiruddin 2013: 573). Higher self-rating on English speaking ability is often associated with taking a private English course, which is perceived as a more effective teaching and learning activity for producing communicative speakers (Dardjowidjojo 2000: 27, Lie 2007: 3).

In line with the communicative approach, the main goal of contemporary ELT in Indonesia is to develop learners' communicative competence for participating in the global community (Badan Standar Nasional Pendidikan, 2006: 165, Lie 2007: 6, Mattarima & Hamdan 2016: 287). Act No. 20 (2003) and Act No. 24 (2009) state that mastery of English is for global competitiveness. However, the standards for process and outcomes stress reading skills, rather than speaking skills (Reg. No. 19, 2005: 18–19, Lowenberg 1991: 129). This seems to have impacted on students' reading competence, so, for example, the surveyed students reported that their reading competence was the highest among other skills: means of 3.37 in 1–5 Likert scales. Assessment on students' competence on reading and writing can be seen in the English National Examination (Reg. No. 19, 2005); this is accompanied with assessment on competence in grammar and well-formedness (Musthafa 2001: 5). This then explains why schools and teachers are highly oriented towards the National Examination. Seven interviewees admitted that all English co-curricular activities were related to the preparation of the National Examination, including the exam try-outs. While in the national context, Bahasa Indonesia is usually the tested subject with higher average score than English, the English's average scores of four participating schools were better than Bahasa Indonesia's, and this was also common in other selective schools in Yogyakarta.

The focus on written language rather than spoken language can be linked to another dimension of ELT in Indonesia. As confirmed by seven principals, English is a medium of accessing scientific knowledge and information and as an educational tool. The surveyed students self-reported their English speaking competence among other skills was in the lowest mean of 3.04, indicating 'Fair' competence. While the teaching-learning in the communicative approach needs the integration of various skills, the purpose of learning a language should be primarily for communication. In this context and to some extent, it is necessary for Indonesia's ELT to join the trend of English teaching in Europe and China, which focus on oral competency (Spolsky & Lambert 2006: 571–572). In the global context, impact of the lack of focus on this skill is learning difficulties for international students from Asia, including Indonesia (Sawir 2005). In this educational setting, and in addition to reading books and other knowledge sources, active engagement in discussion and class participation is a significant factor influencing academic success.

3.2 *Which English best suits Indonesian learners?*

This question is significant because in Indonesian educational context, there has been no consensus of which English is agreed upon for students to learn at school (Martin 2016). However, it is generally assumed that the standard forms of three native Englishes, i.e., British, American, and Australian, are used as the reference.

From the perspective of diglossia, the determination to teach Standard English at school in Indonesia seems reasonable. Different from the L form which is commonly acquired without speakers' paying explicit attention to grammatical norms, the H form is usually learnt formally (Ferguson 1959: 331, Hudson 2002: 7). However, it must be noted that in Indonesia's context, colloquial English is not widely spoken as an everyday language and there are not many native speakers. Even though most of the surveyed English teachers in Yogyakarta used English for the language of instruction as reported through the student and teacher surveys and interviews with school authority representatives, other research also revealed that there was still a significant number of English teachers in other areas being not confident to speak English (Lie 2007: 7–8, Musthafa 2001: 5).

This implies that most first learners learn English as a written text language without adequate exposure to oral language. They have to learn a Standard English without sufficient practice in speaking the language in everyday settings, which is naturally less formal in form.

This makes them focus on learning grammatical and well-formed expressions. As a result, their language learning is more about constructing formally correct forms rather than producing informally common and fluent everyday language. This situation continues to their higher level of education, making it difficult for them to equip themselves with oral communicative competence. It is understandable if six years of English learning do not enable most of them to speak the language well, even for everyday conversations.

3.3   *Two phases of EFL teaching and learning: a proposed new perspective*

Against this complicated backdrop, this study proposes that the teaching and learning of EFL in Indonesia is divided into two phases. The earlier years of education, such as primary and junior high schools, should focus on general English and oral communication; in later years, such as in senior high school and higher education, the focus of English teaching can shift to academic or other specific purposes (see also Agustien et al. 2004: 8, Panggabean 2015). Informal writing will be most applicable at the lower level while reading and writing academic texts will be more suitable at the higher level.

ELT practice in primary or junior high schools should not be strictly limited to Standard English. There should be a place for the use of non-standard English, and so acknowledge and validate the learners' diverse linguistic backgrounds (see also Hamie, 2012: 76, Mukminatien 2012: 224, Panggabean 2015: 35–37). The acceptance of local English as a legitimate means of communication among first English learners in Indonesia would enhance the implementation of the communicative approach in producing active speakers. However, it is necessary to conduct research on the features of Indonesian-English (Kirkpatrick 2010, Lauder 2008: 18, Panggabean 2015: 37–38).

In the first phase, English teachers have two main roles, that is as facilitators and as participants within the teaching-learning groups (see Breen & Candlin 2001: 17). They should:

1. give everyone opportunities to practice speaking the language in communicative activities, especially those which are interactive;
2. build students' confidence in speaking English fluently among themselves;
3. understand that code-mixing is a natural part in communication among Indonesian speakers, who are mostly multilingual (Kirkpatrick 2010: 8);
4. avoid correcting grammar while students are first learning to speak English, as this action might discourage them;
5. maximise language exposure in real-life contexts by speaking English most of or all of the time and also provide authentic, meaningful communication events (Musthafa 2001: 5; 2010: 123)

Creating a fun and relaxed English learning atmosphere is crucial to encouraging students' confidence in speaking. In this way, students will find English learning enjoyable and be motivated to learn more in the next higher level. In short, teachers must create interesting and meaningful learning experiences. The perception that learning and using English is difficult (as reported by 1037 of the surveyed students) might significantly hinder their English learning achievement. Students' declining motivation towards English, for example due to unfavorable teachers and perception of English as a difficult lesson, must be anticipated (see Lamb 2007: 766, Panggabean 2015: 35–36). Prior learning experience and beliefs about language learning are essential for learner success (Sawir 2005: 578).

Even though the use of the local English variety is acceptable among students, it is recommended that teachers have a high level of accuracy and proficiency in English. High proficiency in English teachers provides role models and overcomes the lack of native speakers (Kirkpatrick 2010: 10, Musthafa 2001: 5). However, such teachers should not expect their students to perform at such a high level. The monolingual yardstick should not be used to measure the result of their students' learning.

At higher levels of education where students are expected to gain more knowledge through English, Standard English-oriented teaching and learning can be appropriately applied. The objective is for students to master academic English, which is stricter in adherence to correct grammar and tends to be focused on writing. At this stage, most students are expected to have basic competence in using English learnt at the previous stage. English communication is still an imperative both for teachers and students.

The teaching of grammar and other aspects of standard usage must be incorporated in that of written communicative skills. Teacher-centred grammar teaching, which is evidenced in many Asian countries including Indonesia (Sawir 2005), must be avoided because it shapes students into passive learners. The balance of activities to improve students' four main language skills needs to be maintained and grammar should not be stressed as if it is the only key to master a language.

Using different perspectives and strategies in Indonesia's ELT means that the outcome standard must also be different. There must be adjustment between the nature of the National Examination in English and the goals that will be achieved. In the first phase, assessment should emphasise communication skills. Tests of oral and written communicative competence must be modified to remove native yardsticks of assessment because the learners' real production models are mainly their teachers and their interlocutors—almost all of whom are not native speakers. Their competence should be properly compared to users of English as their second or foreign language (see Cook 1995: 93–94, Cook 2012, Doyle 2015, Franceschini 2011: 348, Kirkpatrick 2010: 10–11, Lamb 2007: 765, Lowenberg 2002: 433, Mukminatien 2012: 228–229). The production target is Indonesian-English, which is comprehensible among non-native speakers in Indonesia and even probably with speakers in the other ASEAN countries. A higher standard of English can be considered for assessing higher-level students with a greater emphasis on academic reading. More sophisticated grammar can be included, but comprehending texts is more pragmatically important.

The division of ELT into the afore-mentioned two stages hopefully gives a clear direction of which competences should be aimed by beginners and advanced learners. A number of positive aspects support the success of these achievable goals. For example, in the context of Yogyakarta the surveyed young people reported that their involvement in English-based activities was dominant among other language-based activities in the past, present and future despite their rare use of English. The students claimed English as a significant language for them. The mean score of 3.72 out of 1–5 Likert-scale indicates that English was more than 'Significant enough' to them. They also reported positive attitudes towards English (mean score of 3.60) even though they perceived it as a difficult language (mean score of 2.67, indicating more difficult than Bahasa Indonesia and Low Javanese). The interviewed principals shared their opinion that English was significant in relation with academic and job purposes as well as living in the global era. Their report on their schools' language teaching and maintenance efforts, and the teachers' reports on facilities indicate that the participating schools have made concerted efforts to fully support the success of ELT. The fact that all the surveyed schools reported having text books, audio-visual equipment and cassettes shows their serious engagement in enhancing the improvement of ELT in Indonesia.

4   CONCLUSION

A significant number of problems have been identified as hampering the successful adoption of English as a compulsory subject in all six years of Indonesian high school. One important issue is the past attention to having a strict emphasis on the use of standard and grammatical English. This expectation that standard variety will be used in the implementation of ELT in Indonesia can be reviewed from various perspectives, including the diglossic situations of a language. Since English is not an everyday language for most Indonesian students, the teaching of Standard English must be preceded by habituation of practicing the language among them in real communicative contexts. It was proposed that two stages of English learning with different stresses on general English and oral competence in the earlier stage and on academic English and reading competence might be a useful solution for a better result of ELT.

It is important to shift the paradigm from focusing on Standard English to give space for non-standard English with junior high school students, who are beginners. The goal would be to assist learners in becoming more confident and fluent in communicating in that low variety, that is, the most common nativised variety of a community within a non-native-English speaking country. Higher requirements for grammar and accuracy in English can be applied at the higher levels of education. This change in ELT's orientation entails the adjustment of teaching practices, classroom activities, and learning materials, as well as learning assessment practices, all of which are already hinted within the communicative approach.

REFERENCES

Act No. 20. 2003. *Undang-undang Republik Indonesia Nomor 20 Tahun 2003 tentang Sistem Pendidikan Nasional 'Act of the Republic of Indonesia Number 20 2003 on National Education System'*. Jakarta: Ministry of National Education.

Act No. 24. 2009. *Undang-undang Republik Indonesia Nomor 24 Tahun 2009 tentang Bendera, Bahasa dan Lambang Negara, serta Lagu Kebangsaan 'Act of the Republic of Indonesia Number 24 2009 on Nation's Flag, Languages, Emblem, and Anthem'*. Jakarta: Ministry of Law and Human Right.

Agustien, H.I R. 2004. Setting up new standards: a preview of Indonesia's new competence-based curriculum. *TEFLIN Journal* 15(1): 1–13.

Agustien, H.I.R., Anugerahwati, M. & Wachidah, S. 2004. *Materi pelatihan terintegrasi Bahasa Inggris 'Integrated training material for teaching English'*. Jakarta: Depdiknas.

Ammon, U. 2010. World languages: trends and futures. In N. Coupland (Ed.), *The handbook of languages and globalization* (1st ed.: 101–122). West Sussex: Wiley-Blackwell.

Badan Standar Nasional Pendidikan. 2006. *Panduan penyusunan kurikulum tingkat satuan pendidikan jenjang pendidikan dasar dan menengah 'Guideline for developing school-based curriculum for primary and secondary levels'*. Jakarta: BSNP.

Block, D. 2010. Globalization and language teaching. In N. Coupland (Ed.), *The handbook of language and globalization*: 287–304. West Sussex: Wiley-Blackwell.

Breen, M.P. & Candlin, C.N. 2001. The essentials of a communicative curriculum in language teaching. In D.R. Hall & A. Hewings (Eds.), *Innovation in English language teaching*: 9–26. London: Routledge.

Celce-Murcia, M. 2001. Language teaching approaches: an overview. *Teaching English as a second or foreign language* 2: 3–10.

Celce-Murcia, M., Dornyei, Z. & Thurrell, S. 1995. Communicative competence: a pedagogically motivated model with content specifications. In *Issues in Applied Linguistics* 6(2): 5–35.

Cook, V. 1995. Multi-competence and the learning of many languages. *Language, Culture and Curriculum* 8(2): 93–98. doi: 10.1080/07908319509525193.

Cook, V. 2012. Multi-competence. *The encyclopedia of applied linguistics*.

Coulmas, F. 2009. Language and economy. In L. Wei & V. Cook (Eds.), *Contemporary Applied Linguistics: Language for the Real World* 2: 28–45. London: Continuum.

Crystal, D. 2003. *English as a global language* (2nd ed.). Cambridge: Cambridge University Press.

Dardjowidjojo, S. 2000. English teaching in indonesia. *EA journal* 18(1): 22–30.

Doyle, H. 2015. Multi-competence, EFL, learning and literacy: a reconsideration. *International Journal of Social Science and Humanity* 5(10): 887–891.

Ferguson, C.A. 1959. Diglossia. *Word, 15*(2): 325–340. doi: 10.1080/00437956.1959.11659702.

Franceschini, R. 2011. Multilingualism and multicompetence: a conceptual view. *The Modern Language Journal, 95*(3): 344–355. doi: 10.1111/j.1540–4781.2011.01202.x.

Hamied, F.A. 2012. English in multicultural and multilingual indonesian education. In A. Kirkpatrick & R. Sussex (Eds.), *English as an International Language in Asia Multilingual Education* 1: 63–78. New York: Springer Netherlands.

Hudson, A. 2002. Outline of a theory of diglossia. *International Journal of the Sociology of Language, 2002* (157): 1–48. doi: 10.1515/ijsl.2002.039.

Kachru, B.B. 1983. *The Indianization of English: the English language in India*. Delhi: Oxford University Press.

Kachru, B.B. 1988. The sacred cows of English. *English Today* 4(4): 3–8. doi: 10.1017/S0266078400000973.

Kachru, B.B. 1997. World Englishes and English-using communities. *Annual Review of Applied Linguistics* 17(March 1997): 66–87. doi: http://dx.doi.org.simsrad.net.ocs.mq.edu.au/10.1017/S0267190500003287.

Kirkpatrick, A. 2010. *English as an Asian lingua franca and the multilingual model of ELT*. Paper presented at the The Hong Kong Association of Applied Linguistics Research Forum, Hong Kong. Revised version of a plenary paper presented at the Hong Kong Association of Applied Linguistics Research Forum, 12 December 2009, Hong Kong Polytechnic University, Hong Kong retrieved from http://www98.griffith.edu.au/dspace/bitstream/handle/10072/42297/73943_1.pdf;jsessionid=B8EE9E3CDC676D4D3EC1D1C12964F3DF?sequence=1

Kirkpatrick, A. 2012. English in ASEAN: implications for regional multilingualism. *Journal of Multilingual and Multicultural Development* 33(4): 331–344. doi: 10.1080/01434632.2012.661433.

Lamb, M. 2007. The Impact of school on EFL learning motivation: An Indonesian case study. *TESOL Quarterly* 41(4): 757–780. doi: 10.2307/40264405.

Latief. (2014, 8 December 2014). Surat keputusan mendikbud menghentikan kurikulum 2013 'Ministrial Decree on Discontinuation of Curriculum 2013', *Compas.com*. Retrieved from http://edukasi.kompas.com/read/2014/12/08/11583761/Surat.Keputusan.Mendikbud.Menghentikan.Kurikulum.2013.

Lauder, A. 2008. The status and function of English in Indonesia: a review of key factors. *Makara, Sosial Humaniora* 12(1): 9–20.

Lengkanawati, N.S. 2004. How learners from different cultural backgrounds learn a foreign language. *Asian EFL Journal* 6(1): 1–8.

Lengkanawati, N.S. 2005. EFL teachers' competence in the context of English curriculum 2004: implications for EFL teacher education. *TEFLIN Journal-A Publication on the Teaching and Learning of English* 16(1): 79–92.

Lie, A. 2007. Education policy and EFL curriculum in Indonesia: between the commitment to competence and the quest for higher test scores. *TEFLIN Journal* 18(1): 01–15.

Lowenberg, P.H. 1991. English as an additional language in Indonesia. *World Englishes* 10(2): 127–138. doi: 10.1111/j.1467-971X.1991.tb00146.x.

Lowenberg, P.H. 2002. Assessing English proficiency in the expanding circle. *World Englishes* 21(3): 431–435.

Madya, S. 2002. Developing standards for EFL in Indonesia as part of the EFL teaching reform. *TEFLIN Journal-A Publication on the Teaching and Learning of English* 13(2): 142–151.

Majhanovich, S. 2014. Neo-liberalism, globalization, language policy and practice. *Asia Pacific Journal of Education, 34*(2): 168–183. doi: 10.1080/02188791.2013.875650.

Marcellino, M. 2008. English language teaching in Indonesia: a continuous challenge in education and cultural diversity. *TEFLIN Journal-A Publication on the Teaching and Learning of English* 19(1): 57–69.

Martin, N. (2016, February 6, 2016). English in Indonesia: is it still a matter of British or American?. *The Jakarta Post*. Retrieved from http://www.thejakartapost.com/news/2016/02/06/english-indonesia-is-it-still-a-matter-british-or-american.html

Mattarima, K. & Hamdan, A.R. 2016. The teaching constraints of English as a foreign language in indonesia: the context of school based curriculum. *Sosiohumanika* 4(2): 287–300.

Mufwene, S.S. 2010. Globalization, global English, and world English(es): myths and facts. In N. Coupland (Ed.), *The handbook of language and globalization* (1st ed.: 31–55). West Sussex: Wiley-Blackwell.

Mukminatien, N. 2012. Accommodating world Englishes in developing EFL learners' oral communication. *TEFLIN Journal* 23(2): 222–232.

Musthafa, B. 2001. Communicative language teaching in Indonesia: issues of theoretical assumptions and challenges in the classroom practice. *Journal of Southeast Asian Education* 2(2): 1–9.

Musthafa, B. 2010. Teaching English to young learners in Indonesia: essential requirements. *Educationist* 4(2): 120–125.

Nunan, D. 2003. The impact of English as a global language on educational policies and practices in the Asia-Pacific region. *TESOL Quarterly: A Journal for Teachers of English to Speakers of Other Languages and of Standard English as a Second Dialect* 37(4): 589–613. doi: 10.2307/3588214.

Panggabean, H. 2015. Problematic approach to English learning and teaching: a case in Indonesia. *English Language Teachin,* 8(3): 35–45. doi: 10.5539/elt.v8n3p35.

Puspitasari, S.N. (2016, 21 March 2016). Tahun Ini, Kurikulum 2013 Diterapkan Secara Nasional '2013 Curriculum will be Implemented Nation-wide This Year', *Pikiran Rakyat*. Retrieved from http://www.pikiran-rakyat.com/pendidikan/2016/03/21/364624/tahun-ini-kurikulum-2013-diterapkan-secara-nasional

Reg. No. 160. 2014. *Peraturan Menteri Pendidikan dan Kebudayaan Republik Indonesia Nomor 160 Tahun 2014 tentang Pemberlakuan Kurikulum Tahun 2006 dan Kurikulum 2013 'Ministrial Regulation No 160 2014 on the Implementation of Curriculum 2006 and Curriculum 2013'*. Jakarta: Ministry of Law and Human Rights.

Reg. No. 19. 2005. *Peraturan Pemerintah Republik Indonesia Nomor 19 Tahun 2005 tentang Standar Nasional Pendidikan 'Government Regulation of the Republic of Indonesia Number 19 2005 on National Standards of Education'*. Jakarta: State Secretary of the Republic of Indonesia.

Ricento, T. 2010. Language policy and globalization. In N. Coupland (Ed.), *The handbook of language and globalization* (1st ed.: 123–141). West Sussex: Wiley-Blackwell.

Richards, J.C. 2006. *Communicative language teaching today*. Cambridge: Cambridge University Press.

Sahiruddin. 2013. *The implementation of the 2013 curriculum and the issues of English language teaching and learning in Indonesia*. Paper presented at the The Asian Conference on Language Learning 2013 Osaka.

Savignon, S.J. 2007. Beyond communicative language teaching: What's ahead? *Journal of Pragmatics* 39(1): 207–220.

Skutnabb-Kangas, T. & Phillipson, R. 2010. The global politics of language: markets, maintenance, marginalization, or murder? In N. Coupland (Ed.), *The handbook of language and globalization* (1st ed., pp. 77–100). West Sussex: Wiley-Blackwell.

Smith, B.D. 1991. English in Indonesia. *English today, 7*(02): 39–43. doi: 10.1017/S0266078400005526.

Spolsky, B. & Lambert, R.D. 2006. Language planning and policy: models. In K. Brown (Ed.), *Encyclopedia of language and linguistics*: 561–575, Elsevier Ltd.

Swaan, A.D. 2010. Language systems. In N. Coupland (Ed.), *The handbook of language and globalization* (1st ed.: 56–76). West Sussex: Wiley-Blackwell.

Yulia, Y. 2014. *An evaluation of English language teaching programs in Indonesian junior high schools in the Yogyakarta Province*. (Doctoral Conventional), RMIT University, Melbourne. Retrieved from http://researchbank.rmit.edu.au/view/rmit:4912 Available from Macquarie University.

Prospective EFL teachers' awareness of varieties of English: Implications for ELT

N. Atma & W. Fatmawati
Universitas Halu Oleo, Indonesia

ABSTRACT: This survey study reports on the prospective English teachers' awareness of the varieties of English. The sample involves English Department students of *Universitas Halu Oleo*, Indonesia. Using questionnaires to collect data, it is found that most of the students who are prospective teachers of English are aware of the status of English as a Lingua Franca. Unfortunately, they still have a lack of awareness of the existence of the varieties of English. Hence, teacher educators need to revisit their classroom practice in order to preparing their students to be cosmopolitan teachers. Finally, strategies for infusing World Englishes in instructional practice are proposed.

1 INTRODUCTION

As English is becoming a global language, it is no longer used solely by Native Speakers (NSs), but also as a means of communication among people who do not share similar first language backgrounds. Further, English has "a unique cultural pluralism and a linguistic heterogeneity and diversity" (Kachru in Al-Asmari & Khan 2014). It means that varieties of English emerge because of the widespread uses and users of English, known as World Englishes. Hence, English is not only the language of NSs but also the language of all people in the world. This fact tells the Non-Native Speakers (NNSs) that they should not be like NSs to be able to communicate internationally using English. As there is a growing number of NNSs using English, it is very possible that when communicating in the international world, the speakers encounter interlocutors speaking with different varieties of English from their own or from the variety they learn.

The worldwide spread of English changes not only the conception of English, but also the ELT paradigm. It has formed a new color of ELT. Seidlhofer (2004) in Ozturk, Cecen & Altinmakas (2009) argues that "if a language is perceived to be changing in its forms and uses, it is reasonable to expect that something in the teaching of it will also change." In relation to this issue, Jenkins (2006) proposes that the shift in the ELT paradigm could be accommodated by raising the awareness of teachers and students of the varieties of English. Heyl & McCarthy (2003 in Gün 2009) state that "a key role for higher education institutions must be to graduate future teachers who think globally, have international experience, demonstrate foreign language competence, and are able to incorporate a global dimension into their teaching". It suggests that teacher training programs especially a TESOL preparatory one is the right path to introduce this new paradigm. Unfortunately, this issue is rarely, if at all, addressed in most of the TESOL preparatory programs (Bieswanger 2008, Gün 2009). Ahn (2014) who examined the awareness of and attitude of teachers of English in South Korea found that teachers' lack of awareness of and familiarity with varieties of English may influence negatively their reactions to other varieties of English which potentially could be a handicap in developing their intercultural communication skills. Ahn (2014) also found that there was a tendency for students with exposure to other varieties of English overseas to have more understanding of other Englishes as well as to hold more positive attitudes to varieties of English than those with no experience with other varieties of English which means "that more exposure, increasing awareness and familiarity may be linked to forming positive attitudes towards varieties of English." Likewise, Matsuda (2003) argues that the students could "devalue their own status in international communication" because of limited understanding about the varieties of English. It indicates that awareness of varieties of English impact not only how the speakers view nonnative varieties, but also on how they view their own status in intercultural communication.

Further, Brown (1993) in Al-Asmari and Khan (2014) states that through the infusion of this issue into TESOL preparatory program, prospective teachers of English could learn and evaluate as to how English is used widely in the world which eventually could also "open up a new landscape of learning for them into which they can see that there are other varieties in addition to gaining knowledge about various models and methodologies of teaching". In addition, by equipping them with the knowledge of world Englishes, they could enrich their skills and familiarity with the varieties of English spoken in the globe which could possibly enhance their comprehension of what is being said by a speaker with a particular accent. As found by Natiladdanon and Thanavisuth (2014), students who have been exposed to different varieties of English could easily understand and identify ASEAN English accents. It indicates that the level of intelligibility and comprehensibility of the varieties is seemingly influenced by the amount of exposure to the varieties. Further, analysis of Spearman's correlation conducted by Ballard (2013) revealed that familiarity with accent is significantly correlated with the speaker's easiness in understanding interlocutors with a particular accent. In other words, familiarity facilitates comprehension. In a nutshell, the more the students are exposed to varieties of English, the more familiar they will be and the easier they understand what is being said.

In addition, by being more informed with the current sociolinguistics landscape of English might probably raise the students' tolerance when speaking with people with different dialects which eventually could foster their understanding that there exists no dominant variety of English (Takagaki 2005). It means that awareness of other varieties of English could probably shape the foundation for the acceptance of language variations. In a nutshell, exposure to varieties of English is crucial which in turn could lead the prospective teachers of English to a better preparation for the global world.

In Indonesia, English is used as a foreign language. It means that referring to Kachru's (1985) concentric model in Al-Asmari and Khan (2014) Indonesia belongs to the expanding circle where English is not used in daily life interactions. Native variety norms as Britain and America are adopted exclusively in most English classrooms in Indonesia. There is a lack of exposure to other varieties. In fact, in international communication, there is no doubt that English is used as a means of communication between NSs and NNSs as well as between NNSs and NNSs.

Many researchers have investigated students' familiarity with World Englishes. Natiladdanon and Thanavisuth (2014) investigated how 20 university students in Thailand perceived the ASEAN English accent. A questionnaire, interview, and listening comprehension test were used to collect the data. The students were asked to listen to ten ASEAN English accents and they had to identify those accents. The findings revealed that six of the participants could recognize five ASEAN English accents because they have been exposed to those varieties. Their attitude towards and amount of exposure are very significant in influencing the students' level of intelligibility and comprehensibility.

Pilus (2013) examined the preference of 34 Malay ESL learners toward British, American, and Malaysian English accent. The data in Pilus' study were analyzed using questionnaires. It was found that the British accent was favored by the students based on their evaluation on the level of correctness, labeling of accent, and model for teaching. Yet, the Malaysian accent was preferred based on the level of pleasant-ness.

Jindapitak and Teo (2012) probed 52 Thai stu-dents of English awareness of and attitudes toward six varieties of English, namely British, American, Indian, Filipino, Japanese, and Thai. The students listened to those English accents and were asked to guess the speaker's country of origin as well as rated those accents on eight stereotypical attributes on a scale of 1 to 7. The findings showed that British and American had higher ratings in almost all the attributes which means that those two varieties were still favored. Moreover, it was found that the most successfully identified accent was Thai.

Coskun (2011) investigated the attitudes of 47 students of the English department toward EIL pronunciation. Using questionnaires and interviews to collect data, Coskun (2011) found that varieties from inner circle countries were regarded as a good model for English teaching.

This study examines prospective teachers' awareness of the varieties of English in general. Besides, it investigates not only prospective teachers' awareness of world Englishes but also suggests possible ways to infuse world Englishes in the classroom. Further, to our knowledge, studies on prospective teachers' awareness of World Englishes in the Indonesian context are still limited. Hence, there is a need to conduct a study on this issue.

2 METHOD

This survey study was conducted at the English Department of *Universitas Halu Oleo*, Indonesia. There were 151 prospective teachers of English participating in this study who were chosen randomly.

The sample prospective teachers were handed a four-point Likert scale questionnaire to be filled in and collected. The scale ranges from Strongly Agree, Agree, Disagree, and Strongly Disagree. The sixteen item questionnaire was adapted from He (2015), Ahn (2014) and Yu (2010). The questionnaire consisted of two parts. The first part asked the students' for background information, such as time spent in learning English, whether or not the prospective teachers ever heard the terms world Englishes and English as a Lingua Franca, as well as purposes of learning English. The second part was focused on the students' awareness of the existence of varieties of English. The themes asked in the questionnaire were the users of English (Item Number 1 and 2), the existence of varieties of English (Item Number 3, 6), exposure to different varieties of English (Item Number 4, 5, 7, 11, 13), acceptability of accent in conversation (Item Number 8, 14, 16), the norm of English (Item Number 9, 10), the benefit of knowing different varieties of English (Item Number 12), and the desire to have native-like pronunciation (Item Number 15). Prior to collecting the data, the questionnaire was piloted with ten prospective teachers who were not involved in the sample of this research to check the item reliability. The result of the reliability analysis showed that the reliability was .793 which means that the items of the questionnaire were reliable enough to collect data. Besides, an analysis of item validity revealed that there were two items which should be removed because the score was only .101 and .067 (<.3). Thus, the number of items was sixteen.

Data collection took around a week. Before distributing the questionnaire, the prospective teachers were informed about the purpose of the study. It took around 25 minutes for them to finish the questionnaire. Frequency distribution and percentages were computed to analyze the data.

3 FINDINGS AND DISCUSSION

3.1 *The users of English*

The first two items of the questionnaire are related to the users of English. The table below shows the frequency and percentage of prospective teachers showing agreement and disagreement to the statements.

Based on the table above, it is obviously seen that only 17.89% of the samples surveyed agreed that English is only used between NSs of English. More than half of them (85.43%) were in agreement that English could often be used between NNSs; one student did not answer Item Number 1, while three students did not answer Item Number 2. This finding is similar with Coskun's (2011) study. It suggests that the samples of this study realized that the use of English is not restricted to those who are NSs. They knew that English is used in multilingual settings. According to Jenkins (2006), the number of NNSs increases outnumbering NSs. Hence, it is very possible for a speaker to encounter NNSs speaking English with different varieties.

3.2   *The existence of varieties of English*

The table below shows the frequency and percentage of prospective teachers showing agreement and disagreement to the statements as regards the existence of varieties of English.

The table above suggests that majority (97.36%) of the prospective teachers acknowledged that there are varieties of English spoken by people around the world. Unfortunately, 95.37% of them considered that native varieties as those used in Britain and America are the major varieties of English in the world. It means that they were aware of the varieties, but they referred the varieties to the native varieties. In other words, they did not have a clear concept about what world Englishes is which corroborates Ahn's (2014) study.

3.3   *Exposure to different varieties of English*

The table below shows the frequency and percentage of prospective teachers showing agreement and disagreement to the statements in relation to exposure to different varieties of English.

Table 1.   Frequency and percentage for items number 1 and 2, respectively.

	Agreement		Disagreement	
Statements	f	%	f	%
English is only used between native speakers of English	27	17.89	123	81.46
English can often be used between non-native speakers of English	129	85.43	19	12.58

Note: f for frequency and % for percentage.

Table 2.   Frequency and percentage for item number 3 and 6, respectively.

	Agreement		Disagreement	
Statements	f	%	f	%
There are varieties of English around the world	147	97.36	4	2.65
British English and American English are the major varieties of English in the world	144	95.37	5	3.31

Note: f for frequency and % for percentage.

Table 3.   Frequency and percentage for item number 4, 5, 7, 11 and 13, respectively.

	Agreement		Disagreement	
Statements	f	%	f	%
Students should learn the characteristics of other varieties of English in addition to American and British English	138	91.40	12	7.95
It is important to learn only native varieties of English	72	47.68	77	50.99
I am willing to participate in English learning program that introduces non-native varieties	130	86.09	19	12.58
Native speaker model should be the only model for English language learners	84	55.63	64	42.38
It is important for the students to be introduced with different varieties of English	141	93.37	10	6.62

Note: f for frequency and % for percentage.

As indicated in the table above, there were 91.40% of the prospective teachers who were in agreement with item Number 4 that students should learn the characteristics of other varieties of English in addition to American and British English. There was one student who did not answer this item. They were aware of the importance of being familiar with the diversity of English. This is consistent with the result of Item Number 5 that only 47.68% of the prospective teachers agreed to learn only native varieties of English. There were two students who did not answer Item Number 5. Moreover, as student teachers of English, they (86.09%) were willing to participate in English learning program that introduces non-native varieties; two students did not respond to this item. It might be caused by their purposes of learning English, namely they want to travel around the world in which it allows them to speak with people with different varieties of English.

Talking about the role model for English language learners, 55.63% of the prospective teachers regarded that NSs model should be the only model for English language learners. There were three students who did not respond to Item Number 11. Early language learning experiences might account for this finding because the students were only exposed to native varieties especially American one. Hence, they have been accustomed with that variety. As found in Yu's (2010) study, lack of familiarity with non-native varieties of English could possibly account for why native varieties are still favored. According to Jenkins (2007) in Soruç (2015), native varieties are valued because of their perceived correctness and intelligibility. Finally, 93.37% of the prospective teachers found that it is necessary for the students to be introduced to different varieties of English. Interestingly, it was found that exposure to varieties of English could positively influence how the students perceive world Englishes (Rousseau 2012). Further, Rousseau (2012) found that there was a statistically significant difference in the students' way in perceiving world Englishes after being given awareness raising activities.

3.4 *Acceptability of accent in conversation*

Table 4 shows the frequency and percentage of prospective teachers showing agreement and disagreement to the statements dealing with whether or not they accept the existence of accent in interaction.

The Table above clearly depicts that the prospective teachers were in agreement to the three items regarding their tolerability to accent. It implies that accent is tolerated as long as it is clear and comprehensible. Two students did not answer Item Number 8. This study concurred Ozturk, Cecen & Altinmakas (2009) and Coskun's (2011) study that the prospective teachers acknowledge the importance of intelligibility despite the fact that their future teaching practices will depend entirely on NSs model.

3.5 *The norms of English*

The table below shows the frequency and percentage of prospective teachers showing agreement and disagreement to the statements regarding who decides the norm of English.

Table 4. Frequency and percentage for item number 8, 14 and 16, respectively.

Statements	Agreement		Disagreement	
	f	%	f	%
In international communication, clearness with accent is acceptable for oral English	135	89.40	14	9.27
It is natural for a non-native English speaker to have an accent in speaking English	130	86.09	21	13.91
The most important thing when speaking English is clear and comprehensible	146	96.69	5	3.31

Note: f for frequency and % for percentage.

The table above indicates that only 23.84% of the prospective teachers surveyed agreed that if English is used differently from British or American English, it must be wrong. There were five students who did not answer Item Number 9. The result is conflicting with item Number 10 where 52.32% of the prospective teachers believed that it is British or American English speakers who have right to decide how English should be. It implies that on one side it is fine to speak differently from NSs. However, on the other side, NSs are those who decide the norm of English. It appears that expanding circle people as Indonesian are norm-dependent whose task is mainly to follow what has been determined by the NSs. Huong and Hiep (2010) found that NSs norms are maintained by Vietnamese teachers of English due to practical reasons, namely time constraint, the availability of materials, and lack of NNSs model based test.

3.6 *The benefit of knowing different varieties of English*

The table below shows the frequency and percentage of prospective teachers showing agreement and disagreement to the statement with regard to the benefit of knowing different varieties of English.

The table shows that majority of the prospective teachers surveyed (93.38%) agreed that knowing the existence of different varieties of English will help mutual understanding; one student did not answer this item. Knowledge about varieties of English could prepare the students to deal with the varieties (Takagaki, 2005). Besides, Natiladdanon and Thanavisuth (2014) found that students who have been exposed to varieties of English could identify and comprehend the varieties well which means that familiarity with varieties could likely facilitate comprehension.

3.7 *Desire to have native-like pronunciation*

The table below shows the frequency and percentage of prospective teachers showing agreement and disagreement to the statement pertaining to desire to have native-like pronunciation.

The table above shows that the prospective teachers (90.73%) were trying to sound like NSs speak. It is paradoxical with the issue of intelligibility mentioned previously. Though the prospective teachers highlight clear and comprehensible accent as found in Item Number 16, they remain to sound like NSs. It implies that clear and comprehensible accent is speaking like NSs. According to Jenkins (2000) in Coskun (2011) the NNSs' ways in speaking is a reflection of their linguistic and cultural background. Thus, they do not need to sound like NSs. Nonetheless, the findings of this study indicate that speaking like NSs seems to be the students' learning goal. It is not surprising because their learning experience including the testing proficiency is NSs oriented. They bear in mind that English is closely related to NSs. Wen (2012) cited in Soruç (2015) states that "students would be extremely proud if they could obtain a nearly native-like accent."

Since most of the prospective teachers surveyed in this study still have a lack of awareness of the existence of world Englishes, there is a need to explicitly infuse World Englishes in the

Table 5. Frequency and percentage for item number 9 and 10, respectively.

Statements	Agreement		Disagreement	
	f	%	f	%
If English is used differently from British or American English, it must be wrong	36	23.84	110	72.85
It is British or American English speakers who have right to decide how English should be	79	52.32	72	47.68

Note: f for frequency and % for percentage.

Table 6. Frequency and percentage for item number 12.

	Agreement		Disagreement	
Statement	f	%	f	%
Knowing the existence of different varieties of English will help mutual understanding	141	93.38	9	5.96

Note: f for frequency and % for percentage.

Table 7. Frequency and percentage for item number 15.

	Agreement		Disagreement	
Statement	f	%	f	%
When speaking English, I want to sound like a native speaker	137	90.73	14	9.27

Note: f for frequency and % for percentage.

instructional practice in order to familiarizing those prospective teachers with the new trend of English. Jenkins (2012) suggests that teachers let the students choose which English to aim for. However, before choosing, students need to be presented with the present sociolinguistic reality of the use of different varieties of English.

Due to the infeasibility of involving speakers of every variety and a lack of materials discussing World Englishes, the internet which provides a lot of models of speakers of English with different language background could be a viable option to be used in the classroom. Teacher educators could raise the prospective teachers' awareness of World Englishes by benefitting from the internet such as You Tube. After exposing the students to You Tube, the teachers could ask the students to discuss the simi-larities and differences between each variety. Like-wise, Matsuda (2003) suggests teachers bring World Englishes to the classroom by showing the students movies and video clips of World Englishes speakers, exchanging e-mail or doing projects that require the students to visit Web sites in various Englishes.

In addition to exposing the students to the varieties of English, teachers could also teach the students strategic competence which aims at helping the students to adjust their speech by negotiating for meaning when communication breakdown occurs (Farrell & Martin 2009), for example the students are taught how to ask the interlocutor to repeats his/her utterance.

4 CONCLUSION

Based on the result of data analysis, it seems safe to conclude that the new landscape of English as World Englishes receives inadequate attention in TESOL preparatory program because the prospective teachers of English surveyed in this study still have restricted awareness of the existence of large numbers of varieties of English. Despite their lack of awareness, the prospective teachers welcome the varieties of English because most of them are willing to participate in English learning programs that introduce nonnative varieties. In a nutshell, it is necessary to bring world Englishes to the classroom in order to familiarize those prospective teachers of English with the knowledge of diverse types of English uses and users as well as to prepare them to be linguistically ready to participate in international communication.

REFERENCES

Ahn, H. 2014. *Researching awareness and attitudes: A study of world Englishes and English teachers in South Korea.* Unpublished Doctoral Thesis. Monash University; Melbourne.

Al-Asmari, A.M. & Khan, M.S.R. 2014. World Englishes in the EFL teaching in Saudi Arabia. *Arab World English Journal* 5(10): 316–325.

Ballard, L. 2013. Students' attitude toward accentedness of native and non-native speaking English teachers. *MSU Working Papers in SLA* 4: 47–73.

Bieswanger, M. 2008. Varieties of English in current English language teaching. *Stellenbosch Papers in Linguistics* 38: 27–47.

Coskun, A. 2011. Future English teachers' attitude towards EIL pronunciation. *Journal of English as an International Language* 6(2): 46–68.

Farrell, T.S.C. & Martin, S. 2009. To teach standard English or world Englishes? A balanced approach to instruction. *English Teaching Forum* 2: 2–7.

Gün, B. 2009. Are teachers fully prepared to teach different varieties of English: A Case Study in Turkey. *English as an International Language Journal* 5: 164–175.

He, D. 2015. University students' and teachers' perceptions of China English and world Englishes: Language attitudes and pedagogic implications. *The Asian Journal of Applied Linguistics* 2(2): 65–76.

Huong, T.N.N. & Hiep, P.H. 2010. Vietnamese teachers' and students' perception of global English. 1(1): 48–61.

Jenkins, J. 2006. Current perspectives on teaching world Englishes and English as a lingua franca. *TESOL Quarterly* 40(1): 157–181.

Jenkins, J. 2012. English as a Lingua Franca from the classroom to the classroom. *ELT Journal* 66(4): 486–494.

Jindapitak, N. & Teo, A. 2012. Thai tertiary English majors attitudes towards and awareness of world Englishes. *Journal of English Studies* 7: 74–116.

Matsuda, A. 2003. Incorporating world Englishes in teaching English as an international language. *TESOL Quarterly* 37(4): 719–729.

Natiladdanon, K. & Thanavisuth, C. 2014. Attitudes, awareness, and comprehensibility of ASEAN English accents; A qualitative study of university students in Thailand. *Catalyst* 9(1): 16–30.

Ozturk, H., Cecen, S. & Altinmakas, D. 2009. How do non-native pre-service English language teachers perceive ELF?: A qualitative study. *English as an International Language Journal* 5: 137–146.

Pilus, Z. 2013. Exploring ESL learners' attitudes towards English accent. *World Applied Sciences Journal* 21: 143–152.

Rousseau, P. 2012. A world Englishes study of Korean university students: Effects of pedagogy on language attitudes. Unpublished Thesis. SIT Graduate Institute; Vermont.

Soruç, A. 2015. Non-native teachers' attitudes towards English as a Lingua Franca. *Hacettepe Üniversitesi Eğitim Fakültesi Dergisi (Hacettepe University Journal of Education)* 30(1): 239–251.

Takagaki, T. 2005. Raising students' awareness of the varieties of English. *English Teaching Forum* 43(2): 4–17.

Yu, Y. 2010. Attitudes of learners toward English: A case of Chinese college students. Unpublished Doctoral Dissertation. The Ohio State University; Columbus.

ELT in Asia in the Digital Era: Global Citizenship and Identity – Madya et al. (Eds)
© *2018 Taylor & Francis Group, London, ISBN 978-0-8153-7900-3*

ELT shift: Necessary matters to be taught dealing with pronunciation among NNS related to English as a Lingua Franca (ELF)

Andy & L. Muzammil
Universitas Kanjuruhan Malang, East Java, Indonesia

ABSTRACT: Considering historical 'superiority' and English as 'capital', Non-Native Speakers (NNS) tend to outnumber Native-Speakers (NS), making English as a Lingua Franca (ELF). Non native-like is less of a sign of incompetence but more of a potential characteristics in its own. English NS videos pronunciation model was an alternative on NNS pronunciation not to deviate too far impeding intelligibility. This study was aimed at investigating pronunciation development and its deviation, the changing and adaptation to promote 'global intelligibility' among all English speakers. The participants were 32 NNS of English from different mother tongue. They accomplished pronunciation test before and after treatment to measure their sounds, stress, and intonation. The scores were analyzed using t-test for correlated samples and it was found that there was significant difference between pre-test and post-test of pronunciation. NNS performed better and deviated less and therefore this model was worthwhile to be included in ELT's consideration.

1 INTRODUCTION

1.1 *Background*

There is an increasing tendency that people around the world start to be more and more familiar with the term 'globalization'; in fact, some of them have really felt the impact in their daily life. This phenomenon is in line with the claim by Burridge & Mulder (1998) that the orientation of the world tends to become global, they assert the term 'global village' to represent world that has become globalised. What can be implied from the notion 'globalization' can be perceived from Kubota's (2002) depiction that is 'local diversity' that tends to be more and more escalated as the impact of 'human contact' beyond 'cultural boundaries' and rapid reciprocity of 'commodities and information'. Therefore, globalization can be interpreted as increasing opportunities for worldwide contact.

The community in the 'global village' demands 'global communication' to stay connected; Block and Cameron (2002) note that 'global communication' needs a shared 'channel' as well as 'linguistic code'—they believe that the applicable code(s) will have been learned by many participants in order to play active role in the 'global village', for other members these codes can just be natively acquired. In terms of the shared 'channel', they argue that the advancement in technology application can support this need. For the shared 'linguistic code' according to Burridge & Mulder (1998) requires a "lingua franca" or "common language".

House (1999) points out that English is 'de facto' an international language (EIL). In terms of English speakers, Kachru (1992) classifies them into three categories: the 'inner circle', the 'outer circle', and the 'expanding circle'. Burridge & Mulder (1998) give the details: the 'inner circle' refers to English native-speakers (NSs), the 'outer circle' refers to countries where English is used as a second language (or ESL), the last circle—the 'expanding circle' refers to countries where English functions as a foreign language (or EFL). They point out that past colonial history plays role in influencing whether English then becomes ESL or EFL in some countries. They also believe that there is steady increase in the number of English speakers in the 'expanding circle'. The interpretation will be that English non-native speakers (NNSs) tend to increase.

In line with Burridge & Mulder (1998), Seidlhofer (2001) argues that use of English globally is "largely" among NNS (English as a lingua franca). Furthermore, she argues that in reality, the description of English does not involve NNSs very much (though they are becoming the majority of English speakers); its central focus is trying to get more and more precise of the description of NSs English. The tendency is still towards description of English as a native language (ENL). She claims that ELF is also worthwhile to have its own description, especially to be used as a reference in approaching English spoken by ELF speakers—NNSs. Seidlhofer advocates the importance of having ENL corpus with ELF corpus as its companion. She claims that research and consideration in the study of English should invite more active role from NNSs. Most of the studies so far seem to neglect the 'rights' of NNSs as English users. Another fact about NNS is mentioned by Jenkins (2006a) in Jenkins et al. (2011) who claims that with the large number of NNS, their pronunciation is different (becomes potential characteristic) and the take-for-granted consideration that non native-like is a sign of incompetence.

In short, there is a shift in terms of the ownership of English from NS realm to NNS worldwide use. Many experts have pointed out the growing predisposition from native-like perfectness to 'global intelligibility', targeting on flourishing communicative competence in a dynamic worldwide contact. It is the part of English Language Teaching (ELT) to take more active role in promoting 'global intelligibility', bearing in mind that local condition affects a great deal of interferences which can somewhat impede understanding between participants of the talk (in English) from different parts of the world.

This paper discusses NNS of English development in their pronunciation and what ELT needs to change and adapt, especially in pronunciation and pragmatics (NNS' accommodation amongst them). The focus is those that are 'teachable' and 'learnable' in terms of training both to the teachers and learners. In addition, many experts begin to agree with the adaption of ELF approaches in ELT worldwide.

1.2 Research questions

1. Do NNS of English develop their pronunciation subsequent to utilizing NS of English pronunciation model?
2. To what extent do NNS of English gain intelligible pronunciation of English as Lingua Franca?

1.3 Hypothesis

1. NNS of English develop their pronunciation subsequent to utilizing NS of English pronunciation model.
2. NNS of English gain intelligible pronunciation of English as Lingua Franca from decreasing deviation, avoiding more misunderstanding, and leading to learnable and teachable approach.

2 LITERATURE REVIEW

2.1 ELF pronunciation

Jenkins (1998) proposes that increasing usage of English as a means of communication worldwide has impact on pronunciation orientation. The 'needs and goals' of English learners tend to shift from being able to speak with a 'native-like accent' and to converse with native speakers (NSs), to using English as ELF. ELF is used for intelligible message-exchange among NNSs.

Jenkins (1998) claims that 'clear-cut alternatives' to current pronunciation teaching method (PTM), which tend to emphasize native-like ability, are lacking. In order to respond to the tendency of the function of English as EIL, Jenkins recommends that adaptation is needed to achieve more practical PTM. This is not easy, she argues that one of the reasons is that PTM gets less attention compared to 'communicative approaches' in English Language Teaching (ELT) curricula. The other 'obstacles' are in terms of the difficulty in trying to satisfactorily 'harmonise' pronunciation of the speakers who consider English as their L2 to promote 'international intelligibility'.

In line with Jenkins (1998), Shibata et al. (2015) also claim great impact of pronunciation to intelligibility in communication. They focus on 'tonicity' ('nuclear tone placement') which they believe to play significant role in delivering utterance meaning. They emphasize on the importance of mastery of 'tonicity' knowledge and practical ability to promote global understanding.

To facilitate their justification of pronunciation teaching, Jenkins (1998) proposes an EIL pronunciation syllabus which she believes can match the demand and need of EIL usage globally—promote intelligibility. She tries to adapt the approach used in majority published pronunciation textbooks, which she believes to be difficult to be totally and effectively taught in ELF context. These materials tend to teach the way NSs' success in conveying the message through uttering—using the 'suprasegmental system (stress, rhythm, and intonation)'; she claims that the suprasegmental' contribution outweigh the one by the segmentals (sounds) to NSs intelligibility.

In order to teach interlanguage speakers, which is her main consideration, pronunciation that can promote intelligibility; then there should be a balance between the segmentals and suprasegmentals. She mentions the three areas of productive focus in teaching pronunciation that are salient to intelligibility in EIL, they are "certain segmentals, nuclear stress (the main stress in a word group), and the effective use of articulatory setting".

In terms of segmentals, Jenkins mentions that emphasis should be given in teaching correct production of English 'core' sounds—this may become the tendency of NNSs' deviation (which is varies based on their L1). In addition, non-core sounds can also be taught which in general are 'vowel quality' and to the consonants /T/ and /°/ – the majority of world's languages do not have them.

The next emphasis is teaching nuclear stress. Jenkins' justification is that there is tendency that EIL learners are generally trained to focus on their 'receptive' goals within a short period; little time allocated to exercise their 'productive' ability. Therefore, EIL learners tend to have limited ability to perform what English fluent speakers usually are able to do—moving nuclear stress from its common position; the aim is to highlight 'extra' meanings.

Jenkins claims that by doing frequent exercises in giving appropriate 'nuclear stress' and producing core sounds that do not deviate too far, EIL speakers are able to avoid potential 'disastrous' for EIL talk.

The last emphasis is 'articulatory setting'. Trying to improve EIL learners' ability in articulatory setting can promote learners' core sounds-production and their ability to manipulate core sounds to generate nuclear stress.

Those three phonological areas above are claimed by Jenkins to be useful and beneficial for teaching pronunciation to EIL learners. Moreover, Jenkins (1998) advocates that EIL should pay more attention to NNSs local norms, than to NSs norms—which she believes to have 'no threat to intelligibility' for other NNS receivers. Such NSs norms are at least in areas: 'word stress', even to formulate reliable rules is not easy—therefore it is not easily learnt; 'features of connected speech'—particularly weak forms, Jenkins notes that lack of weak forms only gives impact to NSs—unlikely to other NNSs; the last are is rhythm, Jenkins argues that stress-timing in English does not need to be done rigidly.

Jenkins (2007) in Deterding (2010: 5–6) displays what 'features of pronunciation' that do not need to be taught, namely "dental fricatives, final consonant clusters, vowel quality (apart from the midcentral vowel), reduced vowels in unstressed syllables, stress-based rhythm, and the pitch movements associated with intonation".

In relation to pronunciation pedagogy, Deterding (2010) states the proposals for ELF-based teaching in China, he finds out that the teachers are attracted to it because it is 'practical', 'achievable', and 'fun'. However, he reminds of possible alert in terms of prioritising which pronunciation features are more important. Moreover, Nikbakht (2010) states current pronunciation teaching with 'interdisciplinary' approach connecting to 'sociopsychological' issues.

Shibata et al. (2015) propose interactive treatment to make the teaching of pronunciation becomes more attractive by using hand gestures to demonstrate tonicity accompanied with power point slides projecting the 'location' and 'movement' of the 'nuclear tones'.

2.2 Misunderstanding among ELF speakers

House (1999) conducts a review of the literature on misunderstanding in ELF communication. Her small empirical study shows that its hypothesis is not true; that 'differences in interactants' pragmatic-cultural norms' does not cause misunderstanding in ELF talk. Seidlhofer (2001) asserts that House' main aim is to emphasize the importance of NNSs' pragmatics skills in communicating in English.

House (1999) summarizes that some of the articles about misunderstanding reviewed tend to describe the following characteristics of ELF talk. First, that ELF talk is short; the reason is that conversation participants feel 'insecure' about their choice of the appropriate norms. It seems that they have no choice but to involve in attempts to adjust their talk.

The other characteristic, which House believes more salient, is that participants in ELF talk tend to adopt a 'Let-it-Pass' principle—they do not have to understand the whole messages that are intended to be conveyed, they only prioritise 'sufficient' understanding which is enough for their current goal of the chat. Explicit efforts to clarify ambiguous utterances seem to be rarely conducted. She points out that this behaviour can conceal the possible sources of misunderstanding. If ELF participants are asked to exchange the exact meaning of the intended message, then House believes these activities can break the commonly taken-for-granted—believed that there is 'mutual intelligibility' in ELF talk. Adding House's 'Let-it-Pass' principle, Jenkins et al. (2011) mention that 'making it normal' strategies also take place forming 'mutual cooperation' in communication among ELF with less consideration on being correct.

The possible cause of 'misunderstanding' in ELF talk is clarified by House (1999) that is 'knowledge frames and interactional norms' of their L1 culture. Moreover, According to her, communication between participants with different cultural background, misunderstanding can be considered as inherent and become an integrated part—inseparable from the communication. Moreover, she acknowledges that the other feature is the tendency that ELF interactants prefer to 'waffle'—trying to convey their intended message by uttering 'too many words'. They feel insecure to chat with more fluent interactants, especially with NSs; they feel that their proficiency is lacking. By being accompanied with other NNSs with 'equal' ability, they have less feeling of being intimidated. In relation to this reality, House claims that the source is ELF interactants' lack of 'discourse attuning' or in her term 'pragmatic fluency'.

The third feature is that ELF interactants' turntaking management tend to be not efficient—their ability to acknowledge clear transition points seem lacking and also no clear job description of how to play role as an addresser or addressee. The result is lack of 'mutual responsibility' as conversations participants. Not understanding of the whole messages that is emphasized but merely to get sufficient understanding is considered adequate.

In terms of 'awareness', Deterding (2010) describes this is central to successful accommodation, that in class activities do no limit itself on NS idioms rather dealing with varies idioms from ESL as well as EFL or ELF countries. Moreover Jenkins, Cogo & Dewey (2011) mention that ELF speakers in their interactions employ varied linguistic features, the purpose is relating to 'cultural identity' and 'solidarity' as well as 'humour' and not to promote understanding among interlocutors.

2.3 ELT with ELF teachable and learnable approach

Jenkins (1998) tries to prompt several reminders to the importance of placing pronunciation at more proper place in English language teaching—not marginalized like in common English teaching curriculum. However, Jenkins et al. (2011) postulate that teaching pronunciation with accommodation skills involves considerably more work. Moreover, Deterding (2010) adds that the other rationale is that huge materials are already made available in native-speaker ones.

There are three phonological areas, namely segmentals, nuclear stress (the main stress in a word group), and the effective use of articulatory setting which are claimed by Jenkins (1998) to be useful and beneficial for teaching pronunciation to EIL learners. The rationale is that they are 'teachable' and also 'learnable'. They are different from most other phonological areas which have complex exceptions and 'fine distinction'—thus not easily learnable and do not have advantaging impact for most EIL contexts. In addition, those three areas proposed by Jenkins can be applied to any learners and contexts.

Additional focus in this paper is pragmatics approach, Jenkins et al. (2011) exemplify such approach as 'signaling of non-understanding' that is how ELF interlocutors 'respond' and 'negotiate' towards 'non-understanding'. They portray strategies employed i.e. 'repetition', 'clarification', 'paraphrasing' and 'self-repair'. In addition to those strategies, there is a strategy which taking the advantage of NNS characteristics that is 'exploitation of plurilingual resources'. As NNS, they have 'plurilingual resources' which are shared among them.

Jenkins (1998) notes that the implications of her proposal to teacher education are: in terms of a model and a norm, and L2 sociolinguistic variation. For the first she recommends that a native norm, what NS English is, should not be treated as the teaching aim; it is 'unrealistic'. In teaching EIL, teachers should position NS English as a model—'points of reference' and guidance. The purpose is to show students, who may be from different L1 background, that they should try not to diverge too far. In macro level, NNS students are encouraged not to move too far apart from each other; this can result in 'international unintelligibility'. While for the teachers, they need to be able to satisfy many of her/his students who are willing to have proficiency which has close proximity with NS norms.

Jenkins et al. (2011) clearly depict ELF that those NNS in EFL who 'failed native speakers' do possess excellent communication skill by employing their 'multilingual resources' (not available in 'monolingual' NS) to give more emphasis on 'successful communication' than the state of being 'correct' (native-like).

In relation to being teachable and learnable, Jenkins (1998) points out that it is necessary to set pronunciation goals which are the best for both teaching and learning; emphasis should be given to matters that are universal, realistically teachable and learnable core, and based on the native model. This is in line with Shibata et al. (2015) who claim that in Japan 'tonicity' is 'teachable' and 'learnable', further work needs to be carried on training teachers to do the teaching.

In the practice of teaching and learning, Gilakjani (2012: 127) suggests that it is needed active participation from both the teacher and learner by setting 'individual teaching' and 'learning goals', by integrating class communication with the course content which promote 'meaningful pronunciation practice'. He suggests that "With this in mind, the teacher must then set obtainable aims that are applicable and suitable for the communication needs of the learner. The learner must also become part of the learning process, actively involved in their own learning."

3 METHOD

The method used in the present study was quantitative approach making use of pre-experimental research design because there was one group taking place to learn pronunciation using NS of English pronunciation model. Due to the existence of one group and the comparison of two data (pre-test and post-test), the test result of both data were analyzed using dependent sample t-test because it compares the same group by doing the test twice, pre-test before the treatment and post test after the treatment.

3.1 *Participants, materials, and treatment condition*

The participants who became the subject of this study were the students of Universitas Kanjuruhan, Malang, Indonesia in English Education Department at semester three. They had

English pronunciation class once a week and had pre-test before the treatment and it lasted for six weeks before doing the post-test.

The materials used for treatment were taken from three different video files of Youtube. The first reference was accessed from A-bit Dotty (2014). This was a compilation of BBC learning English's well-known pronunciation clips. It included all the sounds found in 'British English' with a basic explanation which was very helpful for beginners. The second one was from Academic Skills, The University of Melbourne (2015). It dealt with stress patterns providing examples and exercise pertaining to word stress used for academic studies from different number of syllables in order to increase English fluency. The last one was accessed from JenniferESL (2017). It dealt with falling intonation in statements and wh-questions, rising intonation with yes/no questions, and fall-rise intonation to express hesitancy and in polite speech.

The rationale behind choosing these three different sources of videos was that, firstly, NNS of English could watch and repeat the sounds after NS demonstration from the video easily. So, these videos were considered to be learnable and teachable as a model to NNS in order to decrease their pronunciation deviation. Secondly, the videos could be accessed and downloaded freely, and thirdly, the lips movement was shown clearly to be a NS of English model.

NNS of English got treatment based on the materials we chose from videos and the activities were done as seen on Table 1.

3.2 *Instruments*

The instrument used in this study was pronunciation test. The test consisted of 20 question and answer items. This test measured the participants' pronunciation including *sound* which covers vowels, diphthongs, and consonants, *stress* which included primary and secondary stress for two-syllables and more than two syllables, and *intonation* which covered rising, falling, and sustain or rise-fall and fall-rise.

In terms of sounds, it included 40 items that cover the most difficult sounds for NNS such as /θ/ and /ð/, /ʃ/ and /ʒ/, /tʃ/ and /dʒ/, and / ɜː/ and / ə/ because they were so distinctive and hard to utter. In terms of stress, it included primary and secondary stress for two-syllables and more than two syllables which created difficulty for NNS because they were not found in their mother tongue (L1) language. In terms of intonation, it referred to pitch variation in the voice such as falling, rising, dipping (fall-rise), and peaking (rise-fall). This test was categorized as producing sound and the sound they produced were recorded and therefore it was said to be valid in terms of pronunciation test since it really measured what learners supposed to be measured.

3.3 *Data collection and analysis*

The data were collected from the students' pronunciation test and the students' performance were recorded using their android-based mobile phone. The recordings were collected and transcribed. It's aimed at making raters able to listen to the participants' performance at a later time after the test was completed. Next, the result of the transcription was scored using Deviation and

Table 1. Treatment condition based on the materials chosen.

Meetings	Activities	Researcher	Learners
1	Administering pre-test	Create the test of pronunciation	Do the test
2	Giving treatment of vowels and double vowels	Demonstrate and give examples of vowel and double vowel sounds	Produce the sounds as accepted as possible
3	Giving treatment of consonants	Demonstrate and give examples of consonants sounds	Produce the sounds as accepted as possible
4	Giving treatment of word stress	Demonstrate and give examples of word stress	Produce the sounds as accepted as possible
5	Giving treatment of intonation	Demonstrate and give examples of intonation	Produce the sounds as accepted as possible
6	Administering post-test	Create the test of pronunciation	Do the test

Non-Deviation or True-False of the sound, stress, and intonation production made by NNS. The score of sound (54 items), stress (35 items), and intonation (40 items) was then converted into 0 to 100 band score by dividing the Total Score from Maximum Score and multiplied by 100.

$$\text{Score: } \frac{\text{Total Score}}{\text{Maximum Score}} \times 100.$$

The pre-test and post-test scores were then stored in SPSS and analysed using dependent sample t-test since it compared one group performance twice or within-group comparison.

4 RESULT AND DISCUSSION

4.1 *Result*

The result of the present study was divided into two parts based on the research questions. The first part was the result of NNS of English pre-test and post-test on pronunciation including sound, stress, and intonation. Table 2 showed the result of the statistical analysis for *sound, stress,* and *intonation*, and Figure 1 showed the mean difference summary of NNS of English learners' pronunciation test used in this study. The result of both Table 2 and Figure 2 is elaborated as follows.

In terms of *sound*, it revealed that the paired sample t-test difference between pre-test and post-test were statistically significant at .05 significance level or 95% confidence because the probability (*p*) due to chance (.000) was lower than *alpha* level (.05), ($p < \alpha$, .020 < .05) and therefore, the null hypothesis was rejected. The mean of post-test was greater than the mean of pre-test (73.63 > 60.90) which means that using NS English sound model could perform better production on pronunciation, in terms of *sound*, than before using the model. In this case, NNS of English learners was able to adapt and adopt the intelligible pronunciation even

Table 2. Pronunciation score comparisons of pre-test and post-test of NNS of English learner.

No.	Variable	Group	N	Mean	Std. Deviation	t	Sig.*
1	Sound	Pre-test	32	60.90	13.73	−11.881	.000
		Post-test	32	73.63	10.30		
2	Stress	Pre-test	32	77.23	6.55	−10.345	.000
		Post-test	32	86.07	5.66		
3	Intonation	Pre-test	32	84.77	3.44	−19.287	.000
		Post-test	32	92.27	3.38		

*Significant was set at .05 level.

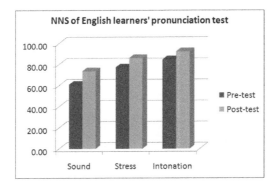

Figure 1. The mean difference summary of NNS of English learners' pronunciation test.

though there were still few deviations after the treatment, namely, to distinguish between sounds / θ / and / t / as in the words 'cloth' which was still pronounced /kl ɔʊt/ instead of /klɒθ/, the word "toothache" is pronounced /'tu:ꞯeɪtʃ/ instead of /'tuθ.eɪk/, the word "health" is pronounced /helt/ instead of /helθ/ and so forth.

With respect to *stress,* it revealed that the paired sample t-test difference between pre-test and post-test were statistically significant at .05 significance level or 95% confidence because the probability (*p*) due to chance (.000) was lower than *alpha* level (.05), (*p* < *α*, .000 < .05) and therefore, the null hypothesis was rejected. The mean of post-test was higher than the mean of pre-test (86.07 > 77.23) which means that using NS English stress pattern could perform better production on pronunciation, in terms of *stress*, than before using the model. NS' stress obviously affected NNS' pronunciation after learning from such stress patterns as two syllables, (••; ••) in service /'sɜ:.vɪs/ and refresh /rɪ'freʃ/, three syllables (•••; •••;) in hand-kerchief /'hæŋ.k ə.tʃi:f/ and collision /k ə'lɪʒ. ə n/, four syllables (••••; ••••) in identify /aɪ'den. tɪ.faɪ/ and literature /'lɪt. ə r.ɪ.tʃ ə r / and the like. So, the stress patterns could be said to be both learnable and teachable to NNS of English learners.

In relation to *intonation,* it revealed that the paired sample t-test difference between pre-test and post-test were statistically significant at .05 significance level or 95% confidence because the probability (*p*) due to chance (.000) was lower than *alpha* level (.05), (*p* < *α*, .000 < .05) and therefore, the null hypothesis was rejected. The mean of post-test was greater than the mean of pre-test (92.27 > 84.77) which means that using NS English intonation pattern could perform better production on pronunciation, in terms of *intonation*, than before using the model. NNS of English *intonation* decreased their deviation from the result of post test in comparison to their pre-test and it lead them to decrease their misunderstanding in question and answer as well.

The second part of the research finding was the extent to which pronunciation was gained pertaining to ELF development learned by NNS of English. This data was obtained from the test of each domain of pronunciation. From the result of the present study, NNS of English learners created more pronunciation deviation in terms of *intonation* than the other variables, *sound* and *stress*. It could be seen clearly from Figures 2a, 2b, and 2c. The only falling intonation that made NNS deviate more as they were accustomed to asking questions using rising intonation in their mother tongue (L1) language which was different from English intonation pattern. In general, questions initiated from Yes/No question mostly have rising intonation, but from Wh-questions have falling intonation. However, NNS of English were still influenced by their mother tongue language.

Exploring further to the result of *sound* including vowels, diphthongs, and consonants, it revealed that the paired sample t-test difference between pre-test and post-test were statistically significant at .05 significance level or 95% confidence because the probability (*p*) due to chance (.000) was lower than *alpha* level (.05), (*p* < *α*, .000 < .05) and therefore, the null hypothesis was

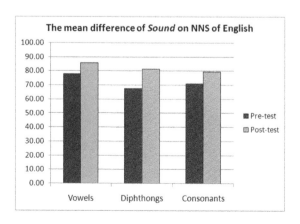

Figure 2a.   The mean difference of *Sound* on NNS of English.

Table 3.   The mean difference of *Sound* on NNS of English.

No.	Variable	Group	N	Mean	Std. Deviation	t	Sig.*
1	Vowels	Pre-test	32	77.93	10.53	−5.805	.000
		Post-test	32	85.74	6.96		
2	Diphthongs	Pre-test	32	67.41	10.41	−9.685	.000
		Post-test	32	81.47	5.08		
3	Consonants	Pre-test	32	71.09	15.04	−9.089	.000
		Post-test	32	79.43	13.22		

*Significant was set at .05 level.

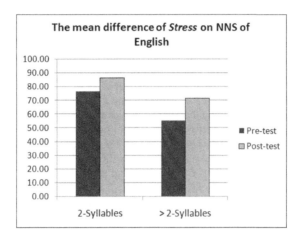

Figure 2b.   The mean difference of *Stress* on NNS of English.

Table 4.   The mean difference of *Stress* on NNS of English.

No.	Variable	Group	N	Mean	Std. Deviation	t	Sig.*
1	2 Syllables	Pre-test	32	76.67	9.12	−9.869	.000
		Post-test	32	86.46	8.55		
2	> 2 Syllables	Pre-test	32	67.41	14.81	−7.588	.000
		Post-test	32	71.56	10.81		

*Significant was set at .05 level.

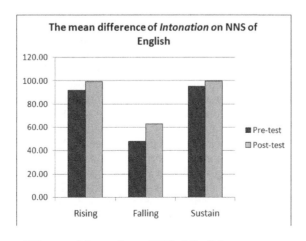

Figure 2c.   The mean difference of *Intonation* on NNS of English.

Table 5. The mean difference of *Intonation* on NNS of English.

No.	Variable	Group	N	Mean	Std. Deviation	t	Sig.*
1.	Rising	Pre-test	32	91.93	1.47	−17.311	.000
		Post-test	32	99.48	2.05		
2.	Falling	Pre-test	32	48.05	17.13	−8.186	.000
		Post-test	32	62.89	16.95		
3.	Sustain	Pre-test	32	95.16	.88	−17.311	.000
		Post-test	32	99.69	1.23		.000

*Significant was set at .05 level.

rejected. As seen on Table 3 that the mean of post-test of vowels, diphthongs, and consonants was greater than the mean of their pre-test (Vowels, 85.73 > 77.93), (Diphthongs, 81.47 > 67.41), and (Consonants, 79.43 > 71.09). It means that NNS of English created less deviation on English sounds in all domains including vowels, diphthongs, and consonants. The extent to these improvements as depicted from Figure 2a was that NNS increased steadily for vowels (85.73–77.93 = 7.81), for diphthongs (81.47–67.41 = 14.06), and for consonants (79.43–71.09 = 8.33).

Next, *Stress* which included investigation on 2 syllables and more than 2 syllables, revealed that the paired sample t-test difference between pre-test and post-test were statistically significant at .05 significance level or 95% confidence because the probability (*p*) due to chance (.000) was lower than *alpha* level (.05), (*p* < *α*, .000 < .05) and therefore, the null hypothesis was rejected. As seen on Table 4 that the mean of post-test of 2 syllables and more than 2 syllables was greater than the mean of their pre-test (2 Syllables, 86.46 > 76.67), (> 2 Syllables, 71.56 > 67.41). It means that NNS of English also created less deviation on English *Stress* both on 2 Syllables and more than 2 Syllables. The extent to these improvements as depicted from Figure 2b was that NNS increased steadily for 2 Syllables (86.46–76.67 = 9.79) and more than 2 Syllables (71.56–67.41 = 16.25).

Finally, *Intonation* which included investigation on *Rising*, *Falling*, and *Sustain*, revealed that the paired sample t-test difference between pre-test and post-test were statistically significant at .05 significance level or 95% confidence because the probability (*p*) due to chance (.000) was lower than *alpha* level (.05), (*p* < *α*, .000 < .05) and therefore, the null hypothesis was rejected. As seen on Table 5 that the mean of post-test of *Rising*, *Falling*, and *Sustain* was greater than the mean of their pre-test (*Rising*, 99.48 > 91.93), (*Falling*, 62.89 > 48.05), and (*Sustain*, 99.69 > 95.16). It means that NNS of English also created less deviation on English *Intonation* for *Rising*, *Falling*, and *Sustain*. The extent to these improvements as depicted from Figure 2c was that NNS increased steadily for *Rising* (99.48–91.93 = 7.55), for *Falling* (62.89–48.05 = 14.84), and for *Sustain* (99.69–95.16 = 4.53).

4.2 *Discussion*

The present study is aimed at answering two research questions (1) Do NNS of English develop their pronunciation subsequent to utilizing NS of English pronunciation model? (2) To what extent do NNS of English gain intelligible pronunciation of English as Lingua Franca? To answer the first research question, pre-test and post test were administered before and after the treatment. It was found that there was significant difference on NNS pronunciation performance between before and after treatment. NNS succeeded to improve and eliminated deviation in terms of sound, stress, and intonation since they were provided with video models which are easily observed and repeated based on A-bit Dotty (2014) BBC English demonstration with lips movement to produce sounds in accordance with their places of articulation. Also, they were provided with clear examples, presented by interesting slides to point out the stress pattern as shown by Academic Skills, The University of Melbourne (2015) make NNS possess clear direction where to practice demonstrating the stress pattern with ease from the model. With respect to intonation, JenniferESL (2017) associated with gestures and hands movement followed by tones that make NNS perceive intonation pattern better than only simply to repeat the sentence pattern.

Despite the need of pronunciation to promote mutual intelligibility across distinct culture and dialect background, intelligible English pronunciation can be encouraged through English NS pronunciation video model. This model should be linked to NNS daily communication. Therefore, to successfully incorporate this pronunciation and pragmatics matter, Jenkins (1998) proposes doing training to NNSs so they become aware of tolerance to possible L2 variation. By doing so, teachers and students get suitable attitudes to tolerate those variation. Being not native-like is just a characteristic for being the member of global English users. This is further supported by Shibata et al. (2015) who state possible drawbacks of doing such training, namely lacking teachers' confidence and not yeat available teaching 'guidelines' dealing with 'what and how to teach'. While for pragmatics, House (1999) states characteristics 'ELF interactants': 'ELF talk is short' (feel 'insecure' and just take part in the talk), 'Let-it-Pass' principle ('sufficient' understanding for the current talk), preference to 'waffle' (uttering 'too many words'), and inefficient 'turntaking management' ('unclear transition points' and 'job description') resulting in short of 'mutual responsibility'.

ELT with EFL approach is a shift in time allotment, as postulated by Deterding (2010) that teaching time allocation is not condensed but the time is better spent to do 'alternative' activities which are more 'productive'. For example, time spent on pronunciation drills can be better spent on more 'productive' tasks. His justification is that most learners cannot reach NS pronunciation, and too much drilling can be unbelievably 'demotivating', 'frustrating' and 'boring'. He proposes alternate approach by developing 'accommodation skills', because it is attainable, 'practical, 'productive' and bring tremendous joy. Moreover, Wach (2011) asserts although native speaker pronunciation is somewhat 'unnecessary' and 'unattainable', for some L2 learners it still is a 'priority'. For teachers, awareness and sensitivity of varieties of choices of 'pronunciation instruction' is valuable to facilitate them in doing adequate preparation.

5 CONCLUSIONS

As far as ELF pronunciation is concerned, Jenkins (1998) postulates three main areas focus: "Certain segmentals, nuclear stress (the main stress in a word group), and the effective use of articulatory setting". While for pragmatics, House (1999) states characteristics 'ELF interactants': 'ELF talk is short' (feel 'insecure' and just take part in the talk), 'Let-it-Pass' principle ('sufficient' understanding for the current talk), preference to 'waffle' (uttering 'too many words'), and inefficient 'turn-taking management' ('unclear transition points' and 'job description') resulting in short of 'mutual responsibitily'.

Jenkins et al. (2011) conclude that ELF main center of attention is on 'miscommunication' and 'the negotiation and resolution' of being unintelligible ('NON-UNDERSTANDING'). They claim that in doing so, EFL interlocutors involve in 'a joint effort' to mutually avoid 'nonunderstanding' among them. NNS also 'constructs identity' by making use of 'resources' attached to certain grup and 'not known' to another group.

Jenkins et al. (2011) are in line with statement of Deterding (2010) related to 'alternative' activities, they mention that there is growing interest in determining the features taken place in EFL interaction and growing evidence of the 'fluidity' and 'flexibility' of ELF communication. According to Jenkins et al. (2011), features that NNS prefer to do 'code-switch' in 'promoting solidarity' and 'projecting cultural identity', in addition they also 'accommodate' vast L1 backgrounds interlocutors which may result in 'error' in native-like domain.

House (1999) claims further that NNSs are lacking 'introductory lubricating element' that the interactants are not capable to do the appropriate commonly-used-way to acknowledge the closing of the talk. In conversation between NSs as well as advanced NNSs, usually the participants prefer to choose the most friendly and polite way in trying to end their chat.

According to Gilakjani (2012), positioning as a 'speech coach' is much preferable than being a checker for correct pronunciation which in the long run will encourage students to improve further. By doing so, learners with own 'unique aims' can manage to do pronunciation learning better.

Relating to the application, Deterding (2010) reveals assessment implementation problem. According to him, a fixed target is not yet available, especially what pronunciation features need to be emphasised. Above all, he succinctly gives better solution by considering the intelligibility of speakers in possible global context that those of being native like correctness.

To sum up, Shibata et al. (2015) believe that elements of intonation is worthwhile in determining meaning and this becomes the lack of proficiency amongst 'foreign learners of English'. Deterding (2010) adds that accommodating listeners need is also worthwhile, and it is 'practical', 'attainable', and 'fun' to teach 'accommodation skills'. The main aim is to be understood in 'global village'. Last but not least, he portrays current presentation using recordings from speakers worldwide, by this then global familiarity of different ways in speaking can be achieved.

ELT needs to adapt ELF approach to the teaching and learning process and adopt ELF emphasis more on understanding and successful communication. ELF interlocutors need to be aware and sensitive to mutually interact and cooperate in order not to deviate too far from the shared norms of being globally understood. Failing to do so can impede understanding and end up in communication problem even breakdown.

REFERENCES

A-bit Dotty. 2014, Aug 16. *RP phonemes: pronunciation tips (BBC learning English)* [Video file]. Retrieved from https://www.youtube.com/watch?v=htmkbIboG9Q

Academic Skills, The University of Melbourne. 2015, May 18. *Speaking Clearly-Word stress* [Video file]. Retrieved from https://www.youtube.com/watch?v=SNmEeNmIxNI&list=PLJSPTc0 K-PlR lz_HgJeIaqmtjMLjQt6UB&index=5

Block, D. & Cameron, D. (Eds.). 2002. *Globalization and language teaching*. London. Routledge.

Burridge, K. & Mulder, J.G. 1998. *English in Australia and New Zealand: An introduction to its history, structure, and use*. Oxford: Oxford University Press.

Deterding, D. 2010. ELF-based pronunciation teaching in China. *Chinese Journal of Applied Linguistics* 33(6): 3–15.

Gilakjani, A.P. 2012. A study of factors affecting EFL learners' English pronunciation learning and the strategies for instruction. *International Journal of Humanities and Social Science* 2(3): 119–128.

House, J. 1999. Misunderstanding in intercultural communication: Interactions in English as a lingua franca and the myth of mutual intelligibility. *Teaching and learning English as a global language, 7389*.

Jenkins, J. 1998. Which pronunciation norms and models for English as an International Language?. *ELT journal* 52(2): 119–126.

Jenkins, J., Cogo, A. & Dewey, M. 2011. Review of developments in research into English as a lingua franca. *Language teaching* 44(03): 281–315.

JenniferESL. 2017, Jan 10. *Falling Intonation – English Pronunciation with JenniferESL* [Video file]. Retrieved from https://www.youtube.com/watch?v=kksfqYcYkeg

_____. 2017, Feb 23. *Fall-Rise Intonation: English Pronunciation with JenniferESL* [Video file]. Retrieved from https://www.youtube.com/watch?v=8 NHa4cVHYBI

_____. 2017, Jan 12. *Rising Intonation—English Pronunciation with JenniferESL* [Video file]. Retrieved from https://www.youtube.com/watch?v=pT6aGkt4czQ

Kachru, B.B. 1992. The second diaspora of English. *English in its social contexts: Essays in historical sociolinguistics: 230–252.*

Kubota, R. 2002. The impact of globalization on language teaching in Japan. *Globalization and Language Teaching: 13–28.*

Nikbakht, H. 2010. EFL pronunciation teaching: A theoretical review. *Journal of Applied Linguistics* 4(8): 146–174.

Seidlhofer, B. 2001. Closing a conceptual gap: The case for a description of English as a lingua franca. *International Journal of Applied Linguistics* 11(2): 133–158.

Shibata, Y., Taniguchi, M. & Date, T. 2015. Teachability and learnability of English tonicity for Japanese junior high school students. *PTLC2015* 5 83. Wach, A. 2011. Native-speaker and NnglisU as a lingua franca pronunciation norms: NnglisU majors' views. *Studies in Second Language Learning and Teaching* (1–2): 247–266.

Wach, A. 2011. Native-speaker and English as a lingua franca pronunciation norms: English majors' views. *Studies in Second Language Learning and Teaching* 1(2): 247–266.

ELT in Asia in the Digital Era: Global Citizenship and Identity – Madya et al. (Eds)
© 2018 Taylor & Francis Group, London, ISBN 978-0-8153-7900-3

Visualizing ideal L2 self and enhancing L2 learning motivation, a pilot study among Chinese college students

C. Zou
Private Hualian University, Guangzhou, China

ABSTRACT: Ideal L2 self, ought to/fear L2 self and L2 learning experiences, the three major components of L2MSS was proposed by Dörnyei (2005) based on self-possible theory. The L2MSS formulated L2 motivation study for the past two decades in SLA field. Literature suggests that vision of ideal L2 self could generate motivational capacity if fitting for the pre-requisites. The current study validates the conclusion of previous literature, the data of the experiment indicated that vision of ideal L2 self will bring forth positive motivation capacity. Through intervention activities of building ideal L2 self, goals of L2 learning become much clearer, achieving significant differences, while intended effort and linguistic confidence will have to be enhanced through longitude study to achieve significant differences. This paper explores the plausibility to provide vision intervention for building Ideal L2 self in English teaching classroom and discuss the motivational capacity that visualization could generate.

1 INTRODUCTION

L2 learning motivation responds to a desire and sustained effort in learning a second language, especially for a relatively long period of time. Motivation is the decisive factor for the success of L2 learning. The dominant model of L2 motivation self system in recent decades proposed by Dörnyei (2005) focused on L2 learners motivating themselves to achieve ideal L2 self. According to Dörnyei (2014), Self-image is the guiding star which generates learners' motivated behavior, but, the future self-image, will not happen automatically, if without a marked increase in extended effort. So far, there are few empirical studies showing that L2 learners' self-image was created or enhanced, either from no vision to have one, or from opaque vision to a clearer one. Magid & Chan (2012) firstly put the theoretical guidelines of visualizing ideal L2 self into practice. They carried out two motivational programs which successfully enhanced learner's L2 motivation, measured by goals, intended effort and linguistic confidence. Based on Magid & Chan's study, this paper displays the empirical study the author conducted in a college in Guangdong, China, to validate the enhancement of ideal L2 self through intervention activities. Variables as goals, intended effort and linguistic confidence are observed through likert scale questionnaires.

2 LITERATURE

2.1 *Possible selves theory and L2MSS L2 motivational self system*

Self-possible theory was proposed by Markus & Nurius (1986) who labeled the self-concept of future dimension as "possible selves". Markus and Nurius distinguished three main types of imagined future selves: individual's ideas of what they might become; what they would like to become and what they are afraid of becoming. People view themselves in the present is not the same as they imagine themselves in the future and there is the gap between future self and current self. The motivational impact of future selves on behavior was explained by

Higgins (1987) with self—discrepancy theory. As Higgins put, people have unease feeling when there is discrepancy between their future self and current real—self. Mind doesn't like inconsistency between the aspired future self and real life one, therefore, desire, motivation is spurred to close the gap between dream and reality. In this sense, possible selves act as future self-guides, moving someone from the present to the desired future.

The L2 Motivational Self System (L2MSS; Dörnyei 2005), partly reflects the self-possible theory. Dr. Zoltán Dörnyei firstly proposed the model of L2MSS (L2 motivation self-system), which as a landmark for the research of L2 motivation and became the dominant model of motivation research in the field of SLA. According to Dörnyei (L2MSS, Dörnyei 2009), the L2 Motivation Self System is made up of three major components:

Ideal L2 self, which refers to one's ideal self. If the person we would like to become speaks an L2 (travelling or doing business internationally), we would have a strong motivation to learn the L2.

Ought to L2 self, which concerns the attributes we believe we ought to have in order to avoid possible negative outcomes, such as we don't want to fail the perceived duties, expectations from parents, friends, and obligations. The obligation which might bear little resemblance with our wishes or will, but we will still fulfill the responsibilities, such as to work hard to get credit for degree and earn necessary certificates.

L2 learning experiences, refers to situation-specific motives, such as the pleasant learning environment and experiences, positive impact of success, and enjoyable quality of a language courses. If a person gains success or pleasure from doing a task, probably he will do it again and perform better.

2.1.1 *Vision*

Ideal self, and ought to self, the two self-guides of possible selves are involved with images and senses. People can 'see' or 'hear' their possible future self (Ruvolo & Markus 1992, as cited in Csizér & Magid 2014). Van der Helm argues that the actual meaning of vision is capturing from three aspects:

1. the future
2. the ideal
3. the desire for deliberate change

Different from the abstract nature of goals, vision involves images, sensory feelings. It describes a vivid picture of how a person might be once he realized his goal, for example, a person's goal is to become a successful singer, and the vision of becoming a singer involves sound, shining costume and applaud, screaming from the fans etc., which is vivid and concrete.

2.1.2 *Mental imagery*

The concept of mental imagery refers to generating an imagined reality that we can see, hear, feel and taste, which is also described as 'visualizing'. The application of guided imagery has been broadly practiced with world-class athletes, for improving confidence, controlling anxiety, preparing for competitive situations and enhancing actual performance (Morris et al. 2005, as cited in Csizér & Magid 2014).

The mechanism behind the effectiveness of visualization is the structure of our brains. When we see something, there are certain neurons in our brain are firing that actually makes record. If we close our eyes imaging that we are looking at the same object again, the exact same neurons are firing again. In other words, the brain can't tell the difference between reality and imagination, which explains why dreams can be so vivid. When we imagine success, we are fooling our mind that it is real and mind doesn't know the difference between the two. If we visualize success again and again and persist with it, mind does not like inconsistency (see in self-discrepancy theory) and therefore, it will bring up the external reality to match the internal schema (Kosslyn et al. 2001).

Thus, L2 learners with a vivid and detailed self-image related to the practice of L2 are more likely to be motivated to take action. Vision of Ideal L2 user seems to be one of the most reliable predictors of learner's long-term intended effort.

As Dörnyei & Kubanyiova (2014) stressed, "Vision is one of the single most important factors with the domain of language learning: where there is a vision, there is a way" (cited in Csizér & Magid 2015, p.11). By imagine what they might become successfully using L2 in the future, L2 learners are likely be motivated to organize more efficient strategies for learning.

2.2 *Empirical studies validating L2MSS*

Dörnyei & Chan's study (2013) investigated 172 grade eight students learning English and Mandarin as target languages in Hongkong. The study identified significant relations between self guides (ideal self and ought-to self) and learners' L2-related learning effort and achievement. Meanwhile, the study also confirmed that mental visualization both visual style and audio style have significant correlation with future self-guided images. A very interesting finding of the study is that in the process of future guides motivating behavior, L2 is independent, that the ideal image related to English is distinct from that of Mandarin, but both of them play active role in the process of motivating. Therefore Dörnyei & Chan (2013) suggested that learner's sensory or image capacity is an important internal resource which can be internally harnessed. Dörnyei & Kubanyiova (2014) provide ample evidence that imagery skills are trainable; therefore, providing imagery training or guided image becomes possible to help students generate visions related to L2 learning.

You et al. (2016) conducted a large-scale, cross-sectional survey in China which investigated among 10,569 students in two different groups: secondary school pupils and university students. The results responded to several intriguing conclusions.

1. Imagery capacity makes a significant contribution to the motivational disposition of Chinese L2 learners, but it depends on initial recognition and activating of imagery skills. There could exit the situation that one has never experienced visualization, esp., L2 related visualization at all. The impact of vivid imagery on the ideal L2 self is twice as strong than that of ought to self, which means ought to selves are often less internalized.
2. Ideal L2 self had a relatively low direct impact on intended effort, rather, ideal L2 self exerted power on attitudes of L2 learning. The finding indicates that visualization experience does not directly and automatically lead to substantial motivational capacity. Attitudes to L2 learning remain the dominant generator and mediator of motivation. For the vision-no group, duties and obligations associated with ought to selves become a substantial driving force.
3. The data also found that among the vision-yes group, the proportion of females was higher than males, indicating that females are more amendable to L2 visualization than their males peers. Females are more likely to expand positively on their visualization experiences than males.
4. The dynamics of one's mental imagery: positive and negative changes in one's imagery affected the person's motivational disposition, which is highly connected with magnitude. Learners who experienced a positive change in their ideal self—image outscored those who experienced the negative change. The largest difference between positive and negative imagery experience was found in vividness of imagery, attitudes toward L2 learning, ease of using imagery which related to learner's ongoing experience. While these three variables have been found to be amendable through teacher's intervention in the classroom (You et al. 2016).

Magid & Chan's (2012) pioneering intervention programs (one in UK; the other one in HK), enhanced learner' vision of Ideal L2 self. The self-imagery activities enhance L2 learners' vision of ideal L2 self and learners became more motivated to learn English and became more confident with English learning. Different from investigations to prove correlation between vision or imagery and L2 learning, The imagery activities used in the study are practical and direct, including, "listing goals, drawing a timeline, developing action plans and imaging feared selves " (Magid & Chan 2012:116). Besides treatment of building vision of L2 self, there are enhancing activities to strengthen the vision, such as listening to the recording of the scripted imagery situations and language counseling, teacher offering suggested strategies for learners to achieve goals. The result of motivational program was very pleasant both in UK and HK and by enhancing their vision of their Ideal L2 self, the young Chinese university students were motivated to learn

English. The success of the two intervention programs firstly put the L2 Motivational Self System theory into practice, which offers inspiration and possibility for the current study.

3 THE CURRENT STUDY

3.1 *Research questions*

Theoretical framework and empirical studies have presented the significant function of vision. In practice, a learner's vision on ideal L2 self may be rather opaque or there could be no vision at all You et al. (2016). The current study observed how the participants' vision of ideal l2 self was enhanced through intervention. If there wasn't any among some participants, could the intervention help to generate? Also, variables of L2 learning such as goals, intended effort and linguistic confidence are to be observed. The likely research questions are as follows:

Q1: What effect will the visualized intervention have on the participant's ideal L2 self?
Q2: How will the participants' ideal L2 self-influence motivation, in terms of goals, intended effort, and linguistic self-confidence?

3.2 *Variables*

3.2.1 *Goals*
When we develop likert scale questionnaire to measure the change of L2 learners' goals before and after the intervention, two aspects of goals are to be concerned, mastery and performance. Ames (1992) summarized that children can adopt two contrasting goal orientations toward learning: mastery orientation and performance orientation. Mastery orientation focus on the mastery of a subject matter, or a certain skill; performance orientation involves getting good praise and demonstrate ability. Learners with a performance orientation place more emphasis on achieving public recognition and learning for the ultimate purpose of attaining high marks rather than for their own personal development (cited in Magid 2011).

3.2.2 *Intended effort & linguistic confidence*
The increases of intended effort or investment to learn a L2 might be due to the positive impact of Ideal L2 self. Goals, intended effort and linguistic confidence are chosen to be observed. Magid & Chan (2012) presented that the participants became more confident and have clearer goals after intervention. Here confidence is observed, to see whether clearer L2 goals in the future will bring forth more intended effort and confidence.

3.3 *Procedures*

The current pilot study offers to test the impact of intervention -- guided visualization of ideal L2 self, to see whether the guided self-imagery will have positive impact on learner's ideal L2 self and thus motivating L2 leaning capacity.

3.4 *Participants*

The pilot study was conducted in a college where 23 participants took part in, first year student in college, English major, averaged 20 years old, and all of them were female due to the fact that there was no male student in this natural class.

3.5 *Instrument*

3.5.1 *Measurement instrument*
The intervention was designed base on the previous study conducted by Magid & Chan (2012), Magid (2011) and Wang & Dai (2015). Two likert scale questionnaires measuring ideal L2 self and motivation capacity were used. The questionnaire of ideal L2 self was

designed based on the previous one (Magid 2011) and altered from four aspects associated with L2 motivation learning, "the most frequent themes associated with Chinese college students' (a college in Shanghai) L2 use are career, living and communicating abroad, entertainment, getting information and knowledge" (Wang & Dai 2015: 50).

3.5.2   *Intervention instrument*

The pilot study used two intervention activities: one is the ideal self image tree which was created by Hock, Deshler, & Shumaker (2006) and practiced by Magid & Chan (2012). The other one was the 'my ideal second language self action plans' which had been performed by Magid (2011) in an intervention program in UK. The action plan intended to put the participants in an urge to set up specific learning plan and set a timetable for achieving objectives.

3.6   *Experiment procedure*

In the beginning of the session, the researcher explained the definition of L2 self in language learning.

Immediately, a consent form about the experiment was handed out to students which provide information about the study (see in appendix B) and get the ethical approval from the participants.

Then, a likert-scale questionnaire of Ideal L2 self was filled in by the students (see in Appendix A); and a likert—scale questionnaire of motivation capacity (Appendix C) concerning goals, intended effort and linguistic confidence was filled in by the participants.

The participants then follow the researcher to close their eyes to imagine their future life related to L2 use in three dimensions: English learning, future career and personal life. The imagination went on for a few minutes.

The researcher asked questions as:

"What kind of person would you like to become in the future?
"from now on to three years, two years or six months?"
"Whom will you live with?"
"How are your friends?"
"What job you might be doing?"
"How is your English at that time? more fluent?"
"Will you become more confident and more successful?"

The questions were associated with L2 in their future work, personal life, social communication and learning. Then the participants opened their eyes, returned to the classroom and wrote down what they just came cross in their mind on the image tree (see Appendix D).

When the participants finished completing the image tree and they took a few minutes break. The other intervention activity was carrying on, a 'my ideal second language self action plans' with participants guided by a scripted imagery (see in Appendix E). The researcher read the script in the classroom and the participants closed their eyes and imagined they were having a successful job interview, after that they were asked to write down the objectives they would like to achieve, steps to take and exact timeline for the action.

Later, the two activities ended. The same questionnaires were filled by the participants. Considering the participants were intermediate or lower level English learners, the questionnaire and the intervention instruments were in both English in Chinese version.

3.7   *Results*

46 questionnaires were collected before the intervention activities and 44 questionnaires were collected after the intervention activities. One of the participants did not hand in the questionnaires after the intervention; One item in a questionnaire was rated with two answers; therefore only 21 participants' data was valid for analysis.

All the questionnaire results were recorded and analyzed with SPSS 19.0. The Cronbach Alpha of the questionnaire I measuring ideal self (Appendix A) is 0.937; the Cronbach Alpha of the questionnaire II measuring motivation capacity (Appendix C) is 0.850.

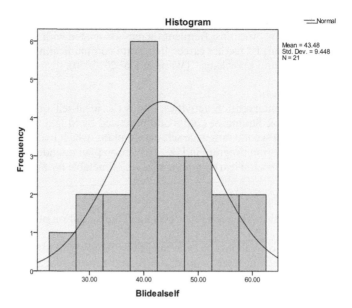

Figure 1.

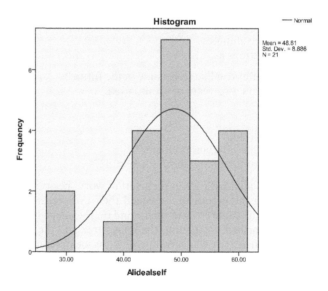

Figure 2.

Non-parametric test is adopted for analysis of significant difference instead of T-test since the data was not normally distributed.

The results of non-parametric test display the significant difference of ideal self between two groups, before intervention and after intervention (See Table 1).

The result (.002 < 0.05) indicates that after intervention, participants' vision of ideal L2 self has been enhanced, achieving significant differences.

The data from Table 2 indicated that variables related to L2 learning motivation and L2 learning goals presented significance after intervention activities. P = 0.005 < 0.05, p = 0.006 < 0.05.

The result (Table 1) indicates the intervention brought significant effect on participants' overall L2 learning motivation capacity, esp. L2 learning goals, while intended effort and confidence show no significant results.

Table 1.   Test statistics.

	AI ideal self – BI ideal self
Z	−3.058[a]
Asymp. Sig. (2-tailed)	.002

a. Based on negative ranks.
b. Wilcoxon Signed Ranks Test.
(BI ideal self refers to before intervention ideal L2 self; AI ideal self refers to after intervention ideal L2 self).

Table 2.

Test statistics[b]

	AI motivation – BI motivation	AI goals – BI goals	AI effort – BI effort	AI confidence – BI confidence
Z	−2.822[a]	−2.729[a]	−1.430[a]	−1.804[a]
Asymp. Sig. (2-tailed)	0.005	0.006	0.153	0.071

a. Based on negative ranks.
b. Wilcoxon Signed Ranks Test.
(AI motivation refers to motivation capacity after intervention, BI motivation refers to motivation capacity before intervention, so is with BI goals, AI goals; BI effort AI effort; BI confidence, AI confidence).

4 DISCUSSIONS

The finding of the current pilot study confirms Magid & Chan's (2012) study that L2 learners' vision of ideal L2 self is trainable and that among 21 participants, there are 15 participants have yielded stronger ideal L2 self vision after the intervention (see Table 3).

4.1 *(Response to RQ1) impact of visualization intervention on ideal L2 self*

RQ 1: What effect will the visualized intervention have on the participant's ideal L2 self?

The results indicated that the intervention activities have significant impact on learners' ideal L2 self (future career, living abroad and communicating with L2 native speakers, entertainment and acquiring information). As Table 1 ($0.002 < 0.05$) presents the significant difference and above 70% participants responded with significant enhancement of vision of ideal L2 self. Appropriate stimulation with vivid pictures and desired future career and life could remind learners that there still exist the dreams unfulfilled.

4.2 *(Response to RQ2) motivational capacities in terms of goals, intended effort and linguistic confidence*

RQ2: How the participants' ideal L2 self influence their L2 learning motivation, in terms of goals, intended effort, and linguistic self confidence?

The study measured three variables, goals, intended effort and linguistic confidence. Of the overall motivation capacity, 15 out of 21 participants responded with positive change (see in Tables 1 and 3), p value = $0.005 < 0.05$, which indicates that there is positive enhancement on the motivation especially L2 learning goals. While intended effort and linguistic confidence showed no significant difference. This could be due to not enough stimulation because there is only one session of vision enhancement. Concerning intended effort and linguistic confidence, less than a half of participants responded with positive results, which is in agreement with You et al.'s finding that, "The ideal L2 self had a relatively low direct impact on intended effort but exerted its power mainly indirectly through the mediation of attitudes to learning" (You et al. 2016:117).

Table 3.

		N	Mean Rank	Sum of Ranks
AI ideal self – BI ideal self	Negative Ranks	3[a]	5.17	15.50
	Positive Ranks	0.15[b]	10.37	155.50
	Ties	3[c]		
	Total	21		

a. AI ideal self < BI ideal self.
b. AI ideal self > BI ideal self.
c. AI ideal self = BI ideal self.

In other words, the participants with more vivid pictures of ideal self-image do not lead to substantial motivational capacity such as commitment for more intended effort, hard work or confidence. The finding is consistent with Dörnyei & Ushioda's (2011) argument that motivation capacity does not happen automatically along with future self-guides, and there are 9 main prerequisites for motivation to happen:

1. The learner has a desired future self-image.
2. The future self is sufficiently different from the currentself.
3. The future self-image is vivid and elaborate.
4. The future self-image is perceived as plausible (possible to come true)
5. The future self-image is not perceived as comfortably to reach. The learner must not believe that the possible self will happen automatically, without a marked increase in expended effort.
6. The future self-image is in harmony with expectations from learner's family, peers or other elements of the social environment.
7. The future self-image is accompanied by relevant and effective procedural strategies towards achieving the goals.
8. The future self-image is regularly activated in the learner's working self-concept. There are frequent and varied reminders.
9. The desire future self-image is offset by a counteracting feared possible self.

4.3 *Pedagogical notions*

L2 learning motivation could be enhanced and could bring positive results to learning. As a teacher teaching English in colleges where English is a compulsory subject, I always confront the situation that the students are de-motivated to learn. Then it came across to me that is it possible we help students build up their motivations to learn, in terms of intrinsically motivated or extrinsically motivated? The characteristic features of intrinsically motivated is self-initiated by choice and largely sustained by inherent enjoyment in the activity. While extrinsically motivated is that learning an L2 for ulterior goals, such as better salary, more prestigious job, and both work better than amotivation (demotivated). In extremely dys-functional cases, individuals may fail to see any internal or external value to their actions—amotivation (Ortega 2009). Such situation happens in the school I worked.

It seems possible that building ideal L2 self among learners is a plausible way to motivate them to learn. The current pilot study adopted two intervention activities to enhance learners' vision of ideal L2 self. Visualization provides a more clear and vivid picture for future learning and the enhancement will generate action to close the gap between possible self and current self.

5 CONCLUSIONS AND LIMITATION

The current study validates the previous literature that vision on learner's ideal L2 self is trainable with intervention activities, accordingly, L2 learning goals become clearer and more specific, however, concerning the impact of ideal L2 self on motivation capacity, the data presents that only vision will not automatically bring forth positive intended effort and linguistic confidence.

There are a number of limitations in this study that should be acknowledged.

5.1 Limitation 1

The current study focuses on one component of the L2 motivational system—ideal self, since it is a small scale pilot study. The vision of ought to self and fear L2 self has not been investigated, which leaves for future study. As the motivation generated by ought to oneself could be quite unique in Chinese context as Dörnyei & Chan (2013) stressed:

"Family duties and obligations play a more important role in shaping students' motivation in Asian-Chinese context than in many western learning contexts" (Shek & Chan, 1999, cited in Dörnyei & Chan, 2012, p. 444).

5.2 Limitation 2

The pilot study only used quantitative method to collect responses from participants, which might be less enough to have a deep understanding of the student's thinking, "a qualitative approach is more sensitive to the evolving dimension of language learning motivation" (Ushioda 2001, cited in Magid, 2011: 71).

"Qualitative data set, allows us to understand the thinking of participants more deeply than solely on the basis of a survey" (p.142–143).

Thus, a combined method of quantitative and qualitative is appreciated to see how participants' thinking and motivation evolved, especially a longitudinal one.

5.3 Limitation 3

The questionnaire used to observe the change of motivation capacity before and after the intervention is the same one, which may have negative effect because the learners have filled in the same questionnaire only one and a half hour ago, and the memory of the item might still be fresh. Should the same questionnaire be used again or should another one be designed (same content, different language) to use is a perplexing issue.

Since the current pilot study offers to test the experiment design, instrument for future study, the limitation will get noticed for improvement.

REFERENCES

Boo, Z., Dörnyei, Z. & Ryan, S. 2015. L2 motivation research 2005e2014: Understanding a publication surge and a changing landscape. *System* 55: 145–157.

Chan, L. 2014. Handbook of imagination and mental simulation. *Innovation in Language Learning and Teaching* 8(1): 94–98.

Dörnyei, Z. 2005. *The psychology of the language learner: Individual differences in second language acquisition.* Mahwah, NJ: Lawrence Erlbaum.

Dörnyei, Z. 2009. The L2 motivational self system. In Z.Dörnyei & E.Ushioda (Eds.), *Motivation, language identity and the L2 self (9–42).* Clevedon, Multilingual Matters.

Dörnyei, Z. 2014. Future self-guides and vision. In Csizér & Magid (Eds.), *The impact of self-concept on language learning.* Bristol: Multilingual Matters.

Dörnyei, Z. & Chan, L. 2013. Motivation and vision: An analysis of future L2 self images, sensory styles, and imagery capacity across two target languages. *Language Learning* 63(3): 437–462.

Dörnyei, Z. & Kubanyiova, M. 2014. *Motivating learners, motivating teachers: Building vision in the language classroom.* Cambridge: Cambridge University Press.

Dörnyei, Z. & Ushioda, E. 2011. *Teaching and researching information (2nd. ed).* Harlow, UK: Pearson Education.

Higgins, E.T. 1987. Self-discrepancy: A theory relating to self and affect. *Psychological Review* 94: 319–340.

Hock, M.F., Deshler, D.D. & Shumaker, J.B.. 2006. Enhancing student motivation through the pursuit of possible selves. In Dunkel, C. & Kerpelman, J. (ed.), *Possible selves: Theory, Research and Application (205–21)*. New York: Nova Science.

Kosslyn, S. M., Thompson, W. L. & Ganis, G. 2001. Neural foundations of imagery. *Nature Reviews Neuroscience* 2 (9): 635–642.

Magid, M. 2011. A validation and application of the L2 motivational self system among Chinese learners of English. (Doctoral dissertation, UK: University of Nottingham).

Magid, M. 2012. The L2 motivational self system from a Chinese perspective: A mixed methodology study. *Journal of Applied Linguistics* 6:69–90.

Magid, M. & Chan, L. 2012. Motivating English learners by helping them visualize their ideal L2 self: lessons from two motivational programmes. *Innovation in Language Learning and Teaching* 6(2): 113–125.

Markus, H. & Nurius, P. 1986. Possible selves. *American Psychologist* 41: 954–969.

Morris, T., Soittle, M. & Watt, A.P. 2005. *Imagey in sport*. Champaign, IL: Human Kinetics.

Ortega, L. 2009. *Understanding second language acquisition*. London: Hodder Education.

Shek, D. T. L., & Chan, L. K. 1999. Hong Kong Chinese parents' perceptions of the ideal child. *Journal of Psychology* 133: 291–302.

Wang, X. & Dai, W. 2015. An empirical study of L2 motivational strategies based on L2 motivation self system. *Foreign Language Education* 36(6): 48–52.

You, C., Dörnyei, Z. & Csizér, K. 2016. Motivation, vision, and gender: A survey of learners of English in China. *Language Learning* 66(1): 94–123.

Participant Questionnaire I

Strongly Disagree	Disagree	Slightly disagree	Slightly agree	Agree	Strongly Agree
1	2	3	4	5	6

(Example) If you stongly agree with the following statement, write this:

I like eating ice-cream very much.   1 2 3 4 5 ⑥

1	I can imagine my self speaking English with clients in fluent English. 我可以想象和外国客户用英语流利地交流。	1 2 3 4 5 6
2	I can imagine myself speaking English with international colleagues. 我可以想象和国外同事用英语交流	1 2 3 4 5 6
3	Whenever I think of my future career, I imagine myself using English. 无论将来的职业是什么，我可以想象用英语交流。	1 2 3 4 5 6
4	I can imagine myself making a speech in English. 我可以想象自己用英语发表讲话。	1 2 3 4 5 6
5	I can imagine myself communicating in English with foreign friends, even boy friends or girl friend in English, as if I were a native speaker of English. 我可以想象我用英语像母语一样和外国朋友，男朋友或女朋友交流。	1 2 3 4 5 6
6	I can imagine myself living abroad and using English effectively for communicating with the locals. 我可以想象自己在国外生活并用英语和当地人交流 。	1 2 3 4 5 6
7	I can imagine myself travelling abroad, using English. 我可以想象自己到外国旅游，用英语实现自由行。	1 2 3 4 5 6
8	I can imagine myself texting with friends or talking with friends on social media with English. 我可以想象自己在社交媒体上用英语发信息或语音，视频。	1 2 3 4 5 6
9	I can imagine myself reading English newspaper or glance English websites without pressure. 我可以想象自己打开英语的报纸或网站时无压力阅览。	1 2 3 4 5 6
10	I can imagine myself watching English movies, programs without referring to the Chinese subtitles. 我可以想象自己看英文电影，节目，美剧英剧无需看中文字幕。	1 2 3 4 5 6

Appendix B

Principal Researcher: Chunyan Zou
Phone: +86 13533126612
Email: C.Y.Zou@student.reading.ac.uk

Participant information sheet

Research Project:

Visualizing Ideal L2 self and enhancing L2 learning motivation, a pilot study among Chinese

college students. 建立理想自我和二语学习动机：中国大学生英语学习试点研究

Researcher's name: Chunyan Zou 研究人员：邹春燕

We would like to invite you to take part in a research study about learning English.
我们欢迎你参加这个关于中国学习者学习英语的研究

What is the study?

The study is conducted by Chunyan Zou, currently a MA student of University of Reading, UK. It aims to investigate the building of vision of ideal L2 self and impact on motivation capacity among Chinese college students. It hopes to make a pedagogical notion for more efficient teaching and learning English in China through enhancing ideal L2 self of learners.

The study will involve learners participating in a session taught by the researcher, and the procedure includes filling in two questionnaires before and after the intervention and follow the guided imagery activity.

Why have I been chosen to take part?

You have been invited to take part in the project because your participation in our project is really important. In the previous teaching the researcher noticed the motivation issues of the students learning English and if students' motivation were enhanced they would learn better. Your participation will test the instrument of the study, which is going to be used for future study, also it will provide pedagogical implication for the researcher as well as for the teachers teaching English in China.

Do I have to take part?

It is entirely up to you whether you participate. You may also withdraw your consent to participation at any time during the project, without any repercussions to you, by contacting the researcher Chunyan Zou Tel: +8613533126612, Email: C.Y.Zou@student.reading.ac.uk

What will happen if I take part?

You will be asked to complete two set of short questionnaire about the ideal self and the motivation capacity. This should take about 10 minutes to complete.

You will follow the researcher during the session she taught, which is going to last for 60 minutes.

What are the risks and benefits of taking part?

The information you give will remain confidential and will only be seen by the researcher. Neither you, or the school will be identifiable in any published report resulting from the study. Information about individuals will not be shared with the school.

Participants in similar studies have found it interesting to take part. We anticipate that the findings of the study will be useful for teachers in planning how they teach English.

What will happen to the data?

Any data collected will be held in strict confidence and no real names will be used in this study or in any subsequent publications. The records of this study will be kept private. No identifiers linking you, the teacher or the school to the study will be included in any sort of report

 **University of Reading**

Principal Researcher: Chunyan Zou
Phone: +86 13533126612
Email: C.Y.Zou@student.reading.ac.uk

that might be published. Participants will be assigned a number and will be referred to by that number in all records. Research records will be stored securely in a locked filing cabinet and on a password-protected computer and only the researcher will have access to the records. The data will be destroyed securely once the findings of the study are written up, after five years. The results of the study will be presented at national and international conferences, and in written reports and articles. We can send you electronic copies of these publications if you wish.

What happens if I change my mind?

You can change your mind at any time without any repercussions. During the research, you can stop completing the activities at any time. If you change your mind after data collection has ended, we will discard your data.

Who has reviewed the study?

This project has been reviewed following the procedures of the University Research Ethics Committee and has been given a favourable ethical opinion for conduct. The University has the appropriate insurances in place. Full details are available on request.

What happens if something goes wrong?

In the unlikely case of concern or complaint, you can contact the researcher Chunyan Zou; Tel: +86 13533126612, email: C.Y.Zou@student.reading.ac.uk

Where can I get more information?

If you would like more information, please contact Chunyan Zou

Tel:+86 13533126612, email: C.Y.Zou@student.reading.ac.uk

We do hope that you will agree to your participation in the study. If you do, please complete the attached consent form and return it to the researcher.

Thank you for your time.

<u>Participant Consent Form</u>

I have read the Information Sheet about the project and received a copy of it. ☐

I understand what the purpose of the project is and what is required of me. All my questions have been answered. ☐

I consent to completing two questionnaires ☐

I consent to the participation in the teaching session ☐

Signed:_____ Date: _____

Participant Questionnaire II

Strongly Disagree	Disagree	Slightly disagree	Slightly agree	Agree	Strongly Agree
1	2	3	4	5	6

(Example) If you stongly agree with the following statement, write this:

I like eating ice-cream very much.   1 2 3 4 5 (6)

1	I have clear goals for improving English. 对于如何提高英语我有具体的目标。	1 2 3 4 5 6
2	I have detailed plan for studying English 对于英语学习现在有详细的计划。	1 2 3 4 5 6
3	I have clear thought about using English in future career. 将来如何在职场上使用英语我有了清晰的想法。	1 2 3 4 5 6
4	I am prepared to extend a lot of effort in learning English. 我准备很努力地学习英语。	1 2 3 4 5 6
5	I would like to spend a lot of time studying English. 我愿意花大量的时间来学习英语。	1 2 3 4 5 6
6	I would like to form good habit of studying English, make time efficient. 我想养成良好的学习英语的习惯，让时间变得有效率。	1 2 3 4 5 6
7	I have confidence in communicating with English. 我现在能自信地使用英语交际。	1 2 3 4 5 6
8	I know confidence is the key to successful and happy English learning. 自信是快乐学习，学好英语的关键。	1 2 3 4 5 6
9	I am not afraid of making mistakes while speaking and using English. 我不怕在使用英语的过程中犯错。	1 2 3 4 5 6

Ideal Self Tree 理想树

Now imagine the ideal you in the future, and put you and your English learning, future career and personal life on the tree. You may also draw small braches indicating your action plan.

现在，请想象一下理想中的你是怎样的一个人？

如何学英语，未来的理想职业是什么？

及美好的情感生活是怎样的？

请把它们写出来，放在意象树的不同位置上，也可以在树枝写上实现理想必须的要素.

The Perfect interview

Close your eyes and imagine that today is the day of a very important job interview in a large, famous, international company that you have been dreaming of working in for a long time. This job could be in any part of the world where you would like to live. You have prepared very well for the interview and as you get dressed, you are feeling really confident that you will do well. As you look at yourself in the mirror, you are happy with how professional and mature you look.

You arrive at the company a few minutes before the interview and are feeling very calm as you wait to be called into the boss's office. When you step into his or her office, you can see that the boss is impressed by your business like appearance, your friendly, confident smile and your firm handshake. He or she asks you to sit down and starts to ask you questions. Although some of the questions are quite difficult, you are able to use your excellent English to answer all of them extremely well. You can see that the boss is pleased and very satisfied with all of your answers. The boss is also impressed by your fluency, grammar, vocabulary, and pronunciation in English. You show him or her that you have so much knowledge, so many skills, and are highly qualified for this job of your dreams. As the interview ends, there is no doubt in your mind that you will get this job. Stay with this feeling of complete confidence as you open your eyes and come back to this room.

My Ideal Second Language Self Action Plans

My objective is: _____

(an objective you want to achieve about English learning, vocabulary, speaking, reading etc.)

What I need to do is: _____

step 1 _____

step 2 _____

step 3 _____

step 4 _____

......

I am going to start this objective on _____ (Write the date.)

I will review my progress on _____ (Write the date.) by

_____ (Write your way to test your progress.)

My objective is: _____ (another

objective that you want to achieve on English learning vocabulary, speaking, reading etc.)

What I need to do is: _____

step 1 _____

step 2

step 3 _____

step 4 _____

I am going to start this objective on _____ (Write the date).

I will review my progress on _____ (Write the date.) by

_____ (Write your way to test your progress).

ELT in Asia in the Digital Era: Global Citizenship and Identity – Madya et al. (Eds)
© 2018 Taylor & Francis Group, London, ISBN 978-0-8153-7900-3

The potential of mobile technology in testing and enhancing L2 word recognition from speech

J. Matthews
University of New England, Armidale, Australia

ABSTRACT: Successful second language (L2) listening comprehension depends on the ability to recognize L2 words in connected speech. Despite this dependence, approaches to developing L2 word recognition from speech (WRS) have received relatively limited interest from researchers. This paper will briefly overview recent research that has begun filling this gap in existing knowledge. First, an approach to testing L2 WRS will be described, and the capacity of these test scores to predict L2 listening test performance will be presented. The design of a simple computer-mediated approach that is effective in the development of L2 WRS will then be overviewed. Next, the potential to integrate and deliver these testing and learning approaches through smartphone technology will be discussed. Lastly, the potential to enhance L2 WRS through mobile-assisted means will be briefly discussed as an example of how integrated technologies hold the potential to change aspects of English teaching in the digital era.

1 INTRODUCTION

Second language (L2) listening is a skill that learners find particularly challenging. In order to comprehend an utterance, L2 listeners must simultaneously process both non-linguistic and linguistic information in real time under considerable time constraints. Accordingly, contemporary approaches to teaching L2 listening are influenced by the idea that successful listening is facilitated through parallel processing involving both top-down and bottom-up components. Top-down processes importantly involve the application of metacognitive knowledge, which involves the listener's awareness of the cognitive processes engaged during listening, and the capacity to exert executive control over these processes (Vandergrift & Goh 2012: 2). Bottom-up processes entail the application of linguistic knowledge to recognise the sequences of meaning bearing units within the speech stream, most importantly words.

Research suggests that L2 listening instruction should actively encourage learners to effectively apply their metacognitive knowledge while listening (Vandergrift et al. 2006). However, there is also an emerging body of empirical evidence which suggests that the development of L2 vocabulary knowledge is also critically important for successful L2 listening comprehension (Matthews 2018). For example, Vandergrift and Baker (2015) investigated the relationship between L2 listening comprehension and a number of variables important to L2 listening, including L2 vocabulary knowledge and metacognition. Vandergrift and Baker (2015) found, from among three cohorts of learners investigated over three separate years, L2 vocabulary knowledge was the strongest correlate with L2 listening comprehension ($r = 0.51$, $p < 0.01$). Other comparable research undertaken within the Asian teaching English as a foreign language (TEFL) context has drawn similar conclusions. Wang and Treffers-Daller (2017) investigated the link between L2 listening comprehension and variables including general language proficiency, metacognitive awareness and L2 vocabulary knowledge among 151 tertiary level students in China. Results confirmed that among the variables measured L2 vocabulary knowledge possessed the strongest correlation with L2 listening comprehension scores ($r = 0.44$, $p < 0.01$).

As L2 vocabulary knowledge is an important construct underpinning successful L2 listening, the systematic development of learners' L2 vocabulary knowledge should have a positive impact on L2 listening comprehension (Vandergrift & Baker 2015: 411). However, any systematic effort to enhance L2 vocabulary knowledge in the support of L2 listening comprehension should emphasise constructs of word knowledge which depend on the ability to recognise the form of words as they occur in connected speech (Matthews 2018, Stæhr 2009). This is key as one of the reasons why L2 learners have difficulty in recognising words from speech, relates not only to a lack of vocabulary knowledge, but also specifically to a lack of knowledge of the words as they occur in the spoken form (Cross 2009). Exemplifying this, Goh (2000) noted during a study involving tertiary level Chinese learners of English that learners often knew words by sight, but were unable to recognise those same words when presented in speech, and that this deficit caused considerable difficulties with L2 listening success.

Recent research emphasises the specificity and strength of the relationship between measures of word knowledge in the aural modality and L2 listening comprehension. Cheng and Matthews (2018) compared the relative strength of the relationships between three forms of vocabulary knowledge and the L2 listening comprehension of 250 tertiary level learners in the People's Republic of China. One of the test formats required test takers to process word knowledge from the aural modality, whereas the other two tests presented test stimulus material only in the written form. Results from multiple regression modelling showed that measures of L2 vocabulary knowledge from the test that depended on the recognition of words in the spoken form could account for 52 percent of the variance observed in L2 listening scores. On the other hand, measures of vocabulary knowledge that were not mediated through the spoken form contributed only a little over one percent to the predictive capacity of the regression models. These results emphasise the need to provide L2 learners with ample opportunities to develop the capacity to recognise L2 words from the aural modality, and the specificity of this capacity in the support of L2 listening comprehension.

The proceeding introduction highlights the importance of the ability to recognise L2 words from speech in facilitating L2 listening comprehension success. Despite this importance, there is a surprising lack of modern and practical tools that can be systematically used to develop L2 word recognition among cohorts of EFL learners. It is argued here that there is strong importance in the development of such tools. This is especially the case as it seems very likely that a limited capacity in L2 word recognition is at the heart of many EFL students' difficulties with L2 listening comprehension. It is further argued that the affordances of smartphones, coupled with their almost ubiquitous presence in the digital era, present a particularly valuable means by which to facilitate better word recognition capacities among language learners. As will be overviewed in the following sections, smartphones have the potential to help language learners develop this capacity through the delivery of integrated learning and testing models. The development of such mobile-assisted tools, which have been tailored to specifically develop L2 WRS, will provide a valuable asset for the efficient development of L2 listening capacities into the future.

2   TESTING L2 WORD RECOGNITION FROM SPEECH

Of central importance to the successful, systematic development of any given language proficiency construct is the implementation of test instruments that adequately measure that construct. Although vocabulary tests are typically presented in the written form only, there are existing test formats that can be used to measure L2 learners' capacity to recognise words from speech. One testing approach that does entail test takers processing word knowledge in the aural modality, and which has been of interest to teachers and researchers in the Asian context for some time is partial dictation (Cai 2013, Coniam 1995, 1998). Partial dictation involves test takers listening to a spoken text, and using their recognition of elements within this spoken stimulus to fill gaps in the corresponding written text that has target words removed from it. This test format is useful in measuring L2 WRS as it requires the test taker to explicitly evidence their recognition of the form of target words as they are enunciated in connected L2 speech.

Test scores from partial dictation tests are strongly associated with L2 listening comprehension scores. Matthews and Cheng (2015) administered a partial dictation test among 167 tertiary level Chinese learners, which measured knowledge of target words from the first, second and third thousand frequency level. Scores on the partial dictation test were strongly correlated with scores on a version of the IELTS listening test ($r = 0.73$, $p < 0.01$), and were able to predict approximately 54 percent of the variance observed in the listening test scores. Partial dictation presents a practical way to test L2 students' capacity to recognise L2 words from speech. This test format enables test developers to conveniently select and systematically test knowledge of important target words, and the resultant data can be used to diagnose areas of weakness and to rationalise targeted interventions. Importantly, partial dictation tests are also able to be automatically administered and scored through use of computational devices, including smartphones (Matthews et al. 2017).

Partial dictation is a useful approach to measuring L2 a learner's capacity to recognise words in speech, and smartphones have the required affordances to facilitate this test type relatively easily. Despite this, there is little sign in the published literature that mobile devices like smartphones have been extensively used to deliver partial dictation tests to L2 learners. It is argued here that the use of mobile phones to deliver these types of tests represents a valuable opportunity to systematically measure and enhance L2 learners' listening success.

3 DEVELOPING L2 WORD RECOGNITION FROM SPEECH

In order to build the capacity to recognise words from L2 speech, it is necessary to ensure that learners have sufficient opportunities to engage with target vocabulary items in the spoken form (Hulstijn 2003). However, facilitating opportunities for learners to be exposed to sufficient levels of spoken language input can be challenging in learning contexts where socially contextualised immersion is extremely difficult. Even though in the digital era it is possible to provide learners with floods of aural stimulus (e.g., podcast, video news texts, etc.), without sufficient scaffolding such exposure is likely to be overwhelming and demotivating for many students. Additionally, when devising learning interventions, it is important that they have the capacity to deliver measurable learning outcomes that reflect key competency benchmarks. In this regard, computer technology has a strong role to play as it can be used to systematically develop L2 WRS among large cohorts of learners. Further, measures indicative of L2 WRS development can be stored and tracked on the device itself and on centralised databases.

Hulstijn (2003) has described the design of a simple computer program which provides learners with multiple opportunities to listen to connected target speech, and further provides learners with the opportunity to reconstruct this speech into the written form. A key feature of the program is that learners can listen to short sections of text as often as they wish through interaction with the computer interface as they attempt to reconstruct the text. Once satisfied with their effort to transcribe the text, learners can click the computer interface and receive feedback on the accuracy of their reconstruction. In order to facilitate noticing of errors in perception of spoken forms, feedback can include the correct target text shown side by side with the learner's effort at reconstruction with discrepancies highlighted (Matthews & O'Toole 2015).

Matthews et al. (2015) used a quasi-experimental research design with 96 tertiary level Chinese learners of English to investigate the efficacy of an elaborated form of the suggestions put forward by Hulstijn (2003). Learners in the treatment groups had the opportunity to use a web application for a period of five weeks. The application facilitated opportunities for learners to repeatedly listen to sections of connected speech, reconstruct the spoken text into the written form, and then receive automated feedback on their reconstruction accuracy. A comparison of word recognition gain scores between those who used the application (treatment groups) and those who did not (the control group) indicated that use of the application was associated with significant improvements in word recognition from speech scores. The results from Matthews et al. (2015) provide a valid starting point from which to base other interventions seeking to systematically develop the L2 WRS capacity of L2 learners.

Models specially aimed at the development of L2 WRS have been articulated in previous research, and these models have been shown to yield measureable improvement in EFL learners' WRS capacities. Previous research describing these models (Hulstijn 2003, Matthews et al. 2015) has employed traditional computers (i.e., desktops & laptops) as the hub for the related learning experiences; however, smartphones also have the capacity to deliver these models (Matthews et al. 2017). Moreover, in recent years ownership and extensive use of powerful handheld computers (viz., smartphones) has become very widespread. Indeed, this ownership and use is also clearly evident among younger cohorts; the same cohorts that are very often the prime focus of broad and institutionalised language development programs. Another key advantage of the mobile-assisted delivery of such learning models is the 'anytime-anywhere' engagement opportunities afforded by these mobile devices.

4 MOBILE-ASSISTED LEARNING AND THE DEVELOPMENT OF L2 WORD RECOGNITION FROM SPEECH

The affordances of smartphones (e.g., Internet connectivity, local and remote data storage capacity, touch screen interface, automated provision of onscreen feedback, etc.) offer ample capacity to deliver both the testing and learning approaches overviewed in previous sections. For example, smartphones can readily facilitate partial dictation tests. Speech samples for the test can be delivered to or stored in the device, and test takers can use headphones to listen to this stimulus. The written components of the partial dictation test can be presented to the test taker on the screen of the smartphone, and the test taker can use the touch screen keyboard to evidence their recognition of the target words. Test takers can move from one test item to the next with "click to continue" panels on the user interface. Similarly, smartphones also have the capacity to deliver the very simple reconstruction task described above (Hulstijn 2003) that has been shown to deliver measurable improvements in L2 WRS among L2 learners (Matthews et al. 2015, Matthews & O'Toole 2015).

A smartphone application which will deliver both the testing and learning modules as described here is currently under development. The application presents opportunities for low stakes, formative testing to be delivered to learners over an extended period. The current testing module proposes to implement partial dictation tests to systematically test word recognition of the 3000 most frequent words of the English language, as this level of knowledge is likely to provide approximately 95% coverage of spoken discourse (Adolphs & Schmitt 2003). As an example, a block of 25 partial dictation test items will take approximately 5 minutes to complete. If undertaken every day for a two-year period this would enable learners to be tested on each of the 3000 most frequent words of the English language six times over. Randomised delivery of the order of target words in the testing blocks would ensure that each testing session was unique. Further, adaptive algorithms can recycle words which are unsuccessfully recognised by test takers. A collection of statistics updated after each test event can record word recognition scores, and provide lists of words which have and have not yet been recognised accurately.

The learning modules can provide a large variety of authentic spoken texts presented to the learner first in full, and then in shorter fragments. A selection of texts which accord with the learning objectives or personal interest of the learners can be used as listening text stimulus. Learners can listen to the speech fragments as often as they wish as they attempt to reconstruct the text through the use of the touch screen on the smartphone. After submitting their attempt at reconstruction, feedback indicating the accuracy of the reconstruction can be automatically supplied. What is suggested is regular, but brief, use of the learning modules. A five-minute session with the learning module followed by a testing session on the testing module, such as that suggested previously, represents a time investment of just ten minutes. Thus, with a time investment of a little over one hour per week, it is suggested that the WRS capabilities of large cohorts can be positively influenced through use of this application. A clear advantage of this type of approach is that L2 WRS development can be allocated as an out of class learning task, and learners can undertake this task at a time that suits them most. There are also administrative and pedagogical advantages of the proposed application. Statistics relating to the learner's interaction with the application can be stored and analysed by teachers and unit coordinators through accessing a back-end database interface. Metrics generated by learner interaction with an application of this type can form an assessable component of online mediated components of blended learning.

In summary, what is envisaged here is the use of smartphone technology to efficiently tackle a significant language learning problem for EFL learners, namely L2 WRS. All the required pieces of the puzzle are on the table: an appropriate test format; an empirically validated learning approach (Hulstijn 2003, Matthews et al. 2015); the capacity to automatically track learner progress and learning outcomes over time; as well as the technological affordance required to integrate and deliver these testing and learning approaches. To effectively harness the potential smartphone technology has in the development of L2 WRS, ongoing efforts in the design, implementation, and evaluation of such learning technology is required. This in turn will necessarily involve collaboration between multiple stakeholders such as teachers, researchers, coders, interface designers and educational management units.

5   A CASE OF INNOVATION AND LANGUAGE LEARNING IN THE DIGITAL ERA

Currently the level of ownership and frequency of use of smartphones among our learners is vast, and this reality presents both opportunities and challenges to the TEFL community. Moving forward into the digital era, an important concern for language teaching professionals is to establish a collective understanding of the aspects of L2 learning which can be effectively enhanced through engagement with the affordances offered by mobile technology. This understanding, coupled with access to effective mobile-assisted language learning technology, represents some vital links in the chain leading toward future best practice in TEFL. One such example has been presented here; mobile-technology has the potential to facilitate interventions which can contribute to the development of L2 WRS. Relatively straightforward smartphone technology can be used to deliver an automated testing and learning intervention for the development of this important component of skilled L2 listening comprehension. As discussed, the use of this type of application not only enables relatively autonomous testing and learning that can take place outside of the classroom, but also enables details of the learner's interaction with the application to be stored and accessed by back-end users for diagnostic and blended assessment purposes. The substantive engagement with this type of smartphone application is predicted to have a powerful and positive influence on the development of L2 listening capabilities in cohorts of EFL learners into the future.

REFERENCES

Adolphs, S. & Schmitt, N. 2003. Lexical coverage of spoken discourse. *Applied linguistics* 24(4): 425–438.
Cai, H. 2013. Partial dictation as a measure of EFL listening proficiency: Evidence from confirmatory factor analysis. *Language Testing* 30(2): 177–199.
Cheng, J. & Matthews, J. 2018. The relationship between three measures of L2 vocabulary knowledge and L2 listening and reading. *Language Testing* 35(1): 3–25.
Coniam, D. 1995. Computerized dictation for assessing listening proficiency. *Calico Journal* 13(2/3): 73–85.
Coniam, D. 1998. Interactive evaluation of listening comprehension: How the context may help. *Computer Assisted Language Learning* 11(1): 35–53.
Cross, J. 2009. Diagnosing the process, text, and intrusion problems responsible for L2 listeners' decoding errors. *Asian EFL Journal* 11: 31–53.
Goh, C.C. 2000. A cognitive perspective on language learners' listening comprehension problems *System* 28: 55–75.

Hulstijn J.H. 2003. Connectionist models of language processing and the training of listening skills with the aid of multimedia software. *Computer Assisted Language Learning* 16(5): 413–425.

Matthews J. & Cheng J. 2015. Recognition of high frequency words from speech as a predictor of L2 listening comprehension. *System* 52: 1–13.

Matthews J., Cheng J., O'Toole J.M. 2015. Computer-mediated input, output and feedback in the development of L2 word recognition from speech. *ReCALL* 27: 321–339.

Matthews, J. & O'Toole, J.M. 2015. Investigating an innovative computer application to improve L2 word recognition from speech. *Computer Assisted Language Learning* 28(4): 364–382.

Matthews, J. 2018. Vocabulary for listening: Emerging evidence for high and mid-frequency vocabulary knowledge. *System* 72: 23–36.

Matthews, J., O'Toole, J.M. & Chen, S. 2017. The impact of word recognition from speech (WRS) proficiency level on interaction, task success and word learning: design implications for CALL to develop L2 WRS. *Computer Assisted Language Learning* 30(1–2): 22–43.

Stæhr, L. 2009. Vocabulary knowledge and advanced listening comprehension in English as a foreign language. *Studies in second language acquisition* 31(4): 577–607.

Vandergrift, L. & Baker, S. 2015. Learner variables in second language listening comprehension: An exploratory path analysis. *Language Learning*, 65: 390–416.

Vandergrift, L. & Goh, C.C. 2012. *Teaching and learning second language listening: Metacognition in action.* New York: Routledge.

Vandergrift, L., Goh, C., Mareschal, C.J. & Tafaghodtari, M.H. 2006. The metacognitive awareness listening questionnaire: Development and validation. *Language learning*, 56: 431–462.

Wang, Y. & Treffers-Daller, J. 2017 Explaining listening comprehension among L2 learners of English: The contribution of general language proficiency, vocabulary knowledge and metacognitive awareness. *System* 65: 139–150.

ELT in Asia in the Digital Era: Global Citizenship and Identity – Madya et al. (Eds)
© 2018 Taylor & Francis Group, London, ISBN 978-0-8153-7900-3

Does exposure to L2 affect cultural intelligence?

Z. Nafissi & N. Salmasi
Alzahra University, Tehran, Iran

ABSTRACT: Despite the emphasis on internationalizing higher education, fewer than 7% of college-level students meet the basic standards for Cultural Intelligence (CQ) (Lopes-Murphy 2014). The present study intended to find the relationship between students' CQ and the learned 2nd language and sought to determine the difference between Freshmen and Senior undergraduates of 5 different language majors. 198 participants were chosen through convenient sampling in a mixed method design in which the CQ conceptual questionnaire (Earley & Ang 2003) was utilized. The four components of CQ (i.e., metacognitive, cognitive, motivational, and behavioral) were analyzed quantitatively leading to no significant difference between freshmen and senior students. However, the cognitive and motivational component analysis showed a significant difference between the Russian and Farsi groups. The results illustrated a significant behavioral component difference between English and Farsi groups. The conclusion is that studying a foreign language proves to be positively correlated with some of the components of CQ.

1 INTRODUCTION

1.1 *Definition*

The world is experiencing a new era of close communication and global interactions. This has resulted in fast-paced, complex and multicultural operations which call for certain skills and abilities. This change, also known as globalization, makes the world seem like a country with one unified culture, nonetheless it remains an immensely varied place. This variety causes more frictions as the people interact more closely with one another.

Almost 20 years ago, a set of skills was recognized among the more effective communicators. These success stories depicted more effective communications and relationships at their work place. Through studies and research, cultural intelligence (CQ) was introduced as a new tool to the business world and distinguished 'leaders' from 'global leaders'.

The importance of CQ was first highlighted among business executives who were mostly looking for effective global leadership to manage the workforce properly. According to Earley & Ang (2003), global leaders with a higher rate of success across international arenas are considered to have a high level of CQ.

Various definitions have been given for Cultural Intelligence, but what all point to is a personal ability or skill through which one can engage, adapt, function, manage and interact appropriately with people in new culture settings (Ang & Van Dyne 2008, Bucher 2008, Earley et al. 2006, Peterson 2004, Thoman & Inkson 2004).

Having a clear definition of CQ paved the way for developing a model for it. The models which were introduced for CQ slightly vary regarding their terminology. Livermore (2011) established a model in which four interrelated elements were shown: CQ drive, i.e. the interest, drive and confidence to adapt to multicultural situations, CQ knowledge, i.e. the understanding about how cultures are similar and different, CQ action, i.e. the ability to adapt when relating and working in an intercultural setting, and CQ strategy, i.e. the awareness and ability to plan for multicultural interactions.

According to Ang & Van Dyne (2008) CQ "is a multidimensional construct which comprises four factors: (1) metacognition CQ, or one's mental capability to acquire and understand cultural knowledge; (2) cognitive CQ, or one's knowledge about cultures and cultural differences; (3) motivational CQ, or one's capability to direct and sustain effort toward functioning in intercultural situations, and (4) behavioral CQ, or one's capacity for behavioral flexibility in cross-cultural interactions". Additionally, Earley & Ang (2003) claim that without having a certain level of all the factors mentioned above one cannot be capable of having a successful international experience.

Another model was put forth by Thomas & Inkson (2004) including three components: knowledge, one's sufficient level of knowledge in order to understand cross-cultural differences; mindfulness, one's ability to monitor and comprehend cross-cultural situations; and behavioral skills, one's ability to adapt their behavior to the cross-cultural situations accordingly.

1.2 The importance of the study

Students who major in foreign languages are mostly seeking jobs in multinational institutions and companies, therefore it is the educators' responsibility to prepare them in a way that enables them to function properly within those cultural settings.

Recent developments in CQ have heightened the need for more discussion about various aspects of culture and language. So far, not enough attention has been paid to foreign languages and how they affect CQ. However, there were studies regarding CQ and its effect on the four language skills (Ervin 1992), on listening comprehension and CQ (Ghonsooly et al. 2013), on interlanguage pragmatics (Tajeddin & Momenian 2012), on the learners' interests in language learning (Tsou 2005) and on how to raise cultural awareness through 'cultural class' (Genc & Bada 2005).

Due to the gap in the literature, this study strived to measure and determine the effect of learning different foreign languages on learners' level of cultural intelligence.

The paper begins with a brief overview of research on CQ. Method and procedure of the study, data collection and data analysis will be explained and the results discussed.

2 LITERATURE REVIEW

2.1 Culture and language

A considerable amount of literature has been published on CQ which can be classified into two main categories: one is leadership, organizational management, globalization and personality traits in multicultural institutions, and another one is language performance of the learners. The first category has conclusively shown that people with higher CQ perform increasingly more effectively than people with lower CQ (Ang et al. 2007, D'Netto & Verghese 2011, Tan & Ang 2012).

The second category distinctively focused on the role culture plays in language learning and the use of language functions (Ghonsooly et al. 2013, Rezaei & Bavali 2017, Tajeddin & Momenian 2012). The idea of dependency of human nature on culture was put forth by McDevitt (2004) who emphasized the mutual relationship between language and culture.

This relationship has gained considerable popularity during the past decades; numerous justifications have been reached through studies on cultural factors and their effects on language learning (Bakhtiarvand & Adinevand 2011, Kitao 2000, Othman & Vanathas 2004).

A large and growing body of literature has investigated CQ using the Four-Factor Model of CQ developed by Ang et al. (2004).

2.2 Cultural intelligence

Considering how different or similar CQ is in comparison with Emotional Intelligence (EQ) (the ability to perceive the emotional states of others and to regulate one's own emotional state in the service of improved interactions, Goleman (1995) or Intelligence Quotient (IQ) defined by Resing & Drenth (2007) as "The whole of cognitive or intellectual abilities required to obtain knowledge, and to use that knowledge in a good way to solve problems that have a well described goal and structure.", two main distinctions can be stated: The assessment of CQ differs greatly from what usually takes place when assessing EQ or IQ. The standardized tests designed to assess them are only mathematical derivations (Mackintosh 1998). Since showing CQ is a cultural phenomenon a standardized test cannot fully capture its essence.

The performance and success of each individual can be different regarding various intelligences. For instance, Earley & Ang (2003) indicated that one who operated well in EQ in their own culture does not necessarily perform well in cross-cultural settings. Having a high CQ however, enables the interlocutors to perform well and appropriate in multicultural environments.

2.3 *Four factors*

Over the past ten years, CQ has developed from a theoretical concept to a measurable construct with strong psychometric properties and evidence of construct validity (Ang, Van Dyne & Rocksuhl 2015).

Ang et al. (2007) stated four factors comprising CQ in their model. These dimensions together create an overall capability to adapt and interact effectively in a culturally diverse situation. The correlation among these factors may not seem very strong; however, they form and shape CQ as a whole. These factors are: motivational CQ, metacognitive CQ, cognitive CQ, and behavioral CQ.

3 METHOD

In most recent studies, CQ has been measured through the Four-Factor Model of CQ, interviews and observations. Therefore, the researchers decided to utilize a questionnaire and a semi-structured interview for collecting the necessary data.

3.1 *Participants*

The initial sample consisted of 200 Iranian female Persian speakers, aged between 17–36, studying for a bachelor's degree in the department of Literature at Alzahra University, Tehran, Iran.

The classes of 2016 (first year students) and 2012 (last year students) in each discipline, i.e. Farsi literature, French translation, English literature, Arabic language and Russian language, were chosen for comparison. Four of these disciplines are foreign languages (L2) and one, Farsi, is the participants' L1, acting as a control group. The participants were chosen through convenience sampling.

3.2 *Instruments*

3.2.1 *Cultural Quotient Scale (CQS) questionnaire*
The 20-item cultural intelligence scale by Ang et al. (2004) was used as the main instrument of the study. The validity and the suitability of the questionnaire has been examined through six studies the first of which led to the scale development, and four studies proved the generalizability of the questionnaire across samples, time, countries, and methods, the last one addressed discriminant and incremental validity of the CQS (Van Dyne et al. 2008).

For ease of administration, CQS was translated into the participants' L1, i.e. Farsi. The back-translation technique was used to validate the reliability of the results and eschew misunderstanding of any kind.

3.2.2 *Interviews*

A semi-structured interview was carried out to enrich the data and obtain an in-depth point of view from the participants. The interviews were conducted with one first year student (freshman) and one final year student (senior) from each discipline. The interviewees volunteered to participate and signed the consent form before conducting the interview.

3.3 *Procedure*

In order to identify the level of CQ among the five chosen disciplines, the participants were asked to complete the questionnaire devised by Ang et al. (2004), which took 15 minutes to be completed. The class instructor and the researcher were both present at the time of data collection.

The questionnaires were distributed and collected in all ten classes by the researcher with her presence during the whole process observing and monitoring the participants.

To enable the participants to complete the questionnaires in the best way possible, first, a short introduction was provided on CQ and the aim of the study, then a brief explanation on the items was provided by the researcher, and participants' questions were answered during the process.

The participants were required to mark the questionnaire if they were willing to participate in an interview regarding the same topic. Among those who marked the interview box, random selection was carried out for the interview.

The interview took place at the time of the participants' convenience inside the university and took almost half an hour.

In an attempt to make each interviewee feel as comfortable as possible, the interviewer started out by talking about the participant's background and personal reasons for studying a language her major.

To control for bias, the interviewer avoided any sort of idea sharing, sympathizing, approval or dismissal of ideas.

The themes and codes were chosen and the frequency of occurrence was manually calculated based on McCracken (1988).

3.4 *Data analysis*

3.4.1 *Quantitative data*

The data gathered from the questionnaires was inputted in the IBM SPSS version 22 and analyzed. One-way between-groups ANOVA statistical technique was used, alongside post-hoc test, Tukey.

The CQ of each major was calculated and the results showed that senior Farsi sank to the bottom of the list, followed quickly by freshman Arabic and Farsi groups.

It is apparent from Table 1 that the control group with no involvement of a second language proved to have the lowest CQ among the participants. This could probably indicate the

Table 1.   Total mean CQ (dependent variable).

Major	Mean	Std. Deviation	N
Farsi2012	86.7826	12.77767	23
Farsi2016	92.1146	14.16172	24
English2012	104.4000	13.20845	20
English2016	94.8095	10.64715	21
French2012	102.9667	14.29344	15
French2016	93.0682	16.61615	22
Russian2012	92.2727	10.47942	11
Russian2016	102.7000	16.19621	29
Arabic2012	93.6667	11.29159	9
Arabic2016	89.8507	13.44334	24
Total	95.3054	14.78351	198

fact that L2 and exposure to L2 does have an effect on having a higher CQ. Table 1 shows the total mean of each discipline.

The equality of all groups regarding metacognitive CQ factor evidently proved no significant difference among them. Therefore, the ability to understand and learn about culture existed in all 4 foreign language groups as well as the control group, Farsi.

Table 2 shows the results of data analysis regarding the metacognitive CQ factor; the groups have been put in order from the lowest to the highest score.

Regarding Cognitive CQ factor, the groups with the lowest score were the Farsi senior group and the Farsi freshman group (Table 4). The Russian freshman group with the highest cognitive CQ factor showed a significant difference at the $p = 0.05$ level (Table 3).

The lowest score for behavioral CQ factor was observed in the Farsi senior group. The English senior group with the highest score showed a significant difference compared with the Farsi senior group at the $p = 0.05$ level (Table 5).

Table 6 shows the between groups comparison and the behavioral CQ factor ranked from the lowest to the highest score.

Although the motivational CQ factor came first in the questionnaire, it has been decided to be dealt with last since the differences were much more significant.

Both French senior and Russian freshman groups showed higher motivational CQ than senior and freshman Farsi groups.

Three groups French senior, English senior and Russian freshman students evidently showed higher motivational CQ than Arabic freshman group.

Table 7 shows the detailed result of the significant results regarding the motivational CQ factor score.

The most striking result to emerge from this data is that the motivational factor was mostly evident in English, Russian and French language learners, therefore it could be concluded

Table 2.   Metacognitive factor, post-hoc Tukey.

Tukey HSD[a,b,c]

		Subset
Major	N	1
Russian2012	11	19.4545
Arabic2016	23	19.7246
English2016	21	20.0000
Farsi2012	23	20.1304
Arabic2012	9	20.8889
Farsi2016	24	21.0417
Russian2016	29	21.3793
French2016	21	21.4762
English2012	20	22.1500
French2012	15	22.8667
Sig.		.128

Table 3.   Russian Freshman and Farsi Senior groups' cognitive CQ factor.

Total cognitive

Tukey HSD

(I) Major	(J) Major	Mean Difference (I-J)	Std. Error	Sig.	95% Confidence interval	
					Lower bound	Upper bound
Russian2016	Farsi2012	5.3124*	1.56415	.028	.3032	10.3217

353

Table 4. Cognitive factor, post-hoc Tukey.

Tukey HSD[a,b,c]

Major	N	Subset 1
Farsi2012	23	21.9565
Farsi2016	24	23.7500
Russian2012	11	24.1818
Arabic2012	9	24.4444
Arabic2016	23	24.5217
French2012	15	24.6000
English2016	21	24.6190
French2016	21	25.3810
English2012	20	27.0500
Russian2016	29	27.2690
Sig.		0.147

Table 5. English and Farsi Senior groups' behavioral CQ factor.

Total behavioral

Tukey HSD

(I) Major	(J) Major	Mean Difference (I-J)	Std. Error	Sig.	95% Confidence interval Lower bound	Upper bound
Farsi2012	English2012	−6.0717*	1.78001	.027	−11.7719	−.3716

Table 6. Behavioral factor, post-hoc Tukey.

Tukey HSD[a,b,c]

Major	N	Subset 1
Farsi2012	23	21.4783
Arabic2012	9	22.1111
French2016	22	23.0909
Arabic2016	23	23.6522
Farsi2016	24	23.9167
English2016	21	23.9524
Russian2012	11	24.4545
Russian2016	29	25.7414
French2012	15	27.3000
English2012	20	27.5500
Sig.		0.071

that the ability to maintain and sustain efforts toward functioning properly in cross-cultural situations stems from second language acquisition. Later on it will be seen from the qualitative data that generally students in these disciplines are the ones who are mostly happy with what they are studying.

The results of all the majors and the motivational CQ factor analysis are shown in Table 8 in more detail.

Table 7. Motivational CQ factor.

Total motivational

Tukey HSD

(I) Major	(J) Major	Mean Difference (I-J)	Std. Error	Sig.	95% Confidence interval	
					Lower bound	Upper bound
Russian2016	Farsi2012	5.0930*	1.28911	0.004	0.9648	9.2211
	Farsi2016	4.9041*	1.27404	0.006	0.8242	8.9840
	Arabic2016	6.0603*	1.28911	0.000	1.9322	10.1885
English2012	Arabic2016	5.4000*	1.41158	0.007	0.8797	9.9203
French2012	Farsi2012	4.9826*	1.53226	0.043	0.0758	9.8894
	Farsi2016	4.7938	1.51961	0.057	−0.0725	9.6600
	Arabic2016	5.9500*	1.53226	0.005	1.0432	10.8568

Table 8. Motivational factor, post-hoc Tukey.

Tukey HSD[a,b,c]

Major	N	Subset		
		1	2	3
Arabic2016	23	22.2500		
Farsi2012	23	23.2174	23.2174	
Farsi2016	24	23.4062	23.4062	23.4062
Russian2012	11	24.1818	24.1818	24.1818
French2016	22	25.2500	25.2500	25.2500
Arabic2012	9	26.2222	26.2222	26.2222
English2016	21	26.2381	26.2381	26.2381
English2012	20		27.6500	27.6500
French2012	15		28.2000	28.2000
Russian2016	29			28.3103
Sig.		0.251	0.053	0.061

3.4.2 Qualitative data

Turning now to interviews on the cultural awareness of the participants, we shall see that the motivation to pursue their major is highest in the English group followed by the French group.

Each interview was conducted in a university classroom in Persian language (participant's L1). Seven open-ended questions were asked, the answers were manually recorded, since the interviewees refused consent for interviews to be audio recorded. Later the questions and answers were translated into English and the emergent themes for each question was coded.

During the interviews some notes were made regarding the attitude and behavior of the interviewees. For the themes to emerge the five stages proposed by McCracken (1988) were followed by the researchers. Table 9 shows the results of the interviews.

The results of the qualitative data are briefly discussed as follows:

1. Educational system as the main reason for studying a major
The high-stake tests: 45% of the students believed that they somehow did not have a choice in choosing their major.
2. Educators:
A few thought they did not gain enough information about the culture through the educators and professors.

Table 9. Themes extracted from the interviews.

Majors Codes	Reasons for studying	Cultural awareness (CA)	Best ways to raise CA	Comparison Source and target culture	Link between the languages	Appropriate function in cross-cultural settings	Motivation and interest in knowing about the culture
Farsi2012	Forced	High	Living the context	Incomparable	Strong	Yes	No
Farsi2016	Interest	Average	Books	Source culture	Weak	Yes	Yes
English2012	Best choice	Low	Living in the context	Incomparable	Strong	No	Yes
English2016	Interest	High	Media	Target culture	Strong	No	Yes
French2012	Interest	High	Media & Living	Incomparable	Strong	Yes	Yes
French2016	Forced	Low	Living the culture	Incomparable	Weak	No	No
Russian2012	Forced	Low	Living in the context	Incomparable	Weak	No	No
Russian2016	Interest	Low	Living in the context	Incomparable	Weak	No	Yes
Arabic2012	Interest	High	Media & Living	Source culture	Strong	Yes	Yes
Arabic2016	Forced	Low	Living the culture	Similar	Strong	Yes	No

3. Confidence
Farsi and Arabic language students had more confidence in being culturally active than other majors.
4. Motivation
The freshmen in English, and Russian languages showed more motivation in learning about the culture of the language they are studying.
5. Language and culture link
60% of the students believed the link between language and culture is very strong.

The cultural awareness result of each group was based on the way they answered the questions about the link between language and culture, as well as the differences between their own culture and the target language culture. The answers which reflected a weak link between language and culture and lack of knowledge about one's culture in comparison with the target culture were considered signs of low awareness.

The different ways that the participants proposed to raise cultural knowledge and intelligence were nearly equal, some insisted on having a firsthand experience rather than reading about it and some stated the importance of media.

The last two columns reflect the motivational and behavioral factors. Some of the answers were in line with the quantitative data analysis, however some others were contradictory to what was found. This could probably be because of the fact that only one participant from each group was interviewed.

4   LIMITATIONS OF THE STUDY

This study like any other study suffers from some limitations. One limitation was having intact classes with unequal number of students. The average of the sample size for each group was 20, however the Arabic group (year 2012) had only nine participants. It is hard to determine to what extent this has affected the results of the study, therefore a larger sample and equal sample size for each group is well-advised. Also the small population under study inhibits the researcher from generalizing the results.

Another major source of uncertainty is in the limited number of participants who took part in the interview and also the method used to calculate the result of the interviews; most probably a computerized software would have had a more objective outcome but due to the limited number of interviewees it was not feasible. Having done the coding manually is subjected to bias and possible errors.

5 DISCUSSION

A strong relationship between CQ and language performance has been reported in the literature (Ghonsooly et al. 2013, Rezaei & Bavali 2017, Tajeddin & Momenian 2012). Students who study languages are seeking jobs at international companies related to inter-cultural settings. Therefore, studying the CQ of language graduates could be of great importance to the future of these students. Previous studies claim that having cultural training will improve an individual's cultural intelligence and perhaps render them more qualified for an international work experience. This study set out with the aim of assessing the students' CQ after studying a second language for four years as their university major. It was also carried out to determine which second language among the four was the most effective in raising the students' CQ.

Most empirical studies focused on what CQ predicts, however the present study focused on whether learning a foreign language can predict a high CQ or not. Since having high CQ positively corresponds to better performance in all different fields (Ang et al. 2007; Ang et al. 2006, D'Netto & Verghese 2011, Ng et al. 2012), it is invaluable to know which components contribute to increasing CQ.

It has been stated that CQ components are steps towards enhancing overall CQ (Dyne et al. 2010). In the present study, the components were compared both as a whole construct, as well as individual variables. The result of this study indicates what may not have been seen in the previous studies. The only CQ component which was not significantly higher after learning L2 was the metacognitive factor. Therefore, it can be claimed that L2 does have an effect; however, the extent of it on CQ is not the same for all the foreign languages under study.

The findings of this study suggest that studying a second language in itself triggers motivational, cognitive, and behavioral factors of CQ. English, French and Russian learners are positively inclined towards learning more about different cultures, especially through active participation in cultural events, learning new languages and interaction with other cultures.

On the contrary, the achievement of educational goals (obtaining a certificate, passing marks, etc.) took preference over cultural intelligence and cultural gains in both Farsi groups. The students in senior Farsi group and Arabic freshmen group with the poorest score on CQ sank to the bottom of the list, followed quickly by Farsi freshman group and Arabic senior group. Both Farsi groups who were not exposed to L2 proved the overarching hypothesis. Both Arabic groups were mostly at the bottom of the CQ table which might be because of the familiarity of the participants with the Arabic culture as a result of shared religion, the abundance of Arabic words in Persian language and the closeness of the two cultures.

Russian students may have higher scores for specific factors, nevertheless senior English group with more experience with this language proved to have the highest cultural intelligence scores, resulting to the fact that learning a second language can have positive effects on learners' CQ.

The significance of the study was mainly in the motivational factor which indicated that the Russian, English and French group scored higher than the Arabic and the Farsi groups. Evidently the Russian freshman by outscoring the Farsi senior group regarding the cognitive factor, and the English senior group by outscoring Farsi senior group in behavioral factor indicate how being exposed to a foreign language can positively affect an individual's CQ.

The result of this study proves there is an urgency and need for course work and academic training on cross-cultural competency (Eisenberg et al. 2013).

The results of the present study only show the female students' CQ, however a similar study which worked on both genders showed that female participants differ significantly from their male counterparts regarding their metacognitve CQ (Khodadady & Ghahari 2011).

Considering the fact that CQ determines success, individuals who seek to improve their CQ should be aware that learning another language will help them in achieving this goal. The present study showed that people who know at least one second language have higher cultural intelligence than people who only know one language, which is why candidates who know at least one foreign language are more likely to get hired. Similar studies resonated with the idea of CQ as a selection tool to identify the best candidates (Ng et al. 2009).

6 SUGGESTIONS FOR FURTHER STUDIES

Suggestions for syllabus designers and material developers can be provided to create new programs and materials in which language learners study the culture as well as the language. Functions of the language can be taught to enhance the behavioral factors rather than only the vocabulary items and grammar. Fostering methods of teaching language functions in different cultural settings with an analysis of the outcome will enhance knowledge of CQ which later can be turned into strategy CQ and action CQ.

Researchers are well advised to conduct a longitudinal study following first year language students and administering a CQ questionnaire each year of the study up to graduation to be able to have a more thorough comparison.

REFERENCES

Ang, S., Van Dyne, L. Koh, C.S.K. & Ng, K.Y. 2004. The measurement of cultural intelligence. Paper presented at the Academy of Management Symposium on cultural intelligence in 21st century, New Orleans, L.A.

Ang, S., Van Dyne, L. & Koh, C. 2006. Personality correlates of the four-factor model of cultural intelligence, *group & organization management* 31(1): 100–123.

Ang, S., Van Dyne, L., Koh, C., Ng, K. Y., Templre, K. J., Tay, C. & Chandrasekar, N.A. 2007. Cultural intelligence: It's measurement and effects on cultural judgment and decision making, cultural adaptation and task performance. *Management and Organization Review* 3: 335–371.

Ang, S. & Inkpen, A. 2008. Cultural intelligence and offshore outsourcing success: A framework of firm-level intercultural capability. *Decision Sciences* 39(3): 337–358.

Ang, S., Van Dyne, L. & Rockstuhl, T. 2015. *Handbook of advances in culture and psychology* 5: 273–322. Oxford University Press.

Bakhtiarivand, M. & Adinevand, S. 2011. Is listening comprehension influenced by the cultural knowledge of the learners? A case study of Iranian EFL pre-intermediate learners. *RELC Journal* 42(2): 111–124.

Bucher, R. 2008. *Building Cultural Intelligence (CQ) nine megaskills.* Upper Saddle River, NJ: Pearson Education Inc.

Earley, P.C. & Ang, S. 2003. *Cultural intelligence: Individual interactions across cultures.* Palo Alto, CA: Stanford University Press.

Earley, P.C., Ang, S. & Tan, J. 2006. *CQ: Developing cultural intelligence at work.* Palo Alto, CA: Stanford University Press.

Eisenberg, J., Hyun-Jung, L., Bruck, F., Brenner, B., Claes, M., Mironski, J. & Bell, R. 2013. Can business schools make students culturally competent? Effects of cross-cultural management courses on cultural intelligence. *Academy of Management Learning & Education* 12(4): 603–621.

Ervin, B.K. 1992. Does knowledge of culture and instruction using thematic units affect listening comprehension. *Reading Psychology Journal* 12: 43–61.

Friedman, T.L. 2005. *The world is flat: A brief history of the twenty-first century.* New York: Farrar, Straus and Giroux.

Genc, B. & Bada, E. 2005. Culture in language learning and teaching. *The Reading Matrix* 5: 73–84.

Ghonsooly, B., Sharififar, M., Sistani, S.R., & Ghahari, S. 2013. Cultural intelligence in foreign language learning context. *Cultus* 47–68.

Goleman, D. 1995. *Emotional intelligence*. New York: Bantam Books.

Hofstede, G. 1991. *Culture and organizations: Software of the mind,* London: McGraw Hill.

Khodaday, E. & Ghahari, S. 2011. Validation of the Persian cultural intelligence scale and exploring its relationship with gender, education, travelling abroad and place of living. *Global Journal of Human Social Science* 11(7): 64–76.

Kitao, K. 2000. Teaching culture in foreign language instruction in the United States. Retrieved from http://icl2.doshisha.ac.jp/users/kkitao/library/article/culture.htm.

Livermore, D.A. 2011. *The cultural intelligence difference: master the one skill you can't do without in today's global economy.* New York: AMACOM, American Management Association.

Mackintosh, N.J. 1998. *IQ and human intelligence*, Oxford: Oxford University Press.

McCracken, G. 1988. *The long interview*. Newbury park, CA: Sage Publication.

McDevitt, B. 2004. Negotiating the syllabus: a win-win situation. *ELT Journal* 58(1): 3–9.

Ng, K.Y., Tan, M.L. & Ang, S. 2009. *Handbook of international human resource management*. Chapter 5. 98–113.

Ng, K.Y., Tan, M.L. & Ang, S. 2012. Culture capital and cosmopolitan human capital: The impact of global mindset and organizational routines on developing cultural intelligence and international experiences in organizations. In A. Burton-Hones & J.C. Spender (Eds.), *The Oxford Handbook of Human Capital*. Oxford University Press.

Othman, J. & Vanathas, C. 2004. Topic familiarity and its influence on listening comprehension. *The English Teacher* 8: 19–32.

Peterson, B. 2004. *Cultural intelligence: a guide to working with people from other cultures,* Yarmouth, MA: Intercultural Press.

Resing, W. & Drenth, P. 2007. *Intelligence: knowing and measuring*. Amsterdam: Publisher Nieuwezijds.

Rezaei, O. & Bavali, M. 2017. The Relationship between cultural intelligence and expressions of gratitude among iranian upper-intermediate EFL learners. *Journal of Studies in Learning and Teaching English* 6(1): 151–174.

Tajeddin, Z. & Momenian, M. 2012. The interface between cultural intelligence and interlanguage pragmatics: The case of gratitude speech act. *Iranian Journal of Applied Language Studies* 4(1): 169–192.

Thomas, D & Inkson, K. 2004. *Cultural intelligence*. Berrett-Koehler Publishers, San Francisco.

Tsou, W. 2005. The effects of cultural instruction on foreign language learning. *RELC Journal* 36(1): 39–57.

Van Dyne, L., Ang, S., & Koh, C. 2008. Development and validation of the CQS: the cultural intelligence scale. In S. Ang, & L. Van Dyne, (Eds.), *Handbook on cultural intelligence: Theory, measurement and application*. 16–38. Armonk, NY: M.E. Sharpe, Inc.

Van Dyne, L., Ang, S., Livermore, D. 2010. Cultural intelligence: a pathway for leading in a rapidly globalizing world. In K. Hannum, B. B. Mcfeeters, & L. Booysen (Eds.), *Leading across differences*. 131–138. San Fransisco: Pfeiff.

Verghese, T. & D'Netto, B. 2011. Cultural intelligence and openness: Essential elements of effective global leadership. *International Review of Business Research Papers*. 7(1): 191–200.

ELT in Asia in the Digital Era: Global Citizenship and Identity – Madya et al. (Eds)
© 2018 Taylor & Francis Group, London, ISBN 978-0-8153-7900-3

Indonesian EFL teachers' identities in written discourse: English or Oriental domination?

R.D. Pratama
Universitas Negeri Surabaya, Surabaya, Indonesia

ABSTRACT: This present study describes Indonesian EFL teachers' multiple identities in written discourse along with the rationales beyond its formations. There were six argumentative compositions composed by six teachers to reveal the forms of multiple identities using an AAIF checklist, while semi-structured interviews were used to reveal the rationales. Using a qualitative approach, results showed that Indonesian EFL teachers exhibited multiple identities formed by negotiating Oriental and English identity which were categorized into two types; multiple identities dominated by Oriental identity and those dominated by English. Another interesting result was that all teachers admitted that Oriental identity could not be shifted easily when composing written discourse. Further, the findings lead to the innovation of appropriate teaching techniques for EFL instructors with Oriental written discourse style to teach L2 writing.

1 INTRODUCTION

Identity reflects one's culture(s) and is mostly formed through three different ways namely appropriation, resistance, and negotiation (Sharifian 2009, Bruce & Rafoth 2016). *Appropriation* aims at totally accepting an intended-culture identity while *resistance* is the contrary (Berman et al. 2001, Swaab et al. 2008, Sharifian 2009, Bruce & Rafoth 2016). Moreover, there is an intersection between them called *negotiation* which typically arises multiple identities (Berman et al. 2001, Swaab et al. 2008, Sharifian 2009). Regardless of either balanced or imbalanced negotiation, multiple identities often happen to those who experience multicultural contacts (Coulthard & Iedema 2008, Wood 2016, Cozart et al. 2017). Thus, one might have single or multiple identities depending on the significant influence of multicultural contacts to identity formation.

In addition, identity is more than the looks of diversity in races, ethnicities, or genders. Rather, it is about a reflection of thinking rhetoric and communication patterns to show their sociocultural communities (Kaplan 1966, Lewis 2006, Lubin 2015). To cope with the principle of thinking rhetoric, Kaplan (1966) and Chovanec (2012) define five groups of thinking patterns based on the dissemination of cultures namely Oriental, English Semitic, Romance and Russian. Moreover, still coping with thinking rhetoric, Lewis (2006) and Lubin (2015) portray 27 communication patterns. Those phenomena also inform that each group carries different identity judgments for the members. For instance, Indonesian EFL speakers are stereotyped as circular thinkers as they are part of Oriental culture, while native speakers with English culture are straight forward (Kaplan 1966, Kuntjara 2004). Therefore, a person's identity and thinking rhetoric are interconnected.

So, how to investigate identity by disseminating a person's thinking rhetoric? Applying written discourse analysis may become an alternative to address the question (Rubin 1995, Truesdell 2014). By knowing the styles of written discourse, it helps to determine identity by relating discourse as a means of the organization of language use in written form to different sociocultural thinking rhetoric which represents diverse identities (Bhatia 2004, Kuznetsova & Umutkulova 2016). Further, dealing with Kaplan's (1966) theory, this principle promotes the rise of several written discourse styles covering Oriental, English Semitic, Romance and Russian written discourse style. Thus, written discourse style then can highlight a writer's identity.

In their study, Kuznetsova & Umutkulova (2016) argue that the investigation of written discourse may work well on argumentative composition. As an academic written discourse, writing argumentative composition deals with Higher Order of Thinking (HOT) or critical thinking skills (Fernsten 2008, Kuznetsova & Umutkulova 2016). In dealing with a systematic and logical composition, there are two elements to consider covering argument traits which consist of claim, reason, evidence and link back; and argumentation with its 9 sub-skills of critical thinking (Warnick & Inch 1994, Fisher 2001, Rieke et al. 2005, Fisher 2009, Bowell & Kemp 2010, Cottrell 2012, Jogja Debating Forum 2012, Pratama & Lestari 2015). By investigating how argument traits are sequentially constructed and permeated in the argument's logic, the written discourse style and the identity writer possesses can be known easily.

As a lot of research has been conducted in investigating EFL teachers' multiple identities, to the best of my knowledge, there is no study revealing identity domination done by EFL users. That is, this present study aims at portraying Indonesian EFL teachers' multiple identities focusing on the identity domination and rationales beyond the formation. In other words, this study also shows why Indonesian EFL teachers have difficulty to deal with international publication and seem effortless in coping with Indonesian Ministry of Research, Technology and Higher Education Law Number 20 Year 2017. At last, it is expected that this study opens a new perspective in how to enhance teachers' writing skills by determining an adequate teaching technique which is in line with English identity and Indonesian EFL teachers' identity.

2 METHOD

This study used six argumentative compositions written by six Indonesian EFL teachers in which they were chosen based on several criteria (see Appendix 1). The different clusters of criteria also aimed at conveying whether identity formation portrayed in written discourse style has nothing to do with school levels and teachers' positions. Data were collected through four steps; collecting argumentative compositions written by six subjects, reading the compositions closely to find argument traits and argumentation skills in order to get the written discourse styles, revealing the identity formation by employing checklist of Argument, Argumentation, and Identity Formation (AAIF) (see Appendix 2), and interviewing the subjects to reveal the rationales beyond the identity formation (interview guidelines in Appendix 3). The data depicted from the results of a checklist and interviews were analyzed qualitatively under the interpretism paradigm through organizing and familiarizing, coding and reducing, and interpreting and representing (Ary et al. 2010).

3 FINDINGS AND DISCUSSION

3.1 *Findings*

3.1.1 *Multiple identities with oriental domination*
Basically, the five subjects knew how to compose an argument by permeating English identity proven by the trend of sequentially structuring argument traits (claim, reason, evidence, and link back). Moreover, it showed an appropriation of the deductive approach which represented the English identity in written discourse, of which is later called as an English written discourse style. However, those phenomena became less apparent than Oriental identity that tends to dominate the subjects' written discourse style. The occurrence of Oriental identity was conveyed by the unsystematic construction of argument traits. For instance, S1 constructed ICR pattern in paragraph 3 and elicited some traits in other paragraphs. The random and incomplete traits proved that the majority of arguments was drawn unclearly and not straight forward (see Table 2). Thus, Oriental written discourse style still dominated the whole argument compositions.

Table 1. Argument traits constructed by S1, S2, S3, S4 and S6.

Paragraph	S1	S2	S3	S4	S6
		Subject codes			
1	$C_1R_1C_2I$	$C_1R_{1.1}C_2C_3R_{2.1}R_{1.2}R_{1.3}$ $C_4R_4R_{2.2}E_4I_4$	CRI	CRE	$C_1R_1C_2R_2I_2$
2	$C_1R_1C_2R_2$	$C_1R_1C_2I_2I_1$	CR	CREI	CR
3	ICR	CREI	$R_{1.1}C_1R_{1.2}$	$C_1R_1C_2R_2$	CREI
4	CRE	CRI	CR	CR	$C_1R_{1.1}C_2R_{1.2}R_2$
5	$C_1R_1C_2R_2C_3I_{1-2}$		$C_1R_1C_2$	CE	CI
6			$CR_{1.1}R_{1.2}$	$C_1R_1I_1C_2$	CRI
7			CRI	CR	CREI
8			CI		CREI
9			$C_1R_1C_2I_2C_3R_3$		
10			CREI		
11			CRE		
12			CR		

Notes: C = Claim R = Reason E = Evidence, I = Inference.
[1]fist particular trait (C, R, E, or I) in an argument.
[2]second particular trait (C, R, E, or I) in an argument.

Table 2. Circular ideas representing oriental identity.

Subject	Argument
S2	Writing an essay is very common in academic life, particularly in colleges (C1). In this level, students are demanded to write and academic writing for writing an essay is student's duty as an academician (R1.1). Writing is the most important things a student does in university (C2). Writing is one of many way of being assessed (C3). Because it is important, every student is demanded to master academic writing skill (Bowker, 2007:5) (R2.1). At university students are expected to write academically (R1.2). How the academicians construct their brilliant ideas systematically into writing as well as the choice of appropriate language and words to be understood by, of course, the assessor, lecture, who expects the best from his students, and further by readers (R1.3). Writing in English requires more skill such as to choose the appropriate words and grammar in line with the English structure regulation (C4). Moreover, it is not enough for the students to have only critical and analytical thinking, the ideas, or to master the writing regulation as well as to set a critical argument but also to have good standard of grammar (R4). However, the fact is that a number of students very struggle to write an academic writing (R2.2). Brown (2000:341) discussed several characteristics of written languages; one of those is that to write a language is very complicated. "Writer must learn how to remove redundancy, how to combine sentence, how to make references to other elements in the text, how to create syntactic and lexical variety, and much more" (Brown, 2000:342) (E4). Hence, writing academically is perceived highly complicated (Jones, Turner & Street, 1999:vi) (I4).

To cope with an unsystematic construction of argument traits, it promoted low argumentation qualities in which it violated the principle of higher order thinking skills (HOTS). The violence also indicated that English thinking rhetoric was not well-implemented. Table 2 shows circular thinking rhetoric which represents Oriental identity. In that S2's case, first, the argument was constructed unsystematically, and tend to, circularly. Second, related to logic, R1.1, R1.2, and R1.3 were irrelevant to claim 1 (C1) since they were repetitive and inadequate enough to justify why writing academic essay should be habituated in college. Another irrational fact appeared as an inference fallacy proven by the occurrence of I4 in

363

concluding previous traits in which it did not accommodate the whole idea stated from the beginning up to the last in S2's argument.

In addition, the above fact indicated an imbalanced distribution of the two identities which unconsciously made one overlap with the others. As a result, there was incomplete English identity transferred to the composition written by the Indonesian EFL teachers. S6 experienced such a situation in that she still could not resist the influence of her Oriental style even by pushing herself hard to consciously reflect English identity on her L2 writing. She believed that it was impossible to totally shift her background identity into another since Oriental written discourse style was her primarily acquired discourse.

> For me it is impossible to delete our background identity when writing composition because we have been living in certain cultural situation. As an English teacher, I always try to seriously focus on how to put English style in my L2 writing. However, I find it difficult. Even I can do so, it must be my Indonesian identity shown as dominating style. I mean, English style is less arise than the Oriental one. (S6, interview 4)

Moreover, lack of L2 writing exposure, especially in argumentative composition which required HOTS, influenced the formation of multiple identities which minorly exposed English identity. In responding to the fact, S2 stated that the more often a writer produced L2 writing, the easier he or she transferred English identity to the L2 writing product.

> I understand that most Indonesian EFL teachers' writing is circular and not directly to the point. This is related to critical thinking mastery. All teachers, including me, also face difficulties to implement critical thinking in writing. (S2, interview 2)
>
> Even when we write under-pressures with impromptu topics, we cannot control how to emerge English style, instead, we only think how to explain such ideas in which the most probably used written discourse is the Oriental ones. That is my problem, and mostly also being others, an unconscious writing problem. (S2, interview 5)

Thus, it could be rationalized that, actually, subjects intended to appropriate English identity but the Oriental one still much more controlled the rhetoric due to difficulty in shifting background identity and the lack of L2 writing using English written discourse style.

3.1.2 *Multiple identities with English domination*

The trend shown in Table 3 described that the deductive writing style was appropriated by S5, of which was also proven through the sequent construction of argument traits. It also indicated that S5 used English written discourse style in composing her composition. Even English identity was found within her composition, uniquely, her second paragraph seemed contradictory to English style in the unsystematic construction of argument traits. Unfortunately, having well-construction of argument traits was not the only determiner of judging the existence of English identity. Thus, HOTS should be employed to administer how straight ahead and logical enough the composition was. Table 4 shows how S5 constructed an argument thru sequent argument traits with HOTS as the argumentation skills. Based on Table 4, the idea was drawn in a straight forward style and no logical fallacy or inaccuracy existed within the argument. Thus, this small interference of Oriental identity lets English written discourse style dominate the whole composition.

Furthermore, the phenomenon of English domination was due to the fact that S5 adopted English style by appropriating English identity in her L2 writing.

> For me, English writing is not only about how I use English as the language. It is more than the language. It is about the thinking style, the accuracy of the language use, and an *English way* I need to master. I always settle my mind in *English way* when writing something. I should shift my Indonesian writing style. Yes, it is really hard but I want my argument to be looked like English style, not Indonesian style. So, I need to acquire English writing style. (S5, interview 3).

Table 3. Argument traits constructed by S5.

Paragraph	1	2	3	4	5	6
Pattern	CREI	$C_1R_1I_1\ C_2R_2E_2$	CREI	CREI	CRE	CRI

Table 4. Sufficient argument to argumentation skills which reflect HOT.

Subject	Argument
S5	In response to pronunciation difficulties, some work has been conducted especially in countries learning English as a foreign language (EFL) **(C)**. For instance, studies conducted to investigate problems with English pronunciation among Thai students and identify key reasons for the problems (Wei & Zhou, 2002; Khamkhien, 2010). The key reasons of the pronunciation problems are such as words directly borrowed from English into the Thai language are pronounced in Thai ways, the Romanization of the Thai language influences English pronunciation, and Thai intonations are applied into English pronunciations. They found that there are English consonants and vowels which appear to be problems for them **(R)**; e.g. words with transcriptions ended with a consonant; consonant clusters; words with/ei/, usually pronounced as/e/; words with/r/, usually pronounced as/l/; words with/v/, usually pronounced as/f/; and words with/z/, usually pronounced as/s/or voiceless, intonation and stress problems **(E)**. This is to say that native language is the most influential factor **(I)**.

To achieve good performance of mastering English writing style in argumentative writing, I always take a challenge for myself namely writing at least one argument in a day. (S5, interview 1).

Actually, the challenge I mentioned before compels me to engage with English style atmosphere and, in the same time, gives me more exposures and habits of using English writing style. This is helpful for me to dominate English style over the Indonesian style. (S5, interview 5).

To enable her totally acquiring the *English way*, she habituated herself to using English written discourse style in every composition she wrote. By having intensive writing practice persistently, she pushed herself in transferring English identity in her L2 writing instead of her Indonesian, or Oriental identity. As a result, English identity, represented by the English written discourse style namely straight forwardness of thinking rhetoric, dominated her discourse product.

3.2 *Discussion*

The phenomena discovered in this study confront the fact that shifting Oriental into English written discourse style is difficult for Indonesian EFL teachers. According to Ha (2008), the West, represented by English style, and the East, represented by the Oriental one, exhibit two repulsive cultures. Those result in an understanding of contrastive identity, English with its straightforwardness while Oriental is circular (Kaplan 1966, Kuntjara 2004). In regards to the differences, Oriental writers indeed have to burn fingers to successfully permeate English style in their written discourse. Moreover, appropriating English identity in a written discourse seems difficult to Indonesian EFL teachers since they have been accustomed to Oriental discourse style. Thus, Indonesian EFL teachers need to give have more pressure in adopting English identity when dealing with written discourse.

The efforts done by Indonesian EFL teachers in trying to appropriate English identity may raise identity formation through negotiation process. In this study, teachers negotiate their background identity with English ones. They want to actualize English-based identity but, at the same time, their background identity too binds them to commit. This case also confirms that identity is a context-dependent mental construct (Leary & Tangney 2012). It can be said that a new identity can be shaped throughout certain moments or contexts, i.e. academic or scientific writing contexts (Leary & Tangney 2012). Henceforth, multiple identity is just an evidence that hybrid identity, a result of identity manipulation or formation, is constructed by corresponding multiple cultures to particular or multiple contexts (Leary & Tangney 2012).

In accordance with multiple identities found in this study, Indonesian EFL teachers still show their Oriental background, of which still dominate the written discourse. However, one unique case portrays that one student can make English dominate her written discourse. This is due to her intensive writing exercises and persistent use of English style permeated within. That phenomenon also confirms that identity is nevertheless a context-dependent mental construct (Leary & Tangney 2012). It means that a writer may possess an English identity in a composition when he or she can apply English written discourse style (Leary & Tangney 2012). In connection with the case of Indonesian EFL teachers' discourse, they may still be interfered with by two situations, which are English and Oriental style, which influence their mental construct and, then, raise multiple or hybrid identities with English domination. Even though so, they still cannot distribute English and Oriental identity fairly. Thus, Gee (2001) in Williams (2005) states that primary discourse learnt by L2 writers more dominates their identity compared to that of multiple secondary discourse learnt afterwards.

To cope with above explanations, a study of culture-based written discourse style can portray how writer's identity is constructed (Kaplan 1966, Kuntjara 2004). The written discourse style is a part of an *identity kit* that influences writer's identity formation (Williams 2005). Moreover, through argumentative writing, the distinctive facts can reveal whether thinking rhetoric possessed by different cultures also determines how one's identity is conveyed through either appropriation, resistance or negotiation. The identity L2 writers are born with, also named as inherit, ethnicity and race may also determine the successful adaptation or adoption of L2 culture (Bruce & Rafoth 2016). This shows how L2 writers' background culture injects much more on them (Leary & Tangney 2012). The sociocultural element such as doctrine to self-belonging influences identity construction portrayed by the used written discourse style (Ha 2008, Kouhpaeenejad & Gholaminejad 2014). Thus, it claims that L2 writer exhibits a different identity depending on what primary culture they possess and what culture habits they deal with.

4 CONCLUSION AND SUGGESTION

Referring to the above discussions, first, knowing the forms of Indonesian EFL teachers' identity helps to understand why English writing is difficult for them. Moreover, identity domination may also confirm the radius of capability in appropriating English written discourse style. Those indeed determine the success of producing good English composition, especially in an argumentative writing. Secondly, it promotes reflection for them in providing a relevant teaching technique and adequate materials in the L2 writing classroom for those who own English and Oriental identity, of which Oriental is dominant. Further, this developed teaching design promotes an easy teaching instruction for L2 writing classroom. Third, it is suggested to investigate whether the portrayal of Oriental domination influences teachers in devising lesson plans to teach writing. As a result, it can be clearly known whether or not teachers' Oriental-dominated identity is transferred to students through the teachers' teaching procedures. As a conclusion, the above ideas may raise awareness for effective instruction of teaching L2 writing based on different cultural contexts.

REFERENCES

Ary, D. *et al.* 2010. *Introduction to Research in Education.* USA: Wadsworth, Cengage Learning.
Berman, A.M. Schwartz, S.J. Kurtines, W.M. & Berman, S.L. 2001. The Process of exploration in identity formation: The role of style and competence. *Journal of Adolescence*, 24: 513–528.

Bhatia, V.K. 2004. *Worlds of Written Discourse*. NY: Continuum.

Bowell, T. & Kemp, G. 2010. *Critical Thinking: A Concise Guide 3rd Edition*. Oxon: Routledge.

Bruce, S. & Rafoth, B. 2016. *Tutoring Second Language Writers*. Logan: Utah State University Press.

Chovanec, J. 2012. Written academic discourse in English: From local traditions to global discourse. *Brno Studies in English* 38(2): 5–16

Cottrell, S. 2005. *Critical Thinking Skills: Developing Effective Analysis and Argument.* NY: Palgrave Macmillan.

Coulthard, C.S.C. & Iedema, R. 2008. *Identity Trouble: Critical Discourse and Contested Identities*. NY: Palgrave Macmillan.

Cozart, S.M. Jensen, T.W. Wichmann-Hansen, G. Kupatadze, K. & Chien-Hsiung Chiu, S. 2017. Negotiating multiple identities in second- or foreign-language writing in higher education(Book Chapter). *Critical Transitions: Writing and The Question of Transfer*, 299.

Fernsten, L.A. 2008. Writer identity and ESL learners. *Journal of Adolescent & Adult Literacy* 52(1): 44–52.

Fisher, A. 2001. *Critical Thinking: An Introduction*. UK: Cambridge University Press.

Fisher, A. 2009. *Berpikir Kritis: Sebuah Pengantar (Indonesian Version)*. Jakarta: Erlangga.

Ha, P.L. 2008. *Teaching English as An International Language*. Clevedon: Multilingual Matters.

Jogja Debating Forum. 2012. *Handbook of Parliamentary Debating*. Yogyakarta: JDF Press.

Kaplan, R.B. 1966. Cultural thought patterns in inter-cultural education. *Language Learning Journal* 16:1–20.

Kouhpaeenejad, M.H. & Gholaminejad, R. 2014. Identity and language learning from post-structuralist perspective. *Journal of Language Teaching and Research* 5(1): 199–204.

Kuntjara, E. 2004. Cultural transfer in EFL writing: A look at contrastive rhetoric on English and Indonesian. *K@ta Journal at Petra Christian University* 6(1): 13–29.

Kuznetsova, T.D. & Umutkulova, A.N. 2016. Fostering academic written discourse in university: From theory to practice. *UDC* (2): 65–70.

Leary, M.R. & Tangney, J.P. 2012. *Handbook of Self and Identity Second Edition*. New York: The Guilford Press.

Lewis, R.D. 2006. *When Cultures Collide: Leading Across Cultures*. London: Nicholas Brealey International

Lubin, G. 2014. Communication charts around the world. UK: Business Insider, retrieved from http://uk.businessinsider.com/communication-charts-around-the-world-2014–3?r = UK?r = US.

MRTHE Law Number 20 Year 2017, retrieved from http://kelembagaan.ristekdikti.go.id/wp-content/uploads/2017/02/PERMEN-NOMOR-20-TAHUN-2017-TENTANG-TUNJANGAN-PROFESI-DAN-TUNJANGAN-KEHORMATAN-SA.pdf.

Pratama, R. & Lestari, L.A. 2015. Analysis of argument and argumentation made by S1students of English department. *RETAIN Journal* 3(2).

Rieke, R.D. Sillars, M.O. & Peterson, T.R. 2005. *Argumentation and Critical Decision Making*. Boston: Pearson Education, Inc.

Rubin, D.L. 1995. Composing social identity in written language. New Jersey: Lawrence Erlbaum Associates, Inc., Publisher.

Sharifian, F. 2009. *English as an International Language: Perspectives and Pedagogical Issues.* Clevedon: Multilingual Matters.

Swaab, R.I. Postmes, T. & Spears, R. 2008. Identity formation in multiparty negotiations. *The British Psychological Society Journals*, 47: 167–187.

Truesdell, D. 2014. Constructing identity in academic writing: A case study on rhetorical awareness in engineering discourse. *STYLUS 6.1*: 38–49.

Warnick, B. & Inch, E.S. 1994. *Critical Thinking and Communication: The Use of Reason in Argument (Second Edition)*. United States of America: Macmillan Publishing Company.

Williams, B.T. 2005. Home and away: The tensions of community, literacy, and identity. *Journal of Adolescent and Adult Literacy*, 49(4): 342–247.

Wood, T.R. 2016. *The Coverage of Race, Ethnicity, and Gender: Multiple Identities in Counseling.* SAGE Publications.

APPENDICES

Subject coding.

Subject	Clusters	Description
S1	Teaches who teach EFL in university level	Subject number 1 in the first cluster who teaches EFL for private university students
S2		Subject number 2 in the first cluster who teaches EFL for state university students
S3	Teachers who teach EFL in high school level	Subject number 1 in the second cluster who teaches EFL for private high school students
S4		Subject number 2 in the second cluster who teaches EFL for public high school students
S5	Teachers who teach EFL in an English Course	Subject number 1 in the third cluster who teaches EFL for one private students
S6		Subject number 2 in the third cluster who teaches EFL for almost 10 students in an English course registered in Governmental Education Office

Content of Argument, Argumentation and Identity Formation (AAIF) checklist.

Indicator	Elements	Numbers in AAIF checklist
Argument Traits; derived from	Claim (existence of claim, claim types and fallacies);	1–7
Warnick & Inch (1994),	Reason (existence of reason, reasoning types and fallacies);	8–21
Bowell & Kemp (2010),	Evidence (existence of reason, evidence types and fallacies);	22–28
Govier (2010) and JDF (2012)	Inference (existence of inference, relevance).	29–30
Argumentation Skills; derived from Warnick & Inch (1994), Cottrell (2005) and Fisher (2009)	Case, related case elements, clarity of problem, assumption, various argument, acceptability of claim, judgment creation, inference, argument creation	31–39
Identity Formation; derived from Sharifian (2009)	Appropriation	40
	Resistance	41
	Negotiation	42

Guides to semi-structured interview.

Question	Objectives of Guiding Questions
1	Confirming subjects' writing habits in composing argument, including but not limited to the frequency of constructing scientific paper
2	Confirming problems in writing argumentative composition, including but not limited to argument construction, argumentation use, language and idea development
3	Confirming subjects' schemata about English written discourse style in argumentative writing
4	Confirming whether subjects' current writing discourse style has reflected English-based written discourse style
5	Confirming what efforts subjects have done to encounter current problems in writing argumentative composition

ELT in Asia in the Digital Era: Global Citizenship and Identity – Madya et al. (Eds)
© *2018 Taylor & Francis Group, London, ISBN 978-0-8153-7900-3*

The construction of imagined identities in two Indonesian English bilingual adolescents

B. Chen & A. Lie
Widya Mandala Catholic University Graduate School, Surabaya, Indonesia

ABSTRACT: Parents in Indonesia believe that English is sonimportant that children should speak the language as early as possible. As a result, there has been a growing number of Indonesian-English bilingual children, which are seen as a threat for eliminating their identity as Indonesian because of their frequent use of English. Thus, this study aimed to find out how bilingual teenagers saw themselves. One male and one female student from a private national school in Grade 11 were the participants. Semi-structured interviews and a questionnaire were administered in this study. The results showed both participants preferred to use English more because they felt proud and more comfortable using it to other English speakers they knew. Nevertheless, they did not dismiss their Indonesian identity since they still actively used Indonesian for communicating with people around them. In conclusion, being bilingual did not automatically hamper participants' identity as Indonesian.

1 INTRODUCTION

As years go by, many Indonesians are now aware that English, as the lingua franca, is extremely important. English has been considered as the key to better education, successful business deals, and prospective career opportunities.

This current trend goes back to the history of English learning in Indonesia. Lauder (2008) explains that English was chosen as the first foreign language of the newly independent country in 1950 because of the international status that English gained over Dutch. The reason why English is favored more is due to the number of speakers who use the language in inner, outer, and expanding circles. Thus, English in Indonesia serves as a compulsory subject for students in secondary and university levels. Today, being able to use English for Indonesians provides a very broad opportunity for success in education, business, and careers. Therefore, middle to upper class parents try their best to educate their children to be able to speak English as early as possible, and this view has raised today's phenomenon of Indonesian English bilingual children in Indonesia today.

As parents try to improve their children's quality of lives, many decide to have their children learn English through different ways. Since many options of English exposure are more varied in this era, some parents send their children to English speaking countries; some also make their children take English courses in the early years of language development. Others prefer to send their children to the so-called 'national plus' schools, meaning that the main language focus in those schools is English instead of Indonesian. As predicted, today Indonesian children particularly in big cities become more fluent in English than their parents' generation.

Though success makes many Indonesian parents proud, it causes a big concern that children nowadays appear to speak more English than Indonesian in their home country. Dixon et al. (2012) conducted a study of 282 Singaporean kindergarteners of three ethnic groups: Chinese, Malay and Indian. A positive effect was found among parents who spoke an ethnic language to their children, while a negative effect was present among parents who spoke English to their children. This study argued that home language was very important to maintain ethnic language for bilinguals. Issues regarding the dominance of English among young generations were also presented in a paper by Ng (2014). Ng argued that the strong emphasis for learning English in the school curriculum and high economic values found in English have caused many younger Chinese Singaporeans to choose English over the Chinese language.

There is also a concern that the dominance of English might lead to another trend: the changing of cultural identity in Indonesian bilingual children. How ones construct identity goes beyond the demographic category (e.g., gender, social status, nationality); language, in fact, has become one of the factors which influence identity construction (Wardhaugh & Fuller 2015). It is argued that these children might replace Indonesian, the local language, with English which will then lead to the changed behavior, their self-perception, and the preferred way to express themselves (Lie 2017). The drive to learn and use English is caused by how they construct their identity when they use the language; they depict and give themselves the new label or identity, or as Norton (2013) proposes the notion of imagined identity. The failure to maintain the mother tongue when learning such a high-power language as English has been investigated extensively in countries where English is the official language or the second language. In Indonesia, this phenomenon is emerging recently along with the growth of international education and the rise of the middle class. However, very few studies have brought up this issue, particularly among Indonesian teenagers.

In order to find out what happened to the identity of the Indonesian bilingual generation, this paper raises some questions:

1. How does the use of English affect identity?
2. How does the identity transformation affect their English learning?

2 LITERATURE REVIEW

2.1 *Identity and language learning*

It is unlikely to separate the construction of identity from the language learning process. Norton (2013), based on Heller's (1987) statement, defines identity as how an individual makes sense of his or her relationship to the world, how the relationship is constructed over time and spaces, and how the person understands the future potential. Wardhaugh and Fuller (2015) see that identities are fluid; it keeps changing through the interaction with others. Identities are not only limited to certain categories, e.g., gender, occupations, or social position. Identities are constructed by many factors, which might be based on social behaviors and discourses, and they can also be constructed through variations of linguistics means. All in all, identity is not something that someone has but something that someone does. There are several expectations and hopes that drive learner to learn second language.

Take Martina's case in Norton (2000) as an example. Martina was an immigrant from Europe with three children with a hope to have a better life. As her English proficiency was little to none, the job offer that she could have was limited and she ended up having a job in a fast food restaurant in Toronto. Due to her limited command of English, she was struggling with cooperating with her Canadian co-workers who used English as their first language. She regarded, in her interview, that her lacking skill in English made her think that she was being 'dehumanized' and seen as 'inanimate "broom"'. With her main motivation to work as a surveyor in Canada, she took ESL courses, practiced her English at her workplace as much as possible, and even asked her child who had better proficiency to teach her English. Based on the stated example before, language learners do change the way they recognize themselves because of the belief in learning and using second language of their choice. Learners may decide to either use or limit themselves from using a particular language in the social network, which gives them the chance to speak with multifaceted considerations. In conclusion, it is necessary to note the reason behind language use by analyzing how people want to be recognized in the society they are currently living in (Norton 2013).

2.2 *Imagined identity*

Norton (2013) defined imagine communities as groups of people that we connect discreetly through our imagination, for examples, communities found in neighborhoods, schools, or workplace. It is believed that imagined identities might be the drive to learn English based on the observation on Mai done by Norton. As Mai—a young adult Vietnamese immigrant—worked in a clothes factory as a lower-class worker, she had an imagined identity as the smart-dressed office worker who was recognized by other workers. To join that community, she noticed that she had to speak and write English. Imagined identity is different from withdrawal from reality (Kanno & Norton 2003). Imagined identity is seen as a hope for future change, not just merely expectation without actions, as (Simon 1992) mentioned by Kanno and Norton (2003) who draw a line between 'wishes', imagination without any possible action, and 'hopeful imagination which represents possible struggles in the future.

2.3 *Bilingualism*

Those who can speak the standard language and the language varieties around them, for example, are considered as bilingual. Some studies have proven that being bilingual brings more benefit than harm to the users. Learning a new language, in fact, can have a dramatic impact on how learners relate with the world and themselves (Dewaele 2014); Cook (2002) as mentioned by Dewaele (2014) claims that having acquired another language alters the L2 user's mind that goes beyond the actual knowledge of the language. Furthermore, Edwards (2003) summarizes that bilingualism is not equal to language loss since there are some arguments saying that increasing the language capacity correlates with the higher sensitivity, enhanced cultural awareness, and even better cognitive flexibility.

There are many definitions to bilingualism. Additive bilingualism sees the addition of the second language not as a threat replacing the first language, but they do not limit themselves to the elite language—the language of the higher rank and prestige in the society. On the other hand, subtractive bilingualism has a different definition: it is when the second language is perceived as being in a competition that it will soon replace the first language, which is seen as minority, low level language (May et al. 2004).

Regardless of the benefits mentioned, there has been a growing concern over bilingualism. Beardsmore (2003) states that there are namely two reasons why skeptical views on bilingualism are present. He further categorizes fears of bilingualism into four categories, two of which will be discussed in this research as follows:

1. Parental fears: The fundamental concern why parents are worried about bilingualism is that learning two or more languages might hamper their children's language learning process.
2. Cultural fears: There is a discrepancy between language and culture that is not easily to be concluded. According to Skutnabb-Kangas (Beardsmore 2003) bicultural bilinguals, additive bilinguals who can appreciate the diversified cultural facets of both groups and does not perceive any frictions in interacting with speakers of either language, might be on the brink of having conflicts with identity, rootlessness, marginality and alienation if the mother tongue and culture are not maintained.

3 METHOD

3.1 *Participants and their profiles*

Two students from St. Louis 1 Senior High School Surabaya were chosen as the participants of this research. They were chosen because both of them are studying in a private school which uses the national curriculum whereby the medium of instruction is mostly Indonesian except for English lessons. The researcher met both participants in their Grade X and observed them on how they used English actively in the English class and at school throughout the year. They were both the researcher's students in Grade XI. Both were born and raised in Indonesia and have never lived in an English-speaking country.

1. Male student: Kent

Kent is the second child in the family. Before studying in senior high school, he went to a 'national plus' elementary and junior high school. He is from Surabaya and lives with his parents and his older sister. His mother is the one who motivated him to study English. She made several attempts to accommodate Kent to study English by sending him to an English course when he was at the primary school level. Though not having the competent English proficiency as Kent claimed in the interview, his mother often asks him to speak in English with her and his sister by initiating a conversation in English. His father, on the contrary, does not speak the language at all and does not seem to be interested in it either. Yet he is not against Kent learning English. His sister, as he claimed, has higher English skills than he does actually, though she does not really speak English with him at home.

2. Female student: Sella

Participants were interviewed using semi-structured questions in order to understand their identity perception. The questions were about participants' English learning milestones, their families' and friends' responses to their choice of language, their reasons for learning English, and their thoughts about their language abilities. The interviews of both participants were recorded. A questionnaire was distributed to the participants' classmates to gain more perspective regarding their bilingual issues. Field observations were done during the English lessons, which took place for 45 minutes per week for a period of 10 weeks in both participants' classes.

3.2 Data collection method

Participants were interviewed using semi-structured questions in order to understand their identity perception. The questions were about participants' English learning milestones, their families' and friends' responses to their choice of language, their reasons for learning English, and their thoughts about their language abilities. The interviews of both participants were recorded. A questionnaire was distributed to the participants' classmates to gain more perspective regarding their bilingual issues. Field observations were done during the English lessons, which took place for 45 minutes per week for a period of 10 weeks in both participants' classes.

4 FINDINGS AND DISCUSSIONS

4.1 How English affect their identity

Both Kent and Sella had almost similar perceptions on why they learnt English: to have a brighter and better future after senior high school. Kent, in fact, said that he finished an entrance test for a college in Germany, and he got accepted. The tests he did were all in English. The program that he would probably take in Germany will be delivered in English for a year before he takes the German course there. He said in the interview saying that the importance of English and how English is used everywhere was what drives him to learn English.

> [Kent's quote]: '…College, I plan to go to Germany Because in Germany there are some programs. One program is for you to learn English, like a collage use English language…. and then you continue in German. This English is important, like to adapt there.'

Interestingly, Sella claimed that she did not see her living in Indonesia in the next 10 to 20 years for her life. She was determined to continue her studies in the United States due to her father's suggestion that she agreed to. Sella said that she could not get into a reputable state university in Indonesia because her outstanding score in her report was in English only, contrary to Kent who got good scores for almost all subjects at school. Thus, she chose to learn English so that she could continue her studies in the United States.

[Sella's quote]: 'Yeah, and for my ultimate goal in life is always go to US university. ...I'm not going to go the other way around, not going to forget my English // I'm 100% sure kalo misale (for example) if I apply here I would not get a good university because of my scores are really bad. But if you go to the university in the US .... I personally think that it's easier for me to get into the university in the US than here.'

When asked about when and where they used English, Kent said that he preferred to use his English for writing captions in social media. He also said that he used English with his best friends when they made a phone call. Kent did not really want to use English at home because he did not really have another person to speak with. He occasionally used English with his sister when they talked about their favorite television show. Sella happened to have a classmate that she could speak English with, unlike Kent. She often mixed Indonesian and English. At home, she did not really use English because her family used Indonesian. She would use English at home when she did not know the Indonesian words. They both used Indonesian every day when they talked to their family, teachers, and non-English speaker friends. Kent claimed that he mostly used Indonesian at home with his family, although he preferred English versions more. Sella had a similar situation with Kent; she used Indonesian with her family at home because she was not used to speaking English at home though she had her father and sisters who could use the language as well. She used her Indonesian when the person she talked to was not a user of English. She used English with other English speakers. In addition, she joined journalistic competitions which were in Indonesian when in junior high school and senior high school. The main reason why they used the two languages that way was because it made them comfortable.

Although they actively use English regularly, they thought they were Indonesian. The main reason was because they felt bonded with Indonesia, where they were born. They concluded that they had a sense of ownership with Indonesia since they had never left the country for a long period. Both said that the food was the main factor that made them love Indonesia. Though both participants regard themselves as Indonesian, Sella had a slightly ambivalent attitude towards her Indonesian identity. She did not feel ashamed of using Indonesian in public because that is the language that she has been using for 16 years living in Indonesia and also Indonesian is the language that connects her with her family and friends. On the contrary, Kent was proud of being Indonesian because of great achievement done by many successful Indonesians in other countries. He stated that he wanted to make Indonesia proud of him through what he will do in the future.

[Sella's quote]: 'Basically, I've talked Indonesian for 16 years of my 16 years life so it's not really that special. There's no special feeling...It's like a normal thing //...it doesn't mean that if I speak fluent in another language and I live in another country then I'm not Indonesian. Like I'm born... I was born here, I'm from here... even if I change my citizenship, ... there will be a part of Indonesia that still lives inside me.'

[Kent's quote] 'Love Indonesia is because.. the culture... The food..Uhm... clothes. The language is number 2 I think, Like the Javanese. // ... Like the way you speak to people here not that polite but it makes you super close to your friend.'

As it is said, identity is fluid and changes over space and time on Wardhaugh and Fuller's (2015) notion. The way Kent and Sella used the two languages showed how they changed their identity, depending on the person they were talking to. They thought of themselves as English speakers when they were surrounded by other English speakers. On other occasions, they perceived themselves as Indonesians since they still need to use Indonesian with other people around them. Kent and Sella also had the imagined identity of being international students who study in other countries. They regarded themselves as being more successful if they studied English starting from Grade XI, which is consistent with Norton's idea of imagined identity (2013). English, to some extent has given them the opportunity to continue their education abroad since the medium of instruction is English. As users of both English and Indonesian, Kent and Sella both perceived themselves as Indonesian who can also speak English. This shows that they could be regarded as additive bilinguals, when learning

English is not a threat to their Indonesian identity, but as a supplement to the way they see themselves, which supports Edward's (2003) claim that bilingualism does not correlate to language loss.

4.2 Their English identity constructed and the effect on language learning

Since Kent and Sella depicted themselves as learners who had more choices for their future studies, they made efforts in developing their English.

Kent used to study in a national-plus school before going to St. Louis 1 which mostly used English as the medium of instruction. His mother also sent him to take English courses before senior high school, though mainly focusing on grammar. At first it was his mother who encouraged him to learn English. It gave him quite a hard time because going to English courses meant that he had less time to play games. When he realized how important learning English was, he made an effort in exposing himself to English through watching anything in English on YouTube, movies, television shows, and sometimes, by reading novels. He often used his friends as benchmarks as they could use English better than him as his motivator; being friends with them made him wants to be as good as them. At the time of the interview, he was preparing to take an English proficiency test by practicing from books. He did not take any English courses because his mother felt that he had the capability to learn for the tests by himself. He actually would like to take a preparation course because he felt that there are some points that need teachers' explanation which he could not comprehend on his own. When he was asked whether he would like to encourage himself or his friends to improve his Indonesian skill, he said that he might need it when he studied in Indonesian and thus needed to make a thesis in Indonesian. Other than that, he said that he did not feel the need to improve Indonesian as he has already been using it every day.

> [Kent's quote] 'No, I think…..Because they (friends) have master it, I guess.'

Sella, by contrast, started studying English in a preschool that used English as the main communication language. She then moved to national schools until senior high school. She managed her English study by going to English courses since there were many options in Surabaya with the addition of the support from parents. She is now taking an English course preparing her for university entrance test requirements in the United States. In addition, she has mostly spent her time learning English and joining English competitions since she was in elementary school. She often watches movies or YouTube videos and reads novels in English as well to improve her English. One question was asked regarding her need to improve her Indonesian skills. She claimed that she might not need to improve her writing because she occasionally joined Indonesian writing competitions. She felt that she needed to improve her speaking skills in Indonesian. Yet she did not think improving her Indonesian at that moment because she focused more on getting admitted to university in the United States.

> [Sella's quote]: 'I don't think I want to improve… I mean I don't know what to improve in my Indonesian. It's not like I'm going to use academically other than schools, so I'm gonna use it for daily usage and most of my Indonesian for daily usage is infiltrated with Javanese. So….. uhmm, no. // I think it's just English, cause I don't know what to improve from Indonesian like you only use it for day-to-day basis'

Due to the imagined identity that they hold on, Kent and Sella were willing to make every effort in their ways to improve their English with the resources that they had (e.g., going to English courses, watching movies or videos in English, reading novels). As Norton mentions regarding imagined identity, both participants try to hold on to their expectations or wishes as speakers of English with better opportunity to get a higher education by practicing their English more.

4.3 Identity when using English as perceived by peers

A questionnaire asking what their classmates thought of Kent and Sella when they used English in class was given to give hindsight of what other adolescents think about English-

Indonesian bilinguals. The class that Kent and Sella were in had 40 students each; only some of them participated in filling out the questionnaire for Kent, so he had 12 questionnaires returned. Sella, on the other hand, had 31 questionnaires resubmitted.

All 12 respondents said that they had heard Kent use his English in class in many emotional situations: happy, sad, angry, or casual. One of his friends confirmed that he used English for chatting on social media; another mentioned that English was used as a replacement for unfamiliar Indonesian words. When asked what they felt hearing Kent use English in class, there were two sides: on the one side they were being really positive, on the other hand they showed disdain. Those who are on the positive sides said that they liked how Kent used his English: he is funny when he speaks English and it made them happy, speaking English with Kent makes them comfortable, they could learn new vocabulary from him, some of his friends knew English and felt okay with his using English. Others had their reasons for disliking Kent and his English: one mentioned that his using English did not fit in the Indonesian culture, two respondents hated his English because they did not like Kent as a person, and the other two said that they just did not like Kent using English in class for indefinite reasons.

In Sella's questionnaire, some of the respondents said that she never or rarely used English directly to them, yet some others claimed that she used English a lot with them when being engaged in normal conversations or explaining something. When it came to lessons and assignments, she used Indonesian. Many claimed that she often mixed Indonesian and English when speaking. One question asked whether they liked how Sella used her English; the majority were in favor of her using English in class, while only 4 people responded negatively and one with a neutral opinion. Most respondents claimed that they liked her accent and pronunciation because they thought her accent was similar to native English speakers. Besides, they could learn new vocabulary from her due to her fluency and saw her as the inspiration for them to learn English; some claimed that it made the class look cool and 'professional' because they had 'a foreigner' in class with them. Those who did not like Sella using English said that her English seemed off in non-English subjects because the lessons they had in schools were delivered in Indonesian and made her sound different from the rest of the class. Some claimed that they did not understand what she said in English and so did not like her using English; another seemed not to like Sella's English because he or she did not like her personally, and the one neutral respondent said that he or she did not mind whatever language she used as long as there was no communication breakdown.

From the questionnaire results, it appeared that the classmates overall accepted bilingualism by being positive with how the two participants of this research used their English. Nevertheless, there are still negative views that cannot be completely ignored. Some of them who dislike Kent and Sella saw their ability to switch between the two languages as a cultural threat, feeling that people should speak Indonesian in Indonesia, not English. It appeared that cultural fears among peers were present in Kent's and Sella's community, the growing concern that conflicts between mother tongue and identity (Beardsmore 2003).

5   CONCLUSION

Equal to the loss of their Indonesian identity. They indeed appeared to spend more time improving and using their English whenever they could as they perceived having a higher education abroad as one way to have a better future. Being born and living in Indonesia for years, which also included being surrounded by people who speak Indonesia, however, are the factors that tie them to their identity as Indonesian. Communicating using either Indonesian or English is just a way to express their thoughts that can make them feel good about themselves. Therefore, being bilinguals should not be seen as a form of betrayal to their mother language and culture but as a chance to explore themselves for greater opportunity and possibilities in the world around them.

This study may be only applied for these two participants involved. It is unlikely that I can claim that bilingual teenagers in Indonesia have the same perception as Kent's and Sella's due to the scarce amount of research done in this field of study. Nevertheless, the results from this research should be the key for further research related to imagined identity in other Indonesian English bilinguals.

REFERENCES

Beardsmore, H.B. (2003). Who's Afraid of Bilingualism? In J.M. Dewaele, A. Housen, & L. Wei, *Bilingualism: Beyond basic principles* (pp. 10–27). Clevedon: Multilingual Matters.

Dewaele, J.M. (2014). Second and additional language acquisition. In L. Wei, *Applied Linguistics* (p. 51). Wiley Blackwell.

Dixon, L., Zhao, J., Quiroz, B.G. & Shin, J.Y. (2012). Home and Community Factors Influencing Bilingual Children's Ethnic Language Vocabulary Development. *International Journal of Bilingualism* 16(4): 541–565.

Edwards, J. (2003). The Importance of Being Bilingual. In J.M. Dewaele, A. Housen, & L. Wei, *Bilingualism: Beyond Basic Principles* (pp. 28–42). Clevedon: Multilingual Matters.

Kanno, Y. & Norton, B. (2003). Imagined Community and Educational Possibilities: Introduction. *Journal of Language, Identity, and Education:* 241–249.

Lauder, A. (2008). The Status and Function of English in Indonesia: A Review of Key Factors. *Makara, Social Humaniora,* 9–20.

Lie, A. (2017). English and Identity in Multicultural Context: Issues, Challenges, and Opportunities. *TEFLIN Journal, 8,* 71–92.

May, S., Hill, R. & Tiakiwai, S. (2004). *Bilingual/Immersion Education: indicators of good practice.* Waikato: Ministry of Education New Zealand.

Ng, C.L. (2014). Mother Tongue Education in Singapore: Concerns, Issues and Controversies. *Current Issues in Language Planning* 15(4): 361–375.

Norton, B. & Toohey, K. (2011). Identity, language learning, and social change. *Cambridge Journal:* 412–446.

Norton, B. (2001). Non-participation, Imagined community, and language learning. In M.P. Breen, *Learners contribution to language learning: new directions in research* (pp. 159–171). New York: Routledge.

Norton, B. (2013). *Identity and language learning: Extending the Conversation.* Bristol: Multilingual Matters.

Wardhaugh, R. & Fuller, M.J. (2015). *An Introduction to sociolinguistics.* Oxford: John Wiley & Sons, Inc.

ELT in Asia in the Digital Era: Global Citizenship and Identity – Madya et al. (Eds)
© 2018 Taylor & Francis Group, London, ISBN 978-0-8153-7900-3

A case study of a seven-year old Indonesian-English bilingual child in a trilingual school

R.Y. Prayitno & A. Lie
Widya Manda Catholic University, Surabaya, Indonesia

ABSTRACT: Additive bilingualism is a process of learning a second language without replacing the first language (Lambert 1975). However, the emergence of bilingual schools which use English as the medium of instruction has created fewer opportunities to speak Indonesian as the first language. This study aimed to investigate a seven-year-old Indonesian child who studied in a trilingual school in Surabaya, Indonesia. Limited exposure to Indonesian through his parents and school has caused him to have low proficiency in the first language. Apart from that, the mother's decision to use more English than Indonesian was mainly driven by the high expectation to prepare her child for competition to possess material resources. English was seen to offer more economic values than Indonesian. Both the school and parents have worked hand-in-hand to create young Indonesians who speak fluent English with the risk of having low proficiency in the first language.

1 INTRODUCTION

1.1 *Background*

Addictive bilingualism is a process of learning a second language without replacing the first language (Lambert 1975). However, the emergence of bilingual schools which use English as the medium of instruction has created fewer opportunities to speak the first language. English is mainly used as the medium of instruction for English, Sciences, and Mathematics. These three core subjects are predetermined by the curriculum and have been the main focus of the school. Thus, many parents are more concerned with their children's performance in these three subjects than other Indonesian-related subjects, such as *Bahasa Indonesia* (Indonesian Language), *Ilmu Pengetahuan Sosial* (Social Studies), or Pendidikan *Kewarganegaraan* (Civics). This phenomenon can be related to subtractive bilingualism which refers to the process of learning a second language at the expense of the first language (Lambert 1975). Some schools have decided to invest less learning time in those subjects which are delivered in Indonesian. Consequently, the decreasing number of lessons for the non-core subjects has caused the children to gain limited access to practice and enhance their knowledge and mastery of Indonesian. The English-speaking environment set by the school also confines the students' exposure to speak Indonesian outside class, such as during lunch and recess; students are mostly found to use English. This phenomenon has created an implication that the language preference has shifted from Indonesian to English for Indonesian students who study in a school, in which English is used as the predominant language. Further-more, this can lead to issues in preserving Indonesian as the first and national language.

The school used as the setting for this current re-search applies three languages as the medium of instruction. For elementary grades 1 and 2, the pro-portion of each instruction is 63% English, 23% Mandarin, and 15% Indonesian. Each lesson can last either 35 or 70 minutes. The total hours of all lessons in a week are 1400 minutes. The reason for using minutes instead of hours is because all lessons in this school are calculated in minutes whereby one period is equal to 35 minutes. This calculation is based on the lessons received by the students per week. The following is the calculation of each medium of instruction in this school (see Table 1):

Table 1. Proportion for English, Mandarin and Indonesian.

Language	Minutes	Percentage (total lessons = 1400 minutes)
English	875 minutes	63%
Mandarin	315 minutes	23%
Indonesian	210 minutes	15%

From this illustration, lack of use in Indonesian as the first language can be overtly seen in class. Also, many students are found to use English when they communicate outside class. As a result, the use of English seems to outweigh Indonesian as the first language. This research aims to investigate this bilingualism phenomenon and the parents' role in the child's language proficiency.

This study on bilingualism focused on investigating the participant's proficiency in Indonesian (L1) and English (L2), and also the parents' investment in the child's language proficiency. Norton (2013) mentions that when learners invest in a language, they believe that this language will provide access to material resources (money, goods and real estate) and symbolic resources (language, friendship and education). However, since the participant was seven years old, the investment was centered from the parents' side. The following are the research questions for this study:

1. How does the participant's speaking proficiency in Indonesian compare to his English proficiency?
2. To what extent does the mother influence the participant's choice in using language?

1.2   Literature review

A theory of additive bilingualism mentions that a second language can be learnt without the subtraction of the L1 and its replacement by the L2 (Lambert 1975). A study of 46 Mexican-American children, who attended and did not attend bilingual pre-school, showed that no loss of L1 proficiency occurred in the children during the bilingual preschool program (Winsler et al. 1999). This study, however, adapted 50:50 two-way immersion programs. Thus, an equal exposure between English and Spanish could possibly occur. The participant in this current research, however, studied in a school which had unbalanced proportion of instructions. Therefore, the results presented by Winslet's study and the current research might not be similar.

Unlike additive bilingualism, subtractive bilingualism occurs when the L1 is gradually replaced by the L2 as the second language is learnt (Lambert 1975). Some studies have found that the failure to preserve the first language occurred when learning a second language (Dixon et al. 2012, Wright et al. 2000). A study was conducted among 282 Singaporean kindergarteners of three ethnic groups: Chinese, Malay and Indian (Dixon et al. 2012). A positive effect was found among parents who spoke an ethnic language to their children, while a negative effect was present among parents who spoke English to their children. This study argued that home language was very important to maintain ethnic language for bilinguals. Another study found that Inuit children in second language classes presented lower levels of heritage-language proficiency compared with Inuit children in Inuktitut classes (Wright et al. 2000). Although they were able to speak in basic conversation for daily use, their first language complexity did not develop in such ways that enabled them to use it for school work.

Norton (2013) presents a concept of investment. When language learners invest in learning a particular language, they believe that the language can provide an access to both symbolic (language, friendship and education) and material resources (money, goods and real estate) (Norton 2013). Other experts also discussed investment and its relation to the parents' expectation on their children. The school where their children study plays an important role in fulfilling this expectation. Many parents believe that educating their children in bilingual schools is an in-vestment for them (Stavans & Hoffmann 2015). Therefore, when learners invest in learning a language, they have a certain belief that this language can provide a wider range of access to these re-sources.

Issues regarding the dominance of English among young generations were also presented in a paper by Ng (2014). In the paper, the author argued that the strong emphasis for learning English in the school curriculum and high economic values found in English have caused many younger Chinese Singaporeans to choose English over the Chinese language. These conditions are similar to those which the re-searcher is intended to explore. The choice of language is influenced by many factors, such as prestige, worthiness and also the value attributed to the language (Stavans & Hoffmann 2015). In Indonesia, the spread of English occurs among middle-class families. Because of the urge to follow trends (Stavans & Hoffmann 2015) or embrace globalization (Lie 2017, Stavans & Hoffmann 2015), many up-per-middle class parents are driven to send their children to bilingual schools which are mostly publicized as having "international curriculum" or "international standard". Many parents are fascinated by such schools because they offer high exposure to English and also international partnerships (Lie 2017).

2 RESEARCH METHOD

2.1 *The participant*

The main participant of this research was a seven-year old Indonesian-English bilingual student who studied in a trilingual school. The participant was at the second-grade level when this research was con-ducted. The reason for selecting this participant was because the researcher had known the participant quite well and had taught him since he was in first grade. Also, based on the information gained from his other teachers, his academic performance in Indonesian-related subjects was low when he was in the first grade.

2.2 *Instruments for data collection*

The instruments used in this research are verbal-fluency task, speaking test and interviews. The verbal-fluency task was used to measure production ability (Linck et al. 2010), while the speaking test was used to assess language proficiency. In the verbal-fluency task, the participant was required to mention as many words as he could in Indonesian and English, based on the three categories (animals, fruits and vegetables). For each category, the participant was given 2 minutes to mention the words: one minute for English, and one minute for Indonesian. The following details the task administration:

To complement the verbal-fluency task, the speaking test was administered to assess the participant's ability to use the language orally to convey meaning. The test required the participant to narrate some stories in Indonesian and English after he watched three videos with no dialogues. One video was used as a trial, while the other two were used as the speaking assessment. Both the trial and the as-assessment were conducted after lunch time, be-tween 2.15 pm and 2.40 pm. Table 3 provides details of the administration:

To support the result of this test, some interviews were conducted with the participant's mother, the nanny, and also some teachers who taught Indonesian- and English—related subjects.

Table 2. The verbal-fluency task.

Categories	Languages (1 minute for each language)
Animals	English-Indonesian
Fruits	Indonesian-English
Vegetables	English-Indonesian

Table 3. Language proficiency test.

	Durations	Languages used to retell the story
Video 1 (Trial)	2 minutes, 40 seconds	English-Indonesian
Video 2 (Assessment 1)	2 minutes, 23 seconds	Indonesian-English
Video 3 (Assessment 2)	2 minutes, 18 seconds	English-Indonesian

Table 4. Verbal-fluency task.

Categories	English	Indonesian
Animals	lion, owl, crocodile, parrot, sharksquid, fish, cats, dogs. Number of words: 9	kucing, anjing, harimau, ikan, burung, tikus, zebra. Number of words: 7
Fruits	apple, pear, watermelon, pineapple melon, grape, banana, coconut. Number of words: 8	apel, jeruk, anggur, pir, pisang melon Number of words: 6
Vegetables	carrot, lettuce, tomato, beans, corn broccoli, nut, potato. Number of words: 8	wortel, tomat, jagung. Number of words: 3

3 FINDINGS AND DISCUSSIONS

3.1 *How does the participant's speaking proficiency in Indonesian compare to his English proficiency?*

3.1.1 *The Indonesian and English production ability (using verbal-fluency task)*
The verbal-fluency task was used to measure the production ability of L1 and L2 (Linck et al. 2010). The L1 here was Indonesian, while the L2 was English. Three categories, which were animals, fruit and vegetables, were selected. The test taker was given 2 minutes for both languages to mention the words, so he had 1 minute to speak for each language. The following is the result of the test:

The result above shows that his production ability in English was better than in Indonesian. In all categories, he mentioned more English words than Indonesian words, although the difference in animals and fruits categories was not as significant as the one in the vegetables group. In the third group, he could only mention three vegetables in Indonesian. Also, the number of words in English was fairly consistent, while the Indonesian declined significantly from six to three. To conclude, his range of vocabulary in English was wider than in Indonesian.

3.1.2 *The English and Indonesian speaking fluency*
The scored by using a rubric adapted from Common European Framework of Reference for Languages (CEFR) (University of Cambridge Local Examinations Syndicate, 2011) and Narrative Scoring Scheme (Heilmann et al. 2010). Three raters were selected to assess the speaking proficiency. The proportions for each cate-gory in the rubric were 20% introduction, 20% cohesion, 30% pronunciation, and 30% vocabulary and grammar. The following are the results of the speaking test:

The results above show that the participant's overall English proficiency was between level 3 and 4 out of 5 levels. His pronunciation was the highest compared to his grammar and vocabulary. His pronunciation was scored 5 by all the raters in Video1 as seen in Table 5, while in Videos 2 and 3 he received either 4 or 5 as seen in Tables 6 and 7. A steady score in pronunciation was given by rater 1 and 3, while rater 2 scored him 4 in Video 2 and 3. Although there was a decline in pronunciation presented by the second rater in Video 2 and 3, it was not significant as it only fell into one level below.

Due to the difficulties in finding the same videos on the internet, the three videos used in the assessment were not one hundred percent alike. However, the durations of the clips were

Table 5. Video 1 (trial English).

	Rater 1	Rater 2	Rater 3
Introduction (20%)	3:0.6	3:0.6	3:0.6
Cohesion (20%)	4:0.8	4:0.8	4:0.8
Pronunciation (30%)	5:1.5	5:1.5	5:1.5
Grammar, Vocabulary (30%)	4:1.2	5:1.5	4:1.2
Score	4.1	4.4	4.1

Table 6. Video 2 (assessment 1 English).

	Rater 1	Rater 2	Rater 3
Introduction (20%)	2:0.4	3:0.6	3:0.6
Cohesion (20%)	4:0.8	5:1	5:1
Pronunciation (30%)	5:1.5	4:1.2	5:1.5
Grammar, Vocabulary (30%)	3:0.9	3:0.9	3:0.9
Score	3.6	3.7	4

Table 7. Video 3 (assessment 2 English).

	Rater 1	Rater 2	Rater 3
Introduction (20%)	3:0.6	3:0.6	3:0.6
Cohesion (20%)	3:0.6	3:0.6	3:0.6
Pronunciation (30%)	5:1.5	4:1.2	5:1.5
Grammar, Vocabulary (30%)	2:0.6	2:0.6	2:0.6
Score	3.3	3	3.3

nearly similar, which was around 2 minutes, but not more than 3 minutes. The complexity of the story in the three videos was not equal. The least complex story was presented in Video 1, while Video 3 contained the most complex one.

Overall, the Indonesian proficiency was lower than the English proficiency. One most noticeable indicator was the low score in grammar and vocabulary, in which he received 1 in both the trial and assessments as seen in Tables 8, 9, and 10. Unlike the results presented in the English assessment, the complexity of the stories did not seem to influence much in the Indonesian language scores. His grammar and vocabulary in Indonesian were significantly lower compared with his scores in English. Even in Video 1, which had the least complex story, he only reached level 1 for grammar and vocabulary.

Another interesting finding to highlight is that his pronunciation scores in Indonesian were as high as his scores in the English pronunciation. This result shows that although he used fewer vocabulary words in the Indonesian language assessment, he still presented good pronunciation skills in Indonesian.

3.1.3 *Interview with teachers*

To support the results of the speaking assessment and the classroom observation, the researcher also conducted interviews with some teachers. However, since the English teacher was the researcher herself, the Science teacher was selected to represent the English-related subjects. Two teachers who taught Indonesian-medium subjects were interviewed regarding the Indonesian proficiency of the participant, the parents' contribution and also the dominance of English in the school. In the interview, the Indonesian teacher expressed her concern about Dylan's vocabulary. Unlike the other 7-year-old Indonesian children, he did not have a wide range of vocabulary which could allow him to attain an optimal proficiency in Indonesian.

"I think Dylan's ability in speaking Indonesian is very limited. He is Indonesian, and he is at the second grade now, but he does not have a wide vocabulary."

Table 8.　Video 1 (trial Indonesian).

	Rater 1	Rater 2	Rater 3
Introduction (20%)	1:0.2	2:0.4	2:0.4
Cohesion (20%)	2:0.4	2:0.4	2: 0.4
Pronunciation (30%)	5:1.5	4:1.2	5:1.5
Grammar, Vocabulary (30%)	1:0.3	1:0.3	1:0.3
Score	2.4	2.3	2.6

Table 9.　Video 2 (assessment 1 Indonesian).

	Rater 1	Rater 2	Rater 3
Introduction (20%)	2:0.4	2:0.4	2:0.4
Cohesion (20%)	2:0.4	3:0.6	2:0.4
Pronunciation (30%)	5:1.5	4:1.2	5:1.5
Grammar, Vocabulary (30%)	1:0.3	1:0.3	1:0.3
Score	2.6	2.5	2.6

Table 10.　Video 3 (assessment 2 Indonesian).

	Rater 1	Rater 2	Rater 3
Introduction (20%)	2:0.4	2:0.4	2:0.4
Cohesion (20%)	1:0.2	3:0.6	2:0.4
Pronunciation (30%)	5:1.5	4:1.2	5:.1.5
Grammar, Vocabulary (30%)	1:0.3	1:0.3	1:0.3
Score	2.4	2.5	2.6

If the statement above is linked with the verbal-fluency task, there seems to be a relationship between the home language and the vocabulary development. Since the parents spoke English to the child, his vocabulary in Indonesian did not seem to develop much. Therefore, this finding is consistent with the findings in the previous study (Dixon et al. 2012). Children raised by parents who used an ethnic language to communicate with them attained higher ethnic vocabulary than children whose parents spoke another language (Dixon et al. 2012).

Another teacher, who taught Indonesian-medium lessons, described extensively with regards to how English had taken over the role of Indonesian in Dylan's everyday life. Furthermore, this condition hampered his ability to speak Indonesian. From this finding, she also mentioned about Dylan's limited proficiency in Indonesian which confirms the result of the language assessment.

"When he does tasks from his book, he has difficulties in understanding the questions, so most of his answers turn out to be wrong."

His Indonesian was not sufficient for academic purposes. He seemed to have difficulties in doing the tasks in his book. This finding is consistent with the previous study of Inuit language (Wright et al. 2000). The proficiency of Inuit language for students in second language classes was not well-developed, thus they faced difficulties as they did their school work.

Unlike the teachers who taught the Indonesian-medium lessons, the Science teacher presented more positive results with regards to the participant's overall performance in Science. This statement contradicts the findings found in Indonesian language class. One of the possible explanations is that his English proficiency was better than his Indonesian proficiency. Therefore, his academic performance in English-related subjects was better than in Indonesian-related subjects.

"His score in Science is good. He can answer the questions in the worksheets and the workbook in-dependently. He does it very well. His home-work's score is also very good, even though he sometimes submits it late, but he always tries to do his best. If I assign projects at home, he also does it well."

According to his Indonesian language teacher, how-ever, Dylan's academic performance in Indonesian was poor. Even though there was an improvement from the first grade to the second grade, it was not significant enough.

"His scores are also bad; his average score is be-tween 50 and 60. There is an improvement, but it is not significant. When he was at the first grade, his average score was 50."

3.2 *To what extent does the mother influence the participant's choice in using language?*

The participant's mother viewed that English would benefit her son's job in the future. She mentioned in the interview that English would be needed by her son as he grew up and had to manage his business or do his job. It was seen to offer economical values, as it is mentioned by Ng (2014). Also, this finding corroborates Norton's statement which said that language can provide access to material resources (Nor-ton 2013). Some of the middle-class parents believe that their children can gain success in this global world through the mastery of English (Lie 2017). The mother expressed her view about the importance of English in business and also in her son's future life:

"English is very important for your future. I think for the future. English is very important for business and commerce. If you can speak English, you can do negotiation and even do lobbying. If my child can speak English, he can have a good job and a bright future ahead."

When she was asked the reason why she spoke English more to her son than the other languages, she mentioned that English is a current trend which she felt responsible to follow, particularly due to her role as a parent.

"Nowadays, English is used everywhere, in business, commerce, negotiation and many more. As parents, I have to stay up to date and follow the trends."

For her, English was viewed as a current trend. Of course, the trend mentioned by her was closely related to the globalized world, and with English, middle-class parents believe that their children would be able to win in the global competition (Lie 2017).

The parents' choice of language is influenced by many factors, such as prestige, worthiness and also the value attributed to the language (Stavans & Hoffmann 2015). When the mother was asked the reason for selecting English over Indonesian as the home language, she mentioned several factors, such as trends, better future and other globalization-related reasons. Thereby, this choice was driven by the current condition as well as the future prospects of the language. Moreover, these two factors seemed to be more associated with English than with Indonesian.

The home languages within the family were Indonesian, English and Mandarin. Although Dylan used them all at home, the nanny stated that English was mainly used by him. He only spoke Indonesian to his nanny and his drivers. She mentioned that his daily language at home was English:

"All his brothers speak fully English with him. They speak English while they are playing. They rarely speak Indonesian. To his mother and father, he also speaks English all the time. He only speaks Indonesian with his two nannies and with the drivers. But his daily language is actually English."

Although he still received first language input from his nanny, it was still far less frequent than English. From this finding, the family did not seem to apply the importance of home language input which is necessary to ensure the child's language development (Dixon et al. 2012). She mentioned that the only situation he spoke Indonesian to her was when he asked her to do something:

"At home, he speaks English. But when he needs anything, he will ask me to do it, and he will speak in one, two, or three words in Indonesian. He speaks Indonesian with me when he asks me to do something. So, whenever he cannot get things or make things by himself, he will speak Indonesian to me."

4 CONCLUSIONS AND SUGGESTIONS

Under the urge of following trends (Stavans & Hoffmann 2015), embracing globalization (Lie 2017, Stavans & Hoffmann 2015) and the need to possess material resources for a better future (Nor-ton 2013), many Indonesian middle-upper class parents were eager to put their children in a dominant English school, and even use English as the main language at home. The minimum input of the first language received from the parents was one of the reasons behind the participant's low proficiency in Indonesian, since parents' language inputs are necessary to maintain the first language (Dixon et al. 2012). In this case, the parents played a significant role regarding the negative effect of subtractive bilingualism which was found in the participant of this study.

Further study is needed to investigate how schools can implement the paradigm of additive bilingualism. Furthermore, many emerging bilingual schools in Indonesia urgently need to revisit their policy regarding the use English as a medium of instruction. The drive to master English does not need to sacrifice the first language. It is advisable that such schools also attempt to preserve Indonesian as the first language by providing more balanced input in L1 and L2.

REFERENCES

Dixon, L., Zhao, J., Quiroz, B.G. & Shin, J.Y. 2012. Home and community factors influencing bilingual children's ethnic language vocabulary development. *International Journal of Bilingualism* 16(4): 541–565.

Heilmann, J., Miller, J.F. & Dunaway, C. 2010. Properties of the narrative scoring scheme using narrative retells in young school-age children. *American Journal of Speech Language Pathology* 19: 154–166.

Lambert, W. 1975. Culture and language as factors in learning and education. In A. Wolfgang, *Education of Immigrant Students.* Toronto: O.I.S.E.

Lie, A. 2017. English and identity in multicultural contexts: issues, challenges, and opportunities. *TEFLIN Journal* 28(1): 71–88.

Linck, J.A., Kroll, J.F. & Sunderman, G. 2010. Losing access to the native language while immersed in a second language evidence for the role of inhibition in second-language learning. *National Institute of Health* 20(12): 1–19.

Ng, C.L. 2014. Mother tongue education in Singapore: concerns, issues and controversies. *Current Issues in Language Planning* 15(4): 361–375.

Norton, B. 2013. *Identity and language learning* (2nd Ed.).. Bristol, UK: Short Run Press.

Stavans, A. & Hoffmann, C. 2015. *Multilingualism.* Cambridge: Cambridge University Press.

University of Cambridge Local Examinations Syndicate. 2011. *Assessing speaking performance at level A2.* Retrieved from http://www.cambridgeenglish.org/images/168617-assessing-speaking-performance-at-level-a2.pdf.

Winsler, A., Diaz, R.M., Espinosa, L. & Rodriguez, J.L. 1999. When learning a second language does not mean losing the first: bilingual language development in low-income, spanish speaking children attending bilingual preschool. *Child Development* 70(2): 349–362.

Wright, S.C., Taylor, D.M. & Judy, M. 2000. Subtractive bilingualism and the survival of the inuit language: heritage-versus second-language education. *Journal of Educational Psychology* 92(1): 63–84.

The teacher's code-switching in ELT classrooms: Motives and functions

D.A. Andawi & N.A. Drajati
Sebelas Maret University, Surakarta, Indonesia

ABSTRACT: The use of code-switching by teachers in teaching English can be found either in students with low or high proficiency. This paper explores the code-switching used by a teacher in teaching English for high-level proficiency students in a senior high school in Indonesia. It investigated types, reasons or motivations, and functions of code-switching in five classrooms. The findings show that (1) the teacher employs two types of code-switching, i.e. situational and metaphorical code-switching. (2) There are eight reasons that motivate the teacher to switch the code. (3) Generally, the teacher employs ten functions of code-switching. The research concludes that the teacher uses code-switching as a strategy in teaching English and it has positive effects on the students' learning. By employing code-switching, the teacher facilitates learning so the learning goal and objectives can be achieved effectively, and the students feel secure thus learn effectively.

1 INTRODUCTION

Using more than one language in teaching English as a second/foreign language is unavoidable. The use of more than one language alternately is called code-switching. The term code-switching is defined by Auer in Nilep (2006: 16) as "the alternating use of more than one language". Those codes are used in the same utterance or 'conversational episode' (Grosjean 1982, Auer 2002). Gumperz (1982) stated that the switch can be analyzed based on its grammatical systems/subsystems in the same turn/exchange/utterance/conversation (p. 59). It is not only a linguistic process but also a psychological process because people have reasons/motivations to switch from one language to another besides alternating two linguistic elements.

Blom and Gumperz (1972) suggested two types of code-switching, i.e. situational and metaphorical code-switching (Gumperz 1982: 60). Situational code-switching happens when "distinct varieties are associated with the changes in interlocutor, context or topic, and is therefore a direct consequence of a diaglossic distribution of the varieties" (Gardner-Chloros 2009: 59). It implies that there is a correlation between the language choice and situation. Metaphorical code-switching happens when "the purpose of introducing a particular variety into the conversation is to evoke the connotations, the metaphorical "world" of that variety" (Gardner-Chloros 2009: 59). It is harder to observe because there is no clue that marks the changeover as the former type does (Gumperz 1982: 98). Wardaugh (2006: 104) said, "metaphorical code-switching has an affective dimension to it: you change the code as you redefine the situation—formal to informal, official to personal, serious to humorous, and politeness to solidarity". It is used to (1) highlight quotation, (2) mark emphasis, (3) indicate jokes, satire, or criticism, (4) redefine new situation, (5) show relationship among participants, (6) convey social meaning, (7) show identities/membership of a group, (8) show whether such activity is formal/informal, (9) show perspective of the speaker, (10) show speakers' position in a speech community, (11) achieve special communicative effect, and (12) give sociocultural framework to others for understanding.

Faerch and Kasper (1984) in Cook (2008) have listed code-switching as one of the psychologically motivated strategies for solving the individual's L2 problems of expression. Cook suggested that code-switching can be used as teacher's strategy in ESL/EFL classroom. She said that communication strategies are naturally used when people encounter a difficulty in communicating his/her intention (2008).

Communication strategy is one of the strategies that teachers can build to achieve effective teaching. The communication process in the classroom is called "instructional communication process" (Richmond et al. 2009: 4). The process is initiated by teachers delivering content/messages, supported by instructional strategies to students. Then, when students give responses, teachers evaluate or give feedback. Instructional strategies are used to help accommodate the different level of proficiency and competence of learners.

The occurrences of code-switching in classrooms have attracted some researchers to understand the process in which code-switching is employed. Some researchers rejected the use of code-switching in second/foreign language classrooms because they believe that code-switching will interfere in the second/foreign language learning of learners (Cummings & Swain in Yao 2011, Ellis in Rahimi & Eftekhari 2011). However, a number of researchers who have conducted research on the use of code-switching in ESL/EFL classrooms suggested that the occurrence of code-switching, will facilitate second/foreign language learning (Greggio & Gil 2007, Zabrodskaja 2007, Ahmad & Jusoff 2009, Then & Ting 2009, Jingxia 2010, Gulzar 2010, Rahimi & Eftekhari 2011, and Yao 2011).

This research proposed three questions, i.e. what type of code-switching performed by the teacher, what reasons motivate the teacher, and what functions implied in every switching in the English teaching and learning. For the categorisation of type of code-switching, the researcher referred to Blom and Gumperz (1972) "situational and metaphorical" code-switching (Gumperz 1982: 60). For the reasons of code-switching, the researcher identified them based on observations and interviews with the teacher and the students. For the functions of code-switching, the researcher used the list of functions that she deduced from the several lists of functions from five previous researchers, i.e. Cameron (2001), Gulzar (2010), Flyman-Mattsson & Burenhult (1999), Greggio & Gil (2007), Jingxia (2010). From the construct, ten functions may be employed by the teacher in classrooms, i.e. explaining concepts, giving instruction, translating, changing topics/classroom procedures, motivating students/drawing students participation, checking understanding, disciplining and controlling, giving feedback, evaluating, and socializing.

This research is different from other previous research in the case of Indonesian context which has various regional dialects as students' native languages. More importantly, it investigates the occurrence of code-switching by a teacher who teaches high-level proficiency learners.

2 METHODS

This research was qualitative in nature and was conducted from January to February 2013 in one of the best senior high schools in an urban area in Indonesia. The research used purposive sampling. It investigated a teacher who had master degree in English Education. The data were mainly taken by observing teaching and learning process, interviewing teacher and students, and analyzing teaching syllabus and lesson plan. The teaching and learning process was recorded and transcribed. All the collected data were analyzed by using Interactive Model of qualitative data analysis technique including data condensation, data display, and drawing conclusion/verification (Miles & Huberman 1994). In data condensation, the significant data were selected and coded. After the coding, the types, reasons, and functions were measured by counting the each occurrence compared to the total occurrences to find the percentage.

3 FINDINGS AND DISCUSSION

3.1 *Types of code-switching*

From the average percentage of occurrence in all classrooms, metaphorical code-switching has the higher frequency than situational code-switching. The class that has the highest frequency of situational code-switching is class X.4 and the lowest frequency is class X.8. The class that has the highest frequency of metaphorical code-switching is also class X.4 and the lowest frequency is also class X.8. The rank of the frequency of occurrence of the two types of code-switching in five classrooms is presented in Table 1 (from the highest to the lowest).

Table 1 shows that the two types of switching in all classrooms have the same rank. It can be seen that the highest level is placed by class X.4 for both types. The lowest level is also placed by class X.8. However, in X.8, the occurrence of situational code-switching is more frequent than in the other classes. It is because the characteristics of the students of X.8 that mostly are the 'excellent' students among others.

When considering the average frequency of occurrence, metaphorical code-switching is more frequently employed by the teacher. As it is noted in the interview transcript, the teacher said that the frequency of metaphorical switching was higher than situational switching. She said that she usually switched the code to tell jokes/intermezzos, to make the situation more relaxing, and to explain concepts.

From the finding, it can be said that the changes of the topics, addressees, and situation contribute less in the occurrence of the teacher's code-switching. For teaching high level proficiency learners, the teacher needs to fall back to students' L1/L2 to keep the students engaged in the lesson. The teacher finds that teaching intelligent students needs more creativity in managing the classroom so they do not get bored easily.

Table 1. The proportion of types of code-switching in all classrooms (highest-lowest).

	Situational (S)		Metaphorical (M)	
Rank	Class	Percentage	Class	Percentage
1	X.4	36.00%	X.4	64.00%
2	X.2	31.67%	X.2	68.33%
3	X.6	44.74%	X.6	55.26%
4	X.3	40.90%	X.3	59.09%
5	X.8	75.00%	X.8	25.00%

Table 2. The connection between the teacher's assumptions and the students' assumptions about the teacher's reasons of code-switching.

Teacher's assumptions	Students' assumptions
1. The students may not understand the instruction because they do not respond to it;	a. Because the students do not give response and they do not concentrate on the lesson. b. To make the students understand the materials/instructions.
2. Among 32 students in each class, the level of students' ability in grasping the material is heterogeneous;	a. To make the students understand the materials/instructions.
3. Translating can be time-consuming;	a. To make the students understand the materials/instructions.
4. Students' will learn effectively if they feel secure;	a. Because the materials will not be understood if the students are stressful. b. To create a close relationship between the teacher and the students.
5. The use of students' home language (Indonesian/Javanese) can increase the students' level of trust to the teacher;	a. Because the materials will not be understood if the students are stressful. b. To create a close relationship between the teacher and the students.
6. The students may not know their errors/mistakes if it is delivered through English.	a. To make the students understand the materials/instructions.

3.2 *Reasons of code-switching*

There are six reasons that motivate the teacher to switch the code. From the interview, the teacher has assumptions that lead her to switch the code. Besides, students also have four assumptions on why the teacher switches the code. Table 2 shows the synchronous assumptions between the teacher and the students on the situations that lead to code-switching

Table 2 shows that the teacher and the students are in the same line. They know what happened in the classroom and what the teacher needs to use as the language of instruction.

Table 3. The connection between conditions when code-switching occurs and the teacher's reasons for code-switching.

Conditions	Teacher's reasons
1. The class is noisy/the students do not concentrate on the lesson;	a. The students may not understand the instruction because they do not respond to it; b. The use of students' home language (Indonesian/Javanese) can increase the students' level of trust to the teacher;
2. The students do not do what the teacher says/instructs immediately;	a. The students may not understand the instruction because they do not respond to it;
3. The students are not/less active;	a. The students may not understand the instruction because they do not respond to it; b. Among 32 students in each class, the level of students' ability in grasping the material is heterogeneous; c. The use of students' home language (Indonesian/ Javanese) can increase the students' level of trust to the teacher;
4. The students do not understand (materials/instruction);	a. The students may not understand the instruction because they do not respond to it; b. Among 32 students in each class, the level of students' ability in grasping the material is heterogeneous;
5. The students' speech is unintelligible or the term/diction they use is not understood by the teacher;	a. The students' speech is unintelligible or the term/ diction they use is not understood by the teacher;
6. The concepts/materials being explained are difficult/important;	a. Among 32 students in each class, the level of students' ability in grasping the material is heterogeneous;
7. When translating words/phrases/sentences;	a. Translating can be time-consuming;
8. There is something funny that occurs in the class;	a. Students' will learn effectively if they feel secure;
9. When building a close relationship between the teacher and the students;	a. The use of students' home language (Indonesian/ Javanese) can increase the students' level of trust to the teacher;
10. When giving instruction;	a. The students may not understand the instruction because they do not respond to it;
11. When correcting the students' errors/mistakes;	a. The students may not know their errors/mistakes if it is delivered through English.
12. When evaluating the students' works/performances;	a. The students may not know their errors/mistakes if it is delivered through English.
13. When praising the students' works/performances;	a. Students' will learn effectively if they feel secure; b. The use of students' home language (Indonesian/ Javanese) can increase the students' level of trust to the teacher;
14. When changing addressees;	a. Students need to be more aware;
15. When checking for students' understanding.	a. Among 32 students in each class, the level of students' ability in grasping the material is heterogeneous; b. The use of students' home language (Indonesian/ Javanese) can increase the students' level of trust to the teacher;

From the interview with the students, the results show that the students have positive comments on the teacher's code-switching. They say that when and how much the teacher switches the code have already been sufficient and eligible for them.

Based on the transcripts of the teacher and the students' dialog in the five classrooms, the conditions when the teacher switches the code raise several motivations for the teacher to switch the code. The breakdown of the conditions that raise teacher's reasons of code-switching is presented in Table 3.

Those fifteen conditions are identified based on the observations of teaching and learning process in five classrooms. The teacher confirms those conditions that motivate her to switches the code. In this case, code-switching performed by the teacher can be categorized as the conscious process because she understands the situation and has control what to use and when. The patterns of the classrooms interactions have been internalized for days even months before the teacher can decide what to use and when.

When discussing the reasons that motivate the teacher to code-switch and the functions of code-switching, the term "reason" and "function" may be used interchangeably by other researchers. According to Flyman-Mattsson and Burenhult (1999), the term reasons and functions are perceived as similar. Their list of reasons/functions of code-switching employed by teachers is: (1) linguistics insecurity, (2) topic switch, (3) affective function, (4) socialising function, and (5) repetitive functions (p. 61). In this research, the term reasons and functions are defined differently. Reason is something that motivates or causes the teacher to do code-switching. The reasons are based on from the conditions that occur in the classrooms.

If the reasons in this research are correlated with the five reasons/functions by Flyman-Mattsson and Burenhult, the first type, linguistic insecurity is not detected as the teacher's reason of code-switching. There is no evidence of teacher's incompetence on the material/subject matter being taught. The second reason, topic switch, is detected as the eight reasons in the Table 3, i.e. students need to be more aware. This topic switch, if it is connected to the functions of code-switching in this research, is changing topic/classroom procedure and disciplining and controlling. Next, affective and socializing functions have to do with the reasons: students' will learn effectively if they feel secure, and the use of students' home language (Indonesian/Javanese) can increase the students' level of trust to the teacher. If it is connected with the functions of code-switching, the functions that belong to affective functions are motivating students/drawing students' participation, socializing, giving feedback, and disciplining and controlling. Lastly, repetitive functions have to do with the reasons: the students may not understand the instruction because they do not respond to it, and among 32 students in each class, the level of students' ability in grasping the material is heterogeneous. If it is connected with the functions of code-switching, the functions that belong to repetitive functions are giving instruction, explaining concepts, giving feedback, checking understanding and disciplining and controlling.

3.3 *Functions of code-switching*

Based on the transcripts of the teacher and the students' dialog in the five classrooms, it shows that the teacher employs all functions of code-switching, but each class has different occurrences of switching. The average occurrences of functions of code-switching in all classrooms are ranked as follow.

1. Giving instruction (19.82%)
2. Giving feedback (18.02%)
3. Checking understanding (15.76%)
4. Socializing (9.91%)
5. Motivating students/drawing students' participation (9.46%)
6. Disciplining and controlling (7.66%)
7. Translating (6.76%)
8. Changing topic/classroom procedure (5.85%)
9. Explaining concepts (5.40%)

As stated above, the occurrences of teacher's code-switching in each classroom are different from those in the other classrooms. The teacher only employs several functions in a classroom. The percentage of occurrences of code-switching in each classroom is presented in Table 4.

The teacher's reasons of code-switching lead her to perform the certain function(s) of code-switching in the pedagogic, managerial and interpersonal aspects. The term function is the manifestation of the teacher's reasons. Thus, if it is joined in a chain, the sequence is the conditions-reasons-functions. In this research, the reasons that motivate the teacher to do code-switching are in the form of teacher's assumptions—something from the teacher's mind—and two others reasons generalized from the observations and data transcripts. The functions are in the form of teacher's actions, e.g. giving instruction, giving feedback, etc. The breakdown of the reasons and the functions the teacher's code-switching is presented in Table 5. Point 7 and 8 of motivations do not come from the teacher's assumptions but generalized from the classroom observation and transcript of the teacher and the students' dialog. The teacher only realizes first to sixth assumptions.

Table 4. The percentage of functions of code-switching in each classroom.

Function	X.6	X.8	X.3	X.4	X.2
1. Giving instruction	41.46	42.86	23.81	6.41	18.67
2. Giving feedback	14.63	14.29	19.05	17.95	20.00
3. Checking understanding	2.41	0.00	28.57	17.95	18.67
4. Socializing	2.41	14.29	0.00	16.67	9.33
5. Motivating students/drawing students' participation	0.00	0.00	19.05	16.67	5.33
6. Disciplining and controlling	24.39	28.57	0.00	3.85	2.67
7. Translating	0.00	0.00	0.00	12.82	6.67
8. Changing topic/classroom procedure	2.41	0.00	0.00	3.85	12.00
9. Explaining concepts	4.88	0.00	9.52	3.85	6.67
10. Evaluating	7.32	0.00	0.00	0.00	0.00

Table 5. Breakdown of the teacher's reasons and functions of code-switching.

Teacher's reasons	Functions of code-switching
1 The students may not understand the instruction because they do not respond to it;	a. Giving instruction b. Checking understanding c. Disciplining and controlling
2 Among 32 students in each class, the level of students' ability in grasping the material is heterogeneous;	a. Explaining concepts b. Checking understanding c. Disciplining and controlling
3 Translating can be time-consuming;	a. Translating
4 Students' will learn effectively if they feel secure;	a. Motivating students/drawing b. students' participation c. Socializing Giving feedback
5 The use of students' home language (Indonesian/Javanese) can increase the students' level of trust to the teacher;	a. Motivating students/drawing students' participation b. Disciplining and controlling
6 The students may not know their errors/mistakes if it is delivered through English.	a. Evaluating b. Giving feedback
7 The students' speech is unintelligible or the term/diction they use is not understood by the teacher;	a. Giving feedback
8 Students need to be more aware.	a. Changing topic/classroom procedure b. Disciplining and controlling

From the occurrence of each type of the teacher's code-switching and the occurrence of each function of the teacher's code-switching in five classrooms, it can be generalized that the teacher does not perform the same frequency of types or functions in different classrooms. The different result is due to the different characteristic, situation, culture of the class, and also type of material and the skill. As proposed by Wardaugh (2006: 106), he said, "Code-switching is not a uniform phenomenon; i.e., the norms vary from group to group, even within what might be regarded as a single community".

When reviewing the research result of Greggio and Gill (2007), there is significant difference in the rank of the occurrences of functions of code-switching. In the Greggio and Gill, the functions of teacher's code-switching in EFL classroom that have high frequency in the pre-intermediate level are: (1) to facilitate/clarify understanding of grammatical rules and structures, (2) to facilitate/clarify understanding of words and expression, (3) to elicit L2 vocabulary and grammatical structures, (4) to call the learners' attention to the correct pronunciation of sounds in English, and (5) to bring about humorous effect. In this research, the first five rank of functions of the teacher's code-switching that have high frequency of occurrences are: (1) giving instructions, (2) giving feedback, (3) checking understanding, (4) socializing, and (5) motivating students/drawing students' participations. To clarify, or in this research is explaining concept, places the ninth rank instead. This suggests that, in the high- level proficient learner, the students have already understood if the teacher explains the materials in English. This also suggests that repeating instructions in Indonesian/Javanese plays more important role in the high-level proficient classrooms.

4 CONCLUSION

After the whole discussion on the teacher's code-switching as a communication strategy, it implies that the use of code-switching by teachers in teaching English as a second/foreign language is not only restricted to low-level proficiency learners but also to high-level proficiency learners. Practically, code-switching can be used as a strategy in teaching English as a second/foreign language. As a strategy, the occurrence of code-switching can be modified so that it will bring success to the students' learning process. In order not to be trapped in the unclear assumptions, English teachers need to make a detailed analysis to the four elements of the occurrence of code-switching in the teaching English stated previously.

It suggests that English teachers have background knowledge on code-switching, especially in the bilingual education environment. It is important for them because their background knowledge and their beliefs/assumptions on code-switching can lead them to the judicious use of code-switching. It also suggests that they understand the characteristics of the learners, conditions of the class, the culture of the class, and the focus of the lesson (materials and skills being taught) so they do not misuse the types and functions of code-switching.

As proposed by Wardhaugh (2006: 106), "Code-switching is not a uniform phenomenon...", the researcher admits that the research findings on the teacher's code-switching in teaching English as a second/foreign language teaching and learning process in this research cannot be generalized/applied to all conditions of classrooms due to the relatively limited data. However, it brings new information about the tendencies and the pattern of teachers' code-switching in an EFL context generally and for high-level proficiency learners especially. Further research is expected to find out the long-term effect of teachers' code-switching on the students language learning and motivation in learning.

REFERENCES

Ahmad, B.H. & Jussof, K. 2009. Teachers' code-switching in classroom instructions for low English proficient learners. *English Language Teaching Journal* 2(2): 49–53. Retrieved on May 13, 2012, from www.ccsenet.org/journal.html/.
Auer, P. (ed). 2002. *Code-switching in conversation: Language, interaction and identity*. London: Routledge.

Cameron, L. 2001. *Teaching languages to young learners*. London: Cambridge University Press.

Cook, V. 2008. *Second language learning and language teaching*. London: Hodder Education.

Flyman-Mattson, A. & Burenhult, N. 1999. Code-switching in second language teaching of French. *Lund University, Dept. of Linguistics Working Papers* 47: 59–72.

Gardner-Chloros, P. 2009. *Code-switching*. New York: Cambridge University Press.

Greggio, S. & Gil, G. 2007. Teacher's and learners' use of code switching in the English as a foreign language classroom: A qualitative study. *Linguagem and Ensino* 10(2): 371–393. Retrieved on February 5, 2012, from http://www.educadores.diaadia.pr.gov.br/arquivos/File/2010/artigos_teses/Ingles/greegio.pdf/.

Grosjean, F. 1982 *Life with two languages: An introduction to bilingualism*. President and Fellows of Harvard College: United States of America.

Gulzar, M.A. 2010. Code-switching: Awareness about its utility in bilingual classrooms. *Bulletin of Education and Research* 32(2): 23–44. Retrieved on February 3, 2012, from http://pu.edu.pk/images/journal/ier/PDF-FILES/2-Malik%20 Ajmal%20Gulzar.pdf/.

Gumperz, J.J. 1982. *Discourse strategies*. New York: Cambridge University Press.

Jingxia, L. 2010. Teacher's code-switching to the L1 in EFL classroom. *The Open Applied Linguistics Journal* 3: 10–23. Retrieved on February 3, 2012, from http://www.benthamscience.com/open/toalj/articles/V003/10TOALJ.pdf/.

Miles, M.B. & Huberman, A.M. 1994. *Qualitative data analysis: an expanded sourcebook 2nd edition*. California: Sage Publication Inc.

Nilep, C. 2006. "Code switching" in sociocultural linguistics. *Colorado Research in Linguistics* 19: 1–22. Retrieved on February 3, 2012, from http://nhlrc.ucla.edu/events/institute/2011/readings/He%20-/%20 Nilep.pdf.

Rahimi, A. & Eftekhari, M. 2011. Psycholinguistic code switching in Iranian university classroom context. *The Journal of Language Teaching and Leaning* 1: 54–63. Retrieved on May 13, 2011, from http://www.jltl.org/jltl/.

Richmond, V.P., Wrench, J.S. & Gorham, J. 2009. *Communication affect learning*. California: Creative Commons.

Then, D.C. & Ting, S. 2009. A preliminary study of teacher code-switching in secondary English and science in Malaysia. *Teaching English as Second Language-Electronic Journal* 13(1): 1–17. Retrieved on May 13, 2012, from http://tesl-ej.org/.

Wardhaugh, R. 2006. *Introduction to sociolinguistics* (5th ed). UK: Blackwell Publishing Ltd.

Yao, M. 2011. On attitudes to teachers' code-switching in EFL classes. *World Journal of English Language* 1(1), 19–28. Retrieved on May 13, 2012, from www.sciedu.ca/wjel/.

Zabrodskaja, A. 2007. Russian-Estonian code-switching in the university[1]. *Arizona Working Paper in SLA & Teaching* 14: 123–139. Retrieved on May 13, 2012, from http://w3.coh.arizona.edu/awp/.

ELT in Asia in the Digital Era: Global Citizenship and Identity – Madya et al. (Eds)
© *2018 Taylor & Francis Group, London, ISBN 978-0-8153-7900-3*

Features of teachers' code-switching in Indonesia: How multiple languages are used in tertiary bilingual classrooms

H. Cahyani
State Politeknik of Malang, Malang, Indonesia

ABSTRACT: This study explores the features of teachers' code-switching in Indonesian tertiary bilingual classrooms in which English, Bahasa, Arabic or Javanese are employed. The observation-and-interview data were collected using ethnographic approach over one semester. Transcripts of classroom interaction were then examined using an Interactional Sociolinguistics perspective. The results show that: (1) the use of blending English words expressed teachers' motivation for communication and teaching, (2) teachers' to-and-fro code-switching —displayed a strategy to make sense of teachers' explanations by elaborating, reinforcing and exemplifying the message, (3) a multilingual practice in which Javanese was featured for quoting somebody else's words and making personal comments to keep the language formal in the classroom. In fact, Arabic was only featured in the restricted expressions for opening and closing the classroom sessions. Overall, these findings describe teachers' translanguaging embarking sociolinguistic, cultural, and pedagogical purposes of the teachers as the speakers.

1 INTRODUCTION

Code-switching is a natural phenomenon that occurs among bilingual speakers. It is an alternating language use where two or more languages are used in a single discourse for the purposes of communication. While traditional views of code-switching saw it as a bilingual deficiency (e.g. Grosjean 1982, Probyn 2009), the current perspectives in multilingualism have seen it as a bilingual asset (e.g. Macaro 2009, Barnard & McLellan 2014). This viewpoint is related to Macaro's continuum of perspectives (2009) which explains the two stances regarding code-switching practice, i.e. '*virtual and maximal position*'. The former believes that mastering a language is best done exclusively in the target language (L2) assuming that more exposures can contribute to learners' comprehensible inputs, whereas the latter speculates that learning language is best done by using first language (L1) since it can help learners bridge their understanding in L2 so that they can gradually develop their L2 in a deliberate way. In other words, the virtual position disagrees with the use of code-switching, while the maximal position acknowledges the benefit of code-switching.

Generally studies in code-switching investigate merely grammar (cf. among others Gardner-Chloros 2009, MacSwan 2012), functions (cf. Moodley 2007, Canh & Hamied 2014), issues between policies and practices (cf. Martin 2005, Andersson & Rusanganwa 2011), and perceptions (cf. Palmer 2009, Then & Thing 2011). Not much research, however, was done to look at code-switching features in a specific context like Indonesia.

Indonesia is a diverse and populous country with over 200 ethnic groups and more than 700 languages (Hadisantosa 2010). It has three classes of spoken languages i.e. Bahasa Indonesia or the national language, local or regional languages—called 'vernaculars' (Nababan 1991), and foreign languages such as English which is currently regarded to be the most important. Even though the main colonial heritage was Dutch, Indonesians did not keep Dutch as an internal language after colonial rule for over 350 years (Gupta 2007).

Today with the demand of globalisation, higher education institution in Indonesia have evolved to develop bilingual/international classes using English as the medium of instruction offering graduates who are not only capable with their skills but also with English communication. Not much study, in fact, investigates classrooms of bilingual programs of how teachers use the language in order to make sense of their teaching (Canh & Hamied 2014). Even no studies have looked at how tertiary level teachers employ code-switching in bilingual program. This study, therefore, aims to investigate the features of teachers' code-switching in order to fill the gap of the research and also to illuminate code-switching studies on how and why such languages are used in a particular context, and for a specific purpose. By using Gumperz' Interactional Sociolinguistics (IS) (1982), this study seeks to find out the implicit meanings of code-switching, of how it is related to social and cultural values of language, and how it is linked to the pattern of code-switching. What we mean by 'features' are the characteristics of code-switching possibly seen from grammatical and behavioral point of view. I argue that language is not merely about linguistic aspects but there are some more contributing aspects that we need to see if we want to describe the features. As an outline, this paper will present the literary works of code-switching features and the theoretical perspective of IS. Then it will articulate research methods and the results which is followed by discussion. Finally, the concluding remarks are dicussed at the end of this paper.

2 LITERARY WORKS

Code-switching research was firstly initiated by seminal works of scholars e.g. John J. Gumperz (1982) working on discourse strategies, and Shana Poplack (1980) researching the grammatical pattern on code-switching among Puerto Rican residents in the US. This section explores some features of code-switching seen in the point of view 'types and sociocultural features' in order to understand how linguistic and non-linguistic components can possibly define the features of code-switching, as well as Interactional Sociolinguistics as the fundamental basis of this study.

2.1 *Types of code-switching*

Poplack (1980) classifies code-switching into types of grammatical code-switching as: intersentential switches, tag switches, and intra-sentential switches. *Inter-sentential switching* occurs at a clause or a sentence level, where each clause or sentence is in one language or another, as in the example below:

> Sometimes I'll start a sentence in Spanish Y TERMINO EN ESPAÑOL (Sometimes I'll start a sentence in Spanish and finish it in Spanish) (Poplack 1980, p. 581).

Tag-switching is the insertion of a tag phrase from one language into an utterance from another language, such as the words: 'you know, I mean, well, etc.'

> e.g. O nee hier's 'n paar goedjies, sorry
> Oh no here-are (truncated) a few thing-diminutive-plural (truncated) sorry
> (Oh no, there are a few things here, sorry)
> (Van Dulm, 2002, p. 64).

Intra-sentential switching takes place within the clause or sentence, regarded as the most complex one. The following example is Punjabi English bilingual in Britain in Romaine 1995 which is presented in Hamers and Blanc (2000):

> *Kio ke six,* seven hours *te* school *de vic spend karde ne,* they are speaking English all the time.
> (Because they spend six or seven hours a day at school they are speaking English all the time)
> (Hamers & Blanc, 2000, p. 260).

So far, research in grammatical aspect of code-switching mostly focuses on the intra-sentential level (MacSwan 2012) and the majority of studies try to explain the irregularities of surface level grammar (Gardner-Chloros 2009).

2.2 Sociolinguistic approach

Generally sociolinguistic approach describes how code-switching is used in relation to 'large overarching issues of language in speech communities' (Seidlitz 2003). This approach links code-switching with sociolinguistic situations. It is connected to factors as to why speakers switch in a specific language, it could be seen in an economic 'market' motivation (Bourdieu 1997) and prestige (Labov 1972). Related to globalisation, this situation reflects English as a language which has economic value and prestige, and which people choose in order to gain those advantages.

A major contribution to the literature by Gumperz (1982) has become the groundwork of code-switching studies and developed key concepts of code-switching. He coined the difference between *situational and conversational code-switching*. Situational code-switching identifies a language shift due to a change of participants, topics or setting which symbolises a direct relationship between language and social interactions (Blom & Gumperz, 1986, p. 116). For example, to illustrate how teachers' change in language can facilitate a shift in activity, Blom & Gumperz (1972) showed an example of formal lectures by teachers in Norway, which was at the beginning done in Bokmål—the standard language, then shifting to Ranamål—the dialect used when they wanted to encourage open and free discussion among students (as cited in Then & Ting 2011). In contrast, conversational code-switching occurs without any change in the social situation, nevertheless it has a social function. Metaphorical code-switching is a subset of conversational code-switching, which enables speakers to evoke a certain mood or to change their status with other speakers. To illustrate, Blom and Gumperz (1986) give as an example when a customer of that community office continued the business transaction with a clerk outside the office to have a more personal and private discussion. There was a shift of relationship from *formal* to *informal* which shows metaphorical code-switching. In short, code-switching has certain features seen from the social factors embedded in speakers' situations where it takes place.

2.3 Interactional sociolinguistics

Interactional Sociolinguistics (IS) investigates how language communicates meaning in interaction, and specifically to see how discourse and context are linked together (Gumperz 1982, 1999, 2008). This enables us to deeply see what participants aim to convey in their communication practice (Gumperz 2008). IS concentrates on how the meaning is made through interaction on culturally different speakers with qualitative analysis and ethnographic investigations; not to mention to consider background knowledge and context which is relevant to the process of interaction in order to access what really happens in communication (Gumperz 2008). IS therefore uses discourse analysis approach to seek relevance both in and beyond the literal meaning of language. This study employs IS to go beyond surface meaning to assess the communicative intention. Presumably, the interpretation using IS may be subjective but this study employs prolonged engagement and ethnographically in-depth analysis.

3 METHODS

This study is following Creswell (2012) in using an ethnographic approach to see the life of the participants by seeing their behavior, culture, and way of life.

3.1 Context and participants

This study took place in a tertiary level of a bilingual program in a vocational higher education, located in East Java, Indonesia. The classroom observations were conducted in Accounting and Business Administration in Computer, and Business courses. English and Bahasa Indonesia were officially used as the medium of instruction which did not have a strict proportion.

Three bilingual teachers of Accounting and Business Administration took part in this research. The consent of the teachers was obtained by first sending an invitational letter/email to the potential participants, then the first three teachers who stated the agreement to participate were chosen to be the participants of this study. The participants consisted of two females and one male and they all had experienced overseas study as well as life in an English speaking country. This is very important to select such participants since code-switching done by competent bilingual speakers is assumed to be 'deliberate', not because of language deficiency. For the sake of data presentation, the teachers are labelled T4, T5, and T6.

3.2 *Data collection and instrument*

The data were collected using audio and video recordings of prolonged classroom observation, semi-structured interview with some stimulated recall, and also a focus group discussion (FGD). The data were gathered over one semester from July to December 2012. Classroom observation was done for six months to avoid an observer's paradox in which participants intentionally changed their behavior when they were observed/recorded. Further, semi-structured interviews with some stimulated recall was aimed to revive the important scenes of code-switching– i.e. teachers' practice of code-switching of why and when they conducted such language shifting in a particular situation (Gass & Mackey 2000). FGD was done in order to gain more perspectives which were not covered in stimulated recall interviews. Therefore, the unexplored ideas can usually come up when involving some participants (Powell & Single 1996, 499) to dig up their perceptions on their code-switching practice.

3.3 *Data analysis*

The data of classroom observation were examined using an IS approach (Gumperz 1982) and were identified into the following categories:

1. Whether inter-sentential or intra-sentential code-switching
2. Whether into or out of English
3. Whether into or out of Bahasa Indonesia
4. Whether into or out of Javanese
5. Whether into or out of Arabic
6. Whether in random patterns of usage or more frequent in particular circumstances, such as: when giving instructions, explaining concepts, etc.

After identifying the category, the data were repeatedly viewed, then some possible themes of code-switching features were identified. At this stage, the researcher can present the data based on the themes shown in the next section.

4 RESULTS AND DISCUSSION

The findings of this study are presented and directly followed by the discussion.

4.1 *The use of blending English words*

The first feature of teachers' code-switching is the use of blending words which expressed teachers' motivation for communication and teaching.
Example 1:
Words with suffix -nya
T6: Tapi sementara masih local, saya lihat banyak sekali local student-nya (*so far I see it still has local characteristics, dominantly local students*).
Example 2:
Words with prefix di-
T4: Silahkan di-shutdown kita lanjutkan minggu depan… atau ada yang

ditanyakan lagi? Tidak ada? (please have the computer shut down and we can continue next week. Any questions? No?)

The introspective data indicated the teachers' reason for using these blending words i.e. (1) they wanted to *teach English vocabulary*, (2) they wanted to *add meaning* (e.g. expressing passive voice), (3) when there was *no equal expression in the first language*, and (4) they found it *practical* to use these words to explain the lesson in some ways.

This phenomenon indicates sociolinguistics aspect of English as a prestigious language (see Labov 1972), and some market motivation (Bourdieu 1997) to display the teachers' social status that teachers are educated and prestigious speakers of language.

4.2 To-and-fro code-switching

The next feature is *to-and-fro code-switching* displaying a strategy to make sense of teachers' explanations. This feature shows how code-switching is done back-and-fro from one language into another. To illustrate, see the following example:

T5:

1. You have to provide me with papers, full paper *jadi full paper untuk saya* (so full paper for me).
2. only me, and you have to bind it *kalian harus menjilidnya.. dan eeh* (you have to bind it and ee*h*).
3. please put your name list on the cover of your paper *jadi kalian tulis nama-nama grup-nya.. kemudian* (you write down the names of the group.. then).
4. don't forget to make a *copy ringkasannya jangan lupa buat summary-nya..* (the summary, don't forget to prepare the summary).
5. just one or two pages and *kopi sebanyak kelas* (copy it as many as the member of the class).
6. times four, jadi kalau yang presentasi empat jadi kalian kopi sebanyak empat belas.. ((thinking)) Sembilan belas (If you have four members, you need to copy it fourteen, nineteen times).
7. Just one or two pages *kalau kalian ndak ada biayanya nanti biayanya minta saya* (If you don't have money, come and ask me) ((smiling)).

The example of *to-and-fro code-switching* indicates a reiteration strategy in order to make meaning. However, it is not necessarily repeating the message since the features expansion was found here. This expansion may function as elaboration, reinforcement, and exemplification. Seen from the grammatical approach, it occurs at an intra-sentential level which is considered *complex*. Furthermore, *to-and-fro code-switching* displays teachers' strategy to support students' understanding of the knowledge and information. This practice endorses Polio and Duff's study (1994) which reported repetition and paraphrase in code-switching can smooth communication, as well as facilitate language acquisition. This, however, is contradicted to Le Van Chan & Hamied's argument (2014) that the reiteration/repetition code-switching showed that teachers *underestimated* their students' language competence.

4.3 Javanese and Arabic code-switching

The last feature indicated *the use of Javanese and Arabic code-switching* conveying Javanese as the vernacular language and Arabic as the language of cultural-religious-priority which were normally featured in the classroom daily communication. To begin, let us see the following example of *Javanese code-switching*.

> T6: In case later on you marry with someone overseas it doesn't mean that you.. well *ganti citizenship seperti itu* (change your citizenship). *Ada istilahnya* permanent resident (there is a term called permanent resident). *Teman saya itu jadi permanent resident di Singapore dia dinikahi sama anak India disana* (just like my friend who is a permanent resident in Singapore. She is married to an Indian and they live there).

Saya pikir, 'Oh awakmu suka nonton film India mangkane akhire rabi ambek Shahru Khan' (I said, 'I know you love Indian movies, therefore you married Shahru Khan').

Javanese code-switching in the above example reveals interpersonal purposes by reporting somebody else's words, and giving a personal comment on something. Javanese is associated with personal bonds and informal activities indicating the language of *we code* (Gumperz 1982) or the language spoken by cultural shared specific group. However, we can notify that Javanese switching occurred only as a short turn briefly to make an impression.

Next, let us move into the example of *Arabic code-switching.*

> T6: *Assalamualaikum warahmatullahi wabarakatuh* (May peace, mercy, and blessings of Allah be with you). Good morning students.
> Ss: Morning
> T6: Today we are going to finish the last week assignment...

Arabic addresses some common expressions for ceremonial purposes such as opening and closing conversations, greeting people, receiving good news, etc. It was used for cultural priority purposes since the majority of people are Muslims. However, non-Muslims sometimes use it to respect Muslims in order to comply with the cultural priority. Unlike Susanto's study (2006, p. 18) which found that the Arabic expressions were used to connect the formal discourse with Islam as a religion during a religious meeting held by the members of Indonesian Islamic association, the Arabic expression found in this study is fairly different. Susanto reported a speaker utters the expression of '*Assalamualaikum*', he/she would expect a response '*Waalaikumussalam*' from the hearers to meet with the religious norms and to receive religious blessing. The present study, in contrast, found that Arabic expression was employed not to directly deal with religious matters, it was rather intended to only engage with the cultural way of communication.

5   CONCLUDING REMARKS

The data of teachers' code-switching demonstrated a switching in a smooth and fluid fashion. The pattern is mostly at the level of intra-sentential which displays teachers' skill in using complex languages, such as in *to-and-fro* and *blending words*. This practice was done in order to *reduce the gap* of the TL and *boost students' comprehension* of the content-subjects. We can identify that teachers occasionally switched (1) when the topic became more complex, (2) when they encountered lexical gaps in the TL, and (3) to emphasise the message. This classroom evidence pinpoints that teachers were engaged in *translanguaging* practice in which shuttling between languages are done in a natural way (see Cahyani et al. 2016). This displays how languages are combined as a unity to achieve effective communication. This study argues that employing multiple languages in the classroom is valuable in order to boost the meaning making process, as well as to make sense the communication which is unique across culture. As an implication, code-switching in the classroom should be seen as *a communication resource* which is not only dealing with the language and pedagogy, but also with the sociocultural norms.

REFERENCES

Andersson, I. & Rusanganwa, J. 2011. Language and space in a multilingual undergraduate physics classroom in Rwanda. *International Journal of Bilingual Education and Bilingualism* 14(6): 751–764.

Barnard, R. & McLellan, J. 2014. Introduction. In R. Bernard & J. McLellan (eds.), *Code-switching in university English-medium classes: Asian perspectives*: 1–9. Bristol: Multilingual Matters.

Blom, J.P. & Gumperz, J.J. 1986. Social meaning in linguistic structures: Code-switching in Norway. In J.J. Gumperz & D. Hymes (Eds.), *Directions in sociolinguistics: The ethnography of communication*: 407–434. Oxford: Basil Blackwell Ltd.

Bourdieu, P. 1997. The forms of capital. In A.H. Halsey, H. Lauder, P. Brown & A.S. Wells (eds.), *Education: Culture, economy, society*: 46–58. Oxford: Oxford University Press.

Cahyani, H., de Courcy, M. & Barnett, J. 2016. Teachers' code-switching in bilingual classrooms: exploring pedagogical and sociocultural functions. *International Journal of Bilingual Education and Bilingualism*: 1–15.

Canh, V.L. & Hamied, F.A. 2014. Codeswitching in universities in Vietnam and Indonesia. In Roger Barnard & James Mc Cellan (eds), *Codeswitching in university English-Medium classes Asian perspectives, Multilingual Matters*. Bristol: Buffalo.

Creswell, J.W. 2012. *Educational research: Planning, conducting, and evaluating quantitative and qualitative research (4th ed.)*. Boston: Pearson Education Ltd.

Gardner-Chloros, P. 2009. *Code-switching*. Cambridge: Cambridge University Press.

Gass, S.M. & Mackey, A. 2000. *Stimulated recall methodology in second language research*. New Jersey: Taylor & Francis.

Grosjean, F. 1982. *Life with two languages*. Cambridge, MA: Cambridge University Press.

Gumperz, J. 1982. *Discourse strategies*. Cambridge: Cambridge University Press.

Gumperz, J.J. 1999. On interactional sociolinguistic method. In S. Sarangi & C. Roberts (Eds.), *Talk, work and institutional order: Discourse in medical, mediation and management settings*: 453–471. New York: Mouton de Gruyter.

Gumperz, J.J. 2008. Interactional sociolinguistics: A personal perspective. In D. Schiffrin, D, Tannen & H.E. Hamilton (eds.), *The handbook of discourse analysis* (pp. 215–228). Massachusetts: Blackwell Publishers.

Gupta, A.F. 2007. ASEAN English on the web. In D. Prescott, A. Kirkpatrick, H. Azirah & I. Martin (Eds.), *English in Southeast Asia: Varieties, literacies, and literatures*: 353–370. Newcastle: Cambridge Scholars Publishing.

Hadisantosa, N. 2010. Insights from Indonesia. In R. Johnstone (Ed.), *Learning through English: Policies, challenges and prospects, insights from East Asia*: 24–46. Manchester: The British Council.

Hamers, J.F. & Blanc, M.H.A. 2000. *Bilinguality and bilingualism*. Cambridge: Cambridge University Press.

Labov, W. 1972. *Language in the inner city: Studies in the Black English vernacular* 3. Philadelphia: University of Pennsylvania Press.

Macaro, E. 2009. Teacher use of code-switching in the second language classroom: Exploring 'optimal' use. In M. Turnbull, & J. Dailey-O'Cain (eds.), *First language use in second and foreign language learning*: 35–49. Bristol: Multilingual Matters.

Macaro, E. 2014. Where should we be going with classroom code switching research? In R. Barnard & J. McLellan (Eds.), Code-switching in university English-medium classes: Asian perspectives: 10–23. Bristol: Multilingual Matters.

MacSwan, J. 2012. Code-switching and grammatical theory. In T.K. Bathia & W.C. Ritchie (eds), *The handbook of bilingualism and multilingualism*: 349–376. New York: John Wiley & Sons.

Martin, P.W. 2005. 'Safe' language practices in two rural schools in Malaysia: Tensions between policy and practice. In A.M. Lin & P.W. Martin (eds.), *Decolonisation, globalisation: Language-in-education policy and practice*: 74–97. Clevedon: Multilingual Matters.

Moodley, V. 2007. Code-switching in the multilingual English first language classroom. *International Journal of Bilingual Education and Bilingualism* 10(6): 707–722.

Nababan, P.W.J. 1991. Language in education: the case Indonesia. *International Review of Education* 37(1): 115–131.

Palmer, D.K. 2009. Code-switching and symbolic power in a second-grade two-way classroom: A teacher's motivation system gone awry. *Bilingual Research Journal* 32(1): 42–59.

Polio, C.G. & Duff, P.A. 1994. Teachers' language use in university foreign language classrooms: A qualitative analysis of English and target language alternation. *The Modern Language Journal* 78(3): 313–326.

Poplack, S. 1980. Sometimes I'll start a sentence in Spanish Y TERMINO EN ESPANOL: Toward a typology of code-switching. Linguistics 18(7/8): 581–618.

Powell, R.A. & Single, H.M. 1996. Focus group. International Journal for Quality in Health Care, (8), 499–504.

Probyn, M. 2009. Smuggling the vernacular into the classroom: Conflicts and tensions in classroom code-switching in township/rural schools in South Africa. *International Journal of Bilingual Education and Bilingualism* 12(2): 123–136.

Seidlitz, L.M. 2003. *Functions of code-switching in classes of German as a foreign language* (Unpublished PhD thesis). The University of Texas.

Susanto, D. 2006. Code-switching in Islamic religious discourse: The role of Insha'Allah. Paper presented at *Rhizomes: Re-Visioning Boundaries Conference of The School of Languages and Comparative Cultural Studies*: 24–25 February, Brisbane, University of Queensland.

Then, D.C.O. & Ting, S.H. 2011. Researching code-switching in teacher classroom discourse: Questioning the sufficiency of informant reports. *Language Society and Culture* 33: 8–18.

Van Dulm, O. 2002. Constraints on South African English-Afrikaans intra-sentential code switching: A minimalist approach. *Stellenbosch Papers in Linguistics Plus* 31: 63–90.

ELT in Asia in the Digital Era: Global Citizenship and Identity – Madya et al. (Eds)
© 2018 Taylor & Francis Group, London, ISBN 978-0-8153-7900-3

Code-switching and code-mixing in bilingual communication: Language deficiency or creativity?

D.A. Nugraheni
Islamic University of Jember, Jember, Indonesia

ABSTRACT: The study aimed to investigate the students' reasons of using code-switching and code-mixing in bilingual communication. Questionnaire exploring the uses of code switching and code-mixing and classroom observation were applied to 24 sixth semester students of English major at a university. The gathered data were then, categorized into two different tendencies: as a language deficiency or creativity of the English language users. The results show no significant difference between the reasons of using code-switching and code-mixing in bilingual communication as the tendency of language deficiency and as the creativity of language users. It means that both reasons become plausible tendencies why students switch and mix code. From the observation, the type of code-mixing congruent lexicalization was the most type found in classroom communication. Further, the result of study could be a basic data for the English teachers/lecturers to take an appropriate action to assist them in their communication strategy.

1 INTRODUCTION

1.1 *What are code-switching and code-mixing?*

Although, the terms of code mixing and code switching have been familiar in bilingualism, the definition between code switching and code mixing is debatable. Code-switching has been defined as the act of alternation of two languages within a single discourse, sentence or their constituents Poplack (1980). According to Bhatia & Ritchie (2004) code mixing refers to the mixing of various linguistic units (morphemes, words, modifiers, phrases, clauses, and sentences) primarily from two participating grammatical systems within a sentence, it is intra-sentential and is restricted by grammatical principles. On the other hand, code-switching occurs when we have inter-sentential alternations when the switch is made across sentence boundaries.

To Claros & Isharyanti (2009) code switching or inter-sentential code alternation occurs when a bilingual speaker uses more than one language in a single utterance above the clause level to appropriately convey his/her intents, while code mixing also called intra-sentential code switching or intra-sentential code-alternation occurs when speakers use two or more languages below clause level within one social situation.

From the definitions above, code switching and code mixing can be distinguished from where the alteration occurs whether it is inter-sentential or intra-sentential.

1.2 *Types of code-switching and code-mixing*

According to Poplack (2004), there are three types of code-switching. The first is tag-switching, which is related to the inclusion of a tag (e.g. *you know, I mean, right*, etc). This type of code-switching is very simple and does not involve a great command of both languages, since there is a minimum risk of violation of grammatical rules.

The second type of code-switching is the inter-sentential switching, which is at the phrase or sentence level, between sentences. The third and most complex type of code-switching is the intra-sentential one. The complexity of this type of switching is explained by the high probability of violation of syntactic rules, as well as the requirement of a great knowledge of both grammars and how they map onto each other.

For the examples mentioned above, it is clearly seen that, in code-switching, there is no adaptation or integration of words or clauses from one language into the other. What occurs is simply a switch in the language.

On the other hand, Muysken (2000) defines three types of code mixing: insertion, alternation, and congruent lexicalization. In his view, insertion occurs when lexical items from one language are incorporated into another. Claros & Isharyanti (2009) gave the examples of three types of code mixing between English and Spanish and between English and Indonesian. The example of insertion between English and Spanish, "*Pero bueno creo que basta con que incluya la pregunta de* enhanced output *más todas las demás*" [Well, I think it is enough if I just include the question of enhanced output]. The example between English and Indonesia is "*Tergantung* team, *terus juga tergantung* event" [It depends on the team and on the event].

The second type, alternation occurs when structures of two languages are alternated indistinctively both at the grammatical and lexical level. The example between English and Spanish, "Just have it in my room like *a niña bonita como debe ser*", [I just have it in my room like a girl pretty as it should be] while between English and Indonesian, "*I mean, ganti ke kalimat laen*" [I mean, change it to another sentence].

The third type, congruent lexicalization refers to the situation where two languages share grammatical structures which can be filled lexically with elements from either language. The example between Indonesian and English, "Gw konek pake cellp gw", [I connected using my cell phone].

2 LITERATURE REVIEW

2.1 *Reasons why switch and mix code*

There are some reasons why people use code-switching and code mixing in communication. According to Hoffman (1991:116), there are seven reasons for bilinguals to switch and mix their languages:

The first is talking about a particular topic. People sometimes prefer to talk about a particular topic in one language rather than in another. The second is quoting somebody else. People sometimes like to quote a famous expression or saying of some well-known figures. The third is being emphatic about something. The fourth is interjection (Inserting sentence fillers or sentence connectors). Interjection can be a short exclamation like: Hey!, Well!, Look!, etc. The fifth is repetition used for clarification that will be understood more by the listeners. The sixth is intention of clarifying the speech content for interlocutor to make the content of his/her speech runs smoothly and can be understood by the hearer. The seventh is expressing group identity.

Most of reasons proposed by Hoffman (1991:116) indicate that the use of code switching and code mixing is the creativity (bilingual strategy) used by speaker or language user in communication. Supported another study, McLellan (2009) has shown that code-mixing is systematic and that code-mixed and code-switched text, far from being deficient, are linguistically extremely sophisticated. He has also convincingly argued that many of the code-mixed texts show a more or less equal amount of grammar and lexis from both languages. In order to be able to produce code switching and code mixing between two languages, the user must be fluent in both languages and they also know how to combine them to create a third code.

Besides Hoffman (1991) & McLellan (2009), Fakeye (2012) admits in his study that preservice teachers code mix and code-switch for various reasons. They are using code alteration in accordance with a variety of situations, language attitude dominance to code mix and switch, and other variables such as social status and age would cause pre-service teacher to alternate codes in their verbal communication.

In another study, Duran, Kan, Khnert, Nett, & Yim (2005) remark that an alternative view of code-switching and code-mixing is to recognize the cultural, social, and communicative validity of the mixing of two traditionally isolated linguistic codes as a third legitimate code. Further, Eunhee (2006) suggests that it is necessary for both monolinguals and bilinguals to understand the cultural, social, and communicative validity factors which become the very possible reasons using code-mixing and code-switching.

Most reasons in the Fakeye's (2012) research finding indicate that the pre-service teacher use code-switching and code-mixing because they try to deliver better meaning related to the society they belong to. In other words, the use the alteration is not because of their lack of language skills but it is as the strategy in bilingual communication.

However, other studies showed quite different reasons why people switch and mix code. According to Blanci & Hamers (2000: 258), 'Code-switching' and 'code-mixing' were considered as signs of incompetence. Study conducted by Malik (1994) discussing code-switching of the language situation in India explained ten reasons for speakers to code-switch. Some of the reasons are because of lack of facility and lack of registral competence.

Similar to Malik's (1994) study, Cahyani (2013) studied code switching in Indonesian tertiary bilingual classrooms. She says that there are three reasons for students to switch code: struggling in using English, concerned that peers may not understand, and expressing solidarity with cultural identity. The first and the second reasons indicate that some students switch code because they lack linguistic knowledge of the target language. They do not know the equivalent words for expressing their ideas in the target language.

The reason employed by the student is he did not know the equivalent words in English. He was afraid if he made mistakes. He thought that it was really hard. Other reasons gotten through interviewing some students: Structuring questions in English related to the topic discussed was not easy, for asking questions, they frequently structure it first before asking it, and in English presentation, they begin with English but in question session, when it gets very complicated, they will switch into Indonesian.

The second reason for concerning peers may not understand is similar to the first reason. Further, Cahyani (2013) explained that her student said that he had difficulty to transfer the content when he delivered in English and he was afraid if his friends could only listen and they could not understand the message.

Moreover, study conducted by Adebola & Babalola (2011) on code-switching and its literacy effects on the acquisition of English Language by Yoruba, showed some reasons for the participants' code switching. They are: switching enables them to discuss freely with their friends and parents at home, it helps them to understand new English concepts better if explained in Yoruba, they do not know the word for it in the other language and that the word is readily recalled in the switched language; and it serves as a status symbol.

The studies conducted by Malik (1994), Cahyani (2013) & Adebola (2011) can conclude that one of the reasons why people switch and mix code is because of language deficiency (lack of linguistic knowledge of the target language). Specifically, from the results of studies above there are two reasons why students use code-switching and code-mixing in bilingual communication; they are because of language deficiency as the lack of linguistic knowledge or as the creativity (bilingual strategy) used by the speaker or language users.

This present study; therefore, investigated the reasons why the students use code-switching and code-mixing in communicating in the classroom activities. To be more specific, I try to answer these two following questions:

1. Do the students use code-switching and code-mixing because of language deficiency or creativity as language users?
2. What types of code-switching and code-mixing are mostly used by the students?

3   METHOD

3.1   *Participants*

Altogether 24 sixth semester students of English major were purposively selected. They had passed courses on English speaking, writing, reading, listening, grammar and vocabulary for two years. The assumption is that they have adequate linguistic knowledge to have a good communication of English in classroom activities.

3.2 Procedures

The data were collected through questionnaire and observation. The students were asked to fill the questionnaire about the reasons why they do code-switching and code-mixing in the classroom communication. The observations were done in two meetings of an English course. The students were observed during teaching learning process to note what type of code-switching or code-mixing were most frequently used.

There are 10 questions in the questionnaire which are in the form of four-point Likert scales ranging from strongly agree (scored 4), agree (scored 3), disagree (scored 2), and strongly disagree (scored 1). The responses of the questionnaire of students' reasons were categorized into two different tendencies: as a language deficiency or creativity of the English language users.

The observations were done in two meetings in Syntax Courses while the students delivered the presentation about the materials. The teaching learning activities were videotaped and the students' conversations during the class were transcribed. From the conversation transcribed, it was coded to determine what type of code-switching and code-mixing most frequently occured.

3.3 Analysis

The questionnaire data were analyzed using descriptive statistics, specifically frequency to determine the mean and standard deviation. The means between questionnaire for both reasons (language deficiency and creativity) were compared using Paired Sample t-test to find difference, then, the result of the data analysis is consulted to the *t*-table of 5% significant level (confidence interval 95%) to know whether the result is significant or not.

4 RESULTS AND DISCUSSIONS

4.1 Item validity and reliability of the questionnaire

The validity and reliability of the questionnaire are examined respectively using the Pearson product moment and Cronbach's alpha by using SPSS program version 20.0.

The result of computation of Pearson product moment was compared to the r-table of $N = 24$ (the total number of respondent is 24) with the 5% level of significance. As we can see from the table, all items in the questionnaire have r*xy* higher than 0.404 so it means that all questions in the questionnaire are valid. Moreover, the item reliability of the questionnaire was calculated using Cronbach's alpha. It is clear from the table that the reliability coefficient 0.747 is higher than 0.70. It means that the reliability was high.

Table 1. Item validity of the questionnaire.

Item validity (N = 24) r table = 0.404	
Items of questionnaire	r_{xy}
Q1	0.440
Q2	0.442
Q3	0.444
Q4	0.471
Q5	0.668
Q6	0.491
Q7	0.763
Q8	0.510
Q9	0.600
Q10	0.692

4.2 Students' reasons in using code-switching and code-mixing

From the results above, we can see that Table 3 has higher total mean (Σ Mean = 15.46) and total lower standard deviation (Σ St.D = 2.736) than Table 4 with the total mean (Σ Mean = 13,54) and total standard deviation (Σ St. D = 3.19). However, the difference between means in the Table 3 and Table 4 was not significant based on statistical analysis (p = 0.073, 0.073 > 0.05). It means that there is no reason used more than the others. Both reasons in using code-switching and code-mixing because of language deficiency and creativity as language users are used by the students. The students might be lack of linguistic knowledge but they also use code-switching and code-mixing as bilingual strategies at the same time.

Although the finding did not show significant difference between both tendencies, this study, therefore, interestingly fill the gap to the difference results of other studies. This study emphasize that both reasons: as language deficiency (Malik (1994), Blanci & Hamers (2000), Cahyani (2013) & Adebola (2011)) or as creativity (Hoffman (1991), McLellan (2009), Fakeye (2012) & Duran et al. (2005) are natural phenomena that happen at the same time in bilingual communication.

Table 2. Reliability of the questionnaire.

Reliability statistics	
Cronbach's Alpha	N of Items
0.747	10

Table 3. Reasons because of language deficiency (lack of linguistic knowledge).

Statements		SA	A	D	SD	St. D
I switch and mix between English and Indonesia because	Freq	8%	75%	17%	–	0.504
I do not know the English words	Mean			2.92		
Code-switching and code-mixing help me to fill the gap in	Freq	4%	92%	4%	–	0.295
speaking when delivering my presentation to the class.	Mean			3.00		
It's easier to speak in Indonesian when I deliver my	Freq	37%	50%	13%	–	0.676
presentation in the class.	Mean			3.25		
I switch and mix English-Indonesian because it's difficult	Freq	42%	50%	8%	–	0.637
to speak in English only.	Mean			3.33		
I use code-switching and code-mixing to add emphasis of	Freq	17%	62%	21%	–	0.624
my presentation to the class	Mean			2.96		

Table 4. Reasons because of bilingual strategy (creativity) as language users.

Statements		SA	A	D	SD	Total
I switch and mix English-Indonesian so others	Freq	8%	79%	9%	4%	0.584
would not understand (privacy)	Mean			2.92		
I switch and mix English-Indonesian to make	Freq	8%	46%	42%	4%	0.717
some jokes in communicating with my colleague.	Mean			2.58		
Among my colleagues I switch and mix	Freq	4%	11%	12%	–	0.588
English-Indonesian to convey intimacy.	Mean			2.54		
Switching and Mixing English and Indonesian	Freq	8%	46%	42%	4%	0.717
leads to the weakness to my English.	Mean			2.58		
Switching and Mixing between English and	Freq	8%	79%	9%	4%	0.584
Indonesian leads to the creativity to use both	Mean			2.92		
English and Indonesian.						

Both tendencies; as language deficiency and creativity are therefore natural process to optimize language performance. As stated by Meuter (2009), in multilingual as well as bilingual communication, the speakers aim to optimize language performance. She admits that language performance optimization requires preparedness to facilitate language switching, sensitivity and responsiveness to language cues, and the ability to maintain a selected language. The reasons why students use code-switching and code-mixing might be due to different tendencies, but the emphasis is that they have the same aim; to maintain language performance and communication.

As the natural phenomena, language deficiency and creativity may happen at the same time. Language deficiency should not be seen solely as a sign of low proficiency, but it is the process that leads the students to use bilingual strategy creatively to maintain their communication. According to Trudgill (1997), it may be difficult to detect, losses being masked by code-switches and it can occur either with heavy linguistic symptoms such as morphological loss or without them (Dorian, 1981; Schmidt, 1985). Moreover, Dorian (1981) points out that in which a variety is abandoned, languages may die without their morphology having altered at all.

4.3 *Observation to the students in classroom activities*

Observation was carried out in two meetings of an English course. While observing the class, the researcher had had a chance to videotape the classroom interactions and the particular circumstances where code switching or code mixing occurred.

From the results of the observations, it was yielded that the type of code-mixing congruent lexicalization as the most type was mostly found. It refers to the situation where two languages share grammatical structures which can be filled lexically with elements from either language. The examples of this code-mixing type are:

Example 1: *Pak, tanya itu yang di*-identify *point yang ke berapa?* (Sir, May I ask you? Which point should be identified?)
Example 2: *Bagaimana kalau dimasukkan di* tree diagram-*nya?* (Sir, what if it was included in the tree diagram?)
Example 3: (between peers) *Ada dua* assigment, *rek!* tree diagram *sama* function-*nya.* (there were two assignments, guys; making the tree diagram and stating its functions)
Example 4: *Pak bagaimana kalau yang* incorrect *di*-indirect object *apakah bisa dibenarkan?* (Sir, what if the indirect object was the only incorrect one, could it be categorized as correct?
Example 5: (between peers) *Ini di*-calculate *semua salahnya?* (Should all the incorrect answers be calculated?

The result of observation indicates that the students found difficulties in making correct complete sentences in English. There were approximately two English words in one utterance. To support the result of observation, I interviewed three students in random. In the unstructured interview, I asked the students why they did not say to their lecturers and peers using complete utterance in English. They answered that they cannot express word in target language because they do not know the equivalent words in English, they were afraid of making mistake, and they are burdened by making grammatically correct sentence.

5 CONCLUSION

Based on the reasons discussed above, it can be concluded that main reason of students' code switching and code mixing can be due to language deficiency (lack of linguistic knowledge). Most of the students cannot express word in target language because they do not know the equivalent words in English, they were afraid of making mistake, and they are burdened by making grammatically correct sentence. This may happen because of inadequate English exposure to the students. At the same time, however, the students believe that they are also creative language users because they do not only use code-switching and code-mixing because they cannot express in the target language, but also to build social community communication such as privacy preferences, conveying intimacy, and emphasize the utterance they want to deliver in classroom activities. Thus, we cannot neglect or view code switch and mix negatively as signs of language incompetency, because both reasons; language deficiency and creativity as language users are plausible reasons that the students at least, if not all, basically understand a more or less equal amount of grammar and lexis from both languages in using code- switching and code-mixing in bilingual communication.

6 RECOMMENDATION

To make students more creative as language users or to accommodate the reason from lacking of linguistic knowledge into creativity of language users, we can create meaningful and beneficial classroom situation by giving more English exposure to the students, use frequently English instruction, and create English-spoken classroom situation. In short, code switching and code mixing are natural and unique phenomena in bilingualism that both because of language deficiency or creativity of language users, they still come up with bilingual communication. But, it can be a more useful strategy in classroom interaction if the tendency is to make meaning clear and to exchange information in an effective way.

REFERENCES

Adebola, O.A. & Babalola, J.A. 2011. Code-switching and its literacy effects on the acquisition of English language by Yoruba / English language bilinguals. *Journal of Education and Practice* 2(5).
Bhatia, J.K. & Ritchie, W.C. 2004. Social and psychological factors in language mixing. In W.C. Ritchie and T.K. Bhatia (eds), *Handbook of Bilingualism*: 336–352. Blackwell Publishing.
Blanci, M. & Hammers, J.F. 2000. *Bilinguality and bilingualism.* Cambridge, U.K: Cambridge University Press.
Cahyani, H. 2013. Beyond a language deficit: Students' code switching in Indonesian tertiary bilingual classrooms. *Paper presented at 8th University of Sydney TESOL Research Network Colloquium in conjunction with Macquarie University.*
Claros, M.S.C. & Isharyanti, N. 2009. Code switching and code mixing in internet chatting: Between 'yes', 'ya', and 'si' a Case Study. *The JALT CALL Journal* 5(3): 67–78.
Dorian, N. 1981. *The life cycle of a Scottish Gaelic dialect.* Philadelphia: University of Pennsylvania Press.
Duran, L., Kan, P.F., Kohnert, K., Nett, K. & Yim, D. 2005. Intervention with linguistically diverse preschool children: A focus on developing home language(s). *Language, Speech & Hearing Services in Schools* 36(3): 251–263.
Eunhee, K. 2006. Reasons and motivations for code-mixing and code-switching. *EFL* 4(1).
Fakeye, D.O. 2012. Motivational factors for code alternation in pre- service teachers' verbal communication in Oyo and Ekiti States. *Asian Social Science* 8(8): 149–154.
Hoffman, C. 1991. *An introduction to bilingualism.* New York: Longman.
Malik, L. 1994. *Socio-linguistics: A study of code-switching.* New Delhi, ND: Anmol Publications Pvt. Ltd.
McLellan, J. 2009. *When two grammars coincide: Malay-English code-switching in public on-line discussion forum texts.* The University of Waikato, Aotearoa, New Zealand.
Meuter, R.F.I. 2009. Language selection and performance optimisation in multilinguals. In Isurin, L., Winford, D., & de Bot, K. *Studies in Bilingualism: Multidisciplinary approaches to Code Switching* 2(41): 27–51.
Muysken, P. 2000. *Bilingual speech: A typology of code-mixing.* United Kingdom: Cambridge University Press.
Poplack, S. 1980. Sometimes I'll start a sentence in Spanish Y Termino en espanol: toward a typology of code-switching. In Wei, L. (ed.), *The bilingualism reader*: 221–256. New York: Routledge.
Poplack, S. 2004. Code-switching: Soziolinguistics. *An international handbook of the science of language,* 2nd ed. Berlin: Walter de Gruyter.
Schmidt, A. 1985. *Young people's djirbal.* Cambridge: Cambridge University Press.
Trudgill, P. 1977. Creolization in reverse: reduction and simplification in the Albanian Dialects of Greece. *Transactions of the philological society* 7:32–50.

ELT in Asia in the Digital Era: Global Citizenship and Identity – Madya et al. (Eds)
© *2018 Taylor & Francis Group, London, ISBN 978-0-8153-7900-3*

English as a medium of instruction: Issues and challenges for Indonesian university lecturers and students

R. Hendryanti & I.N. Kusmayanti
Telkom University, Bandung, Indonesia

ABSTRACT: This study explored issues and challenges that emerged in English medium instruction classes offered by five study programs in a university in Bandung, Indonesia. Data were collected from a series of interviews with thirty lectures and focus group interviews attended by 50 students. English language ability was a common problem perceived by both parties. Heterogeneity of students' English competence, the problematic focus of teaching content over language, and the inability to elaborate, improvise, and insert humor as icebreakers have been reported as specific problems experienced by the lecturers. In addition, lecturers' pronunciation problems, lack of clarity, and monotonous teaching strategies were perceived as issues by students. Implications and suggestions for lecturers' professional development and students' EFL competence are presented.

1   INTRODUCTION

1.1   *The use of English as a medium of instruction in higher education institutions*

The use of English as a Medium of Instruction (EMI) has become a global phenomenon (Dearden 2014). The adoption of EMI in many educational contexts in both native English speaking (NES) and non-NES countries is one of the consequences following the internalization and globalization era (Coleman 2006, Doiz, Lasagabaster & Sierra 2011) as well as expansion in education (Wilkinson 2012). Early EMI context can be traced back to the European content-based integrated learning movement, content-based teaching and bilingual education in NES contexts (Vu & Burns 2014).

In the European context, Wilkinson (2012) states that in the early 2000s, ranking organizations became a trend and thus stimulated higher education institutions to offer degree programs through English. As cited by Wilkinson (2012), Wächter and Maiworm identified three dominating reasons underlying the offering of EMI courses in a university. The first reason relates to the effort of drawing the interest of international students. The second reason is to provide opportunities to domestic students to equip themselves with competencies required by the global market. The third reason is anchored to a university's target to place itself to the highest quality they could result in comparison to other institutions in the country. This phenomenon quickly reached other non-NES countries, thus largely widening the spread of EMI in universities all over the world.

However, the fast growth of EMI is not linear with the success of EMI usage in various higher education contexts. While minor problems exist in the implementation of EMI in universities within the NES countries, substantive issues arise in conjunction with the usage of EMI in non-NES higher education contexts. Vu and Wu (2014) explained that the variation of EMI's implementation greatly depends on the position of the English language within the contexts, i.e., English as the first, second, and foreign language. In contexts where English is the first language of most people and becomes the language of instruction in various levels of education, minor issues exist regarding the integration of English language and content subjects and the role of language and content teachers (Davidson & Williams 2001, Davison

2006). On the other hand, whereby the government or educational institutions mandates the usage of English as the medium of instruction in contexts where English is the second or foreign language, substantive problems regarding language policies and the implementation of the policies involving EMI teachers and students call for more in-depth research (Vu & Burns 2014).

1.2 *Issues and challenges of EMI implementation in higher education*

Studies on EMI's implementation have presented problems faced by both students and lecturers.

Hellekjær (2010) investigated the issue of students' comprehension of lectures in EMI. Three hundred and sixty-four Norwegian and 17 German students participated in the study and were asked to self-report regarding their comprehension towards lectures conducted in English and in their first language. In terms of attending the EMI lectures, both groups reported that it was difficult for them to understand the lectures due to the lecturer's unclear pronunciation and inability to take advantage of meta-discursive cues to help students be aware of what the lecturer was up to, as well as the students' unfamiliarity of specific vocabulary. Using Cummins' (1979) distinction of language proficiency, Basic Interpersonal Communication Skills (BICS) and Cognitive Academic Language Proficiency (CALP), Doiz, Lasagabaster and Sierra (2012) posit that non-NES students' mastery of interpersonal communication does not always guarantee their success in learning within the EMI context.

Moreover, Hamid, Nguyen and Baldauf Jr (2013) found that the implementation of EMI in ten Asian countries is "fraught with difficulties and challenges" (p. 11). Among the problems are the shortage of competent lecturers who have high levels of expertise in academic knowledge and English (Shohamy 2012), questionable learning outcomes achieved by students in terms of academic content and English (Shohamy 2012), and inappropriate teaching methodology regarding the use of EMI in content courses (Sert 2007).

In line with the findings in Hamid et al. (2013), Tan (2011) discovered that the Malaysian mathematics and science teachers in her study did not view themselves as having the responsibility of teaching the linguistic aspects. They believed that language is a mere means of communication. Tan suggested that EMI teachers should be trained to recognize the significant role of language in facilitating students' content learning. Within the European higher educationcontext, Airey (2012) explored the linguistics situation in Swedish universities in which English and Swedish were used in the teaching and learning of physics involving ten physics lectures from four Swedish universities. When it comes to the teaching of physics through EMI, none of the lecturers considered themselves responsible for helping students acquire the linguistic aspects of the course. The study underlined that the absence of lecturers' awareness toward the instrumental role of the socialization of language of physics had contributed to students' low comprehension, particularly, when the course was offered in English.

With regard to teaching methodology, the findings in Lin's study (2012) underline the importance of using students' first language in the transition process of moving toward the idea of an EMI total immersion. She promotes the pedagogical potential of "linguistic processes of 'packing' and 'unpacking' English science texts" (p. 88) in content learning. Interesting findings regarding an EMI lecturer's limited informal register of speech in English, compared to the lecturer's first language speech register, was apparent in Thøgersen's (2013) study. Thøgersen (2013) recorded the lecturer when giving seminars of the same content and objectives, two times in English and three times in Danish and found that the lecturer used informal spoken register of Danish, but spoke more formally in English. Further, the study revealed that the use of informal Danish corpus facilitated students' comprehension of the disciplinary topics taught, while the formal use of English contributed to the lecturer's failure of providing a comprehensible lecture. This research called for the need of providing discourse training to EMI lecturers.

Issues and challenges as evident in the studies discussed may also occur in other EMI programs in non-NES higher education contexts. However, the approaches needed to address the problems may be different and unique to the present contexts, especially when particular EMI policies are involved. Upon reviewing studies on EMI-related policy, Vu and Burns

(2014) posit that there is a need for research involving individual EMI actors, i.e., teachers and students, taking part directly in the EMI implementation. It is in this context that the present study was conducted.

This paper examines the implementation of EMI in undergraduate programs offered by a private university in Bandung, Indonesia. We begin by briefly discussing the EMI context in Indonesia. By using interview data, we investigated central issues and challenges facing by both lecturers and students. Based on the findings, a recommendation to promote EMI lecturers' teaching expertise and improve students' readiness for EMI course are put forward.

1.3 *EMI in Indonesian higher education*

The expansion of education and the trend of ranking organizations in European higher education in the early 2000s (Coleman 2011, Wilkinson 2012) also impacted Indonesian higher education institutions. The number of universities in Indonesia offering content courses in English through the internationalization of certain degree programs keeps on increasing. A vision to be a world-class university has been widely embraced and has entailed an expansion of EMI into an Indonesian university's strategic plan.

Historically, the offering of EMI programs in Indonesia can be traced back to the 1990s when MBA programs were offered by business schools (Ibrahim 2001). Further, Ibrahim (2001) highlighted that rapidly growing universities such as University of Indonesia, Trisakti University, and Atmajaya Catholic University took the step of developing international programs in which English is the medium of instruction. However, unique to Indonesian context, the international programs do not mean that the programs are intended for international students. Dewi (2017) explains that typically, international programs are similar to the regular programs regarding the students' country of origins, i.e., Indonesia. Students enrolling in the international programs are domestic students who meet certain English language proficiency and academic qualification criteria.

The fact that most of the lecturers and students in the EMI programs are Indonesian has posed unique issues and challenges in the process of teaching and learning. Unfortunately, there is a dearth of research investigating various aspects of EMI implementation in Indonesia. The only study was conducted by Dewi (2017), in which she investigated the perceptions of Indonesian lecturers toward EMI through a mixed method study. Findings of her study shows that Indonesian lecturers' perceptions of EMI are complex, involving not only the linguistic aspects but also the issues of national identity and sentiments towards English. She also highlights the need for more empowerment for students so that they can be internationally competitive. Dewi's (2017) findings need to be followed by more studies investigating aspects embedded in the effectiveness of EMI implementation in Indonesian higher education institutions. The present study is expected to contribute to parts of this call.

2 RESEARCH METHOD

2.1 *Context of the study*

The university in which this study took place has set its goal to be a world-class university and had initiated its international programs in the year of 2013 by offering EMI-based undergraduate degrees in Telecommunication Engineering, System Information, Informatics, ICT Business, Business Administration, and Industrial Engineering. Most, if not all, of the lecturers and students involved in the programs are Indonesian. Only one lecturer, out of 97 lecturers, is a NES lecturer. Meanwhile, only 7 out of 489 students enrolling in the program per academic year of 2016/2017 are international students coming from non-NES country such as Malaysia, Bangladesh, Tajikistan, South Korea, and Vietnam. From the point of view of language usage, the university publishes an English only policy regarding the medium of instruction in classes. Preliminary and informal research we did indicated that the running of the programs has been followed by multiple problems, one of which relates to the language of instruction and pedagogical issues. This study is intended to be one of the efforts in entangling the problems through the identification of issues and challenges perceived by lecturers and students.

2.2 Research questions

The lecturer interviews and focus group interviews with the students were aimed at answering the following questions:

1. What are the language and non-language issues perceived by Indonesian EMI lecturers and students in the classrooms?
2. What are the challenges faced by the EMI lecturers and students in the classrooms?

2.3 The participants

Thirty lecturers participated in the interviews and fifty students attended the focus group interviews. Each of the five departments holding the EMI programs was represented by a group lecturers and students as shown in Table 1. The lecturers hold master's and doctoral degrees in their field of studies with five of the total lecturer participants obtaining their master 's degrees from a university in a NES country. With regards to the student participants, one student is from South Korean, one is Vietnamese, and the rest of the students are Indonesian.

2.4 Data collection instruments

The semi-structured interviews with the lecturers were conducted by both authors and one senior lecturer assisting with the data collection. The questions were focused on exploring lecturers' classroom teaching experiences emphasizing on the issues and challenges they faced in class, the approaches they took to overcome the challenges. Each lecturer was interviewed individually in either English or Indonesian as preferred by the lecturer. Prior to the interviews, the interviewers conducted a simulation, making sure that every interviewer was able to use the interview protocol appropriately. The focus group interviews with the students were led by the first author, focusing on stimulating the students to share their classroom experience regarding the use of EMI. The focus group interviews were conducted 6 times, in which each group interview was attended by 5–10 students.

2.5 Procedures

Prior to the interviews, online surveys were administered to all lecturers and students of EMI programs from five departments. At the end of the study information sheet, the authors invited the survey participants to provide their contact emails and phone numbers for follow-up interviews. Participants of this research are those who shared their contact information and responded to the interview invitation. Each lecturer interview was approximately 30. minutes long and each focus group discussion took place in about 40 minutes to one hour. With the participants' consent, the interviews were audio recorded and transcribed for qualitative coding using a constant comparative method (Cresswell 2007) to examine the key themes.

Table 1. Number of lecturer and student participants.

Department	Lecturer	Student
Telecommunication engineering	6	8
System information	6	6
ICT Business	6	14
Business administration	6	12
Industrial engineering	6	10
Total	30	50

2.6 Findings

2.6.1 Language issues for EMI students and lecturers

Two themes regarding the language issues were identified: (1) lecturers' self-efficacy in using English and (2) student's English ability. In terms of lecturers' self-efficacy, most lecturers who were assigned to teach an EMI class for the first time, did not feel confident with their English-speaking ability, even though they met the language requirement for the teaching position. Their lack of confidence was mainly due to the fact that English is not their first language.

> *Well, I think I have to improve my English. I often felt unsure of what to say in class* (Lecturer 1).

Ability to elaborate on a difficult topic was also apparent as an issue regarding language self-efficacy. A calculus lecturer reported that:

> *I felt more comfortable when teaching in a regular class [a non-EMI class]. In the international class, I felt like I could not be flexible in using the language. Sometimes, I did not know how to explain the topic. Quite in contrary with when I was in the regular class…. I can talk about anything using my Indonesian* (Lecturer 3).

Another lecturer expressed his frustration of not being able to use informal register of speech in English.

> *Yeah, [in regular classes] I taught my students through posing a question or spontaneous and humorous comments. Unfortunately, I could not do the same in my international classes. Students seemed to think that everything I said was always something serious. I could not make jokes in English* (Lecturer 15).

The second theme in this category is lecturers' perception of students' English ability. Most of the lecturers reported that many of their students could not understand their explanations in English.

> *… When I asked my students to restate my explanation in their own words, in English, they often asked if they could just do it in Indonesian. Many times, I had to compromise because I did not want to get stuck in certain things. I have to manage my class time* (Lecturer 1).

Students were aware of such issues. However, not all of them thought that their English was a big problem. One of them explained that lecturers should not worry too much.

> *I know that all of them [lecturers] can speak English well, but they worry too much… they worry that we can't absorb the material. That's why they sometimes translated what they said into Indonesian* (Student 1, FGD 3).

In addition to the low English proficiency of some students, lecturers also felt that differences in students' English competence were also challenging. An algorithm lecturer described the situation in his class as follows.

> *Well, the thing is some students could get what I said quickly, but some needed more time to digest. Some did not seem to get my explanation [in English] Even when I made a joke… some students did not understand why their classmates laughed* (Lecturer 2).

2.6.2 Non-language challenges for EMI students and lecturers

The first theme of challenges relates to the language and content trade-offs. Lecturers often found it problematic when they had to decide which should be addressed first: the academic content or the linguistic aspects of the content. A lecturer of information systems, for example, argued that content should be the priority of a subject lecturer

> *To me, the substance [of content] is the most important thing…. A student joining international classes… passing the standard scores for English proficiency, but unable to grasp the substance of certain content will even create a bigger problem* (Lecturer 13).

The second theme relates with lecturers' teaching strategies. Students reported that lecturers' lack of interesting teaching strategies had made some of them loose interest. The example of uninteresting teaching strategy was traditional lecturing where lecturers spent most of their time explaining the topics as reported by student 2.

> *When the lecturer just said the material, when they are only telling us about the material without asking... Without asking or without any activities* (Student 2, FGD 3).

Another student from the same focus group interview added.

> *Students sitting at the back, they were all sleeping. We used to have "sleeping" gank. Only those sitting in the front were awake* (Student 3, FGD 3).

The language and content trade-offs and lack of teaching strategy seem to call for lecturers' professional development in teaching EMI courses.

2.6.3 *Expected solutions to the issues and challenges*

Although they are confronted by the issues and challenges in their classes, both students and lecturers showed positive responses when asked about suggestions of solutions. A student expressed his expectation, demanding reciprocal efforts from both students and lecturers.

> *... Well, the bottom line is that both sides should be aware of the importance of English. It would be better if there is "a way" to help lecturers and also students.... But, the most important thing is that lecturers should take the lead, because they are in the position of educating... Right, like... becoming our role model* (Student 3, FGD 5).

A lecturer teaching an EMI calculus class for the first time hoped that she could observe her colleagues teaching the same subject using EMI prior to her first classes.

> *Emm... actually, I'd like to sit-in in other classes and observed how my senior colleagues teaching their classes. I am not confident teaching my subject although I have read all the materials. I need real examples. Unfortunately, none of my colleagues allow me to visit their classes* (Lecturer 15).

3 DISCUSSION

The expansion of EMI in higher education institution will likely to continue. However, it is worthy to note that it entails caution to the problematic issues and challenges. In the context of this study, the major language challenge as perceived by lecturers resonates with Thøgersen's (2013) study. The lecturers' skills of teaching in the first language, in which they are able to use informal register of speech to facilitate their students' learning does not transfer automatically when they are to teach in English. They are aware that to be successful EMI lecturers, they do not only need academic expertise, but they also need to have the linguistic tools instrumental to their students' learning. This implies that the lecturers are in need of language training designed specifically for teaching content courses in EMI.

Issues of student's language ability, particularly in relation to the students' comprehension toward lectures and lecturer's perception that students in EMI classes should be responsible for their own English learning are in line with previous studies in Asian and European contexts (Tan 2010, Airey 2012). Similar to the mathematics and science teachers in Tan (2010) and physics lecturers in Airey (2012), teachers in this study felt responsible for teaching the linguistic aspects pertaining to their courses. To them, the academic content is more important than the language aspects. They are unaware that language has an important role in facilitating students' content learning (Tan 2010). This implies that the lecturers in this study need training in content-related language awareness.

The issues regarding lecturers' lack of teaching strategy as reported by both students and teachers are also key challenges highlighted in this study. Students reported that they lost interest in classes with "inappropriate teaching methodology" (Sert 2007) and a lecturer expected to be able to observe other EMI lecturers. This finding shows that lecturers in this study demand practical training in EMI teaching approaches.

4 CONCLUSION AND SUGGESTIONS

To be a successful EMI lecturer, one needs to possess a combination of linguistic, academic, and pedagogic competence (Shohamy 2012). Unfortunately, Shohamy (2012) also noted that not many EMI instructors have all elements of the combination. In this study, the lecturers experienced difficulties in various areas of EMI teaching. Based on the findings, this study suggests a number of implications. First, in addressing lecturers' lack of English proficiency, the lecturers need to be supported in leveraging their specific English language skills such as the ability to use informal English registers. This can be done by providing English courses or visiting scholar programs to NES countries.

In addition, the second suggestion relates to enriching the lecturers' pedagogical knowledge and skills instrumental to EMI teaching practices. Doiz et al. (2012) encourage EMI program holders to assist their lecturers with effective teaching strategies that encourage students' active participation and reduce teacher's talk time. This can be done through a teacher training series involving the integration of academic content and language such as training in "linguistic processes of 'packing' and 'unpacking' English science texts" (Lin 2012: 88). In addition, organizing best practice teaching shares among lecturers may be efficacious as well.

REFERENCES

Airey, J. 2012. "I don't teach language": The linguistic attitudes of physics lecturers in Sweden. *AILA Review* 25: 64–79.

Coleman, H. (ed). 2011. *Dreams and realities: Developing countries and the English language*. London: British Council.

Coleman, J.A. 2006. English-medium teaching in European higher education. *Language Teaching* 39(1): 1–14.

Creswell, J.W. 2007. *Qualitative inquiry & research design (2nd ed.)*. Thousand Oaks: Sage.

Davison, C. & Williams, A. 2001. Integrating language and content: Unresolved issues. In B. Mohan, C. Leung & C. Davison (eds.), *English as a second language in the mainstream: Teaching, learning and identity*: 51–70. Harlow, UK: Pearson.

Davison, C. 2006. Collaboration between ESL and content teachers: How do we know when we are doing it right? *International Journal of Bilingual Education and Bilingualism* 9(4): 454–475.

Dearden, J. 2014. *English as a medium of instruction-a growing global phenomenon*. British Council.

Dewi, A. 2017. English as a medium of instruction in Indonesian higher education: A study of lecturers' perceptions. In B. Fenton-Smith, P. Humphreys, and I.Walkinshaw (eds), *English Medium Instruction in Higher Education in Asia-Pacific*: 241–258. *Multilingual Education* 21. Cham: Springer.

Doiz, A., Lasagabaster, D. & Sierra, J.M. (2012). Future challenges for English-Medium instruction at the tertiary level. In Doiz, A., Lasagabaster, Sierra, J.M. (eds.), *English-medium instruction at universities: Global*: 213–221. Bristol: Multilingual Matters.

Doiz, A., Lasagabaster, D. & Sierra, J.M. 2011. Internationalisation, multilingualism and English-medium instruction. *World Englishes* 30(3): 345–359.

Hamid, M.O., Nguyen, H.T.M. & Baldauf Jr, R.B. 2013. Medium of instruction in Asia: Context, processes and outcomes. *Current Issues in Language Planning* 14(1): 1–15.

Hellekjær, G.O. 2010. Lecture comprehension in English medium higher education, *Hermes – Journal of Language and Communication Studies* 45: 11–34.

Ibrahim, J. 2004. The implementation of EMI (English medium instruction) in Indonesian universities: Its opportunities, its threats, its problems, and its possible solutions. *k@talama* 3(2): 121–138.

Lin, A. 2012. Multilingual and multimodal resources in genre based pedagogical approaches to L2 English content classrooms. In Leung, C. & Street, B.V. (eds.). *English: A changing medium for education*: 79–103. Bristol: Multilingual Matters.

Sert, N. 2008. The language of instruction dilemma in the Turkish context. *System* 36(2): 156–171.

Shohamy, E. 2012. A critical perspective on the use of English as a med um of instruction at universities. In Doiz, A., Lasagabaster, D. & Sierra, J.M. (eds.), *English-medium instruction at universities: Global challenges*: 196–212. Bristol: Multilingual Matters.

Tan, M. 2011. Mathematics and science teachers' beliefs and practices regarding the teaching of language in content learning. *Language Teaching Research* 15(3): 325–342.

Thøgersen, J. 2013. Stylistic and pedagogical consequences of university teaching in English in Europe. In H. Haberland, Lønsmann, D. & Preisler, B. (eds.). *Language alternation, language choice and language encounter in international tertiary education*: 181–199. Dordrecht: Springer.

Vu, N.T. & Burns, A. 2014. English as a medium of instruction: Challenges for Vietnamese tertiary lecturers. *The journal of Asia TEFL* 11(3): 1–31.

Wilkinson, R. 2012. English-Medium instruction at a Dutch university: Challenges and pitfalls. In Doiz, A., Lasagabaster, D. & Sierra, J.M. (eds.), *English-medium instruction at universities: Global challenges*: 3–26. Bristol: Multilingual Matters.

ELT in Asia in the Digital Era: Global Citizenship and Identity – Madya et al. (Eds)
© 2018 Taylor & Francis Group, London, ISBN 978-0-8153-7900-3

EFL learners' opportunities and problems in literacy strategy implementation

N. Christiani
Ciputra University Surabaya, East Java, Indonesia

M.A. Latief
State University of Malang, East Java, Indonesia

ABSTRACT: Literacy awareness in Indonesia has grown increasingly nowadays as many people finish their senior high school level as reflected in reading and writing skills. This study employed mind mapping in the teaching of reading and writing to EFL learners in the English Department. The learners reveal and share their opportunities and obstacles. Eight learners learned reading and writing using mind mapping successfully. Individual structured interviews were held at the end of the fifth meeting. The learners agreed that it becomes a helpful tool to understand main ideas and supporting details of passages, to comprehend the text easily, and to avoid plagiarism. However, they still had problems in deciding keywords, timing to read, the lack of vocabulary, and drawing images or symbols. This research highlights the opportunities and obstacles encountered by the EFL learners in implementing mind mapping as a strategy for developing literacy skills.

1 INTRODUCTION

1.1 *Literacy awareness*

Literacy universally represents the ability to read and write as well as developing an awareness of learning strategies and performances. Based on its conceptualization, literacy talks of a common skill or aptitude, being able to read and write and social construct (Wallace 2002). English as a Foreign Language (EFL) learners occupy their literacies to transforming knowledge and experience that involves the symbolically-mediated skills of abstraction and reasoning in structuring and solving the various problems the learners confront in their everyday lives (Wells 1987 in Rahayu & Arrasyid 2016). To foreign language education, literacy is reflected by reading and writing skills which are helped by the learners' learning strategies. According to Chamot (2005), a learning strategy is clear and goal-driven with clear procedures which are used repeatedly to be a conscious awareness within the learners. There are two major reasons on the importance of learning strategies in the second language learning and teaching. First, the metacognitive, cognitive, social, and affective processes have been involved in language learning. Second, it is obvious that the strategies help the less successful learners become better language learners (Grenfell & Harris 1999 in Chamot 2005).

1.2 *Reading-and-writing learning strategy*

The goals of this research are to define the EFL learners' opportunities and problems in their literacies learning strategies, i.e. reading-and-writing learning strategy. Learning strategy instruction on reading-and-writing can develop the learners' awareness, model a teacher in his or her strategic thinking, make the learners practice with new strategies, build the learners' self-evaluation by themselves, and ease to practice in transferring strategies to a new task (Oxford 1990, Grenfell & Harris 1999, Harris 2003, Chamot 2005). Thus, the hypotheses of this research are the EFL learners have beneficial opportunities to improve their reading-and-writing literacies using mind mapping, and they might have known their drawbacks in using mind mapping.

Reading is a learning process of acquiring experiences on the text that allows the reader to discover, comprehend, and clarify the thoughts of written messages. The process of generating ideas is developed through many kinds of strategies, such as meta-cognitive strategies, coordinating the use of multiple strategies, and pre-reading, whilst-reading, post-reading, and follow-up reading (Chamot 2005). The learners need to use their strategies in all reading sentences as processes of extracting and constructing meaning through interaction and involvement with the written language. That is called comprehending the reading text (Christiani 2017).

1.3 *Mind mapping*

The research on mind mapping was discovered by Buzan (1974) on the strategy of reading-and-writing skills. As a learning tool to develop learners' skills, mind mapping can play two roles in teaching and the learning process: the role as schemata for reading and as outlining in writing. The researcher used mind mapping to study how far this tool can develop the learners to be critical readers and thinkers (Ellozy & Mostafa 2010, Christiani 2014). The first role of mind mapping in reading can be useful for recognition, assimilation, intra-integration, retention, recall, and communication processes promoted by Buzan (1974). These advantages help learners to expand their focus on their reading and speed-up their perceptions towards the organized information. In integrating the reading-writing learning processes relationships, Krashen (1984) states that reading is the appropriate input for acquisition of writing skills because it is generally assumed that reading passages will somehow function as primary models which writing skills can be learned. By comprehending the readings, learners are given ideas, insights and information which can develop learners' writing skills. Thus, as the second role, mind mapping can improve their writing skills as well as their writing quality (Chan 2004). As a visual diagram, mind mapping is used to record and organize information in a way which the brain finds captivating and easy to process (Buzan: 32). In other words, mind mapping makes thinking become visible. It works, as a thought organizer, in accordance with the brain work mechanism to outline what the learners plan to write and how to structure their writings. Indeed, mind mapping assists learners in comprehending a reading text and in composing a worth writing.

The foundations of mind mapping focus on the keywords, images/symbols, colorful branches, and start from a central image. In addition, the laws of mind mapping are the use of landscape clean paper, the curved branches, single keywords/headlines, and images/symbols. The main topic is mentioned as the central image consisting of words and images. The main ideas that radiate out from the central theme of a mind map are known as Basic Order Ideas (BOIs). A simple way to work out Basic Order Ideas (BOIs) is to consider some questions about the specific objectives; information or knowledge needed; key questions of who, what, when, where, why, how, and which; the most important categories to look at, and the chapter headings. These primary concepts are responsible for shaping and guiding the process of association by setting the basic framework and hierarchy from which ideas can be extended. The BOIs are clockwise-starting from right and circling to the left. The branches consist of keywords, images, symbols, and/or codes which are written on the associated line, and show the main ideas/topics of paragraphs, chapter headings, or chapters. Then, the branches of main ideas/topics are followed by supporting ideas that are placed as sub-branches. The last is the correlation. Once ideas are displayed in the mind mapping form, patterns of thought can be easily examined, revealing similarities and linkage information in different parts of the map (Christiani 2017).

In consequence, the research discovers the literacy strategy implementation by combining the mind mapping strategy and the reading-and-writing learning strategy. This is called reading-to-mind mapping-to-writing (R-MM-W) (Christiani 2017). See Table 1 for the teaching procedure of reading-to-mind mapping-to-writing (R-MM-W).

Table 1. Teaching procedure of Reading-to-Mind Mapping-to-Writing (R-MM-W).

Scenario activities stages	Teacher activities	Learners activities
Pre-reading activities	1. Greets the learners	1. Pay attention to the lecturer's instruction.
	2. Reviews how to get meaning from the context.	2. Respond to the lecturer's instruction.
	3. Distributes the reading text A.	3. Scan the reading text A.
	4. Builds learners's vocabulary on the topic by matching.	4. Pay attention to the lecturer's ice-breaking instruction.
	5. Explains the lesson aims of today.	5. Answer the meaning of given words from the context.
Whilst-reading activities	6. Previews the topic of today by giving questions.	6. Answer the preview questions topic of today.
	7. Teaches the learners how to identify main idea and supporting details of paragraph 1.	7. Learn how to identify main idea and supporting details of paragraph 1.
	8. Asks the learners to read the reading text.	8. Read the reading text.
	9. Distributes an exercise to recognize the reading structure: titles and paragraph topics.	9. Do the exercise on recognizing reading structure: titles and paragraph topics.
	10. Asks the learners to match the questions on the left with the answers on the right.	10. Match the questions to the answers.
	11. Asks learners to summarize the reading text using MM.	11. Summarize the reading text in MM.
	12. Asks the learners to do the reading comprehension to recognize main ideas and supporting details based on their MMs.	12. Do the reading comprehension to recognize main ideas and supporting details based on MM.
Post-reading activities	13. Give brief explanation about the next activity.	13. Pay attention to the lecturer's instruction.
	14. Asks the learners, individually, rewrite the reading text using their previous MM.	14. Rewrite the reading text using previous MM.

Source: Christiani (2017).
Notes: MM means Mind Mapping.

This teaching procedure is developed in a classroom action research (CAR) to explore, find, and produce the strategy of R-MM-W activities on EFL learners' literacy skills, i.e. reading and writing skills. CAR is aimed at developing an innovative instructional strategy that can help enhance the success in learners' English learning (Latief 2013). Therefore, the purpose of this research is to describe the EFL learners' opportunities and problems or obstacles in implementing R-MM-W strategy as their literacy strategy development.

2 METHOD

2.1 Classroom Action Research (CAR)

As aforementioned, the method of this research is a classroom action research (CAR) as R-MM-W strategy has not as yet been developed. Many studies that have been published use mind mapping either in the reading (Goodnough & Woods 2002, Moi & Lian 2007) or writing skill (Peterson & Snyder 1998, Chan 2004, Al-Jarf 2009). This strategy of R-MM-W was constructed to find the format, to try it out, to revise it if it does not reach its target, and to test it again to find the right format. CAR is required to determine the correct format. After the CAR is completed, the Strategy of R-MM-W was studied.

The CAR design followed Kemmis and McTaggart (1988) consists of four steps: (1) planning the action, (2) implementing the plan, (3) observing the action, and (4) analyzing the data obtained during the action and making a reflection on the result of the observation. The four main steps were designed to find and determine the correct format of the teaching procedure of R-MM-W strategy. In consequence, having CAR could direct the researcher to create the strategy of reading-to-mind mapping-to-writing (R-MM-W).

2.2 *The research method*

Eight learners were involved in this research. They were in the second semester at School of Foreign Language and Literature (*Sekolah Tinggi Ilmu Bahasa dan Sastra*-STIBA) 'Satya Widya' Surabaya, East Java. They were taking the reading subject entitled "Reading and Mind Mapping". In the first meeting, the learners were introduced to what mind mapping was and how to use it as a strategy of R-MM-W. They were given a five-paragraph reading text to be read and then summarized using mind mapping. After that, based on their mind maps (the original reading text was collected), the learners answered seven to eight reading comprehension questions. Next, after collecting the questions and the answers of the reading comprehension activity, the learners were asked to rewrite the reading passage based on their mind maps.

This research used a list of interview questions. According to Latief (2013), interviews can also be used to collect data on factual information as well as information on people's attitudes. Five questions were used to explore the EFL learners' opportunities and problems in implementing the strategy of literacy skills called reading-to-mind mapping-to-writing (R-MM-W). The first question asked about how mind mapping helped the learners to understand the reading text. The second asked about how the learners construct their mind mapping for every text given, whether they found it easy or difficult. The third question asked about the other skill or activity the learners were doing, i.e. rewriting. It was about how mind mapping helped the learners to rewrite the reading text based on their mind mapping. The fourth question asked about what the learners liked best about creating mind maps. This question led the learners to answer and explain more about their opportunities to apply the reading-to-mind mapping-to-writing strategy. The fifth question asked about what the learners liked least about creating mind maps. This final question directed the learners to respond and clarify more about their problems using the R-MM-W strategy. These questions were utilized to inquire about the learners' implementation of the strategy of R-MM-W after they practiced using it from the second to the fifth meetings. Thus, after the fifth meeting, the learners were interviewed one-by-one.

The interview is planned and structured carefully from defining the objectives, developing questions, validating the questions, selecting the subjects, interviewing, and analyzing (Latief 2013). The interview at the beginning aims at identifying the usefulness experienced by the learners in understanding the reading text. Hence, the questions were then developed to delve into the learners' perceptions on the mind mapping activities. Moreover, the questions were addressed to know the learners' reading opportunities and obstacles towards the strategy of R-MM-W. The interview questions developed were then validated by experts to help improve the quality of the questions. Next, after the subjects to be interviewed were selected, the interview was scheduled. The interview session was held successfully by using a voice recorder in a smart phone. The last procedure was analyzing the interview answers.

3 DISCUSSION

3.1 *Opportunities of implementing R-MM-W*

The results of the interview revealed two kinds of perceptions of implementing R-MM-W as a strategy of developing the learners' literacy skills, the opportunities and the problems/obstacles. The opportunities that the learners experienced were categorized into three opportunities.

Firstly, they found mind mapping helpful to identify the main ideas and the supporting details of each paragraph of the reading text. Six out of eight learners mentioned it. Secondly, the learners comprehended the texts easily because the colorful branches and the use of keywords. Four out of eight learners expressed about how the color in developing mind mapping could improve their vocabulary skill. Thirdly, the last opportunity or advantage using mind mapping as a strategy in improving reading and writing skills is for avoiding plagiarism. According to four learners, by using mind mapping in rewriting, they could use their own words. This activity would train them to be able to paraphrase what they had read to their own writing.

3.2 *Problems of implementing R-MM-W*

The second kind of learners' perception towards R-MM-W strategy was the problems or the obstacles they faced. There were four views about employing the strategy. Five out of eight learners stated that they found it difficult to decide the keywords. They realized that determining the keywords of a sentence, two sentences, and/or more than two sentences became their weaknesses as they lacked vocabulary. The second problem was found in drawing the images or symbols of the keywords. Three of the learners felt that they were not able to describe the keywords by illustrating them in images or symbols. The third problem was found in drawing the branches. Somehow, the learners were not able to consistently draw the branches in the right laws of mind mapping. The main branches should be drawn thicker than the first sub-branches. Then, the second sub-branches were thinner than the first sub-branches. This regulation in some way made the learners hard to follow. Three out of eight learners were not able to do it. The fourth problem was related to the time as five learners did not have an adequate amount of time to finish reading. Because of the lack of vocabulary, the learners needed more than 10 minutes to read and understand the reading text. Five out of eight learners described this problem.

3.3 *Findings of the research*

The opportunities and the problems encountered by the learners showed that there were responses towards the new strategy of R-MM-W. The strategy of R-MM-W needed to be drilled more frequently so that the learners' literacy skills, i.e. reading and writing skills, could be developed. The learners also needed to improve their vocabulary skills by reading a lot. They could make their own dictionary called a self-dictionary. When they were reading a reading text and found difficult words, they could write them on their self-dictionary by adding the meaning and an example sentence. Afterwards, the learners needed more time to comprehend the reading text, to summarize it, to answer the questions of reading comprehension, and to write the reading text again. They might need to be trained to read, read, and read. When they were able to comprehend the reading text, they would be able to summarize it, and to do the reading comprehension questions. Moreover, they would be able to rewrite the reading text. Next, the learners and the teachers needed to work together in practicing and paraphrasing. The skill of paraphrasing was quite difficult to apply. Learners had to exercise paraphrasing from one sentence first, then combining two or three sentences to make into one sentence, and to make a paragraph into one or two sentences based on their understanding. Last but not least, the learners needed to do a "follow-up strategy activity". It was an activity to keep on or to go along the topic of the reading text, which could be implemented on the learners' real-life situation.

The findings of this research in the form of statistical significance has been reported in Christiani's (2014) journal article. In this paper, the report is related to the result of interviewing the EFL learners as the subjects of this research after they have implemented the strategy of reading-to-mind mapping-to-writing (R-MM-W).

4 CONCLUSION

EFL learners need to be encouraged to read English texts and to practice new strategies to develop their literacy skills in reading comprehension and writing. Some strategies that can be used by teachers to enhance the learners' reading and writing ability/skill are reading-to-mind mapping-to-writing (R-MM-W) ones. The learners are suggested to keep on reading when they find difficult words that they do not understand. Using their self-dictionary could help them to later on go back to the words and find the meaning and additionally, write them in sentences as examples so the meaning of the difficult words will stay longer in their memory. EFL learners must accustom themselves to continuous reading from the popular books they like to the academic ones. This kind of interest could foster them to adjust to a type or typical texts of academic reading, quite different from popular reading. Lastly, after having a self-dictionary, EFL learners have to review and learn from it daily or three to five times a week. This could assist them to help their long-term memory on the meaning of difficult words. Later, when those words come up in other reading texts, they will remember them easily.

REFERENCES

Al-Jarf, R. 2009. Enhancing freshman students' writing skills with a mind mapping software. Paper presented at *The 5th International Scientific Conference—eLearning and Software for Education*. Bucharest, April 09–10, 2009.

Buzan, T. 1974. *Use your head*. England: BBC Publication.

Buzan, T. 2012. *Mind mapping: Scientific research and studies*. www.iMindMap.com.

Chamot, A.U. 2005. Language learning strategy instruction: Current issues and research. *Annual Review of Applied Linguistics* 25: 112–130.

Chan, W. 2004. The effectiveness of using mind mapping skills in enhancing secondary one and secondary four students' writing in a CMI school. University of Hong Kong, *Masters Dissertation*. http://hub.hku.hk/handle/123456789/31749?mode=full&submit_simple=Show+full+item+record.

Christiani, N. 2014. Reading-to-write in the classroom: The use of mind mapping as schemata and as outlining. *Journal Humaniora, Sains, Pendidikan dan Pengajaran PROSPECTS* 4(2): 53–59.

Christiani, N. 2017a. Teachers' strategies in teaching EFL learners reading skill. Proceedings of *The 8th National English Language Teachers and Lecturers*, pp. 155–159; held on October 30th, 2016. Malang: State University of Malang Press.

Christiani, N. 2017b. The effects of reading-to-mind mapping-to-writing activities on EFL learners' literacy skills. Unpublished Dissertation. Malang: Graduate Program in State University of Malang.

Goodnough, K. & Woods, R. 2002. Student and teacher perceptions of mind mapping: A middle school case study. Paper presented at *The Annual Meeting of American Educational Research Association*. New Orleans. 1st to 5th April 2002.

Grenfell, M. & Harris, V. 1999. *Modern languages and learning strategies: In theory and practice*. London: Routledge.

Harris, V. 2003. Adapting classroom-based strategy instruction to a distance learning context. *TESL-EJ*, 7(2). Retrieved from http://www-writing.berkeley.edu/TESL-EJ/ej26/al.html.

Kemmis, S. & McTaggart, R. 1988. *The action research planner*. (3rd Ed.). Victoria: Deakin University.

Krashen, S.D. 1984. *Writing: Research, theory, and applications*. Oxford: Pergamon.

Latief, M.A. (2nd ed.) 2013. *Research Methods on language learning: An introduction*. Malang: UM Press.

Moi, W.A.G. & Lian, O.L. 2007. Introducing mind map in comprehension. *Educational Research Association (Singapore)*, Study conducted at Compassvale Primary School.

Oxford, R.L. 1990. *Language learning strategies: What every teacher should know*. New York: Newbury House.

Peterson, A.R. & Snyder, P.J. 1998. Using mind maps to teach social problems analysis. Paper presented at *The Annual Meeting of the Society for the Study of Social Problems*. San Francisco, CA. Aug 1998.

Rahayu, A. & Arrasyid, F.I. 2016. Exploring writing practices in EFL classroom: A case study at English Department IAIN Syekh Nurjati Cirebon. *ELT-Echo* 1(1).

Wallace, C. 2002. Local literacies and global literacy in *Globalization and language teaching* edited by David Block & Deborah Cameron. Canada: Routledge.

Wells, G. 1987. Apprenticeship in Literacy. *Interchange* 18(1–2): 109–123.

ELT in Asia in the Digital Era: Global Citizenship and Identity – Madya et al. (Eds)
© *2018 Taylor & Francis Group, London, ISBN 978-0-8153-7900-3*

An explanatory study on the needs of skill-integrated coursebook for listening and speaking classes

S.K. Kurniasih, B.Y. Diyanti & L. Nurhayati
Yogyakarta State University, Yogyakarta, Indonesia

ABSTRACT: This study aimed at providing the sophomores of the English Language Education Department, at Yogyakarta State University, with ample materials to enhance their listening skills that in the end will contribute to the improvement of their speaking skills. The study gathered information on the students' needs via online questionnaires. The results suggested that the students agreed on the integration of the learning materials between listening and speaking. They affirmed that the materials obtained in Listening class will contribute to their speaking skill improvement. Furthermore, students were more interested in learning through audio visual materials than audio materials alone. The students were likely to prefer entertaining materials such as film clips, songs, or talk shows as the input texts. An interesting fact was revealed that printouts from which students can get some information and references about useful expressions or conversation gambits was needed. In other words, students need a course book that meets their needs and maintains their interest as well.

1 INTRODUCTION

1.1 *Background*

English language skills generally are regarded as either receptive (listening and reading) or productive skills (speaking and writing). Speaking skills are considered more difficult and complex to be mastered. Therefore, sufficient meaningful input texts are required to help students express themselves correctly and properly. It means that a student can master the speaking skill if they get enough exposure to the language through listening activities. Students of the English Language Education Department are expected to be English Language teachers who have a good command of English including the linguistic, sociolinguistic, discourse, and strategic competences so that they will teach the language properly. Consequently, the exposure and practice in the learning process has to be sufficient. In addition, language skills are integrated in use. Interacting with others, a learner will not use a sole skill. Therefore, integrating skills in the learning process will produce beneficial results. Listening skills as one of the receptive skills are the basis of other skills in learning English as a second or foreign language (Nunan 2015).

To this day there is not documented coordination among the teachers of Listening and Speaking classes. Therefore, the research was conducted to create well-documented files of the coordination, and to produce a course book for the two related courses: Listening for Academic Purposes (LAP) and Speaking for Academic Purposes (SAP). Besides, the two courses are the highest level of the skill learning classes. At this phase of the study, sophomores need to be equipped with the skills to speak in formal academic contexts like conferences and seminars.

This article aims at describing findings of preliminary research in developing teaching materials for the integrated skills of listening and speaking. The objective of the study is to make a needs analysis and prepare the Lesson plans of LAP and SAP in integration.

1.2 *Literature review*

There are three indicators of good speaking competence i.e. fluency, accuracy, and appropriateness. According to Koponen (1995) in Luoma (2004) fluency is indicated by good flow of speech in normal speed, "a lack of excessive breaks", fillers, and hesitation markers, the length of the utterance, and connectedness. Accuracy is shown in pronunciation accuracy at the word level, stress placement and rhythm, as well as intonation (Luoma 2004). Accuracy can also be regarded in grammar, speech syntactical structure, and word choice and format. Appropriateness refers to whether or not the expressions and the responses are matched with the speech context. The speech context and with whom one has a conversation and the topic of the conversation determine the formality level of the expression selection.

Richards (2008) explains that talk can be categorized into interaction, transaction, and performance. Performance talk or presentational speech is the focus of this research. Shrum and Glisan (2005) define Presentational speech as one-way communication as someone speaks in front of audience. In a presentational speech, a speaker can express his idea or show research findings to attract the audience's attention. Public speaking such as a presentation skill is categorized as planned and non-interactive because it takes a speaker who has prepared his message and passes it on to the audience. Moreover, Richards (2008) states that performance speech has some features; they: a) focus on the message and audience, b) have predictable organization and order, c) prioritize the form and accuracy, d) have similar language features as the written language, d) are often in the form of monologue, e) take specific speaking skills to use proper format, deliver information in an organized way, involve the audience, use correct pronunciation and grammar, use appropriate vocabulary, and suitable openings and closings.

A study conducted by Vidal (2003) found a strong link between intensive academic listening (e.g. listening to lectures) and vocabulary and EFL proficiency enhancement. Furthermore, Richards (2008) states that listening acts as an input text or a data provider for language learners. He also suggests that listening is the process of facilitating learners to understand spoken discourse. In listening activities like noticing and building language awareness, students can learn the use of spoken discourse and how an intention can be revealed through particular language functions. Using an audio input talk as performance can be done as follow: 1) watch a video performance in the form of a speech or presentation, 2) deconstruct linguistic and organizational features, 3) organize speech/presentation script (individually or in groups), and 4) facilitate student practice.

2   RESEARCH METHOD

This study is categorized as explanatory as it is aimed at describing the needs analysis of a bigger Research and Development. The research subjects were fifth semester students who had taken LAP and SAP the previous semester. The data collection instruments were questionnaires and interviews. Thirty-nine students participated as the questionnaire respondents and four lecturers who were teaching the LAP and SAP were interviewed. The data collected was about the problems in learning the two courses, the types of input texts and media, and the kinds of learning activities and tasks. The data were analyzed using descriptive statistics.

3   FINDINGS AND DISCUSSION

3.1   Findings

The data analysis showed the following results. In terms of the learning problems, as many as 56.4% student respondents claimed that they did not have any constraints in learning LAP, while 43.6% of the respondents stated the opposite. Even though the percentage of the students having difficulty learning the material in LAP class was higher, the difference from the ones having no difficulty is small. It means that the number of students having constraints in learning is still high. The students perceived that the causes of the difficulty were: thick accent of the speakers (61.5%), lack of vocabulary (53.8%), lack of interest in listening to academic materials (23.1%), limited knowledge of the course subject (15.4%), and limited grammar proficiency (10.3%). On the other hand, the lecturer respondents thought that most students taking LAP class had problems in vocabulary mastery. Another problem revealed is that many students complained about the speech rate of the speakers on the audio used in class even though it was not to the lecturer's perspective. Moreover, students could not maintain their focus in listening to long duration audio (e.g. lectures). In the lecturer's view, other factors that caused the problems for the students were limited and of limited interest to the academic topics discussed in class.

In addition, as many as 41% respondents articulated the challenges they had when they had to speak in an academic context which was lack of vocabulary. Some others (28.2%) pointed out that lack of background knowledge of the topics discussed in class can hamper their speaking fluency. The remaining respondents differed equally (each was 15.4%) and revealed that limited grammar knowledge and pronunciation mastery were their biggest problems. Similar to the previous data of students' challenges in speaking in academic context, a large number of the respondents (79.5%) admitted having challenges and constraints in developing their speaking skill in SAP class. Twenty-three students (59%) mentioned that the main problem they had in SAP class was poor knowledge of useful expressions. Two other problems that were also mentioned were difficulty of developing ideas (51.3%) and limited vocabulary mastery (48.7%).

On the aspect of wants, the most preferred media in learning listening skills were authentic video (41%), learning video (33.3%), authentic audio (20.5%) and learning audio. The types of authentic audio needed were: songs (30.8%), radio talk (25.6%), English news reading (15.4%), lectures recorded from seminars and conferences. Meanwhile the type of authentic video needed was: Clips (33.3%), radio talk/interview (25.4%), English news reading (15.4%) and lectures recorded from seminars and conferences (10.3%). The lecturer respondents had similar ideas about the type of audio/video needed to aid the learning and enhancement of listening skill in class. Authentic audio/video of social events, as well as official speech were other types that the students did not point out but were added by the lecturers.

In addition, the factors that contribute to the success of using video in the LAP class were pronunciation and tempo (15.4%), model of the video (66.7%), and sound and picture quality (17.9%). Similar to the students' ideas, lecturers thought that those factors affected student learning. Other factors were believed to play important roles as well i.e. interesting topics and suitable duration. However, what the students considered important but they did not get from the video was a list of useful expressions (76.9%), and phonetic transcription (20.5%) whereas they were beneficial for the improvement of their speaking skill in SAP.

Furthermore, the lecturers suggested that the materials learned in LAP should be related to the materials given in SAP and to support the speaking skill improvement. In other words, the learning materials in both the classes should support each other. In this case LAP materials should contain language use and useful expressions which the students could use in producing utterances in SAP class. Vocabulary related to the topic the students would discuss in SAP class should be provided in LAP class as well to help the students get ready.

Responses given on the question related to the affecting factors of the success of listening skill improvement using videos in LAP were that 66.7% of students claimed that they got some benefits from the clear pronunciation and tempo of speech of the speakers in the video. And, as many as 17.9% respondents stated that the quality of the sound and pictures of the video affected their listening skill development. 10.3% and 5.1% respondents respectively said interesting topics and clarity of the material were important factors.

Students' opinions are interlinked with another question about whether or not the materials in LAP should be related and integrated with the materials in SAP so that they support the students' speaking skill development. Almost all respondents (97.4%) suggested that the materials of both the courses should be linked. A further question revealed more information on what materials the students expected to get so that the materials of both the courses support each other. As stated earlier on this paper, mostly the respondents (94.9%) believed that the materials of LAP should cover language use and useful expressions as exposure which help students get prepared to produce accurate and proper utterances in their performance in SAP. The rest of the students stated similar opinions that both the courses should make the students become accustomed to using particular expressions in iterative practices.

In light of some reasons, students could do well in LAP class. They are: note taking while listening (53.8%), drawing mind maps while listening (48.7%), listening to audio followed by rewriting the text in their own words (33.3%), doing exercises to activate their schemata/ framework before listening (23.1%) and listening audio followed by answering comprehension questions (30.8%). In the same way, the lecturer suggested that those activities could help students improve their listening skills.

Moreover, students suggested some class activities that could help them enhance academic speaking ability; they were Role Play (35.9%) and communicative games (20.5%). Whereas, only 10.3% of the respondents considered presentation delivery advantageous. The findings reflected students' poor understanding of the target and objective of the course (SAP) which focuses on developing individual speaking skill i.e. presentation.

Regarding the activities of vocabulary building, the students mostly (71.8%) wanted to read a text followed by identifying word meaning based on the context either using a diction- ary or not, others (48.7%) preferred matching words and their synonyms, and the rest favored matching words and their equivalents in Indonesian (35.9%). More specifically, the types of exercise the students preferred for improving their speaking skill were pair work (69.2%), small group work (56.4%), and individu work (48.7%). Regarding the material organization, students wanted to have examples and model texts (59%), guided exercises (59%), and vocab- ulary discussion/explanation (56.4%).

From the point of view of the lecturers, the data showed that students experienced chal- lenges in LAP class in different degrees. Similar to the fact revealed by students, according to the lecturer, the limiting factor in enhancing listening skills was limited vocabulary. Con- sequently, students had difficulty being tuned in to talk, in terms of words and expressions, held by the model speakers in the video as a learning medium. Besides videos, audio for learning was also used. Both the learning media show news reading, lectures recorded from actual seminars and conferences, also audio recorded from class lectures. There are some considerations to be put into account in selecting authentic learning media. Those aspects are picture and sound quality, correct pronunciation and appropriate tempo, interesting topic and appropriate duration (not longer than 15 minutes).

3.2 *Discussion*

LAP and SAP courses are meant to equip students with receptive and productive skills that enable them to comprehend academic texts and communicate ideas orally in an academic forum. Table 1 includes the description of each course.

It is clear from the table above that some aspects have supported one another while other aspects have not. The objective, for example, is very different. However, both LAP and SAP have one in common that both focus on formal academic contexts. Hence, integration is pos- sible. Based on the needs analysis, the specification of the developed product is as follows:

The next stage after determining the specification of the product is designing the course grid (CG), which is a blue print of the product. The product would adapt a genre-based approach as proposed by Hammond, et al. (1992): BKOF, MOT, JCOT, and ICOT. The structure of the materials would be like this.

1. Ice breaking: this part aims to develop a learning situation which is conducive. Types of activities would be games or other activities that could boost students' motivation and grab their attention.
2. Bkof (building knowledge of the field): activities provided in this phase include exploration of words and key expressions, brainstorming about the text, predicting and many more.
3. Mot (modelling of the text): this phase aims to inform the students about functions, struc- ture, aims and lexico-grammatical features of the text. Students would be given texts ranging from authentic to adapted texts. Students work with texts, explore and de-construct them
4. Jcot (joint construction of the text): in small groups or in pairs, students work with some new texts, trying to use gained skilled and knowledge to comprehend the text and produce a new one.

Table 1. Course description.

Listening for academic purposes	Speaking for academic purposes
Objective: To equip students with knowledge and skills to understand advanced academic texts used in varied academic forum such as seminar, lecture, meeting etc. Materials: varied types of functional text	Objective: To develop communication competence especially in academic activities (oral formal academic discourse) Materials: Informative and persuasive speeches and academic presentation on ELT, linguistics or literatures.
Class Activities: note taking, summarising, concluding implicit meaning, practising listening, discussion, Types of work: independent, pair and group Assessment: class participation, assignment, midterm exam and final exam.	Class Activities: role play, simulation, group discussions, and presentation. Assessment: class participation, assignment, midterm exam and final exam.

Table 2. Product specification.

Criteria	Finding	What does it mean
Correlation	✓ The LAP – SAP correlation is low and nor clear.	✓ Integration of LAP-SAP materials is needed.
Vocabulary	✓ Students perceived that their vocabulary mastery is low. Activities to improve vocabulary mastery are needed.	✓ Pre teaching new vocabulary ✓ Providing sufficient vocabulary learning tasks ✓ Promoting independent vocabulary learning ✓ Making the clear target of vocabulary mastery level
Text types	✓ Students find it hard to understand certain English accents, as the result they cannot comprehend the text well. ✓ Academic text should become the priority. ✓ Glosarrium is perceived important.	✓ Providing graded texts ✓ Providing varied speeds and difficulty level (easy, medium, difficult) ✓ Considering to introduce/accommodate certain accents (to deal with world Englishes issues) ✓ Providing word bank/list of words/expressions
Learning activities	✓ Students think mind mapping, note taking and rewriting are useful activities	Providing some useful and helpful activities such as Listen and take a note, k mind mapping, note taking, rewriting, etc.
Media	✓ The media should be interesting and useful	✓ Using video and audio in LAP
Topic	✓ Topic suggested in the curriculum are perceived too general and old fashioned and not challenging	✓ Providing challenging topics on the area of IT, education, social issues, culture, environment, popculture, literature
Types of feedback	✓ Students perceive feedback very important	✓ Peer feedback ✓ Self reflection ✓ Feedback from lecturer.

5. Icot (independent construction of the text): in this stage, students work with some new texts, trying to comprehend the text and produce a new one independently.
6. Feedback: in this stage students reflect on their learning process, identifying their strengths and weaknesses and sharing their next learning plan in order to achieve the learning objectives.

One of the problems in listening class is the teaching strategy that is used. In many cases, teachers tend to test the students instead of teach them. This is also mentioned by Schmidt (2016) who said that a number of listening practice in the class "focuses on testing listening, not teaching it." Therefore, the developed product should address this issue well. Pre-listening activities would become paramount. In this step students would learn some key vocabulary and expressions that they would need to process as they listen to the input text. This is expected to be a useful scaffolding to help them comprehend the text.

4   CONCLUSION

Needs analysis is one significant step in an R&D study. In this study, it can be concluded from the needs analysis that the materials' integration of Listening for Academic Purposes (LAP) and Speaking for Academic Purposes (SAP) is perceived as important. Some important information pertaining to students' needs, lacks and wants in the teaching learning process are also identified, namely types of text, learning activities, types of media, interaction and assessment. Materials for LAP should be integrated and related to those given in SAP. Students should be exposed to varied types of LAP texts, later on they are expected to be able to produce similar texts in certain activities provided in SAP. This study has resulted in a course grid that would be used as the basis for developing the integrated materials. The course grid was designed based on the result of needs analysis. Considering the importance of this integration, it is recommended to continue the study in order to develop learning materials that integrate LA and SAP.

ACKNOWLEDGEMENT

This research is fully funded by Faculty of Languages and Arts, Yogyakarta State University, 2016.

REFERENCES

Bailey, K.M. 2003. Speaking. In D. Nunan (ed.), *Practical English language teaching*: 47–65. New York: The McGraw Hill-Companies. Inc.

Brown, H.D. 2001. *Teaching by principles: An interactive approach to language Pedagogy (2nd ed)*. New York: Addison Wesley Longman Inc.

Borg, W.R. & Gall, N.B. 2003. *Educational research: An introduction (7th ed)*. New York: Pearson Education Inc.

Burns, A. 2001. Analysing spoken discourse: Implication for TESOL. In A. Burns & C. Coffin (eds), *Analysing English in a global context: A reader*: 123–148. London: Routledge.

Kurniasih, S.K. & Diyanti, B.Y. 2009. *Teaching Material Kits Using Authentic Video for Speaking III in English Education Department, Yogyakarta State University. 8th Asia Computer Assisted Language Learning (ASIACALL) Conference Proceeding*.

Luoma, S. 2004. *Assessing speaking*. Cambridge: Cambridge University Press.

Miccoli, L. 2003. English through drama for oral skills development. *ELT Journal* 57(2): 122–129.

Miles, M.B., Huberman, A.M. & Saldana, J. 2014. *Qualitative data analysis: A method source book*. Thousand Oaks: Sage.

Nunan, D. 2015. *Teaching English to speakers of other languages: An introduction*. New York: Routledge.

Richards, J.C. 2008. *Teaching listening and speaking*. Cambridge: Cambridge University Press.

Shrum, J.L. & Glisan, E.W. 2005. *Teacher's handbook: Contextualized language instruction. (3rd ed.)*. Boston: Thomson Heinle.

Shumin, K. 2002. Factors to consider: developing adult EFL students' speaking abilities. In J.C. Richards, & W.A. Renandya (eds.), *Methodology in language teaching: An anthology of current practice*: 204–211. Cambridge: Cambridge University Press.

Skehan, P. 2001. Comprehension and production strategies in language learning. In C.N. Candlin & N. Mercer (eds), *English language teaching in its social context: A reader*: 75–89. London: Routledge.

Skehan, P. 1998. *A cognitive approach to language learning*. Oxford: Oxford University Press.

Tenenbaum, G. et al. 2001. Constructivist pedagogy in conventional on campus and distance learning practice: An exploratory investigation. *Learning and Instruction* 11: 87–111.

Thornbury, S. 2005. *How to teach speaking*. Edinburg Gate: Pearson Education Limited.

Vidal, K. 2003. Academic listening: A source of vocabulary acquisition? *Applied Linguistics* 24(1): 56–89. Oxford: Oxford University Press.

Wilson, J.F. et al. 1990. *Public Speaking as a liberal art*. Massachusetts: Allyn and Bacon.

ELT in Asia in the Digital Era: Global Citizenship and Identity – Madya et al. (Eds)
© 2018 Taylor & Francis Group, London, ISBN 978-0-8153-7900-3

Indonesian teacher's beliefs and practices on teaching listening using songs

N.A. Fauzi
Sebelas Maret University, Surakarta, Indonesia

ABSTRACT: The primary aim of this study was to reveal teachers' beliefs and practices on teaching listening using songs for high school students. Songs are one of the materials listed in the syllabus of the recent curriculum to be presented in EFL class for high school students in Indonesia. Therefore, teachers are asked to use songs in their class. English language teachers' opinions were collected through an interview. The results demonstrated that teachers have strong beliefs about the pedagogical value of teaching listening using songs for high school students. However, finding showed that teachers had difficulty in applying an appropriate strategy to teach listening using songs. In fact, in many teacher training programs there were no specific discussion of teaching listening using songs. Therefore, such programs are needed by teachers to be able to teach listening using songs. By having sufficient competence, the learning goal in general will be achieved successfully.

1   INTRODUCTION

1.1   *Background of the study*

The different curriculum brings many new aspects in the classroom learning process. Teachers have to be able to execute it well in the classroom. In this study, the researcher portrays the curriculum changing in Indonesia, especially in EFL for high school students. Dealing with the materials, there is something interesting in the newest syllabus compared to the previous one. In the former curriculum, only students of language and cultural program have songs in their English class. However, in the present curriculum, the Ministry of Education and Culture (Kemdikbud 2016: 26) states clearly that songs are provided in the syllabus not only for students of language and cultural programs but also for students of natural and social science. Therefore, it is interesting to find out whether teachers are able to execute it well in the classroom.

In the attachment of the regulation, it is clearly written that songs are presented for both cognitive and skill aspects. Learning a song, one must listen to it carefully. Therefore, songs are closely related to listening. It is based on Kirsch (2008) who states that listening activities should be based on meaningful, appropriate, and authentic texts (e.g., a story, song, or poem) that are able to assist students' listening skills

It is believed that the listening skill is essential in the language learning process. Linse (2005) considers the teaching of listening skills as foundation to the development of other language skills. Having good listening skills, will help students learn speaking, reading, and writing better. Moreover, Richards (2008) believes that listening comes to be seen as an interpretive process. It means that by listening to a certain type of material, one will be able to interpret, and then hopefully explain and discuss the meaning behind the material provided.

In the class, teachers are the key to making the learning atmosphere better for students. Since songs are learning content in the syllabus, it is undeniable that teachers are now asked to be able to teach English using songs especially in the listening section. In fact, not all teachers have sufficient experience of teaching English language using songs since, previously, not every high school in Indonesia has a language and cultural program. For some schools, this is a new thing. In fact, not all teachers have a good understanding about songs. However, the syllabus asks the teachers to bring songs as the material presented in the class.

Rokeach (1968: 113) defined beliefs, circularly, as any simple proposition, conscious or unconscious, inferred from what a person says or does, capable of being preceded by the phrase, 'I believe that ....' In addition, Fauziati (2015: 54) states that it (belief) is accepted as true by the individual, and is therefore imbued with emotive commitment; further, it serves as a guide to thought and behavior. In conclusion, teachers' beliefs can powerfully shape both what teachers do and, the learning opportunities the learners receive. Therefore, the extent to and manner in which teaching listening using songs is promoted in language learning classrooms will be influenced by teachers' beliefs about that. Further, teacher education is more likely to have an impact on teachers' practices when it is based on an understanding of the beliefs teachers hold (Borg 2009).

This research focuses on these questions: (1) what teachers believe in teaching listening using songs for high school students and (2) how they apply a certain strategy in teaching listening using songs in the EFL class.

1.2 Theoretical framework

In term of using songs in improving listening skill, Tegge (2015) concludes that by listening to a song, L2-learners can display short- and long-term memory of the linguistic form of longer connected text, even if they engage in a predominantly meaning-focused learning session and even if they are unaware that they will be tested on their word-for-word memory of the target text. It can be said that songs successfully facilitate the learners in listening. Another research conducted by Salcedo (2002) proves that the students who heard songs scored significantly higher than students who heard spoken text in two out of three trials. Both of the earlier studies inform that teaching listening using songs in the language class has a crucial benefit for the students.

Mustafa Sevik (2011) explains that songs are beneficial in teaching English for young learners. One of his findings is that the EFL teachers would use songs more often if they were able to have easy access to songs. He shows the fact that songs are not given the necessary attention on a systematical basis in Turkey.

Those studies mentioned above conclude that using songs is one of recommended ways in teaching listening. The researcher will pay attention to what teachers believe about teaching listening using songs and how they implement teaching listening using songs in the classroom. The design of this study is a case study method.

Rokeach (1968: 113) defined beliefs, circularly, as any simple proposition, conscious or unconscious, inferred from what a person says or does, capable of being preceded by the phrase, 'I believe that ....' Williams and Burden (1997: 53) stated that teacher beliefs are defined as what teachers make sense of the world around them, particularly regarding the views about education and how these views themselves come to be shaped.

Therefore, teachers' belief is a mental state, of conceptual representations which signify to its holder a reality, influencing what one knows, feels, and does so that it may be consciously or unconsciously held, and guide one's actions that, as teachers, they build up over time and bring with them to the classroom.

Borg (2009: 1) clearly states, "Teacher cognition research is concerned with understanding what teachers think, know and believe." He explains that the nature of teacher cognition has a close relationship to teachers' own experiences as a learner; what and how teachers learn during teacher education; and teachers' instructional practices. Therefore, in order to understand teachers' beliefs, it is necessary to study all those aspects mentioned.

Orlova (2003) states that it is possible to suggest that among the methodological purposes with songs used in class, it is possible to rank the following: practicing the rhythm, stress and the intonation patterns of the English language, teaching vocabulary and grammar, developing listening comprehension, writing skills, and speaking. For this last purpose, songs and mainly their lyrics are employed as a stimulus for class discussion.

Having a belief in teaching listening using songs means teachers believe that the use of songs will ease students' process of listening in terms of differentiating sounds, catching words, understanding pronunciation, phrases, sentences, grammar, gist, and even a certain culture emerged in there. Likewise, Sarıçoban and Metin (2000) say that songs are one of the most enchanting and culturally rich resources that can easily be used in language classrooms. They believe songs are precious resources to develop students' abilities in listening, speaking, reading and writing. Moreover, songs can also be used to teach a variety of language items such as sentence patterns, vocabulary, pronunciation, rhythm, adjectives, and adverbs.

Based on their beliefs, teachers would prepare and choose a song on a certain purpose for their listening class. One of the examples is when a song is used in listening class in terms of distinguishing minimal pairs. A song entitled "*Valerie*" by Amy Winehouse can be selected because in the lyrics, there are "*think*" and "*thing*" which are almost similar in sounds and not familiar in Indonesian. The sounds are "*think*" /θɪŋk/ and "*thing*" /θɪŋ/.

Firstly, students have to repeat after the teacher how to pronounce some words. Those words, including "*think*" and "*thing*", are part of the lyrics going to be filled in the blanks provided in the song. And then, the song is played once while students have to listen to it carefully. Then, on the second play, students have to fill in the gaps by choosing the words provided in the box. The two minimal pairs, "*think*" and "*thing*", are available there. By doing so, teachers encourage students to be more aware of different words, meanings, sounds and how to pronounce them correctly.

For teaching listening in order to enrich vocabulary, teachers may use Madonna's "*Hung up*" with some phrasal verbs such as: to be *hung up* on someone, *keep on* doing something, and *wait on* someone. Firstly, students should listen to the song once. Then, they have to try to work out the meanings of the underlined expressions from the context. Next, teachers should play the tape two more times in order to help students be able to match them with their definitions provided on the same worksheet.

Another song that can be used to introduce vocabulary is "*Paint it, black*" by The Rolling Stones. It is a good means of introducing idioms of colour such as: 'to have green fingers' or 'to paint the town red'. Teachers are advised to use this song as an opportunity to demonstrate different ways to organize phrasal verbs in students' vocabulary notebooks, e.g. as a spider diagram around the verb (or around the particle) or divided into lexical areas such as relationships.

In terms of connected speech, teachers can introduce their students to:

1. Elision (when a sound in a word disappears) such as the following example found in "*Rehab*", by Amy Winehouse: '*You won't know, know, know*'.
2. Weak forms (certain sounds are less stressed in some words) such as the schwas used in "*Where is the love*" by The Black eyed Peas: '*I think tha whole world's addicted ta tha drama*'.
3. Linking (when final consonants join with the vowel of the following word) such as in *Help*, by The Beatles: '*Now I fin dI've changed my min dan dopene dup the doors*'.
4. Assimilation (when a sound is influenced by the sounds before or after it) such as in Chumbawamba's "*Tubthumping*", which is an excellent song to practise many of the pronunciation areas mentioned above, as well as sentence stress. Assimilation is illustrated by the following chorus sentence: '*I get knocked down bud I ged up again*'. For further informations, teachers may visit: http://www.onestopenglish.com/section.asp?docid=155160.

For the main idea of the song, "*Cupid*" by Amy Winehouse can be used as the material. First, the teacher asks students whether they know the meaning of the word "*cupid*". Then, they will have a little discussion on it. After that, the teacher plays the song once. The students have to listen to the song carefully. On the second play, the teacher gives some questions to lead students catching the main idea of the song. While students are listening to the song, they have to answer some questions by choosing the correct options. Teachers are advised to play the song, at least, twice in order to make students feel sure about the answer. Both the song and the lyrics are available and can be downloaded at this web address: https://www.esolcourses.com/content/topics/valentinesday/listening/listening.html.

Those explanations above show that there are many ways in using songs in teaching listening. From the very beginning, teachers are advised to choose the song on purpose. A certain song is prepared to teach a certain skill. Therefore, the song used in the listening class can be a really helpful tool for students' learning process.

2 RESEARCH METHOD

The participants were selected as they are teachers of a favorite state high school in Surakarta (Indonesia) and the school has applied the recent curriculum for three years. They are teacher An, Sd, and Pr. A classroom observation was conducted to find out the teachers' practices on teaching listening using songs in the class. After that, there was an interview with each of participants in order to find out what the teachers think in particular about teaching listening using songs.

This research is in form of a qualitative design. Miles and Huberman (1984: 21–22) declare that data analysis is divided into four parts, namely data collection, data reduction, data displays and drawing conclusion.

3 FINDING AND DISCUSSION

3.1 *Teachers' beliefs in teaching listening using songs*

To answer the first problem, the main data is taken from the questionnaire and interview. Three teachers state that they like songs. They believe songs are benefical in teaching listening, however, every teacher has a different opinion on that.

The first is teacher An. She underlines that songs are useful in terms of introducing new vocabulary to students. She believes that by using songs in the class, students are encouraged to add new words, phrases, idioms, etc. Consequently, she always has to prepare a song that can help to improve her students' vocabulary. She usually chooses a song from a famous singer that is not very popular among students so that students will feel the challenge in answering the questions. She adds that she could see students do like the activity done in listening using songs. They are much more motivated in asking or answering something related to the song. Although she has not sang along with students in the class very often but she states that she likes English songs very much. She spends much of her time listening to popular English songs. All the answers given by teacher An shows that she believes that songs are a benefical tool to be used in teaching listening.

Secondly, teacher Sd, is a little bit different. She says she likes music but when she was asked about what kind of music she likes, she answers it too generally that any kinds of music will do good for her. She honestly says that she is not too keen on English songs. About her beliefs in songs as listening material, she explains that music is fun for students. She states that by listening to a song, students know how to pronounce English words well. It is because she believes that by listening to a song, students' hearing will be more sensitive of English sounds. However, she admits that she has difficulties in preparing a certain song for students. Further, she says that she tends to play the song she likes and knows best for the students without considering the trend.

Last but not least is teacher Pr. She has her own answer. She says she believes songs give many advantages for students. However, she is rarely using songs in listening classes. When she was asked whether she likes English songs or not, she answers that she prefers Indonesian's songs. She usually plays a recent English popular song twice or three times, in the class, and then asks the students to answer some questions based on the lyrics of the song given. The main point is, according to her, students are able to understand the message of the song properly.

3.2 *Teachers' practises in teaching listening using songs*

To answer the second problem, the main data is taken from the observation. Three teachers are observed. All the activities done in the classroom was written. That is because the purpose is to know how they practise a certain strategy in their listening class using songs.

The first is teacher An. Her belief is that song is useful in term of introducing new vocabulary to students. Therefore, before the teaching learning process, she always prepares a certain song that, she thinks it will help to improve her students' vocabulary. She chooses "*Ironic*" by Alanis Morissette for teaching listening in order to enrich vocabulary. There are some phrasal verbs such as; *sneaking up on you, everything blows up,* and also some figurative languages such as "*It's like ten thousands spoons ...*". Firstly, students have to merely listen to the song carefully. Then, they have to try to work out the meanings of the underlined expressions from the context. These underlined expressions obviously have connections with the words around. Teacher An plays the tape three times in order to make students be able to fill in the blanks. Answering the question of from whom she has the skill of teaching listening using songs, she said she almost never had an example of teaching listening using songs before. Although she has a lack of experience in teaching listening using songs, her loving English songs makes her able to do it in a proper way.

Secondly, teacher Sd, she believes she likes music but she admits that she is not too keen on English song. She honestly says that. Further, she explains that when she was in her college, she never had her lecturer discuss how to teach listening using songs in front of class. In the observation, it was found that she chose "*Goodbye*" by Air Supply. This song was very popular in the past. Not many students have known the song before. Those are the reasons given by Ms. Sd when the researcher asked her why she chose the song. First, she plays the song once and all the students have to pay attention to it. Then, she hands out a paper with uncomplete lyrics of the song for each student. After that, she plays the song once again while the students are filling the gaps provided on the paper. She states that by listening to a song, students know how to pronounce English well. In fact, she rarely discusses the pronunciation with students. Mostly the teacher asks the students to fill in the gap and discuss the message of the song. Answering the question of from whom she has the skill of teaching listening using songs, she said she ever had one or two examples of teaching listening using songs from her lectures at college. However, she had not given enough theory on it, therefore, she said that she learned it by herself.

The last is teacher Pr. Although she says she believes songs give many advantages for students, she rarely uses song in listening class. She even admits that during one semester, she usually only plays songs two or three times. Even in front of the class, she looks uncomfortable when singing along with the students. Probably because she told us before that she prefers Indonesian songs. In the observation, she chose "*Frozen*" by Demi Lovato to be played in the class. After she has done with her song "*Frozen*", she asked the students, in groups of four, to play their favorite songs in front of the class. After that, she asks the group to discuss the songs with others. In terms of experience in teaching listening using songs, teacher Pr also says that in the past she almost never had a lecture on that. She admits to having a lack of experience of teaching listening using songs for high school students.

Table 1. Findings.

Teachers	Believe in song to	Way to choose song	Teaching practices
An	increase vocabulary	By choosing a certain song for a certain reason (to increase vocabulary)	Used some steps (discussing new word/phrase/idiom) in increasing vocabulary
Sd	pronounce English well	By choosing song that she likes dan knows best	Used some steps (gap filling) to pronounce the words, however, she rarely discusses how to pronounce the words well
Pr	understand the main idea	By choosing a popular song she likes	Used a strategy to (plays the song at least three times) for the students to be able to understand the main idea

3.3 *Discussion*

From the table above, it is clear that all the teachers believe in songs for teaching listening for high school students. Teacher An believes in song to increase vocabulary, teacher Sd believes in song to pronounce well, while teacher Pr does not specifically state in what skills are songs useful in teaching listening for high school students. She mainly thinks that songs are beneficial in teaching listening.

In term of preparing the song, teacher An seems to have a better preparation compared to others. She finds a song which can be used as a tool to increase students' vocabulary.

Teacher Sd also tries to choose the appropriate song, however, the song seems to be old fashioned. That is not wrong actually, but choosing a popular song probably will draw students' attention more. Also, there should be a different strategy used if it is to improve students' pronunciation. The activities should push the students to pronounce certain words. It is because she rarely discusses the pronunciation while the students are filling the gaps.

Teacher Pr chooses the song she likes to present in front of the class. Moreover, she seems to consider her students' preferences by choosing recent popular songs. It can be seen that she tends to use songs to assess the main idea or the message in the song only, however, she should be clear when she gives instructions to students when asking them to understand the main idea. It is because if the instructions do not fit the purpose of listening using songs, students will fail to understand the real purpose of the lesson, the song will just be entertainment in the listening class.

4 CONCLUSION

This study is not without any limitations. Therefore, in drawing the conclusion there are several limitations that should be kept in mind. Firstly, the study was done only within a period of 4 weeks in three different classes. Secondly, most of the classroom practice analysis was done using the observation checklist and field notes. The analysis would be more thorough if supported with complete classroom discourse recordings and transcriptions. Thirdly, this study was also guided by general research questions which aim to find out the teachers' beliefs and practices on teaching listening using songs for high school students. More in-depth studies are still needed to improve this small-scale study. Nevertheless, the study indicates several considerations of teachers' beliefs and practices to present the song as the material in listening in an interesting atmosphere in the classroom.

Overall, the results of the study show that there is a congruent relationship between teachers' beliefs and practices on teaching listening using songs. Teacher An believes that listening using songs is beneficial in increasing vocabulary, she chooses a song which has some new words for the students to learn in the class. Then she applies the steps to enrich vocabulary. Teacher Sd believes that songs can improve students' pronunciation. She presents the song with some difficult words to be imitated by students. Teacher Pr believes that by using songs in listening, students are easily able to understand the main idea. She chooses a popular song and plays the song at least three times so students can catch the meaning. However, the presence of an appropriate teaching method and strategy in teaching listening using songs is needed to reach the goal of the learning process. Findings showed that teachers had difficulty in practising an appropriate strategy to teach listening using songs. It was mainly due to their educational background. In addition, not many of them had had prior experiences of teaching listening using songs. In fact, in many teachers training programs there was no specific discussion of how to teach listening using songs. Therefore, such programs are needed so that teachers are able to teach listening using songs well. By having sufficient competence, the learning goal in general will be succesfully achieved.

REFERENCES

Borg, M. 2001. *Teacher's belief.* ELT Journal. 55 (April 2001). Oxford University Press.

Borg, S. 2009. Introducing language teacher cognition. Retrieved 17 August 2017 from http://www. education.leeds.ac.uk/research/files/145.pdf.

Fauziati, E. 2015. *Teaching English as a foreign language: principle and practice.* Surakarta: Era Pustaka Utama.

Kementerian Pendidikan Dan Kebudayaan. 2016. Silabus mata pelajaran Sekolah Menengah Atas/ Madrasah Aliyah/Sekolah Menengah Kejuruan/Madrasah Aliyah Kejuruan (SMA/MA/SMK/ MAK): Mata pelajaran Bahasa Inggris. Jakarta: Direktorat PSMA.

Kirsch, C. 2008. *Teaching foreign languages in the primary school.* London: Continuum.

Linse, C.T. 2005. *Practical English language teaching: Young learners.* New York: McGraw-Hill.

Miles, M.B. & Hubberman, A.M. 1984. *Qualitative data dnalysis: A source book of new methods.* California: Sage Publication.

Richards, J. 2008. *Teaching listening and speaking.* New York: Cambridge.

Rokeach, M. 1968. *Beliefs, attitudes, and values: A theory of organization and change.* San Francisco: Jossey-Bass.

Williams, M. & Burden, L.R. 1997. *Psychology for language teachers: A social constructivis approach.* Cambridge: Cambridge University Press. http://www.onestopenglish.com/section.asp?docid=155160.

ELT in Asia in the Digital Era: Global Citizenship and Identity – Madya et al. (Eds)
© 2018 Taylor & Francis Group, London, ISBN 978-0-8153-7900-3

More than just vocabulary search: A bibliographic review on the roles of corpora of English in 21st century ELT

S. Simbuka
Institut Agama Islam Negeri Manado, Manado, Indonesia

ABSTRACT: This paper examines the literature on the roles of corpus linguistics on 21st century ELT. The analysis focuses on answering the question posed by Römer (2010): "How far have we come, where we are now in terms of direct and indirect pedagogical corpus applications?" It was found that online corpora of English, such as the BNC and the COCA have been utilized beyond the traditional role for 'vocabulary search'. These corpora have now had additional role as rich resources for computer and web-assisted research of linguistics patterns in ELT. Discrepancies between various linguistic features as covered in ELT textbooks with corpus findings of naturally occurring English was found as the main theme in the pedagogically-oriented indirect corpus approach. Meanwhile, direct application of corpus linguistics on ELT is the Data-Driven Learning (DDL) which advocates inductive and self-regulated learning by examining concordance lines produced by computer software specially designed to assist ELT.

1 INTRODUCTION

English language learners and teachers may have been familiar with computer-aided language learning and online dictionaries or encyclopedias to search for the meanings and uses of new vocabularies. Large collections of language samples stored in computers or online sites known as "language corpora" such as the British National Corpus (BNC), the Corpus of Contemporary American English (COCA) and the Bank of English (BoE) have been rich resources for these educational purposes in addition to their original function as resources for linguistics studies. Little has been known that there are more resources for learning and researching learning offered by these corpora beyond vocabulary searches.

2 METHOD

The current study utilizes the search tools on the Pennsylvania State University's library website and Google Scholar as data collection tools to collect research articles available online. Proceedings, books and book chapters, research reports were also included as the source for of the bibliographical data. The search keywords were "corpus studies" and "corpus and pedagogy" followed by "Southeast Asia" or names of individual Southeast Asia countries. The search came back with 21.000 entries comprising citations of all entry types mentioned earlier. Since thousands of these records were irrelevant to the exact search terms, a manual selection was conducted. The search results were reduced into 26 titles that perfectly matched the search terms as samples to be reviewed and presented in this paper.

A theory-driven deductive way of analyzing the collected and selected papers was used for the purpose of identification of the major themes of the reviewed studies. This review of the articles and proceeding papers were presented based on Römer's (2010) thematic categorization of pedagogy-related corpus research.

3 CORPORA AND PEDAGOGY

Owing to the main aim of Corpus Linguistics to present naturally occurring language based on empirical examinations of 'real language, the impact of corpus linguistics toward second and or foreign language teaching has consequently been closely related to providing 'more empirical input' for language learning (Flowerdew 2012). The seminal works of John Sinclair (Sinclair 1987, 1991, 2004 as cited in Campoy, Cubillo, Belles-Fortuno & Gea-Valor, 2010) on dictionary making had paved the ways of proving higher quality and finer elaboration of language in its use for learners and teachers alike (Campoy et al. 2010).

The application of Corpus Linguistics into ELT is generally categorized into indirect and direct application (Römer 2010). The first category is related to the role of corpus linguistics in providing highly reliable reference works, such as dictionaries and corpora. Corpus linguistics has also overtly or covertly informs syllabus development (known as the lexical syllabus) and ELT materials. On the other hand, some advocates of corpus linguistics have ventured into developing teaching and learning of ELT based on the inductive nature of corpus analysis in Data-driven Learning, henceforward DDL (Flowerdew 2012, 2015, Römer 2010).

3.1 Direct application of pedagogically-oriented corpus approach research

Römer (2010) recommended that studies on DDL should aim to reveal teacher-corpus interactions and learners-corpus interaction. However, in this bibliographical study it was found that only the last theme was the interest of many recent corpus studies conducted in the Asian context of ELT. These researches advocated the application of corpus data into classroom-based practices in order to demonstrate the effectiveness of this approach to learning as compared to conventional language learning. Some studies addressed English for general purposes utilizing general corpora such as the COCA and BNC as their main teaching materials. Smaller sized-specialized corpora, on the other hand, were the staple resource for programs in EAP and ESP. The researchers showing the claimed success of DDL are listed below:

Chujo, Kobayashi, Mizumoto & Oghigian (2016) claimed that DDL may be more effective than traditional approach to teaching English grammar for Japanese EFL learners, when two resources of web-based corpus tools were combined. The findings showed that DDL program utilizing two free-wares (keyword in context/KWIC tool from WebParaNews, and a lexical profiling tool, the LagoWordProfiler) that are based on a parallel corpus of English and Japanese (ParaNews) was even more effective than when a single corpus tool was used.

Flowerdew (2015) combined deductive tasks derived from the genre-based approach with inductive concordancing tasks of corpus approach to assist postgraduate students in writing the Discussion session of their theses. The DDL program was conducted in two steps i.e. 1) analyzing discussion section samples to identify the move structure patterning followed by corpus tasks of using search strategies for identifying useful lexico-grammatical patterns for particular rhetorical functions; 2) identifying variations of move structure coupled by concordancing tasks focusing on problematic areas of the students' own drafts of discussion section. The researcher suggested some free corpora for use in advanced ESL- EAP programs.

Flowerdew (2016) continues her interest in this DDL topic by designing and implementing a writing module developed from a combination of corpus-based findings on learners' corpus with the Swalesian genre approach. The study examined the effectiveness of this module in developing postgraduate students' skill in writing grant proposals. The researcher outlined tasks requiring students to match the lexico-grammatical patterning to specific move structure. The findings also revealed novice writers' language reuse from corpus resources and the identification of ELF-type language in academic writing.

3.2 Indirect application of corpus linguistics: Corpus studies to support ELT

3.2.1 Corpus and ELT textbook

The main theme in the pedagogically-oriented corpus approach studies has been the discrepancies between various linguistic features as they are covered in ELT textbooks with corpus findings. Römer (2010) listed research as early as the ones in the 90-s that examined the coverage of grammatical categories such reflexives by Barlow (1996), on linking adverbials by Conrad (2004), and on irregular verbs by Grabowski & Mindt (1995), modal verbs by herself (Römer 2004, 2006). Findings of these studies suggested that each of the respective categories of English language presented in many EFL course books were lesser in frequency count when compared to the English forms that occur naturally.

More recent studies in an Asian context that are based on the frequency and collocation analysis of the corpora of ELT textbooks as they are compared to massive corpora of English continued this theme in order to show the very similar issue faced by ELT textbooks/course books/materials stakeholders still exist. Most of these studies reported that the issue of miss-match between the language content presented in many ELT (ESL and EFL) textbooks/course books and other types of materials was still true especially in the context of locally produced EFL textbooks development. The authors of many of these textbooks were found to rely heavily on their intuition rather than to base their decision on selecting and sequencing the language content of their ELT textbooks on corpora of "real" language use.

Many studies contrasting the corpora of ELT textbooks against major corpora focused on examining specific grammatical forms, some of these studies were summarized below:

Based on the data of 1200 concordance lines randomly selected from the academic genre in COCA, Phoocharoensil (2017) reported the discrepancy between the reference corpus and ELT textbook in Thailand in terms of linking adverbials (LA). The findings pointed out that "thus" was the most frequently occurred LA in written academic genre, whilst "so" was markedly frequent in spoken genre. Both were reported to be underrepresented in the examined ELT textbook.

Zarifi (2012) showed that the treatment of phrasal verbs in Malaysian EFL textbooks has been intuitively-driven rather than empirically-proven on the basis of their actual representation in the natural data recorded in the reference corpus. The researchers also pointed out that textbooks/materials developers were often faced one of the main problems in selecting language items to be presented in their material e.g. phrasal verbs given the enormous number of this form in English.

Yoo (2009) investigated the mismatch between on indefinite articles presented in six ESL textbooks published by internationally acknowledged companies that are used in Korea and the corpus of naturally existing (standard) English.

Recent corpus approach studies have also ventured beyond analysis of grammatical forms, focusing on several other concerns such as vocabulary, text difficulty and tests corpora. Some of these studies are:

Chujo & Genung (2003) compared the vocabulary of representative texts and materials used by students in junior and senior high school (JSH) which was English for general purposes (EGP) and the semi-ESP and ESP programs in a college of industrial technology. Their findings indicated a large gap between the vocabulary level of EGP and ESP, meanwhile the semi-ESP vocabulary materials were not effective to close up the gap.

Chen (2016) utilized a very sophisticated quantitative analysis called variability neighbor clustering in measuring text difficulty level and development in ELT textbook series used in Taiwan senior high school. The result of this particular study indicated that one of the analyzed textbook was found to show the best reflection of an expected progression of text difficulty. The learners-users of this textbook series were assumed to benefit from learning from materials with appropriate increasing level of text difficulty in both vocabulary and structure.

Comparing the corpus of an English entrance exam and English textbooks used in junior high school, Tai & Chen (2015) found discrepancy between test and textbook in terms of the investigated marked-structure (relative, adverbial, and passive clauses). The marked structures were found to appear in much higher frequency in the textbooks then in the test corpus. They found that it is not surprising that the teachers were more likely textbook-oriented, rather than test-oriented.

These studies confirmed that there is an intertwining connection between syllabus and ELT materials demonstrating how corpus approach has contributed indirectly to materials development. This contribution is delivered by means of providing research findings mostly on evaluation of the language content as compared to 'the real language'. In other words, the corpus studies of this short recommend "what to teach and when to teach it" (Römer 2010). The accuracy of the language presented in materials can be addressed by making use of corpus research using methods to examine the 'keyness of keywords of subject-specific texts (Baker et al. 2013). The extent of the authenticity of ELT textbooks can be verified by referring and comparing them to corpus of authentic English compiled empirically by experts in this field (Römer 2004). The frequency and range of the lexical items are key information for the selection of vocabulary in ELT textbooks (Flowerdew 201, Harwood 2013, Mukundan & Kalajahi 2016, Römer 2010).

Major publishers of ELT textbooks such as Cambridge University and Oxford University Press have also acknowledged this contribution and have begun to incorporate corpora as rich sources of vocabulary for their textbook products (Alavi & Rajabpoor 2015). To administrators and teachers, the afore-mentioned studies uniformly recommended these parties will equally benefit from the data of corpus approach studies on ELT materials.

3.2.2 Studies on earners' corpora to inform ELT/SLA

Flowerdew (2014) noted that by 2014, research on learners' corpora had been almost twenty-five years old. Now spanned almost twenty eight years of research learners' corpora are still rich resources for studying areas for development for ESL/EFL learners towards achieving even better performance in English. The main issue being explored in this type of studies is the extent to which ESL/EFL learners' mastery of English or use of English in writings resembles the corpus of native speakers of English. These studies obviously have taken the perspective of the British structuralist-main stream school of corpus linguistics such as Randolph Quirk. The main works of these experts had been developing corpus of English produced by its native speakers and use it as the basis for teaching the grammar of English targeting native-speaker like proficiency for ESL/EFL learners (Flowerdew 2012). Comparing learners' corpora to the "standard English" ones have been popular in several Southeast Asian countries. Some of the notable studies are listed below:

Sung & Kim (2016) analyzed Korean learners' corpora of three English/EFL proficiency levels to examine the production patterns of transitivity and particle placement features of the English phrasal verbs (PV) against the corpus produced by native speakers of English. The result revealed that the advanced learner's corpus showed the most similar characteristics with the reference corpus, whilst the basic and intermediate learners corpora were on the opposite direction.

Ha (2015) also compared learners' versus native speakers' corpus when investigating the use of English linking adverbials in Korean learners' corpus. The findings showed that the Korean learners' over-used most of linking adverbials in all semantic categories, mostly in the sequential and additive categories.

Abdul Aziz & Jin (2012 in Barlow, Basturkmen & Li, 2012) reported an analysis of learners' corpus consisting of argumentative essays composed by college students in Malaysia using Antconc 3.2.1, a freeware concordance program. On the basis of learners' use of metadiscourse in their argumentative essays, the study revealed that linguistic variables and non-linguistic variables, specifically gender identity are related in shaping learners' ESL learning and production. A similar study was conducted by Rustipa (2014) in an Indonesian context, contrasting learners' corpus with BAWE and resulted in very similar findings.

Using English as L1 corpus as the norm for judging collocational competence of ESL learners of Malay L2 background, Abdullah & Mohd. Noor (2012 in Barlow et al., 2012) examined learners' actual use of verb-noun collocations in their writing which eventually reflect the quality of their writing.

Taking a different stand point from the afore mentioned studies Kobayashi (2016) did not compare the native speakers' competency head to head with ESL/EFL learners'. The researcher as aware that there is criticism that this practice is theoretically fallacious (Bley-Vroman 1983 as cited by Kobayashi 2016). The study reported the differences in rhetorical preferences i.e. the use of metadiscourse makers among East Asian versus Southeast Asian learners of English.

Drawing on the International Corpus Network of Asian Learners of English (ICNALE) i.e. essays as the data source for the study, Abdul Aziz and Mohd. Don (in Barlow et al. 2012) investigated ESL learners' overuse of be + verb construction using Antconc 3.2.1

Although these studies were indirectly linked to pedagogy, the results were still valuable for ESL practitioners to incorporate learners' corpus as one of the tools to identify learners' factor in designing and planning an ESL programs. The studies exemplified above confirmed (Reppen 2009) statement on the overall contribution of corpora and corpus linguistics to language teaching, especially to learners who stated that:

> *"One of the principle goals of language instruction is to provide learners with the opportunity to interact with authentic materials that will enhance their learning and help them move along to along to language fluency. Corpus linguistics and the use of corpora in the classroom can help move learners towards this goal." (p. 213).*

3.2.3 Identification of specific linguistics features (keywords, word frequency list) for ESP, EAP

Studies that argued for the merit of creation of specific vocabulary list for ESP have been around since the 90-s. One of the earlier studies was conducted by Sutarsyah, Nation & Kennedy (1994) that pointed out a single text in economy had a small number of words that occurred in high frequency, a character that differentiate economic texts with general academic texts of various field. The implication for ELT was clear that ESP learners will benefit from uniquely crafted ESP vocabulary lists.

In the Southeast Asian context, some works continued the legacy of finding more developed methods and tools for generating more thorough field specific ESP vocabulary lists to help ESP teachers with minimum technical knowledge on that specific field. Some of the studies under this theme are:

Kwary & Jurianto (2017), for example, proposed a method for selecting words and a creating a word list based on the authors' analysis of the claims made by the currently available word lists. Differences in the corpora and the source texts were pointed out as the cause for the differences in the coverage of the analyzed word lists. Kwary's works have been consistent in this topic that can be traced back to his proposal of a hybrid method for identifying technical vocabulary for ESP using corpus keywords tools (Kwary 2011). The hybrid method was a combination of the keyword analysis method and the systematic classifications method, two of four methods known for identifying keywords in a corpus.

Before that, Kwary (2006) demonstrated the generation of a technical vocabulary wordlist and Web-based materials for teaching and learning ESP from a practical perspective. The author showed that teachers with minimum level on computer knowledge can use web-based materials created with 3 programs, which can be delivered and/or learned at any computer equipped with any browser.

Abudukeremu (2010) studied the frequency, coverage and distribution of academic vocabulary in Islamic academic research articles. It was found that due to its general nature, AWL did not include some words that occurred in the analyzed articles. The researcher then addressed this issue by actually developing a specific corpus of Islamic academic research articles or IARA (Abudukeremu 2010). He recommended that EFL learners and teachers should pay more attention to specific lexical items in academic articles.

The implications of the afore mentioned studies examining "what kind of vocabulary is suitable for specific ESP program" cannot be dismissed into merely providing linguistic input to ELT materials development. As recommended by these studies, further research exploring their linkage to pedagogy were still an open window for educational linguists to ponder into other aspects such as designing effective tasks for vocabulary learning based on the corpus data, as well as the assessment issues.

4 CONCLUSION

Beyond their preliminary function as mere providers of vocabulary learning for ESL/EFL learners, English language corpora have much more to offer for ELT. The studies reviewed in this article have demonstrated that corpora offered both direct and indirect contributions to ELT. The proponents of DDL whose research reports are reviewed here have strived to offer alternative programs to teaching ESL/EFL that are directly based on the data of general or specialized corpora. Other articles examined in this current paper suggested indirect roles of corpora in terms of their role as rich resources of "real or naturally occurring" English language content for textbooks and materials developers, diagnosis of learners' area of development in mastering ESL/EFL. Last but not least is the importance of researching and building vocabulary list grounded on corpus data for the enhancement of ESP and EAP. As a matter of fact, corpora and pedagogy-related corpus linguistics research offer ELT learning and research opportunities more than just vocabulary search.

REFERENCES

Abudukeremu, M. 2010. *A corpus-based lexical study of the frequency, coverage and distribution of academic vocabulary in Islamic academic research articles*. International Islamic University Malaysia.

Alavi, S. & Rajabpoor, A. 2015. Analyzing idioms and their frequency in three advanced ILI textbooks: A corpus-based study. *English Language Teaching* 8(1): 170–179. https://doi.org/10.5539/elt.v8n1p170.

Baker, P., Gabrielatos, C. & Mcenery, T. 2013. Sketching muslims : A corpus driven analysis of representations around the word "muslim" in the british press 1998–2009, (October 2012), 255–278. https://doi.org/10.1093/applin/ams048.

Barlow, M., Basturkmen, H. & Li, Q. (eds.). 2012. Abstracts of the first asia pacific corpus linguistics conference. In *Proceedings of the First Asia Pacific Corpus Linguistics Conference*: 1–190. Auckland, New Zealand: The University of Auckland, New Zealand.

Campoy, M.C., Cubillo, M.C.C., Belles-Fortuno, B. & Gea-Valor, M.L. 2010. *Corpus-based approaches to English language teaching*. London, New York: A & C Black.

Chen, A.C.H. 2016. A critical evaluation of text difficulty development in ELT textbook series: A corpus-based approach using variability neighbor clustering. *System* 58: 64–81. https://doi.org/10.1016/j.system.2016.03.011.

Chujo, K. & Genung, M. 2003. Vocabulary-level assessment for ESP texts used in the field of industrial technology. *English Teaching* 58(3): 259–274.

Chujo, K., Kobayashi, Y., Mizumoto, A. & Oghigian, K. 2016. Exploring the effectiveness of combined web-based corpus tools for beginner EFL DDL. *Linguistics and Literature Studies* 4(4): 262–274. https://doi.org/10.13189/lls. 2016.040404.

Flowerdew, L. 2012. *Corpora and language education*. Palgrave Macmillan.

Flowerdew, L. 2014. Learner corpus research in EAP : Some key issues and future pathways. *English Language and Linguistics* 20(2): 43–60.

Flowerdew, L. 2015. Journal of English for academic purposes using corpus-based research and online academic corpora to inform writing of the discussion section of a thesis. *Journal of English for Academic Purposes* 20: 58–68. https://doi.org/10.1016/j.jeap.2015.06.001.

Flowerdew, L. 2016. English for Specific purposes a genre-inspired and lexico-grammatical approach for helping postgraduate students craft research grant proposals. *English for Specific Purposes* 42: 1–12. https://doi.org/ 10.1016/j.esp.2015.10.001.

Ha, M. 2015. *Linking adverbials in first-year Korean university EFL learners â€ᵀᴹ writing: a corpus-informed analysis*. https://doi.org/10.1080/09588221.2015.1068814.

Harwood, N. 2013. English language teaching textbooks content consumption production. *Journal of Chemical Information and Modeling* 5. Springer. https://doi.org/10.1017/CBO9781107415324.004.

Kobayashi, Y. 2016. Investigating metadiscourse markers in Asian Englishes: A corpus-based approach. *Language in Focus* 2(1): 19–35. https://doi.org/10.1515/lifijsal-2016-0002.

Kwary, D.A. 2006. *Creating a technical vocabulary wordlist and web-based materials : the first step for teaching and learning ESP*.

Kwary, D.A. 2011. A hybrid method for determining technical vocabulary. *System* 39(2):175–185. https://doi.org/10.1016 /j.system.2011.04.003.

Kwary, D.A. & Jurianto. 2017. Selecting and creating a word list for English language teaching. *Teaching English With Technology* 17(1): 60–72.

Mukundan, J. & Kalajahi, S.A.R. 2016. Developing reading materials for ESL learners. In *Issues in Materials Development*: 65–74. Rotterdam, Boston, Taipei: Sense Publisher.

Phoocharoensil, S. 2017. Corpus-based exploration of linking adverbials of result : Discovering what ELT writing coursebooks lack. *The Southeast Asian Journal of English Language Studies* 23(1): 150–167.

Reppen, R. 2009. English language teaching and corpus linguistics: Lessons from the American National Corpus. In P. Baker (Ed.), *Contemporary studies in linguistics: contemporary corpus linguistics*. London: Continuum.

Römer, U. 2004. A corpus-driven approach to modal auxiliaries and their didactics. *How to Use Corpora in Language Teaching*: 185–199. https://doi.org/10.1075/scl.12.14rom.

Römer, U. 2006. Pedagogical applications of corpora: Some reflections on the current scope and a wish list for future developments. *Zeitschrift Für Anglistik Und Amerikanistik*, 54(2): 121–134.

Römer, U. 2010. Using general and specialized corpora in English language teaching:past, present and future. In M.C. Campoy, M.C.C. Cubillo, B. Belles-Fortuno & M.L. Gea-Valor (Eds.), *Corpus-based approaches to English language teaching*. London, New York: Continuum.

Rustipa, K. 2014. Metadiscourse in Indonesian EFL learners ' persuasive texts: A case study at English Department, UNISBANK 4(1): 44–52. https://doi.org/10.5539/ijel.v4n1p44.

Sung, M.C. & Kim, H. 2016. Tracing developmental changes in L2 learners ' structuring of phrasal verbs : A corpus study of native and non-native argumentative essays. *The Southeast Asian Journal of English Language Studies* 22(2): 151–166.

Sutarsyah, C., Nation, P. & Kennedy, G. 1994. How useful is EAP vocabulary for ESP? A corpus based case study. *RELC Journal* 25(2): 34–50.

Tai, S. & Chen, H. 2015. Are teachers test-oriented ? A comparative corpus- based analysis of the English entrance exam and junior high school English textbooks. *Critical CALL-Proceedings of the 2015 EUROCALL Conference, Padova, Italy*: 518–522. https://doi.org/10.14705.rpnet. 2015.000386.

Yoo, I.W. 2009. The English definite article : What ESL/EFL grammars say and what corpus findings show. *Journal of English for Academic Purposes* 8(4): 267–278. https://doi.org/10.1016/j.jeap.2009.07.004.

Zarifi, A. 2012. *Phrasal verbs in Malaysian ESL textbooks* 5(5), 9–18. https://doi.org/10.5539/elt.v5n5p9.

ELT in Asia in the Digital Era: Global Citizenship and Identity – Madya et al. (Eds)
© *2018 Taylor & Francis Group, London, ISBN 978-0-8153-7900-3*

Hyland's model of argument in ESL writers essay

W.H. Osman
Universiti Malaysia Sabah, Malaysia

ABSTRACT: Persuasive writing is used in the academic world to convince readers to change their views, attitude towards an issue or idea. It is used in writing proposal, critical analysis report, and papers. To be able to persuade or argue an issue well in the written mode, it is important to use the appropriate rhetorical structure to achieve the writers' objective. This paper examined rhetorical structures used by five ESL writers in their essays by means of Ken Hyland's Model of argument (1990) as the tool of analysis. The findings help in explaining the common and uncommon rhetorical structure used based on Hyland's model. The implications are useful for academic writing educators and syllabus designers as more focus activities can be given to areas that are least used by ESL students and this will help learners be better persuasive writers.

1 INTRODUCTION

Writing is an important skill in the academic world. Most universities and learning institution has made written assessments as part of course evaluation and graduation requirement. As mentioned by Bruce (2010), in the last few decades, focus has been on the need to prepare ESL to cope with language requirements and also writing requirements of higher institutions.

Learners at higher institutions write assignments for many reasons and among the common reasons are to persuade, to report, to review and to summarise. Among the many goals of writing, persuasive writing is considered among the most difficult. As reported by Applebee, Langer & Mullis (1986), even native speakers of English in America found persuasive writing difficult. As highlighted by many prominent researchers in the area of ESL such as Ferris (1994) & Crowhurst (1991), non-native speakers of English found it difficult to produce a competent piece of argumentative paper because of linguistic and rhetorical issues. Hyland (1990) has also highlighted that ESL writers lack thought structure to organise content when writing argumentative essays.

Many academicians in the field of education, and applied linguistics have agreed that persuasive writing and the identification of structure and linguistic element of ESL writers' work is significantly important and there are still areas that need to be looked into. In view of these issues and queries, this present study aims to contribute to the data for ESL's persuasive essays. It hopes to look into Malaysian ESL writers' writing of persuasive essay and the rhetorical structure used.

1.1 *Rational of study*

In studying persuasive and argument genre, there are a few scopes that are commonly researched on such as the writing process and the difficulties of writers, the teaching process and also genre analysis. Among the common research is on text analysis. Many researches have been conducted and many have stated among the reasons for conducting research on written text is the motivational drive to teach students to write effectively (Schneider & Connor 1990, Hyland 1990). Schneider & Connor (1990: 411–412) also said that 'Text analyses of written products have been shown to complement research on writing processes and are needed for an integrated theory of writing'.

In view of the reasons given by previous researchers in the same area, this present study is also needed and important to assist educators and learners to discover what are the argumentative structure commonly used by ESL writers in Malaysia. From the finding, then it is hoped that a more appropriate, meaningful and useful writing module can be designed.

Another reason for this present study is that previous studies have also shown that an effective writing is produced when the writers managed to engage with the readers. Thus, structure, organisation and the vocabulary used are very crucial to determine the success of the piece of written text and the success of the reader reading it (Hyland 2002, Salager-Mayer 1998, Zahra et al. 2014).

2 LITERATURE REVIEW

2.1 *Persuasive essay vs argumentative essay*

There are many definitions of persuasive and argumentative essay. Thomson (2000) states that argument is the presentation of conclusion which are supported by information and reasons. Zainoddin & Galea (2016) defined argument as "… the reason(s) a person gives in support of a claim".

The notion of argument focuses more on rhetorical theories which put forward the elements of persuasion (Gilbert 2005). This further supports what Hyland mentioned earlier "… academic writing as an interactive accomplishment is now well established. A writers' development of an appropriate relationship with his or her readers is widely seen as central to effective academic persuasion as writers seek to balance claims for the significance, originality and correctness of their work against the convictions and expectations of their reader" (2002). Rescher (1998) had difficulty in separating between argumentative and persuasive text because there is a need to identify the relationship between rational argumentation, rhetoric and dialect and their influence on the interpretations of argument structures and functions. In short, argument involves persuasion and it has to be done in a well-developed organisation in order for the argument to be clear and logic.

Among the few purposes of argumentation is to persuade (Meiland 1989, Connor 1987, 1990, Blair 2004). According to Crowhurst (1990: 349), argumentative essay is "the kind of writing that the writers take a point of view and support it with either emotional appeals or logical appeals". With all that has been said by previous researchers in the field of rhetoric, composition and argument, in this present study the term persuasive text or essay will be used more often than argumentative text or essay. This is because the researcher believes that the word persuade or persuasive is more general and easily fit into argumentative text. In this study too, both word; persuasive and argumentative will have the same meaning.

2.2 *Ken Hyland's model of argument*

There are a few different models for argumentative essay analysis but for this present study, Hyland's 1990 model will be used. Hyland defines argumentative essay "… by its purpose which is to persuade the reader of the correctness of a central statement" (Hyland 2003: 68). He uses the genre analysis approach by using the terms stage and moves. Genre and moves are important elements because Hyland (2003: 18) has defined genre as "… abstract, socially recognised ways of using language for particular purposes" and moves as defined by Bhatia (2001: 84) are "…rhetorical instruments that realise a subset of specific communicative purposes associated with a genre". Ken Hyland's Argumentative Essay Model has a three stage structure; Thesis, Argument and Conclusion and each stage has its' moves.

The first stage of an argumentative essay is the thesis. In this stage, there are 5 significant moves; gambit, information, proposition, evaluation and marker. The first move, gambit, is not to give information but functions as an attention grabber. The second move, information, gives general information related to the topic or issue being written on. The general information which Hyland calls 'universal features' are taken from "…definitions, classifications, descriptions, critiques or straw man arguments". The third move is the central move of the thesis stage. Proposition move provides a specific point which 'defines the topic and gives a focus to the entire composition.". However Hyland highlighted that not all proposition move are clear cut as the example given. Competent and experience writers may write the proposition move in the same sentence or as a continuation from the information move. It can also be written in the form of a gambit. After the proposition move, Hyland said that a writer may have the evaluation move which is optional. Evaluation move is a positive comment about the proposition. This is primarily because it is the base of our education system. The last move, marker, is the signpost to indicate the direction of the whole essay.

The second stage is the argument stage and it has four moves; marker, restatement, claim, and support. This stage focuses on the grounds for the thesis and is usually repeated indefinitely depending on the points or main ideas of the proposition. The first move which is the marker connects the argument to the proposition. There are two ways to write this marker move. The first is with the use of listing signals such as firstly and next. The other method is with the use of transition signals such as the use of adverbial connectives and conjunctions (Hyland 1990). The second move, restatement, is not always available but it is significant because it functions as a reminder of the subject. The third move in this argument stage is the claim move which is the central move in this stage. Hyland has identified three common persuasion methods in this claim move. The first is when the reader is expected to share the same views on the proposition as the writer. The second method is when the writer generalizes based on facts or expert opinion. The last method to write a claim is when the writer gives an opinion with little regard to contrasting view. The last move in this second stage is the support move and Hyland has mentioned that this move is 'indispensable second part to the claim in the tied pair of moves" (1990: 73). It functions to prove the relevance of the claim and the proposition and is an "explicit reinforcement for the claim and can comprise several paragraphs appealing to several sources of evidence" (Hyland 1990).

The last stage is the conclusion stage and it has four moves; marker, consolidation, affirmation and close. According to Hyland (1990), conclusion is not only a summary or review but it is there in an essay to "consolidate the discourse and retrospectively affirm what has been communicated". This is achieved via the marker move for example the use of words such as thus, therefore and to conclude. The second move, consolidation is the central part of the conclusion stage and it is achieved when the writer refers back to the content of the argument stage and relates it to the theme and proposition. Another two moves in stage three is the affirmation and close moves. Affirmation is optional but for academic purposes for example in exam essays, it is usually available. Affirmation move is when the proposition is mentioned again. The last move, close is opposite of move 2 (consolidation). It is a move where the writer "looks forward to unstated aspects of the discussion by widening the context" (Hyland 1990: 74).

3 METHODOLOGY

This study uses a qualitative study with descriptive statistics to ensure the explanation is clear and justified. Samples are taken from a group of ESL writers attending English for Reading and Writing (ERW) Module in a public university in Malaysia. The requirement to enter this particular module is that they have obtained either Band 1 or 2 for their Malaysian University English Test (MUET). MUET is an English proficiency test which is largely used for admission into Malaysian public universities. The result is shown as Bands and there are 6 bands; Band 1 (very limited user) and Band 6 (highly proficient user).

Students who enter this university with MUET band 1 and 2 result, they need to sit for 4 English Language module and this ERW module is one of it. It is usually taken by students in their third semester and after they have taken module 1 and 2; Communicative English Grammar and Oral Communication.

In this module, students are exposed to reading and writing in English and the materials used in this module are at the intermediate level. They are taught a few different genres such as cause and effect and persuasive. For this present research, only the persuasive genre essay is used. The essays used were produced as part of an English writing class assessment task. The writers were asked to choose a topic in their area of study and to persuade readers to agree or like their topic or issue. They were given one week to complete the task. The writers were allowed to submit a draft and then improve on the essay and submit a final draft for evaluation purposes. For this research purposes, only the final draft was analysed.

This paper is part of a larger research and for the purpose of this paper, only five ESL writers' persuasive essays were used. The five essays were chosen randomly from one of the classes which the language instructor had agreed to participate in the research. When this study was conducted, there were 47 classes consisting of 35 students each and there were 18 language instructors. The class was chosen only with the consent of the language instructors. There were 12 language instructors who were willing to participate in this research.

The researcher employed Ken Hyland's Model of argument (1990) as the tool of analysis in identifying the rhetorical structure realised in the students' essays. The essay where labeled with the stages and moves highlighted in Hyland's 1990 model and the linguistic elements to support the stages and moves were underlined and colour coded. After the identification of stages, moves and linguistic elements, the data were then tabulated.

4 RESULT

The five sample essays written by Malaysian ESL writers were analysed by looking at the structure and selected language features used to compose an argumentative essay. The result will be presented according to the stages which are thesis, argument and conclusion. The examples taken from the samples will be in the original form which includes the grammar mistakes.

The students were required to write a minimum of 5 paragraphs with a minimum of 350 words. However, out of the 5 samples, 1 has 8 paragraphs (R1) and the other four have the minimum number of paragraphs which is 5 paragraphs. As for the number of words, R1 has the most number of words (720 words) and R2 has the least number of words (345 words). Table 1 shows the data for the title and number of words written. Looking at R1 and R4, it can be said that the number of paragraphs does not determine the length of a paper. R4 has only 5 paragraphs but was able to write 624 words which is only 96 words less than R1 that has 8 paragraphs.

In summary, all the five essays fulfilled the requirement of the written task. The following sections will identify in detail the moves of each stages based on what has been designed by Ken Hyland (1990).

4.1 *Stage 1: Thesis stage*

This stage functions to introduce the proposition to be argued. It is usually the first paragraph of an essay. Hyland (1990) model of argument has identified 5 moves in this stage. Based on the 5 essays analysed in this present study, all had Move 1 (gambit), Move 3 (proposition) and Move 5 (marker). Only one had evaluation (R3).

Sample sentence for M1 (Gambit) are as follow:

> Technology is a kind of advancement that invented or created by human being. (R1: Sentence 1). Advertisements are located everywhere. (R3: Sentence 1).

As mentioned earlier, there is one sentence that has two moves; M1 (gambit) and M2 (information) and this is found in R2. The sentence is as follow:

> First impressions are important (M1) *once it formed, it would be difficult to change, so how to achieve a good impression is very important (M2)*. (R2: Sentence 1)

Table 1.　Respondents' essay.

Respondent	Topic & Issue	No of Para & words	No of sentences PerPara
R1	Technology – Bad and good of technology	8 Para & 720 words	p.1–3 sent. p.2–5 sent. p.3–8 sent. p.4–7 sent. p. 5–7 sent. p. 6–7 sent. p. 7–7 sent. p. 8–3 sent.
R2	Psychology – First impression is important	5 para & 345 words	p. 1–2 sent. p. 2–6 sent. p. 3–6 sent. p. 4–5 sent. p. 5–1 sent.
R3	Psychology – Why do we need to help people	5 Para & 480 words	p. 1–4 sent. p. 2–9 sent. p. 3–7 sent. p. 4–9 sent. p. 5–4 sent.
R4	Marketing – Advertisement is bad	5 Para & 624 words	p. 1–6 sent. p. 2–8 sent. p. 3–11 sent. p. 4–11 sent. p. 5–8 sent.
R5	Psychology – Being a successful person	5 Para & 391 words	p. 1–4 sent. p. 2–5 sent. p. 3–5 sent. p. 4–5 sent. p. 5–2 sent.

Table 2.　Stage 1 – Thesis.

Respondent	M1 – (Gambit)	M2 – (Information)	M3 – Proposition	M4 – (Evaluation)	M5 – (Marker)
R1	✓		✓		✓
R2	✓	✓ in M1 (gambit) sentence	✓		✓
R3	✓		✓	✓	✓
R4	✓	✓	✓		✓
R5	✓		✓		✓

The third move; proposition move (M3) is compulsory and is found in all the five responses. A clear example of M3 is found in R3; 'It has helps us a lot in our life. But, it will also bring bad impact to us (R3: Sentence 2 & 3). Here, it is clear the stand or proposition is that technology has negative impact on mankind.

There is one move that is found in only one essay. The move is called evaluation (M4). M4 functions to give positive support to the proposition (M3). For example;

> There are many reasons why helping each other is good for everyone (M3). Not only give a great sense of satisfaction, but this satisfaction leads to the sense of belonging (M4). (R3: Sentence 2 & 3)

M5 (marker) is not always present but as Hyland (1990: 71) mentioned it is always present in examination scripts (. Thus, this may be the reason why all five respondents have this move.

449

An example of the marker move (M5) is 'Basically, there are many ways on how to be a successful person in our life' (R5: Sentence 4).

4.2 Stage 2: Argument stage

Stage 2, argument stage is the body of the essay. It discusses the grounds for the thesis. It has four moves; marker, restatement, claim, and support. This stage is usually written repeatedly and in a few paragraphs because this stage focuses on the proposition and the supports.

All five essays had M1 (marker), M3 (claim) and M4 (support). However as for M2 (restatement), all except for R2 had it. As mentioned by Hyland (1990), M2 is most often only available in essays written for exam purposes and it functions as a reminder to the reader regarding the proposition.

Even though R1, R3, R4 and R5 have restatement (M2), however for R1 it is not found in all the paragraphs. Out of the 6 paragraphs of the argument stage (S2), paragraph 4 and 7 does not have M2.

> Lastly, technology will affect one's health (M1). Radioactive elements that bring out by the advancement of technology like computer will affect one's health (M3). For example, people who are addicted in playing games or watching dramas right in front of the computer for whole day will caused health problem like gastric, heart attack and many more (M4). Electronic technology will leads one to have short-sightedness (M3). For example, electronic technology like mobile phones and computer need our eyes to focus. Within the long period, it will cause our eyes to have short sightedness (M4). Health problems will occur if ones of not use the advancement of technology wisely (M3). (R1: paragraph 7)

4.3 Stage 3: Conclusion stage

This is the last stage of an argumentative essay. Stage 3 has four moves; marker, consolidation, affirmation and close. According to Hyland's model, consolidation (M2) is a compulsory move in Stage 3. However, R1 and R2 have omitted M2 from their writing. All the four moves were found in R3 and R4. M3 and M4 are missing from R5. According to Hyland,

Table 3. Stage 2 – Argument.

Respondent	M1 – (Marker)	M2 – Consolidation	M3 – (Affirmation)	M4 – (Close)
R1				✓
R2				✓
R3	✓	✓	✓	✓
R4	✓	✓	✓	✓
R5	✓	✓		

Table 4. Stage 3 – Conclusion.

Respondents	M1 – Marker	M2 – (Restatement)	M3 – Claim	M4 – Support
R1	✓	✓	✓	✓
R2	✓		✓	✓
R3	✓	✓	✓	✓
R4	✓	✓	✓	✓
R5	✓	✓	✓	✓

M2 (consolidation) is achieved when the points and ideas of argument are mentioned again in Stage 3 (Conclusion). However for R1 and R2, the sentences written are towards M4 (close) which Hyland described as present when a writer writes on a wider context of the argument.

The sentence in R1's essay is 'Technology plays an important role in our lives. Therefore, we must use the advancement of technology wisely instead of misuse it. We must be able to aware about its dangers'. Here R1 has used M4 (close) in 3 sentences and they are all in an advising and warning tone. For R2, M3 has only one sentence and it is in the tone of an advice, 'How to make a good first impression is very important, so I think if you fulfil these conditions, you can have good first impression.'

There are two respondents (R3 and R4) who used all the four moves in their essay. R3 has constructed one sentence for each move and the total number of sentences for Stage 3 is four.

> In conclusion, helping others really is a 'win-win' situation (*M1*).The person we kindly helped is now much better off and now we have raised our self-esteem (*M2*). For that reason, it can lead a good life and get satisfied by helping one another. If the kindness is based and it carries on, it continues to multiply forever (*M3*). This makes the world a better place to live (*M4*). (R3: Paragraph 5)

R4 has eight sentences in the Stage 3 paragraph with one sentence for M1, three sentences for M2, three sentences for M3 and one sentence for M4.

> In short, advertisers are very tricky to get people's attention both in print and on screen (*M1*). They use many kinds of strategies to manipulate our minds. No advertisements are more effective than one that makes you feel something because emotion and memory are tightly linked. Most of the tricks work because they speak directly to our psychology (*M2*). We should not blame lies to the advertisers because the problem is caused by our human attitude in shaping (*M4*). Thus, we as a wise buyer should know about how to differentiate between the necessary and unnecessary things. These tricks also let us think logically about the certain products in advertisements. It really help us in making a right decision before we purchase something (*M3*). (R4: Paragraph 5)

5   DISCUSSION AND CONCLUSION

This present study was to study the rhetorical structure of argumentative essays produced by a group of ESL writers in a Malaysian public university. Another purpose is to use the model proposed by Hyland to analyse the stages and moves. The finding from this study is that Hyland's model of argument does fit in Malaysian ESL writers style of writing. However, it is discovered via informal discussion with the language instructor and a few of the students who attended this module, the end product of the students' essay is because they follow rigidly to the structure taught. Most of them said that they may not be able to produce such a well-structured persuasive essay structure if they were not taught and reminded of the structure and also if the essay is longer.

This paper is only a small report of the finding of a bigger research and it is conducted as a pilot study to a larger study. It must also be reminded that the essays that were used for this study, are the final draft and this means that the students have made correction and gone through consultation on their writing. The finding of this study may be more interesting if the students writing were authentic; where the first drafts are analysed and they were not drilled on the format. Thus, this can be future studies that can be conducted to obtain more in-depth data on ESL writing and issues they face.

It is hoped that the whole study will contribute to the teaching and learning of academic essays especially argumentative writing in the Malaysian context.

REFERENCES

Applebee, A.N., Langer, J.A. & Mullis, I.V.S. 1986. *The writing report card: Writing achievement in American schools*. National Assessment of Educational Progress. Princeton, NJ: Educational Testing Service.

Bhatia, V. 1993. *Analysing genre: Language use in professional settings (Applied linguistics and language study)*. London: Longman.

Blair, J.A. 2004. Arguments and their uses. *Informal Logic* 24(2):137–151.

Bruce, I. 2010. *Academic writing and genre. A systematic analysis.* London: Continuum International Publishing Group.

Connor, U. 1987. Research frontiers in writing analysis. *TESOL Quarterly* 21: 677–696.

Connor, U. 1990. Linguistics/ rhetorical measures for international persuasive student writing. *Research in the Teaching of English* 24(1): 67–87.

Crowhurst, M. 1990. Teaching and learning the writing of persuasive discourse. *Canadian Journal of Education* 15 (4): 348–359.

Crowhurst, M. 1991. Research review: Patterns of development in writing persuasive/argumentative discourse. *Research in the Teaching of English* 25(3): 314–338.

Ferris, D.R. 1994. Lexical and syntactic features of ESL writing by students at different levels of L2 proficiency. *TESOL Quatertly*, 28(2): 414–420.

Gilbert, K.M. 2005. Argumentation in students' academic discourse. In D. Hitchcock (Ed.), The uses of argument (First ed., 129–138). Ontario Canada: Ontario Society for the Study of Argumentation.

Hyland, K. 1990. A genre description of the argumentative essay. *RELC Journal* 21: 66–78.

Hyland, K. 2002. Directives: Argument and engagement in academic writing. *Applied Linguistics: Oxford University Press* 23(2): 215–239.

Hyland, K. 2003. Second language writing. Cambridge: Cambridge University Press.

Meiland, J.W. 1989. Argument as inquiry and argument as persuasion. *Argumentation* (3): 185–196.

Rescher, N. 1998. The role of rhetoric in rational argumentation. *Argumentation* 12: 315–323.

Savager-Mayer, F. 1998. 'Language is not a physical object.' *English for Specific Purposes 17 3*: 295–301.

Schneider, M. & Connor, U. 1990. Analysing topical structure in ESL essays: Not all topics are equal. *Studies in Second Language Acquisition, 12: 04, USA: Cambridge University Press* 411–427.

Thomson, A. 2000. Critical reasoning: A practical introduction. New York: Routledge.

Zahra, Z., Radha, M.K.N. & Tengku, N.R.T.M.M. 2014. The importance of text structure awareness in promoting strategic reading among EFL readers. *Procedia – Social and Behavioural Sciences* 118: 537–544.

Zainoddin, S.R. & Galea, S.R. 2016. Effects of training in the use of Toulon's model on ESL students' argumentative writing and critical thinking ability. *Malaysian Journal of Languages and Linguistics* 5(2): 114–133.

ELT in Asia in the Digital Era: Global Citizenship and Identity – Madya et al. (Eds)
© *2018 Taylor & Francis Group, London, ISBN 978-0-8153-7900-3*

Investigating students' perceptions of blended learning implementation in an academic writing classroom

F. Indratama, N.A. Drajati, D. Rochsantiningsih & J. Nurkamto
Sebelas Maret University, Surakarta, Indonesia

ABSTRACT: This case study explores students' perceptions of learning Academic Writing using a Blended-Learning approach. Along with the educational world's demand to publish manuscripts into Scopus or Web of Science journals, teaching Academic Writing is an urgent concern for educators. In addressing the challenge of teaching Academic Writing, technology has been introduced to complement the teaching and learning processes. The combination of in-class learning and online learning is called blended learning. The main subjects of this study are Master's students majoring in the English Education Department. Data are collected through interviews and questionnaires. The data results indicate that students need more advice on understanding and following Blended Learning activities before they can engage in them. It is suggested that a tutor needs to focus on providing more guidance that could significantly improve the value of Blended Learning such as students exploring knowledge from outside the classroom.

1 INTRODUCTION

A higher education environment is challenged to face new circumstances for more effective teaching and learning strategies. In this case, new technology is a solution to be applied in the teaching and learning of a foreign language. The recent technologies create many opportunities to renew the old findings, to conduct new research, and to establish the belief in which teaching-learning strategies are carried out (Betty 2010). Several ways should be done to encourage the use of new technology in a classroom such as improving technological facilities in a university and applying an interesting method in the teaching process.

A higher education environment, specifically a university, needs to improve the quality of recent advancements. They need to prepare several things to welcome this ICT development by using the internet and online learning. Every element of the university setting has to be aware of those advancements. All students, lecturers, and staff need to be aware of the recent updates in addressing challenges in education. Importantly, the students need to be technology literate so they can compete with other students around the world.

In addressing the challenges of ICT development in the educational field, the use of technology has been introduced to complement the traditional teaching and learning process. Bonk and Graham (2006) state that the mixture of conventional teaching-learning, face-to-face learning, and computer-mediated (online learning) can address the teaching learning challenges in higher education. The combination of traditional learning and online learning is called a Blended Learning approach. Geta and Olango (2016) mentioned that in traditional learning, lecturers and students tended to have human-human interaction, while online will focus on students-material interaction.

In teaching and learning writing for academic purposes, both the lecturer and students are facing a great challenge. Writing the English language is considered difficult even in a university setting, it is stated by Brown (2004) that writing is complex written product that includes some processes such as thinking, drafting, and revising. Writing itself is regarded as an important skill to be mastered by someone to express his/ her feeling to others in an

English-written context. Kirby and Crovitz (2013) state that writing is uniquely acts of creation that do not solely learn about the aspects that are embedded in its study but also learn about habits of the mind, strategic thinking, many self-expressions, and self-awareness. On the level of intermediate and advanced, the writer must be concerned about the rhetorical matters of unity, organization, coherence, and grammatical accuracy. On the intermediate or advanced level, students are asked to create a piece of academic writing in the form of an article for a journal. Murray and Moore (2006) stated that Academic Writing is much more complicated than writing since the students are working on the continuous process that involves reflection, improvement, development, progress, and fulfillment of various types of writing in varying lengths.

Due to the difficult process of learning Academic Writing, joining an academic online session will be helpful for both students and lecturers. Blended Learning is the the best answer to solve the problems that have arisen in the Academic Writing classroom. The students will get a good understanding of the material supported by online teaching-learning sessions. As explained by Macdonald (2008), blended learning offers enormous opportunities to develop self-directed learners, provides a good foundation for lasting learning, gives wider choices for the students to learn and many options of teaching approaches. Furthermore, it offers wider reflection compared with face-to-face learning. Some strategies and concepts are provided in terms of the teaching and learning process. It enriches the conventional learning process with a variety of activities, tasks, programs, and material discussions.

The online learning process that is popularly used nowadays is the MOOC (Massive Open Online Course). It is targeted for an unlimited number of participants from every country and it is open access via the web. MOOCs provide many activities, tasks, programs, materials (both video and document/print based), gives an opportunity to discuss the material with all the participants and encourages reflective learning on what they have learned. Nowadays, MOOCs are associated with top universities in the world, including Coursera, edX, Udacity, and Canvas.

Several studies have examined the implementation of blended learning in writing and some are focusing on students' writing challenges. In Tuomainen (2016) in a paper entitled *A Blended Learning Approach to Academic Writing and Presentation Skills,* the author described the implementation of Blended Learning in teaching Academic Writing and presentation skills. He focuses on exploring Business and Economic students' perceptions about using Blended Learning. He found that it is difficult in teaching EAP for non native speakers of English at the university level in countries such as Finland. Lecturers or tutors often seek the most effective and flexible manner in order to teach ESP and EAP courses while still concentrating on giving valuable knowledge and practice for students. Therefore, he uses Blended Learning since it provides flexibility for students. The result of the study showed that the Blended Learning Approach has captivated students' attention in their learning and has made them recognize the role of Blended Learning in encouraging them to learn more flexibly and independently. Serag in the *International Journal of Arts & Science* (2011) in his paper entitled *Teaching Academic Writing and Oral Presentation Skills: A Japanese Framework for Understanding the Learning Motivation Process,* states that his students lack proficiency in Academic Writing and have low motivation for learning English.. It was found that the students believe English plays a secondary role in scientific research. In this study, Serag applied online learning to help his students to overcome these problems. Serag investigated his students' perceptions toward the research publication assignment in the international conference and peer-reviewed journal assignment in order to understand the learning motivation process of Academic Writing and Oral Presentations.

There have been some discussions related to the implication of blended learning in educational fields and whether the students perceive it postively or negatively. Since there is a regulation in Indonesia asking the Master's students to publish an article in a national or international journal, there is a challenge that these students be technology literate. Thus, it encourages the lecturer to use a Blended Learning Approach in his/her teaching. Therefore, Blended Learning implementation raises the researcher's curiosity about the phenomena of students' perceptions of Blended Learning implementation,

2 METHOD

The researcher used an academic writing course in the first semester for master's students in one of the universities in Surakarta for data collection. The participants were 30 students (10 males and 20 females). 23 students were aged between 19–24 years old, 6 students were from 25–34 years old, and the remainder was between 35–44 years old. Because the target population was an available class, the sampling method was convenience sampling. All students were freshmen in a different range of age, gender, and origin. Not all data of students were used for this paper. This research was conducted using a qualitative approach with interviews. Fraenkel and Wallen (2000) state that qualitative research is a "research study that investigates the quality of relationships, activities, situations, or materials". In this research, the researcher used a qualitative case study method. The data were collected by using questionnaires and interviews to find out students' perceptions toward the implementation of Blended Learning. The main purpose of the questionnaire was to get students' opinions and impressions about the use of Blended Learning in Academic Writing class. In addition, the researcher used a semi-structured interview protocol as guidance to conduct the interviews in the field. The purpose of the interviews was to know what students perceived during the implementation of the Blended Learning approach. After the researcher interviewed the students, the data of interviews were transcribed and analyzed to know students' perceptions using Blended Learning in an Academic Writing course.

3 DISCUSSION

This study investigates the Blended Learning Approach in Teaching Academic Writing for students learning development as well as the implementation and students' perceptions of this approach. Data were collected from questionnaires, and interviews with 8 participants enrolled in the English Education Department. Questionnaires were given to know students' opinions of Blended Learning, an open-ended interview was used to provide more insight about students' perceptions of blended learning implementation in the Academic Writing classroom.

The study was conducted with graduate students in one of the universities in Surakarta and was developed in line with the learning objectives of that university. The Academic Writing course is taken by the graduate students in the first semester to give them knowledge and skills in designing a scientific article in English. In the course of study, the students are expected to be able to write a research article according to the correct principles of writing scientific articles. At the end of the contract, the students are asked to produce a manuscript and publish the manuscript into a Scopus-indexed or Web of Science Journal. The contract of the study contains the identity of the subject, time allocation, standard competence, basic competence, indicators of students' achievement, learning procedures, learning resources, and assessment. On the basic competence, the students are asked to follow online learning of Academic Writing from Oregon University. Then, the lecturer asks the students to understand and practice how to paraphrase, cite, avoid plagiarism, follow library study, and use technology in their learning. After that, in face to face learning, the students practice how to write a manuscript which includes an abstract, a literature review, methodology, findings, discussion, conclusion, and references. Next, the students are asked to proofread with their friends, and the last step is they are asked to submit the manuscript to a Scopus-indexed or a Web of Science Journal.

The Academic Writing course met 18 times. In order to Table 1 facilitates the understanding of the Blended Learning activity in the Academic Writing classroom.

In the first meeting, the lecturer explains to the students the activities of the Academic Writing classroom. The students are asked to join the MOOC in three months, to make a blog, and to follow the class provided by the university library that consists of two meetings. In the second meeting, the lecturer gave the students a handout about "Narrowing Topics for Research". On the handout, the students are asked to think about what topic they are

Table 1. Blended learning activity.

Object	Description	Activity
Space	The setting where Academic Writing course took place (in the classroom)	One lecturer with 30 master students and enough space for that number of students.
Activities	Some activities related to the topic of discussion are presented during the teaching and learning session	In the first meeting, the lecturer asks the students to follow MOOC and join online Academic Writing Course. The students have to follow every activity provided in MOOC. The second task in Academic Writing subject is the students are asked to make a blog and post their summary of some journals on it. The students have also give comments on their friends' work to build their critical thinking. The third task in the application of Blended Learning Approach is the students are asked to go to the library. The lecturer asks the students to follow a class provided by university library that discusses about journal publication.
Time	When the activities took place	Academic Writing class started at 8.00 and ended at 9.45.
Goals	The learning objective of Academic Writing subject	In the end of the meeting, the students are expected to have critical thinking, understand how to paraphrase, make summary of writing, know the research ethics in writing scientific article/journal, and know how to make references (especially APA style).

interested in and what they will do with the topic they have chosen. The lecturer also asks the students to find 13 references that include ten journals and three books related to their topic of interest. The purpose of this activity is to build reflective learning for students' reading.

In the third meeting, the lecturer asks the students to write an abstract. The students have to decide what journal they will target so they can adjust their format of writing. While the students are taking the Academic Writing class every Thurday, they also must join the online class of Academic Writing, make a blog, and engage in library study. They learn how to produce a scientific journal article by following every activity in the online course (MOOC). In the blogging activity, they apply their knowledge from online learning and face-to-face learning. Meanwhile, in library study, the students learn how to get good references (e-book and journals) for writing a scientific article.

Meanwhile, in the beginning and at the end of the meeting, the researcher collects the data through questionnaires. Table 2 shows the data of the questionnaire:

The data in Table 2 indicates that the majority of the students believe that face-to-face learning is not enough to make them able to write a scientific piece of writing. They also believe that blended learning can support and encourage their academic writing. Few of them show disagreement toward the use of the Blended Learning Approach in the Academic Writing classroom. They prefer to learn Academic Writing from their teacher rather than learn from both the teacher and material supported by online media. To get more students' responses, interviews with participants were undertaken by the researcher. The outcome of the students' interviews can be seen in Table 3.

Based on the interview data, most students admit that blended learning is beneficial for them, in terms of their writing skill mastery. Besides the positive responses, there are also some negative responses which show disagreement toward the implementation of blended learning in the classroom. Through an open-ended interview, it is found that the students who don't like the use of blended learning in the Academic Writing classroom are the ones who

Table 2. Questionnaire (Blended learning implementation in academic writing).

No	Question	Yes	No
1.	Do you think face to face learning will help you to develop your skill in Academic Writing?	30	
2.	Have you ever consult with your lecturer about your problems in Academic Writing?	29	1
3.	Do you think face to face learning is enough to enhance your knowledge in Academic Writing?	6	24
4.	Have you followed courses in which course materials and resources have been delivered online (i.e. within an integrated virtual learning environment)?	30	
5.	Have you known MOOCs phenomenon before participating Academic Writing course?	8	22
6.	Do you think reading material in MOOC gives you a positive impact on your Academic Writing?	30	
7.	Do you think having discussion and quiz in MOOCs give you a positive impact on your Academic Writing?	30	
8.	Do you have any obstacle in participating MOOCs?	15	15
9.	Do you think that blogging is a tool for learning?	29	1
10.	Do you think that giving peer feedback or comment is one of ways to develop critical thinking?	30	
11.	Is there any difficulties in summarizing and paraphrasing an article?	28	2
12.	Have you ever joined library study conducted in the library near you?	25	5
13.	How important is library study to support your Academic Writing literacy?	29	1
14.	Do you think library study guides you on finding good journals?	30	
15.	Can you integrate the information you got from library study to Academic Writing activity?	28	2

Table 3. The outcome of students' interview.

No.	Question	Answer
1.	What is your impression learning Academic Writing related to MOOCs, blogging, and library study?	• It enhances one another • Full of benefit • It is beneficial for my learning • Nice. It is helpful • They enhance each other • Those this are so helpful for us in enhancing our ability in Academic Writing since it eases us in gaining information and references
2.	What are your suggestions to improve writing skill related to MOOCs, Blogging, and Library Study?	• For MOOC, it will be better if the instructor does not provide key answer for the tests. So, we can learn more. Blogging, it be better if we post our own writing and have our friends comment on it. and for library study, the duration is not enough and it will be better if we have the real writing activity during the session • More practice less reading material and constructive feedback • Practice a lot and guidance from the advisor • Teacher has to keep giving guidance to the students • Good writing comes from good reading • Students need to get proper instruction using them

(Continued)

Table 3. (*Continued*).

No.	Question	Answer
3.	If you are a teacher, will you do the same teaching method by using MOOCs, Blog, and Library Study in Academic Writing course? Please give the reason!	• I think integrated those kind of learning strategy is a good option. But, surely every strategy has its own weakness, so it is our duty to minimize the weakness by evaluating those methods • Yes, I will. Because it can enhance the learning • Yes. They help the teacher a lot in teaching • Yes. Because they can enhance students' Academic Writing ability • I prefer to implement one or two of them separately because it will reduce students' confusion about their learning activity, task, material during the learning process • Yes, I will. Nowadays the teacher are demanded to optimize the use of technology in language learning
2.	What do you think when the lecturer use Blended Learning in Academic Writing teaching and learning process?	• I think it is difficult to find the relationship between the media used in Blended Learning. Related to the integration between online learning and offline learning, I think it is needed to give more advice or guidance • It is really useful but sometimes it makes me confuse, for example this month we study MOOC, next month library study, and next month blogging. All of the activities makes me confuse but maybe if there is a clear concept from the beginning, it will be better. • I think by providing extra guidance to all class member will be really helpful.

prefer real communication with the lecturer rather than communicating with people through a virtual world. Meanwhile, when asking students' thoughts about Blended Learning implementation, the majority of students feel difficulty in integrating some media or techniques of learning in Blended Learning activities. They get confused easily and they admit that they need more guidance from the lecturer in learning Academic Writing through an online course. In this case, it can be clarified that the students do not get sufficient guidance prior to their activities. In addition, this may also be a reflection of a different assumption between the lecturers and students as regards their level of understanding in the activity.

4 CONCLUSION

This paper investigates the perception of master's students in an English Education Department. A combination of in-class learning and online learning is implemented in teaching the students' Academic Writing. The Online course of Academic Writing, online article posting assignment, library course, and face-to-face learning are implemented. Based on research discussion, the majority of students claim that Blended Learning activities in Academic Writing classroom does not contain enough guidance, or they have insufficient understanding of Blended Learning activities, so they could not follow the activities accurately during the learning process. The students tend to have expectations about receiving more guidance but unfortunately are not enough given. It may happen because students are perceiving themselves to be a customer, with certain expectation, and if those expectations are not met, it could effect their dissatisfaction which affects their intake of study.

To provide students with the best opportunity to improve their valuable knowledge, it is important for the lecturer to be aware of students' responses during Blended Learning implementation. It is best to provide students with approriate guidance rather than simply teaching them and scoring their work. The lecturer needs to ensure that she/ he is close with the students so the students are free to consultwith lecturers about their problems. This strategy can help to improve communication between lecturer and students and develop a student-centred aproach in teaching and learning which will encourage deeper learning (Weaver nd).

It is supported by Garrison and Vaughan (2008) that there are three main guidelines for conducting blended learning. In the first stage, the lecturer needs to develop students' openness to one another to make them interact comfortably in the Academic Writing classroom. Then, to establish students' cognitive abilities, the lecturer must pay attention to the course content that will be taught. Finally, the last stage of blended learning is to make sure the distribution between face-to-face learning and online learning are supporting each other in enhancing students' Academic Writing.

REFERENCES

Beatty, K. 2010. *Teaching and researching computer-assisted language learning. London*: Pearson Education.

Bonk, C.J. & Graham, C.R. 2006. *The handbook of blended learning: Global perspective local design.* San Francisco: John Wiley and Sons.

Brown, H.D. 2004. *Language assessment: Principles and classroom practices.* New York: Longman.

Creswell, J.W. 2012. *Educational research: Planning, conducting, and evaluating quantitative and qualitative research.* Boston: Pearson Education.

Fraenkel, J.R. & Wallen, N.E. 2000. *How to design and evaluate research in education.* San Francisco: McGraw-Hill.

Garrison, D.R. & Vaughan, N.D. 2008. *Blended learning in higher education: Framework, principles, and guidelines.* San Francisco: Jossey-Bass.

Geta, M. & Olango, M. 2016. The impact of blended learning in developing students' writing skills: Hawassa University in Focus. *African Educational Research Journal* 4 (2): 49–68.

Gyamfi, S.A. & Gyaase, P.O. 2015. Students' perception of blended learning environment: A case study of the university of education, Winneba, Kumasi-Campus, Ghana. *International Journal of Education and Development Using Information and Communication Technology (IJEDICT)* 11(1): 80–100.

Heigham, J. & Croker, R.A. 2009. *Qualitative research in apllied linguistics: A practical introduction.* London: Palgrave MacMillan.

Kirby, D.L. & Crovitz, D. (Eds.). 2013. *Inside out: Strategies for teaching writing.* Portsmouth. Heineman.

Lalima. & Dangwal, K.L. 2017. Blended learning: An innovative approach. *Universal Journal of Educational Research* 5 (1): 129–136.

MacDonald, J. 2008. *Blended learning and online tutoring: Planning learner support and activity design.* USA: Gower Publishing Company.

Madsen, H.S. 1983. *Techniques in testing: Teaching techniques in English as a Second Language.* New York: Oxford University Press.

Murray, R. & Moore, S. 2006. *A handbook of academic writing: A fresh approach.* New York: Open University Press.

Serag, A. 2011. Teaching academic writing and oral presentation skills: A Japanese framework for understanding the leanring motivation process. *International Journal of Arts & Science* 4(11): 337–346.

Tuomainen, S. 2016. A blended learning approach to academic writing and presentation skills. 3(2). doi: 10.1515/llce-2016.

Weaver, M.R. (nd). Do students value feedback? Students Perceptions of Tutor's Written Responses, 1–12.

Part IV: Transforming TEFL in a fully digital world

ELT in Asia in the Digital Era: Global Citizenship and Identity – Madya et al. (Eds)
© 2018 Taylor & Francis Group, London, ISBN 978-0-8153-7900-3

Intercultural language teaching and learning in digital era

A.J. Liddicoat
University of Warwick, Convenrty, England

ABSTRACT: The contemporary communication allows language learners to have immediate access to other languages and cultures. In such communication, models of intercultural interaction assuming language learners use their languages to communicate with native speakers are being challenged and languages are being used as lingua franca. This means that communication ability with linguistically and culturally different others has become a key need for contemporary communication. Therefore, we need to reconsider what interculturally capable means and what abilities learners need to develop. The nature of intercultural communication today shows that developing intercultural capabilities needs to be different from learning about another culture. This article argues that learners need to be aware of both languages and cultures as meaning resources and that intercultural capabilities involve understanding of self and other as meaning makers and interpreters. It also explores some of the consequences of such a view for developing contemporary language teaching and learning.

1   ONLINE INTERCULTURAL COMMUNICATION

The development and increasing use of new communication technologies have dramatically expanded the opportunities for language learners to engage in intercultural exchanges (Rasmussen et al. 2006). Online communication largely occurs in social spaces where linguistically and culturally diverse participants interact with each other, often using languages in addition to their primary language of communication. In such communication, participants, although they may come from diverse cultures and speak diverse languages typically come together to communicate about shared interests and social media can create shared communities of interest that are globally constructed, which function in many ways like local community groups. In such contexts, languages, most frequently, but not exclusively English, are used as lingua francas to facilitate communication across the languages present in the community and hybrid language practices frequently emerge that give space for the complex linguistic repertoires of participants (Leppänen & Piirainen-Marsh 2009, Wodak & Wright 2006).

Such development in contemporary practices of communication mean that intercultural interactions have the potential to be everyday experiences and that intercultural communication is a feature of life even for people who have never left their home communities. This reality has consequences for how language educators consider the role of intercultural learning. In more traditional approaches to language teaching, the development of intercultural abilities was seen as an additional, and even optional, part of understanding that could be developed later, or when the learner had to deal with a target language community during travel (Damen 1987). It was often considered that intercultural learning could be deferred until the learner had completed 'basic' learning of grammar and vocabulary. The changing nature of human communication in the modern era, however, means that such assumptions no longer hold. Intercultural interactions can happen at any point in language learning and is likely to occur in unstructured social activities in which learns engage voluntarily for their own personal reasons. Thus, even a very beginning learner of a language may need to have quite sophisticated intercultural abilities to facilitate spontaneous, personally chosen forms of communication, and without the ability to negotiate intercultural differences may experience such communication negatively (Chase et al. 2002).

Developing contemporary practices of communication also throw light on other assumptions about the place and nature of intercultural capabilities in language education. In particular, it calls into question the idea that intercultural capabilities consist in knowing about another country in which the target language is used. What is needed in online communication is not a knowledge of a country, as such things are rarely central to the interactions that take place. In fact, in communities of shared interest, the content of communication is much more likely to be something about which all participants in the communication have similar knowledge. Communication is not with abstract entities like nations and cultures and participants in communication are not communicating a representatives of their nation or culture. Instead, communication is with *individuals*, and these have diverse experiences of languages and cultures that they bring to communication. In online contexts, the main need of communicators is not knowledge about cultures but rather practices that allow them to communicate with individuals who may not share their assumptions about the processes and practices of communication itself as a form of meaning making (Liddicoat & Scarino 2013). Moreover, especially in the case of English, languages are used as lingua francas and the idea that intercultural communication occurs between a native speaker and a non-native speaker of the target language, which is so central to how language education is constructed, is a very flawed one (Kirkpatrick 2014). Again, the study of cultures and countries is highly problematic as a form of preparation for intercultural encounters; a knowledge of Britain, for example, will be of little help in an English language interaction between someone from Indonesia and someone from Japan.

Communication in online environments creates new needs for language learners, who more than ever need also to be intercultural learners and also new contexts for language and intercultural learning to occur.

2   CONSEQUENCES OF LANGUAGE EDUCATION

The evolution of contemporary communication practices for language education has consequences for how language educators understand the basic constructs that shape the field, in particular, they require a rethinking of the understandings of language and of culture and how these are viewed as the content of learning.

Conceptualisations of language need to expand beyond traditional constructs of grammar and vocabulary and of communication as represented through the four macro-skills of speaking, listening, reading and writing (Liddicoat & Scarino 2013). While such constructs are undeniably a part of language ability, they represent a narrow view of language. In particular, such ways of understanding language favour the idea that languages are discrete, separate systems and they main relation between learners' languages is one of interference. Such views of language miss the very role that human languages play in human life; languages are used to express meanings to others and understand their meanings in return. Grammar, vocabulary and macro-skills are things that allow meanings to be exchanged, but it is meaning that is at the heart of language. Moreover, meanings do not exist only within languages. A person's meaning making practices and meaning making potential lie not in particular languages but in the whole repertoire of languages and this repertoire is a complex inter-related one, not an accumulation of discrete language systems (García & Li Wei 2014). Ultimately, language is something that is individual, personal and created in and through communication rather than simply as an autonomous system of codified and conventionalised norms (Shohamy 2007). Moreover, language is a culturally contexted meaning-making practice; the meanings that we create and interpret and made and understood within both a context of situation and a context of culture (Halliday 1973, Malinowski 1923). This means that language and culture need to be thought of as in relationship as they function together in the creation and interpretation of meanings (Liddicoat 2009).

Conceptualisations of culture similarly need rethinking. Culture has often been understood in terms of what Bayart (2002) calls *culturalism*, a view that represents cultures as monolithic, essentialised and static and adopts a national culture focus as the core way of understanding culture, especially in education. This means that cultures are often viewed as homogenous and unvarying within nations and the study of the nation is considered to be the central aim of culture teaching and learning. In situations of interaction between individuals, such national cultures may have little relevance for understanding the meaning-making practices of participants (Risager 2007). In such contexts, culture is experienced as contingent, created and highly variable, involving individual participation in purposeful social life (Abdallah-Pretceille 1986). Moreover, this contingent, created, variable culture has a symbolic dimension; that is, it imbues behaviours, including language use, with meanings and the full meaning of communication cannot be understood only from the linguistic form of the communication, but needs to also take into account the context of situation and a context of culture in which and for which the communication occurs.

Such rethinking points to a new focus in intercultural teaching and learning in language education. In the past, the focus of culture teaching has been on learning about the other. This is the approach to culture teaching that has been adopted in some established teaching approaches that focus on literature or some other area of cultural studies, such as French *civilisation*, German *Landeskunde* or Japanese *nihonjijou* (Byram 1989, Hasegawa 1995). The learner has been positioned as an observer of difference rather than as a participant in linguistic and cultural diversity. In intercultural communication, however, it is participation that is central and the key focus for leaning is not about the other but about oneself in relation to diversity. It is important to understand one's own reactions, perspectives, expectations, etc. in communication and from understanding of self, one can move to understanding of another.

These reconceptualisations of language and culture reveal that intercultural communication not something that is additional to communication, but a constituent part of it. All communication involves coming to understand and be understood by others who do not share exactly the same knowledge, expectations, practices and meanings. It always involves reciprocal processes of meaning-making and interpretation, but these processes may be made more complex and brought closer to the surface when communication is between people who have been socialised in quite different cultural contexts. This means that intercultural capabilities need to be understood as something which is needed at all points in communication not only as something a special case characterised by meaning breakdown.

3 TEACHING FOR EXPLORATION

If we start from the perspective that intercultural communication is a process of meaning making and interpretation that occurs between individuals, that language is both collective and personal and that culture is contingent and variable, intercultural learning cannot be viewed as a set body of knowledge about language, culture and communication that an individual needs to acquire (Liddicoat & Scarino 2013). This is because it is impossible to teach all of any culture because cultures are variable and diverse and also because it is impossible to know which cultures a learner may need to engage with in the future. Anything that we can teach in the classroom is inevitably only a partial picture of a language and culture and unless we acknowledge that in our own teaching then we run the risk of developing stereotypical views of the cultures we are teaching and of their people. Instead, learners need to explore meaning making as it occurs and to work from experiences of meaning making to understandings of themselves as communicators and of the roles played by languages and cultures in the ways they create and respond to meanings (Liddicoat & Scarino 2013). Intercultural learning involves processes of discovery form experience, whether that experiences is an interaction with a linguistically and culturally different other, or with a text. This process of discovery is not simply a learning process is actually the real world application of intercultural capabilities; that is, intercultural capabilities involve making sense out of instances of communication as they happen and realising any differences in perspectives that may be shaped by what is communicated and what is understood. This requires personal interpretation of experiences of communication. It involves understanding of oneself as a communicator and of the processes of communication. As both a learning process and as a communicated capability, it requires a process of thinking through experiences to learn from them that involves constantly readjusting interpretations as new experiences provide more information about meaning making practices and recognising that there is no 'right answer', given that there are multiple valid understandings, but only thoughtful interpretation.

As the ability to learn from one's own experiences of language and culture as they are encountered when one tries to create and interpret meanings is an important element for intercultural communication, learning about culture and the language classroom needs to involve a considerable element of learning how to learn. Learning how to learn about culture means that as people engage with new aspects of cultures variable to develop their knowledge and awareness and find ways of acting according to their new learning.

One way of developing such abilities is through an interconnected set of activities (See Figure 1) involving:

1. noticing cultural similarities and differences as they are made evident through language;
2. comparing what one has noticed about another language and culture with what one already knows about one's own and other languages and cultures;
3. reflecting on what one's experience of linguistic and cultural diversity means for oneself: how one reacts to diversity, how one thinks about diversity, how one feels about diversity and how one will find ways of engaging constructively with diversity; and
4. interacting on the basis one's learning and experiences of diversity in order to create personal meanings about one's experiences, to communicate those meanings, to explore those meanings and to reshape them in response to others. (Scarino & Liddicoat, 2009, p. 23).

The process of noticing has been shown to be important for language learning in general (Schmidt 1993) and is equally central to leaning intercultural capabilities. In intercultural language teaching and learning, learners need come to notice cultural similarities and differences in practices of making and interpreting meaning as they are made evident through language in use. When experiencing something new, learners need to examine the new information in their own terms and seek to understand what it is they are experiencing and their own reactions to it. However, it cannot be assumed that learners will automatically be able to notice such things as noticing is an activity that occurs in a framework of understandings which regulate what can and should be noticed. Teachers' questions are therefore important in helping

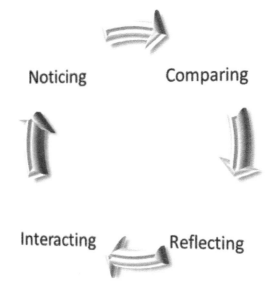

Figure 1. Interacting processes of intercultural pedagogy (Liddicoat & Scarino 2013, Scarino & Liddicoat 2009).

students develop the sophistication of their noticing and to become independent noticers of lived experiences language and culture. Such questions include questions such as:

1. What do you notice here?
2. What do you think is important in this?
3. What is new here?

Such questions aim at identifying information that is relevant for learners' purposes in understanding and experience of meaning making and interpretation.

When learners have noticed something in their experience, it then becomes available to them for further work. One basic process that learners' can then draw on in relation to their noticing is comparison, in which students identify relationships between different pieces of information, such as similarities and differences. The process of comparison involves comparisons between the learners' existing culture and the target culture and also between what learners already know about the language and culture they are learning and their new experiences of meaning making. Comparisons, however, do not only have to focus on the content of an experience, they can also be comparisons of reactions: either their own reactions to different aspects of meaning making or the reactions of different learners to the same phenomenon. Again the process of comparison needs to be supported by teachers' questions, such as:

1. What is similar? What is different?
2. What does X add to Y?
3. How does this fit with what you already know?
4. Have you seen anything like this before?
5. Do other people think the same way about this?

Comparison in turn provides a resource for reflection and reflection as a classroom process is a core element of developing interculturality (Kohonen 2000). Reflection is a complex and multifaceted activity. It is a process of making sense of experience. The aim is not to come up with a correct answer about the experiences but rather that the learner makes personal sense of experiences. It is a question of understanding one's own reactions and interpretations of experience: there is no "the right conclusion" as different people will interpret the same experience differently because of differences in their prior experiences and understandings. This involves the learners in reflecting on what their experience of meaning making and interpretation in a context of linguistic and cultural diversity means for them: how they react to differences in meaning making or interpretation, how they think about diversity, and how they will find ways of engaging constructively with the diversity they have experienced.

Reflecting also involves learners in gaining insight into the ways their knowledge has adapted or been changed as a result of new experiences. The aim is to build an ever increasing depth and sophistication of understanding through an explicit focus on how their knowledge of themselves, of others and of the ways that languages and cultures influence process of communication. Some examples of teachers' questions that can support processes of reflecting include:

1. What do you think about…?
2. Why do you think that…?
3. What do you know now that you didn't know before?
4. How do you see this differently?

Interacting focuses on two things. The first is engaging with others to develop understanding; learners discuss ideas with peers and teachers and develop new insights through talk. To do this learners can communicate their new learning with others (in speech, writing, image, etc.). Secondly interacting means drawing on knowledge gained through reflection on experiences to engage in interactions with others. To do this that they need to have thought through the consequences of their new understanding for their future ways of using language through their reflections. Realising that there are consequences of differences in meaning making practices does not mean that learners must assimilate to the meaning making practices of others; the aim is not to develop 'native-like' practices but rather to understand the practices for others and develop ways of compensating where one's own practices are different from those of their interlocutors. It is about making personal decisions that allow one to engage well with diverse others while acknowledging the legitimacy of one's own practices and their connection with one's sense of self.

While it is useful to think of these processes as having noticing as a starting point, they are not really linear but rather all processes may be co-present in any moment of experience. Noticing may involve within itself an initial comparison; comparison may include making sense of the comparison, etc. Moreover, noticing is not always the starting point; a comparison of things that have been noticed may lead to noticing of something else; reflection may lead to new noticings and comparisons, etc. These processes are ultimately an unending cycle of growing knowledge and understanding. What is important is that all of the processes are engaged in learning and that learners come to draw on these processes to understand their experiences both in and out of class.

4   RESOURCING INTERCULTURAL LEARNING

Teaching for exploration has consequences for the sorts of materials that are used in language teaching and learning (Liddicoat & Scarino 2013). Most materials in textbooks present information in ways that do not support process of noticing, comparing, reflecting and interacting, and where they do present cultural information, they do so in a very static nation-centred way. This means that it is necessary to consider other ways of resourcing intercultural learning. A resource for intercultural learning needs to enable access to and insights about the role of language and culture in meaning making and interpretation. Such a resource will not only relate to the target language but also needs to be able to connect to students' existing practices of meaning making. For most teachers, resourcing learning from an intercultural perspective on language learning requires more than a textbook and it is common for teachers to supplement, or even replace, textbooks with other materials more relevant to their own learners and their teaching goals.

Selecting a resource involves an evaluation and the evaluation needs to be made in relation to the purpose and goals of teaching and learning and also to one's theories of learning and ethical positions. A resource needs to be thought of as an experience in language use for learners; that is the resource needs to be something in which learners can notice how meanings are created in the language and consider how they interpret and react to those meanings. In considering a resource it is important to consider what resource contributes to developing practices of meaning-making and interpretation and awareness of languages and cultures and their relationship to meaning making. It is also important to consider the opportunities for exploration that the resource provides and how it allows learners to make connections with their own lives and experiences. As a central aim for learning is developing connections between experiences and building complexity and sophistication of understanding. This requires resources to link together in a way that allows students to draw connections across resources.

Intercultural leaning requires authentic materials; materials designed for communication among members of a cultural group that uses the language (Liddicoat & Scarino 2013). It is in such texts that learners can encounter ways of making and interpreting meanings that are used by speakers of the language and which are different from their own. Resources that are too much assimilated to the learners' own culture may actually prevent opportunities for such learning (Kramsch 1987). Authentic materials, because they are not designed for learners, may need to be adapted for use in the classroom by:

1. providing additional language support, for example a glossary, explanation of terms
2. providing additional information relevant to understanding the resource, e.g. additional resources
3. showing different aspects of the same basic issue
4. providing scaffolding to assist in using the resource (Scarino & Liddicoat 2009: 61).

Authentic materials gain value when assembled into collections—groups of materials that focus on a similar phenomenon and show differing perspectives on that phenomenon. Such collections encourage learners to make connections between the various resources they experience and seek for similarities and difference in meaning making practices (Liddicoat & Scarino, 2013). Moreover, when a single instance of meaning making in another language is presented, it can lead to essentialising and stereotyping; a single instance is seen as representative and typical. A collection of differing perspectives shows the variability within any cultural group and emphasises the need to engage with complexity and multiple perspectives.

Authentic materials need to be current; meaning making practices change over time and what may have been true of the past may not be true of the present. In the digital age, accessing collections of contemporary materials has been made relatively easy as technology provides teachers and students with a vast range of contemporary material in the language both design for and about communities. This material makes the language and its communities available both in and out of class and can draw on their own uses of online communication in teaching and learning and allow them to pursue their own interest and agendas in the target language community.

In reality, what is done with materials is more important than what the materials are. Many different materials can support the processes of noticing, comparing, reflecting and interacting and it is much more important to consider how materials are used.

5   CONCLUDING COMMENTS

Contemporary communication requires learners to understand the processes of meaning making and the ways that language and culture contribute to how meanings are created and interpreted, and to reflect on themselves are participants in diversity in terms of:

1. what they bring to meaning making.
2. how they interpret the meanings of others.
3. how they respond to the meanings of others.

Such abilities are fundamental to language use, not additional or independent 'skills'. Language teaching and learning in the digital age has made such learning more important and more immediate than it was in the past. In order to prepare language learners for the realities of internationalisation and the ease and ubiquity of intercultural communication, language education needs to engage actively with the development of intercultural capabilities.

REFERENCES

Abdallah-Pretceille, M. 1986. *Vers une pédagogie interculturelle*. Paris: Economica.
Bayart, J.-F. 2002. *The illusion of cultural identity*. Chicago, IL: University of Chicago Press.
Byram, M. 1989. *Cultural studies in foreign language education*. Clevedon: Multilingual Matters.
Chase, M., Macfadyen, L., Reeder, K. & Roche, J. 2002. Intercultural challanged in networked learning: Hard technologies meet soft skills. *First Monday* 7(8). Retrieved from doi:DOI 10.5210/fm.v7i8.975.
Damen, L. 1987. *Culture learning: The fifth dimension in the language classroom*. Reading, MA: Addison-Wesley.
García, O. & Li Wei. 2014. *Translanguaging: Language, bilingualism and education*. London: Palgrave Macmillan Pivot.
Halliday, M.A.K. 1973. *Explorations in the functions of language*. London: Edward Arnold.
Hasegawa, T. 1995. Bunkakenkyuu no shoruikei kara mita 'Nihonjojoo'. *Gaikokujinryuugakusei no tame no 'Nihonjijoo' kyooiku no arikata ni tsuite no kisoteki choosa kenkyuu*: 51–66.
Kirkpatrick, A. 2014. Teaching English in Asia in non-Anglo cultural contexts: Principles of the 'lingua franca approach'. In R. Marlina & R.A. Giri (Eds.), *The pedagogy of English as an international language*: 23–34. Dordrecht: Springer.
Kohonen, V. 2000. Student reflection in portfolio assessment: making language learning more visible. *Babylonia* 1: 13–16.

Kramsch, C. 1987. Foreign language textbook's construction of foreign reality. *Canadian Modern Language Review* 44(1): 95–199.

Leppänen, S. & Piirainen-Marsh, A. 2009. Language policy in the making: An analysis of bilingual gaming activities. *Language Policy* 8(3): 261–284. doi:10.1007/s10993–009–9130–2.

Liddicoat, A.J. & Scarino, A. 2013. *Intercultural language teaching and learning*. New York & Oxford: Wiley-Blackwell.

Liddicoat, A.J. 2009. Communication as culturally contexted practice: A view from intercultural communication. *Australian Journal of Linguistics* 29(1): 115–133.

Malinowski, B. 1923. The problem of meaning in primitive languages. In Ogden, C.K. & Richards, I.A. (eds.), *The Meaning of Meaning*: 296–336. New York: Harcourt Brace and World.

Rasmussen, K.L., Nichols, J.C. & Ferguson, F. 2006. It's a new world: Multiculturalism in a virtual environment. *Distance Education* 27(2): 265–278. doi:10.1080/01587910600789696.

Risager, K. 2007. *Language and culture pedagogy: From a national to a transnational paradigm*. Clevedon, UK: Multilingual Matters.

Scarino, A., & Liddicoat, A.J. 2009. *Language teaching and learning: A guide*. Melbourne: Curriculum Corporation.

Schmidt, R. 1993. Consciousness, learning and interlanguage pragmatics. In G. Kasper & S. Blum-Kulka (eds.), *Interlanguage pragmatics*: 21–42. New York: Oxford University Press.

Shohamy, E. 2007. *Language policy: Hidden agendas and new approaches*. London & New York: Routledge.

Wodak, R. & Wright, S. 2006. The European Union in cyberspace: Multilingual democratic participation in a virtual public sphere? *Journal of Language and Politics* 5(2): 251–275. doi:doi:10.1075/jlp.5.2.07wod.

ELT in Asia in the Digital Era: Global Citizenship and Identity – Madya et al. (Eds)
© *2018 Taylor & Francis Group, London, ISBN 978-0-8153-7900-3*

Developing multiliteracies for EFL learners in the digital era

W. Lei
Graduate School of Research Institute of Petroleum Exploration and Development, CNPC, China

ABSTRACT: The multimodal resources: linguistic, audio, visual, gestural and spatial are always complementary and overlapping. Multiliteracy pedagogy put forward by New London Group has expanded the traditional views of literacy to various multimedia forms. This study explores the development of multiliteracies in EFL teaching and learning in the digital era. By the application of descriptive-explanatory method, document analysis, and comparison, this paper introduces the benefits of multimodalities in TEFL from four aspects, and significance of multiliteracy pedagogy in EFL learning in seven areas. Then, it elaborates on the research about the methodology of developing multiliteracies for EFL learners. Six aspects of how to facilitate the implementation of multiliteracy pedagogy is discussed further. Finally, it concludes how educators incorporate the multiliteracy pedagogy focusing on critical reflection, empirical reasoning, collective intelligence, and metacognition to promote learners' critical thinking and cross-cultural awareness in the digital era.

1 INTRODUCTION

Traditionally, literacy referred to reading and writing of printed text, while in the digital era, with various modes of communication and growing linguistic and cultural diversity, literacy development evolves from traditional textual literacy to digital media literacy and EFL learners are exposed to new forms of literacy and communication that are increasingly multimodal. Multimodalities integrate a number of modes to make meaning in literacy teaching and learning. Multiliteracies refer to the ability to creatively apply information and communication technology to interpret the information provided by multimedia critically, by means of language, visual, audio and other forms of multimodalities. The pedagogy of multiliteracies put forward by New London Group has expanded the traditional views of literacy to include the various multimedia forms available. It refers to the ability to understand the meaning that various modes make through reading, viewing, understanding, internalizing, feeding back, producing and interacting by means of multimedia. Multiliteracy pedagogy entails linguistic, visual, audio, gestural and spatial modalities by the use of visual, hearing, tactile, olfactory, gustatory and other senses. As complements to unimodality, multimodalities in TEFL, such as tone, intonation, sound speed, music, visual arts, color, dress, dance; facial expressions, eye contact, gestures, postures and PPT, charts, maps, graphics, network and other non-physical symbols can improve teaching efficiency, attract more attention, express emotions, feelings and make teaching materials easier to get across. Multiliteracies overcome the limitations of traditional approaches by emphasizing how negotiating the multiple linguistic and cultural differences in our society is central to the pragmatics of the working, civic, and private lives of learners (New London Group 1996).

The digital era has made EFL teaching and learning shift from lecture-based learning (LBL) into project-based learning (PBL), with more focus on developing learners' comprehensive application skills in English. The multiliteracy teaching approaches make the curriculum requirements comprised of "language + culture + application skills", adhering to learner-centered principle with more emphasis put on learners' learning by doing. The multilieracy acquisition of basic language skills, cultural quality and application ability can expand EFL learners' knowledge and provide a variety of options to improve their cultural literacy and self-learning ability. It has gained more and more popularity that the more capable teachers are of using the multiliteracy pedagogy, the more and faster improvements learners will make in learning.

2 BENEFITS OF MULTIMODALITES IN TEFL

2.1 *To act as complements to single modal teaching*

Multimodalites can compensate for the insufficiency of single modal expression. For instance, if words cannot express fully, body languages, paralanguages, visual or audio materials etc. can help to make more sense.

2.2 *To attract more attention*

The mixed-up modalities can stimulate learners' more interest and encourage them to participate in class more.

2.3 *To express feelings*

Undoubtedly, a single modality cannot adequately express feelings, and the use of another modality may help, such as the use of photographs to reproduce the scene, the appropriate tone to render atmosphere.

2.4 *To facilitate teaching and learning*

Multimodalities can make teaching materials more learner-friendly. Textual contents cannot fully explain rather abstract, general or complicated results or theory, the application of the graphs, charts or flashes, etc. can help learners to understand. Multimodalities can be used to improve teaching quality by emphasizing particular teaching contents and improve the relationship between teachers and students and mobilize students' enthusiasm to learn so as to maximize teaching efficiency.

3 SIGNIFICANCE OF MULTILITERACY PEDAGOGY

From these different modes of representations, it's known that EFL learning is more than reading and writing and multiliteracies should be integrated for meaning-making and exchange of feelings, ideas and culture in learning. Literacy evolves from traditional literacy, media literacy, computer literacy to the latest info media literacy (digital literacy), according to the mainstream communication means used in each era. Digital literacy is the ability to locate, organize, understand and analyze information via digital technology. To foster EFL learners' competence as required in the digital era, the increasing use of the multiliteracy pedagogy has dramatically changed the traditional EFL teaching and learning in the following seven aspects.

3.1 *Ubiquitous learning*

With access to software, applications and network, learning can be ubiquitous. The digital technology has made it possible for EFL learning life-long and life-wide without the confinements of space or time. Integrating outside learning into the classroom can be an essential tool with which to make students' learning experiences more active and beneficial (Seidman & Brown 2006).

3.2 *Personalized education tailored to meet learner's individual interests and needs*

Nowadays, individual traits are becoming more and more prominent. Learners cannot be evaluated by uniform standards; whereas, individual differences should be recognized, such as learners' subjectivity. Learners have their own interests, motives, determination and targets, which are also brought into EFL learning. Teachers should teach with learners' different languages, discourse and register as individual language learning resources, rather than setting the unified standards for all learners. Differentiated learning is conducted to meet learners' individualized interest and needs.

3.3 *Learner-oriented teaching and learning*

Teachers no longer control but facilitate classroom teaching, with learners playing a more active role in learning. The purpose of multiliteracy pedagogy is to give learners the opportunity to access the evolving language in the real situations, such as in the workplace, the authority branches and the community etc. Learners learn the related knowledge before class by themselves, then, present ideas, exchange thoughts, discuss and solve problems under the guidance of teachers in class.

3.4 *Multimodal pedagogy*

In the digital era, people express or obtain meanings pretty often with multimodalities through mass media, multimedia and electronic hypermedia. The multimodal teaching approach expands the connotation and scope of the traditional reading and writing to a diversity of culture. It emphasizes teaching in the context of cultural pluralism and world connectivity, with the information not only from the printed text, but from many other media. Multimodal pedagogy takes learners' positive, dynamic meaning construction of new information as the priority.

3.5 *Fostering autonomous learning ability with digital technology*

Learners' ability of self-study, information gaining, internalization and evaluation is urgently needed in multiliteracy pedagogy. They are encouraged to be autonomous learners who are able to take responsibility for their own learning (Richards 2015). Learners should initiatively seek for information, locate and access information, evaluate information, synthesize information to solve practical problems for active and efficient EFL learning. Multiliteracy pedagogy can fully mobilize learners' initiative as well as creativity, and develop their multiliteraices so as to achieve SLA.

3.6 *Critical thinking*

Critical thinking enables learners to see the world from multiple points of view, distinguish facts from factoids, reality from fiction, and anticipate alternate outcomes. To develop learners' critical thinking enables them to critique what they have got to form a subjective assessment. Language learning is conducted in specific social and cultural contexts, and learners should be critical and reflective in information input and output.

3.7 *Collective information sharing and teamwork*

Collaborative intelligence is shared widely in the digital era. PBL allows learners to be involved in an active learning experience for the purpose of solving problems in groups (Brown 2007). Learners brainstorm in the pair work, group discussion, and workshops, etc. to fulfill the assigned task with the shared information. Learners become more open to cooperative learning and innovative teaching methods (Strayer 2012).

4 METHODOLOGY OF MULTILITERACY PEDAGOGY

The following four teaching strategies to cultivate learners' multiliteracies advocated by New London Group provide enlightenment for the reform of TEFL as well as strategic guidance on how to conduct multiliteracy pedagogy.

4.1 *Situated practice*

Multiliteracy pedagogy requires learners to be immersed in what they have already known or experienced to explore the unknown. Teachers should take learners' cognitive ability and knowledge background into full consideration. Personalized teaching plan can be designed based on the characteristics of learners to construct new knowledge system. Immersion instruction is rather difficult to realize for TEFL, so teachers can use alternative teaching resources, such as videos, images, recordings, audios, etc. to simulate the real situation. PBL is an effective teaching approach. In "Learning by Doing", teachers can assign multiple teaching tasks to learners to meet the needs of teaching and learning, such as classroom presentation, PPT presentation, panel discussion, debates, dubbing, imitating, video-making, and etc. For example, when it comes to "community service", students are assigned the video-making task of their own local community service. About 1/3 of the class time is allocated for the teacher to impart the knowledge, 1/3 of the class time is for the presentation for every group and the final 1/3 will be the time for the teacher and students to comment, assess, propose suggestion for the improvement in both language and contents. Learners are motivated to be involved in all learning activities. Video-making is considered as an ideal task to cultivate learners' multiliteracies because it can not only simulate the real-life scene, but also push learners to mobilize multimodal semiotic resources, such as audio, visual, language, body language, digital technology etc.

4.2 *Overt instruction*

As the designer and organizer of the classroom activities and language importer, teachers should be qualified for using a variety of semiotic resources in a scientific and effective way, clearly and accurately describing the teaching contents, form and function of the discourse practice activity to cultivate learners' ability to expand and deepen their language knowledge. In the multimodal teaching mode, teachers' role is mainly manifested in three aspects:

1. Teachers should make full use of multimedia resources, selecting, categorizing and processing English materials. With learners' language foundation, interests, life experience and teaching contents as the starting point, teachers design and organize classroom teaching activities to help students give full play to their imagination and creativity.
2. Teachers should select appropriate multimodal discourse materials to make learners understand the meaning constructed by nonverbal components in the discourse, interdependence of modalities and how to achieve meaning-making through interaction, which helps to cultivate learners' awareness and ability of multiliteracies.
3. Teachers assign projects, allocate tasks to learners based on the teaching contents; instruct students to learn online, to consult materials and write papers with access to library resources and network resources; and help students improve their networking application technology and self-learning ability. Thus, overt instruction has set up a higher standard for English teachers in that they should improve not only their professional skills, but also their ability to obtain information, to use network as a teaching tool, to integrate teaching resources, and to facilitate classroom teaching in network environment. The sequence of situated practice and overt instruction is not fixed. If instruction is needed before the implementation of a certain learning task, overt instruction goes before situated practice. And vice versa, overt instruction goes after the situated practice to summarize the guiding knowledge.

4.3 *Critical framing*

Critical framing exists in all the procedures of teaching. It plays a significant role in the cultivation of learners' critical thinking and creativity. It pushes learners to reflect on teaching and learning from a more objective and critical perspective. Thus, learners gradually gain their ability of critical thinking and creative application of their knowledge.

4.4 *Transformed practice*

It refers to learners' practice to internalize knowledge acquired by multiliteracies to integrate multimodal semiotic resources creatively for meaning-making in different contexts. It is not the end of multiliteracy pedagogy; however, it is converted into situated practice again to drive teaching into a new round of cycle. In this way, the cultivation of learners' multiliteracies is gradually realized in an escalating cycle.

5 DISCUSSION

How to facilitate the implementation of multiliteracy pedagogy:

5.1 *Changing teachers' EFL teaching philosophy*

EFL learning is no longer confined to the cramming of language itself, but a significant process for learners to gain their critical learning ability to actively explore knowledge, construct information, analyze, interpret, internalize, compare and absorb multiculture to innovate knowledge. The meaning construction is jointly expressed by texts, pictures, sounds and other symbolic modes in teaching, media, network, communication. The society tends to be multimodal. Thus, EFL teaching should be multiliteracies related too. While adjusting their role in the classroom, teachers are supposed to change their teaching philosophy, aiming to build up learners' science and technology literacy, cultural literacy, political literacy and other multiliteracies. Teachers and students take the initiative to explore knowledge, actively construct new knowledge system and innovate knowledge by means of understanding, comparing, absorbing multiculturalism and sublimating thoughts. The target of teaching is to cultivate learners' multicultural communication awareness by developing their critical thinking of analysis, explanation, generalization and statement. The study has extended from a single language-oriented one to a multimodal communicative one, so as to achieve the purpose of exploring the meaning making in social practice; comprehensively and accurately interpreting the target of multimodal discourse generated from the interaction of two or more semiotic modes of communication including language, dynamic and static visual images, architecture, electronic media, film and print, etc. (O'Halloran 2004).

5.2 *Changing teaching and learning approaches*

To cultivate learners' multiliteracies, teachers are supposed to diversify the teaching approaches, rather than rigidly adhere to textbooks only. Audio, video, film clips, PPT presentation, self-made DVs and other means can be introduced into classroom teaching to lead learners to meaning remaking with acquired learning strategies. The application of big data in education has contributed to the emergence of CALL, web-based EFL instruction, like flipped classes, MOOC and microlectures, which is changing the traditional educational model. CALL deals with the use of computers, software, and online learning materials for teaching and learning a second language (Chapelle & Jamieson 2008). CALL can be seen as an approach to language teaching and learning in which teachers use the computer as an aid to present, reinforce, and assess materials that students learn (Davies 2016). In the flipped classroom, learners can set their learning pace on their own to conform to their study. Teachers can have a full mastery of the problems encountered by learners individually, based on the data gathered from learners' homework performance. The classroom is no longer the place for teachers to impart new knowledge, but the place for learners to solve problems or make experiments and etc. The rise of MOOC pushes the learning model of reconstructed education to be popularized quickly to higher education by the use of video. The credits gained by taking MOOC can gradually be brought into the orthodox education. As the response to the flipped classroom, microlecture is the mini class enriched by teaching videos. The accumulation of microlectures leads to microlecture groups and the application of microlecture groups will lead to new application data, which will benefit the innovative application of the analysis, discovery and prediction of big data.

5.3   Changing teachers' role

In a multimodal teaching setting, undoubtedly, teachers have changed from the controllers of the traditional classroom to the facilitators in the classroom teaching, that is, to guide learners to use a variety of semiotic resources and multimodal media means to construct knowledge and improve learners' critical thinking of multimodal information. Teachers' former dominant role has been transformed into a guiding one, aiming to convert the traditional classroom teaching centered on knowledge imparting to the teaching mode centered on learners' knowledge construction on their own in the network environment. Because the society has progressed from the oral age, reading and writing age into the hypertext era, it increasingly heads for multimodalities, with texts, images, sounds and other symbolic modes increasingly used to make joint meaning in media, network and communication. Thus new requirements and challenges for classroom teaching appear. Teachers should not be content with the traditional way to nurture learners' reading and writing ability only; whereas, they are responsible for improving their own multiliteracy awareness and ability as well as learners'. Teachers are supposed to design multimodal teaching pedagogy based on learners' academic background in a scientific way to satisfy learners' needs to develop multiliteracies. Working collaboratively on development of the curriculum, common assessments, and guided notes fosters a bond among the teachers and stimulates their professional growth as well (Kathleen 2012).

5.4   Changing teaching materials

In the digital era, teaching materials have changed from once text-centered to web-based. With the development of ICT in language teaching and changed teaching approaches, learners can have an easy access to a variety of multimodal learning materials, such as multimedia graphics, audio, video and other online teaching materials, such as MOOC, microlecture etc. Meanwhile, students should update their learning strategies timely to fit in with the development of the teaching materials.

5.5   Changing learners' role

Learners' role changes from passive to active. In the past, learners learned English mainly by reading, but nowadays in the situated practice, under the guidance of teachers, EFL learners take an initiative to participate in the cognitive process to describe the diversity of language, culture and multiple communication means. Through multimodal pedagogies, learners are recognized as remakers and transformers of the representational resources available to them in the ESL classroom (Stein 2000). For example, in a group study of English speech, interviews, short plays, etc., students play different roles in different situations to understand textual meaning and use their acquired knowledge and personal experiences to analyze and understand the learning contents critically. Learners should make great efforts on their own initiative to give a deep insight into diversified semiotic resources and identify how a variety of texts, images, colors, sounds, and other modalities are closely joined to make the overall meanings. In the era full of pluralistic information, it is important that learners learn language knowledge and technology under the multimodal circumstance. What's more important is that learners learn language for the sake of the mastery of multiculture; master meaning potentials of various symbols and learn to use technology for the sake of meaning-making; moreover, while learning, make full use of information channels to drill independent learning ability.

5.6   Adjusting teaching and learning evaluation system

In the past, a final exam was the most important means to evaluate learners' academic performance, in most cases, with learners' language competence as the core of the exam. While in the digital era, the highlight of teaching and learning evaluation should be shifted from only the score results to both the learning process and learning outcomes, with multiliteracies added into the evaluation system. Learners' multiliteracies should be assessed by their multimodal representation, e-learning, collaborative learning and mixed-up learning abilities in their own academic assessment system. Their multiliteracies can be assessed by means of classroom performance, learners' self-mutual assessment, final exam and so on. In addition, with CALL widely employed, web-based online assessment technology increasingly comes into spotlight.

6 CONCLUSIONS

In the digital era, the intense tendency of regional diversity and world connectivity has made EFL multimodalities and multiliteracies increasingly noticeable and significant in cross-community, cross-culture, and cross-nation exchanges. The use of multiliteracies and ICT undoubtedly improves education and social practices (Pullen & Cole 2009). EFL learning is no longer just the acquisition of traditional reading and writing ability, but the acquisition of multiculture in communication. Dramatic changes have taken place in the nature of language learning. With a large number of new options for multimodal communication to realize meaning construction, the multimodal discourse theory provides a strong support for the choice of classroom teaching modes. For the age of interactive multimodality, multimedia and multi-skilling, different modes and media play crucial roles in communication (Kress. G. & Van Leeuwen. T. 2001). Pedagogy of multiliteracies overcomes the weaknesses of traditional language-centered teaching model, highlights the use of various symbolic resources to acquire language and culture, and emphasizes the significance of learners' comprehensive English competence. Teachers can choose the appropriate teaching situation and teaching materials according to learners' needs, obtain certain auxiliary conditions, and adopt multi-literacy pedagogy to optimize teaching. Big data has transformed empirical teaching model into a data-service one, which helps teachers to have a better understanding of learners according to their individual micro-performance. With the analysis of every learner's data, teachers can constantly adjust teaching plans to make education personalized to meet every individual's needs. EFL learning in the future will be based on big data of the digital era and teachers are supposed to follow the trend to take full advantage of the digital era to further improve EFL teaching and learning.

However, some problems also arise.

1. Many learners lack digital literacy. They trust online information unconditionally without their own critical thinking, in other words, they haven't cultivated the ability to assess the quality of online information. There is a long way to go for learners to learn to judge whether information source is reliable or not.
2. Some learners lack the thirst for knowledge. Because they can have easy access to all the materials needed, they are likely to have less desire to explore knowledge by themselves, and just resort to the already-existing source offered by others on line, which leads to their retrogressive learning ability.
3. Some learners excessively depend on search engines, not making good use of printed matters and library, which spoils their study habits.
4. The digital era makes it much easier for learners to plagiarize rather than exert their own efforts honestly, which deteriorates academic ethics.
5. More qualified teachers are needed

EFL teachers should improve both their theoretical knowledge and practical experience to guarantee holistic and effective professionalism in order to meet learners' needs in the digital age from both cultural and technical aspects.

To sum up, in the digital era, how teachers incorporate the multiliteracy pedagogy focusing on critical reflection, empirical reasoning, collective intelligence, collaborative teamwork, metacognition and cross-cultural awareness is still in urgent need of further serious study and discussion for TEFL.

REFERENCES

Brown, H.D. 2007. *Principles of language learning and teaching (5th ed.)*. New York: Pearson Education, Inc.

Chapelle, C.A. & Jamieson, J. (Eds.) 2008. *Tips for teaching with CALL: Practical approaches to computer assisted language learning. New York: Pearson Education, Inc.*

Davies, G. 2016. *CALL (computer assisted language learning)*. Retrieved from https://www.llas.ac.uk/resources/gpg/61.

Kathleen F. 2012. *Upside down and inside out: Flip your classroom to improve student learning*. Learning and leading with Technology 6: 12–17.

Kress. G. & Van Leeuwen, T. 2001. *Multimodal discourse. The modes and media of contemporary communication*. London: Arnold.

New London Group. 1996. A pedagogy of multiliteracies: Designing social futures. *Harvard Educational Review* 6 (1): 60–93.

O'Halloran, K.L. 2004. *Multimodal discourse analysis: Systemic functional perspectives*. London: Continuum.

Pullen L.D. & Cole R.D. 2009. *Multiliteracics and technology enhanced education*. New York: Information Science Reference.

Richards, J.C. 2015. *Key issues in language teaching*. Cambridge: Cambridge University Press.

Seidman, A. & Brown, S.C. 2006. Integrating outside learning with the classroom experience: The student learning imperative. *Education* 127(1): 109–114.

Stein P. 2000. Rethinking resources: multimodal pedagogies in the ESL classroom. *Tesol Quarterly* 34 (2): 333–336.

Strayer, J.F. 2012. How learning in an inverted classroom influences cooperation, innovation and task orientation. *Learning Environments Research* 15(2): 171–193.

ELT in Asia in the Digital Era: Global Citizenship and Identity – Madya et al. (Eds)
© 2018 Taylor & Francis Group, London, ISBN 978-0-8153-7900-3

Exploring the contribution of the school culture and the learner factors to the success of the English e-learners

R.C.Y. Setyo
Universitas Islam Lamongan, East Java, Indonesia

Suharsono & O. Purwati
State University of Surabaya, East Java, Indonesia

ABSTRACT: The aim of the study is to explore the contribution of the school culture and the learner factors to the success of the students in learning English with e-learning Quipper School. By using an ethnographic case study design and six successful e-learners as the subjects of the study, the fundamental finding was the high academic performance culture of the school critically contributed to the students' motivation to succeed e-learning. In the learner's factor aspects, the students' motivation became the most critical success factor that contributed to the success of the students in the national e-learning competition and in learning English through e-learning. The use of the ethnography for classroom research studies is still new in Indonesia. Hence, it will give a big implication to change the mindset of the Indonesian researchers to apply an ethnographic approach and it also influences the government policies to support the e-learning implementation.

1 INTRODUCTION

One of the main issues faced by English teachers of developing countries is a low literacy on computer and internet skills. Indonesia is not an exception. If their literacy on the main teaching tools of e-learning instructions is low, there is a strong indication that most teachers do not apply e-learning in teaching English. However, a case of the successful e-learning learners in learning English in Indonesia is interesting to be explored. This school is located in a village but their students successfully won a national e-learning competition in 2014. Interestingly, the e-learning winners were also successful in their English skills after learning English with e-learning Quipper School. Quipper School is an online learning plat-form or learning management system that engages students in learning and supports teachers in class management at elementary, junior high, and high schools (Quipper School 2017).

Of course, the success phenomenon of a school in a village like this rarely happens in Indonesia. Hence, by using the Critical Success Factors (CSFs) approach and the ethnographic case study methodology, this research paper is aimed to explore the contribution of the school culture and the learner factors to the success of the students in the e-learning competition and the English e-learning.

The computer and internet are powerful teaching tools for teachers (Lee, Jor & Lai 2005) and portant media for students to use in learning (Taylor 2006). The use of these tools has significant effects on language in general (Crystal 2001), on second language classroom (Dudeney & Hockly 2007), and on English language teaching (Noytim 2006). It is in line with Eagleton & Dobler (2007) who found that the computer and internet literacies are essential for the middle school students. Brooks (2007) said that to understand the skills that comprise technology literacy for students, teachers must become technology literate first. However, most English teachers in Indonesia have a crucial problem of a low literacy in using the computer and the internet (Son, Robb & Charismiadji 2011). Moreover, MarkPlus Insight Netizen

Survey (2014) found that 95% users in Indonesia accessed the Internet from notebooks, tablets, and cellular phones. Internet usage is the highest in the age group between 15 and 19 years. It means most of the users are the middle and high school students.

The implementation of e-learning in Indonesia is urgently needed, even though it is facing some main issues related to access and quality of internet, its regulation, budget, infrastructure, and human resources (Ali 2005), no standard in the contents (Sulistyo 2007), low quality of teacher (Son et al. 2011) and low independence level of students to learn (Kusumo et al. 2012). In fact, not many schools use e-learning for teaching and learning process, even schools in big cities.

In this study, e-learning is defined as instruction delivered via electronic media and supported with digital learning content and services in computer, communication and internet technology to create, deliver and facilitate learning, anytime and anywhere (Mason & Rennie 2006, Govindasamy 2002). Meanwhile, e-learning Critical Success Factors is the critical factors that must be done to make students successfully and effectively learn English through e-learning activities (Howell 2010, Zainon et al. 2008).

2 RESEARCH METHOD

2.1 *Research design*

Ethnographic case study in this research is well-defined as a method for doing research to portray a particular contemporary phenomenon or a case in a particular culture-sharing group of an educational system by deeply observing and interviewing the everyday experiences of individuals (Creswell 2009, Wiersma 1995). An ethnographic case study design was applied in this study because exploring a unique case and culture of SMPN 2 Sumberpucung, Malang needed a holistic analysis based on the experiences of the successful e-learners of this school. Ethnography deals with a culture. Meanwhile, e-learning is the result of a social process (Brown 2002) and a school culture (Ali et al. 2016). The social process and school culture can be explored easily by using this ethnographic case study design. Since many data are taken from the internet and social media that related to the subjects of the study, a virtual ethnography (Hine 2001) was also used to collect the data.

The term "a case" comprises an individual, class-room, school, or program (Fraenkel, Wallen, & Hyun 2012). A case study is also associated with a particular phenomenon. Marriam (1998) stated a case study as "an intensive, holistic description and analysis of a single instance phenomenon or social unit." A representative definition is from Yin (2009 & 2011) who defines it as a strategy for doing research which involves an empirical and in-depth investigation of a particular contemporary phenomenon or a case in its real life world context using multiple sources of evidence, for an instance, in classroom activities.

Moreover, questionnaires were also given to the subjects (participants). The use of a questionnaire in ethnographic research was supported by Bernard (2002) who said that the questionnaire data could illuminate and validate many of data that the ethnographer had collected during participant observation. The combination of Ethnographic case study and survey data produced more insight about e-learning Critical Success Factors (CSFs) and identificated clearer patterns of how the subjects became successful in e-learning and in learning English.

2.2 *Subject of the study and setting of the institution*

The subjects of the study were six successful digital-native students of SMPN 2 Sumberpucung Malang. They were successful in e-learning as well as in the English learning (English e-learners). In the end of 2014, there were two national e-learning competition held by Quipper School management. The first was an Inter-Quipper Class Competition (October 27 – November 2, 2014). In this event, surprisingly, SMPN 2 Sumbepucung became the second winner of the school that conducted a quipper class. Moreover, three students of this school earned the first, sixth, and eighth winners of the best students (Quipper School 2015a). Subject R became the first winner of the SMP and SMA category competition. It means she could beat the contestants not only from the junior high school but also from senior high school level. She became the first winner in the national level.

The second competition was the End of Year Competition 2014 held in December 1–7, 2014. There were two events competed. They were an interclass competition for SMP category (Junior High School) and an inter-quipper class for SMP category. Surprisingly, all best ten students of the SMP category competition were swept out by the students of SMPN 2 Sumberpucung. More surprisingly again, this school became the first winner in the inter-quipper class competition for SMP category (Quipper School 2015b).

Meanwhile, Subject W, Subject M, and Subject A were first, sixth, and seventh runner up of the national e-learning competition in the junior high school level category. The other subjects were Subject I who had the most fluent English speaking skill of the school and Subject F who got the first runner up of the National Examination Tryout Competition for Malang Raya level in 2017.

Meanwhile, the setting of the institution is in an SMPN 2 Sumberpucung in Malang. Based on the data from *Data Pokok Pendidikan Dasar dan Menenah* (Main Data on Basic and Secondary Education), Education and Culture Ministry, this school has 1028 students, 50 teachers, 6 staffs The number of the ninth grade students is 319, eighth grade 352, and seventh grade 357. It seems that the numberof the students increases in every year. All students study in the morning, from 6.45 am up to 13.15 pm. The extracurricular lesson is from 14.00–17.00 pm. The subjects taught are based on the 2013 Curriculum. This school is a national standard school that has become one of the pilot project schools to implement the 2013 Curriculum since 2014.

2.3 *Data collection method*

The data needed were technically obtained by observation and then data triangulation was conducted with an in-depth interview, questionnaire, and documentation. The questionnaires were adapted from Son et al. (2011) & Selim (2007) to have a complete description of the prior knowledge of the subject and to identify patterns of how the subjects became successful in e-learning and in learning English.

2.4 *Data analysis procedure*

Creswell (2008) divides data analysis in an ethnographic case study into five parts: (1) data managing, (2) coding and developing themes, (3) describing, (4) interpreting, and (5) representing. Coding is a crucial aspect of analysis (Basit 2003) after organizing the data. Creswell adds that a description of etnography is to describe from general picture to the specific setting in which an event or events take place. He suggests a broad-to-narrow description in analyzing e-learning Critical Success Factors (CSFs) of the learners. The coded data were categorized based on the kinds of Critical Success Factors and the kinds of data collection instrument. The process of establishing codes and themes had implications for descriptive reporting and theory building.

3 FINDING AND DISCUSSION

3.1 *School culture and a high achievement performance school*

By using the ethnographic method and a long study in the field, that was from 21 February 2015 up to 31 March 2017, it could be explored that SMPN 2 Sumberpucung had a high academic-performance culture. Based on the observation and an in-depth interview with the research subjects, with the data being triangulated to the interviews with the vice headmaster, head of student affairs, English teachers, homeroom teacher, another student, the results of the analysis showed that there was a strong indication that the achievements of this school was influenced by the school culture.

The combinations of the history of this school as the school built by the alumni of Tentara Genie Pelajar (TGP), the traditions of winning in many academic and non-academic competitions, teachers' attitudes and beliefs, principal's policies, school structure, school curriculum, and school regulations contribute to create a unique culture as a high academic-performance school. It can be seen that in 2016, there were 32 achievements in the district, province, and national level. They were 18 achievements in 2012, 20 in 2013, 31 in 2014, and 25 in 2015.

Exploring of the traditions, beliefs, system of the school, personal connections and relationships in the school portrays the holistic description of the high academic performance culture of the school. The description opened and related the understanding, significance, and meaning of the school culture to the success of the students this school, especially the success in e-learning. Based on the description of the school culture, the critical success factors from the learners' factors could be explored.

3.2 *Quipper school and school culture*

The success of the students and the institution of SMPN 2 Sumberpucung in the national e-learning competition was influenced by the success of this school to implement Quipper School during the class and after the class. However, most teachers in this school used Quipper School for enriching the lesson materials and assessments. Quipper School is a learning platform (Learning Management System) that lets teachers and educators set and track assignments, answer students' questions, push out feedback and grading, and monitor individuals' learning progress via Internet. Quipper School can be accessed through personal computers, laptops, tablets, and smartphones, where internet is available. Quipper School is always on or available to students anywhere they have an internet connection. So whether they are at school, at home, or at an internet café, students can access this service.

The success of the students in e-learning was contributed by the students' prior knowledge in a computer and internet literacy. All subjects (students) agreed that using a computer was joyful and comfortable. Besides, they also agreed that a computer was important to improve their foreign language learning. Dealing with QS, they thought that their computer and internet competency helped them to operate QS because both of them had an email address to make a QS account and log in Quipper School. They also felt comfortable to open Quipper School up to 3–4 times per week and in one hour in average. In addition, the frequency of opening web search engines, blog, and wiki influenced them to learn independently. They were more confident and faster to open and do the quizzes on QS. All subjects had a good internet and computer literacy.

Their good rate of the internet and computer literacy could be crosschecked from their responses in the questionnaire. All of the six students had laptops and internet access at home, so they usually did the tasks given by their teachers in QS at home. The open wi-fi at school also supported them to learn, do quizzes, or do assessments at school. The implementation of QS brought a new learning environment. Many students did not go home early, even up to late afternoon, because they used the free wi-fi hot spot to do the tasks given by their teachers. They learned together or learned individually. The e-learning culture spread widely in this school.

The literacy of using computer and internet leads their e-learning literacy. It can be seen that they could apply Learning Management System of Quipper School at school; they could use learning materials from Web to help you learn English; they could you use online test for their English; and they could use an asynchronous method to learn, such as using emails. The Figure 2 below shows the influence of the prior knowledge of the students' e-learning technical competency towards the success of the students in learning English by using e-learning.

Meanwhile, the relationship between the school culture and student's motivation for the success in e-learning is shown in Figure 1.

Figure 1.

The indication of the students' motivation as one of the main factors that contributed to the successful students in learning English through e-learning was supported with the following literature. Jacobson (2009) found that motivation was one of the most powerful elements for achievement outcomes in school systems. The students' motivation influenced the students to get many achievements in many events. Meanwhile, Macneil, Prater & Busch (2009) found that the school culture and school climate of feeling comfortable to study influenced a student motivation to study. Simply, the school culture gave a contribution to the students' motivation and the students' motivation led to the success in e-learning.

3.3 *The student motivation as the most critical success factor in the e-learning activities and in the English e-learning*

Based on the result of the interviews and questionnaire, there was a strong indication that the students' motivation became the most critical success factor that contributed to the success of the subjects (digital native students) to win the e-learning competition and to improve their English skills. Thus, the high motivation of the students not only lead the students to be successful in the e-learning competition but also to be active to learn English by using the QS e-learning.

The e-learning critical success factors from the learner factors showed that the students' motivation was the most critical factor that contributed to the success of the digital native students in the QS e-learning. All subjects of the research stated that the motivation was the most critical factor that contributed to their success in the QS e-learning. The English teacher, homeroom teacher, IT instructor and the vice principle also agreed that the motivation became the main factor in this case.

The finding of the students' motivation as the main critical success factor was supported by the finding in the questionnaire analysis. The questionnaire from six subjects put the student's motivation as the main factor. Chart 1 showed that student motivation was the most critical factor and then it was followed by the prior knowledge, e-learning student's self-efficacy, and student's interaction and collaboration. The finding of putting student motivation as the main success factor is in line with Selim (2007) who stated that the instructor characteristic and student characteristic are the main success factor in e-learning activities.

If I compare the results of the observation and interview with the result of the questionnaire, it seems that the result of questionnaire also support the logical orde of the successful learner factors. The successful students had a high motivation to learn English through the QS e-learning because they had a prior knowledge of the technical competencies needed to operate the e-learning, such as a computer and internet competency. Since they had a good computer and internet competency, they had a high self-efficacy to succeed any exercises or quizzes in the QS e-learning. Then, one of the strategies to accomplish the quizzes was by doing an interactive and collaborative learning. These critical success factors were from the learner's perspective factors that contributed to the success of the digital native students in the e-learning.

Moreover, Figure 2 above shows that the prior knowledge of the e-learning technical competency is the second main critical factor that contributes to the success of the student in the e-learning. Then, it is followed by the student's interactive and collaborative learning as the third main critical factor. The last main factor is the e-learning student's self-efficacy.

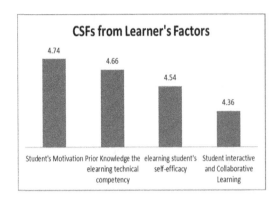

Chart 1.

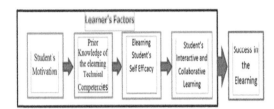

Figure 2.   The flow chart of the learners' factors that contributed to the success in the e-learning.

4   CONCLUSION AND SUGGESTION

4.1   *Conclusion*

The use of the ethnographic case study to explore the critical success factors in e-learning is still new in Indonesia. That is why there is a fundamental result of the study that cannot be found in other research studies. The fundamental result is the contribution of the school culture to the success of the students in learning English with e-learning. The other crucial results are there are four most critical success factors that contribute to the success of the English e-learners. They are the students' motivation, the students' prior knowledge on computer and internet literacy (e-learning technical competencies), the students' interactions and collaboration, and the e-learning students' self-efficacy. The big implication of the study is able to change the mindset of the Indonesian researchers in doing an ethnographic approach at school (such as a classroom ethnography) and able to influence the policy of the government in applying e-learning instructions in Indonesian schools.

4.2   *Suggested*

This finding is one of the crucial findings in my dissertation entitled "An Ethnographic Case Study of the Critical Success Factors of the Digital-Native Students in Learning English With E-Learning Quipper School". The next researchers should explore the critical success factors from the institution factors and outcome factors that influence the success of the students in learning English through e-learning.

REFERENCES

Ali, M. 2005. E-learning in the Indonesian Education System. *Asia-Pacific Cybereducation Journal* 1(2): 15–24.
Ali, N., Sharma, S. & Zaman, A. 2016. School Culture and School Effectiveness: Secondary Schools in Pakistan. *Malaysian Online Journal of Educational Management* 4(4): 50–65.

Basit, T.N. 2003. Manual or Electronic? The Role of Coding in Qualitative Data. Analysis Institute of Education. Manchester Metropolitan University. *Educational Research* 45(2): 143–154.

Brooks, Y.S. 2007. *The Digital Age Literacy for Teachers: Applying Technology Standards for Everyday Practice*. Oregon: International Society for Technology in Education (ISTE) Publications.

Brown, J.S. 2002. Learning in the Digital Age. *The Internet & the University: Forum 2001* edited by Devlin, M. et al. Published as a joint project of the Forum for the Future of Higher Education and EDUCAUSE.

Creswell, J.W. 2008. *Educational Research: Planning, Conducting, and Evaluating Quantitative and Qualitative Research*. New Jersey: Pearson Education, Inc.

Creswell, Jhon W. 2009. *Research Design: Qualitative, Quantitative, and Mixed Methods Approaches*. New Jersey: Pearson Education, Inc.

Crystal, D. 2001. *Language and the Internet*. Cambridge: Cambridge University Press.

Dudeney, G. & Hockly, N. 2007. *How to Teach English with Technology*. Edinburgh Gate Harlow Essex: Pearson Education Limited.

Eagleton, M. & Dobler, E. 2007. *Reading the Web: Strategies for Internet Inquiry*. New York: The Guilford Press.

Fraenkel, J.R., Wallen, N. & Hyun, H. 2012. *How to Design and Evaluate Research in Education*. (Eighth edition). New York: McGraw-Hill Companies, Inc.

Govindasamy, T. 2002. Successful Complementation of E-learning Pedagogical Considerations. *Internet and Higher* Education 4: 287–299.

Hine, C. 2000. *Virtual Ethnography*. University of Surrey: Sage Pub. Inc.

Howell, M.T. 2010. *Critical Success Factors Simplified: Implementing the Powerful Drivers of Dramatic Business Improvement*. New York: Taylor and Francis Group.

Jacobson, K. 2009. The Charactheristics and roles of the motivation attributes on High School Students' academic achievement and the implication for Michigan High Schools in the Era of the Merit Core Curricula. *Thesis*. Master of Art in Education. Northern Michigan University.

Kusumo, N.S.A.M., Kurniawan, F.B. & Putri, N.I. 2012. eLearning Obstacle Faced by Indonesian Students. *Proceedings: The Eighth International Conference on eLearning for Knowledge-Based Society: 23–24 February 2012, Thailand*.

Lee, C.F.K., Jor, G. & Lai, E. 2005. *Web-based Teaching and English Language Teaching: A Hong Kong Experience. Hong Kong*: The Chinese University Press.

Macneil, A.J., Prater, D.L. & Busch, S. 2009. The Effects of School Culture and Climate on Student Achievement. International Journal. *Leadership in Education* 12(1): 73–84.

MarkPlus Insight. 2014. *Indonesia Consumer Survey 2014*. http://markplusinsight.com/article/detail/33/women-cast-strongest-influence-in-household-buying-decisions. *Retrieved on 2 September 2016*.

Marriam, Sharon B. 1998. *Qualitative Research and Case Study Application in Education*. San Fransisco: Jossey-Boss, Inc. Publishers.

Mason, R. & Rennie, F. 2006. *E-learning the Key Concept*. New York: Roudlege.

Noytim, U. 2006. The Impact of the Internet on English Language teaching: A case Study at a Thai Rajabhat University. *Dissertation*. Thai Rajabat University.

Ordóñez, A.C. 2014. Predicting International Critical Success Factors in E-learning: A comparison of Four Universities from China, Mexico, Spain and USA. *Dissertation*. Universitat Oberta de Catalunya.

Quipper School. 2015a. Pengumuman Kompetisi antar Kelas Quipper School. http://indonesia.quipper-school.com/post/102602547992/pengumuman-kompetisi-antar-kelas-quipper-school. Retrieved on 5 February 2015.

Quipper School. 2015b. Pengumuman Kompetisi Akhir Tahun Quipper School http://indonesia.quipper-school.com/post/105257779587/pengumuman-kompetisi-akhir-tahun-quipper-school. Retrieved on 5 February 2015.

Quipper School. 2017. *https://school.quipper.com/en-PH/index.html*.

Selim, H. M. 2007. Critical Success Factors for E-learning Acceptance: Confirmatory Factor Models. *Science Direct: Computers & Education* 49: 396–413.

Son, J.B., Robb, T. & Charismiadji, I. 2011. Computer Literacy and Competency: A Survey of Indonesian Teachers of English as a Foreign Language. *CALL EJ* 12(1): 26–4.

Sulistyo, B.L. 2007. IT and Education, the Case study of E-learning in Indonesia. *Paper* presented in Korea-ASEAN Academic Conference on Information Revolution and Cultural Integration in East Asia, Ho Chi Minh city, Vietnam, January 25–26.

Taylor, J. 2006. *Information Literacy and the School Library Media Center*. London: Libraries Unlimited.

Wiersma, W. 1995. *Research Methods in Education: An Introduction (6th ed.)*. Boston: Allyn and Bacon.

Yin, R. K. 2009. *Case Study Research: Design and Methods (5th ed.)*. Los Angeles: Sage Publication, Inc.

Yin, R. K. 2011. *Qualitative Research from Start to Finish*. New York: The Guilford Press.

Zainon, O., Masrom, M. & Rahiman, R.. 2008. E-learning Critical Success Factors: the Student's Perspective in Salleh, M.F.M. (ed). *E-learning Issues in Malaysian Higher Education*. Kualalumpur: UTM Press.

ELT in Asia in the Digital Era: Global Citizenship and Identity – Madya et al. (Eds)
© *2018 Taylor & Francis Group, London, ISBN 978-0-8153-7900-3*

Perception and ICT usage of students and lecturers of the English study program of the Faculty of Teacher Training and Education, Tridinanti University

Y. Hendrety
Tridinanti University, South Sumatra, Indonesia

ABSTRACT: This study examined the perception and ICT usage of students and lecturers of English study program of FKIP University of Tridinanti. It investigated how lecturers perceived ICT in teaching, whether or not lecturers used ICT in teaching, how lecturers used ICT and how students perceived ICT and responded to the use of ICT in classrooms. This study utilized a descriptive qualitative method which involved 16 lecturers and 50 students in the academic year of 2016/2017 as the samples. A questionnaire was used to collect the data. The findings revealed that the majority of lecturers and students tended to perceive ICT positively. Some other lecturers and students did not perceive and respond positively on ICT due to a lack of training, comprehension, supporting facilities and financial support. In conclusion, it was found that both lecturers and institution needed a lot of improvements to support a more effective ICT usage.

1   INTRODUCTION

Information and Communication Technology (ICT) is defined as the effective use of equipment and programs to access, retrieve, convert, store, organize, manipulate and present data and information (Gay & Blades 2005). The huge developments which were led by the introduction of information and communication technologies (ICT) not only make people share knowledge faster but also create many challenges in all sectors including the educational sector (Alassaf 2014). Further, Casal (2007) states that education is the first and the best key area for ICT applications. ICTs can provide alternative possibilities for education. The purpose of ICT in education is generally to familiarize students with the use and workings of computers, and related social and ethical issues. Khan (2011) also says similar idea; he says that the use of different information communication technologies has become inevitable for students in learning. By using modern information communication technologies, students can retrieve their required information within a short time.

In addition, Dudeney & Hockly (2007) mention that computers and language teaching have walked hand in hand for a long time and contributed as teaching tools in the language and second language classroom. It means that technology usage in the classroom becomes increasingly important. Some reasons why ICT will become a normal part of English language teaching practice in the coming years are: 1) internet access is becoming increasingly available to learners, 2) younger learners are growing up with technology, and it is natural and integrated part of their lives, 3) English, as an international language, is being used in technologically mediated contexts, 4) technology, especially the internet presents new opportunities for authentic tasks, and materials, as well as access to a wealth of ready-made ELT materials, 5) internet offers excellent opportunities for collaboration and communication between learners who are geographically dispersed, 6) technology is offered with published materials such as course books and resource books for teachers, 7) learners increasingly expect language schools to integrate technology into teaching, 8) technology offers new ways for practicing language and assessing performance, 9) technology is becoming increasingly mobile. It can be used not only in academic setting but also at home and everywhere and 10) using a range of ICT tools can give learners exposure to and practice in all of the four main language skills.

Considering the importance of ICT integration in classroom, the writer was interested to investigate Perception and ICT Usage of Students and Lecturers of English Study Program of Faculty of Teacher Training and Education Tridinanti University.

1.1 *Perception and ICT usage in learning*

Information and communication technology (ICT) is generally viewed as a modern instructional tool that enables educators to modify the teaching methods they use in order to increase student learning. The use of ICT in education aims to improve the quality of teaching and learning as well as democratize access to education. To remain globally competitive, it is essential for any university to change the traditional way of delivering education in order to respond to the rapidly changing conditions in technology and society (Lee & Yeap 2009, in Chitanana 2014).

Ammanni & Aparanjani (2016) state that there are some positive effects when ICT is integrated with English language teaching and learning, which include: 1) the required information can easily be found, 2) e-learning makes learners become more innovative 3) the information provided by the ICT help students to compete with this competitive world, 4) integrating multimedia with English lessons can motivate and provide bored students with exciting new ways to learn, 5) ICT provides current and authentic sources which can make students and teachers to work together, 6) ICT also improves the learner's interaction and verbalization involvement in collaborative learning and 7) ICT enables students to be independent learners. On the other hand, they also claim that ICT has also some disadvantages such as: 1) online learning reduces human interaction, 2) unnecessary websites may be opened by students to play games or to watch movies, 3) ICT usage requires self-discipline and self direction and 4) ICT usage requires good infrastructure and trained man power in teaching and learning.

Dealing with perception on ICT, Alassaf (2014) states that there are several claims from lecturers in Jordanian universities about their unwillingness to use educational technologies in which many lecturers believe that educational technologies are major threats for them which will make a key shift in the common vision of the lecturers as being the only source of knowledge, thus marginalizing their role.

Further, Gay et al. (2006), Galanouli & McNair (2001) & Zare-ee (2011) mention that perceptions about ICTs are affected by many factors such as the users' experiences, lack of resources, professional training, institutional support and time. Another factors also include the faculty, gender and academic qualification,. Furthermore, many studies indicated that positive perceptions don't mean high levels of ICT use; this is because the use of ICT is also affected by the previous factors that affect the perception.

Abu Qudais et al. (2010) mention that to develop positive perceptions, suggestions were provided by educators such as increasing lecturers' motivation, because it is believed that motivation and perceptions are related to each other. Other recommendations were provided such as supporting and resourcing educational institutions, and providing effective ICT training (McCormick 2004).

Kember et.al. (1997) in Sheard & Carbone (2008) state that a number of studies have shown that educators' perception of their students as learners influences their understanding of teaching roles and responsibilities. This may reflected in the educational environment they provide. An educator's perception of student motivation, interests and capabilities may influence their interactions with students, their teaching approach and the way they present the curriculum. Further, Greening (1998) in Sheard & Carbone (2008) says that investigating students' and educators perspectives may be useful for informing curriculum design or pedagogical approaches and may also help address misconceptions about course content or the teaching and learning environment.

Realizing the influence of lecturers' perception on ICT and their ICT use in classroom, it is very significant to investigate the perception and ICT usage of students and lecturers of English study program of Faculty of Teacher Training and Education Tridinanti University.

This study illustrated how lecturers and students perceive the ICT and they used ICT development which becomes the basis for and improvement for the institution in general, that is the University and the study program especially. Moreover, considering the process of teaching and learning at English study program at FKIP university of Tridinanti which is directed to the ICT based learning, it is crucial to conduct the study as it investigated the perception of both students and lecturers on ICT as well as evaluated ICT usage which could be give benefits for English study program evaluation to do some improvements in the area of teaching and process.

2 RESEARCH METHOD

This study was aimed at investigating how lecturers perceived ICT in teaching, whether or not lecturers used ICT in teaching, how the lecturers used ICT in their classroom, how students perceived ICT and how students responded to the use of ICT in their classroom. Descriptive qualitative research was used as the research method. Cresswell (2005) mentions that qualitative research is a type of educational research in which the researcher relies on the views from participants. Then, he describes and analyzes these words for themes, and conducts the inquiry in a subjective, biased manner. The sample was all students and lecturers at the odd semester in the academic year of 2016/2017. There were about 16 lecturers and 50 students at the odd semester that became the sample of the study. Questionnaire which consisted of 18 open ended questions was used as the instrument. It was a lecturer-made questionnaire which was designed to answer the research questions. To validate the questionnaire, an was asked to provide feedback and modification where necessary. Some comments were given on the language used, question order, the ambiguity and also the need for additional questions. The modified questionnaire was also trialled to students out of the chosen sample before distributing the questionnaire to improve the rigor of the instrument and estimate the time needed in the process of collecting data. Since it is a descriptive qualitative research, the researcher analyzed the data by the process of selecting and classifying them on the basis of the research questions. The researcher then made interpretion and finally drew conclusion based on the interpretation.

3 FINDINGS AND DISCUSSION

The finding revealed that lecturers tended to perceive ICT positively. Using ICT meant the use of technology which was functioned to manage, manipulate, transfer, access, deliver, send and save data and information. It was used to ease communication process among people. Mostly, using ICT was considered to be very important considering the benefits given to the learning process. Moreover, ICT gave students opportunity to find information by themselves. There was only one lecturer mentioning that ICT was important especially when she was absent, ICT could be used to facilitate the learning process. One other mentioned that ICT use was not really needed in classroom considering that some students had not had laptop and also because the network system did not support them.

Further, mostly, lecturers mentioned that ICT contributed in some ways, they were: 1) improving learning quality, 2) helping them visualize ideas, 3) helping them perform more interesting materials. For example, YouTube can be used to show the students how to apply fishbowl technique. ICT was assumed to help lecturers achieve learning objectives, stimulate students' motivation and involvement and even achieve a successful learning. Kinds of ICTs used by them were video, laptop, internet, projector, picture, power point, LCD, YouTube, online journal, online translation, Google/chrome, learning application like Cartoon-online for writing activities, sound system, e-journal, blog for writing and sharing activities, online website, BBC news, podcast and YouTube for listening activities, email, social media, flash disk, CDs, DVDs and online and offline dictionary.

In relation to the use of ICT in language learning, Dudeney & Hockly (2007) mention that blogs, wikis and podcast are computer tools which allow people to connect, communicate and collaborate online. Using blog in language learning especially provides a 'real-world' tool for learners to practice their written English as well as a way of contacting learners to others. Another type of ICT that can be used is internet—based project work. It is used with some reasons such as: 1) encouraging cooperative learning and stimulates interaction, 2) giving students a more 'real-world' look and feel and provides greater motivation for learner and 3) encouraging critical thinking skills in which they have to transform the information to achieve a given task.

Yunus (2007) shares similar idea, he says that ICT provides a variety of learning opportunities for students to learn language. The Internet and the World Wide Web provide supplemental language activities which can help students with additional practice in specific areas of language learning. These include reading tests and comprehension questions, grammar exercises, pronunciation exercises, vocabulary tests, cloze tests, and so fort. Students can search the Web such web sites for their own learning. This can help them to enhance their English language learning.

Dealing with perception in using ICT, two lecturers said that they kept up with ICT very well; they tried to be as maximum as possible in using ICT in class. They realized that there were some benefits of using ICT and knew how to use the ICT. Most of the lecturers kept up enough with ICT. The two lecturers added that ICT development became potential for improving the quality of education. Quite often they got new information/application on ICT from students; they exchanged information about ICT with students. There was only one lecturer who did not keep up with ICT; he taught manually. The lack of comprehension, supporting facilities, insufficient network system and ICT variation were reasons why it was difficult for them to be always up to date with ICT development. The above finding is in line with Dudeney & Hockly (2007) stating that educators often feel fear, unconfident and insecure when they are dealing with technology. It is due to their limitation in comprehending and operating the technology itself.

Mostly, lecturers were accustomed to using ICT. They mostly used cell phone and gadget to get an access to ICT. They used email to check assignment from students. Also, they used it for personal uses like doing research and society service, browsing for finding information about knowledge and technology development, blog, traveloka, grab car, WIFI and internet for teaching materials, journal, reference and update information. In short, they mostly used ICT to support their work, for entertainment and social interaction with laptop, internet and cell phone.

The findings showed that most lecturers tended to integrate the use of ICT in learning; as in basic grammar and basic speaking which used video. Then, interpretive listening, interpretive reading and complex English grammar were taught using LCD and internet access for grammar exercises. Second Language Acquisition was delivered using LCD and internet access like YouTube. Seminar on TEFL was taught using the integration of LCD, YouTube, and learning application like British online learning. Interpretive listening used internet, laptop, projector and speaker. Interpretation was delivered with the use of laptop and projector. Basic listening used laptop, speaker and LCD. Sociolinguistics was taught using laptop and LCD, Introduction to Research Method used laptop and LCD and seminar on literature was taught using the integration of laptop and LCD.

Other subjects also integrated ICT. They were pronunciation which was delivered using laptop, hp, LCD, speaker. Speaking for group activities used laptop and LCD. Writing II used laptop and LCD. Pragmatics was taught using laptop LCD and cellphone. Interpretive listening used cellphone and speaker. Morphology was delivered with the integration of laptop, LCD and online dictionary. EYL used laptop and LCD. ICT for English literacy was taught using laptop, LCD, blog and internet connection and Extensive reading with laptop and internet connection but not very often.

Also for subject such as basic reading was taught using network to get access to the web or blog. Basic English grammar was taught using network to web and blog as the sources. Basic writing was delivered by integrating network to web blog. Basic speaking used web of blog as reference. Morphology was taught using LCD projector, e-book, and website. Curriculum and material development was taught using LCD, website and learning blog. ICT for

English literacy was delivered by integrating blog, LCD, website. Then, Seminar on literature was taught using laptop, and internet connection. Literary appreciation and CCU were also integrated with the use ICT but the lecturers did not mention the kinds of ICT they used, and writing I was not integrated with the use ICT.

The finding revealed that some lecturers mentioned that the use of ICT in classroomsom during the semester was effective. Some other mentioned that the use of ICT in classrooms during the semester was not effective due to unsupportive condition, such as problems on the LCD (its number and performance), bad signal and bad network system. Also, Good sound system is not available. One lecturer mentioned that he delivered his lesson manually without involving any ICT usage in classroom. Further, lecturers mostly took the benefits of using ICT. It was used to ease the learning process in class, give an access to up to date information, entertain, and make them sociable. Also, it stimulated the exploration of new knowledge. In accordance with these ideas, Oliver (2002) claims that the role of ICT in higher education in 21st century. He said that ICT offers a student centered learning, it supports in knowledge construction, distance education, and learning at any time.

Dealing with the skill of lecturers in using ICT in classroom, students tended to respond positively on the use of video in listening class. With good network system, teaching materials could be packaged and delivered interestingly. It could increase students' motivation, comprehension and interest. It also enriched lecturers' teaching sources and helped them explain the lesson. It gave benefits to both students and lecturers. Further, it was found that some lecturers were mostly skillful in using ICT. Some others were skillful enough and only one who admitted that he was not skillful in using ICT in classroom.

The findings showed that listening and speaking class needed much ICT support. Speaking class needed audio while listening class needed audio laboratory. In Seminar on TEFL, students were expected to download the learning method. Then, institution also needed to provide books as teaching sources as listed on the curriculum, provide computer and internet connection in classroom in order that students could make the theory into practice, repair and do maintenance with LCDs. General subject especially needed much attention related to the use of ICT. Lecturers should optimize the use of ICT and choose the appropriate ICT which may help achieve the learning objective.

Another findings showed that study program should provide laboratory and regulate learning pattern involving the use of ICT in delivering material by all lecturers. Then, it should be evaluated every semester for improvements. Moreover, study program needed to: 1) provide an ICT training for lecturers about using ICT as teaching media, optimize ICT usage and regulate to all lecturers that integrating ICT usage is a must for all subjects, 2) provide rooms with computer, LCD, AC, good internet connection, software and hardware, sufficient WIFI connection, hot spot, and up to date computers, 3) provide a link or webpage in which both students and lecturers can find any academic information needed in it and they can get access to it wherever they are, 4) do facilities improvement at computer subject especially and add more LCDs, 5) provide computer and printer at library. Library is operated manually and conventionally. It needed audio and PC corner which must be developed into an ICT-based library to support online learning by providing a multimedia computer library and availability of e-book and e-library.

In accordance with the vision and mission of English study program, it was expected that learning process could be an ICT-based learning. ICT could be used with supporting facilities such as no more cable error, low internet connection and black out. Study program should have webpage and blog connected with students, lecturers and even Universities. It also needs to use online journal. Even though majority of the lecturers tended to have a positive perspective towards ICT usage, a few of them tended to have different idea. In relation to this, Dudeney & Hockly (2007) mention that lack of confidence, facilities and training resulting in an inability to see the benefit of using technologies in the classroom.

From the questionnaire, it was found that students perceived ICT as a developing, sophisticated tool which made people easily to communicate, find information, ease human work in all fields, make the lesson in class becomes interesting and creative, proceed and deliver information using ICT such as laptop, LCD, Ppt, word, internet, blog, email and website.

ICT integration was really important. It helped both students and lecturers and made them became more active and got focused on the lesson. It was used to prepare the lesson and present materials interestingly.

Using ICT gave much contribution on the successful learning process. It saved time, gave more illustration for students to get a better understanding and added more variation in learning process. Students felt that the use of ICT was still minim; it also depended on the readiness of the lecturer and institution. The example of ICT uses were LCD projector, internet, sound system, WIFI, blog, website browsing, video, audio, speaker, Ppt, gadget.

The findings showed that 19 students kept up with the ICT development, 19 students kept up enough with the ICT development and 12 students did not really keep up with ICT development. 43 students mentioned that they were accustomed to using laptop, hp, email, YouTube, blog, for finding information, reading news, doing their assignment and enjoying entertainment and pleasure. 7 other students mentioned that they were not accustomed to using ICT. Reasons for not being keep up with ICT were laziness, unsupportive condition, a difficulty to understand the ICT, no supporting facilities in class, not much exposure to the ICT use, limited WIFI connection, ignorance on ICT development, comfortable feeling to stay oldish, the expensiveness of ICT, not having much time due to part time students, the complexity of ICT, lack of financial support, no training in using ICT and no obligation regulated in using ICT.

Meaning that eventhough the majority of the students tended to perceive ICT positively, but still a few of them tended to have different point of view. As it is stated by Luambano & Nawe (2004) that majority of students did not use internet due some reasons such as, the insufficient number of computers with internet and lack of facilities and skills in using ICT.

The findings revealed that most of the students tended to respond positively to the use of ICT. 32 students mentioned that ICT use had been effective already and presentation had been done well. Most lecturers had already used laptop and LCD. Students mostly got some benefits from ICT usage. They understood more about how to use the ICT and got more information, got accustomed to using ICT. Further, learning process became easy and interesting by using chatting application and video call to practice speaking, YouTube for listening and email for submitting assignment. It gave positive effect to the learning process in general. 2 students mentioned that ICT was not really useful. If not used wisely it would give bad impact to students. Most students responded positively on the use of ICT in classroom. They were enthusiastic and hoped that it would always be developed. Only 1student felt that ICT use was still minim. It was also found that in using ICT there were 7 very skillful lecturers, 31 were skillful enough lecturers, others said that they were skillful and some others were not.

In contrary, 18 others tended to respond to the use of ICT in the classroom negatively. They mentioned that the use of ICT in classroom was not effective yet because there were some subjects which did not integrate any ICT usage. Computer subject especially used old fashioned computers with low WIFI connection. Both lecturers and students did not make use the online dictionary. Lecturers still relied on books much. The number of the computer in Computer subjects was very minim. One computer was operated by three students. Then, the lecturer of Computer subject also only gave theoretical lesson without giving any further explanation on the application.

Some suggestions related to the use of ICT in classroom were: 1) be more communicative in delivering information, 2) all subjects needed to do improvements dealing with the use of ICT, 3) Philosophy subject needed to be made more interesting by not just using books and 4) Extensive reading subject should also integrate the use of ICT.

Institution, especially study program needed to optimize the use of ICT. It needed to improve and develop facilities available such as strong WIFI connection and steady LCDs. It also needed to upgrade computer lab, and do maintenance and service on facilities. Classrooms with WIFI, projector, audio, tape recorder, and good sound system were needed. Some other expectations dealing with the use of ICT at English study program were to improve and optimize the use and the skill of using ICT itself. Explore more ICT applications, not just using Powerpoint and word since using interesting ICTs can promote students' motivation.

It also needs to have broadcasting radio, add computer availability, keep up with changes and provide more computers and books as sources in library.

In brief, the majority of the students tended to respond positively to the use of ICT in classroom, while some others did not say the same. Even most of them perceived ICT positively but their response towards ICT usage in classroom quite different. In relation to this phenomenon, Alassaf (2014) claims that the positive perceptions do not mean high levels of ICT used due to the fact that ICT used is also affected by many other factors such as the users' experiences, lack of resources, professional training, institutional support and time might explain the the cause of the different point of view.

4 CONCLUSION AND SUGGESTION

In order not to stay behind in the global competition, the university should replace traditional ways of delivering materials to the integration of ICT usage. For the English study program FKIP University of Tridinanti especially, where ICT-based learning becomes the goal in teaching and learning model. On the basis of the finding, it was found that the majority of lecturers tended to perceive ICT positively. Most of them tended to use ICT and use them integratedly in classroom. They commonly used laptop, LCD, internet connection, Powerpoint, blog, YouTube and email. Students also shared similar idea, they tended to have positive perception on ICT and respond positively on the use of ICT. Some other lecturers and students did not perceive and respond positively on ICT. It tended to be caused by a lack of training, comprehension, supporting facilities available or nonconducive atmosphere to get exposed to the ICT development and financial support which then created an insecure feeling towards ICT developments which resulted inability to see the benefit of using technologies in the classroom.

Both lecturers and students shared the same idea dealing with some improvements needed to do for the institution, they were: 1) provide an ICT training for lecturers about using ICT as teaching media, optimize ICT usage and regulate to all lecturers that integrating ICT usage is a must for all subjects, 2) provide rooms with computer, LCD, AC, good internet connection, software and hardware, sufficient WIFI connection, hot spot, and up to date computers, 3) provide a link or webpage in which both students and lecturers can find any academic information needed in it and they can get access to it wherever they are, 4) do facilities improvement at computer subject especially and add more LCDs, 5) provide computer and printer at library. Library is operated manually and conventionally. It needed audio and PC corner which must be developed into an ICT-based library to support online learning by providing a multimedia computer library and availability of e-book and e-library.

In conclusion, positive perception on ICT of both lecturers and students is not enough. For an effective ICT usage, it needs to be supported by the readiness of both lecturers and institution. Therefore, it is suggested that the institution pay attention to these factors to improve the learning process and achieve the vision and mission of study program as well.

REFERENCES

Abdulfatteh, H.A. 2014. Effective strategies on using ICT for teaching and learning undergraduate level at Jordanian Universities. *Journal of Education and Practice*. ISSN 2222-288X, 5(3) retrieved from www.iiste.org/Journals/index.php/JEP/article/download/10721/10926, accessed on March 21, 2017.

Abu Qudais, M., Al-Adhaileh, M., Al-Omari, A. 2010. 'Senior faculty members' attitudes in Jordanian Universities towards using information and communication technology', *International Arab Journal of e-Technology* 1(4): 135–141. [Online]. Retrieved from http://www.iajet.org/iajet_files/vol.1/no.4/Senior%20Faculty%20Members%20Attitudes%20in%20Jordanian%20Universties%20towards%20Using%20Information%20and%20Communication%20Technology_doc.pdf accessed on March 27, 2017.

Ammanni, S. & Aparanjani, S. 2016. The role of ICT in english language teaching and learning. *International Journal of Scientific & Engineering Research* 7(7): 1–7. Retrieved from https://www.ijser.org/

researchpaper/THE-ROLE-OF-ICT-IN-ENGLISH-LANGUAGE-TEACHING-AND-LEARN-ING.pdf, accessed on March 23, 2017.

Casal, R. C. 2007. *ICT for education and development*. Info 9 (4).

Cresswell, J. W. 2005. *Educational research: Planning, conducting, and evaluating quantitative and qualitative research.* Upper Saddle River, N.J: Merrill.

Chitanana, L. 2014. A change in university lecturer's perception of e-learning tools for instructional delivery at Midlands State University: From techno-phobic to technology savvies. ISSN 2223-7062 *Proceedings and report of the 7th UbuntuNet Alliance annual conference*, 83–98 retrieved from https://www.ubuntunet.net/sites/default/files/uc2014/proceedings/chitananal.pdf accessed on February 12, 2017.

Dudeney, G. & Hockly, N. 2007. *How to teach English with technology* (with CD ROM). Pearson-Longman. ISBN 978-1-4058-5308-8.

Gay, G. & Blades, R. 2005. *Information technology for CXC CSEC*. Oxford University Press, Oxford, UK.

Galanouli, D. & Mcnair, V. 2001. 'Students' perceptions of ICT-related support in teaching placements', *Journal of Computer Assisted Learning* 1 (7): 396–408.

Gay, G. Mahon, Sonia, Devonish, D. Alleyne, P. & Alleyne, G. 2006. 'Perceptions of information and communication technology among undergraduate management students in Barbados', The University of the West Indies, *Barbados. Journal of Education* 2(4): 6–17.

Khan, Shakeel Ahmad, Bhatti, Rubina & Ahmad Khan, Aqeel. 2011. Use of ICT by Students: A survey of faculty of education at IUB. Library of Philosophy and Practice. *(e-journal). Paper 677.* Retrieved from http://digitalcommons.unl.edu/cgi/viewcontent.cgi?article=1751&context=libphilprac accessed from April 02, 2017.

Luambano, I. & Nawe, J. 2004. Internet use by students of the University of Daree es Salaam. *Library Hi Tech News* 21(5): 13–17.

McCormick, R. 2004. 'Collaboration: The Challenge of ICT'. *International Journal of Technology and Design Education* (14), pp. 159–176.

Oliver, R. 2002. The role of ICT in higher education for the 21st century: ICT as change agent for education. Available: http:///elrond.scam.ecu.edu.au/oliver/2002/he21.pdf.

Sheard, Judy & Carbone, Angela 2008. ICT teaching and learning in a new educational paradigm: lecturers' perceptions versus students' experiences. Retrieved from. http://crpit.com/confpapers/CRPITV88Sheard.pdf. accessed on April 10, 2017.

Yunus, Md, M. 2007. Malaysian ESL teachers' use of ICT in their classrooms: expectations and realities. *RECALL: The Journal of EUROCALL* 9(1): 79–95. Retrived from https://www.cambridge.org/core/journals/recall/article/malaysian-esl-teachers-use-of-ict-in-their-classrooms-expectations-and-realities/A5F320B1BCD1F4316031285F1E3E29E6, accessed on March 25, 2017.

Zare-ee, A. 2011. University teachers' views on the use of information communication technologies in teaching and research. *Educational Technology* 10(3): 318–327.

The story of "Julie": A life history study of the learning experiences of an Indonesian English language teacher in implementing ICT in her classroom

D.S. Ciptaningrum
Yogyakarta State University, Yogyakarta, Indonesia

ABSTRACT: This paper examines the experiences of an English language teacher in learning the integration of Information and Communication Technology (ICT) in a contemporary Professional Development (PD) and how the experience influences her pedagogical practices. The relationship between the socio-cultural factors underlying the construction of the teacher's conceptions and pedagogical practices with ICT can be revealed using a life history interviews as the technique of data collection. A zoom model in the data analysis indicates that despite hands-on practice on good integration of ICT, she found some challenges in her English language classroom implementation after the program. The culture and ethos of school as an organisation influence the sustainability of change in her pedagogical practice. This implies that strategies of school ICT integration need to account for the complexities of other factors around teachers' work and life in order to reach stronger sustainability of change in teachers' pedagogical practices.

1 INTRODUCTION

Governments across the world have developed policies to integrate ICT in their educational context. These policies range from allocating expenditure on ICT facilities for its schools and teacher training on the use of ICT to strategies of ICT implementation (UNESCO 2007). Indonesia also implements similar strategies to integrate ICT in its schools. Schools are given ICT equipments (Maruli 2008, Maulia 2010, Ministry of National Education 2010) and various programs on ICT professional development are provided for Indonesian teachers (Belawati 2005, Burns 2010, LPMP 2011) in order to encourage them to change their professional practices by integrating ICT in their classroom effectively.

Despite years of mandatory ICT training for Indonesian teachers, ICT is still mainly used for supporting teachers' administrative tasks and as tools for information presentation (Hoseanto et al. 2008, Sari & Tedjasaputra 2008, Surjono & Gafur 2010). Teachers' training and professional development are essential for the successful usage of ICT in education. However, these opportunities for teachers to learn effective use of ICT should be an ongoing process that is not only promoting computer literacy, but it also needs to model ICT as effective teaching and learning tools. In addition, sufficient enabling socio-cultural factors which are context—specific should be put into place to ensure teachers' ICT utilization in constructivist manner.

This study is a part of a bigger study which investigates the ICT learning experiences of an English language teacher in Yogyakarta, Indonesia, who had experienced learning ICT in contemporary (high quality) teacher professional learning context. Studies in the effectiveness of the contemporary ICT PD (e.g. Beckett et al. 2003, Holland 2001, Keller et al. 2008) did not measure the real change in teachers' practices after the programs had finished. Most studies also used self-report data as the basis of evaluation in Likert-scale type of questions. What they actually measure is the participants' level of confidence or their perceptions of the activities offered in the program (Lawless et al. 2002, Schrader & Lawless 2004). The impact of these high quality ICT PDs towards teachers' everyday pedagogical practices needs further investigation.

Little is known about the process and outcomes of teacher learning to use ICT as tools for enhancing English language learning in Indonesia and the complex socio-cultural factors that influence this learning processes and outcomes. Using life history interview, the stories of the teacher were located within their wider social and historical context, and pays attention to social relations of power. The results of the interviews were analyzed using the zoom model (Pamphilon 1999) to interpret the complex and dynamic relationship between the teacher's ICT learning processes and the outcomes in her use of ICT in her pedagogical practices. By analyzing this relationship, the socio-cultural factors underlying the construction of these teachers' conceptions and pedagogical practices with ICT can be revealed.

2 TEACHER PROFESSIONAL DEVELOPMENT IN ICT

Technology related teacher professional development shows a movement from one-size-fits-all type of workshops that focus on showing teachers how to use the technology hardware and software (Denning & Selinger 1999) to those that are conducted over time with the element of follow-up learning and feedback (Cole et al. 2002, Holbein & Jackson 1999, Kariuki et al. 2001, Mulqueen 2001, Orrill 2001) as well as mentoring and reflection (Jamissen & Phelps 2006). The reasons for this shift are based on the literature in the area of teacher PD in general (e.g. Borko 2004, Sykes 1996, Cole 2004, Fullan 2007) that the former model to teacher PD fails in meeting the teachers' ongoing pedagogical needs and is separated from the classroom context. Similar finding is also present in the area of ICT teacher PD (Daly et al. 2009; Gross et al. 2001). The later approach adds topics on how to integrate technology into classroom instruction (e.g., Angeli & Valanides 2009; Koehler et al. 2007, Koehler & Mishra 2005).

One of the models that is used in technology-based PD is train-the-trainers (Gonzales et al. 2002, Martin et al. 2003). This cascade model is aimed to reach a wider audience by training a group of teachers who will train their colleagues upon the completion of the program. This model is based on the assumption that teacher instructors know well about the complexities of day-to-day classroom practices. Teachers learn from people who 'understand' them; thus, making teacher instructors a more relevant and credible source of learning (Howard et al. 2000). However, if the training is conducted in the traditional approach (one-off type of training with minimum or no feedback component and is delivered mostly in lecture mode or traditional teaching), the result of such training cannot influence changes in teachers' practices.

Another model is also applicable by the use of a mentoring or coaching model in the program (Cole et al. 2002, Holbein & Jackson 1999, Jamissen & Phelps 2006, Kariuki et al. 2001, Margerum-Leys & Marx 2004, Mulqueen 2001, Orrill 2001). The benefit of this model is teachers are provided with technical support and expertise at the personal and collegial level aimed to solve specific problems experienced by the teachers. This model has increased teachers' confidence and developed teachers' knowledge in using technology. The coaches or the mentors and the teachers experience how the technology becomes the tool in the process of teaching and learning.

Many PD programs use design-based components in the curriculum where the participants need to construct artefacts (such as online courses, digital video, or podcasts) to be used in their own classroom (Angeli & Valanides 2009, Beckett et al. 2003, Cole et al. 2002, Keller et al. 2008, Koehler et al. 2004, Koehler & Mishra 2005, Koehler et al. 2007, Mulqueen 2001). One example of the later approach in teacher ICT PD was reported by Koehler et al. (2007). By using design approach as the framework of the PD, they recorded gradual growth in the learners' technological pedagogical content knowledge (TPACK) over the 15 weeks period of the course. Similar studies that implemented design approach in different contexts (Koehler & Mishra 2005) had been proven to be effective in increasing the participants' level of TPACK. Angeli and Valanides (2009) also used two design tasks in a pre-service primary teacher education course conducted in one semester. The result from repeated measures within-subject effect showed that the participants' ICT-TPCK (similar construct with TPACK) was improved.

In the context of foreign language learning in Indonesia, the QUIPNet project and the BRIDGE program is considered as a PD for both English and Indonesian language teachers to integrate ICT. Considering how these two programs were held, the design approach is implemented in the QUIPNet project and the BRIDGE program. Queensland Indonesia Project Internet (QUIPNet) provided Indonesian English language teachers and Australian Indonesian language teachers to use ICT to link Indonesian students with Australian students in Queensland in a tandem e-learning project. This program was supported by MOEC and funded by the Queensland Office of Premier and Cabinet. This project facilitated students to extend the use of language beyond the confines of the classroom (Hoven & Crawford 2001).

Building Relationships through Intercultural Dialogue and Growing Engagement (BRIDGE) is a similar event which has been conducted since 2008. So far, this project has involved 96 Australia-Indonesia schools and 380 teachers. Participants use ICT to communicate and discuss topics that could improve their intercultural awareness while practising English (BRIDGE Australia-Indonesia School Partnerships, n.d.). An exchange program is conducted early (Indonesian teachers came to Australia and vice versa) where the teachers collaborate to design the teaching and learning processes. Trainings to support online collaborative projects are provided for both the Indonesian and Australian teachers in each country which include the development of online resources. Grants to support the implementation of the program are also available. In addition, some Indonesian schools receive computer hardware and related support to join the program. Students from both countries are involved in project-based learning using video and images to work on a project, for example, that depicts 'a day in the life' of a student, and other cultural topics. They showcase the result of their work on their wiki/blog project which provides an opportunity for both Australian and Indonesian students to share their thoughts on their friends' work. They also conduct teleconferences to have synchronous communication on certain topics. Thus, these two programs are examples of contemporary, high quality, ICT PD for English language teachers in Indonesia.

3 YOGYAKARTA ENGLISH LANGUAGE TEACHERS' EXPERIENCE IN JOINING BRIDGE PROGRAM

In 2011, Julie's schools were selected as one of the 6 schools from Yogyakarta to join BRIDGE program. This program, which was established in 2008, is initiated by Australia-Indonesia Institute and the Asia Education Foundation and it is funded by Myer Foundation and AusAID. It is a partnership program between Australian and Indonesian schools and its principal aim is to increase intercultural understanding between Indonesia and Australia. The initial stage of the program is to send Indonesian teachers to Australia for professional learning program. There, Julie learnt about Australian culture and the ICT tool to support the program implementation and they spent some time at the partner school to share knowledge on Indonesian culture and planned for the future collaboration activities with the Australian teacher. At the end of her stay in Australia, there was a time to reflect on her experience in Australia and prepared for online collaboration which would be conducted at a later time. It was in this program that Julie learnt about Skype and Wiki because the online collaboration between Indonesian and Australian students would be conducted in the form of teleconference using Skype where Indonesian students interviewed Australian students about Australian culture using English language and Australian students interviewed their Indonesian friends about Indonesian culture using Indonesian language. After teleconferences were completed, the students were divided into groups comprises of mixed Indonesian and Australian students, using any means of communication (e.g., Skype, email, or IM) they worked together to design a website (i.e. wiki spaces) about Indonesian and Australian culture.

This type of ICT learning that was experienced by Julie in the BRIDGE program showed the application of the principles of learning by design approach (Koehler & Mishra 2005) where it used design-based components in the curriculum and required the participants of this program to develop an artefact suitable to be used in their context to elicit the students' foreign language production.

4 JULIE'S STORIES OF HER PEDAGOGICAL PRACTICES WITH ICT

At the time of the interview, Julie worked at schools which had a status of RSBI or International-standard pioneer state school. In The National Education Act year 2003, article 61, it is stated that all municipalities and districts in Indonesia have to have at least one RSBI school (Ministry of National Education 2003). Provincial and regional ministry of education provide RSBI schools with significant amounts of extra money to help them increase their capacity building. Therefore, RSBI schools had enjoyed more ICT infrastructure compared to the other schools.

In addition to the bigger budget they received from the central government in their capacity as RSBI schools, Julie's school also received additional supports from the government in terms of ICT equipment. Pelangi Primary School (Julie's school) received 20 computers from the ICT Utilization Project for Educational Quality Enhancement (EQEP) program and 15–20 more computers from the local education government office. Thus, access is not a problem in her school.

Julie realised that ICT should be practiced in the context of English language learning and teaching, mostly for its multi-media capability, to motivate students. According to Julie, ICT "can convey idea through visual and audio-visual media much better." She also stressed the importance of "games", "stories" and "cartoon" to help students in learning "the tenses" and "type of verbs" in English. The "sophisticated" capability of ICT made English language lessons "easier for the students", "motivated them" and would prevent them from thinking that English was so difficult.

Besides underlying the convergence of audio and visual technology as the feature of ICT to support the affective factors in students' learning, what is interesting in Julie's accounts is the perception that ICT in English language learning and teaching works best in reading and listening skills only, and its role is to improve the students' mastery in grammar and vocabulary. For Julie, lessons on listening were best conducted using ICT. She preferred to have listening activities in the classroom using their laptop and portable speakers. She also used ICT to teach "the most commonly confused, the English idiom" since it could assist students to visualise the context which could stick to their memory. In her opinion, English idiom belongs to the list of English vocabulary that the students needed to memorise. Julie did not use ICT during exams, or when teaching reading if the materials are available on the textbook. "...... it (ICT) wasn't necessary, because the book was enough. For example, I didn't use ICT during group-work. I also didn't use ICT during writing activity."

Julie had been using the Internet so far as a source of learning and teaching materials, for communication, or for administrative purposes. When she had some time to spare, she sometimes looked for some reading texts of different genre for teaching purposes, read general news, or news related to recent educational policy. Julie sometimes emailed their partner teacher in the BRIDGE program and vice versa to set up the learning agenda of their students. However, due to her school activities and slow Internet connection, she preferred using text messages. Students were usually asked to browse the Internet to look for the topic of the lesson and then they were given a set of questions that they should find the answers in the Internet.

Julie's narratives reveal several reasons on her use of ICT. The first reason relates to affective factors such as increasing students' motivation and interest in learning English. The second reason is to assist her in teaching certain English language skills like Listening and Reading, especially to help with the mastery of Vocabulary and Grammar. Besides using ICT for communicative purposes, another common reason is to present her learning material. Finally, she used ICT as an information bank, to look for specific information.

Thus, even though Julie's school enjoys more ICT facilities compared to the other mainstream schools in Yogyakarta—and the fact that she had various learning experiences in ICT, there was low usage of ICT and its uses were generally limited to teacher-centred instruction.

The capability of ICT in facilitating foreign language cultural import to complement negotiation of meaning in the classroom (Blake, 2008; Tudini, 2015) has not been fully realised either in Julie's classrooms.

5 "THIS PROGRAM IS ACTUALLY VERY USEFUL, BUT..."

It has become a challenge for English language teachers to provide learning environment where their students can engage in contextualised and meaningful conversation to develop their communicative skills. The synchronous communication facilitated by the Internet tools like Skype and other Internet Messengers give ways to the creation of such learning environment where students can have oral or written conversations with native speakers of English. Hence, students' writing, reading, and speaking skills can be developed. The asynchronous tools like email can extend this communication practice (Warschauer, 1997). In addition to enhancing English language learners' communicative skills, this kind of learning environment can also improve learners' cultural awareness which is imperative in preparing them to the life in the 21st century where countries in the world become interdependent.

The process of developing teachers' knowledge on ICT integration in The Australia-Indonesia BRIDGE Project program can be said to have incorporated the TPACK framework in the language learning context since teachers from both countries work collaboratively to design and facilitate meaningful language learning activities based on socio-constructivist philosophies that used ICT to represent linguistic and cultural concepts in order to develop learners' language competence by considering the learners' context to cultivate the sharing of knowledge and the creation of new knowledge (Olphen 2008).

Julie considered the BRIDGE program as the most effective ICT training for her. While the other ICT PD that she had participated were "still so abstract", The BRIDGE program was "related to real life", and it had "real practice". It had improved her knowledge on "how to use ICT in the real teaching". Even though JULIE had practiced the example of effective ICT integration in English language learning context in The BRIDGE program, she was unsure whether she would be able to repeat similar instruction in her future English language lessons due to unreliable Internet connection at her school, different schedules, and the lack of support in terms of time and technical assistance.

As a part of the BRIDGE program activities that she had attended, Julie and her students had tried to conduct a Skype meeting with their partner school in Australia. The Skype meeting was supposed to be held at the school but after a few attempts they were not successful because "the Internet connection was too slow". She tried again when her class had a study tour visiting a local science museum and it was successful, her students could use Skype to have a conversation with their Australian friends. The time and schedule differences between Australia and Indonesia were problematic as well. When Julie's school hour was already over, her sister school in Australia was still having classroom activities. Their different school holiday schedule presented another problem.

Julie and her students also conducted a Wiki project with their partner school in Australia. Her students needed to form groups with the Australian students and they could use any means of communication to contact each other to get the work done. Facebook was a cheap alternative to texting or regular phone calls, but Julie's school prohibited the use of cellular phones and blocked Facebook from the school's Internet access.

Julie was aware that ICT was potential in English language learning and appreciated all the ICT trainings that she had attended in contributing to improving her knowledge about ICT for teaching and learning. Actually she was eager to practice herself using Macromedia Flash or Lectora, for example, to be fluent in using these software to develop her own multimedia English language learning material. However, it was hard to find time to do those practices. The same with Moodle and Thinkquest, after the training finished, she did not continue her Moodle and Thinkquest projects. On one hand, she was feeling uncomfortable about this but on the other hand, she had a lot of other responsibilities to fulfil. She summed it up in her remarks, "So ... there are so many problems... The programs are actually brilliant, but... because of my busy schedule [helpless tone]...

Julie had to teach 24 hours a week. She also had to teach Mathematics and Science using English because English should become the language of instruction in Math and Science subjects in RSBI schools. Moreover, she had to complete all the administrative work like lesson planning, developing test items material, and marking. Because she was the only English language teacher who had the civil-servant status, she was the coordinator for English language lessons. This means that she had to organise the teaching schedules and the extra English lessons for the students in the afternoon after school hours. She was recently appointed as the school's Treasurer who was responsible to organise the flow of the school's incomes and expenses. The school's principal often asked her to represent the school in out of town's assignments since she was still single and did not have family responsibility yet. With all of these obligations and so many meeting agenda every week, she wished she had more than 24 hours in a day.

The BRIDGE program had a clear goal toward student achievement. It was longer in duration and spread over several phases so there was a constant follow up of the program. It also facilitated teachers to be actively engaged in relevant activities and they were given autonomy to design and choose related topics according to their contexts. Most of the program's activities promoted collaboration and community building while at the same time provided access to ICT for learning and teaching (BRIDGE Australia-Indonesia School Partnerships, n.d.; Indonesian Teachers Building Bridges of Learning and Friendship in Australia together with Australia sister-schools 2009).

6 FACTORS INFLUENCING TEACHERS' PEDAGOGICAL PRACTICES WITH ICT

Julie's accounts yield an important finding that she had been engaged in an ICT PD (i.e. The BRIDGE program) which was considered as an effective ICT PD according to the theory of teacher professional learning (Garet et al. 2001, Guzey & Roehrig 2009, Lloyd et al. 2005, Margerum-Leys et al. 2004). The learning activities were designed to allow its participants to connect facts in a conceptual framework and organise the knowledge to facilitate understanding and to be applied to new situations. Thus, they were facilitated "to take control of their own learning by defining learning goals and monitoring their progress in achieving them" (Bransford et al. 2004: 18). Besides being learner-centred, activities were also designed to accommodate a sense of community where the participants worked together by building each other knowledge, and involved in mutual dialogues to solve problems. Julie mentioned that opportunities for reflections in and outside the program were also provided. The ability to reflect is necessary in the process of evaluation and critique as the highest educational objective according to Bloom's taxonomy. Deep learning also occurs as a result of reflection and it is through the use of reflection that learners are enabled to work with meanings toward the attainment of transformative learning (Moon 1999).

Julie's professional learning program in this project also reflected the application of TPACK framework (Mishra & Koehler 2008; van Olphen 2008) and ICT in language learning (Blake 2008, Felix 2003, Kern et al. 2008, Tudini 2015, Warschauer et al. 1996). The participants of this project also learn how to operate software like Wiki and Voki, and to upload video files to Youtube. ICT here was used as a tool to help learners engaged in collaborative activities that addressed individual student's learning style, needs, and interest which required them to communicate using the target language.

However, this kind of learning experience is not powerful enough to ensure that such pedagogical practice will sustain in Julie's English language classrooms. This is because ICT implementation in school requires teachers to change their classroom practices, thus, it is closely related to the change management issues and teacher ICT PD is only one factor which needs to be considered among the other related factors in managing such change.

Tearle (2004) proposes that ICT implementation in school needs to use a different approach. It is no longer sufficient to direct strategies of ICT implementation towards ensuring that all teachers in all curriculum areas understand how to connect pedagogies with ICT to enhance learning in their classroom. Rather, ICT implementation in school should also be seen as a case of managing change with its associated complexities. In addition to the generic change management issues, namely the culture and ethos of school as an organisation, the attitude of all the school members and the characteristics of the process or model through which change is being managed, and the specific individual factors need to be widely considered.

7 CONCLUSION

Julie had attended various ICT PD. One of these PD reflected the principles of contemporary PD and adhered to TPACK framework which could facilitate English language learning of their students. However, ICT tended not to be used in ways that could develop students' skills in critical thinking and collaborative work to find, analyse, and synthesise resources in order to solve real world problems which could lead to students' improvement on their communicative English language skills. Thus, this study confirms the findings of previous studies (Hoseanto et al. 2008, Sari & Tedjasaputra 2008, Surjono & Gafur 2010). Julie's experience which showed how difficult it was to implement the result of her learning in her real context supports the studies of Tearle (2004), which pointed out the complexities of other factors around teachers' work and life in affecting ICT implementation in teachers' pedagogical practices. The culture of the school is one of the factors which determines for pedagogical change to happen and sustain. It is a culture that demands obedience which results in limited freedom and creativity of the teachers to integrate ICT in their pedagogical practices. Indonesian government should revisit its strategies of school ICT integration. There needs to be no more standardised, top-down replicable programs within the technocentric paradigm. A shift toward a holistic and ecological paradigm is crucial in this matter. ICT implementation strategies need to be sensitive and really address the social, economic, and environmental factors of the school.

REFERENCES

Angeli, C. & Valanides, N. 2009. Epistemological and methodological issues for the conceptualization, development, and assessment of ICT–TPCK: Advances in technological pedagogical content knowledge (TPCK). *Computer & Education,* 52: 154–168.

Beckett, E.C., Wetzel, K., Chishlom, I.M., Zambo, R., Buss, R., Padgett, H. et al. 2003. Supporting technology integration in K-8 multicultural classrooms through professional development. *TechTrends* 47(5): 14–17.

Belawati, T. 2005. *UNESCO meta-survey on the use of technologies in education: Indonesia ICT use in education.* Retrieved from http://www.unescobkk.org/fileadmin/user_upload/ict/Metasurvey/indonesia.pdf.

Blake, R.J. 2008. *Brave new digital classroom technology and foreign language learning.* Washington, DC: Georgetown University Press.

Blumenfeld, P.C., Marx, R.W., Soloway, E. & Krajcik, J. 1996. Learning with peers: From small group cooperation to collaborative communities. *Educational Researcher* 25(8): 37–40.

Borko, H. 2004. Professional development and teacher learning: Mapping the terrain educational researcher. *Educational Researcher* 33(8): 3–15.

Bransford, J.D., Brown, A.L. & Cocking, R.R. 2004. *How people learn: brain, mind, experience, and school.* Washington DC: National Research Council.

BRIDGE Australia-Indonesia School Partnerships. (n.d.). Retrieved from http://www.indonesia.bridge.edu.au

Brookfield, S. 1985. *Self-directed learning: From theory to practice.* San Francisco: Jossey-Bass.

Burns, M. 2010. 17,000 islands, 1 GOAL. *JSD the Journal of the National Staff Development Council* 31(1): 18–23.

Cole, K., Simkins, M. & Penuel, W.R. 2002. Learning to teach with technology: Strategies for inservice professional development. *Journal of Technology and Teacher Education* 10(3): 431–455.

Cole, P. 2004. *Professional development: A great way to avoid change.* Retrieved from http://www.edstaff.com.au/docs/Peter%20Cole%20-%20PD%20A%20great%20way%20to%20 avoid%20change.pdf.

Daloz, L.A. 1986. *Effective teaching and mentoring.* San Francisco: Jossey-Bass.

Denning, T. & Selinger, M. 1999. Patterns of change and innovations in pre-service education. Paper presented at the Annual Conference of SITE '99 (Society for Information Technology & Teacher Education), San Antonio, Texas.

Eraut, M. 2007. Learning from other people in the workplace. *Oxford Review of Education,* 33(4) 403–422.

Felix, U. 2003. An orchestrated version of language learning online. In U. Felix (Ed.), *Language learning online: Towards best practice* (pp. 7–17). Exton, Pa.: Swets & Zeitlinger.

Friedman, T.L. 2005. *The world is flat: A brief history of the twenty-first century.* New York: Farrar, Straus and Giroux.

Fullan, M.G. 2007. Change the terms for teacher learning. *Journal of Staff Development* 28(3): 35–36.

Garet, M., Porter, A., Desimone, L., Birman, B. & Yoon, K. 2001. What makes professional development effective? Analysis of a national sample of teachers. *American Education Research Journal* 38(4): 915–945.

Gonzales, C., Pickett, L., Hupert, N. & Martin, W. 2002. The regional educational technology assistance programs: Its effects on teaching practices. *Journal of Research on Technology in Education* 35(1): 1–18.

Gross, D., Truesdale, C. & Bielec, S. 2001. Backs to the wall: Supporting teacher professional development with technology. *Educational Research and Evaluation* 7(2): 161–183.

Guzey, S.S. & Roehrig, G.H. 2009. Teaching science with technology: Case studies of science teachers' development of technology, pedagogy, and content knowledge. *Contemporary Issues in Technology and Teacher Education* 9(1): 25–45. Retrieved from http://www.citejournal.org/ vol9/iss1/science/article1.cfm.

Holbein, M.F. & Jackson, K. 1999. Study groups and electronic portfolios: A professional development school inservice project. *Journal of Technology and Teacher Education,* 7(3): 205–217.

Holland, P.E. 2001. Professional development in technology: Catalyst for school reform. *Journal of Technology and Teacher Education* 9(2): 245–267.

Hoseanto, O., Tobing, R.L. & Widiatmika, I.M.A.A. 2008. *Teachers' readiness for teaching with ICT.* Paper presented at the Simposium Tahunan Penelitian Pendidikan. Retrieved from http://puslitjaknov.org/data/file/2008/makalah_poster_session_pdf/ObertHoseanto_teachers%20readiness%20 for%20teaching%20with%20ICT.pdf.

Hoven, D. & Crawford, J. 2001. *Networking and communicating: Technological applications and implications for learning of Indonesian and EFL.* Paper presented at the AALA 2001. Retrieved from http:// eprints.qut.edu.au/509/1/509.pdf.

Howard, B.C., McGee, S., Schwartz, N. & Purcell, S. 2000. The experience of constructivism: Transforming teacher epistemology. *Journal of Research on Computing in Education* 32(4): 455–462.

Jamissen, G. & Phelps, R. 2006. The role of reflection and mentoring in ICT teacher professional development: Dialogue and learning across the hemispheres. *Teacher Development: An International Journal of Teachers' Professional Development* 10(3): 293–312.

Kariuki, M., Franklin, T. & Duran, M. 2001. A technology partnership: Lessons learned by mentors. *Journal of Technology and Teacher Education* 9(3): 407–417.

Keller, J.B., Hixon, E., Bonk, C.J. & Ehman, L. 2008. Professional development that increases technology integration by K-12 teachers: The influence of the TICKIT Program. *International Journal of Instructional Tech & Distance Learning* 5(3): 3–22.

Kern, R., Ware, P. & Warschauer, M. 2008. Network-based language teaching. In N.V. Deusen-Scholl & N.H. Hornberger (Eds.), *Encyclopedia of language and education.* New York: Springer.

Koehler, M.J. & Mishra, P. 2005. Teachers learning technology by design. *Journal of Computing in Teacher Education* 21(3): 94–102.

Koehler, M.J., Mishra, P. & Yahya, K. 2007. Tracing the development of teacher knowledge in a design seminar: Integrating content, pedagogy, and technology. *Computers & Education* 49: 740–762.

Koehler, M.J., Mishra, P., Hersey, K. & Peruski, L. 2004. With a little help from your students: A new model for faculty development and online course design. *Journal of Technology and Teacher Education* 12(1): 25–55.

Krajcik, J.S., Blumenfeld, P.C., Marx, R.W., Bass, K.M., Fredricks, J. & Soloway, E. 1998. Inquiry in project-based science classrooms: Initial attempts by middle school students. *Journal of the Learning Sciences* 7: 313–350.

Lave, J. & Wenger, E. 1991. *Situated learning: Legitimate peripheral participation.* New York: Cambridge University Press.

Lawless, K.A. & Pellegrino, J.W. 2007. Professional development in integrating technology into teaching and learning: Knowns, unknowns, and ways to pursue better questions and answers. *Review of Educational Research* 77(4): 575–614.

Lawless, K.A., Kulikowich, J.M. & Smith, E.V., Jr. 2002. *Examining the relationships among knowledge and interest and perceived knowledge and interest.* Paper presented at the annual meeting of the American Educational Research Association.

Lloyd, M., Cochrane, J. & Beames, S. 2005. *Dynamic not static: Characteristics of effective teacher professional development in ICT.* Paper presented at the AARE Conference. Retrieved from http://scholar.google.com.au/scholar?q=Dynamic+not+static%3A+Characteristics+of+effective+teacher+professional&hl=en&btnG=Search&as_sdt=2001&as_sdtp=on.

LPMP Jogja. 2011. *Fasilitas LPMP Prov. D.I. Yogyakarta.* Retrieved from http://lpmpjogja.org/index.php?option=com_content&task=view&id=127&Itemid=95.

Margerum-Leys, J. & Marx, R.W. 2004. The nature and sharing of teacher knowledge of technology in a student teacher/mentor teacher pair. *Journal of Teacher Education* 55(5): 421–437.

Martin, W., Culp, K., Gersick, A. & Nudell, H. 2003. *Intel teach to the future: Lessons learned from the evaluation of a large-scale technology-integration professional development program.* Paper presented at the annual meeting of American Educational Research Association, Chicago, IL.

Maruli, A. 2008, May 13. Tarif internet turun 20–40 persen Juli 2008. *Antaranews.com.* Retrieved from http://www.antaranews.com/view/?i=1212222193&c=TEK&s=.

Maulia, E. 2010, December 11. Ministry's program to get schools online meets with criticism. *The Jakarta Post.* Retrieved from http://www.thejakartapost.com/news/2009/11/12/ministry%E2%80%99s-program-get-schools-online-meets-with-criticism.html.

Mezirow, J. 2009. Transformative learning theory. In J. Mezirow & E.W. Taylor (Eds.), *Transformative learning in practice: Insights from community, workplace, and higher education:* 18–31. San Francisco, CA: Jossey-Bass.

Ministry of National Education. 2010. *Rencana strategis pendidikan 2010–2014 [Strategic plan in education 2010–2014].* Jakarta.

Ministry of National Education. 2003. *Undang-undang Sistem Pendidikan Nasional nomor 20 tahun 2003 [The act no. 20/2003 about the national education system].* Jakarta.

Mishra, P. & Koehler, M.J. 2008. *Introducing technological pedagogical content knowledge.* Paper presented at the Annual Meeting of the American Educational Research Association.

Moon, J. 1999. *Reflection in learning and professional development: Theory and practice.* London: Kogan Press.

Mulqueen, W.E. 2001. Technology in the classroom: Lessons learned through professional development. *Education* 122(2): 248–256.

Orrill, C.H. 2001. Building technology-based, learner-centered classrooms: The evolution of a professional development framework. *Educational Technology, Research and Development* 49(1): 15–34.

Pamphilon, B. 1999. The zoom model: A dynamic framework for the analysis of life histories. *Qualitative Inquiry* 5(3): 393–410.

Papert, S. & Harel, I. 1991. Situating constructionism. In I. Harel & S. Papert (Eds.), *Constructionism: Research reports and essays* 1985–1990: 1–11. Westport, CT, US: Ablex Publishing.

Sari, E. & Tedjasaputra, A. 2008. Exploring potentials and challenges of mobile ICT for learning in Finland and Indonesia. *International Journal of Mobile Learning and Organisation* 2(2): 103–118.

Schrader, P.G. & Lawless, K.A. 2004. The knowledge, attitudes, and behaviors (KAB) approach: How to evaluate performance and learning in complex environments. *Performance Improvement* 43(9): 8–15.

Surjono, H.D. & Gafur, A. 2010. Potensi pemanfaatan ICT untuk peningkatan mutu pembelajaran SMA di Kota Yogyakarta. *Cakrawala Pendidikan* 29(2): 161–175.

Sykes, G. 1996. Reform of and as professional development. *Phi Delta Kappan* 77: 465–467.

Tearle, P. 2004. A theoretical and instrumental framework for implementing change in ICT in education. *Cambridge Journal of Education,* 34(3): 331–351.

Tudini, V. 2015. Interactivity in the teaching and learning of foreign languages: What it means for resourcing and delivery of online and blended programmes. *The Language Learning Journal.* Retrieved from http://dx.doi.org/10.1080/09571736.2014.994183.

UNESCO. 2007. *Initiating and managing SchoolNets.* Retrieved from http://www2.unescobkk.org/elib/publications/111/.

Van Olphen, M. 2008. TPCK an integrated framework for educating world language teachers. In AACTE (Ed.), *The handbook of technological pedagogical content knowledge (TPCK) for educators.* New York: Routledge.

Vygotsky, L.S. 1962. *Thought and language.* Cambridge, MA: MIT Press.

Vygotsky, L.S. 1978. *Mind in society: The development of higher psychological processes.* Cambridge, Mass: Harvard University Press.

Warschauer, M. 1997. Computer-mediated collaborative learning: Theory and practice. *Modern Language Journal* 81(3): 470–481.

Warschauer, M., Turbee, L. & Roberts, B. 1996. Computer learning networks and student empowerment. *System* 24(1): 1–1.

ELT in Asia in the Digital Era: Global Citizenship and Identity – Madya et al. (Eds)
© *2018 Taylor & Francis Group, London, ISBN 978-0-8153-7900-3*

Faculty's attitudes towards the shift to blended learning, challenges faced and its impact

K.K. Aye
Swinburne University of Technology, Sarawak, Malaysia

ABSTRACT: Like other higher education institutions, the institution that the researcher is with is adopting Blended Learning (BL) to primarily address the issues of 21st century students' learning and engagement. Using Graham, Woodfield and Harrison's (2013) three institutional BL adoption stages, this qualitative study explores BL impact on student learning, challenges faced, and faculty's attitudes towards this institutional shift to BL through the lens of an educator, student and administrator during BL exploration and implementation in the researcher's undergraduate and postgraduate classrooms. Through personal reflection notes, participant observation and informal discussions with people involved, this study shows that while BL adoption has significantly positive impact on student learning, a systematic ongoing institutional support and recognition is crucial for the faculty's acceptance of BL by helping them overcome challenges such as anxiety, time management and capacity to seek and select appropriate ICT resources.

1 INTRODUCTION

Pressing challenges of earning 'enhanced institutional reputation' in this increasingly competitive market by a range of cost-effective course offerings which reach out and provide optimal learning experience to 21st century netizen students, potential benefits of ICT and the need for human touch in language learning have led more and more institutions, including Australian universities, to adopt blended learning (BL) (Garrison & Vaughan 2007, Loch & Borland 2014). Although successful BL implementation is significantly determined by an overarching institutional BL strategy, structure and support, this paper argues that attitudes of faculty staff towards this transformative pedagogical approach and challenges that they face during BL adoption should be paid equal attention to because, as pointed out by Linden (2014: 79), better learning is, in fact, an outcome of 'the implementation, active learning strategies embedded in pedagogy and course redesign' which academics takes charge. This study aims to provide a clear picture of BL transformation from an academic perspective which in turn is hoped to be able to inform institutions for the successful BL implementation and growth while fulfilling the very promises BL assumes to give to the higher education sector.

Also known as mixed-mode learning, blended learning (BL) is a hybrid of the traditional face-to-face instruction and technology-assisted learning activities which takes advantage of the best attributes of both and creates a conducive learning environment whereby an interactive student-centered collaborative learning takes place inside and beyond classroom (O'Byrne & Pytash 2015, Vaughan 2007).

The structural make-up of these two modes still vary depending on the subject nature or individual academic staff's familiarity with technology, as rightly pointed out by Linden (2014: 75) that it constitutes 'a continuum with minimal online activities on one end and minimal face-to-face activities on the other end' (cf. Peterson & Horn 2016). However, according to Vaughan (2007), once successfully combined, this flexible learning in terms of time or location promotes student satisfaction, improved student learning outcomes, better student-lecturer interaction and increased student engagement and institutional opportunities for enhancing institution reputation and broader course offerings with reduced operation costs (see also Salamonson & Lantz 2005). Vaughan's study (2007) also reveals challenges faced by students, faculty and administration, some of which include student's time management, responsibility for learning, technical problems, academics' time commitment, lack or insufficient professional development support, risks of losing instructor's predominant role in and control over the course, BL strategic alignment with institutional vision, mission and priorities, and faculty's resistance to this transformational shift (see also Linden 2014).

Integral to this learning transformation is learning technology, at the heart of which is the course learning management system (LMS), the tools of which allow asynchronous and synchronous communication, course management which ranges from integration, distribution and delivery of collaborative and interactive course learning materials of any kind, usage tracking and (automated) assessments to evaluation and reporting (see also Black et al. 2007). A flipped classroom is an instructional BL strategy, a reversal of the traditional pedagogic approach in which text-based or ICT based learning materials are accessed in student's own pace anywhere before the class while working on advance concepts and collaborative problem-based learning takes place in face-to-face classroom (Tucker 2012).

Given significance of institutional BL strategies, infra structure and support mechanisms, using data collected from 6 institutions implementing or adopting BL, Graham et al. (2013) outline three stages that these institutions go through: (1) an 'awareness/ exploration' stage in which administrator's awareness of BL leads to limited support given to individual academic staff to employ BL in their class without any stated BL overall design; (2) an 'adoption/ early implementation' stage whereby new policies and practices are piloted based on a BL strategy to support BL implementation; and (3) a 'mature implementation/ growth' stage in which BL is operated and directed by well-established BL strategies, structure and support.

BL research highlights the significance of 'development of a single, university-wide blended strategy' (Engert 2004 cited in Torrisi-Steel & Drew 2013). Some underlying frameworks or models for BL implementation reported in literature include behaviorism, cognitivism and constructivism (Ahmad M. Al-Huneidi & Schreurs 2012, Beutelspacher & Stock 2011 cited in Torrisi-Steele & Drew 2013). Salmon (2000), for example, proposes five-stage model online learning which starts with 'access and motivation' followed by 'online socialization, information exchange, knowledge construction' and ends with development.

With course learning objectives in mind and focus on education over technology, this innovative pedagogy requires insightful redesigning of the course formerly offered in face-to-face mode, replacing certain amount of class time with computer-based technologies that engage students so that authentic personalized learning could take place. This points to the pivotal role of academics who champion this transformational task, as their awareness, understanding and acceptance of BL strategies and technologies, and skills in learning technology will make institutional BL implementation successful though it is in the capacity of institutions which can empower academics with targeted BL capacity and capability building training.

Given the fact that members of an organization can choose whether to adopt any innovation, Roger (2003) categorizes innovation adopters into five: (1) innovators who make up 2.5% of adopters with considerable technical knowledge who pioneer a new innovation; (2) early adopters with some technical know-how who adopt innovation with greater discretion than innovators and constitute 13.5%; (3) early majority representing 35% of adopters who adopt a new innovation given the convincing evidence of its value and well-founded recommendations from others; (4) late majority representing approximately 34% of adopters who are less comfortable with technology and adopt an innovation only out of peer pressure and necessity; and (5) laggards constituting 16% who resist adopting an innovation as much as they can, possibly given their strong dislike for or discomfort with technology. The population composite of 5 categories of innovators suggests successful implementation of any innovation requires buy-in from the early majority.

Using Graham et al.'s institutional BL adoption framework (2013) and Roger's five innovation adopter categories (2003), findings of Porter and Graham's study (2016) with Brigham Young University full-time and part-time instructors suggest 'the availability of sufficient infrastructure, support in technology and pedagogy, BL evaluation data, the alignment of faculty and administrators' purposes' are the factors influencing all adopters' BL adoption decision. Their findings points to significance of early adopters' course evaluation outcomes to secure the buy-in from the early majority, and institutional support and training for the late majority and laggards which make up 51% of the total adopters.

As other Australian universities, Swinburne University of Technology as well as its international Sarawak Campus is mandated to adopt BL. As part of Swinburne Transformation Learning Unit which spearheads digital learning, using Blackboard learning management system, Salmon et al. (2015) developed the Carpe Diem learning design process MOOC (massive open online course) to expose Swinburne academics to authentic course design process as a student and course designer and this is viewed by participants as 'a valuable, relevant, experiential and authentic learning experience' (see also Gregory & Salmon 2013).

Research has been carried out for more than a decade to feed into this popular instructional approach. A review of literature carried out in 2011 by Torrisi-Steele & Drew (2013) on 827 BL research articles reveals that 69.4% of research focus on different ways of macro- and micro level BL implementation, 25.63% on students, that is, student experience, BL acceptance and impact, and only 4.96% on academic practice which includes faculty professional development, implementation of blended technology and differing degree of faculty's use of blended technology. Note that, while current statistics are yet to be available, these five-year-old statistics still point to scant academic attention paid to faculty, the front-liners of this transformational learning.

As such, using the three-stage institutional BL adoption framework by Graham et al. (2013), this study investigates faculty's attitudes and challenges faced in each stage and impact as a student, educator and administrator through reflection and analysis of the researcher's BL adoption stages along with the Swinburne Sarawak BL implementation process. In this study, the researcher is self-categorised as an early adopter who has some knowledge of technical know-how, but is willing to take risks to try better pedagogical practices. Evaluation data from an early adopter like the researcher, as the findings of Porter & Graham (2016) highlight, will motivate early majority adopters which make up 35% to willingly redesign and implement BL delivery of their courses. With the institutional support and training, these early majority's step is, in turn, hoped to be taken up by the rest of the adopters.

2 METHOD

This preliminary qualitative study was conducted at Swinburne University of Technology, Sarawak Campus that the researcher has been with since 2009. It is an international campus of Swinburne University of Technology, Australia, with the student population of approximately 4,000 registered either in undergraduate courses such as engineering, business, design, computing and science or postgraduate courses by research or coursework. There are currently 187 full-time academic staff and 168 non-academic staff. The Blackboard Learning Management System has already been in use since its inception in Malaysia although the degree and purpose of its usage among the faculty varies.

As stated earlier, this study situates the researcher's BL personal journey in the BL adoption framework by Graham, et al. (2013). Data were collected during each stage through (1) personal reflection notes; (2) participant observation; (3) informal face-to-face or online discussions with course mates and students involved. These data were analyzed and categorized into (1) benefits of BL and (2) challenges and issues faced during the journey as a student, a lecturer, and administrator.

3 DISCUSSION

This section will start with the institutional strategy, structure and support provided in each stage of the researcher's BL implementation which is followed by benefits gained and end with challenges faced and some suggestions. It will end with an overview of the benefits and challenges across these three groups.

3.1 *Awareness or exploration*

As part of institutional support, Academic Practice Team was established in March 2013 at Swinburne Sarawak to provide targeted academic staff teaching and learning development through workshops conducted by internal or invited academics. Some workshops worth mentioning at this stage include (1) workshops conducted by Melbourne Learning Trans-formation Unit to introduce designing online courses and activities to academics; and (2) workshops conducted by Sarawak staff on teaching and learning technologies, for example, Blackboard training in the beginning of each semester.

As attempts to explore new pedagogic practices, the researcher attended the following workshops: (1) Introduction to Carpe Diem and Five-stage model E-moderating face-to-face workshops conducted by Professor Gilly Salmon (7–8 May 2013) attended by 20 academics; (2) A 5-week online Carpe Diem—Learning Design Facilitator Training Workshop (10 March–17 April 2014); (3) A 5-week E-moderating online course using '5 stage model' on how to execute and structure E-tivities for online environment (28 April–30 May 2014); (4) Swinburne Digital Aquarium—Flipped Classroom (17 June 2014) as an observer; and (5) "SAMR Model: Using iPad for Teaching and Learning" (14 May 2014). The first four work-shops allow the researcher with administrative duties at that time to discern them from the perspectives of a student, lecturer cum course designer and administrator.

3.1.1 *Reflection through student lens*

Benefits that the researcher gained as a participant of these online courses include (1) opti-mal learning experience through the use of interactive and thought-provoking videos and online activities, (2) opportunities to learn in own pace, time or location though required to meet deadlines given by the facilitator and course mates working in groups, (3) collaborative learning through student-student and facilitator-student networks; (4) varying achievements of learning outcomes given different time-management skills, and (5) broadening networks for life-long learning.

Challenges or issues that the researcher recognized as a student include (1) familiarity with the online learning environment and the Blackboard tools to access materials in the beginning of the online course, (2) successful completion of the course as some course mates left half-way due to workload as academics, and (3) technical problems when uploading or downloading files or during synchronous collaborate sessions.

3.1.2 *Reflection through educator lens*

As modelled by these courses, experience as a participant/student and course designer instilled in the researcher awareness that, if the course is designed using appropriate online activities with pedagogical outcomes in mind, and facilitators have all the required skill sets, redesigned courses in which these computer-assisted activities and traditional class-room are complementary to each other can lead to (1) student-centered collaborative learning whereby students are responsible for their own learning with an overall student's better achievement of learning outcomes; (2) motivation to use existing Online Education Resources (OERs) (learnt from the facilitator and course mates) for course redesign; and (3) drive for ongoing search for new approaches and learning technologies.

Though being motivated, through an informal discussion and online discussions with course mates and the researcher's own personal reflection, an educator cum course de-signer had the following challenges: (1) fear for or concern of the possible loss of teacher role or full control over the subject; (2) time commitment that designing and administering online activi-ties require which would possibly be added to the staff's already heavy workload; (3) perceived anxieties to cope with acquisition and deployment of new learning technologies; (4) course reforms and transition processes which call for institutional support in providing pedagogic and learning technologies or support from colleagues with technical knowledge; (5) some reservation about the possibility of positive learning impact that the online course would have in comparison with significant amount of time committed (especially for students with time management and attitude problems).

3.1.3 *Reflection through administrator lens*

Challenges or issues that administration needs to address during BL implementation gleaned by the researcher as an academic with administrative responsibilities include (1) institutional support—infra structure, technical support and staff professional development workshops tailored to the specific needs of each faculty; (2) university's recognition of staff's effort working on online or blended courses; (3) allowance for lighter workload to leave time for course transformation; and (4) achieving buy-in from academic staff who may resist to changes possibly either due to lack of awareness of the advantages of using technology in education or their discomfort with technology or their teaching philosophy which values face-to-face interaction and teaching.

3.2 *Adoption or early implementation*

In this stage, the university required 20% of the sub-jects of each program to be transformed into BL on a voluntary basis. To facilitate this process, faculty digital technologists were appointed to provide necessary technical support and consultation while workshops on BL design continue.

The following are the BL adoption tasks that the researcher took during her early imple-mentation stage: (1) working with a Melbourne learning design team and Sarawak teaching team for the BL de-livery of one compulsory subject that international students are required to take, as the researcher was one of few academics who attended the training in the first stage; (2) convening and delivering an undergraduate core communication subject in BL mode designed by a Melbourne convener which used (a) weekly face-to-face and online tutorials posted on Wikis which serves as a platform for students to upload their work and for the lecturer to give feedback, (b) videos online and during face-to-face tutorials, and (c) major authentic assess-ments which require students to use information technologies; (3) BL transformation of three postgraduate subjects that the researcher was teaching which involved redesigning paper-based weekly assessments and projects to become online based assessments and digital or online feed-back and using the flipped classroom whereby recorded lecture slides and short YouTube video clips related to the topic were uploaded for students to go though in advance of the class and class time was used for students to go through hands-on experience to solve real-world problems.

3.2.1 *Reflection through student lens*

Student feedback from both undergraduate and postgraduate subjects were positive. Informal discussions with students taking these subjects highlight the following benefits that students have: (1) learning outcome achievement through real-world problem-based assessments for both groups of students; (2) interactive, collaborative and meaningful learning which took place on Blackboard discussion board and wikis or inside the classroom; and (3) fun learn-ing which motivates students for life-long learning. Students of all types were found to show preference for shorter video clips which enable them to better understand abstract concepts or complicated processes to longer ones.

On the other hand, challenges that students faced in this stage include: (1) managing time to complete reading tasks before coming to class and failure to do so prevented them from active participation in classroom problem-solving activities; (2) technical problems upload-ing assignments or tasks, especially big files, during system downtime or maintenance; (3) technical problems uploading tutorial answers which required international phonetic sym-bols which were not supported by the Blackboard system at that time; and (4) familiarity with online environment, which necessitates the lecturer's consultation or support.

3.2.2 *Reflection through educator lens*

Convening and delivering the undergraduate subject designed by a Melbourne Convener allowed the researcher to have a taste of a real sample of the subject designed in BL mode and to foresee some potential issues and solutions. Working with a teaching team with diverse backgrounds points to the re-searcher that this paradigm shift will be a success in collaboration with other academics with diverse backgrounds.

Redesigning three postgraduate subjects allowed the researcher to apply what she had learnt from the previous stage. Evidence of successful learning reflected through better positive student feedback resulted in the researcher's empowerment and enhanced confidence in deploying learning technologies and drive to seek new and better technologies to keep improving the materials used for the subjects.

However, some issues existing at this stage include: (1) amount of time spent to look for short and comprehensive video clips from different sources to motivate millennial students with shorter attention span and creating activities which students can relate to; (2) redesigning processes which require some expertise in pedagogic practices and learning technologies; and (3) students especially those with family or workplace commitment who did not finish the learning materials in advance of the class. As highlighted previously, the first two challenges can be overcome if the lecturer as the course designer can work with a teaching team rather than working alone.

3.2.3 *Reflection through administrator lens*

The researcher's experience working with the Melbourne learning design team and Sarawak teaching team, the majority of whom are not comfortable with learning technologies allowed the researcher to see the following issues that necessitate institutional attention: (1) capacity-building training needs to be tailored to those with anxiety problems or those who would not like to leave their comfort zone, and to those teaching subjects of different nature to achieve buy-in from all academics; (2) a needs assessment is required to figure out what technical support students need earlier before the delivery of the subject; and (3) arrangements to ensure the redesigned course is compatible with IT infrastructure and network connectivity of the institution and those of the countries or regions students are in.

3.3 *Mature implementation or growth*

As stated earlier, depending on the familiarity with technology, not all academics make full use of Blackboard learning tools though training work-shops have been provided before every semester at Swinburne Sarawak. In addition, the system by which individual academics organize content materials differ and this discrepancy sometime confused students. As such, at this stage, as a university-wide strategy and as a Sarawak consistent approach to BL using Blackboard, a generic Blackboard template was created for use in Sarawak sometime in 2016.

The new user-friendly template enables students to get the information at a click of mouse. It has an organization system that introduces topics that each week covers, the lesson plan which allows students to see what they are expected to learn and do in each week and in what order and provides text-based or digital learning materials. This Sarawak consistent approach to BL is hoped to minimize student's confusion in looking for materials, thus producing optimal learning experience.

In July 2016, a group of academics from 3 faculties were introduced to the new template and trained how to make the best use of Blackboard learning tools for the BL delivery of subjects. In addition, Swinburne Sarawak asked for volunteers to receive the flipped classroom training and the researcher was one among them. These academics were asked to pilot this template in one of the subjects they were teaching in 2016 Semester Two. Semester-end feedback of students taking these subjects was then obtained. Their positive feedback on this trial has led to the campus-wide prescription of this generic blackboard template starting from 2017 Semester 1 and each academic staff is required to use this generic template in at least one of the subjects that they teach. Options of face-to-face workshops and webinars are available to staff to acquire skills to use the prescribed template.

The researcher was one among few academics who tried out the new template. The researcher also volunteered to use the Swinburne's generic BB template in all the postgraduate subjects taught. At this stage, with the suggestion of the trainers, to address the issues of students coming to the class without going through learning materials, the researcher added in some quizzes for students (with some marks allocated as incentive) to interact with learning materials to make activities more meaningful to them.

3.3.1 *Reflection through student lens*

Through observations and informal discussions with students, benefits that students have gained at this stage of Swinburne BL growth include (1) students' satisfaction with the new template, especially those students who had had negative BB experience; and (2) a better understanding of the concepts through short video clips together with text-based learning materials which are enhanced by classroom activities. It is interesting to note that it took time for the researcher's students to get used to the new tem-plate due to their prior familiarity with her organization system in the previous semesters.

3.3.2 *Reflection through educator lens*

The researcher currently is still in in the beginning of her journey towards mature implantation, going through the cycle of redesigning, trying out, evaluating and redesigning. Challenges faced at this stage are more or less the same as those faced in the second stage.

Findings of this study suggest that BL benefits both students and lecturers: student-centered meaningful learning resulting in optimal learning experience and better achievement of learning outcome for the former and empowerment, enhanced confidence and professional development for the latter. On the other hand, time management, familiarity with and ability to use technology are challenges that both groups face. It is the institution support that enables both groups to reap these benefits and overcome challenges. Besides, collaborative course redesign is hoped to help ease the burden of academic in this process.

4 CONCLUSION

This paper argues that a better understanding of academics' attitudes towards and acceptance of BL implementation and challenges faced during different BL implementation stages is significant as it is academics who champion course reform which involves embedding interactive collaborative online and class activities in pedagogy and implementing them.

Using three BL implementation stages by Gra-ham et al. (2013) and self-categorising as an early adopter, through this paper, the researcher has reflected on challenges faced as a student, an educator and administrator at each BL implementation stage.

The significant issues that the academics have had throughout these three stages are revolved around the process of changing their mindset and being open to innovation, making oneself familiar with learning technologies and innovative pedagogic practices, choosing appropriate tools to complement traditional classroom to make learning meaningful to students; and amount of time devoted to these processes in addition to routine academic responsibilities.

To achieve successful BL implementation, institutions need to be fully aware of challenges faced by educators and reasons behind these issues so that ongoing targeted supports which are well aligned with an institutional consistent strategy and infra structure can be provided for the empowerment of academics who spearhead this process. In addition, evaluation data by the researcher as an early adopter, as suggested by Porter & Graham (2016)'s findings, may well convince early majority adopters to confidently participate in institutional BL implementation.

Findings of this preliminary study, however, are based on experience of an individual educator together with other people involved in her journey. As such, a large scale research into this aspect is recommended for a more comprehensible input into BL implementation processes.

REFERENCES

Ahmad M.A. & Schreurs, J. 2012. Constructivism-based Blended Learning in Higher Education. *Ijet* 7(1): 4–9.

Black, E.R., Beck, D., Dawson, K., Jinks, S. & DiPietro, M. 2007. The Outside of the LMS: Considering Implementation and Use in the Adoption of an LMS in Online and Blended Learning Environments. *TechTrends* 51(2): 35–39.

Dias, S.B. & Diniz, J.A. 2014. Towards an Enhanced Learning Management System for Blended Learning in Higher Education Incorporating Distinct Learners' Profile. *Educational Technology & Society* 17: 307–319.

Garrison, D.R. & Vaughan, N.D. 2007. *Blended Learning in Higher Education: Framework, Principles, and Guidelines.* San Francisco, CA: Jossey-Bass.

Gregory, J. & Salmon, G. 2013. Professional Development for Online University Teaching. *Distance Education* 34(3): 256–270.

Linden, K.V.D. 2014. Blended Learning as Transformational Institutional Learning. *New directions for Higher Education*: 75–85. Willey Online Library. doi: 1002/he.20085.

Loch, B. & Borland, R. 2014. The Transition from Traditional Face-to-Face Teaching to Blended Learning—Implications and Challenges from a Mathematics Discipline Perspective. In Hegarty, B., McDonald, J. & Loke, S.K. (eds.) *Rhetoric and Reality: Critical Perspectives on Educational Technology. Proceedings ascilite Dunedin 2014*: 708–712.

O'Byrene, W.I. & Pytash, K.E. 2015. Hybrid and Blended Learning: Modifying Pedagogy across Path, Pace, Time and Place. *Journal of Adolescent and Adult Literacy* 59(2): 137–140. doi10.1002/jaal.463.

Peterson, P.E & Horn, M.B. 2016. The Ideal Blended-learning Combination. *Education Next, Stanford* 16(2).

Porter, W.W. & Graham, C.R. 2016. Institutional Drivers and Barriers to Faculty Adoption of Blended Learning in Higher Education. *British Journal of Education Technology* 47(4): 748–762.

Roger, E.M. 2003. *Diffusion of Innovations.* New York, NY: Free Press.

Salamonson, G. & Lantz, J. 2005. Factors Influencing Nursing Students' Preference for a Hybrid Format Delivery in a Pathophysiology Course. *Nurse Education Today* 25: 9–16.

Salmon, G. 2003. *E-moderating: The Key to Teaching and Learning Online.* London: Kogan Page.

Salmon, G., Gregory, J., Dona, K.L. & Ross, B. 2015. Experiential Online Development for Educators: The Example of the Carpe Diem MOOC. *British Journal of Educational Technology*.

Torrisi-Steele, Geraldine & Drew, S.. 2013. The Literature Landscape of Blended Learning in Higher Education: The Need for Better Understanding of Academic Blended Practice. *International Journal for Academic Development* 18(4): 371–383.

Tucker, B. 2012. The Flipped Classroom: Online Instruction at Home Frees Class Time for Learning. *Education Next* 12(1): 82–83.

Vaughan, N. 2007. 'Perspectives on Blended Learning in Higher Education'. *International Journal on E-Learning* 6(1): 81–94.

ELT in Asia in the Digital Era: Global Citizenship and Identity – Madya et al. (Eds)
© *2018 Taylor & Francis Group, London, ISBN 978-0-8153-7900-3*

The incorporation of Facebook in language pedagogy: Merits, defects, and implications

T.N.T. Dung & L.T.N. Quynh
Ho Chi Minh City University of Economics and Finance, Vietnam

ABSTRACT: Along with the increased emphasis on the 21st-century educational concepts comes the inevitable outdatedness of the traditional 'chalk-and-talk' instruction, and the growing popularity of integrating social networking sites into the teaching-learning process. The current article provides an in-depth discussion on the utility of Facebook in the modern English-as-a-Foreign-Language (EFL) classroom. Facebook has been recognized as a promising tool, with a broad array of user-friendly features, for language teachers to break out of the conventional classroom and provide EFL learners with more authentic teaching approaches, highly interactive environment and flexible timing. A number of certain difficulties may, however, possibly arise, concerning teachers' capacity to integrate English learning tasks into this social virtual world, the informal nature of this website and students' manner. In light of such opportunities and challenges, a number of pedagogical implications are offered to EFL teachers who wish to efficiently exploit Facebook to establish an English learning cyber-community.

1 INTRODUCTION

The new setting of EFL teaching and learning has been characterized by the decline of lecture-based approaches and the infiltration of technological tools. Along with the availability of various modern engines, the recent prevalence of social media sites has substantially appealed to a large number of researchers in language education, e.g. Arnold & Paulus (2010), Terantino & Graf (2011), Wang (2013), Kamnoetsin (2014). As Sebastian & Martinsen (2015) stated, more and more studies have been focused on 'the exploration of social networking communities and their potential to enhance the traditional paradigm of language teaching and learning.'

Even though the information and communication technologies (ICTs) have been widely appreciated in the field of ELT, this cannot always guarantee the positive effects of these modern tools in every classroom. Adopting such a sense, Harrison & Thomas (2009, as cited in Clark & Gruba 2010: 164) indicated that the pedagogical assumptions behind the application of social networking sites (SNSs) to learn foreign languages have been called into question. From the careful examination of the existing relevant literature and the descriptive data gained from students' questionnaire responses, this paper, therefore, aims to identify the appreciable values as well as defective features related to the employment of a particular social networking site, i.e. Facebook, in language classrooms. Constructive suggestions in light of the findings are also put forward as references for interested practitioners.

In order for these research objectives to be well achieved, three primary questions are accordingly formulated to guide this study:

1. How beneficial is the employment of Facebook in the ELT domain?
2. What are the downsides of utilizing Facebook in language education?
3. In what way can EFL teachers optimize the application of Facebook-based activities in their language teaching practice?

2 FACEBOOK'S UTILITY IN FOREIGN LANGUAGE EDUCATION

2.1 *Essential conceptions*

The use of such SNSs as Facebook has its solid grounds in important conceptual frameworks and bears a strong association with some related notions.

The curriculum for Net generation of students are derived from social and learner-centered views of learning, such as the sociocultural theory initiated by Vygotsky (Terantino & Graf 2011). According to Scott & Palinesar (2013), the sociocultural ideology 'has been taken into consideration in the design of online distance education technologies' because digital tools help to create multimodal literacy, new skills and habits of mind. Also underlying the educational use of SNSs is Jerome Bruner's constructivism, which describes both of the learners' mental schemes in their cognitive growth (Brooks & Brooks 1999) and the social nature of learning through the scaffolding process.

In addition, young generation has nowadays become highly aware of the magnitude of being digitally literate, i.e. being able to 'participate in a range of critical and creative practices that involve understanding, sharing, and creating meaning with different kinds of technology and media' (Hague 2010). The second relevant key term is computer-mediated communication (CMC). According to Sumakul's (2014) synthesis from other previous studies, CMC serves as 'a good tool in language learning' by providing learners with 'an effective and fun way in learning English.'

2.2 *Existing studies*

According to a statistical report after the first quarter of 2016, the total number of monthly active Facebookers already reached over 1.6 billion, with an increase of 15% year-over-year (Facebook 2016), revealing a large picture of Facebook as one of the most commonly-used SNSs. The effectiveness of Facebook in teaching English as a foreign language has been widely recognized upon the general findings that Facebook allows students to receive information instantaneously, develop their competence through exposure to fellow's posts, and have chances for more student-centered language production as well as EFL communicative practice.

In other relevant educational areas, English-for-Specific-Purposes learners can, for example, improve their professional knowledge via the combination of in-class instruction and peer assessment on Facebook (Shih 2013). The effects of applying Facebook as a strategy training tool was also explicated by Alias, Manan, Yusof, & Pandian (2012), who confirmed the participants' approval of Facebook Notes for promoting the use of language learning strategy among college undergraduates. Sebastian & Martinsen (2015) also synthesized various valuhues related to Facebook group, i.e. fostering students' genuine contributions as well as maintaining the connection between the virtual and face-to-face spaces. Those studies, just to name a few, can be considered concrete evidence for the existent qualities of Facebook in real-life education.

3 ADVANTAGEOUS ASPECTS

As an exemplar of the 21st-century social networks, Facebook can be utilized to promote both learner autonomy (Promnitz-Hayashi 2011) and cooperative learning by allowing individuals to freely share knowledge and interact with others (Shih 2013) with low stress and high engagement (Kamnoetsin 2014). It allows the users to easily upload, observe, share, comment on statuses, documents, photos or videos, and enlarge their social contacts as well. For ELT theorists and practitioners, this SNS is hence able to create the expressive capacity for students to work in a community of practice, where they can construct new knowledge and improve their language skills via the comments from authentic audience (Suthiwartnarueput & Wasanasomsithi 2012) and teachers' necessary facilitation.

In addition to this dynamic delivery of feedback, Facebook also provides an engaging format for informal conversations in the target language, which stimulates students' linguistic production and gives them great access to authentic materials (Terantino & Graf 2011). Furthermore, as the short time of in-class instructions and textbook practice can never suffice, the provision of 'additional venues for interaction' is then especially essential for EFL learning (Arnold & Paulus 2010: 189), which perfectly explains the recent emergence of Facebook-based activities for, in Sebastian & Martinsen's (2015) words, breaking down 'the physical barriers of the traditional classroom.' From the affective angle, activities on Facebook can support EFL learners with low proficiency by giving them more comfort to take part in the lesson and forge closer relationships with fellow students (Promnitz-Hayashi 2011).

Conclusively, Facebook provides 'a target-language-friendly interface' in a format familiar to students, as well as encourages 'multi-dimensional conversation, both among students and between students and the instructor', allowing for a richer and more engaging learning experience (Terantino & Graf 2011).

4 ADVERSE EFFECTS

As Facebook is not originally designed to be an educational tool, it is completely understandable to have a few critical remarks towards the incorporation of Facebook in language classrooms.

One of the most recognizable drawbacks discussed by many researchers is relentless distractors crowding on the site's interface. Some Facebook features, like inbox messages or newsfeed notifications, even contribute to students' inability to concentrate on their academic tasks (Yunus et al. 2012, as cited in Kamnoetsin 2014: 35). Moreover, the possibility of students' improper cyber-behavior is not to be overlooked. Chartrand (2012) brought up the issue of privacy infringement as students may use their English and get to talk openly about their own and others' personal affairs (Terantino & Graf 2011).

Even though all of those obstacles are just relative enough not to prevent students' participation in learning activities on Facebook, it is still apparent that making the implementation of ICTs in general, and Facebook in particular, academically beneficial is by no means a simple task for both language instructors and learners.

5 METHODOLOGY & ANALYSIS

5.1 *Research design*

The design for this study is primarily descriptive, adopting a cross-sectional survey to collect data. This descriptive survey approach lends itself well to the research questions, which are to unveil the pros and cons of Facebook-based activities from students' perspectives. Data was gathered from the participants, basing on their previous and current experience without any experiments involved.

5.2 *Participants and context*

The target population for this study was all EFL learners. However, given the actual research context, purposive sampling was applied in order for the researchers to effectively acquire their targeted sample. In fact, the sample comprises 74 Facebook users who were at the time of the survey all English majors at Ho Chi Minh City University of Education. Along with the fact that the respondents range from freshmen to seniors, all survey respondents have already experienced a significant number of different English classes and instructed by different lecturers as well. This makes replies from the sample more varied and better representative of the target population.

5.3 Research instrument

The instrument employed in this study was a researcher-designed questionnaire which was created and administered online using Google Forms, a free tool to establish user-friendly Web-based surveys. Distinctive features of this internet-mediated data gathering device include flexible submission time, accessible online data storage, and automatic formation of statistical summary.

The survey consists of 13 questions grouped into three sections A, B and C, namely 'General Information', 'Your own Facebook activities', and 'Others' Facebook activities relevant to English teaching and learning' respectively. More specifically, the questionnaire includes 11 multiple-choice items and 2 questions designed on the Likert scale, which attempts to ascertain the respondents' opinions on the issue under current investigation.

5.4 Data collection and analysis

The researchers first solicited volunteers for their participation in the survey questionnaire. A request and an introduction of the study, i.e. the purpose and its process, was made known to the potential respondents. They were then provided with a link leading to the secure online questionnaire for them to complete and submit by the stated deadline. The web-based survey was opened on June 25th and closed on July 3rd, 2017. Thanks to the automatic conveniences of Google Forms, all of the responses were saved for later analysis and reference.

Once the survey was officially closed, the researchers then proceeded to the analysis of the descriptive data obtained from 74 responses to the online questionnaire. The values of mean and percentage were mostly exploited for more insight into the participants' viewpoint toward the reality of how Facebook has been used in language pedagogy, the effectiveness of particular Facebook-based activities, as well as their further expectations. Noticeable statistics was then taken to be, in the next part, visually described in form of bar charts.

6 OUTSTANDING FINDINGS

From the investigation into the questionnaire items which relevantly address the three major issues stated in the research questions, this current section goes to present the prominent revelations from this study. As previously discussed, Facebook offers a broad array of interactive activities which are likely to be of certain value for EFL learners. Figure 1 below demonstrates some concrete Facebook acts related to the language learning process.

Overall, four out of seven activities surveyed, namely (a), (d), (e), and (g), were widely exploited among the surveyed Facebook users. Obviously, the top popular Facebook acts were reading English posts and sharing English videos. Meanwhile, the other two activities (a and g), which involves producing oral and written language, attracted well over half of the

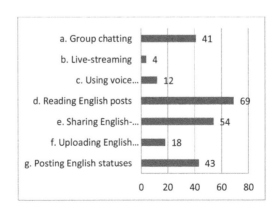

Figure 1. Students' current habit of using English-learning Facebook activities (Question B3).

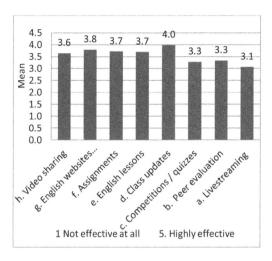

Figure 2.   Levels of effectiveness of some Facebook-based activities (Question C4).

participants each. These figures indicate that activities on SNSs relating to receptive skills, engaged more students than those of productive ones.

However, Facebook is not without problems. The survey result reveals that being distracted by various features on Facebook was regarded the greatest downside. Lack of facilities, however, did not appear to bother many participants.

When asked to evaluate the efficiency of different English-related practices done by their English teachers on Facebook, the majority of participants reported being positively impressed. It is encouraging to note that the popular activities usually applied by EFL teachers received positive feedback as the means are all above 3.0. The top effective act went to 'Announcing class' activities and upcoming events'. Other well-managed Facebook activities were the items e, f, g and h. However, more active and interactive methods, particularly Livestreaming English lessons, Organizing English contests along with Peer evaluation, did not gain the popularity they should deserve, with the means just hovering around 3.0.

Also shown in the questionnaire, nearly fifty out of seventy-four respondents welcomed the idea that teachers should continue to share more useful English resources for self-study. Interestingly, although having humble experience with such activities, nearly half of the respondents would like more English competitions to be organized. Coming as little surprise, merely 23 learners wanted to receive extra homework on this SNS.

In general, the vast majority of subjects (95%) advocated the further exploitation of Facebook's functions for English learning purposes, implying an eager embrace from English learners to Facebook as a beneficial tool in the domain of EFL education.

7   PEDAGOGICAL RECOMMENDATIONS

It is worth raising some concerns for language teachers to take into account before packing Facebook into his suitcase for innovative EFL teaching experiences. The first worry of all is that a large portion of users might easily be distracted by what is shown on the user interface. What is more, learners' personal identity and vulnerability to criticism should also be considered so that poor achievers and socially awkward students could feel comfortable demonstrating their language use. Another concern is students' unwillingness to accomplish assignments given online even though they give them the sense of purpose to join Facebook activities as well as guidelines and self-study materials supplied online by teachers. Last but not least, while Facebook is initially known as a means of communication, the practice of oral English on this SNS is being downplayed and shunned.

Based upon the awareness of what has been so far presented, this section aims to provide some concrete implications to ELT practitioners. For starters, language teachers can easily create a Facebook group as a convenient medium for making 'a connection with students about assignments, upcoming events, useful links, and samples of work (Suthiwartnarueput & Wasanasomsithi 2012). Setting themselves as administrators, teachers are completely able to control the participation of group members, announce course-related new updates, share meaningful authentic materials, provide students with opportune assistance via instant messaging, and so on. ELT practitioners, can also organize mini workshops and then livestream them on Facebook. Moreover, as there are different characteristics and requirements involved in different teaching areas, Facebook's specific implications also vary accordingly.

7.1 Receptive skills

Dealing with such EFL skills as Reading or Listening, teachers can, for example, post necessary materials or extra exercises as a link to another page or a compressed file for direct download. The function of 'comment' also comes to work when students request and then receive further elaboration on some points in the answer key. Particularly for the Listening skill, language teachers can turn Facebook into a place for their students' extensive practice by sharing videos. To exploit this kind of practice to the fullest, a few 'after-you-watch' tasks can also be uploaded along, with a view to checking comprehension and ensuring students' attentiveness in practicing Listening on the social networking environment.

7.2 Productive skills

The utilization of Facebook for Speaking and Writing is of greater diversity. This social network can be exploited as a platform for task submission since it allows written assignments or audio recordings to be posted directly through statuses or shared links, along with the support of 'hashtag' tool for teachers to easily control their students' fulfilment of homework. Thanks to Facebook, the exchange of feedback has also become more convenient and multidirectional. Specifically, not only the instructor but also other classmates and social friends of the learner can now evaluate one another hitting 'like' button, sharing interesting well-written statuses, commenting, or even sending private inbox messages. In order to boost learners' motivation further, EFL teachers can additionally award some bonuses to students whose academic posts receive the greatest number of 'likes' or 'shares', or alternatively to those who give comments of highest lexical and grammatical quality to a certain study-related status. However, the use of bonuses should be cleverly considered so that the negative competition between classmates is reduced to the minimum.

8 CONCLUSION

From both conceptual and experiential perspectives, the current article has shed some light on both the challenging aspects and tremendous opportunities related to the application of Facebook as a facilitative instrument in the 21st century language classroom. Since social networks are not born to be educational by nature, Facebook may distract learners with continuous newsfeed notifications or inbox messages. Psychologically, the invisible teacher-student distance can be much shortened via friendly online environment, which requires class members' awareness of cyber-manner in order for private zones not to be violated. By no means can such controversies negate the meritorious qualities involved in the use of this SNS in language teaching. In fact, the interactive design of this social network can turn the academic process into an enjoyable experience via the potential construction of an online learning community where information, feedback and support can be conveniently shared among the collaborative members.

Considering those pros and cons, Facebook, have still functioned as a motivation-provoking platform for ELT in global contexts. Providing that language teachers judiciously consider and properly employ the wide-ranging implications related to this SNS, the injection of Facebook-based elements into the language education arena will be absolutely valuable, especially when the conventional teaching paradigm cannot guarantee the full satisfaction of learners' needs, and Facebook has increasingly infiltrated the entertaining and academic life of digital generations.

REFERENCES

Alias, A.A., Manan, N.A.A., Yusof, J. & Pandian, A. 2012. The use of Facebook as Language Learning Strategy (LLS) training tool on college students' LLS use and academic writing performance. *Procedia—Social and Behavioral Sciences* 67(2012): 36–48.

Arnold, N. & Paulus, T. 2010. Using a social networking site for experiential learning: Appropriating, lurking, modeling and community building. *Internet and Higher Education* 13(2010): 188–196.

Brooks, M.G. & Brooks, J.G. 1999. The courage to be constructivist. *Educational Leadership: The Constructivist Classroom* 57(3): 18–24.

Chartrand, R. 2012. Social networking for language learners: creating meaningful output with web 2.0 tools. *Knowledge Management & E-Learning: An International Journal* 4(1): 97–101.

Clark, C. & Gruba, P. 2010. The use of social networking sites for foreign language learning: An autoethnographic study of *Livemocha*. In C.H. Steel, M.J. Keppell, P. Gerbic & S. Housego (Eds.), *Curriculum, technology & transformation for an unknown future. Proceedings ascilite Sydney 2010* (164–173). Retrieved from http://ascilite.org.au/conferences/sydney10/procs/Cclark-full.pdf.

Facebook, Inc. April, 2016. *Facebook reports first quarter 2016 results and announces proposal for new class of stock*. Retrieved April 29, 2016, from http://www.prnewswire.com/news-releases/facebook-reports-first-quarter-2016-results-and-announces-proposal-for-new-class-of-stock-300258749.html.

Hague, C. 2010. *"It's not chalk and talk anymore": School approaches to developing students' digital literacy*. Bristol: Futurelab.

Kamnoetsin, T. 2014. Social media use: A critical analysis of Facebook's impact on collegiate EFL students' English writing in Thailand (Doctoral Dissertation, Seton Hall University, 2014). *Seton Hall University Dissertations and Theses (ETDs)*, Paper 2059.

Promnitz-Hayashi, L. 2011. A learning success story using Facebook. *Studies in Self-Access Learning Journal* 2(4): 309–316.

Scott, S. & Palincsar, A. 2013. *Sociocultural theory*. Retrieved June 20, 2016, from http://www.education.com/reference/article/sociocultural-theory/.

Sebastian, P.L. & Martinsen, R.A. 2015. Facebook as a virtual learning space to connect multiple language classrooms. *The IALLT Journal* 45(1): 44–69.

Shih, R. 2013. Effect of using Facebook to assist English for Business Communication course instruction. *The Turkish Online Journal of Educational Technology* 12(1): 52–59.

Sumakul, D.T. 2014. Facebook Group in An EFL Grammar Classroom. In X. Deng & R. Seow (Eds.), *Alternative Pedagogies in the English Language and Communication Classroom*: 69–75. Singapore: Center for English Language Communication, NUS.

Suthiwartnarueput, T. & Wasanasomsithi, P. 2012. Effects of using Facebook as a medium for discussions of English grammar and writing of low-intermediate EFL students. *Electronic Journal of Foreign Language Teaching* 9(2): 194–214.

Terantino, J. & Graf, K. 2011. In the classroom: Using Facebook in the language classroom as part of the net generation curriculum. *The Language Educator*. Retrieved April 15, 2016, from https://www.actfl.org/sites/default/files/pdfs/TLEsamples/TLE_Nov11_Article.pdf.

Wang, S. 2013. Intermediate-Level Chinese language learner's social communication in Chinese on Facebook: A mixed methods study (Doctoral Dissertation, University of South Florida, 2013). *Graduate Theses and Dissertations*. Retrieved April 15, 2016, from https://scholarcommons.usf.edu/etd/4606.

ELT in Asia in the Digital Era: Global Citizenship and Identity – Madya et al. (Eds)
© *2018 Taylor & Francis Group, London, ISBN 978-0-8153-7900-3*

Reading enjoyment in the digital age: How does it differ by parents' education, self-expected education, and socio-economic status?

N.H.P.S. Putro
Yogyakarta State University, Yogyakarta, Indonesia

J. Lee
The University of New South Wales, Sydney, Australia

ABSTRACT: While reading enjoyment has been found to differ by gender and major, little is known about how students' enjoyment in reading across multiple-modality differs by their parents' education, self-expectation of highest education attainment, and socio-economic status (SES). This study aims to explore how undergraduate students of different parents' education background, self-expectation of highest education, and family SES enjoy reading from different modalities or modes. The respondents in this study were 993 undergraduate students in an Indonesian university. Exploratory factor analysis and confirmatory factor analyses were used to examine the structure of reading enjoyment. Subsequently, *t-tests* and Anova were conducted to find out if there are differences in student's enjoyment by their parents' education, self-expectation of highest education attainment, and Socio-Economic Status (SES). An interesting pattern of relationships emerged with respect to father's education, student's self-expectation of their highest education, and SES. The paper is concluded with implications for future research on the psychological meaning of reading enjoyment.

1 INTRODUCTION

Recent studies show that reading online has been extensively adopted as an alternative mode of reading instead of reading in print settings (Bawden 2008, Bibby et al. 2009, Buzzetto-More, Guy & Elobaid 2007, Leu et al. 2004). Many people in developed nations even consider reading in digital environments as the main method of reading (Martin 2008, Woody et al. 2010). It has also been well documented that social media have become one of the most important vehicles for communication as well as for sharing news and academic information among today's youth (Junco 2012, Kirschner & Karpinski 2010).

As multimodal literacy becomes more widespread (Walsh 2010), a great deal of previous research into reading enjoyment has focused on how the reading enjoyment across multiple modality differs by gender and/or major of study. These studies have revealed how female students in general have better reading attitude and habits than their male counterparts (e.g., Clark 2012, Clark & Akerman 2006, Clark & Foster 2005, Clark & Rumbold 2006, Gambell & Hunter 2000, NCES 2003, Stokmans 1999) and how students majoring in education were likely to report being less enthusiastic about reading than students majoring in other fields (e.g., Applegate & Applegate 2004, Chen 2007, Jeffres & Atkin 1996, Karim & Hasan 2007, Liu 2006).

While reading enjoyment has been found to differ by gender and major, little is known about how students' enjoyment in reading across multiple-modality differs by their parents' education, self-expectation of highest education attainment, and socio-economic status (SES). A study investigating this gap is important since extant studies suggest that reading attitude may also be related to parents' education (e.g., Chen 2007, Chen et al. 2011), self-expectation of highest education attainment (e.g., Mullen et al. 2003), and socio-economic status (e.g., Chall & Jacobs 2003, Clark & Akerman 2006). Therefore, the present study aims to explore how undergraduate students of different parents' education background, self-expectation of highest education, and family SES enjoy reading from different modalities or modes.

2   DIFFERENT TYPES OF READING MODES IN THE DIGITAL AGE

A large and growing body of literature has well documented that students read from two main modes, i.e., reading in print settings and reading in online or digital environments (Boyd & Ellison 2008, Coiro 2011, Martin 2008, McKenna et al. 2012). In these studies, reading in print settings, has been associated with reading of any types of texts that are printed on paper (Coiro 2011). These texts range from short sentences to long texts presented in the non-digital format (Conradi et al. 2013, Foltz 1992, 1996, McKenna et al. 2012) and reveal information in a linear format (Foltz 1992, 1996, Kim & Jung 2010, Rockinson-Szapkiw et al. 2013). Reading online, on the contrary, is associated with non-linear screen-based reading of texts that are available (e.g., online newspapers) or obtained (e.g., e-books) through the Internet (Coiro 2011, Park & Kim 2011, Sandberg 2011). The texts range from those utilizing closed-ended hypertexts to those of a more complex, open-ended information system involving hyperlinks and hypermedia (Coiro & Dobler 2007, Hill & Hannafin 1997).

In addition to reading in print and reading online, current literature also indicates that social media or social network site is another important mode of reading that current young generation increasingly adopt. A social network site has been defined as a web-based service that allows individuals to create a particular profile within a bounded system whereby people share a list of other users with whom they are connected and exchange information with others within the bounded system (Boyd & Ellison 2008: 211).

3   READING BY GENDER, AGE, AND MAJOR OF STUDY

Just as the three modes of reading have been consecutively and continuously adopted by current young generation in this digital age, a great deal of recent studies has focused on how reading from the three modes of reading differs by several contextual correlates. Most of these studies seem to be acknowledging gender, age, and major of studies as important correlates of enjoyment in reading.

With respect to gender, the majority of these studies consistently show that female students possess better reading attitude and habits than their male counterparts (Clark 2012, Clark & Akerman 2006, Clark & Foster 2005, Clark & Rumbold 2006, Gambell & Hunter 2000, NCES 2003, Stokmans, 1999). Clark & Burke (2012), for instance, reported that female students enjoyed reading more than male students and had a more positive reading attitude. The gap became wider with the students' year level. Similarly, studies in the US by McKenna et al. in 2012 found that female students showed better attitude in reading from printed materials while male students reported better attitude in reading from online sources. (McKenna et al. 2012).

Regarding students age, studies on students' reading enjoyment across different age groups have revealed inconsistent results. Much of the research on school-aged students suggests that reading attitude typically worsens over time (e.g., Chall & Jacobs 2003, McKenna et al. 1995, Sainsbury & Schagen 2004) In contrast, findings from studies where age is considered isomorphic to year level confirm the trend for undergraduate students with more seniority to develop better reading attitude than their younger counterparts (e.g., Chen 2007, Gallik 1999).

In the case of major of study, college students' reading interest has been shown to vary widely according to the majors they are studying. Students majoring in education and social studies were likely to report being less enthusiastic about reading than students majoring in other fields (e.g., Chen 2007, Jeffres & Atkin 1996, Karim & Hasan 2007, Liu 2006). Other research showed that students majoring in the humanities and arts tended to read classics and fantasy novels more than students majoring in other fields (e.g., Gilbert & Fister 2011) and that students majoring in human science had better reading attitude than those majoring in information and communication technology (e.g., Karim & Hasan 2007).

4 PARENTS' EDUCATION BACKGROUND, SELF-EXPECTATION OF HIGHEST EDUCATIONAL ATTAINMENT, AND FAMILY SES AS IMPORTANT CORRELATES OF STUDENTS' READING ENJOYMENT

While the majority of studies have investigated how reading across multiple modes differs by gender, age, and major of study, very little was found in the literature on how reading enjoyment differs by parents' education background, self-expectation of highest educational attainment, and family SES. Prior studies have noted the importance of these contextual correlates of reading enjoyment.

Parents' educational background is one of the correlates of reading enjoyment and has been claimed to indirectly relate to reading achievement (e.g., Chen 2007, Chen et al. 2011). Parents with lower educational levels, especially those with no university education, are more likely to live in poverty and have higher unemployment rates. These parents are also found to be less likely to read to their children when they are young, which in turn influences later reading enjoyment. Thus, college students of parents with higher education levels were likely to enjoy reading more than those of parents with lower educational background (Chen 2007). In the same vein, Chen et al. (2011) found that the level of parents' education and the parents' reading attitudes were related to the reading attainment of fourth-grade students in Taiwan.

With respect to students' self-expectation of highest educational attainment, the literature review failed to identify any data on the association between reading enjoyment and self-expected education. Studies by Mullen et al. (2003) and Stolzenberg (1994), however, indicated that educational continuation after college is strongly related to students' academic achievement during their bachelor degree (GPA) and parents' education level. Given the significant role of reading enjoyment in students' academic attainment as reflected in their GPA (e.g., De Naeghel et al. 2012, Hughes-Hassell & Rodge 2007), it is possible to argue that undergraduate students' self-expectation of highest educational attainment is also related to their reading enjoyment.

Considering family SES, little research to date has investigated the correlation between undergraduate students' reading enjoyment and SES. As yet, it has mostly been conducted with samples of elementary, middle or high school students (e.g., Baker & Scher 2002, Kirsch et al. 2002). Young learners from lower SES were reported to read less for enjoyment than those from higher SES (Clark & Akerman, 2006), especially from fourth grade onward (Chall & Jacobs 2003). For instance, a study by Chall & Jacobs (2003) showed that, in general, learners from higher SES families tend to score significantly higher on reading tests than learners from lower SES families. These gaps become larger with age. This is due to the fact that low SES students are likely to be further delayed as they enter low quality schools which do not adequately support students to improve their enjoyment in reading. Thus, it is expected that undergraduate students coming from low family SES also possess lower reading enjoyment than those from higher family SES.

Together, these studies provide evidence that the reading enjoyment of undergraduate students is significantly related to the parents' educational background, self-expectation of educational attainment, and family SES. However, it is not known whether students' enjoyment in reading from different modes differ by these variables. Do students expecting to pursue a PhD degree, for instance, enjoy reading online more than their peers wishing to pursue a master degree? This study aims to explore this lacuna.

5 METHOD

5.1 *Participants*

This study's participants were undergraduate students in an Indonesian university. A total of 993 undergraduate students volunteered to participate in the study. The survey data was collected from them between the 17th of August and the 16th of November in 2014. Parents' educational backgrounds were divided into mother and father's education background, each has five categories, i.e., *(1) No school; (2) Primary School; (3) Junior high school; (4) Senior high school;,* and *(5) University.* About 31% of the participants' mothers and 36% of the participants' fathers had university graduates. Self-expectation of highest education has three categories, i.e., *(1) Finishing university; (2) Master degree after university;* and *(3) PhD degree.* About 39.7% of the students were expecting to pursue a master degree and 35.6% were expecting to pursue a PhD degree. Family SES has four categories, namely *(a) Low-income: US$1,035/year or less (n = 259, 26.1%); (b) Lower middle-income: US$1,036 to $4,085/year (n = 490, 49.3%); (c) Upper middle-income: US$4,086 to $12,615/year (n = 240, 24.2%);* and *(d) High-income: US$12,616/year or more (n = 4, 0.4%).*

5.2 *Measures/variables*

A total of forty six of the reading enjoyment scale were developed for this study. The survey items were written in a way that includes a particular reading mode. The survey respondents were asked to rate their enjoyment in reading in three different formats, i.e., reading in print settings, reading online, and reading through social media. All items were measured on a 5-points response categories, ranging from "*Strongly Disagree*" (1) to "*Strongly Agree*" (5) with the middle point of "*Neither Disagree nor Agree*" (3).

5.3 *Statistical analysis*

The main analyses of the present study were exploratory factor analysis (EFA), confirmatory factor analysis (CFA), and analysis of variance (ANOVA). In many runs of EFAs we tried to reduce the items that showed the standardized factor loadings lower than .50 to select the items that have strong relationships to the corresponding factors. Then, CFA was used to confirm the measurement model(s) suggested by the EFA and to further investigate a potential hierarchical structure of the reading interest dimensions. *Mplus* version 7.2 (Muthén & Muthén 1998–2012) was used for both the EFA and CFA results reported in this study. The maximum likelihood estimation with robust standard errors (MLR) was used to adjust for non-normality of the survey responses of the data, as suggested in Bentler (2005). As the model fit indices, the Comparative Fit Index (CFI > .90), Tucker-Lewis index (TLI > 0.90), Root Mean Square Error of Approximation (RMSEA < 0.05), and Standardized Root Mean Square Residual (SRMR < 0.05) were used to indicate a good model fit (criteria cut-off scores indicated, also see Byrne (2006)). In addition, a ratio of 1/3 or less between the degrees of freedom (*df*) and chi-square statistics (x^2) was used as an acceptable model fit criterion (see Wang and Wang (2012)) instead of the significance of x^2.

We also performed analysis of variance (ANOVA) tests to examine the mean difference by sub-groups. ANOVA tests are used to compare the mean scores between more than two groups. In the present study, the group differences were examined by: (a) parents' education background (i.e., mother and father's education); (b) self-expectation of highest educational attainment, and (c) family SES. These analyses were performed to provide an understanding of how students' reading interest differs by the student's characteristics. The results of the post-hoc analysis were also used to examine how the scores in the reading enjoyment differed by which groups.

6   RESULTS

6.1   *Nature of reading enjoyment*

Many runs of exploratory factor analysis led to the final set of 9 items which converged into three factors. This 3-factor model yielded an excellent fit to the observed data in the final EFA run ($x^2 = 6.59$, df = 12, $x^2/df = 0.6$, RMSEA = 0.00, SRMR = 0.01, CFI = 0.99, and TLI = 0.99). Similarly, confirmatory factor analysis (CFA) showed that the 3-factor model yielded a very good fit ($x^2 = 27.50$, df = 24, $x^2/df = 1.15$, RMSEA = 0.01, SRMR = 0.02, CFI = 0.99, and TLI = 0.99). The standardised factor loadings of the CFA results are presented in Table 1, together with the Cronbach's α of each factor.

The first factor represents enjoyment of reading printed materials. It is about good feelings, happiness, and the pleasure the students experience from reading in print mode. All three items show high loadings on this factor, ranging from 0.65 to 0.84. The Cronbach's α = 0.80 is also reasonably high. The second factor is labelled as enjoyment in online reading. Key terms for this factor include "favourite activities" and "feeling good", and "try to find time to read". Substantial factor loadings were shown in the three items, ranging from 0.53 to 0.85. The Cronbach's α = 0.82 of this scale is also reasonably good. The last factor is interpreted as enjoyment in social media reading. Key terms are "favourite activities" "reading for hours", and "enjoy". The items' factor loadings were all substantial, ranging from 0.65 to 0.84. It also shows a reasonably good internal consistency with the Cronbach's α = 0.76.

6.2   *Analysis of relationship—differences by father's educational background*

The ANOVA tests suggest that there is no relationship between father's education background and the students' enjoyment in reading in print settings. However, a significant difference in

Table 1.   Confirmatory factor analysis on reading enjoyment.

Item	Factor 1	2	3	Cronbach's α
1. I enjoy reading in print settings.	0.84			0.80
2. Reading in print settings makes me feel good.	0.76			
3. I feel happy if I receive a book as a present.	0.65			
4. Reading online is one of my favourite activities.		0.85		0.82
5. Reading online makes me feel good.		0.79		
6. I always try to find time to read online for enjoyment.		0.53		
7. Reading from social media sites is one of my favourite activities (e.g. Facebook, WhatsApp).			0.84	0.76
8. I enjoy reading through social media sties.			0.67	
9. Once I read social media sites (e.g. Facebook, WhatsApp), I keep reading for hours.			0.65	

Table 2.   One-way ANOVA of the reading enjoyment by Father's education.

		Sum of squares	df	Mean square	F	Sig.
Enjoyment in online reading	Between Groups	11.90	5	2.38	3.50	0.00
	Within Groups	671.39	987	0.68		
	Total	683.29	992			
Enjoyment in social media reading	Between Groups	5.02	5	1.00	2.48	0.03
	Within Groups	400.23	987	.41		
	Total	405.25	992			

enjoyment in online reading was found when analysed by father's education ($F[5, 987] = 3.50, p = 0.00, \eta^2 = 0.02$). Higher levels of enjoyment in online reading were also reported among students of fathers with university education ($M = 0.10, SD = 0.83$) compared to students of fathers with primary school education ($M = -0.12, SD = 0.85$) or no schooling ($M = -0.59, SD = 0.84$).

The omnibus F-test also showed a significant difference in enjoyment in social media reading when analysed by father's education ($F[5, 987] = 2.48, p = 0.03, \eta^2 = 0.01$). Students of fathers with university education reported higher levels of enjoyment in social media reading ($M = 0.07, SD = 0.62$) compared to the students of fathers with junior high school education ($M = -0.15, SD = 0.63$).

6.3   Analysis of relationship—differences by mother's educational background

The results from ANOVA tests on the reading enjoyment by mother's education showed no significant relationship between mother's education and the enjoyment the undergraduate students get from reading in print settings, reading online and social media reading.

6.4   Analysis of relationship—differences by self-expectation of highest educational attainment

Enjoyment in reading in print settings differed significantly when analysed by students' self-expectation of their educational attainment level ($F[3, 989] = 11.39, p = 0.00, \eta^2 = 0.03$). Students wishing to pursue a Ph.D. degree ($M = 0.10, SD = 0.71$) and students expecting to do a Master's degree ($M = 0.04, SD = 0.63$) reported higher levels of reading enjoyment in print settings compared to students expecting to finish an undergraduate degree and not pursing any further schooling ($M = -0.21, SD = 0.69$). There was no difference between students wishing to pursue a Ph.D. and students expecting to do a Master's degree ($p = 0.58$). Interestingly, there is no significant relationship between student's enjoyment in digital reading (online and social media) and their self-expectation of highest educational attainment.

6.5   Analysis of relationship—differences by family SES

ANOVA results revealed a significant difference in students' reported enjoyment in online reading when analysed by SES ($F[3, 989] = 3.76, p = 0.01, \eta^2 = 0.01$). Students from the upper

Table 3.   One-way ANOVA of the reading enjoyment by students' self-expectation of highest educational attainment.

		Sum of squares	df	Mean square	F	Sig.
Enjoyment in reading in print settings	Between Groups	15.64	3	5.21	11.39	0.00
	Within Groups	452.81	989	0.46		
	Total	468.45	992			

Table 4.   One-way ANOVA of the reading enjoyment by Socioeconomic Status (SES).

		Sum of squares	df	Mean square	F	Sig.
Enjoyment in online reading	Between Groups	7.70	3	2.57	3.76	0.01
	Within Groups	675.59	989	0.68		
	Total	683.29	992			
Enjoyment in social media reading	Between Groups	5.41	3	1.80	4.46	0.00
	Within Groups	399.84	989	0.40		
	Total	405.25	992			

middle-income category reported higher levels of enjoyment in reading online ($M = 0.10$, $SD = 0.81$) compared to students from the low-income category ($M = -0.14$, $SD = 0.83$). No other group differences were observed with respect to enjoyment in online reading by SES.

7 DISCUSSION

The results from ANOVA tests were somewhat consistent with the idea that enjoyment in reading from multiple modes was perceived differently by undergraduate students. In the case of reading online and reading through social media, the results reflected the relationship between fathers' education level and enjoyment in digital reading. This finding is consistent with the findings of Hargittai (2010), who found a positive relationship between father's education level and students' Internet use; that is, students of father's with college education were found to have better digital and virtual skills than others. One possible explanation for this is that fathers have an important role in reading and other literacy-related activities (Clark 2009). Fathers with university education have been found to play an important role in encouraging students to get the most from online resources and social media, particularly by developing new media skills and technological fluency (Barron et al. 2009). They also provide motivation and intellectual stimulation to their children to read (Nicholas & Fletcher 2011), for instance by supplying facilities (e.g., PC or laptop) and access to online resources and social media at home.

In addition to father's education, family SES also turned out to be a significant correlate of undergraduate students' enjoyment in both reading online and social media reading. This finding is in line with previous studies claiming that use of Internet and social network sites is associated with SES; that is, young adults from high SES families are likely to derive more benefit from accessing Internet for both reading online and social media sites such as *Facebook* (Brooks et al. 2011, Ellison et al. 2007, Perrin 2015, Valenzuela et al. 2009). This result may be partly explained by the fact that access to the Internet requires users to purchase computer hardware and software, to have fast and reliable Internet connectivity and to pay for data usage. Thus, students from high SES family backgrounds are likely to have more access to the internet. This raises important equity considerations if students from low-income families are to obtain the benefits that social media provide in relation, for instance, to information search and the opportunity to exchange course-related ideas with friends.

While enjoyment in reading online and social media reading is related to both fathers' education and family SES, the results from ANOVA tests revealed that enjoyment in reading in print settings is only related to self-expectation of highest education attainment. This indicates enjoyment in reading in print is significantly related to education-related variable. One possible explanation for this finding is that reading in print is a preferable format when in-depth comprehension is the objective (Liu 2005; Mangen et al. 2013, Tanner 2014). This in-depth comprehension is likely needed for learning purposes. Reading in print settings is also believed to be more conducive to human learning as people are generally more familiar with print than online reading sources (Ackerman & Goldsmith 2011). One implication of this finding is that reading in print settings will not be replaced by other reading modes (not any time soon, at least), particularly when the reading is for academic purposes.

Together, these findings indicate that parent's education, self-expectation of highest level of education, and family SES are important factors of reading enjoyment in particular settings. Specifically, self-expectation of highest educational attainment is an important correlate for enjoyment in reading in print, whereas parents' education (i.e., father education) and family SES are essential correlates of digital reading, i.e., reading online and social media reading.

Although significant effects were found for the reported indicators of students' reading interest in relation to both demographic and educational variables, the effect sizes were quite small and explained no more than 3% of the variance. This indicated that the demographic and educational variables incorporated in this study did not play a substantial role in the differences in students' reading enjoyment. Regardless of the small effects, the findings discussed in this section suggest several implications for research and practice.

These findings have at least two sets of educational implications for practitioners. First, that reading enjoyment is significantly related to self-expected highest level of education, parents' education, and family SES suggests that educators, facilitators, and policy makers at university level need to be aware that an individual student's reading interest is tied to his or her demographic and educational background. Second, students from low SES family background are disadvantaged in relation to digital reading (i.e., reading online and social media reading) because they lack access to necessary equipment and other resources. Continued efforts must be made to make online reading materials more accessible to students of lower family SES.

There were also significant differences in students' enjoyment in social media reading when analysed by their SES ($F[3, 989] = 4.46, p = 0.01, \eta^2 = 0.01$). The result from Tukey post hoc tests revealed that students from the upper middle-income category enjoyed social media reading ($M = 0.12, SD = 0.59$) at a greater level, compared to students from the low-income ($M = -0.08, SD = 0.61$) and students from lower middle-income ($M = -0.02, SD = 0.67$) categories.

REFERENCES

Ackerman, R., & Goldsmith, M. 2011. Metacognitive regulation of text learning: on screen versus on paper. *Journal of Experimental Psychology: Applied* 17: 18–32. doi: 10.1037/a0022086.

Applegate, A. J., & Applegate, M. D. 2004. The Peter effect: Reading habits and attitudes of preservice teachers. *The Reading Teacher* 57: 554–563. doi: 10.2307/20205399.

Baker, L., & Scher, D. 2002. Beginning readers'motivation for reading in relation to parental beliefs and home reading experiences. *Reading Psychology* 23: 239–269. doi: 10.1080/713775283.

Barron, B., Martin, C. K., Takeuchi, L., & Fithian, R. 2009. *Parents as learning partners in the development of technological fluency.*

Bawden, D. 2008. Origins and concepts of digital literacy. *Digital literacies: Concepts, policies and practices* 17–32.

Bentler, P. M. 2005. EQS 6 structural equations program manual. Encino, California: Multivariate Software, Inc.

Bibby, R. W., Russell, S., & Rolheiser, R. 2009. *The emerging millennials: How Canada's newest generation is responding to change & choice.*: Project Canada Books.

Boyd, D. M., & Ellison, N. B. 2008. Social network sites: Definition, history, and scholarship. *Journal of Computer-Mediated Communication* 13: 210–230. doi: 10.1111/j.1083–6101.2007.00393.x.

Brooks, B., Welser, H. T., Hogan, B., & Titsworth, S. (2011). Socioeconomic status updates: Family SES and emergent social capital in college student Facebook networks. *Information, Communication & Society* 14: 529–549. doi: 10.1080/1369118X.2011.562221.

Buzzetto-More, N., Guy, R., & Elobaid, M. 2007. Reading in a digital age: E-books are students ready for this learning object? *Interdisciplinary Journal of E-Learning and Learning Objects* 3: 239–250.

Byrne, B. M. 2006. *Structural equation modeling with EQS: Basic concepts, applications, and programming:* Lawrence Erlbaum Associates.

Chall, J. S., & Jacobs, V. A. 2003. The classic study on poor children's fourth-grade slump. *American educator* 27: 14–15.

Chen, S. Y. 2007. Extracurricular reading habits of college students in Taiwan: Findings from two national surveys. *Journal of Adolescent & Adult Literacy* 50: 642–653. doi: 10.1598/JAAL.50.8.3.

Chen, S. Y., Chang, Y. J., & Ko, H. W. 2011. The influence of parental education level, parental reading attitude, and current home reading activities on students' reading attainment: Findings from the PIRLS 2006.

Clark, C. 2009. Why fathers matter to their children's literacy. *National Literacy Trust.*

Clark, C. 2012. Boys' Reading Commission 2012: A review of existing research conducted to underpin the Commission. *National Literacy Trust.*

Clark, C., & Akerman, R. 2006. Social inclusion and reading: An exploration. *National Literacy Trust.*

Clark, C., & Burke, D. 2012. Boys' Reading Commission. A review of existing research to underpin the Commission. London: National Literacy Trust.

Clark, C., & Foster, A. 2005. Children's and young people's reading habits and preferences: The who, what, why, where and when. *National Literacy Trust.*

Clark, C., & Rumbold, K. 2006. Reading for pleasure: A research overview. London: National Literacy Trust.

Coiro, J. 2011. Predicting reading comprehension on the Internet: Contributions of offline reading skills, online reading skills, and prior knowledge. *Journal of Literacy Research* 43: 352–392. doi: 10.1177/1086296 × 11421979.

Coiro, J., & Dobler, E. 2007. Exploring the online reading comprehension strategies used by sixth-grade skilled readers to search for and locate information Internet. *Reading Research Quarterly* 42: 214–257. doi: 10.1598/RRQ.42.2.2.

Conradi, K., Jang, B. G., Bryant, C., Craft, A., & McKenna, M. C. 2013. Measuring adolescents' attitudes toward reading: A classroom survey. *Journal of Adolescent & Adult Literacy* 56: 565–576. doi: 10.1002/JAAL.183.

De Naeghel, J., Van Keer, H., Vansteenkiste, M., & Rosseel, Y. 2012. The relation between elementary students' recreational and academic reading motivation, reading frequency, engagement, and comprehension: A self-determination theory perspective. *Journal of Educational Psychology* 104: 1006. doi: 10.1037/a0027800.

Ellison, N. B., Steinfield, C., & Lampe, C. 2007. The benefits of Facebook "friends:" Social capital and college students' use of online social network sites. *Journal of Computer-Mediated Communication* 12: 1143–1168. doi: 10.1111/j.1083–6101.2007.00367.x.

Foltz, P. W. 1992. *Readers' comprehension and strategies in linear text and hypertext.* (Doctoral Dissertation), University of Colorado.

Foltz, P. W. 1996. Comprehension, coherence, and strategies in hypertext and linear text. *Hypertext and cognition* 109–136.

Gallik, J. D. 1999. Do they read for pleasure? Recreational reading habits of college students. *Journal of Adolescent & Adult Literacy* 42: 480–488.

Gambell, T., & Hunter, D. 2000. Surveying gender differences in Canadian school literacy. *Journal of Curriculum Studies* 32: 689–719. doi: 10.1080/00220270050116941.

Gilbert, J., & Fister, B. 2011. Reading, risk, and reality: College students and reading for pleasure. *College & Research Libraries* 72: 474–495. doi: 10.5860/crl-148.

Hargittai, E. 2010. Digital na(t)ives? Variation in internet skills and uses among members of the "net generation"*. *Sociological inquiry* 80: 92–113.

Hill, J. R., & Hannafin, M. J. 1997. Cognitive strategies and learning from the World Wide Web. *Educational Technology Research and Development* 45: 37–64. doi: 10.1007/BF02299682.

Hughes-Hassell, S., & Rodge, P. 2007. The leisure reading habits of urban adolescents. *Journal of Adolescent & Adult Literacy, 51,* 22–33. doi: 10.2307/40015543.

Jeffres, L. W., & Atkin, D. J. 1996. Dimensions of student interest in reading newspapers. *Journalism and Mass Communication Educator* 51:15–23.

Junco, R. 2012. Too much face and not enough books: The relationship between multiple indices of Facebook use and academic performance. *Computers in Human Behavior, 28,* 187–198. doi: 10.1016/j.chb.2011.08.026.

Karim, N. S. A., & Hasan, A. 2007. Reading habits and attitude in the digital age. *The Electronic Library, 25,* 285–298. doi: 10.1108/02640470710754805.

Kim, J. H.-Y., & Jung, H.-Y. 2010. South Korean digital textbook project. *Computers in the Schools, 27,* 247–265. doi: 10.1080/07380569.2010.523887.

Kirsch, I., De Jong, J., Lafontaine, D., McQueen, J., Mendelovits, J., & Monseur, C. 2002. *PISA Reading for Change: Performance and Engagement Across Countries: Results from PISA 2000*: OECD Publishing.

Kirschner, P. A., & Karpinski, A. C. 2010. Facebook® and academic performance. *Computers in Human Behavior, 26,* 1237–1245. doi: 10.1016/j.chb.2010.03.024.

Leu, D. J., Kinzer, C. K., Coiro, J. L., & Cammack, D. W. 2004. Toward a theory of new literacies emerging from the Internet and other information and communication technologies. *Theoretical Models and Processes of Reading, 5.*

Liu, Z. 2005. Reading behavior in the digital environment: Changes in reading behavior over the past ten years. *Journal of Documentation, 61,* 700–712. doi: 10.1108/00220410510632040.

Liu, Z. 2006. Print vs. electronic resources: A study of user perceptions, preferences, and use. *Information Processing & Management, 42,* 583–592. doi: 10.1016/j.ipm.2004.12.002.

Mangen, A., Walgermo, B. R., & Brønnick, K. 2013. Reading linear texts on paper versus computer screen: Effects on reading comprehension. *International Journal of Educational Research, 58,* 61–68. doi: 10.1016/j.ijer.2012.12.002.

Martin, A. 2008. Digital literacy and the 'digital society'. *Digital literacies: Concepts, policies and practices, 30,* 151–176.

McKenna, M. C., Conradi, K., Lawrence, C., Jang, B. G., & Meyer, J. P. 2012. Reading attitudes of middle school students: Results of a U.S. survey. *Reading Research Quarterly, 47,* 283–306. doi: 10.1002/rrq.021.

McKenna, M. C., Kear, D. J., & Ellsworth, R. A. 1995. Children's attitudes toward reading: A national survey. *Reading Research Quarterly,* 934–956. doi: 10.2307/748205.

Mullen, A. L., Goyette, K. A., & Soares, J. A. 2003. Who goes to graduate school? Social and academic correlates of educational continuation after college. *Sociology of Education*, 143–169.

Muthén, L. K., & Muthén, B. O. 1998–2012. *Mplus User's Guide. Seventh Edition.* CA: Muthén & Muthén Los Angeles.

NCES. 2003. The Nation's Report Card: Reading Highlights 2002 *National Center for Educational Statistics* (Vol. 524, pp. 2): National Center for Educational Statistics.

Nicholas, K., & Fletcher, J. 2011. What role does a father play in influencing a child's reading ability? *Institute of Education, University of London, 6*, 8.

Park, H.-R., & Kim, D. 2011. Reading-strategy use by English as a second language learners in online reading tasks. *Computers & Education, 57*, 2156–2166. doi: 10.1016/j.compedu.2011.05.014.

Perrin, A. 2015. Social media usage: 2005–2015. Washington, DC: Pew Research Center.

Rockinson-Szapkiw, A. J., Courduff, J., Carter, K., & Bennett, D. 2013. Electronic versus traditional print textbooks: A comparison study on the influence of university students' learning. *Computers & Education, 63*, 259–266. doi: 10.1016/j.compedu.2012.11.022.

Sainsbury, M., & Schagen, I. 2004. Attitudes to reading at ages nine and eleven. *Journal of Research in Reading, 27*, 373–386. doi: 10.1111/j.1467–9817.2004.00240.x.

Sandberg, K. 2011. College student academic online reading: a review of the current literature. *Journal of College Reading and Learning, 42*, 89–98. doi: 10. 1089/10949310 41774613.

Stokmans, M. J. W. 1999. Reading attitude and its effect on leisure time reading. *Poetics, 26*, 245–261. doi: 10.1016/S0304-422X(99)00005-4.

Stolzenberg, R. M. 1994. Educational continuation by college graduates. *American Journal of Sociology*, 1042–1077.

Tanner, M. J. 2014. Digital vs. print: Reading comprehension and the future of the book. *SLIS Student Research Journal, 4*, 6.

Valenzuela, S., Park, N., & Kee, K. F. 2009. Is there social capital in a social network site?: Facebook use and college students' life satisfaction, trust, and participation. *Journal of Computer-Mediated Communication, 14*, 875–901. doi: 10.1111/j.1083-6101.2009.01474.x.

Walsh, M. 2010. Multimodal literacy: What does it mean for classroom practice? *Australian Journal of Language and Literacy, 33*, 211–223.

Wang, J., & Wang, X. 2012. *Structural equation modeling: Applications using Mplus:* John Wiley & Sons.

Woody, W. D., Daniel, D. B., & Baker, C. A. 2010. E-books or textbooks: Students prefer textbooks. *Computers & Education, 55*, 945–948. doi: 10.1016/j.compedu.2010.04.005.

ELT in Asia in the Digital Era: Global Citizenship and Identity – Madya et al. (Eds)
© 2018 Taylor & Francis Group, London, ISBN 978-0-8153-7900-3

'Read-to-Me' story books: Parent-child home English reading activities

D.R. Meisani
Indonesia University of Education, Bandung, Indonesia

ABSTRACT: Both teachers and parents play a crucial role to open avenues for the success of children's learning. This idea indirectly indicates that besides at school, children need to gain positive support that parents should be able to provide at home. In the context of foreign language learning, learners, especially the early ones, require multi exposures to the target language so that understanding of its meaning and use can be developed. As the English time at school is limited, it is advantageous if parents can also take a part in supporting children's English learning. Given the situations, this current study was aimed at investigating how parents in Indonesia, who mostly do not speak English, can support children's English learning by conducting parent-child home reading activities using downloadable audio English books. The findings revealed parents' positive responses towards their experiences in using the books for several reasons, especially due to the 'read-to-me' feature.

1 INTRODUCTION

1.1 *Burning issues*

Young children's ability to read and write is often seen as the precursor of their academic performance. Dealing with this, it is common to see children in their very early age to be taught to read, write and even count to prepare them for the formal education. This has been a trend as well in Indonesia to have children start schooling from the very early age. As Rhyner (2009) posits that a child's experiences as an infant, toddler, and preschooler are critical to the acquisition of knowledge and skills that the child can draw on to facilitate academic success, the number of Early Childhood Education Schools in Indonesia perfectly embodies this idea.

Related to this, besides teachers, parents also play a crucial role to open avenues for the success of children's learning. Both teachers and parents should be knowledgeable about who children are, how they learn successfully, and under what particular conditions their potentials can be then explored and developed. This idea indirectly indicates that besides at school, children need to gain positive support that parents should be able to provide by creating home learning environment. As Duncan et al. (2007) suggests, a child's success in school is strongly influenced by the knowledge and skills that he or she acquires outside the school. Although knowledge and skills are the goal of the learning activities, what should be emphasized by teachers and parents is how children spend their time meaningfully during learning and gain eloquent experiences through the activities—not solely insisting on what they can do after being taught or given the activities.

Dealing with English for young learners in Indonesia, the controversy among decision makers about the idea of offering English at elementary schools (Setiasih 2012) and the challenges of teaching English for Indonesian young learners and the insufficient knowledge and ability of Indonesian teachers of English (Hamied 2010) are considered as gaps in which this present study took into account by fostering the involvement of parents to support children's English learning.

As preliminary studies, a survey by administering a web-based questionnaire had been conducted involving 78 parents of the students studying at a private elementary school in Malang, East Java, Indonesia. The results found that parents are generally aware of the importance of involvement in their children's literacy development and believe that they should participate in a number of home and school-based activities. Despite this, their actual level of involvement in their children's English language studies was somewhat limited.

Regarding the young learners' requirements of parents' involvement and on the other side, the parents' incapability of using English language, this study recommended that a positive interference should be given. Audio books which can be free downloaded and read and listened through smart phone were used as means to support parent-child English reading activities at home. Hence, besides being intended to find out the challenges that parents face to support their children's EFL learning, this present study was also aimed at investigating the use of audio books by parents and children to support the English learning at home.

1.2 *Purpose of the study*

Based on the background elaborated above, the following objectives for the current study are set up. They are:

1. To find out the challenges that parents face to support their children's EFL learning;
2. To investigate the use of audio books to support parent-child English reading sessions at home.

2 RESEARCH METHOD

2.1 *Research design*

This current study applied mixed-methods by collecting and analyzing quantitative data gathered from the questionnaires and interpreting the results into qualitative study (Creswell 2003).

2.2 *Setting*

This study was administered at an Integrated Islamic Elementary School, in Malang, East Java—one of the private schools that offers English subject as a compulsory subject starting from grade 2. This school that was founded in 2003 has become one of favorite elementary schools in Malang, East Java, and earned predicate 'A' from the National Elementary School Accreditation Board.

2.3 *Questionnaire*

To collect the data, two sets of web-based questionnaires were used. The first questionnaire which was modified from Al-Mahrooqi (2016) was implemented in the preliminary study, the second was designed to gather further data based on the findings of the first questionnaire.

The first questionnaire contained two sections. Section one related to participants' attitudes about parental involvement in their children's English learning. This section was divided into five parts: benefits of involvement, parent involvement activities, personal reasons for non-involvement, teacher-related reasons for non-involvement, and school/ administration's reasons for non-involvement. The second section explored the frequency with which parents engaged in eight activities related to their children's English language learning.

The second questionnaire was designed to investigate how parent-child home English reading activities were conducted and how audio books were used to support the activities. The questionnaire which was also filled out by parents of young learners consisted of four parts: participants' data, parents and children's English skills, home reading activities, and home English learning and English reading activities.

2.4 *Interview*

For the succeeding stage, a follow-up interview with the parents was conducted. It was done to explore in more detail the parents' responses towards the questionnaires. The interview was, with the participants' permission, audio recorded and field noted.

2.5 Participants

The questionnaire was administered to parents of students aged between 7 to 12 years old who were studying at the Private Integrated Islamic Elementary School, Malang, East Java. The first questionnaire was filled out by 78 parents. Even though the questionnaire was answered by either the mother or the father, the questions required the data from both father and mother. Random sampling was administered to generalize the population (Malik & Hamied 2016). Of the participants who completed the demographic section of the questionnaire, 20 were male (26%) and 58 were female (74%).

In terms of parents' levels of education and occupation, the parents were asked to mention both father and mother's educational background. Twelve fathers and 16 mothers graduated from senior high school, 55 fathers and 58 mothers finished their bachelor degree, and 11 fathers and 4 mothers accomplished their master's degree. The vast majority of participants, (n = 78 pairs of parents) were currently working, only one mother who was a housewife. The participant parents were the ones who had children studying at elementary school, while the number of children in each family was as follows: one (n = 19; 24%), two (n = 43; 55%), three (n = 13; 17%), four (n = 3; 4%).

Concerning the family income, as the study was conducted in Malang, East Java, thus the local minimum wage of Malang was considered as the standard. Twenty-three respondents (29.5%) reported a total family monthly income of between less than 1 million rupiahs to two and a half million rupiahs, the other fifty-five (70.5%) informed that they earned more than two and a half to more than ten million rupiahs a month.

Next, out of the 78 parents who filled out the first questionnaire, there were 41 of them aged between 25 to 52 years old who were willing to fill out the second questionnaire—seven of them (17.1%) were fathers and 34 (82.9%) were mothers.

3 FINDINGS AND DISCUSSION

3.1 Challenges in supporting children's EFL learning

Participants were asked to indicate on a 5-point Likert-type response scale their level of agreement with a series of items across five categories. Responses ranged from strongly agree to disagree and had a middle option of neutral. Interpretations of item and category means are: strongly disagree (1.00 < average < 1.79), disagree (1.80 < average < 2.59), neutral (2.60 < average < 3.39), agree (3.40 < average < 4.19), and strongly agree (4.20 < average < 5.00).

The first questionnaire contained seven categories related to parents' involvement to children's learning that included: benefits of involvement, parents' involvement activities, teacher related reasons for non-involvement, personal reasons for non-involvement, school/administration reasons for non-involvement, parents-children home reading activities, and frequency of parents' involvement in children's English studies. The Table 1 shows the mean scores from the responses of each category.

From these findings, three major reasons why parents' involvement towards children's English study was slightly limited were found. The obstacles in choosing suitable materials

Table 1. Overall means of the categories in questionnaire I.

No	Category	Mean
1	Benefits of involvement	4.53
2	Parents' involvement activities	4.18
3	Teacher-related reasons for non-involvement	2.68
4	Personal reasons for non-involvement	2.85
5	School/administration reasons for non-involvement	2.88
6	Parents-child home reading activities	4.17
7	Frequency of parents' involvement in children's English studies	3.33

for assisting their children's English learning were mostly selected. The other two were parents' lack of knowledge about teaching English to children and low English proficiency. The Table 2 displays the percentage of each reason.

As it is a fact to know that Indonesian parents do not speak English, including the parents as the subjects in this research, they admitted that the three mentioned problems hindered their involvement. Yet, it is fascinating to know that they had done some efforts to cope with those hindrances and attempted to still actively assist their descendants in learning English. The most frequent efforts done by parents are: studying their children English books, watching TV shows in English, and setting English language mode in their mobile phone. Table 3 demonstrates the percentage of each item.

More detailed questions were given to find out what parents had done for their kids to support their English learning. Five activities were captured to be done by the respondents, such as: helping their students do the English assignment was the majority of the parents' answer. Others were financing private tuition in English, giving commands, providing learning facilities, and instilling a positive attitude towards English learning. Table 4 shows the percentage of each answer.

Dealing with the data obtained, one of the previous related research states that as one of the low GDP countries, Indonesia has the lowest level of parental investment and involvement which is associated with students' lowest reading literacy score (Sui-chu 2009). In fact, exposing children to a home environment rich in literacy opportunities is beneficial to young children's literacy and language development. Furthermore, regarding the reasons of parents' limited involvement, workshops are to be designed to accommodate and acknowledge parents on how to support children's learning and how to create home literacy environment. Besides, parent-child home reading activities are to be proposed as the sustainable means to support children's literacy development, as well as parent-child purposeful interaction.

3.2   The use of audio book

As being elaborated in the previous section, parents' supports significantly bring positive effects on children's learning. Not only the school, but students themselves, parents' supports

Table 2.   Reasons for parents' limited involvement towards children's English learning.

No	Reason	N	%
1	Low English proficiency	78	37
2	Lack of knowledge about teaching English to children	78	45.2
3	Obstacles in choosing suitable materials	78	49.3

Table 3.   Parents' efforts to be able to assist children's English learning.

No	Activity	N	%
1	Setting English language mode in their mobile phone	78	57.5
2	Watching TV shows in English	78	39.7
3	Studying their children English book	78	20.5

Table 4.   Parents' supports to children's English learning.

No	Activity	N	%
1	Financing private tuition in English	78	14.6
2	Giving commands	78	24.4
3	Instilling a positive attitude towards learning English	78	36.6
4	Providing facilities	78	48.8
5	Helping do the assignment	78	61

and educational facilities, also determine significantly to success of students' English literacy (Setiasih 2012; Duncan et al. 2007). Dealing with English as a foreign language learning, parent-child book reading is the activity which is considered to be involved in early vocabulary development. Renandya (2015) also recommends that through extensive reading, ESL/EFL skills and components, like grammar and vocabulary should be learned and improved inductively.

However, regarding the challenges the parents face to support children's EFL learning, the parents' involvement become hardly fulfilled. Dealing with this, this study saw the advantages provided by the use of technologies, in this case smart phones, to foster early reading skills. It was proposed that parents download English audio books for kids from the Play Store or App Store in their smart phones to be used as the media to conduct home reading activities together with their children.

From the second questionnaire focusing on the use of audio books which was filled out by 41 fathers and mothers, the following findings were gained. From all of the participants, 35.7% of them read with child at home regularly, 35.7% of them sometimes did it, and 7.1% of them never did it. Hence, related to the audio books, the data revealed that 32 participants (78%) did not use audio book and 20 of them (48.8%) were willing to try English audio books from their smart phones.

Further investigation found that some of the books parents downloaded were iStoryBooks, Read & Play, My First Books, and The Bedtime Book. In the interview, they shared the benefits of using the audio books, they are: the book are free downloadable, with the feature 'read-to-me', parents who do not know English can use the option and listen to the story, so both parents and children can learn English together (pronunciation, vocabulary, grammar), parents can learn how to read stories to children, the books provide activities as the follow-up after reading the stories, such as educative games, coloring, and singing songs, and most importantly, while reading or listening the stories using the audio books, interactions occur between parents and children discussing about the plot, the characters in the stories, and the English words. In short, the respondents in majority gave positive impressions towards the use of audio books for English reading activities at home, although some were still worried and considered about the negative sides of gadget for children.

4 CONCLUSION AND SUGGESTIONS

The findings of the study revealed that parents were aware of the importance of being involved in their child's English learning and were willing to help. However, it was found that they faced difficulties to support their children to learn English at home so that their involvement were slightly limited. the data revealed that the difficulties to select suitable materials for their children's English learning at home were the major reason of their minor involvement (49.3%). It was followed by their lack of knowledge about English teaching to children (45.2%) and their low English proficiency (37%). To deal with these handicaps, the data from the questionnaire captured that the participating parents had done efforts, like: studied their children English books (57.5%), watched TV shows in English (39.7%) and set English language mode in their mobile phone (20.5%).

From these findings, the use of English audio books was proposed to parents to support their participation in children's English learning. Positive responses were gained from 20 parents who were willing to try to use the books they downloaded in their smart phones, like: iStoryBooks, Read & Play, My First Books, and The Bedtime Book. Besides helping parents to read with the 'read-to-me' feature provided in the application, the books were also very useful as the means to stimulate meaningful communications between parents and their child while having the story time that indirectly lead to child's language acquisition and academic success.

Finally, according to the results of data analysis, it can be implied that parents' awareness and understanding about early literacy, in particularly English, are the main ideas that should be taken into account. Although most of the parents who became respondents in this study agreed that their involvement for their children's learning were crucial, many did not know how to help their offspring and some even did not do that. In addition, the fact that today's children are digital native cannot be avoided where what parents, teachers, or the care givers can do is to take the benefits the technologies offer. What occurred in this study, when options were given to use smart phones and utilize the application of audio books in the phones, some were worried about the bad effects of letting the children use smart phones. In this case, parents were required to be given understandings that the children would not be exposed by the use of smart phones too much; their intense involvement to use the audio books in the smart phone for reading together with children is the core point, so children are well guided to use the device wisely.

Furthermore, considering the length of time in conducting the current study that may affect the comprehensiveness of the results of the research, longitudinal study is recommended to be done in order to investigate the better forms of home-based supports. Last of all, as Kirkpatrick (2012) who proposes English as a lingua franca, posits local culture should be included in ESL/EFL learning, parents are encouraged to also introduce stories that contain local culture. Not only do young learners learn the foreign language and culture of others, but they also uphold their own culture and raise the values it brings through the stories they read.

REFERENCES

Al-Mahrooqi, R. et al. 2016. Omani parents' involvement in their children's English education. *SAGE Open*: 1–12. DOI: 10.1177/2158244016629190.

Creswell, J.W. 2003. *Research design: Qualitative, quantitative, and method approach.* California: Sage Publication, Inc.

Duncan, G.J. et al. 2007. *Children's early academic and attention skills best predict later school success, according to analysis of large-scale studies.* http://www.apa. org/news/press/releases/2007/11/school-readiness.aspx.

Hamied, F.A. 2010. EFL assessment in Indonesia: National exams and quality education. In Spolsky et al. *Language Assessment in Asia: Local, Regional or Global?*, 2010. Asia TEFL.

Kirkpatrick, A. 2012. English as an Asian lingua franca: A lingua franca approach and implications for language education policy. *Journal of English as a Lingua Franca* 1(1): 121–140.

Malik, R.S. & Hamied, F.A. 2016. *Research method: A guide for first time researchers.* Bandung: UPI Press.

Renandya, W.A. 2015. Reading in a foreign language: What else is important besides skills and strategies? In Hamied, Fuad Abdul. et al. 2015. *Developing indigenous models of english language teaching and assessment.* Denpasar: Udayana University Press.

Rhyner, P.M. 2009. *Emergent literacy and language development: Promoting learning in early childhood.* New York: The Guildford Press.

Setiasih, L. 2012. *The role of out of school literacy activities in promoting students' English literacy.* Unpublished Dissertation. Indonesia University of Education, Bandung.

Sui-chu, E.H. 2009. *The diversity of parental involvement and investment on children's learning across the pacific RIM.* 7th International Conference of the European Research Network about Parents in Education. ISBN 978-91-86238-82-2.

ELT in Asia in the Digital Era: Global Citizenship and Identity – Madya et al. (Eds)
© *2018 Taylor & Francis Group, London, ISBN 978-0-8153-7900-3*

Utilizing iBooks in teaching EFL reading comprehension

D.S. Suharti
Muhammadiyah University of Tangerang, Banten, Indonesia

ABSTRACT: This research was conducted to reveal the implementation of utilizing iBooks in teaching EFL reading comprehension and the benefits the challenges gained by teachers and students. It was a case study which involved qualitative data collecting techniques such as observations, interviews, and documents examination. Data were collected from 32 participants: one of them is the researcher as an instructor, the main participant observer. The instructor used the iBooks application in iPad for helping the students in learning English as a Foreign Language (EFL) reading comprehension. The result shows that iBooks had altered the teaching and learning experience of teachers and students through a new respective teaching EFL reading. It acknowledged the gained benefits as it could assist instructor to teach EFL reading easily and help the students to read the EFL text in different and pleasant ways. Further challenges and drawbacks are discussed in the remaining sections.

1 BACKGROUND OF THE RESEARCH

Reading comprehension has been believed to be significant for long-term academic success as stated by Dickinson *et al.* (2012). However, to comprehend the reading texts in English students need a process. English language learners in an EFL context, such as Indonesia, do not have much exposure to foreign language use. This is a problem to solve since successful English language acquisition by students of a second or a foreign language needs a condition that the students are exposed to the language in large amounts of comprehensible input in a relaxed setting as argued by Harmer referring to Krashen (2007).

The factors of reading comprehension are considered as two types, namely reader and text factors. Both the background knowledge that readers carry to the reading process and the strategies they employ while they are reading as well as their motivation and engagement during reading are built-in as reader factors. Whereas text factors comprise the author's thought, the words the author takes to state the ideas, and how the ideas are structured and presented. Thus, both factors concern comprehension (Thompkins 2010).

Particularly, the researcher found that students have misunderstanding that reading well means to know every word and figure out its meaning from the printed text; thus, they look for every unfamiliar word up, and translate sentences word-by-word. They choose to pay no attention to the meaning of the context and as a result they surrender in comprehending the passage.

A line with this misconception, Booth & Swartz (2004) cite that stressed foreign language readers habitually make less effort in finding the gist of what they have been reading, or they prefer to disregard making meaning of the reading totally and surrender in dissatisfaction. Based on the researcher's survey on "Reading in English as a Foreign Language", adopted from Mikulecky & Jeffries' (2007) idea to know the students reading ability, given to 144 students, most students had difficulty in understanding a text as a whole for they discovered quite number of unfamiliar words in the text and they did not know what to do to comprehend the text. Another finding was that the students had some troubles when they were taking reading tests. This showed that many students still found difficult to comprehend the reading texts.

Accordingly, they feel that English text is very hard to comprehend for they have no strategy to read English texts well. The students do not have background knowledge about the text when reading so they find it difficult to identify the topic of the passage. Furthermore, they lack vocabularies and reading practice. As a result, they feel bored with learning to read texts. Thus, they may need to learn about how to comprehend reading EFL text so they can improve their reading comprehension strategy.

It is not to say that there are not ways of improving teaching EFL reading comprehension, but teachers very often teach their students in monotonous ways. Teachers mostly use the printed teaching materials with English Module and presentation when teaching reading. This situation tend to make the learning activities monotonous and boring. And therefore teachers need specific ways of addressing the problems of teaching reading.

Besides, it is critical that students gain more from reading for the gist and reading a lot of material than from identifying every word and figure out its meaning from the difficult paragraphs (Krashen 1982, Harmer 2007, Mikulecky & Jeffries 2007). Foreign language teachers also find it necessary to develop a fresh teaching approach that can stimulate students' interest in English language learning (Fang 2010). They must think about new effective ways to create a better foreign language teaching and learning environment that is supported by multimedia technologies.

The role of Information and Communication Technology (ICT) in teaching and learning of EFL promotes: 1) learner-centered, self-directed, and organized learning directed to increase independence of students as language learners; 2) creative and interactive work; 3) direct feedback; 4) teacher to update content continuously; 5) distributions the roles of teacher and learner; 6) faster access to attain materials (Ravichandran 2000, Marzban 2008, Hartoyo 2012).

Teaching English as a foreign-language can take benefit from using a computer. The application of computers in the learning process will enhance people's language learning. Certainly, a computer is a tool and medium that facilitates people in learning a language, although the effectiveness of learning depends totally on the users (Richards & Renandya 2002, Hartoyo 2006).

Although the strengths of Computer Assisted Language Learning (CALL) can be included as providing motivation and independence for learners, companionable learning style and time adaptable learning, creative and interactive work, immediate feedback, teacher updating content of teaching materials, distributions the roles of teacher and learner, and easy access to attain materials yet, a number of considerations must be given to the weaknesses of CALL, for instance less handy equipment, low resolution screens causing difficulty in reading a long text, high cost of education, lack of trained teachers as well as limited auxiliary teaching function which leads inadequate facility of computers to cope with unpredicted situations (Fang 2010, Hartoyo 2012).

Now there is a transformation of education by a sophisticated tool named iPad. Tech-Terms. Com. (2011) defined that the iPad is a tablet computer developed by Apple. Furthermore, Cabot (2010) declared the iPad as teaching tool has several uses in the classroom. It is due to the obvious—materials, video, and reference materials in teachers' fingertips. For students, it has been praised as a valuable tool for autonomous learning. In addition, Melhuish (2010) noted that the way m-learning with iPad can be integrated into effective, evidence-driven, innovative practices, so that the learner is empowered and enriched by the learning experience. It means that learning with iPad is very potential to determine the successful learning in the future by intensifying the students' activities from the media in order to develop their English language learning. A portrait of the possibility of the iPad as a response tool and may be useful in helping teachers make decisions about whether the iPad or a similar tablet may be an appropriate tool for their literacy goals. As literacy teachers begin to select technologies that are practical learning tools for their classrooms, mobile devices such as the iPad deserve particular consideration as Hutchison, Beschorner, & Schmidt-Crawford (2012) believed.

The iPad one-to-one program uses technology that is already a big part of students' lives to make them more excited about learning as Apple.com (2013) informs. It provides teachers teaching tools in the classroom with the obvious—materials, video, and reference materials in teachers' fingertips and for students, iPad has been valued as a beneficial tool for their autonomous learning. And the iPad has many applications to assist teaching learning EFL, one of them is iBooks. Utilizing iBooks as learning media in reading comprehension EFL learning deserve a consideration in assisted the learning. iBooks transforms the simple act of reading into simply delightful learning experience.

This research examines how the implementation of utilizing iBooks for teaching EFL reading comprehension for EFL students is. The research includes investigating its potential benefits and challenges of that implementation faced by teachers and students in teaching and learning EFL reading. Hence, hopefully the goal of teaching and learning EFL reading comprehension can be achieved.

2 METHOD

This interpretive qualitative research used a case study method. This research was conducted at. The researcher notices that this college is one of alternative college which utilizing iPad, iBooks, in their teaching and learning activities which fits with the research conducted by the researcher. The research participants are the researcher as participant observer, her coworker as non-participant observer, and 30 students, the second-year students of in even semester of academic year 2013/2014 are selected purposively. And it held from April 15 to June 1, 2014. This research constitutes the important aspect of a case study that requires extensively, multiple sources of information, such as observations, interviews, documents, and audiovisual materials (Cresswell 2009: 175). The research employs a set of method collecting data such as observations, interviews, documents examination.

The observation was managed to get a picture of the utilizing iBooks in teaching EFL Reading Comprehension. The observation was held from April 15 to June 1, 2014. The subjects were observed seven times in a class. The research uses both participant and non-participant observer. And all activities were noted in field notes.

Interviews are conducted among the subjects' research: the researcher herself as the main participant who is the instructor or the teacher in the project study as well as 30 students who are selected in this research. These participants were coded as R#1 up to R#31. This research employed an open-ended interview.

Documents Examination were employed to gain the data; report of students' assignments submission from iDu English class and a form of journal entries from their English 2 iBooks sent by email during the courses made by students as well as audiovisual materials in a form of videotapes of the students' task, students' iMovie reading comprehension presentation which were uploaded to YouTube.

3 FINDING AND DISCUSSION

3.1 Findings

3.1.1 The implementation of utilizing iBooks in teaching EFL reading comprehension.
Based on the data of the research; the observation, interview, and documents examination, the researcher revealed a description of the implementation of utilizing iBooks in teaching EFL reading comprehension.

All respondents, the main participant (coded as DSS), non-participant (coded as NSRR), and 30 student participants, had demonstrated the prospect of the implementation of utilizing iPad in teaching EFL reading comprehension. Based on the observation based data, it is proven that utilizing iPad in teaching EFL reading comprehension deserves as new model of teaching EFL reading comprehension assisted by the current technology device like iPad with its appropriate applications can support all activities reading phases, namely pre-reading, during (active) reading, and post reading phases which is initiated by Dowhower (1999). By each of these phases' strategies, students are skilled how comprehension strategies are employed while reading in different sections of text. Thus, students should become independent and automatic use of strategies. The iPad can be used effectively for curricular integration rather than technology integration as Hutchison et al. (2012) recommended.

The pre-reading phase covers some activities including teacher's creations to make her students have a full engagement with the text. Teacher realized that it must be conditioned an environment in class which supported full engagement with the text for students. English 2 iBooks which is made by the teacher in their iPad supports this situation as indicated in the result of observation 1 by DSS (2014). Those activities are included to Lead-in activities which are proposed by Harmer (2007), he points out its basic methodological model procedure for teaching receptive skills.

Observation 1. The Result of Observation Field on Utilizing iBooks in Teaching EFL Reading Comprehension Project Study

Date: April 15th, 2014 8th Reading Comprehension
Time: 09.40 – 11.20
Topic: Human Memory
Observer: DSS (Researcher as participant)
Period: First Observation
During the pre-reading phase
Note the facilities and applications used! And for each statement, write T (true) or F ((false) and give your comments if it is necessary

In the second phase activities, active reading is continued by Teacher direct comprehension task, Students read for the task, and Teacher directs feedback (Harmer 2007). In these activities the use of English Book 2 is to meet the needs of her students a model of application that allowed students to do many practice learning outside of school as Harmon (2011) found that it should be taken with iPads in English class, it was creating applications which meet the students' needs.

This model of teaching allowed students to do a lot more to learn outside of school. And these findings are similar to previous research conducted by McMinn & Li (2012) that is the role of this technology was a learning assistant device rather than the core of face-to-face classes. They, the researcher and McMinn and Li revealed the use of iPads enhanced the effective negotiation of meaning as well as the use of iPads offered teachers to provide feedback to students. However, the different is found McMinn and Li believed on the use of iPads prompted collaborative peer feedback while the main participant here adds the use of iPads also encouraged autonomous learners.

Third phase activities, post reading, it comprises the activities which is proposed by Harmer (2007), Teacher directs a text-related task step. The main participant, teacher used iMovie app in iPad to make reading activity interesting as Donoghue (2009) supported this idea, he asserted that one of the principles of reading is students need to see that reading is an enjoyable interest. And A collaboration research groups at the Universities of York, Oxford, Lancaster and Sussex (2013) cited in ESRC Seminar Series Reading Comprehension that the goal of receptive skills, both reading and listening: is to comprehend the passages. They said that meaning-based representation models are common to reading comprehension: they are also the creation of successful comprehension of spoken talk. The researcher anticipated the task related task in a form of creation of reading comprehension of spoken talk by the use of the iMovie which proposed by Apple com (2013) previously.

Based on the interview data finding, from 30 participants of students, there are 28 students have positive thought towards utilization of iPad in learning EFL reading comprehension and only 2 students have negative thoughts of it. The positive thought towards utilization of iPad in learning EFL reading comprehension; iPad eases their efforts to comprehend English reading text as R#7 said that iBooks facilitated learning English reading comprehension for the flexibility: one could learn anywhere and the features in the iPad, iBooks, which assisted one to comprehend English as well as made him easier utter its sentences. In line with Assia (2012) in the previous research states the important role ICT, especially computer/internet play in assisting EFL teachers introduce innovation in the reading classroom and engaged

No.	Description	True/False	Note the facilities and applications used & comment
1	Teacher involves students with the topic of the reading	True	Before started teaching EFL Reading Comprehension by using iPad, iBooks, researcher gave some explanations about how to work with English 2 iBooks app. The explanations were showed to students by Apple TV, and they were accessible in iDu Class. Then directly she and the students implemented it, using the iBooks by her and themselves since they have their own iPads. After that she asked the students about the topic of the reading.
2	Teacher tries to stimulate their schema or knowledge of the reading topic	True	Researcher showed the students picture and short movie from her English 2 iBooks related to the topic in projector by Apple TV and asked their opinion about them. She tried to elicit students' knowledge about "Human Memory" as the reading topic.
3	Teacher gives them a variety of clues, such as pictures, headlines, video etc.	True	Researcher showed the picture of "The Human Memory" and the short movie about "Human Memory from her English 2 iBooks which were showed by Apple TV.
4	Teacher doesn't give them a few words or phrases as key words from the text	False	Researcher gave students a few words as the key words from the text that is whether they still remember about the subject of the study they had when they were in Senior High School, how they were and asked and recalled them about their hobby, how they did their hobby.
5	Teacher does not ask them to guess what these might specify about its content.	False	Students are asked to guess the contents of the topic by showing the picture and the short movie about Human Memory from her English 2 iBooks which were showed by Apple TV.
6	Teacher persuades a general discussion of the topic	True	Researcher manipulated the students' knowledge about the topic by asking whether their knowledge about their hobby were related to long memory or short memory.
7	Teacher asks students to make their own questions for the reading topic	True	Students asked to think some questions of the reading topic what might they know about the text and students asked about what is human memory, how is the memory working, and how many types are human memory?
8	Students doesn't has a full engagement with the text	False	Then students had a full involvement with the text. Each of them was busy reading and working with their English 2 iBooks.

students actively in the fruitful skill of both intensive and extensive reading that is it can strengthen students reading competency and make them enjoy the reading act.

Established on the interview data finding, it reveals the applications they used in using iBooks to assist them learning EFL reading comprehension: 26 students used English Book 2 (iBooks), then 21 Google Translate, 18 KamusPro, 13 iMovie, 10 Keynote, 6 Dictionary and

6 also Safari browser, 4 Pages, 3 iDu, 2 Speak menu, 1 YouTube, and 1 Dropbox. It means that most students are familiar with the applications on the iPad which are assisted them in their EFL reading comprehension learning.

Considering the interview data finding, it is found from the researcher as a main participant (coded as R#31), that it is an interesting breakthrough for education development in teaching EFL reading comprehension as she said. It is similar to McMinn & Li (2012) found that iPad implementation in a TBLT classroom had positive outcomes. When the instructors were planning for an iPad-based lesson, they prepared not only differently but also more carefully to achieve learning objectives easily. Thus, the role of this technology was a learning assistant device rather than the core of face-to-face classes.

Found in interview data, it shows that the applications teacher used on the iPad such as iBooks, Dictionary, KamusPro, Speak menu, and iMovie as well as virtual learning, iDu Class, are to assist her teaching English reading comprehension as she stated. It means that the applications cited are really applied to help her to teach EFL reading comprehension.

Thus, teaching EFL reading comprehension using iBooks can apply in the situation that each of the teacher and students are assisted with iPad completed by those applications which had been explained. It is in line with Lee (2012) he believed that iPads are tolerable. One of the important insights was the instructors considerately iPad, in the classroom, by every-one had a personal iPad to utilize. And also Department of Education in Melbourne, Victoria, Australia (2012), in their writing article entitled Why the iPad; iPad Features; iPads for Education/ iPads Educational Features, they believe one of some educational reasons for using the iPad in education is the iPad defines as an individual tool and practically valued to operate as a one to one, anywhere, anytime learning device.

Built on the documents examination data finding, the researcher portrays information about how teacher and her students implemented the utilization of iPad in teaching learning EFL reading comprehension. The researcher as a main participant, as a teacher, built lessons in iDu class and reading comprehension materials in iBooks.

3.1.2 The benefit gained by teacher and students

The conclusion of the answers of the interview questions about the advantages which the researcher as a main participant (coded as R#31) gained in teaching English reading comprehension using the iBooks, as she said that the teaching EFL reading comprehension using iPad, iBooks, was an interesting breakthrough in the world of education for its applications which supported the teaching by Dictionary, KamusPro, Speak menu, and iMovie. Moreover, Lee (2012) believed that instructors can intend different methods to incorporating the iPads in conduct their pedagogy.

From 30 participants of students, there are 28 students have positive thought towards utilization of iBooks in learning EFL reading comprehension and only 2 students have negative thoughts of it. The positive thought towards utilization of iBooks in learning EFL reading comprehension elaborates as R#7 said that iBooks eased their efforts to comprehend English reading passage. Thus those findings mentioned previously are similar to McMinn & Li (2012) found. They revealed the use of iPads enhanced the effective negotiation of meaning.

3.1.3 The advantages students gained

All participants (30 students) believed that there were many apps in iPad, iBooks, assisting EFL reading comprehension learning as R#1 said. It is similar to Department of Education in Melbourne, Victoria, Australia (2012), They said that one of some educational reasons for using the iPad in education is the use of diverse apps make students are able to select the type of creation they build to express their comprehension. There were 26 students convinced that it was simpler, easier to learn, and effective learning EFL reading comprehension by using iBooks such as R#18 said. 12 students asserted that it was efficient for it helped them; to respond the materials faster as R#26 believed, to support them to do their English language assignments as R#12 cited, to know quickly the meaning of words or sentences as well as read the text properly as R#20 mentioned, to translate the words that he does not know and he can hear the voice of those words by selecting and tapping Speak menu as R#10 found, to save their time as R#19 showed, for not necessary to bring a dictionary to look for the meaning of the word as R#24 stated, for cost saving as R#23 said, for not depressed to bring a lot of books as R#3 and R#5 asserted.

It is as Mitchell (2012) supported that set learning goals to address with the help of iPads range from vocabulary acquisition to presentation skills to paraphrasing. She believed the advantage of three crucial workings of the iPad for its portability, its connectivity, and its multimodality. These features can help create meaningful learning opportunities, including creating multimodal digital product and analyzing sources found online. There were 3 students said that it was practical such as R#22 and R#23 believed. And 2 students admitted that iPad made the learner become creative as R#2 claimed that iPad assisted the students to enhance their creativity as well. Those are supported by Melhuish & Falloon (2010) observed that the way m-learning with iPad can be integrated into effective, evidence-driven, innovative practices, so that the learner is empowered and enriched by the learning experience.

Moreover, Department of Education in Melbourne, Victoria, Australia (2012), also used iPad in their teaching learning activities, for it is rich multimedia and data visualization techniques. In line with this Lee (2012) added that iPads are tolerable for providing students the autonomy to be stimulated in multimedia innovations.

3.1.4 *The advantages the teacher gained*

The teacher does not need to carry heavily books or textbook and dictionary because the applications are already on the iPad. The documents and tasks can be uploaded to iBooks by the teacher and synchronized onto the iPad by the student and vice versa. In line with this finding Lee (2012) believed that iPads are tolerable for handiness and easiness of use assisted instructors concentrate on their reading materials and information in new habits, iPad enables students develop projects outside the classroom, into their community.

Department of Education in Melbourne, Victoria, Australia (2012) also state two educational reasons for using the iPad in education namely flimsy and handy, simply carried in the school bag and to and from class and heavy schoolbooks could be replaced by virtual eBooks and these can be updated in a timely fashion. It is sufficient. By tapping the select word, she and her students could define the meaning of difficult words easily by Dictionary app which they had downloading and speak them up by selecting and tapping Speak menu so they knew how to pronounce them correctly. Moreover, it makes teacher ease to teach her students EFL reading comprehension for they can easily record their works and share them via email in the iBooks.

iMovie app really helps her to redirect comprehension text-related tasks to the students in different way and interesting. Hence, students can express their summary of the text differently and with fun.

Assisted by the iPad, she could ask her students to submit their works via BL102 iDu class, as soon as she announced them in iDu. She could monitor students works wherever and whenever she was by looking at incoming email reply as well as in BL102 iDu class. It is similar to Department of Education in Melbourne, Victoria, Australia (2012). They believe one of some educational reasons for using the iPad in education is the students can access to current information that contains text, sound, images and interactivity wherever, whenever they exist.

3.1.5 *The challenges found by teacher and students*
3.1.5.1 The challenges teacher faced
Considering the interview data finding, it is revealed the challenges teacher faced as below:

1. The internet is slow or even non-existent service.
2. Knowing her students has conversations with their friends through social media networking or they just look at the update activities there.

It is the different findings with previous research conducted by Department of Education in Melbourne, Victoria, Australia (2012) they did not revealed challenges such as these evidences. And also by Mitchell he believes connectivity allows users of iPad to access materials from around the web, simplifying dictionary searches, research, etc. It also tolerates users to publish on the web more effortlessly.

3.1.5.2 The challenges students found

From 30 participants interviewed it is revealed that although there were 27 students believed that there were some challenges found during the use of iBooks in their learning EFL reading comprehension, there were 3 students discovered that there was no challenge in using it as R#14 believed. There were 11students found a trouble in internet connection/Wi-Fi as R#27. 8 students admitted that they had to be focus or become autonomous learner as R#26 claimed. This is in line with Cabot (2010) who affirmed that the iPad as teaching tool has several uses in the classroom for the obvious—materials, video, and reference materials in teachers' fingertips. And in students' side, it has been praised as a valuable tool for autonomous learning. 6 students faced iPad hang/error as R#16 said, 4 students discovered low battery for example R#9 said. It is different with Department of Education in Melbourne, Victoria, Australia (2012). They believe one of some educational reasons for using the iPad in education is the iPad can be used throughout the entire school day due to a 10-hour battery life device. That condition is due to the findings that and other is when there are few of her students have conversations with their friends through social media networking or they just look at the update activities there. It makes them not focus to the instructions in the classroom. And consequently, it triggers low battery.

Furthermore, there were 3 students did not accustom to apply the apps as R#21 asserted. 2 students revealed it was costly as R#8 claimed. It is not similar with Lee as he believed that iPads are tolerable for regain to praising or moderately priced apps. And the last, a student admitted that he was tired for looking at iPad often as R#25 said. They are different findings with Department of Education in Melbourne, Victoria, Australia (2012). They did not revealed challenges such as these evidences.

3.2 *Discussion*

3.2.1 *The implementation of utilizing iBooks in teaching EFL reading comprehension*

Considering the need of the strategy teaching reading comprehension, the researcher revealed in this research that the main participant conducted her teaching with three phases of comprehension which is initiated by Dowhower (1999) he suggests teachers can teach strategies most effectively through explanation and modeling, guided student practice, and independent student practice. They can be applied in three phases of comprehension: the pre-reading phase, the active reading (during reading) phase and the post reading (after reading) phase. By each of these phases' strategies, students are skilled how comprehension strategies are employed while reading in different sections of text. Thus, students should become independent and automatic use of strategies. Hutchison et al. (2012) recommended the iPad can be used effectively for curricular integration rather than technology integration. Along with Lee (2012) also believed that instructors can intend different methods to incorporating the iPads in conduct their pedagogy. Here the researcher as main participant initiated the use of iBooks as her assisted tool of teaching EFL reading comprehension as a new model of teaching EFL reading comprehension can support all activities reading phases as elaborated by researcher below.

Those activities are included to Lead-in activities which are proposed by Harmer (2007), he points out its basic methodological model procedure for teaching receptive skills. There are five steps: Lead in, Teacher direct comprehension task, Students read for the task, Teacher directs feedback, Teacher directs a text-related task. And by giving students clues such as picture and video related to the text in the English 2 iBooks app, providing them a few words or phrases as key words, persuading them to guess what these might specify about text's content by showing the picture and short movie about the text, influencing them for a general discussion of the topic by attempting to ask them to make their own questions for the reading topic, all those activities are to assist her students the ways how to read successfully. This strategy namely Intensive reading is proposed by Harmer (2007). It comprises reading skills such as skimming and scanning: using a quick survey of the text to get the main idea, identify text structure, confirm or question predictions. What to add here that is the researcher provided the students a few words or phrases as key words, persuading them to guess what these might specify about text's content by showing the picture as well as the short movie.

After pre-reading activities, Lead-in activities, the teaching continued with second phase activities, active reading. It is continuing the basic methodological model procedure for teaching reading as teaching receptive skills as stated by Harmer (2007) previously: beginning by Lead-in then next continued by Teacher direct comprehension task, Students read for the task, and Teacher directs feedback as the active reading activities. In these activities the use of English 2 iBooks as mentioned previously is to meet the needs of her students a model of application that allowed students to do many practice learning outside of school as Harmon (2011) found that it should be taken with iPads in English class was creating applications that meet the needs of students underserved should be done. A model that allowed students to do a lot more to learn outside of school.

Apple.com (2013) states that teachers can create their own interactive materials or iBooks with iBooks Author and it works best for the students since it sets in by their own teachers who know well about them. By this application, teacher directs some kind of a comprehension task in order that they would read the text. For instance, the participant researcher (2014) asserted in the interview that teacher reminded the students to apply English 2 iBooks in their iPad to comprehend the text. In intensive reading, in order to get students to read actively in class, teachers require creating interest in topic and tasks. Therefore, the teacher's roles when asking students to read intensively namely: organizer, give them clear instructions about the goal and the time of the instructions, as Harmer (2007) believes.

Teacher asks students to read the text. Teacher really knew that after explaining the tips to understand the text, she invited the students to read the text in their English 2 iBooks as the non-participant, NSRR (2014) said in the interview. Here teacher's role as observer, observe their progress when they are reading as Harmer (2007) thinks. And the tips to understand the text in this iBooks are adapted from JamesESL (2008) in Reading Comprehension in English http://www.engvid.com/ he believes there are three steps to comprehend reading text; first step, read quickly and underline the words that a reader doesn't know, second, reread, use dictionary, and summarize each paragraph, the last step read it again and summarize everything. The teacher has the same idea with James, both believed this strategy, by reading the English text over and over; readers will learn words, phrase, and ideas. They will read it faster and finally they will understand, comprehend the text.

Teacher asks students to do some endeavors to get a general understanding of the text. Teacher asked students to use some applications in iBooks, English 2 iBooks, as well as Dictionary, KamusPro or Google Translate so they could comprehend the text easily as the participant researcher, DSS (2014) asserted in the interview.

Teacher reminds students to check the answers. For example, the non-participant, NSRR (2014) said teacher had to give feedback to their students so they knew whether they had good work or not by utilizing English 2 iBooks app in iPad reviewed their work through their email by projector connected by Apple TV. Here the teacher's role as feedback organizer, lead a feedback discussion when they have finished the task to ensure whether they have done it effectively or not, prompter, notice language feature within the text after students have read it as Harmer (2007) considers. And to give students an immediate assessment of their knowledge, teachers can built-in review questions in the iBooks so they comprehend where to focus more study time as Apple.com (2013) asserts.

Students are promoted to be autonomous learners. Only a few students acquired more chances to collaborate. Teacher made their students busy with their own work by using English 2 iBooks app in iPad as DSS (2014) claimed. It is in line with Harmon (2011) found that it should be taken with iPads in English class was creating applications that meet the needs of students, a model that allowed students to do a lot more to learn outside of school.

Thus, these research findings are similar to previous research conducted by McMinn & Li (2012) that is the role of this technology was a learning assistant device rather than the core of face-to-face classes. They, the researcher and McMinn and Li revealed the use of iPads enhanced the effective negotiation of meaning as well as the use of iPads offered teachers to provide feedback to students. However, the different is found McMinn & Li (2012) believed on the use of iPads prompted collaborative peer feedback while the main participant here adds the use of iPads also encouraged autonomous learners.

Built on the observation data finding, after active reading activities the teaching continued with third phase activities, post reading, it comprises the activities which is proposed by Harmer (2007), he points out the last basic methodological model procedure for teaching receptive skills: Teacher directs a text-related task step. In this step the main participant, teacher used iMovie app in iPad to make reading activity interesting as Donoghue (2009) supported this idea, he asserted that one of the principles of reading is students need to see that reading is an enjoyable interest. And A collaboration research groups at the Universities of York, Oxford, Lancaster and Sussex cited in ESRC Seminar Series Reading Comprehension (2013) that the goal of receptive skills, both reading and listening: is to comprehend the passages. They said that meaning-based representation models are common to reading comprehension: they are also the creation of successful comprehension of spoken talk. The researcher anticipated the task related task in a form of creation of reading comprehension of spoken talk by the use of the iMovie which proposed by Apple com previously.

Lee (2012) also believed that the iPad2 has some supplementary multimedia qualifications, one of them is movie editing. Students developed into distinctive creators, published their work to YouTube, and explored outside—the-classroom learning occasions. Thus again here iPad, iBooks supports autonomous learner. And all these activities in three phases of reading noted by observers and recorded the facilities in the classroom such as projector and Apple TV and also applications used in the iPad; iBooks, Dictionary, KamusPro or Google Translate, and iMovie.

The three phases' EFL reading comprehension learning activities assisted by those various apps in iPad proposed due to pay great intention to two important reading factors as suggested by Thompkins (2010), he believed that there are two factors of reading comprehension; reader and text factors. Reader factors are both the background of readers' knowledge that they take to the reading process and the strategies they use while they are reading as well as their motivation and engagement during reading. Still, text factors comprise the author's thought, the words the author takes to state the ideas, and how the ideas are structured and presented. Then, Chard & Santoro (2008) cited that to comprehend a reading text, the reader requires conscious and continuous effort to understand the meaning of what they read. Excellent readers are accustomed to use strategies to comprehend the text. He will realize when utilize such strategies, passionately observe what he is read, recognize its structure, and easily determine the main idea of the passage.

In brief, the employment of these three phases of comprehension: the pre-reading phase, the active reading (during reading) phase and the post reading (after reading) phase as endorsed by Dowhower (1999), and the necessity for instructors to intend those strategies to incorporating the iPads and their apps in conduct their pedagogy as Lee (2012) also believed can help students to become independent and automatic use of the strategies. When students have the ability to use strategies independently, then the learning outcomes that is the comprehension of the reading text comes naturally.

From the interview data finding, it shows that from 30 participants of students, there are 28 students have positive thought towards utilization of iBooks in learning EFL reading comprehension and only 2 students have negative thoughts of it. The positive thought towards utilization of iPad in learning EFL reading comprehension means that iBooks eases their efforts to comprehend English reading text. iBooks facilitated learning English reading comprehension for the flexibility: one could learn anywhere and the features in the iPad which assisted one to comprehend English as well as made him easier utter its sentences (Interview: R#7).

In short, iPad provides a variety of apps which let students gain a different learning experience and quite enjoyable due to they can express their comprehension of the EFL reading text in different and pleasant way. In addition, it is in line with Assia (2012) in the previous research states the important role ICT, especially computer/internet play in assisting EFL teachers introduce innovation in the reading classroom and engaged students actively in the fruitful skill of both intensive and extensive reading. Thus, it can strengthen students reading competency and make them enjoy the reading act.

Established on the interview data finding, it reveals the applications they used in the iPad to assist them learning EFL reading comprehension: 26 students used iBooks, then 21 Google Translate, 18 KamusPro, 13 iMovie, 10 Keynote, 6 Dictionary and 6 also Safari browser, 4 Pages, 3 iDu, 2 Speak menu, 1 YouTube, and 1 Dropbox (Interview: R#1-R#30). It means that most students are familiar with the applications on the iPad which are assisted them in their EFL reading comprehension learning.

Furthermore, it clarifies the data on how students used the applications in iPad such as iBooks, Speak menu, KamusPro, Google Translate, Keynote, iMovie, Youtube, iDu in learning EFL reading comprehension. It revealed also the use of Pages, Safari, and Drobox apps (Interview: R#1, R#5, R#17, R#19, R#22, R#23). It means that besides they are recognizable with the applications they also knew how to use those apps.

After that, considering the interview data finding, it is found from the researcher as a main participant (coded as R#31), her thought of teaching English reading comprehension using the iPad that it is an interesting breakthrough for education development in teaching EFL reading comprehension (Interview: R#31). It is similar to McMinn & Li (2012) found that iPad implementation in a TBLT classroom had positive outcomes. When the instructors were planning for an iPad-based lesson, they prepared not only differently but also more carefully to achieve learning objectives easily. Thus, the role of this technology was a learning assistant device rather than the core of face-to-face classes.

Another data it shows that the applications she used on the iPad such as Dictionary, KamusPro, Speak menu, and iMovie as well as virtual learning, iDu Class, are to assist her teaching English reading comprehension using iBooks (Interview: R#31). It means that the applications cited are really applied to help her to teach EFL reading comprehension.

Moreover, it clarifies how she used the applications in iPad while she was teaching EFL reading comprehension as she claimed below:

First in presenting the EFL reading comprehension materials, she used iBooks application which she designed by herself for teaching. That is English 2 (BL102) iBooks. As Apple.com (2013) mentions iPad inspires creativity and hands-on learning with features of educational tool such as iBooks. Besides, she proved that it transformed the simple act of reading into simply delightful learning experience. She also could create the interactive materials with iBooks Author and it worked best for her students for it set in accordance to her objective teaching learning activities as Apple.com stated about iBooks (2013).

It is proved that the iBooks has many advantages, it can give not only picture but also video. The picture and short video in the iBooks were utilized as her pre-reading activity to involve her students predicting about the topic of the passage. In addition, both she and her students could define easily the difficult words just by select the word and click define and immediately arouse the definition of that word (before this they had already downloaded Dictionary app in the iBooks). Besides those apps, students used KamusPro. This is similar to as Apple.com (2013) explains hesitant with unfamiliar words is common to occur when reading new texts or learning new subjects. Therefore, in iPad students can look up words by using the dictionary integrated in iOS. They could quickly access to definitions and commonly used phrases to help with grammar, spelling, and pronunciation—still when they are offline. What to add here is Kamus Lengkap Pro, it could work either online or offline (No internet connection required), as iTunes in Apple.com (2013) cited.

And what more is Speak menu in the iPad. Teacher gave an explanation how to use it. Students selected or blocked the words and tapped Speak menu to know the correct pronunciation. As Apple.com (2013) elaborates iBooks supports VoiceOver, Speak Selection, and closed-captioned videos to facilitate all kinds of learners.

Furthermore, in the iBooks the students recorded their notes by highlighting or underlining the words and then tapped the picture of note thus they could easily write down their difficult words and ideas of each paragraph as well as the answer of the questions given after they read the text. The notes eased the students to study the passage and to share their works after reading via email and this made the teacher ease to get and evaluate their works immediately. As Apple.com (2013) explains multicolor highlighting, notes, search, study cards, and the glossary such features facilitate students be better organized and better prepared. To give students an immediate assessment of their knowledge, teachers can built-in review questions, so they comprehend where to focus more study time.

To redirect comprehension text-related tasks teacher asked the students to use iMovie app. Before that students had to prepare the presentation by using Keynote app. This application assisted them to show their iMovie reading comprehension presentation. And their video presentations were uploaded to YouTube. This way makes them practice to read aloud, summary everything about the text that they had in the classroom so they learnt the EFL reading comprehension differently and interesting. As Apple.com (2013) offers iMovie can also assist reinforced chronological ordering skills, and provide students the opportunity to employ visual-spatial powers and build up their storytelling skills.

For the announcements and the submission of students' assignments, she applied iDu class which was provided by the college especially for iLearning classes that used iPad in their teaching and learning activities. As advocated by Perguruan Tinggi Raharja (2013) iDu, abbreviated from iLearning Education, is a learning system that is developed by Raharja College to facilitate campus community and students in conducting lectures. It is a learning media in which the students are assigned and encouraged to ask, response, think, create and present as well as be active autonomously through the applications used in the iPad.

All the works demonstrated without any difficulty in the classroom for the class was equipped by projector which was connected to Apple TV so the teacher or students could show their works easily at the projector, as Apple com (2013) cites in its writing article entitled Apple-Education-Special Education-iOS. Apple com (2014) in its writing article entitled What is Apple TV proposes that by Apple TV one can show what is on one's Mac or iOs device such as iPad in your HDTV with AirPlay effortlessly.

These clarifications show that teaching EFL reading comprehension using iPad can apply in the situation that each of the teacher and students are assisted with iPad completed by those applications which had been explained. It is in line with Lee (2012) he believed that iPads are tolerable. One of the important insights was the instructors considerately iPad, in the classroom, by every-one had a personal iPad to utilize. And also Department of Education in Melbourne, Victoria, Australia (2013), in their writing article entitled Why the iPad: iPad Features; iPads for Education/ iPads Educational Features, they believe one of some educational reasons for using the iPad in education is the iPad defines as an individual tool and practically valued to operate as a one to one, anywhere, anytime learning device.

Built on the documents examination data finding, the researcher portrays information about how teacher and her students implemented the utilization of iPad in teaching learning EFL reading comprehension. The researcher as a main participant, as a teacher, built lessons in iDu class and reading comprehension materials in iBooks, and from 13 students it is found samples data students' iBooks assignments report submission from iDu English class and a form of journal entries from their English 2 iBooks sent by email during the courses, as well as samples data students' iMovie assignments report submission from iDu English class in a form of audiovisual materials or videotapes, students' iMovie reading comprehension presentation which were uploaded to YouTube. Moreover, the information contained in these documents is explained in the next following explanation.

Based on the data of documents examination finding, it is confirmed that iPad can be used to teach EFL reading comprehension. For example, a sample of lessons in iDu, a virtual class which was provided by Raharja College for teaching and learning as well as a sample of Reading Comprehension Material in iBooks, a multi touch textbook on technology which was created by the researcher as main participant to assist her teaching EFL reading comprehension.

In addition, after the iDu class description, the documents data finding reveals samples data report of students' iBooks assignments submission from iDu English class and a form of journal entries from their English 2 iBooks sent by email during the courses made by students are identified from subjects' research. They are 7 students who were selected in this research. These documents are samples data about how students implement the utilization of iBooks in learning EFL reading comprehension, and the example of the journal entries from one of the subjects' research as it was worked by #AW.

Those documents examination findings as supported by Hutchison et al. (2012). They recommended the iPad can be used effectively for curricular integration rather than technology integration. Moreover, Lee (2012) also believed that instructors can intend different methods to incorporating the iPads in conduct their pedagogy.

Thus, it is proven that utilizing iBooks in teaching EFL reading comprehension deserves as new model of teaching EFL reading comprehension assisted by the current technology device like iBooks in iPad with its appropriate applications can support all activities reading phases, namely pre-reading, during (active) reading, and post reading phases as asserted by Dowhower (1999), as well as the tips or strategies to comprehend the text as proposed by JamesESL (2008).

3.2.2 The benefits gained by teacher and students in implementing iBooks in their EFL reading comprehension

Marzban (2008) investigated the effect of CALL on the quality of students' reading comprehension. And he found that there was a significant difference in the means and he could assume that such differences could not be by accident. And Hutchison et al. (2012) saw a valuable lesson about how iPads can be used to improve the instruction. Accordingly, they had developed a register of features helped iPads for teaching literacy and special considerations for integrating iPads or similar tablets into curricular. They recommended the iPad can be used effectively for curricular integration rather than technology integration.

It is strengthened from the interview data finding, it can be inferred the answers of the interview questions about the advantages which the researcher as a main participant (coded as R#31) gained in teaching English reading comprehension using the iPad.

From the finding, it shows her thought of teaching English reading comprehension using the iPad that it is an interesting innovation for education development in teaching EFL reading comprehension as she said that the teaching EFL reading comprehension using iPad was an interesting breakthrough in the world of education for its applications which supported the teaching such as iBooks, Dictionary, KamusPro, Speak menu, and iMovie. Moreover, Lee (2012) believed that instructors can intend different methods to incorporating the iPads in conduct their pedagogy.

Established on the interview data finding, it shows that from 30 participants of students, there are 28 students have positive thought towards utilization of iBooks in learning EFL reading comprehension and only 2 students have negative thoughts of it. The positive thought towards utilization of iBooks in learning EFL reading comprehension elaborates as R#7 said that iPad eased their efforts to comprehend English reading passage. Thus those findings mentioned previously are similar to McMinn & Li (2012) found. They revealed the use of iPads enhanced the effective negotiation of meaning.

Other important information data on the advantages students gained in learning EFL reading comprehension using the iPad shows as follow:

All participants (30 students) believed that there were many apps in iPad assisting EFL reading comprehension learning as R#1 said. It is similar to Department of Education in Melbourne, Victoria, Australia (2012), they say one of some educational reasons for using the iPad in education is the use of diverse apps make students are able to select the type of creation they build to express their comprehension.

26 students convinced that it was simpler, easier to learn, and effective learning EFL reading comprehension by using iBooks (Interview: R#18).

12 students asserted that it was efficient for it helped them to respond the materials faster (Interview: R#26), it also supported students to do their English language assignments (Interview: R#12), students felt they can know quickly the meaning of words or sentences as well as read the text properly (Interview: R#20), student can translate the words that he does not know and he can hear the voice of those words by selecting and tapping Speak menu (Interview: R#10), it is saving their time (Interview: R#19), they do not necessary to bring

a dictionary to look for the meaning of the word (Interview: R#24), it is cost saving (Interview: R#23), they do not need to bring a lot of books (Interview: R#3 and R#5). This is as Mitchell (2012) supported that set learning goals to address with the help of iPads range from vocabulary acquisition to presentation skills to paraphrasing. She believed the advantage of three crucial workings of the iPad for its portability, its connectivity, and its multimodality. These features can help create meaningful learning opportunities, including creating multimodal digital product and analyzing sources found online. In addition, 3 students said that it was practical (Interview: R#22 and R#23).

And 2 students admitted that iPad made the learner become creative (Interview: R#2). Those findings are supported by Melhuish & Falloon (2010) observed that the way m-learning with iPad can be integrated into effective, evidence-driven, innovative practices, so that the learner is empowered and enriched by the learning experience. It means that learning with iPad is very potential to determine the successful learning in the future by intensifying the students' activities from the media in order to develop their English language learning. And moreover as Department of Education in Melbourne, Victoria, Australia (2012) also endorsed by iPad the information is represented with rich multimedia and data visualization techniques. In line with this Lee (2012) added that iPads are tolerable for providing students the autonomy to be stimulated in multimedia innovations.

In addition, the data also shows the advantages that teacher gained in teaching EFL reading comprehension using the iBooks such as she supposed below:

She does not need to carry heavily books or textbook and dictionary because the applications are already on the iPad. In line with this finding Lee (2012) believed that iPads are tolerable for handiness and easiness of use assisted instructors concentrate on their reading materials and information in new habits, the course works could be handed on paperless, and the portability, tiny and lightweight iPad enables students develop projects outside the classroom, into their community. And also Department of Education in Melbourne, Victoria, Australia (2012) say two of some educational reasons for using the iPad in education are flimsy and handy, simply carried in the school bag and to and from class and heavy schoolbooks could be replaced by virtual eBooks and these can be updated in a timely fashion. The documents and tasks can be uploaded to iBooks by the teacher and synchronized onto the iPad by the student and vice versa.

It is sufficient. By tapping the select word, she and her students could define the meaning of difficult words easily by Dictionary app which they had downloading and speak them up by selecting and tapping Speak menu so they knew how to pronounce them correctly.

And it makes teacher ease to teach her students EFL reading comprehension for they can easily record their works and share them via email in the iBooks.

iMovie app really helps her to redirect comprehension text-related tasks to the students in different way and interesting. Hence, students can express their summary of the text differently and with fun.

Assisted by the iPad, she could ask her students to submit their works via BL102 iDu class, as soon as she announced them in iDu. She could monitor students works wherever and whenever she was by looking at incoming email reply as well as in BL102 iDu class (2014). It is similar to Department of Education in Melbourne, Victoria, Australia (2012). They believe one of some educational reasons for using the iPad in education is the students can access to current information that contains text, sound, images and interactivity wherever, whenever they exist.

Concerning these findings, it can be concluded that the advantages in utilizing iBooks in teaching EFL reading comprehension are good news in English education. Utilizing iBooks in teaching EFL reading comprehension can be one of new ideas in a teaching model in the classroom in order to follow the development of technology which assists EFL teaching and to improve the teaching itself.

The Challenges Found by Teacher and Students in implementing iBooks in Their EFL Reading Comprehension

Based on the interview data finding, it can be concluded the answers of the questions about the challenges she gained in teaching English reading comprehension using the iBooks. Although most of the students have positive thoughts in learning EFL reading comprehension using the iBooks but they are a few of the students have negative thoughts of learning English reading comprehension using the iBooks. Such as R#4 believed that learning EFL reading comprehension assisted by iBooks so far is quite efficient and easier but with the ease of it make the user spoiled by the iBooks itself. It means that one who uses the iBooks in his EFL reading comprehension learning has an obstacle for the iBooks makes the user inconsistent by it.

Considering the interview data finding stated previously, it is revealed the challenges teacher faced as she thought below:

The most challenge is that if the internet is slow or even non-existent service.

And other is when there are few of her students have conversations with their friends through social media networking or they just look at the update activities there. It makes them not focus to the instructions in the classroom (interview: R#31).

It is the different findings with previous research conducted by Department of Education in Melbourne, Victoria, Australia (2012) they did not revealed challenges such as these evidences. And also by Mitchell (2012) he believes connectivity allows users of iPad to access materials from around the web, simplifying dictionary searches, research, etc. It also tolerates users to publish on the web more effortlessly.

Furthermore, the interview data finding also describes the challenges faced by students in learning English reading comprehension using the iBooks. From 30 participants interviewed it is revealed that although there were 27 students believed that there were some challenges found during the use of iBooks in their learning EFL reading comprehension, there were 3 students discovered that there was no challenge in using it such as R#14 believed. And those challenges found are as follow:

11students found a trouble in internet connection/Wi-Fi as R#27 stated (Interview on Utilizing iBooks in Learning English as a Foreign Language (EFL) Reading Comprehension Q.5 at R#27, 2014).

8 students admitted that they had to be focus or become autonomous learner, for example, R#26 claimed (Interview on Utilizing iBooks in Learning English as a Foreign Language (EFL) Reading Comprehension Q.5 at R#26, 2014). As Cabot (2010) affirmed that the iPad as teaching tool has several uses in the classroom for the obvious—materials, video, and reference materials in teachers' fingertips. And in students' side, it has been praised as a valuable tool for autonomous learning.

6 students faced iPad hang/error as R#16 said (Interview on Utilizing iBooks in Learning English as a Foreign Language (EFL) Reading Comprehension Q.5 at R#16, 2014).

4 students discovered low battery for example R#9 said (Interview on Utilizing iBooks in Learning English as a Foreign Language (EFL) Reading Comprehension Q.5 at R#9, 2014). It is different with Department of Education in Melbourne, Victoria, Australia (2012), they believe one of some educational reasons for using the iPad in education is the iPad can be used throughout the entire school day due to a 10-hour battery life device. That condition is a line to the findings that and other is when there are few of her students have conversations with their friends through social media networking or they just look at the update activities there. It makes them not focus to the instructions in the classroom (Interview: R#31). And consequently it triggers low battery.

3 students did not accustom to apply the apps as R#21 asserted (Interview on Utilizing iBooks in Learning English as a Foreign Language (EFL) Reading Comprehension Q.5 at R#21, 2014).

2 students revealed it was costly as R#8 claimed (Interview on Utilizing iBooks in Learning English as a Foreign Language (EFL) Reading Comprehension Q.5 at R#8, 2014). It is not similar with Lee (2012) as he believed that iPads are tolerable for regain to praising or moderately priced apps.

And the last, a student admitted that he was tired for looking at iPad often as R#25 said (Interview on Utilizing iBooks in Learning English as a Foreign Language (EFL) Reading Comprehension Q.5 at R#25, 2014). The findings of students not accustomed to apply the apps, students' thought that the iPad was costly, a student tired for looking at iPad often are the different findings with Department of Education in Melbourne, Victoria, Australia (2012). They did not revealed challenges such as these evidences.

Considering these findings, it can be concluded that challenges in utilizing iBooks in teaching and learning EFL reading comprehension are something inevitable. Good Wi-Fi access connection and adequate trainings for the teaching learning EFL reading comprehension using iBooks become somewhat that is mandatory in order to make this teaching occurred successfully.

4 CONCLUSIONS AND SUGGESTIONS

The implementation of utilizing iBooks in teaching EFL reading comprehension has some benefits; It supports autonomous learners. It also affords teacher and students with online accessibility for they can interact each other anywhere and anytime easily.

Some challenges in the implementation of utilizing iBooks in teaching EFL reading comprehension; Teacher should be mastered all matters relating to iBooks and others supported applications used in the iPad. It is found that the most challenge for teacher as well as students is that if the internet is slow or even non-existent service. And other is due to social media networking or the update activities from it, makes few students not focus to the instructions in the classroom. Teacher must also have enough time to explain well to the students when they encounter problems.

Finally, utilizing iBooks in teaching EFL reading comprehension is a breakthrough thought in the teaching of EFL reading comprehension that utilizes new technologies which can assist and motivate students in EFL reading comprehension. It is proven that utilizing iBooks in teaching EFL reading comprehension deserves as new model of teaching EFL reading comprehension assisted by iBooks with its supportive applications can support all activities reading phases, as well as the tips or strategies to comprehend the text. Hence, iBooks transforms a simple act of reading EFL text to more enjoyable and challenging.

Furthermore, to achieve maximum results in the teaching of EFL reading comprehension using the iBooks, there are some suggestions that can be given as follows: Students must give enough opportunity or training to properly understand how to use the iBooks and other applications supported, not only in the classroom but also outside the classroom, such as Speak Selection, KamusPro and iMovie apps on iPad which are utilized in teaching learning EFL reading comprehension using the iBooks as well as to access iDu, their virtual class to submit their assignments.

Then, the teacher as students' counselor should provide motivation to her students who are not autonomous in learning EFL reading comprehension by using this iBooks. Teacher should play an active role as well as possible. First as an organizer, meaning that she has to prepare the materials well using iBooks and the applications supported such as Speak Selection, KamusPro and iMovie apps on iPad which are used in teaching learning EFL reading comprehension as well as to access iDu, their virtual class to submit their assignments. Besides, when asking students to read intensively she should be able to give them clear instructions. Next, as an observer, he should examine students' progress when they are reading. And do not miss the role as the prompter, notice language features within the text after students have read it. And the teacher role is also as feedback organizer. She should lead a discussion of feedback when they have finished the task from their sent email to ensure whether they have done it effectively or not.

Equally important, the college properly provides training program which prepare the teachers to use iBooks with other applications that supports the utilization of iBooks in their curricular education system with a good enough internet connection for their community so they can easily perform their tasks properly and help their students to improve their English.

REFERENCES

Apple-Education-Special Education-iOS. Retrieved on November 28, 2013, from http://www.apple.com/education/special-education/ios/.

Apple in Education. Apple in Education Profiles: Creating New Possibilities in The Classroom with iPad. Apple-Burlington High School Profile. Retrieved on April 30, 2013 from http://www.apple.com/education/profiles/burlington/.

Apple in Education: The Device that Changed everything is Now Changing theClassroom. Apple-Education-iPad makes the perfect learning companion. Retrieved on April 30, 2013 from http://www.apple.com/education/ipad/.

Assia, Miss. BENETTAYEB 2012. ICT and Reading: In the Technology- Enhanced Extensive Reading Classroom. *Revue academiques des sciences socials et humaines* 8(2012): 3–6. Hassiba Ben- Bouali University of Chlef, Algeria. Retrieved on June 14, 2013 from http://www.univ-chlef.dz/ratsh/RATSH_AR/Article_Revue_Academique_N_08_2012/article_18.PDF.

Booth, D. & Swartz, L. 2004. *Literacy techniques: Building successful readers and writers* (2nd ed.). Ontario, Canada: Pembroke Publishers Limited. Some names are shoetened but others are NOT …… issue of consistency.

Cabot, J. 2010. *Teaching with The iPad-First Day*. Gadgetell LLC & North American Publishing Company (NAPCO) Spring Garden Street, 12th Floor | Philadelphia, USA. June 16, 2010: 1. Retrieved on May 4, 2013 from http://www.teleread.com/ipad/teaching-with-the-ipad-first-days/.

Chard, David J. & Santoro, Lana E. 2008. *What is reading comprehension and why is it important? A Reading First Quality Brief*. US: Department of Education.

Dickinson, David, K., Griffith, Julie, A., Golinkoff, Roberta M. & Hirsh-Pasek, Kathy. 2012. *How Reading Books Fosters Language Development around the World*. Child Development Research, 2012(2012): 15. Retrieved on October 17, 2015, from http://www.hindawi.com/journals/cdr/2012/602807/.

Donoghue, Mildred, R. 2009. Language arts: Integrating skills for classroom teaching; reading; principles, approaches, comprehension, and fluency. Chapter 6. *Sage Publications*: 158–161.

Dowhower, Sarah L. 1999. *Comprehension strategy framework. The reading teacher*. April, 1999. Karen Haag: Sarah Dowhower—LikeToRead.com: 2–3. Retrieved on November 2, 2013, from http://www.liketoread.com/Resources/Dowhower%20Comprehension%20Framework.pdf.

Fang, L. 2010. Using multimedia to motivate EFL students' interest in English language learning. *Paper Presented in a Seminar Paper Research in University of Wisconsin-Platteville*. Apr 14, 2010. Retrieved on May 5, 2013 from http://minds.wisconsin.edu/handle/1793/39124?show = full.

Harmer, J. 2007. *The practice of English language teaching*. 4th Ed. completely Revised and Updated. Harlow: Pearson Education Limited.

Harmon, J. 2011. *Unlocking literacy with iPad: A teacher research project*. Euclid City Schools, Ohio. 5–6. Retrieved on June 17, 2013 from http://www.throughstudentseyes.org/ipads/Unlocking_Literacy_with_iPad/iPads_files/Unlocking_Literacy_iPad.pdf.

Hartoyo. 2006. I*ndividual differences in computer assisted language learning (CALL)*. Semarang: Pelita Insani Semarang Press.

Hartoyo. 2012. *ICT (Information and Communication Technology) in language learning*. Semarang: Pelita Insani Semarang Press.

Hutchison, A., Beschorner, B. & Schmidt-Crawford, D. 12 Jul 2012. Exploring the use of the iPad for literacy learning. Article published online: *The Reading Teacher* 66(1): 23, September 2012. Retrieved on May 10, 2013 from http://onlinelibrary.wiley.com/doi/10.1002/TRTR.01090/pdf.

iPad Definition. Update: March 9, 2011. TechTerms. Com. Retrieved on May 4, 2013, from http://www.techterms.com/definition/ipad/.

iPad: Your New Favorite Way to Do Just About Everything. Apple-iPad-Built-in apps. Retrieved on May 04, 2013 from http://www.apple.com/ipad/built-in-apps/.

Krashen, Stephen D. 1982. *Principles and Practice in Second Language Acquisition*. University of Southern California: Pergamon Press Inc.

Lee, A. 2012. iPads for Teaching and Learning: Technology Enhances the First year Experience. *Summer* 2012. Minneapolis, MN: University of Minnesota. Retrieved on November 28, 2013, from http://www.cehd.umn.edu/pstl/PsTLposts/SummerPOSTS–2012.pdf.

Marzban, A. 2008. *Using CALL in EFL reading comprehension classes: English language teaching conference*. Azad University Ghaemshahr, Iran: Rodehen Branch. Retrieved on June 17, 2013 from http://faculty.ksu.edu.sa/aljarf/Documents/English%20   Language%20Teaching%20Conference%20-%20 Iran%202008/Amir%20Marzban.pdf.

McMinn, S. & Li, Y. 2012. Enhancing Interactions with Mobile Devices in Language Classrooms. International Conference. "ICT for Language Learning" (5th ed). *The Hong Kong University of Science and Technology* 3–5. Retrieved on June 17, 2013 from http://conference.pixel-online.net/ICT4 LL2012/common/download/Abstract_pdf/150-IBT28-ABS-McMinn-ICT2012.pdf.

Melhuish, K. & Falloon, G. 2010. Looking to the future: M-learning with the iPad: Computers in New Zealand Schools: Learning, leading, technology. *Computers in New Zealand Schools Published*

Journal 22(3) Retrieved on May 10, 2013 from http://researchcommons.waikato.ac.nz/bitstream/handle/10289/5050/Looking%20to%20the%20future.pdf?sequence=1.

Mikulecky, Beatrice S. & Jeffries, L. 2007. *Advance reading power: Extensive reading, vocabulary building, comprehension skills, reading faster*. White Plains, NY: Pearson Education. Inc.

Mitchell, K. 2012. *iPads for students learning. TESOL Connections*. Retrieved on November 25, 2013 from http://newsmanager.commpartners.com/tesolc/issues/2012-07-01/3.html.

Ravichandran, T. 2000. CALL in the Perspective of Interactive Approach: Advantages and Apprehensions. Proceedings: National Seminar on CALL, Anna University, Chennai, 10–12 February 2000, 82–89:1–2. Retrieved on May 17, 2013 from http://home.iitk.ac.in/~trc/call.pdf.

Renandya, W. A. & Richards, J.C. 2002. *Methodology in anguage teaching: An anthology of current practice*. Cambridge: Cambridge University Press.

The ESRC Seminar Series Reading Comprehension: From Theory to Practice. Collaboration research groups at the Universities of York, Oxford, Lancaster and Sussex. 2013.

Tompkins, G.E. 2010. Reading comprehension factors. *Pearson Allyn Bacon Prentice Hall*. Updated on Jul 20, 2010. Retrieved on December 20, 2013, from http://www.education.com/reference/article/reading-comprehension-factors/.

What is Apple TV. Retrieved on August 30, 2014, from https://www.apple.com/appletv/what-is/.

Why the iPad: iPad Features; iPads for Education. Department of Education in Melbourne, Victoria, Australia. 2012. Retrieved on November 25, 2013, from http://www.ipadsforeducation.vic.edu.au/why-ipad/ipad-features.

ELT in Asia in the Digital Era: Global Citizenship and Identity – Madya et al. (Eds)
© 2018 Taylor & Francis Group, London, ISBN 978-0-8153-7900-3

The effectiveness of online brain-writing compared to brainstorming as prewriting strategies in teaching writing to students with high frequency and low frequency of Language Learning Strategies (LLS)

D. Hermasari
Yogyakarta State University, Yogyakarta, Indonesia

ABSTRACT: The article examined two prewriting strategies, Online Brain-writing and Brainstorming, to students with High Frequency (HF) and Low Frequency (LF) of LLS by means of Oxford's Strategy Inventory of Language Learning (1990). The study applied a 2×2 factorial design to the data collected from 60 EFL college students. ANOVA test showed that online brain-writing was significant for both groups of students with ρ .000. Brainstorming, however, was only significant for HF of LLS students with ρ .000, but insignificant for LF of LLS students with ρ .059. The mean score of Online Brain-writing to students with HF of LLS was higher than Online Brain-writing to students with LF of LLS. Brainstorming also resulted in higher mean difference for students with HF of LLS compared to that of students with LF of LLS. Future research might consider using a different method to enhance the generality of the results.

1   INTRODUCTION

Over decades, the use of prewriting strategies has been investigated for its effectiveness to help students' writing in different kinds of contexts (King 1990, Kellog 1990, King 1991, McAlister 1999, Vincent 2002, Coskun 2005, Aaron et al. 2006, Firkins 2007, Bush & Zuidema 2012, Morris 2012). Becoming fully aware that writing is not simply a matter of correct usage and mechanics yet more to the process of conveying ideas to the audiences, many teachers find prewriting strategies useful to help students in developing ideas. Through prewriting strategies, teaching thinking strategies essential to effective written communication becomes the main concern to serve students a planning stage. This planning stage in a form of prewriting strategies is believed to be able to promote the next stages of writing process, leading to better quality of students' writing.

2   LITERATURE REVIEW

2.1   *EFL writing*

Writing in EFL context is regarded as a fundamental skill, owing to the fact that it requires thinking, forces students to organize their ideas, and needs a good command of the knowledge to be written on. On that account, many researchers in EFL writing contends that writing is one of the most difficult language skills to master (Kurt & Attay 2007, Latif 2007). This issue deals with the major difference between expert and EFL writers in their use of planning stage; Asmari (2013) points out that experts develop far more elaborate and integrated goal networks than novice do. Good writers recognize the essence of the prewriting phase, viewing it as rehearsal in which preparation comes from daydreaming, sketching, note-taking, reading, conversing and writing itself. To encounter this problem, EFL teachers keep on trying to find an effective method of teaching writing.

2.2 Technology and writing

The notion of "digital natives" was defined by Prensky (2001) as "native speakers' of the digital language of computers, video games, and the Internet". Thus, students who were born when computers, video games, and the Internet were already part of their daily life are considered as digital natives. Herring (as quoted by Bloch 2011) proposed the term computer-mediated discourse (CMD) as "the communication produced when human beings interact with one another by transmitting messages via networked computers" (p. 67). There are two areas of CMD: synchronous which refers to interaction in real time (which more resembles oral language, such as in chat room) and asynchronous discourse for example the interaction found in email and blog comments.

Bloch (2008), as a techno-realist, regards the fear of failure in implementing a technology in writing class as understandable fact due to all existing considerations, i.e. plagiarism, students' unlimited time expectation to teachers, the nature of technology itself, teachers' roles, etc. Zhang & Barber (2008) argue that it is crucial when incorporating technology in the language learning process that the relationship between activities in the use of technology itself and the learning pedagogy be carefully considered.

To give a perspective in the technology use, Warschauer (1997) proposed the special features of online communication, i.e. text-based and computer mediated, many-to-many, time- and place-independent, usable across long distances, and distributed via hypermedia which provide impressive array of new ways to connect learners. From the context of sociocultural learning theory, these features of online learning is viewed as having potential use for collaborative language learning.

2.3 Prewriting strategies

In the prewriting phase, a writer gathers ideas by looking for sources through several strategies. Thus, the aims of the prewriting process for EFL students is to be familiar to the characteristic of writing target (its organization and its language features) and come up with ideas to write. Several strategies done as prewriting activities are: brainstorming, mind-mapping, survey, observation, and guided-discussion. As consequences, these varied prewriting strategies have been implemented in research on that area, for example the ones by Emig (1971) and Morris (2012). Hashempour argue that being familiar with various types of prewriting strategies helps students to become strategic writers (Hashempour 2015).

2.4 Brainstorming

Brainstorming was firstly introduced by 'The Father of Brainstorming', Alex F. Osborn, in his book 'Your Creative Power', published in 1952. Osborn mentioned that this technique began in his advertising agency in 1939. The technique, which refers to the oral generation of ideas by a group, provides a space for a group of people to gather and generate as many ideas as possible to find solution to a problem (Takagi, N. 2013). Being well-known, the technique also spread in the world of teaching, where creativity became essential. A Large number of education practitioners (Brown & Paulus 2002, Bolin & Neuman 2006, Ang et al. 2013) started using brainstorming in the classroom to stimulate students' creativity and to serve collaborative work among students.

Despite its advantages, teachers found some drawbacks in conducting brainstorming. One of the drawbacks is the time allotment of the activity. Group brainstorming conducted in the writing class takes time. Besides, brainstorming might inhibit creativity of silent students since they have a tendency to be reluctant in expressing ideas through spoken conversation. As the result, the brainstorming process is frequently dominated by one or two individuals. In addition to these inhibitory factors, Smith (1995) argues that interactive brainstorming groups tend to display two main tendencies. The first tendency is that groups typically tend to lower their idea-generation performance during later periods of the brainstorming session. This may reflect reduced availability of ideas, reduced motivation in time, or some degree of cognitive inhibition. To face the drawbacks, many variations of brainstorming, then, came into being. Brain-sketching and brain-writing are two of these variations which might be alternatives over traditional brainstorming to cater the specific needs of classroom condition.

2.5 Online brain-writing

Brain-writing, which is defined as a method of brainstorming in a form of writing, tries to encourage more uniform participation within a group. This technique is also designed to generate numerous ideas in a short amount of time. During the process, the participants are allowed to write new ideas, combine other ideas, adapt ideas to new areas, modify ideas into alternative approaches, and add to the ideas. Silent students get more advantages using this technique in a way that they have a chance in expressing ideas through written media. In addition, Takagi (2013) reported that the majority of students, the participants of the research comparing brainstorming and brain-writing, responded by choosing brain-writing over brainstorming for its effectiveness in gaining ideas.

As technology become inevitable, the collaborative language learning in a form of online brain-writing, or also known as electronic brainstorming, has become an alternative to traditional brainstrorming. Students are grouped and joined the brain-writing in the provided virtual space like website or e-learning portal. Using this technique, students are no longer restricted to time boundary. They can be active in the group brain-writing session whenever they are available. Here, the moderator task is to make sure that participants keep participating. The rules or steps of brain-writing also apply in electronic brain-writing. The number of ideas in each post should be defined to give every student equal participation. A study done by Michinov shows that the use of online brain-writing is superior to traditional brain-writing (Michinov 2012). He further explains the advantages of using online brain-writing compared to the traditional one are: increasing the task focus (participants do not see each other), reducing redundancy, and improving students' performance in generating ideas.

One case study conducted by Litcanu, et al. resulted in a conclusion that Brain-writing is preferred compared to brainstorming since the former method do not impose dominant member to perform better and also provided more thinking time for individual member (Litcanu et al, 2015).

2.6 High frequency and low frequency of Language Learning Strategies (LLS)

Apart from strategies applied by teachers, the time limitation suffer by EFL learners needs to be encountered to better reach students' performances. For that reason, other factors influencing the students' level of proficiency require more attention, especially the ones which raises students' autonomy so that time limitation in class can be substituted by their autonomy outside the class. One among those factors specified to EFL students is the frequency of Language Leaning Strategies (LLS) used by the students. LLS has been investigated by several researchers among the world.

Several studies show that HF of LLS is proven to lead to high students' proficiency (e.g. Lan 2005 and McMullen 2009). In addition, Giffiths (2003) in his research found that the frequent use of a large number of language learning strategies is reported by the most proficient learners. Further, he suggested teachers to encourage students to use more strategies in their learning process to improve their proficiency. Thus, the investigation of students' level of LLS was found to be useful to support teaching and learning process. As a follow up of the findings, to further know the essence of LLS investigation, some practitioners started to have training on LLS. They believe that the strategies are teachable and by teaching the strategies they expect their students to have better language proficiency.

To get insightful understanding, researchers on LLS (Fazeli 2011, Chamot 2004, McMullen 2009) suggest more studies to investigate its influence in different contexts and situations. Thus, responding to the suggestion, the coming study is investigating the comparison of the use of different prewriting strategies by also considering the level of LLS in EFL context.

3 METHODOLOGY

This study was done to 60 second-semester EFL students of Yogyakarta State University in 2016. Two classes are chosen for their similarity of conditions; both classes learn English as compulsory subjects and both classes are majoring Dance Education. 30 students were the subjects of the study by random sampling method. This study applied quantitative approach which involved factorial design and questionnaire. The use of factorial design was to analyze two independent variables (one treatment variable and one moderator variable) in the experiment. There were 2 forms of data; i.e. students' questionnaire results on the frequency of language learning strategies results, and students' pretest and posttest scores which were collected from students' writing projects.

The study used a quasi-experimental design. The design of this study is a modified version of Tuckman's (1999) model of a 2×2 quasi-experimental design with pretest-posttest. There were two experimental groups in this design: the experimental group 1 receiving online brain-writing as the treatment and the experimental group 2 (in the original model, this later group is called control group) receiving traditional brainstorming as its treatment. Both groups are given a pretest and a posttest. The existence of pretests aimed to control the threats to internal validity. The pretest was also important to find out whether the treatment improves students' scores by comparing them to the posttest results. The study applied random assignment to determine the control and experiment groups to minimize the bias factors in this study. The researcher also applied the inter-rater agreement method in assessing the students' essays to have the scores valid and reliable.

The subjects of the study were 60 students of Yogyakarta State University. Those 60 students were from two different EFL classes; the students learn English as a compulsory subject. The students' ages typically ranged between 17–20 years old. They have learned English since grade 4 elementary school. They are familiar with grammatical features, such as tenses, noun, adjectives, and verbs. They also have learned many kinds of text genres, such as narrative, descriptive, recount, and exposition. However, review text which requires the skill of delivering arguments is something new and challenging for them. The students were to write a review on art performance: "Tron Dance" both in pretest and posttest. The researcher using interrater agreement analyzed the students' writing using ESL Composition Profile (Jacobs et al. 1981).

To investigate students' level of LLS frequency, students fill out on-line SILL questionnaire. There were 50 items of Linkert scale questionnaire that later indicates students' frequency of using Language Learning Strategies.

4 FINDINGS AND DISCUSSIONS

4.1 *The significance of online brain-writing compared to brainstorming on English writing skills of students with HF and LF of LLS*

The first objective is comparing the significance of online brain-writing and brainstorming on English writing skill of students with HF and LF of LLS. According to the test statistic using paired samples t-test, the significance scores (ρ value is below 0.005) for four groups were as follows.

The above table shows that online brain-writing to students with HF of LLS compared to that of students with LF of LLS are similarly significant in improving students' writing skills with ρ value .000. On the other hand, the use of brainstorming resulted in different significance for HF of LLS compared to that for LF of LLS. When brainstorming is applied for HF of LLS, the test proves that the technique is significant in improving students' writing skills with ρ value .000. While for LF of LLS students, brainstorming technique fails to improve students writing skills with ρ value .059.

The result shows that the frequency of LLS influences the effectiveness of the use of pre-writing techniques. When students have HF of LLS, the uses of both techniques are proven

Table 1.   The significance (ρ value) of online brain-writing and brain-storming on English writing skill of students with HF and LF of LLS.

Group	HF of LLS	LF of LLS
Online Brain-writing	.000	.000
Brainstorming	.000	.059

Table 2.   The mean difference of online brain-writing and brain-storming on English writing skill of students with HF and LF of LLS.

Group	HF of LLS	LF of LLS
Online Brain-writing	14.83	13.13
Brainstorming	13.96	9.53

to be significant. While the LF students struggle with the use of brainstorming as prewriting strategies; it is proven by the insignificant ρ value .059. The findings support the previous research on students' frequency of LLS done to Saudi EFL students which proves that the more strategies used by the students, the better the writings (McMullen 2009).

The findings of the current study also prove that the use of online brain-writing is more effective compared to brainstorming in improving students' writing skills. More clarity will be further discussed by investigating the mean differences of the four research groups.

4.2   *The mean differences of online brain-writing compared to brainstorming on English writing skills of students with HF and LF of LLS*

The second objective of the study is comparing the mean difference of online brain-writing and brainstorming on English writing skill of students with HF and LF of LLS.

Comparing the mean differences between online brain-writing and brainstorming for the HF of LLS, the numbers show a gap; 14.83 for online brain-writing compared to 13.96 for brainstorming. When both treatment are given to the LF of LLS students, the main difference gap is even bigger; 13.13 for online brain-writing and 9.53 for brainstorming. Those gaps infer that online brain-writing is more effective compared to brainstorming in improving students' writing skills.

The findings support the study by Litcanu et al. which shows that brain-writing method is preferred compared to brainstorming because it increases the number of generated ideas (Litcanu et al. 2015). By writing down the ideas on line, participants are able to think thoroughly while also being comfortable with the time allotment; therefore, they are able to gain more fruitful ideas.

Similarly, it is reasonable to suppose that online brain-writing is superior to brainstorming as also concluded by a study done by Michinov. The former technique offers more time and focus to pay attention to other group members' ideas (Michinov 2012).

The result of the study is also in line with the study conducted by a study in Indonesian context. From the paired samples t-test both studies inferred that brain-writing could improve students' writing skill (Purwati & Trainingand 2017). Students post test scores in both studies show improvement which were shown by the mean differences.

However, it contradicts the findings of Hashempour who suggests that the use of brainstorming, and its sub-categories including brain-writing, do not have any significance towards EFL learners writing development (Hashempour 2015). He suggested to include another important factor such as the effect of other strategies to enhance the generality of the findings. This article includes the frequency LLS as another important factor and resulted in different findings.

By using combined variables: the prewriting strategies and the frequency of LLS, this research should be considered as the first attempt to better understand the influence of both frequency of LLS and the type of prewriting strategies to students' writing scores. Overall, the present results extend the previous studies demonstrating indirectly that brain-writing boosts students' creative thinking skills (Naser & Almutairi 2015, Oishi 2015).

5 CONCLUSION

Based on the above findings, it can be summed up that both online brain-writing and brain-storming played a significant role in improving students' writing skills. However, the frequency of LLS influences the effectiveness of both techniques. By dividing the group into two minor groups, HF of LLS students and LF of LLS students, it is also found that online brain-writing is more effective compared to brainstorming; online brain-writing is proven to be significant in improving the writing skills of students with both high and LF of LLS, while brainstorming is only significant in improving the writing skills of students with HF of LLS. The mean difference results also show that online brain-writing is superior to brainstorming.

Better mean differences gained by online brain-writing technique might be the result of better focus towards task assignment, minor influence from dominant participants, and better encouragement to autonomous learning compared to that of brainstorming technique.

As a response to suggestions from researchers of LLS (Fazeli 2011, Chamot 2004, McMullen 2009) to conduct more studies to investigate its influence in different contexts and situations, this current study examines the use of LLS in Indonesian context. It can be concluded that students' familiarity to LLS needs to be awakened. It has been shown from the research that students have been using several LLS among 50 listed items without realizing that they are actually applying strategies to improve their English skills. Therefore, training LLS to EFL students in Indonesia should help students' learning process.

This study has some limitations. First, in obtaining the samples, the selection of area, groups or clusters, university and classrooms were not randomly selected. Second, it only measures the effectiveness of both techniques from the paired samples t-test without investigating students' preferences between those two techniques which can be done by interviews. Third, the current study gained the result by having different time allotment for both techniques since the nature of online brainstorming is to give the freedom of space and time to the students.

In future prospective researches, it is suggested, especially in Indonesian context, that having a large number of participants with random sampling techniques will result in more fruitful findings. Future researchers might also consider having a mixed method of study in comparing those two strategies to get more precise results. Having more subjects to apply the two strategies is also encouraged to make the data more valid and reliable. Giving varied types of prewriting strategies other than the two techniques used in this research is also suggested in order to know the effectiveness of prewriting strategies. Lastly, selecting a good instrument to observe a particular skill is very important, for instance using academic writing task for advance students might show a better comparison of those two strategies.

REFERENCES

Ang, et al. 2013. Effects of gesture-based avatar-mediated communication on brainstorming and negotiation tasks among younger users. *Computers in Human Behavior* 29: 1204–1211.
Asmari, A.R.A. 2013. Investigation of writing strategies, writing apprehension, and writing achievement among Saudi EFL-major students. *International Education Studies* 6(11): 130–143.
Bloch, J. 2011. *Technologies in the second language composition classroom.* Ann Arbor: The University of Michigan Press.
Bolin, A.U & Neuman, G.A. 2006. Personality, process, and performance in interactive brainstorming groups. *Journal of Business and Psychology*, 20(4): 565–585.
Bush, J. & Zuidema, L. (ed.). 2012. Professional writing in the English classroom. *English Journal* 102(2): 138–141.
Brown, V.R. & Paulus, P.B. 2002. Making group brainstorming more effective: Recommendations from an associative memory perspective. *Current Directions in Psychological Science* 11(6): 208–212.

Chamot, A. U. 2004. Issues in language learning strategy research and teaching. *Electronic Journal of Foreign Language Teaching* 1(1): 14–26. https://doi.org/10.1017/ S0261444808005612.

Coskun, H. 2005. Cognitive Stimulation with Convergent and Divergent Thinking Exercises in Brainwriting: Incubation, Sequnce Priming, and Group Context. *Small Group Research* 36: 466.

Fazeli, S.H. 2011. The Exploring Nature of Language Learning Strategies (LLSs) and their Relationship with Various Variables with Focus on Personality Traits in the Current Studies of Second/ Foreign Language Learning. *Theory and Practice in Language Studies*, 1(10), 1311–1320. https://doi.org/10.4304/tpls.1.10.1311–1320.

Firkins, A. et al. 2007. Teaching writing to low proficiency writing students. *ELT Journal* 61(4): 341–352.

Giffiths, C. 2003. Language leaning strategy use and proficiency. The Relationship between Patterns of Reported Language Learning Strategy (LLS) use by Speakers of Other Languages (SOL) and Proficiency with Implications for the Teaching/Learning Situation, A Thesis. Department of Education: University of Auckland.

Hashempour, Z. 2015. The effect of brainstorming as a pre-writing strategy on EFL advanced learners' writing ability. *Journal of Applied Linguistics and Language Research* 2(1): 86–99.

Kellog, R.T. 1990. Effectiveness of prewriting strategies as a function of task demands. *The American Journal of Psychology* 103(3): 327–342.

King, A. & Rosenshine, B. 1993. Effects of guided cooperative questioning on children's knowledge construction. *The Journal of Experimental Education* 61(2): 127–148.

Latif, M.A. 2007. The factors accounting for the Egyptian EFL university students' negative writing affect. *Essex Graduate Student Papers in Language & Linguistics* 9: 57–82.

Litcanu, M., Prostean, O., Oros, C. & Vasile, A. 2015. Brain-writing vs. brainstorming case study for power engineering education. *Procedia – Social and Behavioral Sciences* 191: 387–390. https://doi.org/10.1016/j.sbspro.2015.04.452.

Manham, L. & Nejadasari, D. 2012. The effect of different pre-writing strategies on Iranian EFL writing achievement. *International Educational Studies* 5(1): 154–160.

McMullen, M.G. 2009. Using language learning strategies to improve the writing skills of Saudi EFL students: Will it really work? *System* 37(3): 418–433. https://doi.org/10.1016 /j.system.2009.05.001.

Michinov, N. 2012. Is electronic brainstorming or brainwriting the best way to improve creative performance in groups? An overlooked comparison of two idea-generation techniques. *Journal of Applied Social Psychology* 42(SUPPL. 1): 1–22. https://doi.org/10.1111/j.1559–1816.2012.01024.x.

Morris, P. 2012. Planning at a higher level: Ideas, form, and academic language in student prewriting. *English Journal* 102(2): 85–92.

Naser, A. & Almutairi, M. 2015. The effect of using brainstorming strategy in developing creative problem solving skills among male students in kuwait: a Field Study on Saud Al-Kharji school in Kuwait City. *Journal of Education and Practice* 6(3): 136–146.

Oishi, T. 2015. Applying brainstorming techniques to EFL classroom. *NII Electronic Library Service*: 121–127.

Oxford, R. 2001. Language learning strategies. In *The Cambridge guide to teaching English to speakers of other languages*. Retrieved from http://proxy.lib.ohio-state.edu/login?url=http://search.credoreference.com.proxy.lib.ohio-state.edu/content/entry/cupteacheng/language learning_strategies/0.

Oxford, R.L. 1990. *Language learning strategies: What every teacher should know*. New York: Newbury House.

Prensky, M. 2001. *Digital natives, digital immigrants*. MCB University Press 9(5).

Purwati, R. & Trainingand, T. 2017. The use of brainwriting strategy to improve the students' writing skills in descriptive text (classroom action research of second grade students at MTS N 1 Susukan in the academic year of 2016/2017). Graduating Paper. IAIN Salatiga.

Smith, S.M. 1995. Fixation, incubation, and insight in memory and creative thinking. In S.M. Smith, T.B. Ward, & R.A. Finke (Eds.), *The Creative Cognition Approach*: 156. Cambridge, MA: MIT Press.

Takagi, N. 2013. Applications of idea-generating techniques to the teaching of argumentative writing. In N. Sonda & A. Krause (eds.). *JALT 2012 Conference Proceedings*. Tokyo: JALT.

Warschauer, M. 1997. Computer-mediated collaborative learning: Theory and practice. *Modern Language Journal* 81(4): 470–481.

Wretzler, W.F. 1962. Brainstorming in the college classroom. *Improving College and University Teaching* 10(1): 34–36.

Gallery Walk for teaching a content course

I. Maharsi

Universitas Islam Indonesia, Yogyakarta, Indonesia

ABSTRACT: Gallery Walk is a learning activity that requires students to visit galleries displaying concept maps (created using e-draw application) on a particular topic while exchanging ideas and discussing related issues being discussed. This paper investigates the use of the Gallery Walk technique in a two-credit Qualitative Research course and how students perceive Gallery Walk to help them understand concepts. Forty-one students participated in this study. Data were collected from reflective notes, observation, and a focus group discussion. The results indicated that Gallery Walk was perceived as being a powerful tool for engaging students' learning and promoting affective and psychomotor learning. High-achievers tended to create net type concept maps and low-achievers demonstrating different ways in providing details to illustrate particular concepts. Although the mean score of the post-test improved significantly, this method failed to make the students obtain the targeted score for content knowledge mastery.

1   INTRODUCTION

To cope well with the 21st century learning skills, students need to be taught how to collaborate and acquire technology-based learning experiences. Mastery on theories as well as practices is indeed necessary for their future professional development. In so doing, learning should be learner-centered and students should be adequately exposed to and involved in contextual learning in which theories and practices are aligned. Johnson (2003) confirms that cooperative learning could be one of the concepts that embed a close relationship between research, theory, and practice. In addition, cooperative learning procedures are built on and characterized by the social interdependent theory (Johnson & Johnson 2002). The social interdependent theory, in addition, postulates that goals of an individuals could be achieved and influenced by the actions of other people (Deutsch 1949). Simply put, cooperative learning can be a promising alternative for learning that combine the notion of research, theory, and practice to help learners achieve their goals of learning. It is also a tool to cope with the 21st century requirements in which collaboration becomes one of the essential constituents.

In the education field, cooperative learning has attracted the attentions of practitioners and researchers over several decades. The studies by Johnson *et al.* (1978), Slavin *et al.* (1984), Gillies & Boyle (2005), Johnson *et al.* (2000), Johnson *et al.* (2013), Alghamdi & Gillies (2017) mentioned some of the rigorous investigations on how cooperative learning activities may work to help learners succeed in achieving their goals. Research findings show that cooperative learning has significantly helped students to increase their academic achievement (Alghamdi & Gillies 2017). Cooperative learning is also perceived to be beneficial in developing students' generic skills (Ballantine & Larres 2005), increase students' motivation and reading ability (Meng 2010), improve students' achievement and retention measure (Tran & Lewis 2012). Some studies also combine the use of technology in classrooms and cooperative learning (Liao *et al.* 2011, Yoshida *et al.* 2014, Neo *et al.* 2009). It is implied that cooperative learning has become an alternative for learning activities that bring many benefits and thus investigation continues.

According to Johnson *et al.* (2000), there are ten modern methods of cooperative learning, namely Learning Together and Alone, Teams-Games-Tournaments, Group Investigation, Constructive Controversy, Jigsaw Procedure, Student Teams Achievement Divisions,

Complex Instruction, Team Accelerated Instruction, Cooperative Learning Structures, Cooperative Integrated Reading & Composition. The Cooperative Learning Structures is the one pioneered by Kagan (Johnson *et al.* 2000). One of the various activities of cooperative learning is Gallery Walk – a learning activity conducted by displaying visuals on galleries where students can learn and discuss the corresponding topic in the galleries (Kagan & Kagan 2009). Studies on the use of Gallery Walk, however, is apparently limited particularly in language learning contexts. Francek (2006) implements Gallery Walk in a science class indicating the benefits of such an activity for being so flexible and engaging that students have opportunities to move around the classroom and generate open-ended questions orally. In comparison, *Schendel et al.* (2008) applied virtual Gallery Walk in K-12 classrooms and finds that the post-research test results indicate significant higher score than the pre-research test results. However, it is important to note that difficult topics and numbers of tasks may influence students' learning gain. In short, it can be implied that the use of Gallery Walk in language learning is quite rare and therefore it needs further investigation in different context and classroom situations.

In this study, Gallery Walk is implemented in Qualitative Research course. Based on the previous class reports and teachers' limited observation, there are initially two problems concerning with the learning of this course. First, students' understanding on the concept of qualitative research is often unsatisfactory as indicated by their final grades. They are often confused with the quantitative inquiry when they begin the undergraduate thesis writing project including research topic, types of data, data collection techniques, and data analyses. In practice, they could not formulate the appropriate research questions for the appropriate research paradigm. In addition, students could not determine types of data that they need for their undergraduate thesis writing project. Second, the previous learning activities of this course involved jigsaw method. To continue with similar cooperative learning platform and to support the learning with more visualization, Gallery Walk may become an alternative as it also involves learning together in groups with visuals as the learning tools. Therefore, it can be highlighted that studies on the use of Gallery Walk in this context is necessary as an attempt to contribute both theoretically and practically.

2 LITERATURE REVIEW

Cooperative learning has been the buzzword for creating active learning environment. Not only does it offer intensive engagement during learning but also it accommodates varied learning styles of learners and multiple intelligences. The cooperative learning term is rooted from the theory of cooperation and competition. Deutsch introduced the basic theory of social interdependent with the concept of "promotively interdependent goals" (an individual achieves goals when the others also attain their goals) and "contriently interdependent goals" (an individual achieves goals when the others fail to obtain theirs) (1949: 133). Johnson & Johnson (2010) argue that the social interdependence theory has several limitations. The social interdependent theory assumes that there is only one goal, it occurs in small groups, the participants have the same power and have self-interests, and the theory lies on the assumption that the persons involved do not have relationship one another. In more practical sphere, cooperative learning is indicated to require students "to work together in small groups to support each other to improve their own learning and those of others" (Jolliffe 2007). Briefly, it can be affirmed that cooperative learning is a type of learning activity that is likely to offer active learning engagement among learners, cater learners' various learning styles, and develop learners' multiple intelligences.

Cooperative learning may work differently across ages, culture, and learning styles (Kagan & Kagan 2009). Therefore, the impact of its use in a particular context of study may be significantly different from the others. As is indicated, cooperative learning may also be applicable for teaching specific content and problem-solving skills. To achieve the goals, there are five basic elements of cooperative learning that should be fulfilled—positive interdependence, face-to-face promotive interaction, individual accountability and personal responsibility, frequent use of interpersonal and small group social skills, frequent, regular group processing of current function (Johnson *et al.* 1991). Likewise, Kagan & Kagan posit that the positive impacts of cooperative learning can be accessed through the PIES principles—positive interdependence, individual accountability, equal participation, and simultaneous interaction along with the extensive range of cooperative activities related to team work, management, class building, and social skills (2009). In other words, to successfully implement cooperative learning, several requirements should be fulfilled involving all students to be actively engaged in face-to-face classroom interactions, group works, and equal and simultaneous participations of all group members.

According to Johnson & Johnson, cooperative learning has three types, namely formal cooperative learning (one to several week period for assignments), informal cooperative learning (few minutes to one class period), and cooperative base group (a semester or a year-long implementation) (2010). In addition, a large number of cooperative learning activities that are proposed by Kagan & Kagan (2009) have been adapted in many learning contexts to match unique condition of a class and one of them is Gallery Walk. Gallery Walk can be defined as a cooperative learning activity in which questions or topics are posted onto the wall around the class. Students are grouped and have to walk around to discuss all topic by moving from one wall to the other. Students can ask many questions, take notes, comments, add information, etc. Gallery Walk is believed to promote higher order thinking, presentation skills, and team building (Hosseinali n. d). It can be assessed through formal evaluation such as oral or written tests. Several forms that can be used for assessment are instructor/students evaluation on group discussion, evaluation on oral reports, written reports, student rubric for group work, student evaluation for gallery walk (Science Education Resource Center Carleton University n.d.). The learning structure of cooperative learning can be divided into two parts—the basic format (three-step interview, roundtable, structured problem solving, luck of the draw, think-pair-share, visible quiz, stand up and share, three-stay one-stray, gallery walk) and the advanced format (value line, jigsaw, within-team jigsaw, responsive written exchanged, paired annotations, send/pass a problem, dyadic essay confrontation, reciprocal peer questioning (Millis n.d.). In short, Gallery Walk involves students' activity to present, question, discuss, and find answers on a particular topic. It is a type of basic cooperative learning that can be modified into reciprocal peer questioning (Millis).

In addition, Gallery Walk has been practiced in various learning activities such as reading comprehension using e-story book (Indriani *et al.* 2015), cooperative technique to teach Mathematics (Barczi 2013), and in science classroom (Francek 2006). It can be implied that Gallery Walk can be applied in any context of learning. The goals of the learning can be adapted for both simple and advanced concepts. The goals, in addition, may also influence the procedures of implementation, materials, the depth and width of learning.

In line with the core of teaching in the 21st century, technology immersion in a learning process can give benefits and meaningful experiences. Information and Communication Technology literacy is included in one of the 21st century skills that learners should acquire (Binkley *et al.* 2012, Framework for 21st Century Learning 2015). Therefore, it is important to note that engaging students' learning with the use of technology is relevant with the 21st century skills and even it is highly recommended for students at higher education. With their sufficient prior knowledge, they can be empowered through active learning which is naturally autonomous.

3 RESEARCH METHOD

This study was conducted to help enhance students' learning processes that encourage students' collaboration and make use of ICT-based instruction. It is deliberately designed as an investigation that quest for exploring the use of a collaborative approach (Gallery Walk) to help students understand concepts better. The use of Gallery Walk strategy is aimed to empower students to read concepts, understand them, and summarize them in the form of mind-map poster or visual presentation. In making the mind-map, students were required to use mind-map application and do the tasks in groups. This activity is expected to sharpen students' understanding on concepts, to function as the scaffolding for the learning to take place, and to leave students to engage in active learning that involve both visual and verbal interactions. Students' exploration and presentation is expected to give more opportunities to generate open-ended questions as a tool to understand concepts better.

This research aims to find answers to the questions: (1) How is Gallery Walk implemented to teach a content course; (2) What is students' perception on the use of Gallery Walk for Qualitative Research course? The participants of this study were 41students of semester 5 of the bachelor degree of English Language Education Department. They took a two-credit semester of Qualitative Research course which met once a week for 100 minutes.

In this course, the students were taught about theories and practices of qualitative research. The theories were taught using Gallery Walk technique while the practices were taught using group work. Data were collected from reflective notes, observation, and a focus group discussion. The Gallery Walk activities were conducted for 7 times (7 topics) with 7 groups presenting their Galleries.

4 FINDINGS

In this study, Gallery Walk concept was introduced in the first meeting with the students. Preparation, procedures, and assessment were also explained. It is expected that all students are prepared and can perform their tasks well. Gallery Walk is conducted as a group work activity because it needs quite demanding preparation such as reading a topic, making a concept map by using *e-draw* application, print it, display it, present it to their classmates, discuss the topic, and answer questions posed by the audience. Because this gallery walk is a group work, all students in a group should be responsible for the gallery walk session from the preparation to the question and answer session. All students had to present their parts of the galleries to their classmates, so all students participated in the activity either as presenters or audience.

Based on a preliminary interview with the students, one student had an experience in using Gallery Walk in the other class the semester before and another student had Gallery Walk in an English course she ever took. The majority of the students have never had experiences in using Gallery Walk. Students enjoy Gallery Walk in this course because of many reasons. Students felts the learning as a fun, active, and interesting activity. It offers varied way of presenting knowledge and understanding it. Students were involved in elaborative and challenging learning by asking questions more clearly, practicing speaking English, and critical thinking. Hence, more interactions among students in the class were generated. Gallery Walk is also perceived as improving the students' presentation skills. On the contrary, some of the students feel that they less enjoy Gallery Walk activity due to insufficient time availability and difficulties to explain concepts. In addition, not all students can explain well therefore the audiences sometimes feel confused. Another situation—when many students visit a gallery—results in less concentration. As a gallery is displayed during the course hours and students keep moving and learning from one gallery to the other, students feel tired because they had to repeat their explanation.

Students perceive that Gallery Walk is helpful to understand concepts because of some reasons. Gallery Walk provides students with eye-catching and relevant pictures on display that help stimulate concentration. In addition, peers are perceived as able to explain concepts more simply. During the Gallery Walk activity, students can ask questions and ask for re-explanations when they do not understand the concepts. However, some other students perceive that Gallery Walk may not be quite helpful because not all presenters explain clearly. Similarly, they feel difficult to focus on the explanations due to crowdedness in the gallery and that sometimes few presenters forget to explain important points.

Gallery Walk is viewed as an activity that is interesting, engaging, interactive, and can increase critical thinking. Presenters help students understand concepts while at the same time they also practice their public speaking skills where they practice organizing materials from general to specific. The quiz, furthermore, helps to motivate students to ask questions because the presenters are their classmates. Feedback from lecturers was given at the end of the session.

The drawbacks of Gallery Walk activities vary. Not all presenters can explain well and give sufficient information to the audience. Galleries are often crowded so that it may be difficult to stay focused. Due to time limitation, understanding concepts are even harder, particularly when the learning situation is a little bit crowded. Presenters also suffer from fatigue as they have to present several times due to the audience's taking turn in visiting the galleries.

5 DISCUSSION

Gallery Walk activity, in this study, can help students understand discipline knowledge through the use of concept map and group discussion—two techniques applied together with Gallery Walk. While Gallery Walk promotes higher order thinking, presentation skills, and team building (Hosseinali n. d), concept map can be used to encourage learning and manage information, and demonstrate students' understanding on relationship of ideas (Chiu & Lin 2012). It can be implied that Gallery Walk is a way to train students to develop students' high order thinking, presentation skills, and team building while at the same time teach students to manage information by making connections of ideas into a visual aid (concept map).

The student participants were also required to make mind-maps using e-draw application. Winitzky *et al.* (1994) argue that there are two types of concept map that students create—the expert and the novice. The experts' concept maps possess several characteristics such as elaborative, complex, interconnected and hierarchical. On the other hand, simpler and less structured concept maps are commonly geared to novices'. Kinchin & Hay (2000) classify concept maps into three types—spoke, chain, and net. The spoke type is described as radial structure with the main topic in the middle and connected to all sub topic while the sub topic is not always connected one another. The chain type is described as a linear sequence with direct concepts are connected above or below the topic based on the sequence. The net type is described as a hierarchical network that represents the connection of topics. In this research, the majority of the mind-map created by the students can be categorized as the novice net type. Those concept maps fall to the net type due to the fact that the topics that they have to present in concept maps include varied aspects and contains many sub topics both directly and indirectly connected to the main topic. Furthermore, the concept-maps fall to the novice because the characteristics of the mind-maps are less elaborative and comprehensive. More relationships of ideas and more important points need to be displayed in the concepts maps.

Gallery Walk may be assessed through group discussion, oral or written reports, and student rubric for group work (Science Education Resource Center Carleton University, n.d.). In this course, students were assessed based on group work, individual written reports, oral presentation during Gallery Walk activity, and participation. This allows students to have opportunities to demonstrate their abilities to work both in team and individually. Students have to show their mastery of the topics through the presentation of the concept maps, their oral presentation, and how they answer questions from their peers.

Many advantages of using concept map software (e-draw) have been identified such as varied, clear, colorful, and interesting designs, highlighted important points, simple operation, and visible keywords. With interesting display of concepts, students are motivated to learn. This finding is also supported by Tabatabaei & Khalili (2014) who find that concept mapping techniques promote meaningful learning such as clearer concepts, relevant knowledge, and motivation to learn. In terms of students' understanding on topics as represented in the concept maps, it is also clear that students who understand concepts make better visualization and organization of keywords. Details are given appropriately without leaving minor information and other technical issues such as color, design, and decoration. Those students with low understanding on the concepts tend to present ideas much simply, contain general points leaving some important details, and ignore visualization. This finding is in line with Wong (1998) who argues that high achievers and low achievers are different when making concept maps. While high achievers differentiate, categorize, and organize concept features, low achievers give less efforts to identify relationship of concepts. It can then be concluded that students' understanding on concepts can be represented by the concept maps that they create and how they explain the concepts to other students. In general, students create concept maps following deductive pattern of organization. This is similarly justified that concept maps can be created following the sequence of concepts such as from the most general to more detailed information or from the major concepts and move to more inclusive concepts (Wong 1998; Novak & Gowin 1984). Simply put, high achievers and low achievers tend to create more salient concept maps with clear relationship of ideas due to the depth of their understanding on the particular topic. Whereas, less brilliant students may create less interesting and comprehensive concept maps.

It can be implied that the learning of Qualitative Research course using Gallery Walk gives benefits and drawbacks to students' learning. It may encourage students to learn and try new experiences in learning, promote autonomous learning, and support team working activities. To a wider extent, Gallery Walk facilitate students' learning in a way that low proficient and less confident students have the opportunities to present in groups and be responsible for their group assignment.

Qualitatively, this study has shown positive notion on the use of Gallery Walk to teach Qualitative Research course. However, statistically this study has not proven successful. The mean score of 50.9 for this Qualitative Research course is not good enough to meet the requirement for knowledge mastery. Students are expected to obtain the minimum score 70 to ensure that the knowledge mastery is good enough to proceed to the next learning goals. To compensate the students' low score and give students more opportunities to learn better, a weekly quiz on one topic is administered to make students more focus on the topic and get better score. The results of the weekly quiz show that students' score rose to 54.90. Although there is a rise in the score, it remains insufficient for good understanding on a topic. It can be implied that there is a problem of learning in terms of understanding theories. This problem may result from several causes. First, students may have difficulties in understanding texts. This commonly relates with difficulties in reading comprehension which roots from limited number of vocabulary and reading speed. Second, students may not be used to take notes, summarize, and make concept maps. Therefore, their reading comprehension remains below the expected level. Third, the test instruments need to be revised and checked for their validity and reliability.

6 CONCLUSION

Gallery Walk implementation in this study has indicated that students learn in fun, engaging activities. In addition, students are able to create concept maps using e-draw application and confidently present their concept maps to their classmates. Although their concept maps are still limited to the novice net type, students can benefit from the process of making the concept maps such as team work experiences and the use of electronic application for making their concept maps. However, it is necessary to note that the result of the statistic test for the knowledge mastery which remains below requirements shows that Gallery Walk can be an interesting medium for learning content course but does not seem to significantly help students with the concept mastery. Gallery Walk is recommended for creating engaging class, yet complication of cognitive load needs to be more carefully anticipated and addressed.

REFERENCES

Alghamdi, R. & Gillies, R. 2017. The impact of cooperative learning in comparison to traditional learning (small groups) on EFL learners' outcomes when learning. *English as a Foreign Language* 9(13): 19–28. https://doi.org/10.5539/ass.v9n13p19.
Ballantine, J. & Larres, P.M. 2005. Cooperative learning : a pedagogy to improve students' generic skills ? *Education & Training*. https://doi.org/10.1108/00400910710739487.

Barczi, K. 2013. Applying cooperative techniques in teaching problem solving. *CEPS Journal* 3(4): 61–78.

Binkley, M., Erstad, O., Herman, J., Raizen, S., Ripley, M., Miller-Ricci, M. & Rumble, M. 2012. Defining twenty-first century skills. In P. Griffin, B. McGraw, & E. Care, *Assessment and Teaching of 21st Century Skills* (17–66). New York: Springer Science + Business Media B.V.

Chiu, C.H. & Lin, C.L. 2012. Sequential pattern analysis: Method and application in exploring how students develop concept maps. *The Turkish Online Journal of Educational Technology* 11(1): 145–153.

Deutsch, M. 1949. *Theory of cooperation and competition*. Human Relations.

Framework for 21st Century Learning. 2015. Retrieved December 20, 2015, from p21.org: http://www.p21.org/our-work/p21-framework.

Francek, M. 2006. Promoting discussion in the science classroom using gallery walk. Retrieved December 23, 2017, from http://www.nsta.org/publications/news/story.aspx?id=52391.

Gillies, R.M. & Ashman, A.F. 2000. The effects of cooperative learning on students with learning difficulties in the lower elementary school. *The Journal of Special Education* 34(1): 19–27. https://doi.org/10.1177/002246690003400102.

Gillies, R.M. & Boyle, M. 2005. Teachers' scaffolding behaviours during cooperative learning. *Asia-Pacific Journal of Teacher Education* 33(3): 243–259. https://doi.org/10.1080/13598660500286242.

Gillies, R.M. & Boyle, M. 2008. Teachers' discourse during cooperative learning and their perceptions of this pedagogical practice. *Teaching and Teacher Education*, 24(5): 1333–1348. https://doi.org/10.1016/j.tate.2007.10.003.

Hosseinali, T. (n.d.). Retrieved January 1, 2016, from http://hwmath.net/References/TeachingStrategies.pdf.

Indriani, L., Estiyowati, R. & Sarwanti, S. 2015. Online gallery walk and e-story book to improve EFL learners' reading comprehension. *The 9th International Conference: Capacity Building for English Education in a Digital Age* (pp. 95–109). Salatiga: Faculty of Language and Literature.

Johnson, D., Johnson, R. & Stanne, M.B. 2000. Cooperative learning methods: A meta-analysis. *Cooperative Learning Methods*, (January 2000).

Johnson, D.W. 2003. Social interdependence: Interrelationships among theory, research, and practice. *American Psychologist* 58(11): 934–945. https://doi.org/10.1037/0003-066X.58.11.934.

Johnson, D.W. & Johnson, R.T. 2002. Learning together and alone: Overview and meta-analysis. *Asia Pacific Journal of Education* 22(1): 95–105. https://doi.org/10.1080/0218879020220110.

Johnson, D.W., Johnson, R.T. & Johnson, R.T. 2010. New developments in social interdependence theory, *Genetic, Social, and General Psychology Monographs*, (May 2014), 37–41. https://doi.org/10.3200/MONO.131.4.285–358.

Johnson, D.W., Johnson, R.T. & Scott, L. 1978. The effects of cooperative and individualized instruction on atudent attitudes and achievement. *The Journal of Social Psychology* 104(13): 207–216.

Johnson, D.W., Johnson, R.T. & Smith, K.A. 1991. *Cooperative learning*. Washington: ASHE-ERIC Higher Education Report.

Johnson, D.W., Johnson, R.T. & Stanne, M.B. 2013. Cooperative learning methods: A meta-analysis (January 2000).

Jolliffe, W. 2007. *Cooperative learning in the classroom: putting it into practice*. London: Paul Chapman Publishing.

Kagan, S. & Kagan, M. 2009. *Kagan cooperative learning. kagan publishing*. California.

Kinchin, I.M. & Hay, D.B. 2000. How a qualitative approach to concept map analysis can be used to aid learning by illustrating patterns of conceptual development, *Educational Research* 42(1): 43–57.

Liao, C., Chen, F. & Chen, T. 2011. Perspectives of university students on cooperative learning by Moodle, *Educational Technology & Society* 5(6): 190–197. https://doi.org/10.4156/jdcta.vol5.issue6.22.

Meng, J. 2010. Jigsaw cooperative learning in English reading, *Journal of Language Teaching and Research* 1(4): 501–504. https://doi.org/10.4304/jltr.1.4.501-504.

Millis, B.J. (n.d.). Cooperative learning structures. Retrieved January 25, 2016, from www2.humboldt.edu/institute/.../CL_Structures_UT_Austin_Revised.doc.

Neo, T., Neo, M. & Kwok, J.W.J. 2009. Engaging students in a multimedia cooperative- learning environment : A Malaysian experience (1978): 674–683.

Novak, J.D. & Gowin, D.B. 1984. *Learning how to learn*. New York: Cambridge University Press.

Schendel, J., Liu, C., Chelberg, D. & Franklin, T. 2008. Virtual gallery walk, an innovative outlet for sharing student research work in K-12 classrooms. *Proceedings – Frontiers in Education Conference, FIE*, 1–6. https://doi.org/10.1109/FIE.2008.4720431.

Science Education Resource Center Carleton University. (n.d.). Starting Point Teaching Entry Level Geoscience. Retrieved Januari 22, 2016, from serc.carleton.edu: http://serc.carleton.edu/introgeo/gallerywalk/assessment.html.

Slavin, R.E., Madden, N.A. & Leavey, M. 1984. Effects of cooperative learning and individualized-instruction on mainstreamed students. *Exceptional Children* 50 (5): 434–443.

Tabatabaei, O. & Khalili, S. 2014. The effect of concept mapping on Iranian pre-intermediate L2 reading comprehension. *Journal of Language Teaching and Research* 5(6): 1368–1380.

Tran, V.D. & Lewis, R. 2012. Effects of cooperative learning on students at an giang university. *International Education Studies* 5 (1): 86–100. https://doi.org/10.5539/ies.v5n1p86.

Winitzky, N., Kauchak, D. & Kelly, M. 1994. Measuring teachers' structural knowledge. *Teaching and Teacher Education* 10 (2): 125–139.

Wong, M.S.L. 1998. An investigation into high-achiever and low-achiever knowledge organization and knowledge processing in concept mapping: A case study. *Research in Science Education* 28 (3): 337–352.

Yoshida, H., Tani, S., Uchida, T., Masui, J. & Nakayama, A. 2014. Effects of Online Cooperative Learning on Motivation in Learning Korean as a Foreign Language, *International Journal of Information and Education Technology* 4 (6). https://doi.org/10.7763/IJIET.2014.V4.453.

ELT in Asia in the Digital Era: Global Citizenship and Identity – Madya et al. (Eds)
© *2018 Taylor & Francis Group, London, ISBN 978-0-8153-7900-3*

Assessing speaking by f2f or using a developed application: Are there any differences?

M.S. Simatupang
Universitas Kristen Indonesia, Jakarta, Indonesia

M. Wiannastiti & R. Peter
Bina Nusantara University, Jakarta, Indonesia

ABSTRACT: To access students' ability in speaking, lecturers normally ask questions in face to face (f2f) mode and the students answer them directly. In class consisting of 40 students or more, it takes time to ask them the same questions one by one. Is there any faster way to do so? This study explored the differences between assessing speaking f2f and using a developed application, i.e. the Bingar Application. The participants of this study were 40 students. They were tested twice with the same questions. The first f2f test was taken in class about 1.5 hours and the second using the Bingar application in the computer lab, lasting only for about 15 minutes. The results showed that 80% of the students answered the questions with no significant differences either by the above testing modes. This indicates that using the Bingar application is more efficient in assessing speaking than by f2f.

1 INTRODUCTION

Teaching English especially speaking with more than 40 students needs special skills to ensure that the process of learning and teaching runs well. Speaking means the verbal use of language to communicate with others (Fulcher 2003). Consequently, it takes several minutes for a student to sufficiently speak his/her ideas with or without preparation so that his/her ideas can be understood fully. In a class with 40 students or more and the time allocation is 2×50 minutes per session, mostly not all students will have their turn to speak adequately. In such a class, a lecturer requires hours in order that the 40 students have sufficient time to speak. In other words, it certainly takes much time for students to present their thoughts orally one by one, especially in big classes. Furthermore, in one assessment, a lecturer needs not only more time to evaluate the students' speaking ability, but also more energy to concentrate to listen to their utterances to evaluate the accuracy, the vocabulary, and the pronunciation. The worst can happen when the lecturer asks the students one by one. It means that the lecturer needs to raise the same questions many times so that all students do not misunderstand them, and they are able to express their thoughts to match with the questions being asked.

To fulfil the needs of reducing time in assessing speaking ability of big class students, this study suggested the use of technology in order that to help us doing the task easily. Technology has been used in all aspect of life, including teaching, learning and assessing. With the advance of technology nowadays, it is possible to save time in evaluating students' speaking skills. This study explores the use of a developed application, called the Bingar application to be used in assessing students' performance in speaking. This study was worth conducting due to the fact that it is time consuming to conduct speaking tests for more than 40 students (f2f). We focus on three ideas to discuss:

1. Technology in teaching English
2. Bingar application
3. Differences between assessing speaking by f2f and using a developed application, that is using Bingar application

2 TECHNOLOGY IN TEACHING ENGLISH

Some studies have been accomplished to use technology in teaching and learning process (See, for instance, Mayora 2006, Sad 2008, Simatupang 2004, Wang 2015). The practical one used in many classes is using computer or laptop with LCD as the means of delivering the materials in the teaching and learning process. The computer also helps lecturers obtain information easily to prepare materials properly before the class (Simatupang 2004). Using power point in delivering the teaching materials is also popular with the intention that the teaching materials are well prepared, interesting, and focus (Simatupang 2005). Wang (2015: 593) explains multimedia technology improves the teaching quality and effect of English linguistics course in universities. Not far difference, Dewi (2005) explained in her paper that online learning is useful to learn a language as a whole or to learn a skill of language. It indicates that the use of technology like computers (hardware) and internet (software) enhances the teaching quality. Technology indeed is needed in almost all aspects of education, including teaching English. Mayora (2006) experienced to the application of Technologically Enhanced Language Learning (TELL) to implement a program that seeks to raise in the students an autonomous attitude toward learning a language and the integration of multimedia technology as a reinforcement of in-classroom activities. The use of technology in teaching English has been developed in many places. The most advanced technology is stated by Sad (2008) who found that using mobile phone technology helped students to communicate better by producing drama activities with mobile phones.

The use of technology has been applied widely in education, starting from gathering the information and materials, preparing the syllabus, delivering the materials to the students, and finally assessing the students. This study was focused on assessing the students' speaking ability. Why should we demand an application to teach English, especially speaking? In this technological era, where everything needs to be done efficiently and practically, an application is compulsory to help lecturers save the time allotted to evaluate students' performance. Moreover, technology supports lecturers to minimize asking the same questions many times to students since the application replaces the lecturers' roles. In traditional classes, a lecturer carries out speaking assessment by ordering the students to deliver their talk one by one until everybody gets their performance. A lecturer carefully does observation while students are involved in speaking activities which can provide useful information of their progress (Nation & Newton 2009). As a consequence, a lecturer needs to fully concentrate to get his/her students ideas.

3 RESEARCH METHOD

This research concerns to find out whether or not there are differences if the students use the Bingar application in their speaking test compared to face to face (f2f) test. In doing the research, there are 40 students of Bina Nusantara University majoring in *Game Application and Technology* who get involved in the speaking test. Firstly they do the test (f2f) by answering two questions:

1. What is your favorite place to visit on weekends? Describe it and explain why it is your favorite place to go.
2. Do you agree or disagree that it is more important for students to study history and literature than to study science and mathematics? Give specific reasons and examples to support your opinion.

The students' responses were recorded to find out exactly what they said. The next week, they had to answer the same questions using the Bingar application and recorded. They did not expect that they would be given the same questions. Consequently, they did not prepare to give answers to similar questions. It was possible that their answers might be better for the second time as long as their speaking abilities were good enough. If their speaking abilities are bad, their answers would not get better. The results were compared to find out the differences between two testing types.

4 FINDINGS AND DISCUSSION

The Bingar application is a desktop application consisting of three types of content and several questions which are played sequentially. The questions vary and depend on the order or the set (Wiannastiti 2016). When this application is used, the students are doing the test together in the lab. Some lab assistants are available to check if there are problems faced during the test. One of the lab assistants explains what to do and how to use the application to make sure that the students understand and are capable to use the application. First of all, they are doing the prerequisite sample question that should be answered after the beep signal and then, they listen to their recorded voice to make sure that the application runs well. Next, the lab assistant told them to listen to the questions of the speaking test and after about 20 seconds they answer the questions orally and at the same time, their voices are recorded. The test takes only 15–20 minutes since all students do the test at the same time. This indicates the efficient time to have one test for all students (depending on the quantity of the computers provided for the speaking test). The results of the tests are evaluated by the lecturers later on, at home or anywhere and at their convenient time. This denotes the flexible time to give scores even though it takes a longer time to get the results for all students.

Results of the analysis of the data obtained from the questionnaires distributed to the students about the Bingar application showed some information about the application. Figure 1 shows the ease with which the students used the Bingar application. It indicates that more than 90 percent of the students agreed that it is easy to start, more than 80 percent agree it is easy to use, more than 80 percent agree it is easy to record voice, more than 80 percent agree it is helpful, and more than 80 percent agree it is easy to check the sound. This implies that students can use the Bingar application with ease.

Figure 2 shows the interface of the application. The interface means the program of the computer that controls the display for the user. More than 70 percent of the students agreed that the Bingar application is simple to operate; 16 percent say neutral because it wass just the first time for them to use the application. More than 80 percent of the students agreed and strongly agreed that the application has clear instruction, provides supportive picture, has easy button click, and overall is it easy to use.

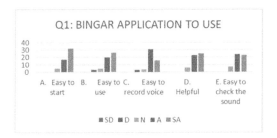

Figure 1.   The use.

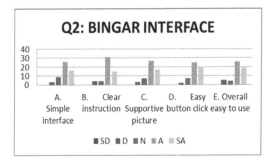

Figure 2.   The interface.

The information in Figure 3 shows the sound system of the Bingar application. Since the test was speaking, the sound system should be of the high quality. The students listened to the questions and directly answered them after the notification. The result shows that in all questions concerning the sound, more than 80 percent students agree that they can hear the instruction clearly, they could hear the questions easily, they could hear their voice clearly, they can hear the pronunciation clearly, and the sound in the application was clear.

The last questions were regarding the time allotted in accomplishing the speaking test using the application. This is essential to figure out since it shows how effective and how efficient is the time to do the test. The information in Figure 4 demonstrates in all questions, more than 85 percent of the students agreed that it is easy to see the preparation time; it is easy to see the respond time; it is easy to see the time allotment; it is easy to see the idle time; and the overall time is clearly seen.

In this research study, each student answered the questions for the speaking test twice: firstly, in the class f2f with the lecturer (recorded); secondly in the lab using Bingar application (recorded). The questions for both tests were the same. The purpose of this research is to identify if there are differences between assessing speaking test by using an f2f (face to face) method and by using the Bingar application.

Assessing speaking through an f2f tests implies taking a great deal of time. If one student needs one minute to listen to the questions from the lecturer, one minute to prepare, and 2 minutes to answer, it requires four minutes for each student. Forty students need 160 minutes or more than 2 hours, plus interrupted time like waiting for the students to approach the front or repeating the instruction. Furthermore, the lecturer requires energy to concentrate in order that s/he can give similar judgment to every student. This can create unfairness to value the students' performance if the lecturer is already tired.

Using the Bingar application in assessing speaking does not require plenty of time. Each student performs the test together in the lab. They listen to the questions and answer the questions all together at the same time without disrupting one another since each of them is using the headset provided in the lab; thus their answers can be recorded all at once. It is enormously practical and easy to use.

The scoring for f2f and Bingar application is formulated based on the Speaking Rubric[i] (see the appendix). The scores are categorized into excellent, good, average, and poor. After the

Figure 3.   The sound.

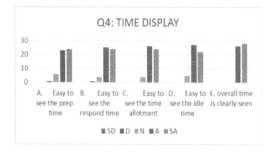

Figure 4.   The time.

entire students got their scores, the grades were compared for each student to see if there are differences in both tests based on the category. For instance, if student A's score for f2f is 75 and for Bingar is 80, the score category is 75–84 (good). It means no different score category for student A. On the other hand, if B's score for f2f is 70 (average) and for Bingar is 80 (good), B's scores of Bingar is higher than of f2f test due to the different category. The results show that 80 percent or 32 students answered the questions with no significant difference category either by using Bingar application or by face to face test. There are 5 students or 12.5 percent answer the questions with better scores by using Bingar application than by f2f[ii]. This is probably because they have heard the questions before. Nevertheless, they did not expect to have the same questions since they are informed to have the second speaking test. Their answers are better possibly due to their high English proficiency. The rest 8 percent or 3 students answered the questions with worse scores by using the Bingar application than by f2f. This indicates that using Bingar application is more efficient in assessing speaking than by f2f. Furthermore, this application is excellent to apply for big classes since one test can be applied to a lot of students.

5 CONCLUSION AND SUGGESTIONS

Assessing speaking for more than 40 students in a class can require a lot of time and energy. To solve the problem, an application is designed so that the speaking test can be completed in fewer tempos. To see if it is applicable, this study is conducted as whether or not the application contributes to the process of speaking assessment. The result reveals that the use of the Bingar application was found to be more efficient since the time used for the speaking test was about fifteen to twenty minutes for all 40 students, and the lecturer could give scores later at his/her convenient time. It is also effective since the result of this research study shows that there were no significant differences between assessing speaking face to face and using the Bingar application.

The use of technology proves that it assists lecturers to enlighten his/her work. The Bingar application is one of the technologies that support speaking tests. It is suggested that the Bingar application or other similar technology should be applied in assessing students' oral communication, especially for big classes. Indeed technology makes assessment easier and efficient.

REFERENCES

Dewi, I.I. 2005. The implementation of information technology in language teaching. *Teflin International Conference* (Proceeding). https://lib.atmajaya.ac.id/Uploads/Fulltext/84146/artikel/Ienneke%20Indra%20Dewi-The%20Implementation%20of%20IT.pdf.

Fulcher, G. 1997. The testing of speaking in a second language. In C. Clapham & D. Corson (eds.): Encyclopedia of Language and Education 7: Language testing and assessment. The Netherlands: Kluwer Academic Publishers. 75–85.

Mayora, C.A. 2006. Integrating multimedia technology in a high school EFL program. *English Teaching Forum* 3: 14–21. http://files.eric.ed.gov/fulltext/EJ1107903.pdf

Nation, I.S.P. & Newton, J. 2009. *Teaching EFL/ESL Listening and Speaking*. Routledge: New York.

Sad, S.N. 2008. Using mobile phone technology in EFL Classes. *English Teaching Forum* 4: 34–40. http://files.eric.ed.gov/fulltext/EJ1096315.pdf

Simatupang, M.S. 2004. The role of computer technology in English teaching. *TEFLIN International Conference 52nd: Cross-cultural communication: TEFL Concerns and Contribution.* https://lib.atmajaya.ac.id/default.aspx?tabID=61&src=a&id=93978

Simatupang, M.S. 2005. Power Point and Creative English Teaching. *International Seminar of Information Technology and English Language Studies (ICELS 3)*: 106–113.

Wang, Y. 2015. Study of application of multimedia technology in English teaching. *7th International Conference on Information Technology in Medicine and Education*: 593–597. https://lib.atmajaya.ac.id/Uploads/Fulltext/204300/Study%20of%20Application%20of%20Multimedia%20Technology%20in%20English%20Language%20Teaching.pdf

Wiannastiti, M. 2016. Assessing speaking for a large number of students by Using Bingar Application. *The 5th English Language Teaching, Literature, and Translation: International Conference* (Proceeding).

APPENDIX

Indicators	Proficiency level			
	Excellent (E) (85–100)	Good (G) (75–84)	Average (A) (65–74)	Poor (P) (0–64)
Ability to perform fluency when talking in English for general topics	Almost fully able to explain in English about a general topic with very few pauses and/or fillers	Mostly able to explain in English about a general topic with few pauses and/or fillers	Generally able to explain in English about a general topic with some pauses and/or fillers	Moderately able to explain in English about a general topic with many pauses and/or fillers
Ability to demonstrate intelligibility when talking in English for general topics	Other people almost fully recognize the speech, & the speech is generally clear in pronunciation	Other people mostly recognize the speech, & the speech is moderately clear in pronunciation	Other people generally recognize the speech, & the speech is somewhat clear in pronunciation	Other people moderately recognize the speech, & the speech is limitedly clear in pronunciation
Ability to demonstrate language use when talking in English for general topics	Almost fully apply varied & appropriate grammar and vocabulary	Mostly apply varied & appropriate grammar and vocabulary	Generally apply varied & appropriate grammar and vocabulary	Moderately apply varied & appropriate grammar and vocabulary

ⁱⁱSpeaking score of f2f and Bingar Application

Student	F2F	Bingar	Student	F2F	Bingar
1	75/G	85/E	21	70/A	70/A
2	80/G	90/E	22	75/G	75/G
3	75/G	85/E	23	60/P	60/P
4	70/A	80/G	24	78/G	75/G
5	80/G	90E	25	90/E	90/E
6	80/G	80/G	26	85/E	85/E
7	70/A	70/A	27	85/E	90/E
8	60/P	62/P	28	95/E	90/E
9	95/E	90/E	29	65/A	65/A
10	90/E	90/E	30	78/G	78/G
11	90/E	85/E	31	75/G	75/G
12	85/E	85/E	32	90/E	88/E
13	75/G	75/G	33	90/E	90/E
14	85/E	85/E	34	85/E	85/E
15	78/G	80/G	35	70/A	70/A
16	78/G	80/G	36	75/G	80/G
17	80/G	80/G	37	80/G	75/G
18	90/E	88/E	38	70/A	60/P
19	90/E	85/E	39	80/G	70/A
20	85/E	85/E	40	70/A	60/P

Author index

Abduh, A. 15
Abidin, M.J.Z. 129
Alwasilah, I.A. 241
Andawi, D.A. 385
Andriyanti, E. 299
Andy 315
Ashadi, A. 249
Atma, N. 307
Aye, K.K. 505

Budiman, A. 197

Cahyani, H. 393
Chen, B. 369
Christiani, N. 417
Ciptaningrum, D.S. 495

Damio, S.M. 93
Devi, D.B. 103
Dhamotharan, M. 103
Diyanti, B.Y. 423
Djohan, R. 143
Drajati, N.A. 385, 453
Dung, T.N.T. 513

Fahriany, F. 173
Fatmawati, W. 307
Fauzi, N.A. 429
Febiani, T.H. 49

Hakim, M.A.R. 129
Healy, S. 65
Hendrety, Y. 487
Hendryanti, R. 409
Hermagustiana, I. 57
Hermasari, D. 555
Hidayati, K.H. 45
Hidayati, N. 235
Hidayati, S. 249
Hsu, H.T. 221

Indratama, F. 453
Istiqamah 135

Jamilah 87
Jannah, M.N. 45

Kadaryanto, B. 49
Karjo, C.H. 143
Korompot, C.A. 119
Kurniasih, S.K. 423
Kusmayanti, I.N. 409

Latief, M.A. 417
Lee, J. 521
Lei, W. 471
Liddicoat, A.J. 463
Lie, A. 369, 377

Maharsi, I. 563
Mahmud, M. 29
Masulah 285
Masyhur 205
Matthews, J. 343
Mauludin, L.A. 113
Meisani, D.R. 531
Muamaroh 21
Mukminatien, N. 293
Mukminatun, S. 249
Muzammil, L. 315

Nafissi, Z. 349
Nation, I.S.P. 275
Ngadiso 79
Nugraheni, D.A. 401
Nuraeni, N. 173
Nurhayati, L. 423
Nurichsania, N.A. 189
Nurkamto, J. 453

Osman, W.H. 445

Peter, R. 571
Pratama, R.D. 361
Prayitno, R.Y. 377
Purwati, O. 479
Putro, N.H.P.S. 521

Quynh, L.T.N. 513

Rachmajanti, S. 189
Rambet, R.D.B. 37
Riazi, M. 161
Rieschild, V. 299
Rizqan, M.D.A. 265
Rochsantiningsih, D. 453
Rosli, N.N. 93
Rosmaladewi, R. 15
Rugaiyah 255

Sahril 29
Salmasi, N. 349
Setiawan, S. 45
Setyo, R.C.Y. 479
Simatupang, M.S. 571
Simbuka, S. 437
Suezawa, N. 229
Sugirin 181
Suharsono 479
Suharti, D.S. 537
Sumardi 235

Tarjana, S.S. 235
Tedick, D.J. 3
Triastuti, A. 161

Utaminingsih, D. 49

Wiannastiti, M. 571
Widyantoro, A. 73

Yujobo, Y.J. 153

Zou, C. 327

For Product Safety Concerns and Information please contact our EU
representative GPSR@taylorandfrancis.com Taylor & Francis Verlag GmbH,
Kaufingerstraße 24, 80331 München, Germany

Printed and bound by CPI Group (UK) Ltd, Croydon, CR0 4YY
08/05/2025
01864327-0015